Management consulting
A guide to the profession

Management consulting

A guide to the profession

Second (revised) edition
Edited by Milan Kubr

International Labour Office   Geneva

Kubr, M.
Management consulting: A guide to the profession (second edition)
Geneva, International Labour Office, 1986
/Guide/, /Management consultancy/, /Management development/. 12.04
ISBN 92-2-105479-9

ILO Cataloguing in Publication Data

Printed in France   JOUVE Paris

CONTENTS

Management consulting

Management consulting

FOREWORD

Management consulting has long been recognised as a useful professional service that helps managers to analyse and solve practical problems faced by their organisations, and to learn from the experience of other managers and organisations. Hundreds of thousands of private businesses and public organisations in both industrialised and less developed countries have used management consulting services, separately or in combination with training, feasibility and market studies, systems design, action research, engineering consulting and other professional services.

The Management Development Programme of the ILO has therefore from its inception in the early 1950s paid considerable attention to the development of management consulting and the promotion of effective consulting practices in member states. Through its technical co-operation projects, the ILO has assisted many of its member states in establishing local consulting services for the various sectors of the economy, and/or developing management consultants and trainers.

To respond to a pressing demand for a comprehensive practically-oriented guide to management consulting the first edition of this book was published in 1976. The book quickly became a basic reference work and learning text on management consulting, used world-wide: the original English edition (which had to be reprinted eight times in ten years) was followed by editions in Japanese, French, Spanish, Portuguese, Serbo-Croatian, Indonesian, and, most recently, in Chinese.

However, there have been many changes on both national and international economic fronts since 1976. Management consultants have made a great effort to keep pace with these changes and respond to new challenges. This effort has resulted in many developments in the consulting profession and the methodology of consulting work: in the size, specialisation and profile of consulting firms; the strategies adopted by these firms; the range and combination of services offered; the marketing of consulting and other professional services; the methods of consultant-client collaboration; the integration of consulting and training; the expansion of consulting in developing countries; and many others.

These developments have stimulated numbers of consultants to writing about their experiences. While there had been an acute shortage of any literature about management consulting before 1976 and the ILO book was, in fact, the first relatively complete work on the topic, a number of books have appeared since 1976, in particular in the United States. Outside the United States, original publications on consulting have remained very scarce.

North American experience has without any doubt played a critical role in fostering the art and science of management consulting. But it is important, too, to consider and generalise the valuable experiences of other countries, in particular if their different socio-economic and cultural environments have generated different approaches to managing organisations and to consulting for management.

The success of the first edition of *Management consulting: A guide to the profession* has encouraged the authors to prepare an updated and substantially revised edition, reflecting the international management consulting scene of the latter part of the 1980s, and giving a balanced picture of interesting new trends in various areas of consulting.

The concept of consulting

In this book management consulting is treated as a *method* for improving management practices first of all. This method can be used by an independent private firm, an internal consulting (or similar) unit in a private or public organisation, a management development, productivity or small enterprise development institute, an extension service, or an individual (e.g. a sole consulting practitioner or a university professor). Even a manager can act as a consultant if he provides advice to his peers or subordinates.

At the same time, however, management consulting has been developing into a *profession*. A growing number of individuals and organisations make consulting their full-time occupation, striving for professional standards in the quality of the advice provided, methods of intervention and ethical principles. Even individuals who do some consulting without being full-time members of the profession can comply with the profession's standards and principles and should be helped to do so.

There is no conflict between these two ways of viewing consulting. Indeed, consulting as a method and consulting as a profession constitute two sides of one coin and a guide such as ours has to deal with both these sides of consulting.

Management consulting is practised in many different ways. These reflect the diversity of the business and management contexts in which consultants operate, the different personalities of clients and consultants, and the various conceptual approaches and intervention methods developed by consultants. Therefore to generalise about consulting and recommend a best way of approaching consulting is difficult and risky. In our book we have opted for an eclectic approach, providing the reader with a comprehensive and balanced picture of the consulting scene, including the different methods, styles, modes or techniques applied, and pointing out their advantages and shortcomings. Thus the reader can make his own choice, consistent with the technical, organisational and human context of his organisation.

However, to say that the authors of this book have no bias whatsoever for any approach to consulting would not be correct. We do have a bias, and a strong one, for a form of consulting in which (i) the consultant shares expertise with the client instead of trying to keep it to himself; (ii) the client participates as closely and intensively as possible in the assignment; and (iii) both parties spare no effort to make the assignment a valuable learning experience. Many different methods and techniques can apply within this broad concept and the reader will have ample opportunity for making choices.

Purpose of the book

The main purpose of the book is to contribute to the upgrading of professional standards and practices in management consulting and to provide information and guidance to individuals and organisations wishing to start or improve consulting activities. The book is an introduction to professional consulting, its nature, methods, organisational principles, behavioural rules, and training and development practices. It also suggests guidelines to consultants for operating in various areas of management. However, it is not intended to replace handbooks and manuals which deal in depth and detail with various management functions and techniques: for this the reader is referred to special sources, some of which are suggested in our selected bibliography. The same point applies to certain special areas of consulting, such as executive search, market studies, advertising or systems design, which are mentioned briefly in this book, but can be studied in detail from special publications.

In summary, the book is intended for:

— new entrants to the consulting profession;
— independent management consultants and consulting firms, bureaux and services;
— consulting departments of national and sectoral institutions concerned with productivity, management development and small enterprise development;
— departments and divisions performing internal management consulting and advisory functions in large private and public organisations, including management services, organisation and methods services, and so on, in governments;
— management teachers, trainers and researchers who may be part-time consultants, and whose work is closely related to that of consultants;
— students of management and business administration taking courses in management consulting or involved in in-plant projects where they can use some consulting techniques;
— managers, businessmen and administrators wishing to use consultants more effectively, or to apply some consulting skills in problem solving within their organisation.

Finally, many principles and techniques described in the book apply to *consulting in general*; hence consultants operating in areas other than management and business may also find it useful and inspiring.

Terminology

The most common terms used in management consulting in various countries are explained in the text of the book. But the meaning and use of two basic terms warrant a definition at this early point:

—   the term *management consultant* is used in the book as a generic term and applies to those persons who perform all or some of the typical consulting functions in the field of management on either a full-time or a part-time basis;

—   the term *client* is also used as a generic term and applies to any manager, administrator or organisation using the services of management consultants in private businesses, public undertakings, government agencies or elsewhere.

Similarly, unless specified otherwise in the text, the term *consulting organisation* applies to any type of organisational unit whose function is to provide consulting services. This term is often used interchangeably with the terms *consulting unit* or *consulting firm*. The job done by a particular consultant for a particular client is normally called *consulting assignment* (*project, case, engagement*).

Plan of the book

The revised edition of the guide is divided into 29 chapters grouped in 5 parts. These are followed by 11 appendices.

Part I (chapters 1-6) presents an overall view of the consulting method and profession. Emphasis is placed on the consultant-client relationship, on the role of management consultants in the process of change and on the principles of professional ethics.

Part II (chapters 7-11) is a systematic review of the consulting process, divided into five major phases: entry, diagnosis, action planning, implementation and termination.

Part III (chapters 12-19) provides an introduction to consulting in various areas of management. The areas covered are general management and corporate strategy, finance, marketing, production, human resources, small enterprises, public enterprises and computer applications.

Part IV (chapters 20-26) deals with the management of consulting organisations. The main aspects examined are a consulting organisation's strategy, marketing of consulting services, cost and fees, assignment management, operational and financial control and structuring of consulting units.

Part V (chapters 27-29) focuses on careers in consulting, the training and development of consultants, and special problems involved in promoting the consulting profession in developing countries.

The appendices provide information supplementing the main text of the book as well as material for a deeper study of consulting methods and communication techniques discussed in various parts of the book. They also include a selected bibliography intended to facilitate an in-depth study of the aspects of consulting treated in this book. Appendix 1 is addressed to clients who want to become more knowledgeable and effective in choosing and using consultants.

Authors and acknowledgements

This book is the result of a collective effort and reflects collective experience.

The first edition was written by the following team: James Dey, George Kanawaty, Milan Kubr, Frederic Latham, Philip Neck, and J. Geoffrey Rawlinson, with contributions from Derek Bowland, Gerry Y. Elliot, W. J. C. McEwan, Alan Gladstone, Colin Guthrie, Alan C. Popham, Edgar H. Schein, P. W. Shay and W. Trevor Utting. Milan Kubr served as technical editor.

The second, revised edition of the book was prepared and edited by Milan Kubr in collaboration with the following co-authors: Alan Gladstone, Colin Guthrie, John Heptonstall, George Kanawaty, Gordon Lippitt, Leonard Nadler, Philip Neck and John Wallace.

Valuable material, ideas or comments were provided by Maurice C. Ashill, Daniel Bas, Bengt Björklund, Kenneth L. Block, George Boulden, Joseph J. Brady, Praxy Fernandes, Stelan Friberg, S. R. Ganesh, John F. Hartshorne, James H. Kennedy, Emile Laboureau, Lauri K. Leppänen, Hans-Åke Lilja, William J. McGinnis, Klaus Molenaar, Lewis S. Moore, Alex Morley-Smith, M. S. S. El Namaki, Robert Nelson, Graham Perkins, Edgar H. Schein, Howard L. Shenson, Carl S. Sloane, Sten Söderman, Fritz Steele, Arthur B. Toan, and Arthur N. Turner.

There are, furthermore, many colleagues in ILO field projects, and in management institutions and consulting organisations with which the ILO has co-operated over the years, whose experience, ideas and suggestions made the publication of this book possible.

The ILO extends its sincere thanks to all co-authors and contributors, including those who could not be mentioned by name. Furthermore, the ILO would be most grateful to readers for any comments and suggestions on how this book could be further improved and its usefulness to the practice of management consulting enhanced.

PART I

MANAGEMENT CONSULTING IN PERSPECTIVE

NATURE AND PURPOSE OF MANAGEMENT CONSULTING

1

1.1 Definition: What is consulting?

There are many definitions of consulting, and of its application to management situations and problems, i.e. of management consulting. Setting aside minor stylistic and semantic differences, two basic approaches to consulting emerge.

The first approach takes a broad functional view of consulting. Fritz Steele defines consulting in this way: "By the consulting process, I mean any form of *providing help* on the content, process, or structure of a task or series of tasks, where the consultant *is not actually responsible for doing the task itself* but is helping those who are." [1] Peter Block even suggests that: "You are consulting any time you are trying to change or improve a situation but have no direct control over the implementation . . . Most people in staff roles in organisations are really consultants even if they don't officially call themselves consultants." [2] These and similar definitions emphasise that consultants are helpers, or enablers, and assume that such help can be provided by persons doing a wide range of different jobs. Thus, a manager can also act as a consultant if he decides to give advice and help to a fellow manager, or even to his own subordinates rather than directing them and issuing orders to them.

The second approach views consulting as a special professional service and emphasises a number of characteristics that such a service must possess. According to Larry Greiner and Robert Metzger "management consulting is an advisory service contracted for and provided to organisations by specially trained and qualified persons who assist, in an objective and independent manner, the client organisation to identify management problems, analyse such problems, recommend solutions to these problems, and help, when requested, in the implementation of solutions". [3] Similar definitions are used by professional associations of management consultants in the United Kingdom, the United States and other countries, as well as by individual consulting firms.

We regard the two approaches as complementary rather than conflicting. Management consulting can be viewed either as a professional service, or as a method of providing practical advice and help. There is no doubt that management consulting has been developing into a specific sector of professional activity and should be treated as such. At the same time, management consulting is also a method of assisting organisations and executives in improving management practices as well as individual and organisational performance. The method can be, and is, applied by many technically competent persons whose main occupation is not consulting but teaching, training, research, systems development, providing technical assistance to developing countries in short-term missions, and so on. To be effective, these persons need to master consulting tools and skills, and to observe the fundamental behavioural rules of professional consulting.

In our book, we have chosen to address the needs of both these target populations. Though it has been written primarily about and for professional management consultants, the needs of any other person who intervenes in a consulting capacity, even though he is not a full-time consultant, are borne in mind.

Some particular features of management consulting need to be emphasised at the outset.

Professional help to management practitioners

Whether practised as a full-time occupation or an ad hoc technical service, management consulting provides professional knowledge and skills relevant to practical management problems. An individual becomes a management consultant by accumulating, through study and practical experience, considerable knowledge of varying management situations, and by acquiring skills needed for problem solving and sharing experience with others: for identifying problems, finding relevant information, analysing and synthesising, developing proposals for improvement, communicating with people, planning changes, overcoming resistance to change, helping clients to learn from experience, transferring management techniques between countries, and so on.

It could be objected that managers, too, need to possess this range of knowledge and skills, and that each management situation is unique. What then can be gained by bringing in a newcomer who is not familiar with a given situation?

Over the years, management consultants pass through many organisations and learn how to use experience from previous assignments in helping their new clients, or their old clients, to face new situations. Because they are exposed to many varying combinations of circumstances, consultants learn how to discern general trends and common causes of problems, with a good chance of finding an appropriate solution; they also learn how to approach new problems and opportunities. In addition, professional consultants continuously keep abreast of management literature and of developments in management concepts, methods and systems, including those taking place in universities and research institutions. Thus they function as a link between the theory and practice of management. Even an excellent manager may find that a management consultant can contribute something new to the organisation.

Advisory service

Consulting is essentially an advisory service. This means that consultants are not used to run organisations or to take delicate decisions on behalf of the managers. They are advisers and have no direct authority to decide on changes and implement them. Their responsibility is for the quality and integrity of their advice; the clients carry all the responsibilities that accrue from taking it. Of course, in the practice of consulting there are many variations and degrees of "advice". Not only to give the right advice, but to give it in the right way, to the right persons and at the right time — these are the basic skills and art of a consultant. The client in his turn needs to become skilful in taking and using the consultant's advice. These points are so important that they will be repeated many times in the text that follows.

Independent service

Consulting is an independent service. A consultant must be in a position to make his own assessment of any situation, tell the truth and recommend frankly and objectively what the client organisation needs to do without having any second thoughts on how this might affect his own interests. This detachment of the consultant has many facets and can be a very tricky matter in certain cases.

Financial independence means that the consultant has no interest in the course of action taken by the client, e.g. in a decision to purchase a particular brand of equipment. The desire to get more business from the same client in the future must not affect the objectivity of the advice provided in a current assignment.

Administrative independence implies that the consultant is not the client's subordinate and cannot be affected by his administrative decisions. While this does not present a problem to autonomous consulting organisations, it is a rather complex, although not insurmountable, problem in internal consulting, as will be shown in section 2.6 below.

Political independence means that neither the client organisation's management nor employees can influence the consultant informally, using political power and connections, political party membership, and similar influences.

Emotional independence means that the consultant preserves his detachment, irrespective of friendship and other emotional affinities that may exist at the beginning or develop in the course of an assignment.

What consulting is not

There is an abundance of case histories of successful assignments carried out by some of the world's best management consultants in order to rescue companies facing bankruptcy, or to give new life to aging firms. They have created a reputation which implies that the consulting business can resolve virtually any management difficulty. However, consultants do not provide miracle solutions to burning issues. It would be an error to assume that, once a consultant is brought in, management can relax because someone else is taking care of the problems. There are situations where nobody can help. And if help is still possible, effective consulting will need difficult, systematic and disciplined work based on analysis of hard facts and a search for imaginative but feasible solutions. Strong management commitment to improving organisational performance and effective client-consultant collaboration are as important to the end result as the quality of the consultant's technical advice.

1.2 Why are consultants used?

Generally speaking, managers turn to consultants if they perceive a need for help in problem solving. The consultant's work begins with some condition judged to be unsatisfactory and/or capable of amelioration; it ideally ends with a condition in which *a change* has taken place, a change that must be seen as an improvement. Directly or indirectly, all changes generated and implemented with the consultant's help should contribute to *improvements in the quality of management* and *in organisational performance or excellence*. These are the overriding objectives of using consultants, although "improved management", "organisational performance", or "organisational excellence" are relative concepts and their precise meaning has to be defined in the context of each organisation concerned.

The main practical reasons which lead managers to seek help from consultants are listed below.

Special knowledge and skill

Consultants may be called in when an organisation is short of people able to tackle a problem with the same chance of success. It may often involve special methods and techniques in which the consultant is an expert. In other cases, the problem submitted may be of a general nature, if the organisation is failing to achieve its principal purpose, and the skills required may concern organisational diagnosis, strategy, planning, co-ordination, information systems, and similar comprehensive issues. Or management may realise that improvements are needed, but the organisation is short of skills for planning, generating and implementing a difficult change process effectively. The consultant can provide these skills, making the client aware of organisational processes and relations, and helping him to define and pursue an appropriate strategy for change.

The fact that an organisation does not possess some knowledge or skill of which it could make good use is not unusual, and is not necessarily a sign of incompetence. The pace of change in the environment and in management technologies is so high, and the needs of organisations so diversified, that even very large and powerful organisations may be short of internal resources for dealing with certain new problems and seizing new opportunities. In such cases management consultants can be of help.

Intensive professional help on a temporary basis

In other situations, the requisite technical skills may be available in the organisation, but senior managers or staff specialists cannot be released for deep and sustained work on a major problem or project. The day-to-day running of business leaves them little time, and it is not easy to deal simultaneously with operational and conceptual issues. Consultants not only provide the time but will leave the organisation once the project is completed.

Impartial outside viewpoint

Even the best people within an organisation may be too influenced by their personal involvement and existing traditions and values to see a problem in its true light and think of feasible solutions. Because he is independent of the client organisation, and unaffected by its culture, a management consultant can provide a fresh viewpoint and be impartial in situations where no member of the organisation itself would be. Some managers have made it a standing practice to use a consultant as a sounding-board and review all important decisions with him before they are taken.

Justifying management decisions

From time to time consultants are approached with a request to undertake assignments and submit reports so that a manager can justify his decision by referring to the consultants' recommendations. In other words, a manager may have determined his aims and have reached his own decision, but wants to be able to say that he is putting into effect suggestions made by an independent consultant.

A consultant who accepts such an assignment is pulled into the hidden and intricate world of in-company politics. His report will have a political role in addition to the technical message it carries. This role may be constructive and useful, for example, if a manager is facing strong resistance to changes that the organisation will have to make anyhow, and needs to refer to the consultant's authority. However, it can also happen that a consultant falls into a trap and provides a report that is misused for in-company politics, and for defending vested individual or group interests. An independent and impartial assessment of every situation helps the consultant to avoid being used as an easy scapegoat.

Learning through consulting

"The only work that is really worth doing as a consultant is that which educates — which teaches clients and their staff to manage better for themselves," said Lyndon Urwick, one of the main contributors to the development of management consulting. In the modern concept of consulting this dimension is strongly emphasised. Many clients turn to consultants, not to find a solution to one distinct problem, but to acquire the consultant's special technical knowledge (e.g. in environmental analysis, business forecasting or using microprocessors for management information) and the methods he uses in identifying problems and implementing changes (interviewing, diagnosis, communication, persuasion, feedback, evaluation and similar skills). Consulting assignments become learning assignments: the purpose is to bring new competence into the organisation and help managers and staff to learn from their own experience. It is often stressed that in this way "organisations are helped to help themselves". This is a two-way exchange, since by helping his clients to learn from experience a management consultant enhances his own knowledge and competence.

The learning effect of consulting is probably the most important one. The choice of the consulting methods and the degree of the client's involvement can increase or reduce this effect. We shall, therefore, pay considerable attention to this aspect in our guide.

Benefits should exceed costs

In addition to the technical and learning dimension there is, too, the financial issue to be considered when consultants are used. Their service is not free, and a major consulting project may be a costly venture. The relationship between costs and benefits is an important factor in deciding on the use of a consultant. In principle, this use is justified only if the benefits are higher than the costs. This looks obvious. However, in many cases the costs and benefits are not properly assessed, and it is not clear whether the assignment was really beneficial from the economic and financial point of view. Further comments on this point will be made later, when the planning and evaluation of consulting assignments are discussed in chapters 7, 9 and 11.

1.3 Who uses consultants?

Management consulting as a professional service and method for implementing change is not confined to a particular type of organisation and economic or business situation. In the course of its development, consulting has been spreading to new areas of human activity, new countries and new regions.

Ailing or excellent organisations?

There was a time when turning to a consultant was viewed as a last resort and an admission of incompetence and inability to handle the situation with the organisation's own resources. Such an attitude still persists in quite a few organisations. So long as business is as usual, spending money on consultants is seen as wasting it. If business deteriorates, the pressure of events may be so strong that reluctantly a consultant is brought in, but it may then be rather late. No wonder that consultants are still regarded by some managers mainly as "trouble-shooters", "company doctors", "business healers" and the like.

This attitude contrasts with the current practice of many well-managed and generally successful business corporations. Although they possess considerable managerial and staff talent, even the largest corporations have made it their normal practice to use management consultants quite regularly. Experience shows that even strong and important organisations have developed many ideas for action and have seized major business opportunities with the help of consultants.

Starting from the quality or level of the situation faced by a client organisation, the consultant may be asked to help to rectify a situation which has deteriorated (corrective problem), improve an existing situation (progressive problem), or create a totally new situation (creative problem).

In a particular enterprise, for example, difficulties may have arisen in marketing. The volume of sales of a product which has been manufactured and sold successfully for several years suddenly drops and this starts causing serious financial difficulties for the organisation. The reasons are not very clear. Everybody agrees that this is an urgent problem calling for immediate action. It is a *corrective problem*. This means that, with almost the same resources, a more satisfactory performance was achieved in the past than is now the case. The problem is clearly defined if it is accepted that restoration of the original condition is all that is required. This is "trouble-shooting" indeed. The solution lies in tracking back the deviations that have taken place, and finding and correcting the reasons for them. But it is more likely that, when doing this, the consultant finds opportunities for ending with something better than the original.

Progressive problems represent another group. They involve the very common task of taking an existing condition and improving it. They may concern partial elements of management, such as accounting and cost control techniques, administrative procedures, or record keeping. For example, a company using historical costing feels that it should switch to standard costing to enhance the accurancy and efficiency of cost control and thus be in a better position to take timely cost-saving measures. The consultant may have models or standards used elsewhere and his main job will be to examine the conditions of their application, determine necessary adjustments, and help to persuade and train the staff affected by an improved procedure. But many progressive problems are less structured and more difficult to tackle. A client organisation may have a good potential for improving performance, but realistic targets have to be set and measures devised in various areas of the operation. The assignment may involve a whole range of technological, structural, personnel, financial, procedural and other changes.

Creative problems provide the consultant with the smallest amount of starting information. There may be little more than a desire for change and some bright ideas. This is often the case when an excellent corporation turns to a consultant. The purpose is not to solve an urgent problem or to prevent potential difficulties, but to find new areas of business, develop new services to customers, experiment with unconventional ways of motivating people, suggest joint ventures with foreign partners, and so on.

9

Needless to say, many assignments include elements of all three types of problem described above. While working on an apparently progressive type in a well-performing company, the consultant may discover that some corrective measures are needed first. Or a corrective problem may require an entirely new, creative approach, otherwise it is no longer possible to stop the process of continuing deterioration. In general, any situation should be seen in the perspective of future opportunities. If called on by an ailing organisation to deal with a corrective problem, the consultant will always ask whether rectification of a deteriorated situation is really what is needed, or whether instead the organisation should not look for new ways of defining its purpose and objectives, and for new strategies and clients. A basically corrective problem may often be turned into a progressive and creative one.

Beyond the business corporation

Management consulting had its origin in private business; the growth and diversification of consulting is interwoven with the development of *the business corporation*, and with the changes in the ways of doing business. As already mentioned, even the largest and most successful corporations find it useful to employ consultants and have become very skilful in using them effectively. There are consulting firms whose clients are mainly the Fortune 500 companies. A great deal of "repeat business" is undertaken: a large corporation, satisfied with the professional know-how and approach of a consulting firm, may turn to it many times over the years. In some consulting firms the volume of repeat business is as high as 70-80 per cent. Many corporations have their "permanent" consultants, use several consulting firms, and have learned how to benefit from the expertise that various consultants are able to offer.

In *a small enterprise*, the decision to use a management consultant may be a difficult one. The owner or manager may find such a professional service expensive, and he often does not see how an outsider could help in his unique situation. Nevertheless, the volume of consulting services provided to small firms has been growing. Some management consultants specialise in problems of small businesses, and in some countries subsidised consulting services are available to smaller firms as part of small-business development programmes.

A prominent trend in management consulting has been a rapid growth in the volume of work done for *the public sector*. Management consultants are increasingly used in central and local government, specialised government agencies and services, and public enterprises. In the United States, for example, several important consulting firms do as much as 30-40 per cent of their business in the government sector and some are worried by their growing dependence on government contracts. The figure is even higher in countries where the share of the public sector in economic activity is very important.

The main reason for this use of management consultants for public sector work is the desire of governments to draw from private business management expertise to raise the efficiency of government machinery and to combat the red tape and other chronic diseases of the public service. On the other hand, independent consultants have to learn enough about public policy and procedures to avoid transplanting concepts and methods that the public sector cannot use. In addition to using independent private consultants, most governments have now established their own consulting services in various forms and under many different names.

Finally, the widening scope for the use of management consulting services is well demonstrated by the growing number of assignments carried out in various *social organisations and agencies*. In their quest for efficiency and better service to clients, the social sectors have found their way to management consultants, who now work for hospitals, health-care administrations, social insurance agencies, universities, school administrations, religious organisations, trade unions, and so on.

The international scene

The use of consultants for work in countries other than their own has been another development trend with many implications. It was started by business corporations operating internationally, and pursued by governments and international organisations. A great deal of management consulting is provided as part of technical assistance projects, bilateral or multilateral. For example, the World Bank is a major user of consulting services, and many consulting organisations work for governments and businesses in developing countries in connection with technical projects financed from loans provided by the World Bank.

Some consulting firms have become real multinationals, with an important share of their income generated by work abroad, and with branch offices or subsidiaries in several countries and continents. More recently, the growing demand for consulting work has encouraged the development of a local consulting profession in the developing countries, in particular in countries undergoing rapid industrialisation.

The general trend

It is clear that demand for management consulting services comes from all sectors of human activity and from all types of organisation, because all are under growing economic and social pressure to improve their management and attain higher standards of performance and efficiency. It would be an exaggeration to say that management consultants influence the course of history. However, they have been the invisible hand behind some extremely important business and government decisions, and their interventions have helped to shape the future of powerful private and public organisations. Their total impact on business and public affairs has been considerable, although it will never be possible to express it in figures. The efforts to increase the professional standards of management consulting services are therefore of interest not only to the direct users of these services, but also to the society in which the users of consulting services operate.

1.4 Fundamentals of the consulting approach

This whole book is about the consulting approaches and methods applied to various types of management and business problems, organisations and environments. Indeed, there is an extremely wide range of consulting approaches, techniques, methods, modes and styles. This diversity is one of the exciting features of management consulting; it allows even clients with very peculiar problems and characters eventually to find a consultant who fits their organisation and personality.

However, consulting exhibits not only diversity but also certain common principles and methods. Some of them are quite fundamental; they are used by the vast majority of consultants. For example, psychological testing is a special fact-finding technique used only in certain personnel selection assignments. Some consultants are even opposed to this technique. In contrast, every consultant uses interviewing and has to be versed in report writing. Interviewing and report writing are fundamental consulting techniques.

In a nutshell, an effective consulting approach suggests how to deal with two critical dimensions of change in client organisations:

(1) *a technical dimension*, which concerns the nature of the management or business problem faced by the client and the way in which this problem can be analysed and resolved;

(2) *a human dimension*, i.e. the relationship between the consultant and the client and the way in which people in the client organisation react to changes, and can be helped to plan and implement them.

For methodological reasons, this text will often deal separately with these two dimensions. In consulting practice they are not separated. Technical and human problems of management and business are inter-linked and the consultant's understanding of this point is one of his principal assets.

How to solve the client's technical problem

First, the consultant helps the client to deal with his problems from a technical point of view. The client expects from the consultant considerable technical expertise in the area involved, e.g. international financial operations, computerised inventory control, staff compensation systems, or strategic planning in the manufacturing of capital equipment. In dealing with the problem in hand the consultant applies a rigorous problem-identification and problem-solving method, which includes collecting, verifying and cross-checking facts, challenging assumptions and impressions communicated by the client, and subjecting all findings to thorough diagnosis. The consultant is equally methodical but also applies a wide range of creative techniques in searching for feasible new solutions, identifying and justifying the best alternative to be chosen by the client, devising action plans for the implementation of the proposals, and helping the client to organise and monitor implementation.

How to relate to the client organisation in planning and implementing changes

The second critical dimension of the consulting approach is an effective consultant-client relationship in planning and implementing changes. This has many facets. The consultant and the client have to clarify their respective roles, making sure that these are complementary, mutually supportive and fully understood by both parties. We shall see that the consultant can choose among several roles (or modes) depending on the nature of the problem and the experience and attitudes of the client. He aims at enlisting the client's collaboration at all stages of the assignment, so that the client participates actively and the final result of the assignment is a joint achievement, not merely the consultant's own.

The ultimate objective is to help the client to make progressive changes in his organisation. In helping to identify and solve specific technical problems the consultant therefore deals with human problems and human aspects of organisational change. Consultants are often called "change agents". This emphasises their helping role in identifying the need for change and in planning and implementing it. Since organisational change involves changing people, the consultant also deals with the psychology of change, helping the client to proceed in a way that does not create resistance to change, and, if necessary, to overcome this resistance.

An overview of the consulting process

The consulting process is the consultant's and the client's joint activity aimed at solving a distinct problem and implementing the desired changes in the client organisation. This process has a beginning (the relationship is established and work starts) and an end (the consultant departs). Between these two points the process can be subdivided into several basic phases. This helps both the consultant and the client to be systematic and methodical, proceeding from phase to phase, and from operation to operation, as they follow each other in logic and in time.

Many different ways of subdividing the consulting process, or cycle as some authors call it, into major phases can be found in literature. Various authors suggest models ranging from three to ten phases.[4] It is useful to use a simple *five-phase model*, including the following major phases: *entry, diagnosis, action planning, implementation* and *termination*. This model, shown in figure 1.1, will be used consistently in our book. Obviously, a universal model cannot be applied blindly to all problems, but it provides a good framework for structuring and planning particular assignments and projects. When applying the model to a concrete situation it is possible to let some phases overlap, e.g. implementation may start before action planning is completed. Or it is possible to cycle back from a later to an earlier stage. Thus evaluation serves not only for a final assessment of the results of the assignment and of benefits drawn from change (termination phase) but also for deciding whether to move back and take corrective measures. Every phase can be broken down into several sub-phases or parallel activities, and so on.

Figure 1.1   Phases of the consulting process

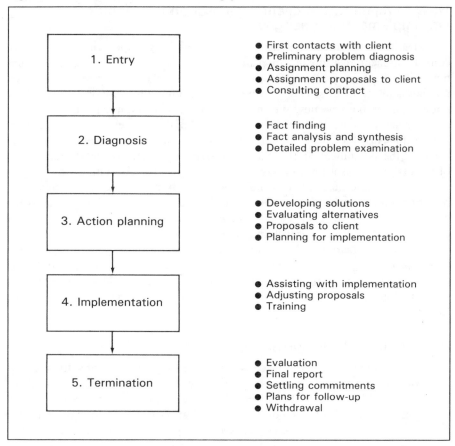

The reader will probably notice that our model of the consulting process is very similar to *problem-solving models*, whose various alternatives can be found in literature. Indeed, consulting *is* essentially a form of problem solving. The differences from other forms of problem solving are explained by the involvement of a consultant. A model of the consulting process also includes activities whereby the consultant enters and leaves the scene, as well as various aspects of the consultant-client interaction in the course of problem solving.

The reader may also have seen various *models of planned organisational change* and may be interested in comparing them with the model in figure 1.1. Here again, the consulting process can be viewed as a variant of the change process, one in which the need for change is identified and specific change measures prepared and implemented with a consultant's help. The process of planned change and the consulting process follow the same basic logic.

The consulting process will be examined in detail in chapters 7-11, but at this point it may be helpful to have short descriptions of its five basic phases.

Entry

In this phase the consultant starts working with a client. This phase includes their first contacts, discussions on what the client would like to change in his organisation and how the consultant might help him, the clarification of their respective roles, the preparation of an assignment plan based on preliminary problem analysis, and the negotiation and agreement of a consulting contract. It is a preparatory and planning phase. Nevertheless, it is often emphasised that this phase lays down the foundations for everything that will follow, since the subsequent phases will be strongly influenced by the quality of conceptual work done, and by the kind of relationships that the consultant will be able to establish with his client at the very begining.

In this initial phase it can also happen that an assignment proposal is not prepared to the client's satisfaction, or that several consultants are invited to present proposals but only one of them is selected for the assignment.

Diagnosis

The second phase is an in-depth diagnosis of the problem to be solved, based on thorough fact finding and fact analysis. During this phase the consultant and the client co-operate at identifying the sort of change that is required. Is the fundamental change problem technological, organisational, informational, psychological or other? If it has all these dimensions, which one is the crucial one? What attitudes to change prevail in the organisation: is the need for change appreciated, or will it be necessary to persuade people that they will have to change? The results of the diagnostic phase are synthesised and conclusions drawn on how to orient work on action proposals so that the real problem is resolved and the desired benefits obtained. Some possible solutions may start emerging during this phase.

Fact finding and fact diagnosis often receive the least attention. Yet decisions on what data to look for, what data to omit, what aspects of the problem to examine in depth and what facts to skip, predetermine the relevance and quality of solutions that will be proposed. Also, by collecting data the consultant is already influencing the client system, and people may already start changing as a result of the consultant's presence in the organisation.

Action planning

The third phase aims at finding the solution to the problem. It includes work on alternative solutions, the evaluation of alternatives, the elaboration of a plan for implementing changes and the presentation of proposals to the client for decision. The consultant can choose from a wide range of techniques, in particular if the client's participation in this phase is active. Action planning requires imagination and creativity, as well as a rigorous and systematic approach in identifying and exploring feasible alternatives, eliminating proposals that could lead to trivial and unnecessary changes, and deciding what solution will be adopted. A significant dimension of action planning is developing strategy and

15

tactics for implementing changes, in particular for dealing with those human problems that can be anticipated, and for overcoming resistance to change.

Implementation

Implementation, the fourth phase of consulting, provides an acid test for the relevance and feasibility of the proposals developed by the consultant in collaboration with his client. The changes proposed start becoming a reality. Things begin happening, either as planned, or differently. Unforeseen new problems and obstacles may arise and false assumptions or planning errors may be uncovered. Resistance to change may be quite different from what was assumed at the diagnostic and the planning stage. The original design and action plan may need to be corrected. As it is not possible to foresee exactly every relationship, event or attitude, and the reality of implementation often differs from the plan, monitoring and managing implementation is very important. This also explains why professional consultants prefer to be associated with the implementation of changes that they have helped to identify and plan.

This is an issue over which there has been much misconception and misunderstanding. Many consulting assignments end when a report with action proposals is transmitted, i.e. *before* implementation starts. For example, in the United States not more than 30 to 50 per cent of consulting assignments include implementation. If the client is fully capable of handling any phase of the change process by himself, and is keen to do it, there is no reason why he should use a consultant. The consultant may leave as early as after the diagnostic phase. Unfortunately, the decision to terminate the assignment after the action-planning phase often does not reflect the client's assessment of his own capabilities and his determination to implement the proposals without any further help from the consultant. Rather it mirrors a widespread conception of consulting according to which consultants do not have to achieve more than getting their reports and proposals accepted by the clients. Some clients choose it because they do not really understand that even a very solid consulting report cannot provide a full guarantee that a new scheme will actually work and the promised results will be attained. Other clients may be happy with it because what they really wanted was a report, not a change. We will return to these questions in chapter 10, suggesting various modes of the consultant's involvement in implementation.

Termination

The fifth and final phase in the consulting process includes several activities. The consultant's performance during the assignment, the approach taken, the changes made and the results achieved have to be evaluated by both the client and the consulting organisation. Final reports are presented and adopted. Mutual commitments are settled. If there is an interest in pursuing the collaborative relationship, an agreement on follow-up and future contacts may be negotiated. Once these activities are completed, the consultant withdraws from the client organisation and the consulting assignment or project is terminated by mutual agreement.

1.5 Relationship to training, research and information

Consulting is not the only service or intervention technique that helps to enhance managerial competence and organisational performance. Training, research and information services pursue the same ultimate objective in assisting management as consulting does, although they have their specific methodological approach. Their relationship to consulting is very close. Consultants make extensive use of training, research and information in working with clients, or in preparing for new assignments.

Consulting and training

Consulting is inseparable from training. As mentioned above, an effective consulting approach has a strong learning dimension. The client learns from the consultant. The consultant learns from the client; this helps the consultant to adjust his approach in the following phases of the assignment, and to accumulate experience for future assignments. The client may not realise it, but he does train the consultant!

Some learning takes place in every consulting assignment, but it may be only modest if it is the consultant who does the job by himself and hands the result over to the client. This is why in our book we will place so much emphasis on a collaborative relationship and on consulting modes that require the client's active involvement. The client does not learn by doing ordinary and routine tasks, but by undertaking, in collaboration with the consultant, meaningful tasks that are new to him, and by being able to see his problems from new angles.

Training is often used as an intervention technique to assist change and help people to cope with changes proposed by the assignment (see section 4.5). The consultant may suggest including distinct training events in the assignment. These can take the form of a seminar on data-collecting techniques, or on new developments in the technical area covered by the assignment. Extensive training programmes may be part of the implementation phase — for example, if major changes are being made in management information and control systems or in marketing strategy and techniques.

Many consulting organisations have gone further than that in offering training services to clients. Experience accumulated through various client assignments is very helpful in designing practically-oriented management training programmes. These can be regular programmes, or ad hoc management seminars and round tables. Consulting experience can be reflected in the programme content (focusing on issues that worry the clients most) and methodology (emphasising methods through which participants improve problem solving and other skills). Consulting reports provide a wealth of materials that can be used in the classroom as case studies, practical exercises, management games, checklists, in-basket exercises, and so on.

While training is an essential intervention technique of the consultant, consulting is very important to the professional trainer. Even if their primary function is not consulting, management training centres and institutes are more and more keen to do some consulting in connection with the training programmes they run. This is necessary for the reasons mentioned in the previous paragraph: to base training above all on practical experience and focus it on issues regarded as priority by the practitioners. In addition, in many situations training is not enough: the participants may get new ideas and learn some new skills, but they need more help if they are to start applying what they have learned. Problem-oriented training workshops can be used to make the participating managers aware of an effective consulting approach, identify problems that need to be resolved, and generate interest in working with a consultant following such a workshop. Management training institutions therefore encourage their training staff to do consulting and adopt various work arrangements to make this possible. Clearly, in these situations the trainers must also become competent in consulting skills.

Consulting and research

Many of the older-generation management consultants liked to stress that they were down-to-earth grass-root practitioners who had nothing in common with the researcher. This dichotomy, however, reflected a poor theoretical preparation of the consultant and a lack of practical purpose on the side of most academics, rather than a substantive conflict between the consulting and the research approach. Indeed, despite their differences (see table 1.1), research and consulting have a lot in common and can be very useful to each other.[5]

In dealing with practical management problems, consultants need to know the results of research and draw from them — for example, before recommending an incentive technique it is better to know whether any research has been made into the use of that technique in conditions similar to those experienced by the client. Consulting organisations increasingly encourage their members not only to be informed about published results of management research, but also to keep in touch with on-going research projects and with the leading researchers.

Research, then, can only benefit from close links with consulting. The data collected in client organisations by consultants can serve wider research purposes. Data from a number of organisations can be used for drawing general conclusions on sectoral or other trends, without infringing confidentiality. On becoming aware of this, many consulting firms have also gone into research. They have a formalised research programme, undertake contract research, and publish books based on their own research, or they co-operate on research projects with universities and individual researchers. Some consulting firms have gained the reputation of being strongly research-based. Business schools and research institutes are increasingly interested in testing and diffusing the results of their research through consulting assignments.

Table 1.1   Factors differentiating research and consulting

FACTOR	RESEARCH	CONSULTING
Problem	Mainly fashioned by researcher; more open-ended, especially in exploratory research	Mainly fashioned by client, sometimes on joint basis
Time scale	Usually flexible	More tight and rigid
End product	New knowledge and new theories + ? better practice	Better management practice
Ownership of information	Usually publicly available	Often confidential
Decision making	Focus may change at researcher's discretion subject to plan	Discretion limited to main task only
Academic rigour	Methodologically tight	Minimum level appropriate to problem
Evaluation	External − by peers in scientific community, policy-makers	Internal − by company

Methodologically, consultants learn a lot from researchers and vice versa. Action research is an example of research that is on the borders of research and consulting; it aims simultaneously at solving a meaningful practical problem and yielding new knowledge about the social system under study. Action research involves changing that which is being investigated; conventional research does not.

Consulting and information

Providing information to the client is one of the main undertakings of a consultant in every assignment. In some instances it is the only or the main contribution expected from him − for example, if the client is keen to compare his performance standards with those of other organisations, using data that the consultant can supply.

Indeed, in many cases it is enough if the consultant finds and presents information that permits the client to reorient work, make an investment decision, or decide that he wants to learn more about organisations achieving better results. Information by itself can have great power and strongly influence people who are information-minded and able to draw conclusions from it.

Consulting firms are depositories of a tremendous wealth of information and many have become real experts in collecting and processing information. Some consulting firms started viewing themselves as specialised data banks, thinking about new ways of working with information and using it to provide new services to clients. This area is now developing rapidly. It includes various types of information services, regular or ad hoc, whereby clients can keep in touch with practical and theoretical developments in areas vital to their businesses.

This is a useful direct service to clients, and a source of new contacts. A client may get new ideas from information thus obtained and ask the consultant to explore them further and help in putting them into effect.

Balanced portfolio of intervention methods

Management consultants tend to be pragmatic in deciding what range of services to offer to clients. Training is so close to consulting that, for reasons already explained, every consultant does some training and is also a trainer. There are valid reasons, too, for linking research and information activities to consulting. In certain cases an alternative choice applies — for example, a manager who has a problem may choose between collecting more information on the problem, attending a training programme where the problem area concerned will be explored in greater depth, or asking a consultant to help in solving the problem.

Practically-oriented training institutions look at their work methods in a similar way. Even if they are primarily in the business of training, and want to stay there, they find it difficult to do effective training without some involvement in consulting, research and information activities. This involvement may take many different forms.

Thus, the problem is not one of consulting *versus* training or other methods of professional help to managers, but one of mastering and applying with imagination a well-balanced portfolio of intervention methods. This does not mean that differences between consultants, trainers, researchers, and others in similar fields would have to disappear. Nevertheless, there is a clear trend towards drawing from other management professionals' methods and expertise, and towards combining the various intervention methods in a way likely to produce the best effect for the benefit of the client.

---

[1] F. Steele: *Consulting for organisational change* (Amherst, MA, University of Massachusetts Press, 1975); p. 3.

[2] P. Block: *Flawless consulting: A guide to getting your expertise used* (Austin, TX, Learning Concepts, 1981); pp. v and 2.

[3] L. E. Greiner and R. O. Metzger: *Consulting to management* (Englewood Cliffs, NJ, Prentice-Hall, 1983); p. 7.

[4] Frequently referred to is the Kolb-Frohman model, which includes the following seven phases: scouting, entry, diagnosis, planning, action, evaluation, termination. See D. A. Kolb and A. L. Frohman: "An organisation development approach to consulting" in *Sloan Management Review*, Vol. 12, No. 1, Fall 1970.

[5] The table is taken from R. Bennett: *Management research: Guide for institutions and professionals* (Geneva, International Labour Office, 1983), p.18. This book is useful to management consultants who want to get a good overview of organisation and methodology . of management research.

RANGE AND SCOPE OF CONSULTING SERVICES

2

2.1 A historical perspective

A historical perspective will help us to understand the present scope, strengths and limitations of management consulting. Where does management consulting have its historical roots? How far back can they be traced? What principal events and personalities have given the consulting business its current shape?

Management consulting has its origins in the industrial revolution, the advent of the modern factory, and the related institutional and social transformations. Its roots are identical with those of management as a distinct area of human activity and a field of learning. Consulting in or for management becomes possible when the process of generalising and structuring management experience attains a relatively advanced stage. Methods and principles applicable to various organisations and situations have to be identified and described and the entrepreneur must be pressed, and motivated, to seek a better way of running and controlling his business. These conditions were not fulfilled until the latter part of the nineteenth century, a period which saw the birth of the "scientific management" movement.

The pioneers of scientific management

There were a number of predecessors of scientific management. One of them was the American manufacturer Charles T. Sampson, who in 1870 reorganised the whole production process in his shoe-making factory in order to be able to staff it by unskilled Chinese labour. One year later, acting in a consulting capacity, Sampson passed on his experience to an owner of a laundry, who accepted the advice and applied the approach previously used by Sampson.[1]

The pioneers of scientific management, including Frederick W. Taylor, Frank and Lillian Gilbreth, Henry L. Gantt and Harrington Emerson, gave a major impetus to the development of consulting. Their technical and methodological approaches to simplifying work processes and raising workers' and plant productivity were not the same and in certain cases even conflicted with each other. However, they all believed in the application of the scientific method to solving production problems. They believed, too, in the benefit of combining several methods for disseminating their scientific approach and making sure that it would be used by the businessman. They were tireless in lecturing, making studies, writing books and articles, organising practical demonstrations, and providing advice in every possible way. Later in his life, Taylor chose to become a full-time management consultant.

These pioneering efforts gave rise to a very important strain in management consulting, one which has strongly marked the profession and influenced its image. Consulting that emerged from the scientific management movement focused mainly on factory and shop-floor productivity and efficiency, rational work organisation, time and motion study, eliminating waste and reducing production costs. This whole area was given the name of "industrial engineering". The practitioners, often called "efficiency experts", were respected for their drive, methodical approach and improvements achieved (which were often spectacular). But their interventions were also feared and detested by workers and trade unions due to their often ruthless approach.

The negative early image of some management consultants has changed considerably over the years. New areas of management and new types of problems were tackled and became a normal part of the consulting business, thus reducing the share of work in production and work organisation. Important changes in the social and labour-relations fields tended to limit the use of techniques unacceptable to the workers; negotiation became an indispensable method of handling many assignments affecting workers' and other employees' interests. However, the positive side of the efficiency expert's image has been very much preserved: consultants continue to be regarded as persons able to find new opportunities for saving resources and raising productivity even where others see none.

Towards a general management approach

The limitations of the industrial-engineering and efficiency-expert approaches have led to a broadened interest in other aspects and dimensions of business organisations, and to the birth of new areas of consulting. One of the first, perhaps the first, consulting firm of the kind known today was established in Chicago in 1914 by Edwin Booz under the name "Business Research Services".

In the 1920s, Elton Mayo, with his Hawthorne experiment, gave impetus to research and consulting in human relations. Important consulting work in human resource management and motivation was started by Mary Parker Follett. Interest in more effective selling and marketing was fostered by people such as the Englishman Harold Whitehead, the author of *Principles of salesmanship* written in 1917. A number of consulting firms were established during the 1920s. These were increasingly able to diagnose business organisations in their totality, treating manufacturing and productivity problems in a wider perspective of sales and business-expansion opportunities.

Consulting in finance, including financing the enterprise and financial control of operations, also started developing rapidly. A number of the new management consultants had a background in accountancy and experience drawn from working with firms of public accountants. One such was James O. McKinsey, a protagonist of the general management and comprehensive diagnostic approach to a business enterprise, who established his own consulting firm in 1925.[2]

In the 1920s and 1930s, management consulting was gaining ground, not only in the United States and in Great Britain, but also in France, Germany, Czechoslovakia and other industrialised countries. Yet its volume and scope remained limited. There were only a few firms, prestigious but rather small, and their services were used mainly by the larger business corporations. The consultant remained unknown to the overwhelming majority of the small and medium-sized firms. On the other hand, assignment requests began coming from governments: this was the start of consulting for the public sector.

Consulting for governments, and for the army, played an important role during the Second World War. The United States in particular understood that the war was a major management challenge and that mustering the country's best management expertise was essential to winning on the battlefield. Also operations research and other new techniques, applied first for military purposes, rapidly found their way into business and public management, adding a new dimension to the services offered by consultants.

The golden years of consulting

Post-war reconstruction, the rapid expansion of business coupled with the acceleration of technological change, the emergence of new developing economies and the growing internationalisation of the world's industry, commerce and finance, created particularly favourable opportunities and demands for management consulting. This is the period in which most consulting organisations that exist today were established and in which the consulting business has attained the power and the technical reputation it enjoys at the present time. For example, PA, the largest consulting firm based in the United Kingdom, had only 6 consultants in 1943, but 370 in 1963 and over 1,300, based in 22 countries, in 1984. The American firm A. T. Kerney employed 49 professionals in 1950 and 500 in 1980. The total number of full-time management consultants was assessed as 50,000 in the United States by the end of the 1970s, three times the number that existed in the mid-1960s. In the United Kingdom, there are about 5,000 management consultants.

In this period, the expansion of management consulting has been impressive by any standard. However, a number of major qualitative changes have also occurred.

Service diversification. To meet their clients' needs and to attract clients from new sectors of economic and social activity, management consultants have developed varying strategies, offering new special services, specialising in particular sectors, or, on the contrary, providing a broad comprehensive package of services to the most demanding clients.

At the forefront of technical progress. In doing this, most management consultants have made it their policy to be associated with the latest developments in management and related fields that can interest their clients, and to offer a new sophisticated service before anyone else can do so. The computer business, the use of microcomputers in production management and accounting, and new communication technologies belong to such areas. Consultants do not hesitate to step out of the management field and deal with technology, communication systems, quality control, equipment design, economic studies and the like if this is of interest to clients and if it can enhance a consultant's competitive edge.

Aggressive business-promotion strategies. Competition in management consulting has greatly increased over the last 20 years. In addition to improving quality, management consultants have increased their aggressiveness in both searching for clients and trying to convince potential clients that they can offer a better service than others. This has brought about many developments in the advertising and marketing of consulting services.

The "Big Eight" come on the scene. A major development has been the new attitude of the Big Eight public accounting firms towards management consulting. Considered for several decades as incompatible with professional accounting and auditing, management consulting started being promoted vigorously by the Big Eight in the early 1960s, producing 15-20 per cent of their income, and in some cases even more, in the 1980s.[3]

Continued internationalisation. All larger and many smaller consulting firms continued to internationalise their operations in searching for new markets, adapting to the changes in international economy, and taking advantage of the new opportunities for consulting in the less developed countries. In larger consulting firms, foreign operations may contribute 30-70 per cent of income. As already mentioned, new consulting firms have been established in developing countries.

Internal consulting. Consulting services provided under various names by internal units within private and public organisations are not a new phenomenon, but their volume and role has increased very considerably in the 1970s and 1980s. The internal consultant has become a regular actor on the management consulting stage.

Progress in the methodology of consulting. Great efforts have been made to increase the long-term benefits derived by clients from consulting assignments, by perfecting the methodologies applied at all stages of the consulting process. Greater emphasis has been placed on clients' active participation in assignments, the development of clients' own problem-solving skills, and on the need for clients to learn from every consulting assignment generally.

Increased clients' competence in using consultants. Many organisations, private and public, have become real experts in using consultants effectively. They have developed their own criteria and methods for selecting consultants, monitoring their interventions, learning from their approach and evaluating results. The progress made by consulting would not have been possible without these improvements on the clients' part.

2.2 Range of services provided

Today's management consulting professionals can be asked to help with any type of management problem in any sort and size of organisation. If new problems appear and new needs are identified, it is more than certain that some management consultant in one country or another will immediately make an effort to become an expert in such a new field.

There have been several attempts to list and classify the areas covered by management consultants.[4] Increasingly, the professional associations of consultants are interested in such lists, both to define areas from which they accept members and to be able to provide information on the types of services available from members. The publicity and information booklets of individual consulting firms normally give complete lists of areas of competence.

Areas and functions of management

A larger consulting firm would normally be able to cover a wide range of areas and functions of management, including general management, financial management, production organisation and management, marketing and sales management, and personnel and human resource management and development. Some consulting organisations have developed and offer expertise in only one or a few of these areas, which may be due to technical reasons, to their limited size, or to a deliberate choice as regards service specialisation. Examples are consulting in corporate strategy and planning, market studies, project management, compensation systems, warehouse management, international business ventures, and so on.

Effective approaches to organisational change

Some consultants emphasise that their main strength is not in a detailed knowledge of a specific technical area or function, but in their ability to share with the client their effective work method — for identifying problems, devising action programmes for organisational change and performance improvement, and making sure that such programmes get implemented. They stress the learning dimension of their interventions, achieved through the closest possible association of the client and his personnel with the consultant's work. Some consultants have developed and offer to clients complete consulting and training methodologies and assistance in applying these packages to various types of situations.

However, effective approaches to organisational change are increasingly offered in combination with special knowledge and skills in areas mentioned in the previous paragraph.

Sectoral focus

Many consultants do their whole business for one sector, or have established sectorally specialised divisions. The reasons are both technical (the need for an intimate sectoral knowledge of technological processes, management and economics), and determined by marketing strategy. As some consultants put it: "If you develop a reputation as a sugar-industry consultant, you get sugar-industry clients." This is quite important in sectors that traditionally regard themselves as different from other sectors (e.g. the construction or mining industries) and are sceptical about the value of advice coming from outside the sector.

The sectoral focus in consulting reflects the structural changes in the economy. Originally, most consultants in the United States worked mainly for industrial and commercial enterprises. In today's consulting, work for the service sectors tends to be very important; this includes clients from banking and insurance, communications, transportation, community development, central and local government administration, general and technical education, health care, libraries, voluntary associations, leisure and entertainment. Similar trends can be observed in other industrialised countries, while in the developing countries most management consulting assignments concern manufacturing, and development projects in industry, energy, agriculture and infrastructure.

New types of service

Sectorally specialised consulting firms often provide their clients with a service package combining management and engineering consulting. In their efforts to be as useful as possible to their clients, management consultants in all countries have developed a number of new services in areas such as technical and managerial training, training of supervisory and office personnel, production and distribution of audio-visual training packages, computing services, collection and distribution of business information, psychological testing, opinion polls for market research, consumer taste surveys, advertising, packaging, sectoral economic and market studies, advice on investment opportunities, statistical work, and so on. Several consulting firms have moved into areas such as choice of technology, technology transfer, patents and licenses, product development and testing, design of control equipment, and similar fields. All these are closely related to management consulting, but some of them are clearly outside its traditional framework. As for the clients, what they are interested in is a helpful service package — and this can often best be provided by crossing the traditional barriers of subjects and disciplines.

2.3 Other consultants

Among the many fields in which consulting services are available, three are particularly close to management consulting: engineering, law and accounting. Not only is there considerable scope for collaboration and co-ordination of services, but management consultants can learn a great deal from the approach of those working in these fields, and perhaps even undertake assignments for them.

Engineering consultants

Engineering consultants (consulting engineers) constitute a vast and diversified sector providing technical expertise in areas such as civil engineering, the construction industry, architecture, land and quantity surveying, town and country planning, project planning and supervision, mechanical engineering, chemical engineering, patent services, computer science and systems and so on.

The link between management consulting and consulting in engineering has traditionally been very close and the boundaries are in many cases blurred. Some engineering consultants also deal with organisation and management questions, particularly in areas such as industrial or production engineering and control, quality management, maintenance, feasibility studies, plant design, or project design, implementation and supervision. On the other hand, production management consultants with an engineering background can deal with various production and productivity improvement problems that are of both a managerial and a technological nature.

New sorts of interdisciplinary possibilities have arisen in connection with the increasing penetration of computer and microprocessor technology into management and production processes; these new technical developments will have a strong impact on the scope of services required from management consultants in the future and can very well increase the area of co-operation and joint efforts between engineering consultants and management consultants.

Legal consultants

The law affects business and management in many respects and the part played by legal advice to management has greatly increased. Such advice may be required on questions governed by company law, labour law, taxation law, civil law and other special areas of legislation. Legal advice becomes critically important in international business, for instance with respect to the legal requirements for opening businesses and those concerned with personnel policies and industrial relations practices of a host country. Numbers of organisations have a permanent legal adviser or counsel; he may be a staff member and operate as an internal consultant. Others rely on outside counsel. In either case there is wide scope for interaction and collaboration.

Management consultants collaborate very closely with legal consultants on many issues with legal aspects and implications. The initiative often comes from the legal side: legal counsel may feel the need for management or financial advice in dealing with a legal problem, and so turn to a management consulting firm, which may or may not already be on contract to a mutual client. However, the management consultant can also perceive the need for legal advice in a given situation and seek consultation with internal counsel or recommend to the client engaging outside legal counsel.

Chartered accountants and auditors

It can be argued that auditing in the narrow sense of the term, that is, checking and certifying accounting records and financial reports, is not consulting. However, it is only a small step to consulting. If an auditor makes a value judgement on the client organisation's records and reports or recommends an improvement — and this is what is increasingly required from him in many countries — he acts as a consultant whether he calls himself a consultant or not. Auditing often prepares the ground for important management consulting projects; this was well perceived by accounting firms when they decided to enter management consulting.

2.4 Generalists and specialists

One of the oldest issues debated by the observers of consulting is whether both generalists and specialists have the right to be called management consultants. Some contend that only an all-round generalist is a real management consultant, while a specialist can be an industrial engineer, a financial analyst, an expert in compensation techniques, or an industrial psychologist, but not a management consultant. Others object to this, pointing out that generalists lack the in-depth knowledge required to solve problems in today's business; therefore to be really useful a consultant must be a specialist.

The history and the current profile of the profession indicate that both generalists and specialists have their place in management consulting. The issue is not generalists *versus* specialists, but how to combine generalist and specialist skills and perspectives to achieve a better total effect. This combination has several facets.

Specialist work viewed from a generalist perspective

To manage an organisation is an interdisciplinary and multifunctional task, and measures taken in one specialist area relate to other areas. Therefore a management consultant will always try to view specific (and often narrow) problems, requiring the intervention of a specialist, in a wider context. To be a good consultant, the specialist has to be able to look at the problem from the generalist point of view. He must be able to apply basic diagnostic and other methods common to all skilled consultants. This is one of the main objectives of theoretical and practical training in a consulting firm.

Generalists and specialists co-operate

It would be unrealistic to require every consultant to be both a complete specialist and a generalist. A few talented and experienced individuals do achieve this. However, in most consulting organisations there is some division of work between those who are primarily specialists (and keep up to date in a special area of knowledge and its applications) and those who are generalists (who deal with several areas of management and focus on their interaction, co-ordination and integration).

The so-called generalists prepare and co-ordinate global assignments requiring combined specialist and generalist interventions. They normally take care of preliminary organisational diagnoses, negotiations with clients, assignment planning and co-ordination, drawing conclusions from specific observations made by specialists, presenting final proposals to clients, and so on. Supervisory and managerial functions in consulting are often in the hands of the generalists.

Some assignments are totally or primarily in the general management field and are undertaken by senior generalists. They concern issues such as corporate policy and strategy, leadership and management style, organisational structure, mergers, turnarounds and the like. Most consulting for small businesses is done by generalists, capable of advising the client on the business in its totality. Clients expect that the generalist will suggest the participation of a specialist consultant whenever such a need is identified, just as they expect that the specialist will exercise self-discipline and refrain from giving advice in areas beyond his special competence.

Trend towards specialisation

In today's management consulting there is a pronounced trend towards greater specialisation. This trend concerns the service specialisation of the consulting firms (of all sizes, including individual practitioners) first of all. Increasingly, clients are interested in working with firms that do not present themselves as *universal* experts in solving business problems, but possess the right specialist knowledge and expertise — e.g. in the industrial sector or functional area concerned. Many firms have started rethinking their profile to comply with this requirement.

Furthermore, management consulting firms have started modifying their internal staff structure, that is, the number and the respective roles of the specialists and generalists employed. There are more and more assignments that clients wish to be undertaken by a specialist, and if a firm does not have full-time employment for such a specialist, it will employ him part-time, or borrow his services from another firm when necessary. However, many of these specialists, highly competent in their technical fields, urgently need to widen their outlook and improve their understanding of the functions of the total organisation.

As for all-round generalists, their role in dealing with interdisciplinary and multifunctional problems will remain important. But there are various degrees of generalisation, and the trend seems to be towards generalists who do not try to deal with all kinds of situations but become proven experts in certain sectors (health, transportation) or types of problems (mergers and acquisitions, diagnosing and assisting organisations in difficulties).

2.5 Main types of consulting organisations

The diversity of the clients and markets served, technical services provided, approaches taken and personalities involved, is reflected in the wide range of types of management consulting organisations. Without going into details concerning their legal set-up and internal structuring, which will be covered in chapter 26, we will now review the main types.

Large multifunctional consulting firms

A consulting firm employing several hundred professionals can be considered as large, but there are a few giants with over 1,000 consultants on their staff. Most of them operate as multinational firms, with branch offices in 20 or more countries. Their size permits them to deal with a wide range of clients and most complex management problems; they are sometimes referred to as "full-service management consulting firms" providing "total service packages". They prefer to serve large clients. They also tend to exhibit some special skills, which makes them different from each other, e.g. they may be known for possessing special sectoral expertise and have important sectorally specialised departments.

Management advisory services of major accounting firms

Management advisory services (MAS) established as divisions of major accounting firms are in fact similar to large multifunctional consulting firms, which they match in size and in level and range of expertise. They benefit from the environment of a major accounting firm in terms of both expertise and assignment opportunities. Some of them emphasise that they are not keen to undertake just any type of assignment, but rather those that "would be expected from a reputable professional accounting firm". This, however, tends to be interpreted very liberally and MAS divisions also operate in areas such as behavioural science, personnel management and career development.

Small and medium-sized consulting firms

This group embraces a variety of organisations, ranging from a few to 50-100 consultants. Obviously a firm small by American standards can be very large in a smaller developing country. Their prevailing technical profiles include:

- general management consulting for small and medium-sized firms in a limited geographical area;
- specialist management consulting services in one or a few technical areas, such as corporate strategy, personnel administration, job evaluation, production control systems, marketing, sales management, office management, and so on;
- consistent specialisation in one or a few industrial or service sectors, e.g. urban transport, textiles, printing industry, insurance.

Special technical service organisations

A number of organisations, usually those with a strong mathematical, computer science, operations research or econometrics background, offer special consulting services in areas such as strategic studies, model building, forecasting of consumer demand, systems analysis and design, plant and office automation, and others. Some of them are also referred to as "think-tank" type organisations. They may be independent, or associated with a computer firm, a technological university, or a research institute.

Consulting divisions in management institutions

To foster local management consulting capabilities and link management teachers and trainers with the world of practice, a number of management and productivity institutes and centres, primarily in developing countries, have established consulting services to private and public organisations. Often this has been done with technical assistance from international organisations and with the involvement of experienced consultancy firms from other countries. The development problems of these "institutional" units will be discussed in more detail in chapter 29.

Sole practitioners

The existence of thousands of sole consulting practitioners demonstrates that, despite competition and aggressive marketing by larger organisations, there is plenty of interest in working with independent consultants. These may be generalists, emphasising their broad management experience, problem-solving and behavioural skills, or specialists working in a narrow technical area. Their strength is in a highly personalised and flexible approach, more difficult to apply consistently in a large consulting unit. The services of a senior individual practitioner will also be less expensive, because he can avoid many of the overhead costs of a larger organisation. Many clients enjoy the opportunity to entrust the whole assignment to a very senior person, one who in a larger firm would probably work as a project leader, supervising the work of several more junior consultants.

Sole practitioners are often informally connected with other colleagues and so can team up to undertake larger and more complex assignments, or can recommend another person for work outside their own area of competence. Most of them consult for smaller enterprises, but even larger enterprises sometimes turn to sole practitioners when there are smaller assignments in particular functional or subject areas.

The problem is that, alongside highly experienced and committed individuals, this group also includes some mediocre consultants and it is not always easy to find out who these are.

The "consulting professors"

While a sole practitioner makes his living from consulting, there are management professors, lecturers, trainers and researchers whose principal job is not consulting, but who are involved in it on a part-time, though fairly regular, basis. They may undertake longer projects and be released for these by their employers for several months, or provide ad hoc advice on management issues which are quite significant, but which do not require extensive consulting time. Some full-time consultants do not regard the "professor" as a real management consultant. This, however, may be a short-sighted view. Experience has shown that outstanding benefits can be drawn from combining teaching with consulting (see also section 1.5). If a professor of management is unable to provide sensible advice on a practical management problem, it is probable that something is also wrong with his teaching.

Non-traditional suppliers of consulting services

A new group of suppliers of management consultant services has emerged in recent years. This group is rather heterogeneous but has one common characteristic: its original and main function is something other than consulting, but consulting is viewed as a profitable addendum to its products and services. The group includes, among others:

— suppliers and vendors of computer and communication equipment;
— computer software houses;
— commercial and investment banks, brokers, insurance companies and other organisations in the finance sector;
— suppliers of equipment and turn-key projects in energy, transportation, drinking water, irrigation and other utilities;
— many other organisations that have turned their internal management service groups into external consulting services.

2.6 Internal consultants

An internal consulting unit is one which is established within an organisation — a national or international business corporation, a public utility, a government ministry or department — to provide consulting services to other units of the same organisation. Definitions and delimitations are not very precise. These services are given many different names, but the term "management services" prevails.[5] They can be found at different places in the organisational structure. Some of them are consulting services in the full sense of the term — they have a mandate to intervene in an advisory capacity at the request of a senior manager, or a unit manager within the organisation. In other cases, consulting is one of the staff functions, and the units concerned are also responsible for developing and maintaining accounting and information systems, records and reporting procedures, organisational circulars, staff development programmes, and other similar functions.

The current trend

The growth of internal consulting has been impressive in recent years. Internal units undertake many types of assignment which used to be given to external consultants. To have some sort of internal management consulting service has become common practice in larger business corporations; multinational corporations have large and versatile consulting units, available both to headquarters and to foreign subsidiaries. These units are staffed with technically competent specialists and generalists, some of whom have experience with external management consulting or accounting firms. The same trend can be observed in government administrations.

Internal consultants started establishing their own professional associations, and several professional bodies of external consultants have recognised them. For example, in 1976, the Institute of Management Consultants in the United Kingdom agreed that the term *independent practice* "shall include consultants engaged as in-house consultants who meet the required standards of knowledge, experience and competence and are free at all times to offer objective and independent advice".

The critics

There are many critics of internal consulting. The main criticism comes from some larger consulting firms, which contend that internal consulting can be a useful staff function, but does not deserve to be called management consulting. They challenge the internal consultants' independence and objectivity and criticise their lack of exposure to different situations in various companies which it is believed leads to in-breeding. Also, it is said, only a large firm or government department can really afford a sufficiently important and competent internal unit for consulting work. This criticism does not seem to be shared by organisations that build up their own internal consulting services.

Why such an interest?

First of all, the rapid growth of internal consulting is a recognition of the power of the consulting approach. It is only logical that, having appreciated the technical and methodological advantages of consulting, businesses and governments want to make more use of this approach. Many of them have found that an internal consulting service is one way of achieving it; for example, consulting is thus made accessible to many internal units and is available for dealing with problems where previously consultants would not have been used.

Further technical reasons for retaining an internal consultant are quick availability, an intimate knowledge of the organisation's internal practices, work and management style, culture and politics (hence sensitivity and a more rapid orientation in any work situation), and confidentiality. Internal consulting is often thought to be more appropriate for problems that require a deep knowledge of the highly complex internal relations and constraints in large organisations. In governments, they may be given priority for national security and interest reasons.

The cost factor is by no means negligible. Because of reduced overheads, travel and other expenses, even a well-paid internal consultant will cost 30-50 per cent less than an external one — if the company has enough employment for him.

Independence and other problems

Independence and objectivity certainly represent a problem in some cases. This occurs if the management of the organisation and the internal consultants fail to clarify the roles and mutual responsibilities of client and consultant within an organisation, if consultants are used for anything that comes into an executive's mind, and if they know that they have to please top management or their direct client instead of giving an impartial view. An internal consulting service which has low status and has no access to top management will not be able to deal with higher-level and interfunctional problems and its recommendations will lack credibility and authority.

If the role and status of internal consulting are properly defined and respected, the independence, objectivity and credibility of this service can be considerably enhanced.

Combining internal and external consulting

The use of internal consultants is not a passing fad, nor will it replace the use of external consultants. The latter will continue to be preferred in situations where an internal consultant does not meet the criteria of impartiality and confidentiality, or lacks expertise. However, it is difficult to contest that internal consulting has a definite role to play, and its obstinate opponents would do well to stop denigrating its potential.

In a growing number of cases, assignments are entrusted to joint teams of external and internal consultants. This is a technically interesting arrangement: it can reduce costs; it helps external consultants to learn quickly about the client organisation; it facilitates implementation; and it contributes to the training of internal consultants.

Many external consultants enjoy this way of working and regard internal consultants as useful technical partners. In many situations it is tactically better if proposals are endorsed by an internal unit, or are presented by this unit, than if they represent only an outsider's view. Internal consultants are more and more involved in defining terms of reference for external consultants, establishing short-lists for selecting consultants, making the selection, negotiating the terms of contracts, discussing recommendations, and monitoring implementation.

An interesting way of increasing the competence and credibility of internal consultants is to involve them in external consulting. For example, some management services units in electricity corporations, railways and other public utilities have developed performance improvement and staff training programmes that are of interest to public utilities in other sectors or countries; and in-company management services units in various sectors have done a great deal of work on project and systems design, consulting and training for projects in developing countries.

Helping relationship within an organisation

Besides the activities of internal consulting units, there are many other opportunities for making effective use of the helping relationship within organisations. Examples are advisory missions of managers and staff to other subsidiaries and plants within a corporation, temporary task and project groups, short-term detachments, and so on. Some of these forms will be described in sections 4.3 and 4.5, when organisational forms and interventions for managing and assisting change are discussed. They are often used in connection with a consulting project carried out by an external or internal consulting unit.

This sort of helping activity is not normally referred to as consulting. However, it tends to produce better results if the individuals involved are familiar with principles and methods of professional consulting.

2.7 The future prospects

The previous sections have reviewed a number of current developments in management consulting. Will these trends continue in future years? It is difficult to predict the future of professional services in areas where change is as dramatic as in technology, business and management. Yet management consultants seem to be increasingly concerned about the future, trying to anticipate new opportunities, avoid past errors and prepare for new roles in helping clients to cope with change.

This shift in the consultants' strategic thinking was triggered off by the world-wide recession at the outset of the 1980s. The recession provided an "acid test": resources for using external consultants became much scarcer in many organisations, clients became more selective and demanding, and assignments that were not addressing basic issues of business strategy and efficiency became difficult to sell. The growth of many consulting firms slowed down, some firms disappeared from the scene, and others had to merge, restructure operations and look seriously into their own efficiency. Once again, the leading consulting firms proved to be adaptable and dynamic enough in changing their service portfolio, organisation and operating methods. All in all, the recession rendered a useful service to the consultants who had to examine critically their real achievements and weaknesses and become aware of conditions under which management consulting can be a prosperous profession in the long term.

An interesting discussion on the current and future trends in management consulting took place at the 1984 conference of the European Federation of Management Consulting Organisations (FEACO). The study submitted to the conference mentioned that in the past "management consulting firms have proven themselves rather poor at predicting change and preparing themselves for change, but very agile in adapting to change when it really takes place".[6] Put in other terms, most firms used to be reactive, not pro-active. Equally interesting are the views of several protagonists of the consulting profession in the United States, compiled by Jim Kennedy in *The future of management consulting*.[7]

By and large, despite some words of caution, an optimistic note prevails in the management consultants' views of the future. The unprecedented pace of environmental change is regarded as the principal factor that will generate a continuing demand for consulting services. There are likely to be literally unlimited opportunities for services helping business and government clients to keep pace with environmental changes, and to adapt organisational strategies and operations to these changes. Services concerned with the application of new computer and communication technologies to management, manufacturing and distribution will be in particularly high demand for many years to come. However, the changes occurring in public policies, international business and competition, financial markets, industrial relations, employment patterns, social legislation, environmental protection and similar, will also create many new opportunities for management consultants.

Consulting approaches and techniques will put ever more emphasis on implementation, on active participation of the client in all stages of the assignment, and on developing the client's own diagnostic and problem-solving abilities. However, there will be many clients whose implementation capabilities are strong enough, and who will be looking mainly for new information, ideas and suggestions on how to make their business more competitive. Helping clients to cope with the information explosion will be a major task of management consulting, in many cases perhaps the principal task.

The growth areas of consulting will also include consulting to small and medium-sized businesses and work for social-service sectors, where the use of consultants was less common in the past. Consultants must be able to follow this trend not only by adapting their service packages and intervention techniques to the needs of these sectors, but also by keeping costs under control. While growing costs of consulting services have already become a matter of some concern to larger business firms, these costs risk becoming prohibitive and make the consultants' expertise inaccessible to many smaller enterprises and non-profit organisations. New formulas for providing consulting and training services will therefore need to be developed in order to slow down the growth of costs and fees. The deterrent example of the rocketing costs of medical services should not be followed!

Finally, management consultants in many countries seem to agree that a successful consulting organisation of the future will exhibit the following characteristics above all:

- it will be *innovative and flexible* in choosing and adapting its service portfolio; acquiring new capabilities; looking for new products and markets; applying new intervention methods; and restructuring operations;
- it will be *committed to high professional standards* in respect of service quality and staff integrity, and in making sure that the client always gets what he is paying for.

With this in mind, the following chapters will guide the reader through the main principles and methods of management consulting.

[1] For a more detailed fine account of the history of management consulting see H. J. Klein: *Other people's business: A primer on management consultants* (New York, Mason-Charter, 1977); and P. Tisdall: *Agents of change: The development and practice of management consultancy* (London, Heinemann, 1982).

[2] See W. B. Wolf: *Management and consulting: An introduction to James O. McKinsey* (Ithaca, NY, Cornell University, 1978).

[3] The "Big Eight" include the following international accounting firms: Arthur Andersen; Arthur Young; Coopers and Lybrand; Deloitte Haskins and Sells; Ernst and Whinney; Peat, Marwick, Mitchell; Price Waterhouse; and Touche Ross. See M. Stevens: *The Big Eight* (New York, Macmillan, 1981).

[4] For example, J. H. Fuchs has listed 100 areas of management consulting competence, grouped under 10 broader headings. See the appendix in J. H. Fuchs: *Making the most of management consulting services* (New York, AMACOM, 1975). The Management Consultants Association in the United Kingdom recognises, for the purpose of membership, 63 fields of consulting activity grouped under the following seven headings: organisation development and policy formation; production management; marketing, sales and distribution; finance and administration; personnel management and selection; management information systems and EDP; economic and environmental studies. There have been several other attempts to classify management consulting services in compiling directories of consultants.

[5] A study of internal consulting reported by R. E. Kelley found that internal consultants worked under 96 different job titles, reported to superiors holding 57 different job titles, and were found in every major function within organisations. See R. E. Kelley: "Should you have an internal consultant?" in *Harvard Business Review*, Nov.-Dec. 1979. On internal consulting, see also K. E. Albert: *How to be your own management consultant* (New York, McGraw-Hill, 1978); and F. Steele: *The role of the internal consultant: Effective role-shaping for staff positions* (Boston, MA, CBI Publishing Co., 1982).

[6] *A study of the management consulting profession 1960-84*, presented by the Finnish national consultants' association (LJK) and the consulting firm Mec-Rastor to the 1984 professional conference of FEACO in Helsinki. The debate at the conference is summarised in J. Marcure: "World-wide developments in management consulting" in *Journal of Management Consulting*, Vol. 1, No. 4, Fall 1984.

[7] J. H. Kennedy (ed.): *The future of management consulting* (Fitzwilliam, NH, Consultants News, 1985). See also J. Berry: "The consultants wake up to human resources" in *Human Resource Management*, Fall 1983; and D. A. Tierno: "Growth strategies for consulting in the next decade" in *Sloan Management Review*, Winter 1986.

THE CONSULTANT-CLIENT RELATIONSHIP

3

The consulting process involves two partners — the consultant and his client. The client has decided to purchase a professional service under certain terms — for example, for an agreed number of days and a daily fee. During this time, the consultant's expertise will be fully available to him, and in theory it should be easy to put this expertise to work on the problem which is of concern to the client. It is fair to assume that both the client and the consultant are keen to achieve the same objective.

The reality is infinitely more complex. The consultant remains an external person to the organisation, someone who is supposed to achieve a valid result in the client organisation without being part of its administrative and human system. Quite independently of its technical relevance and quality, the consultant's advice may or may not be understood and accepted by the client. Rejection can take many forms. The history of consulting records thousands of assignments whose excellent reports have been buried in managers' desks and never implemented, although they were formally accepted. This underlines the critical importance of creating and maintaining *an effective consultant-client relationship.*

Experience shows that building this relationship is not easy. To achieve success, both consultants and clients ought to be aware of the human and other factors that will affect their relationship, and of the errors to be avoided when working together on the assignment. They must be prepared to make *a special effort* to build and maintain a relationship that makes the effective intervention of an independent professional possible. There is no alternative.

3.1 Defining expectations and roles

To begin with, the client and the consultant may look differently at both the expected outcome and the ways of carrying out the assignment. The client may have only a vague idea of how consultants work and he may be slightly suspicious — possibly he has heard about consultants who try to complicate every issue, require more information than they really need, ask for more time in order to justify longer assignments, and charge exorbitant fees. But even if there is no suspicion, there is a risk of misunderstanding.

Joint problem definition

First, the problem for which the consultant was brought in needs to be well defined. A manager who wants to call for a consultant's help should not merely recognise a need for such help, but define the problem as he sees it, as precisely as he can. In many organisations, top management would not even consider using consultants unless presented with a clear description of the problem.

Before accepting the assignment, the consultant must be sure that he can subscribe to the client's definition of the problem. With the exception of the most simple and clear cases, he wants to be able to reach his own conclusion as to what the problem is and how difficult its solution might be.

There are many reasons why the consultant's definition of the problem might differ from the client's. Frequently managers are too deeply immersed in a particular situation, or have created the problem themselves. They may perceive the symptoms but not the real issue. They may also prefer the consultant himself to "discover" certain significant aspects of the problem.

Comparison of the client's and consultant's definition of the problem lays down the basis of sound working relations for the whole duration of the assignment. It requires discussion. Both the consultant and the client should be prepared to make corrections to their initial definition of the problem and to agree on a joint definition. But this joint definition should not be considered as final. Once the assignment has started, detailed diagnostic work may uncover new problems and impose a redefinition of what was originally agreed.

Results to be achieved

Secondly, the consultant and the client should clarify what the assignment should achieve and how this achievement will be measured. This may require an exchange of views on how each party regards consulting, how far the consultant should go on working on an agreed task, and what his responsibility to the client is. As mentioned in section 1.4, there is often a misunderstanding about the consultant's role in implementation. He may be keen to participate in it but, from previous assignments undertaken by other consultants, the client may be used to receiving reports with action proposals, and to deciding on implementation only after the consultant has left. If possible, the consultant will try to be involved in implementation. If cost is what worries the client, the consultant's presence during implementation can be a light one (limited to short visits from a team leader, to review meetings for discussing the progress of implementation, and similar).

The consultant's and the client's roles

Thirdly, it is important to determine how the assignment will be conducted by the two parties. What roles will be played by the consultant and what by the client? What will be their mutual commitments? Who will do what, when, and how? Does the client want to obtain a solution from the consultant, or does he prefer to develop his own solution with the consultant's help? Is the client prepared to be intensely involved throughout the assignment? Are there specific areas that the consultant should cover himself without trying to involve the client? And vice versa? These and similar questions will clarify the client's and the consultant's conception of management consulting and of the roles that can be effectively played by consultants. The answers will define the strategy to be followed in order to make the assignment a success by both the client's and the consultant's standards.

During the assignment, many unforeseen events may occur and new facts may be uncovered so that it becomes necessary to review the original definition of expectations and roles. Both the client and the consultant should be alert to this possibility and be flexible enough to adjust their contract and work arrangements. For example, the client's staff may find at some stage that they can easily produce information or action proposals that the consultant was originally supposed to work out. Insisting on keeping to the initial definition of roles, although changed conditions require a new definition, may prove to be counter-productive.

3.2 Collaborative relationship

Different situations and client expectations lead to different definitions of the consultant's roles and intervention methods. Sections 3.4 and 3.5 will review a number of roles from which to choose. Nevertheless, whatever choice is made, the overriding objective should always be the creation and maintenance of *a true collaborative relationship*. This is a golden rule of consulting. The degree and form of client-consultant collaboration will differ from case to case, but there should always be a strong spirit of collaboration, characterised by a shared desire to make the assignment a success, by trust and respect, and by an understanding of the other partner's technical and human roles.

Some clients imagine that by actively collaborating with the consultant they would actually do the job themselves, paying the consultant a handsome fee for nothing. The consultant who insists on his client's collaboration is compared to "the guy who borrows your watch to tell you the time". Often the real will to collaborate is tested at the fact-finding stage. The client feels that he should not give the consultant all the data requested and even instructs his staff to withhold information. This shows that the need for active collaboration is not automatically perceived by every client and that various misconceptions may have to be dispelled.

In some countries the client's reluctance to give the consultant all information on the state of the business cannot be interpreted as a misunderstanding of consulting, or as the client's unwillingness to establish a collaborative relationship. Accounting and financial information may be regarded as strictly confidential by a local business and the consultant should not ask for it unless the assignment is in the area of finance. Clearly, it is not possible to provide sound advice on financial matters without having access to financial data . . .

The modern concept of consulting methodology assumes strong client collaboration for the following main reasons:

(1)   There are many things that the consultant cannot do at all or cannot do properly, if the client is reluctant to collaborate. This happens if the consultant is refused information or cannot exchange ideas with the right people.

(2)   Often higher management is unaware of all the competence existing in the organisation, and important strengths may be concealed from it. Through collaboration, consultants help clients to uncover and mobilise their own resources.

(3)   Collaboration is essential so that the client associates himself fully with the definition of the problem and with the results of the assignment. Consultants emphasise that their client must "own" the problem and its solution. The reason is that human systems often reject changes proposed from the outside. By collaborating on a solution the client is more likely to be committed to it and will not put all the responsibility on the consultant. This commitment will be not only rational, but also emotional. We all know that we tend to have different attitudes towards projects into which we have had to put long hours of hard work and a lot of energy, and to those which we are asked to apply without ever having been consulted on them.

(4)   Most importantly, unless the client collaborates in the assignment, he is unlikely to learn from it. Learning does not occur by defining terms of reference and accepting or rejecting a final report, but by joint work at all stages of the assignment, starting with problem definition and diagnosis, and ending with the implementation and the assessment of the results actually obtained.

3.3 The client system

With whom, then, and how, will the consultant collaborate? The client, in the widest sense of the term, is the organisation which employs the services of a consulting unit. There we have an institutional relationship. That is why many consultants can indicate in their references that their clients included IBM, BP or another important firm. But there are also clients in a narrower sense of the term — individuals or groups of persons in the client organisation who initiate the bringing in of the consultant, discuss the job with him, collaborate in the course of the assignment, receive reports and recommend to higher management whether or not to accept them, and so on. Often a number of managers, supervisors, staff members, workers and liaison officers will be directly involved in the assignment at its various stages, or affected by the conclusions reached. Here the consultant-client relationship is personalised and will be affected by psychological and other factors.

It should be noted that in professional advisory services the consultant-client relationship is always personalised. There may be a formal contract between the consulting firm and the organisation using its services. However, the delivery of the service occurs in a direct contact between persons acting on behalf of the two organisations. This is fundamental. A really productive relationship cannot be fully guaranteed by any legal contract between organisations; it will depend on the abilities and attitudes and on the "psychological contract" between the individuals directly involved.

Management consultants know that in working with client organisations they can discover highly complex and recondite relations. They can face conflicting expectations, hopes and fears, respect and disrespect, confidence and distrust. Information may be readily offered or deliberately concealed or distorted. Consultants refer, therefore, to "client systems", taking a systems view of the client organisation and trying to map out the network of relationships in which they are going to operate. This may show that the client system embraces only a part or an aspect of the client organisation. Within the client system, the consultant needs then to determine:

(1) who holds the real power for making decisions related to the assignment (at all stages);

(2) who has the main interest in the success or failure of the assignment;

(3) whose direct collaboration is essential.

Many consultants make the mistake of automatically considering and treating the man at the top as their main client. This upsets those people who know that they will have the main responsibility for implementing the conclusions reached, and that it is their work that will be affected, not that of the top manager. On the other hand, it may also be a great mistake to leave out the higher level manager, forgetting to keep him informed, and to ask for his guidance or support only when this becomes necessary.

During the assignment, the consultant continues to explore the client system and improve his understanding of the roles played by various persons. He does this because he cannot be sure that his original assessment of roles was correct, and also because assignments are living processes and shifts in role can occur at any moment. The appointment of a new manager can change the course of the assignment quite dramatically.

Some situations may be particularly intricate — e.g. if the consultant does not really know who the main client is and whom he should try to satisfy first of all. This may happen if top management recruits the consultant, but leaves it solely to a functional department to handle the job, if a consulting assignment is recommended and sponsored by a bank as a precondition of a loan to its client, or if a ministry sends consultants to a public enterprise. In these and similar situations, the consultant needs to clarify whether he is supposed to act as an inspector, an auditor, an informant, or a real management consultant. He should find out who "owns" the problem and is keen to be helped — this person or organisation will be his main client.

3.4 Behavioural roles of the consultant

This section examines the concept of the consultant's behavioural roles (consulting modes), very popular in literature on consulting. It tries to show, in a condensed form, the most typical and frequent consulting behaviours, and describe how the consultant relates to the client, what inputs he makes, and in what way and how intensively the client participates. It emphasises that the roles assumed depend on the situation, the client's expectations and the consultant's profile.

There is no shortage of different descriptions of consulting roles. We have found it useful to make a distinction between *basic roles*, which include the resource and the process role, and *a further refinement of the role concept*, in which many more roles or sub-roles can be visualised in order to facilitate the understanding of the various intervention modes used in consulting.

Basic roles: the resource and the process role

In *the resource role* (also referred to as an expert or content role), the consultant helps the client by providing technical expertise and doing something for and on behalf of the client; he supplies information, diagnoses the organisation, undertakes a feasibility study, designs a new system, trains staff in a new technique, recommends organisational and other changes, comments on a new project envisaged by management, and the like.

Management does collaborate with the resource consultant, but this collaboration may be limited to providing information on request, discussing the progress made, accepting or declining proposals, and asking for further advice in implementation. Management does not expect the consultant to deal extensively with the social and behavioural aspects of the change process in the organisation, although the consultant will have to be aware of these aspects.

In *the process role*, the consultant as the agent of change attempts to help the organisation to solve its own problems by making it aware of organisational processes, of their likely consequences, and of intervention techniques for stimulating change. Instead of passing on technical knowledge and suggesting solutions, the process consultant is primarily concerned with passing on his approach, methods and values so that the client organisation itself can diagnose and remedy its own problems.

Expressed in simpler terms, while the resource consultant tries to suggest to his client *what* to change, the process consultant suggests mainly *how* to change and helps the client to go through the change process and deal with human problems as they arise. Edgar Schein describes his detailed model of process consultation as "a role of activities on the part of the consultant which help the client to perceive, understand, and act upon process events which occur in the client's environment".[1] Appendix 7 gives a detailed description of a process consulting assignment. While any consulting involves some collaboration with the client, the process approach is a collaborative approach *par excellence*.

Choosing between the basic roles

In past years, "pure" resource or expert consulting used to be quite common. In today's consulting practice, it tends to be confined to those situations where the client clearly wants to acquire, in one way or another, special technical expertise, and does not want the consultant to deal with organisational change. In most situations, the two roles should be seen as complementary and mutually supportive. This is possible thanks to progress in the competence of management consultants: today even technical specialists intervening in a relatively narrow area tend to have some training in the behavioural aspects of organisational change and of consulting, and are keen to help in implementation. On the other hand, the "pure" behavioural scientists, the traditional protagonists of process consulting, have come to the conclusion that the possibility of their helping in organisational change would remain modest if they did not improve their understanding of technical, economic, financial and other factors and processes in client organisations. Thus, more and more consultants feel comfortable in both roles.

Nevertheless, it is possible to refer to situations, or to phases in assignments, where one or the other approach predominates. A consultant may start his assignment as a resource consultant in order to acquaint himself with the client organisation and demonstrate to the client that he is a real expert in his technical field. He can then act more and more as a process consultant, trying to involve the client in looking for solutions likely to be internalised by the client system. Temporarily he will switch back to the role of resource consultant to provide missing technical knowledge so that the process of change does not stop.

In choosing his role, the consultant must not forget that it constitutes a "communicating vessel" with the client's role. Both the consultant and the client should feel competent and comfortable in their respective roles and believe that they have made the right choice. No one should try to play a role which is alien to his nature and in which he will be less effective.

3.5 Further refinement of the role concept

Reducing the various consulting processes to two basic roles or modes is a simplification that is conceptually useful, but disregards a number of situational variables. For practical purposes it is also instructive to visualise a greater number of consultative roles along a *directive* and *non-directive* continuum, as shown in figure 3.1.[2] By directive we mean these behaviours where the consultant assumes a position of leadership or initiates activity. In the non-directive role he provides data for the client to use or not to use. Here again the situational roles are not

Figure 3.1 Description of the consultant's role on a directive and non-directive continuum

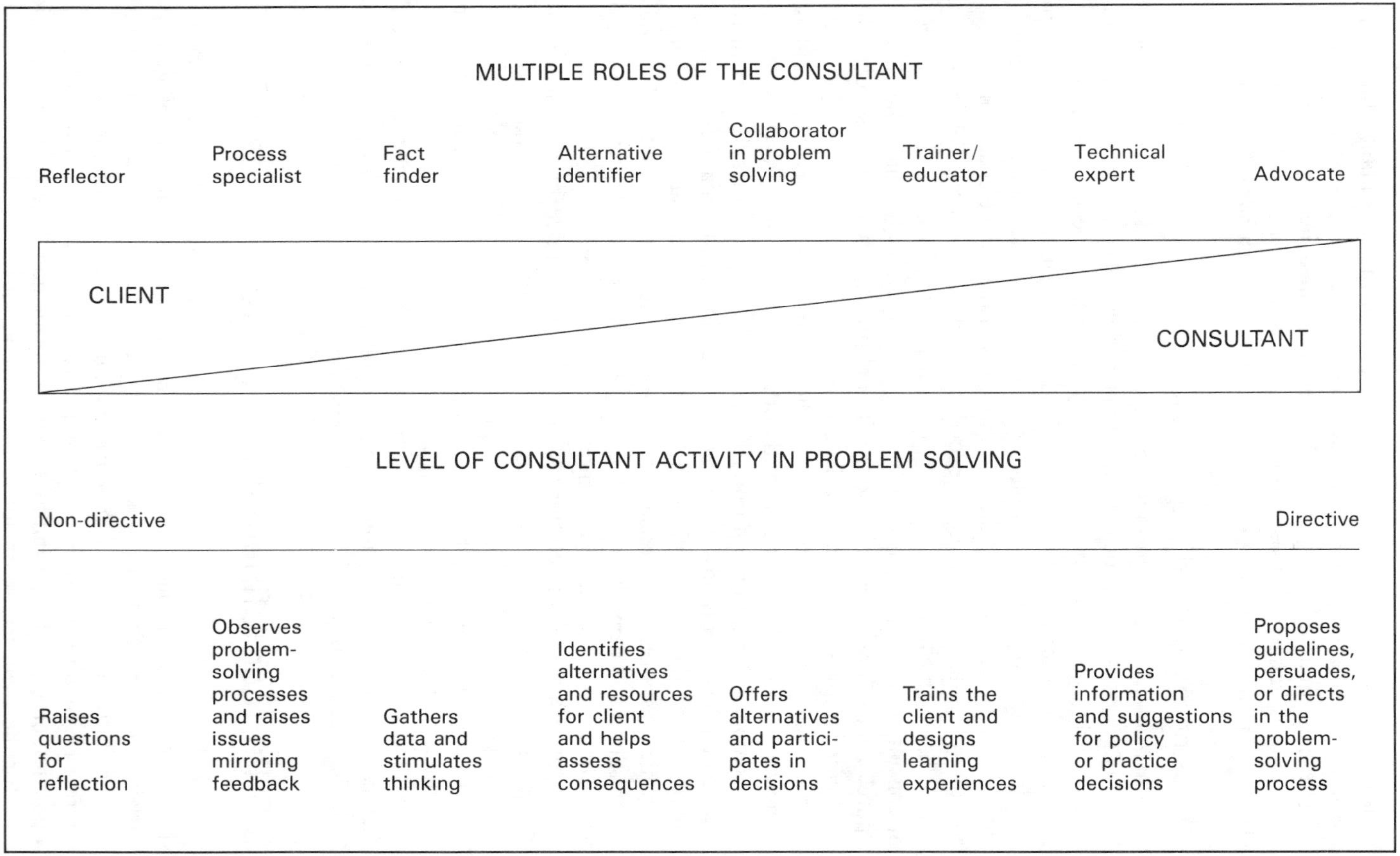

MULTIPLE ROLES OF THE CONSULTANT

Reflector	Process specialist	Fact finder	Alternative identifier	Collaborator in problem solving	Trainer/ educator	Technical expert	Advocate

CONSULTANT

CLIENT

LEVEL OF CONSULTANT ACTIVITY IN PROBLEM SOLVING

Non-directive .... Directive

Raises questions for reflection	Observes problem-solving processes and raises issues mirroring feedback	Gathers data and stimulates thinking	Identifies alternatives and resources for client and helps assess consequences	Offers alternatives and partici-pates in decisions	Trains the client and designs learning experiences	Provides information and suggestions for policy or practice decisions	Proposes guidelines, persuades, or directs in the problem-solving process

mutually exclusive and manifest themselves in many ways in a particular consultant-client relationship. These roles are "spheres of influence" rather than a static continuum of isolated behaviour. Let us examine these different role choices in response to a client's needs.

Advocate

In an advocate role, the consultant endeavours to influence the client. There are two quite different types of advocacy:

- *positional or "contact" advocacy* is a role which tries to influence the client to choose particular goods or to accept particular values;
- *methodological advocacy* is a role which tries to influence the client to become active as problem solver, and to use certain methods of problem solving, but is careful not to become an advocate for any particular solution (which would be positional advocacy).

In this role, the behaviour of the consultant is derived from a "believer" or "valuer" stance on content or a methodological matter.

Technical expert

One of the roles adopted by any consultant is that of technical specialist or expert. As mentioned above, the more traditional role of a consultant is that of an expert who, through special knowledge, skill and professional experience, is engaged to provide a unique service to the client. The client is mainly responsible for defining the objectives of the consultation. Thereafter the consultant assumes a directive role until the client is comfortable with the particular approach selected. Later in the relationship the consultant may act as a catalyst in helping to implement the recommendations he has made. Either the external or the internal consultant may be a resource (content) specialist in the client's problem, or a process specialist advising how to cope with a problem and how to implement change. This particular role brings out the consultant's substantive knowledge.

Trainer and educator

Innovative consultation frequently requires the consultant to initiate periodic or continuous training and education within the client system. In this aspect of the helping relationship, the consultant can play a role in bringing to bear the learning process that can best be employed, critically and creatively, depending upon the situation and the need. The consultant may design learning experiences, train or teach by imparting information directly. In a sense, this work requires the consultant to possess the skills of a training methodologist and developer of others' potential.

Collaborator in problem solving

The helping role assumed by the consultant uses a synergistic (co-operative) approach to complement and collaborate with the client in the perceptual, cognitive and action-taking processes needed to solve the problem. The consultant helps to maintain objectivity while stimulating conceptualisation during the formulation of the problem. Additionally, he must help to isolate and define the real dependent and independent variables that influenced the problem's cause, and will ultimately influence its solution. He also assists in weighing alternatives, aids in sorting out salient causal relationships which may affect alternatives, and synthesises and develops a course of action for an effective resolution. The consultant in this role is involved in decision making as a peer.

Alternative identifier

There are direct costs associated with decision making. While the value of a decision is dependent upon the attainment of a given set of objectives, in selecting an appropriate solution to a problem the consultant can normally propose several identifiable alternatives, along with their attendant risks. The alternatives, either because of economic or other identifiable implications, should be discovered jointly by the client and the consultant. In this helping relationship, the consultant establishes relevant criteria for assessing alternatives and develops cause-effect relationships for each along with an appropriate set of strategies. In this role, however, the consultant is not a direct participant in decision making, but a retriever of appropriate alternatives facing the decision maker.

Fact finder

As we know, fact finding is an integral part of any consulting assignment, both for developing a data base and for resolving intricate client problems. But the consultant's role can be confined to fact finding. In this case he will influence the client system by choosing the sources of data, using a technique that will get the client more or less involved in gathering and examining data, and presenting data to the client in a way that will show where and why improvements are needed. In this role the consultant is functioning basically as a researcher.

Process specialist

This is the "pure" process role as discussed in section 3.4. The consultant focuses chiefly on the interpersonal and intergroup dynamics affecting the process of problem solving and change. He must bring all his role skills to bear on helping the client. He works on developing joint client-consultant diagnostic skills for addressing specific and relevant problems in order to focus on *how* things are done rather than on *what* tasks are performed. Furthermore, the consultant helps the client to integrate interpersonal and group skills and events with task-oriented activities, and to observe the best match of relationships. In this role, an important function of the consultant is to provide feedback.

Reflector

When operating in the mode of a reflector, the consultant stimulates the client to make decisions by asking reflective questions which may help to clarify, modify, or change a given situation. In utilising this attribute, the consultant may be an arbitrator, an integrator, or an emphatic respondent who experiences jointly with the client those blocks which provided the structure and provoked the situation initially. In this role the consultant finds himself being an "overseer" as well as a "philosopher".

3.6 Methods of influencing the client system

Whether the consultant likes to admit it or not, he exercises *personal influence* on the client system in adopting any one of the behavioural roles described in the previous sections. The consultant has to influence people in order to obtain information, gain confidence and respect, overcome passive resistance, enlist collaboration, and get his proposals accepted and implemented. This section will therefore review some general methods of exercising personal influence.[3]

To exercise personal influence on the client is not in conflict with a professional approach. The consultant has committed himself to helping to change management practices and organisational performance, and this may be impossible without influencing certain people. The purpose is *to energise and activate the client* in his own interest, *not to manipulate him* in the interest of the consultant. Nevertheless, the consultant must realise that his influence on some people may be quite strong and that by exercising this influence he takes on himself considerable technical and moral responsibility. The consultant will be able gradually to transfer this responsibility to the client by developing his knowledge and his problem-solving skills. This will help the client to recognise when and in what sense he is being influenced, and make his own judgement on whether there are any alternatives.

Various methods are available and it is difficult to say in advance which one will produce the desired effect. These methods reflect the fact that people's attitudes and decisions have both rational and irrational (emotional) motives. In one case it may be enough to show the client a few meaningful figures and he will be able to draw practical conclusions from them. In another case the client will be so impressed by the consultant's personality, which inspires confidence, that he will immediately trust the advice he receives without examining the reasons behind it. Here again, experience is the best guide in making the right choice and combining the methods as appropriate.

Demonstrating technical expertise

The consultant should consider whether he enters the client organisation as a technical expert enjoying prestige, or, on the contrary, as someone totally unknown. Demonstration of theoretical knowledge and practical expertise appeals mainly to technically oriented individuals who are themselves experts in the consultant's field. This can be done in informal discussions, by passing on information on developments in theory, new techniques and equipment, successful firms or projects in which the consultant was himself involved, and in similar ways.

Technically superior findings or proposals submitted by the consultant may speak for themselves and influence the client's stance.

Exhibiting professional integrity at work

The consultant's behaviour at work is closely observed by the client, whose attitude can be influenced by the way in which the consultant exhibits commitment, integrity, a methodical approach and efficiency. These are demonstrated at various stages and aspects of the assignment — the way of going about collecting information, self-discipline and perseverance in fact finding, the ability to discover pitfalls about which the consultant was not informed by the client, persistence in looking for a better technique, rational use of time, tact in handling delicate matters, and the like. A powerful effect can be achieved if people see that the consultant is prepared to share his knowledge and work method with them.

Using assertive persuasion

This widely applied method uses the force of logical argument to convince the other person that what you want them to do is the right, correct, or effective action to take. As a rule, new ideas or suggestions are put forward followed by reasons for and against, as the consultant presents arguments, facts, or data to support his position. The method is most effective when the consultant is perceived as knowing what he is talking about and seen as relatively objective; he should, too, know enough about the other person's situation to speak to specific needs. However, assertive persuasion tends to be overused in the practice of consulting and people often think of it as synonymous with influence.

Developing a common vision

A common vision is a shared picture of where you are headed, what you are trying to accomplish, and why it would be worth while for others to help. Articulating exciting possibilities includes generating images of what the future of the organisation could be like if such and such a course was followed. In addition, the consultant can influence people by showing enthusiasm for what is to be done and where that action will take the organisation. The method tends to be more effective when the consultant must influence a number of people and generate collective commitment to action. It does not work if it is not clear what the other person can actually do towards achieving a common vision. In contrast to assertive persuasion, common vision tends to be the least utilised influence mode.

Using participation and trust

This method implies recognising and involving others by asking for their contributions and ideas, giving them credit for an idea, and building on what others have proposed. This is accompanied by sharing feelings with others and being open about one's own mistakes, shortcomings and lack of knowledge. The purpose is to develop an atmosphere of collaboration and co-responsibility for achieving a common goal. The other person involved must believe that your interest in participation and mutual trust is genuine and not just a facade, and that collaborating with you is really the right way to achieve the desired results. Attempts at one-way influence and control should be avoided. Also, participation is hard to achieve when the situation is such that it is not really in the other person's best interest to co-operate. This method is absolutely essential in collaborative consulting styles that emphasise the client's active involvement and his "ownership" of the problem, as well as of the solutions representing the final outcome of the assignment.

Using rewards and punishments

Consultants normally do not control the same kinds of rewards and punishments that are available to management in the client organisation. Nevertheless, they can influence people by giving or taking away from them certain things which seem desirable. It could be a public acknowledgement (e.g. in a meeting) of a person's competence, achievement, or exceptional contribution to the assignment. Enhancing someone's self-esteem is a reward. Omitting to invite someone to a meeting he would probably like to attend, or withholding some information from him, could be a punishment. Rewards and punishments which do not motivate people, which are out of proportion to the importance of the issue involved, or which are chosen arbitrarily, produce little effect and should be avoided.

Using tensions and anxieties

Although it is not always realised, tensions and anxieties do play some role in consulting. Often, the very presence of the consultant creates tensions because there are speculations about the hidden causes of his presence and about possible outcomes that could upset the status quo and affect the positions and interests of individuals or whole groups. The tensions that exist in the organisation can be exploited in collecting information to obtain a true picture of the situation. Interdepartmental competition can be used in choosing the unit in which to start applying a new method in order to demonstrate its feasibility to other units. In generating and strengthening desire for change, it may be useful to explain what would happen to the organisation and/or to the individual if the necessary change is resented or delayed, thus creating a state of anxiety. It may be enough to produce data showing that the organisation already is or is likely to be in difficulties (see also section 4.4). Here again, a wrongly focused and excessive use of tensions and anxieties will produce negative rather than positive effects. Also, the consultant must be careful not to become involved in internal power struggles and be perceived as their instrument.

[1] E. H. Schein: *Process consultation* (Reading, MA, Addison-Wesley, 1969); p. 9.

[2] The figure is adapted from G. Lippitt and R. Lippitt: *The consulting process in action* (La Jolla, CA, University Associates, 1978); p. 31.

[3] The description of assertive persuasion, common vision, participation and trust, and rewards and punishments, is taken and adapted, with acknowledgement of the origin, from chapter 8 in F. Steele: *The role of the internal consultant: Effective role shaping for staff positions* (Boston, MA, CBI Publishing Co., 1982), which refers to a model developed by R. Harrison and D. Berlew. The reader should refer to Steele's book for a more detailed discussion of the topic.

CONSULTING AND CHANGE

4

Change is the *raison d'être* of management consulting. If diverse consulting assignments have any common characteristic, it is that they assist in planning and implementing change in client organisations. Organisational change, however, is full of difficulties and pitfalls. Often the very behaviour of those who strive to make changes generates resistance to change and brings the whole process to a standstill. To avoid this, every management consultant needs to be aware of the complex relationships involved in the change process and know how to approach varying change situations and help people to cope with change.

This chapter is, therefore, particularly important for understanding the nature and methods of consulting and of the consultant-client relationship. Throughout the chapter the consultant's point of view and intervention methods will be emphasised. However, they will be reviewed in the wider context of changes occurring in society, in organisations, and in individuals, and related to the managers' roles in generating and managing organisational change. The chapter provides some notions of the theory of organisational change, and also practical guidelines for planning and implementing changes.

4.1 The nature of change

The concept of change implies that there is a perceptible difference in a situation, a person, a work team, an organisation, or a relationship, between two successive points in time. How does this difference occur, what are its causes, and what does it mean to a manager or a consultant? To answer these and similar questions, we will first look at the various levels and dimensions of change and at the relations between them.

Environmental change

There is nothing new about change: it has always been a feature of the very existence and history of mankind. We all know that without change there is no life and that human efforts to obtain better living conditions imply coping with change. There is a new phenomenon, however: the unprecedented depth, complexity and pace of technological, social and other changes occurring at the present time. Today's organisations operate in an environment which is continually changing. The ability to adapt to changes in the environment has become a fundamental condition of success in business, and, in a growing number of cases, a condition of mere survival.

It is not the purpose of this chapter to examine current development trends or predict future changes in the business and social environment. Many excellent publications are available which attempt to do this from various angles.[1] They show that today the processes of change concern all aspects of human and social life, both nationally and internationally. The scope of environmental changes differs from country to country and from region to region, but certain changes are global and affect societies world-wide. For example, a new legal text concerning the employment of expatriate managers in a developing country is a change in the local environment of business, while changes in the prices of crude oil, or in information and communication technologies, affect businesses virtually throughout the world.

Of course, no business or other organisation is sufficiently large and diversified to be directly and immediately affected by all changes in the national and international environment. The practical question is what to regard as the external environment of a particular organisational unit, and what this unit should do to keep abreast, not of environmental changes at large (which could be an unmanageable and inefficient task), but of those changes that sooner or later will affect its operation.

This question is increasingly difficult to answer, not only in countries which are developing particularly fast, such as Japan or the United States, but also in other countries. Many managers are totally perplexed when they realise that their organisation can be affected by forces − economic, social or political − which they would previously never have considered when making business decisions.

And this is where management consultants can step in to render an extremely valuable service to their clients. It is very probable that making clients aware of the new nature of environmental changes, and helping them to react to these changes effectively, will be the most important and forward-looking area of management consulting in the last years of this millenium.[2]

Organisational change

Organisations do not change for the sake of change, but because they are part of a wider process of development and have to react to new environmental changes, constraints, requirements and opportunities. They are continually forced to adapt to the environment within which they exist and operate. But more than that − businesses and other organisations also generate changes in their external environment, for example by developing and marketing new products and technologies that become dominant and widely adopted. Thus they modify the technological environment nationally and internationally.

Change can concern any aspect or factor of an organisation. Therefore it can involve:

- changes in the basic set-up of the organisation (nature and level of business, legal set-up, ownership, sources of finance, international operations and impact, diversification, mergers, joint ventures);
- changes in tasks and activities (range of products and services provided, markets served, clients and suppliers);
- changes in technology used (equipment, tools, materials and energy used, technological processes, office technology);
- changes in management structures and processes (internal organisation, work flow, decision-making and control procedures, information systems);
- changes in organisational culture (values, traditions, informal relations, influences and processes, management style);
- changes in people (management and staff employed, their competence, attitudes, motivations, behaviour and effectiveness at work);
- changes in organisational performance (financial, economic, social: showing how the organisation relates to the environment, fulfills its mission and tackles new opportunities);
- changes in the image of the organisation in business circles and in society.

Change in people

The human dimension of organisational change is a fundamental one. For it is people in the organisation — its managerial and technical staff and other workers — whose behaviour ultimately determines what organisational changes can be made and what real benefits will be drawn from them. It is so because organisations are human systems above all. People must understand, and be willing and able to implement, changes which at first glance may appear purely technological or structural, but will in fact affect people in some way.

In coping with organisational change, people have to change, too: they must acquire new knowledge, absorb more information, tackle new tasks, upgrade their skills, and, very often, modify their work habits, values and attitudes to the way of doing things in the organisation. Change in values and in attitudes is essential. There probably cannot be any real change without a change in attitude.

It is important to recognise that in an organisation this requirement relates to everyone, starting with the top manager. Those who want their subordinates and colleagues to change must be prepared to analyse and change their own behaviour, work methods and attitudes! This is a golden rule of organisational change.

But how do people change? What internal processes bring about behavioural change? Many attempts have been made to describe the change process by means of models, but none of these descriptions has been exhaustive and fully satisfactory. In particular, different people change in different ways, and every person has many unique features that influence his willingness and ability to change. The influence of the culture in which a person has grown up, and lived, is paramount, as will be explained in chapter 5.

Social scientists tend to agree that a useful concept of change in people is one developed by Kurt Lewin.[3] It is a three-stage sequential model, whose stages are referred to as "unfreezing", "changing", and "refreezing".

Unfreezing postulates a somewhat unsettling situation as it is assumed that a certain amount of anxiety or dissatisfaction is called for — there must be a need to search for new information if learning is to take place. Conditions which enhance the unfreezing process usually include a more than normal amount of tension leading to a noticeable need for change — for example, an absence of sources of information; removal of usual contacts and accustomed routines; and a lowering of self-esteem amongst people. In some instances, these pre-conditions for change are present before the consultant arrives on the scene. In other instances, the need for change is not perceived and has to be explained if unfreezing is to occur — for example, by making it clear what will happen if the organisation does not change.

Changing, or the movement towards change, is the central stage of the model, in which both management and employees start practising new relationships, methods, and behaviours. The sub-processes of changing involve two elements:

— *identification*, where the people concerned test out the proposed changes, following the external motives presented to them (e.g. by management or a consultant);

— *internalisation*, where individuals translate the general objectives and principles of change into specific personal goals and rules. This process may be quite difficult, usually requiring a considerable effort by the changee, and a great deal of patience, creativity and imagination on the part of the consultant in assisting the change, to convert the external (general) motives to internal (specific and personal) motives for accepting the change proposed.

Refreezing occurs when the changee verifies change through experience. The sub-processes involved require a conducive and supportive environment (e.g. approval by responsible management) and are usually accompanied by a heightening of self-esteem as a result of a sense of achievement derived from task accomplishment. During the initial stages of the refreezing step it is recommended that continuous reinforcement of the required behaviour (by means of rewards, praise, and so on) should be carried out to accelerate the learning process. At later stages, intermittent or spaced reinforcement is recommended to prevent extinction of the newly acquired behavioural patterns. Eventually the new behaviour and attitudes are either reinforced and internalised, or rejected and abandoned.

It will be seen that change in a particular person takes place at several levels: at the knowledge level (information about change, understanding its rationale), the attitudes level (accepting the need for change and a particular measure of change both rationally and emotionally) and the behavioural level (acting in support of effective implementation of change).[4] The relationship between change

Figure 4.1 Time span and level of difficulty involved for various levels of change

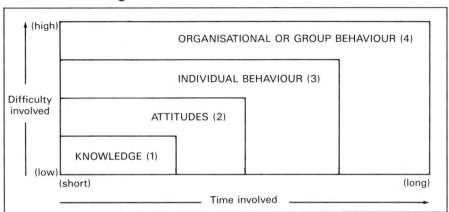

in people and organisational change is set out in a diagram in figure 4.1.[5] It shows *four levels of change*: (1) knowledge changes, (2) attitude changes, (3) individual behaviour changes, and (4) group or organisational behaviour changes. A hierarchy of difficulty is experienced in effecting change when moving from level (1) through to level (4). The relative levels of difficulty and time relationship are also indicated in the diagram.

It is essential to keep in mind that environmental change affects change in individual persons within an organisation. For the environment is not something that "starts behind the factory gate", but permeates the whole organisation. People "bring it with them" when they come to work. Changes occurring in the environment of an organisation may facilitate or hamper change in people working within this organisation. A frequent problem is that of individuals who are simultaneously exposed to so much change and stress, both at work and in their social and family life, that they are not able to cope and so break down. On the other hand, certain environmental changes, such as an increased penetration of new information and communication technologies into all areas of human life, greatly facilitate the changes that have to be planned and implemented by the management of organisations.

Resistance to change

The history of mankind has taught us that, after all, people are remarkably adaptable, can cope with change and generally accept it as a natural fact of life. Why, then, is change in people so often the bottleneck of organisational change? Why is "change" such a frightening word for many people?

People resist and try to avoid changes that will leave them worse off than they are now in terms of job content, conditions of work, workload, income, personal power-base and the like. This is understandable. But a great deal of resistance may be met even if the proposed change is neutral, or beneficial to the persons concerned. While there are many reasons for this, psychological and others, the following appear to be the most important:

Lack of conviction that change is needed. If people are not properly informed and the purpose of change not explained to them, they are likely to view the present situation as satisfactory and an effort to change as useless and upsetting.

Dislike of imposed change. In general, people do not like to be treated as passive objects. They resent changes that are imposed on them and about which they cannot express any views.

Dislike of surprises. People do not want to be kept in the dark about any change that is being prepared; managerial decisions bringing about important changes tend to be resented if they come as a surprise.

Fear of the unknown. Basically, people do not like to live in uncertainty and may prefer an imperfect present to an unknown and uncertain future.

Reluctance to deal with unpopular issues. Managers and other people often try to avoid unpleasant reality and unpopular actions, even if they realise that they will not be able to avoid these for ever.

Fear of inadequacy and failure. Many people worry about their ability to adjust to change and maintain and improve their performance in a new work situation. Some of them may feel insecure, and doubt their ability to make a special effort to learn new skills.

Disturbed practices, habits and relations. Following organisational change, well-established and fully-mastered practices and work habits may become obsolete, and familiar relationships may be altered or totally destroyed. This can lead to considerable frustration and unhappiness.

Lack of respect and trust in the person promoting change. People are suspicious about change proposed by a manager whom they do not trust and respect, or by an external person whose competence and motives are not known and understood.

Some of these causes of resistance to change stem from human nature. However, they are reinforced by life experience (e.g. by positive or negative consequences of past changes). People who have experienced a great deal of unnecessary change (e.g. frequent but useless reorganisations), or to whom harm was caused by changes presented to them as beneficial, tend to become very suspicious about any further changes. This is very important. Causes of trouble are often sought in inherent resistance to change, although they lie elsewhere — for example, in poor choice of new technology, or poor organisational conditions for its application. In such cases, resistance to change is only a symptom, and its cause has to be discovered and removed.

There are then differences in the character of individual persons so far as resistance to change and the ability to cope with change are concerned. Unfortunately, but not surprisingly, those who are in greatest need of change often resist it more than anybody else. This may mean individual persons (both workers and managers), groups, organisations, and even whole human communities. Managers and consultants must be well aware of this; some specific suggestions will be made in section 4.4, which discusses how to gain support for change.

Change is not an end in itself

In this chapter, we are emphasising that organisations and people alike must be prepared and able to change in order to survive and prosper in an environment that is constantly changing. Yet the reader should not gain the impression that we are obsessed by change and trying to idealise it.

Change in organisations is not an end in itself, but only a means to adjusting to new conditions and sustaining or increasing competitiveness, performance and effectiveness. If an organisation can achieve its objectives without disturbing the established product and service lines, procedures and relationships, there may be no need for changes, at least in the short term. Certain changes are quite costly (e.g. if a successful product is phased out and replaced by a new product at the wrong moment). Some managers suffer from chronic "reorganisation disease": they feel that to be active, and to be seen as such, they must reorganise their enterprise or department at least once a year. Many consultants do not have the courage to tell the client that the best solution is to leave things as they are, especially if the work is being done for a client who obviously is very keen to change something.

In a world where technological, social and other changes are occurring at an unprecedented pace and frequency, managers and consultants must not overlook that both people and organisations are badly in need not only of change, but also of stability and continuity. Striking the right balance between change and stability, and helping the client to maintain this balance throughout the organisation, is therefore one of the vital tasks of the consultant.

4.2 Some basic approaches to change in organisations

How is change generated and implemented in an organisation? Several basic approaches will be reviewed in this section.

Unplanned change

In every organisation a great deal of *evolutionary, natural change*, occurs. A typical example is the aging of equipment and people, which has both negative, problematic aspects (e.g. the need to repair, modernise and replace equipment, or the need to replace managers who have lost dynamism and drive), and positive aspects (technical and managerial competence acquired by years of practical experience). These changes take place independently of the management's will. While they cannot really be planned, they can and must be considered in planning the organisation's future. It is possible to plan measures for preventing and removing negative consequences of evolutionary change.

A great deal of unplanned change is not of an evolutionary nature. It occurs because organisations must react to new situations. A manufacturing firm may be compelled by competition to drastically reduce its prices. A strike may force an organisation to raise wages, and the like. Such a change is *adaptive or reactive*. The organisation has not planned and, quite often, has not foreseen its necessity until very late in the day. But the organisation makes the change in order to respond to some events and trends which may be threatening it, or, on the contrary, which offer an unexpected new opportunity.

Planned change

It is a sign of poor management if an organisation confines its total change effort to making unplanned changes. Where this happens, it is a demonstration of unwillingness or inability to look ahead and prepare the organisation for reacting to future opportunities and constraints at the right moment. Planning does not completely eliminate the need for unplanned changes. However, it helps the organisation to prepare itself properly for changes that can be anticipated, and minimises the number of situations where hasty changes have to be made in an atmosphere of panic. More than that, the planning of change enables the organisation to "create the future" (e.g. through technological development or by launching new products and services), and establish and attain challenging development objectives. Therefore, planned change can be *pro-active*.

Some typical questions addressed in planning change are:

- What changes are occurring in the environment? What will be their implications for our organisation?
- What changes should we make in order to achieve our development objectives, improve our performance, increase our share of the market, etc.?
- What undesirable changes will occur in our organisation if we do not take timely steps to prevent them?
- What sort of and how much change are we able to manage?
- What sort of and how much change will our people be able to absorb and support?
- Should we implement change in stages?
- What will be the relations between various changes that we intend to make? How will they be co-ordinated?
- What should be our time horizon and timetable for implementing change?

The last question is crucial. Both organisations and individual people can absorb only a limited amount of change over a certain period of time, and this absorptive capacity is not the same in different countries, organisations, and individuals. A careful pacing of change is therefore one of the main skills needed in managing change, and a critical dimension of its planning.

Imposed change

In organisations, a great deal of change is imposed by management. Frequently this causes unhappiness and resentment, in particular if persons affected by such changes believe that they should have been consulted, or at least informed beforehand. If change is initiated from a position of power and imposed, it could be inherently volatile; it may disappear with removal of the power source, or in the absence of appropriate punishments and sanctions.

Yet we cannot say that every imposed change must be bad. There are emergency situations where discussion is impossible and delaying a decision would be suicidal. There are regulatory and administrative measures which will affect many people, but which are of minor importance and do not justify long discussion and consultation. Also, imposed change is considered to be more effective when dealing with dependent rather than independent persons. In general, the attitude to imposed change is very much influenced by culture, education, access to information, the existence of alternatives, and other factors.

A manager should think twice before deciding to impose a change. He should do it only if he is firmly convinced that there is no alternative — if, for example, he was unable to gain the support of the group, yet he feels that a change is inevitable. But he should always take the trouble to explain why he has chosen to impose a change.

Participative change

People in different national and organisational cultures do not feel the same way about change that is presented to them as an accomplished fact, and imposed on them without prior discussion or consultation. However, the trend towards participative change is ever more pronounced in most parts of the world. People want to know what changes are being prepared, and to be able to influence changes that concern them. Managers and administrators, on the other hand, are increasingly aware of this fundamental demand and react to it by adopting a participative approach to change.

A participative change process is slower and more time-consuming and costly than imposed change, but it is considered to be long lasting. In addition, participative change helps management to draw on people's experience and creativity, which is difficult to do if change is imposed.

There are different levels and forms of participation in the change process, depending on the nature and complexity of the change itself, on the maturity, coherence and motivation of the group, and on the relationship between management and employees.

At the first level, the manager or the consultant informs the staff concerned about the need for change and the specific measures that are being prepared.

At the second level, consultation about change takes place in the course of the change process — for example, in identifying the need for change, and in checking whether people would react negatively to the measures proposed. Suggestions and criticism are solicited and management may reconsider its plan for change on the basis of these.

At the third level, management seeks active involvement of the staff in planning and implementing change by inviting them to participate in defining what to change and how to do it, and in putting the agreed changes into effect. This is normally done through working parties, task forces, special committees, staff meetings and other methods discussed in section 4.5.

Negotiated change

In many situations change requires negotiation. This takes place when two or more individuals or groups discuss together the measures to be introduced, and the benefits and costs to the parties involved. This may lead to a compromise that neither party considers to be an ideal solution. However, the probability of support by those concerned, and hence the probability of implementing the agreement reached, is enhanced.

There are, then, changes that require negotiation between management and trade unions representing employees. These sorts of changes may be determined by law, through collective bargaining, or by any other joint agreement, formal or informal.

Managers and consultants should be particularly alert to the desirability of a dialogue with the workers' and other employees' representatives, not only in cases explicitly stipulated by laws or formal agreements, but also in preparing any other changes that may affect the interests of people in the organisation and where trade union support may be essential.

4.3 Managing the change process

After having examined the commonly used basic approaches to organisational change we will now turn to the management of the change process. Although it may be self-evident to many readers, we want to start by underlining that change must be managed and that managing change is a fundamental management function in every organisation. For again and again managers and consultants make the same mistake: special organisational and administrative measures may be taken to prepare and introduce important changes, but senior management, absorbed by daily business and policies, fails to provide leadership during the change process. Change requires leadership, and it is quite natural that this should be provided by those managers who have the principal responsibilities in operating the organisation. This leadership is necessary even if an important role in the change process is assigned to a management consultant.

Some general principles

It is, of course, impossible to provide a simple blueprint on how to handle organisational change in all situations, though some useful rules can be mentioned.

First, there is the need to harmonise change measures and processes with normal activities and management processes of the organisation. There may be competition for scarce resources: some people may be wanted both for planning or preparing a change and for running current business. The problem is particularly acute and delicate in organisations undergoing major changes — e.g. in mass production, where a transition to a new product or new technology requires a major restructuring of production processes and workshops, and the question is how to achieve this without substantial losses in production and productivity.

Secondly, management has to determine the specific change measures requiring its leadership, and decide on the degree and form of its direct involvement in such measures. The difficulty of the measures and their importance to the organisation's future is the main criterion. In a larger organisation, senior managers cannot themselves be involved in all changes, but there are certain changes which they must manage personally, or they must find a suitable way, explicit or symbolic, of providing and demonstrating management support. Reinforcing messages from the leaders are a key stimulus in a change effort.

Thirdly, various change processes within the organisation need to be harmonised with each other. While this may be easy in a small and simple organisation, it may be quite difficult in a large and complex one. Often various departments work at similar problems (e.g. introducing new information processing technology). They may come up with proposals that do not fit general management policy and standard procedures, or present excessive resource requirements. Or one department develops superior proposals, and other departments will have to be convinced that they should give up their current system or their new proposals and accept the best proposal developed by another unit. These are situations where higher management has to intervene with tact.

Fourthly, managing change includes dealing with its various aspects — technological, structural, procedural, human, psychological, political, financial, and so on. This is perhaps the basic and most difficult management responsibility related to organisational change; because the change process involves specialists who often try to impose their limited view of a complex and multidisciplinary problem.

Fifthly, managing change involves decisions on the use of various approaches and intervention techniques that help to make a good start, proceed systematically, cope with resistance, gain support and get the change implemented. These will be reviewed in the following sections.

The role of innovators and change agents

Experience shows that a change effort requires a successful start. Making a correct decision on what to change and assigning responsibilities is not enough. There must be people who have critical and innovative minds, enjoy experimenting, can visualise the future, believe that change is possible, and influence others, not by talking about change, but by demonstrating what can be achieved. These "innovators", "prime movers", "champions" or "intrapreneurs", as they are sometimes called, may be in managerial jobs, but often they are design engineers, marketing specialists, project co-ordinators, skilled workers and other staff members.

Organisations which are keen to change must encourage innovation, experiments and entrepreneurship. To management this means not only tolerating departures from routine and tradition, and admitting that this is not possible without some risk, but deliberately employing innovators, giving them chances, observing their work, and referring to their example in showing what the organisation is able to achieve.

Innovative and entrepreneurial individuals or teams play a prominent role in successful strategies for organisational change. They are the organisation's principal change agents. Often it is in their unit that change will start. Some of them will become managers of new units responsible for new product lines or services, co-ordinators of change projects, or trainers and internal consultants helping other units in making the necessary changes.

Different roles are played by two basic types of change agents: those whose interest is and remains predominently technical, and who may produce excellent technical ideas without being able to convert them into business opportunities, and those who are mainly entrepreneurs and leaders and can help management to generate and implement changes that require the active involvement of many people, individually or in groups.

A strategy for organisational change may rely entirely on internal capabilities and on managerial and specialist staff members who can play the role of change agents. An alternative is to bring in a change agent from outside as a consultant. This is an important managerial decision affecting the whole approach to the change process. For the consultant will not only be contributing some missing technical competence and an alternative viewpoint, but, as we know, he will be influencing, by his presence and by the action he takes (and sometimes refrains from taking), the behaviour of those concerned in change (including possibly the behaviour of the very person who has invited him). The main factors to consider are:

- the consultant's profile (his technical knowledge and personality: he must be acceptable to and respected by people whom he is supposed to help to change);
- the mode of consulting to choose (as discussed in chapter 3, there are various modes; the question is, which mode is likely to stimulate change in a particular human system).

Structural arrangements for managing change

Since the manager bears the main responsibility for managing change in his organisation or unit, he may decide to take charge of a specific change effort personally. In many cases, no special structural arrangements are made, and the manager and his staff work on defining and implementing change proposals, handling their other duties simultaneously. This is not an unwise approach provided it works. It underlines that the change is significant to the management hierarchy and will not be treated as a "side assignment" carried out by a group of staff specialists or consultants.

In the practical life of organisations, however, the use of special structural arrangements for handling change is required for certain specific reasons:

(1)   the regular organisational structure may be fully oriented towards current business and could not cope with any additional tasks, either for technical reasons or owing to high work-load;

(2)   more importantly, rigidity, conservativism and resistance to change may be strongly rooted in the existing structure and it would be unrealistic to expect that this structure would generate and manage change;

(3)   in some cases it is desirable to introduce change in steps, or to test it on a limited scale before making a final decision;

(4)   change may start spontaneously in one part of the organisation and management may decide to encourage it, but to proceed to a wider application in several stages.

Organisational practice has recourse to a wide variety of special arrangements for planning and implementing changes. They may be ad hoc and temporary, and cease to exist once a change process has been completed, or they may constitute the nucleus of a future regular structure.

Special projects and assignments are a very popular form. A person or unit within the existing structure is given an additional special task as a temporary assignment. He may be given some additional resources for this, but basically he has to use resources existing within the current structure. For mobilising resources and taking decisions that are beyond his authority, the project manager or co-ordinator would, of course, turn to the general manager who appointed him. This is, in fact, a transitional arrangement between a normal and special structure.

Task forces and working parties are frequently used as temporary groups, either at one stage of the change process (e.g. to establish the need for change and develop alternatives), or throughout the whole process for its planning and co-ordination.

Selecting the members of a temporary group is extremely important. They should be people who can and want to do something about the problem that is the focus of the change. The members of the group must have time to participate in group work. Task forces often fail because they are composed of extremely busy people who give priority to running current business before planning future change.

The group should also have a defined life. A possibility is to introduce the use of the "sunset calendar" — that is, at a predetermined point the group will cease to exist unless there is a management decision to continue it. This avoids the possibility of the group slowly disintegrating as more and more members absent themselves from meetings.

The group may use a convener. This could be the consultant or somebody designated by management, after discussion with the consultant. The convener is not the chairman of the group, but just the person who gets it moving initially. The group may decide that they do not want a regular chairman and might even rotate the role of the convener.

As far as possible, the expected output of the group should be identified. It should bear a direct relationship to the problem and be amenable to review.

Experiments are used to test a change measure on a limited scale, e.g. in one or two organisational units, and/or over a limited time period, say several months. For example, flexible working hours or a new scheme of bonuses may first be applied on an experimental basis in selected departments and workshops.

A true experiment involves pre- and post-test control design. Two (or more) units or groups are used. They should exhibit the same or very similar characteristics (which may be very difficult to achieve and prove scientifically). Data are collected about both groups. Some change is then made in one group (experimental group) but not in the other (control group). Once the change has been made, further observations or data collection are made. The data collected before and after the change in both groups are compared. However, as the famous Hawthorne experiments illustrated, it is possible in a field experiment that some other variable is influencing performance.[6]

Pilot projects are used to check on a limited scale whether a new scheme, involving considerable technological, organisational or social change and, as a rule, important financial resources, is feasible, and whether adjustments are necessary before introducing the scheme on a larger scale. A great deal of experience is normally drawn from a properly prepared and properly controlled pilot project and in this way the risk involved in an important new scheme is minimised.

In drawing conclusions from the evaluation of pilot projects certain mistakes are made again and again. In order to demonstrate that the proposed change is justified and feasible, management and consultants tend to pay special attention to a pilot project (e.g. by assigning the best staff to it, or by intensifying guidance and control). The pilot project is thus not executed under normal but under exceptionally favourable conditions. Furthermore, it is assumed that the conditions under which a pilot project is undertaken can be replicated for a larger programme. Often this is not possible, for a number of reasons. Hence learning from a pilot project also includes an unbiased review of conditions under which it succeeded.

New organisational units are often established if management has made up its mind to go ahead with a change measure (e.g. develop and start marketing a new service) and decides that adequate resources and facilities must be fully assigned to it right at the outset. As a rule, this would be done if the need for change has been well documented, and the importance of the change envisaged justifies an underutilisation of resources which may well occur in the first period after the establishment of the unit.

New forms of work organisation involve the people concerned in redesigning and restructuring their own work. An outside consultant, a manager, or a staff specialist, can act as a catalyst, but it is the group itself that decides on the new organisational design. This approach emphasises group work rather than individual work and places more responsibility on the group, reducing the need for traditional active supervision.

Harmonising the change cycles

From a manager's or a consultant's point of view, it is essential to realise that change in people and organisational change do not necessarily follow the same change cycle and may occur over different periods of time. The unfreezing — changing — refreezing cycle, described in section 4.1, has to be related to the organisational change cycle, i.e. establishing the need for change — action planning — implementation — evaluation, making sure that there is proper co-ordination in timing, technical work content and management emphasis. For example, management may regard the need for change as fully established. But has the process of unfreezing started? Do people realise that change is inevitable? Do they support management's decision to start a major change effort? Or management may view the implementation phase of change as completed, but have people adopted the new method or relationship, and are they going to use it on a permanent basis?

4.4 Gaining support for change

One of the principal messages of this chapter is that effective change is best achieved if it enjoys the support of the people involved. This can be a very complex matter. Managers and consultants may feel uncertain about their ability to mobilise support for the change envisaged. Owing to errors made by management, the existing support may be lost and give way to resistance; to redress the situation may then be quite difficult.

As mentioned in section 4.2, inviting people to participate actively in a change effort at all its stages is a useful general method for gaining support and reducing resistance. It helps to create an atmosphere in which people feel they are the "owners" of a change proposal: the idea comes neither from the top, nor from an external person, but from within the group. If things go wrong, the group does not seek a culprit from without, but examines the causes and willingly helps in redefining the proposals.

However, there are some other aspects and methods. A number of comments on how to gain and retain people's support for change will be made in this section, and in section 4.5 which discusses intervention techniques for assisting change.

Arousing attention to the need for change

Undeniably there must be unlimited methods of drawing the attention of individuals and groups to the need for a change. The reader should refer to section 3.6 where various methods of influencing the client system are discussed. However, two proven methods are of particular interest to consultants.

The most effective manner of arousing immediate attention occurs when people become *anxious*. In special cases the introduction of a state of extreme anxiety is undeniably effective — for example, a building will be cleared very promptly if it is reported that a bomb has been placed in it. However, results show that the continued use of the heightened anxiety approach tends to be self-defeating. Recipients eventually ignore such threats, especially if the alleged events do not occur.

Notwithstanding that, the use of minimal anxiety is effective as an attention-arousing device which can be sustained over a long period. A particularly successful combination is to use an anxiety state to draw attention to specific needs (i.e. the unfreezing process described in section 4.1) and to follow up by providing a solution meeting these needs.

The second method is called *the two-step information process*. The underlying idea is that the acceptance and effective introduction of change occurs as the result of a multiplier effect in the flow of information.

Detailed research findings suggest that people most likely to experiment and be influenced by new approaches possess certain characteristics. These individuals, labelled as "isolates", are inclined to be highly technically oriented; to read widely on their chosen subjects; to attend meetings and conferences frequently; and to travel in order to investigate new schemes. They may be considered by their group to be something akin to "cranks". Surprisingly, they are not likely to influence other members of their group directly.

Nevertheless, the activities of these technically-oriented isolates are kept under constant observation by a second type of person who possesses characteristics similar to those of isolates but, usually owing to widespread interests in other fields, does not have the same amount of time available to experiment and test new methods in any considerable depth. This second type of person, identified as an "opinion-leader", has considerable influence over the group, and even beyond it. In addition to acknowledged technical expertise, this type of person usually has considerable civic and social standing.

In tracing the life-cycle of the adoption of new procedures, it seems that the new scheme is first investigated, along with other possible choices, by the isolate and is eventually chosen over other alternatives because of its proven technical superiority. At a later stage the opinion-leader adopts the new idea once he is convinced that the isolate has firmly decided on this new approach. Subsequently an "epidemic" phase erupts as the followers of the opinion-leader also adopt the new approach. Therefore, when introducing change a strong case can usually be made for emphasising the highly technical aspects of the new approach in order to attract and convince both the isolates and the opinion-leaders who should under normal circumstances assist in influencing the other members of the group.

Getting support for specific proposals

Once the audience's attention has been aroused, and interest created in seeking change, then comes the time to develop a desire for the change proposal.

In presenting information to enhance the selection of a given proposal in preference to alternative schemes, it is often necessary to mention some negative aspects of the proposed scheme in addition to the more beneficial ones. Similarly, the positive and negative aspects of existing or alternative schemes should also be presented. This technique of providing all aspects of the case under review is referred to as an "inoculation" effect; it weakens any counterproposals likely to arise at a later date. Experience has shown that an effective manner of presenting information where proposal B is intended to displace proposal A is to employ the following sequence:

(1)   present a complete listing of all the positive and beneficial aspects of proposal B;

(2)   mention the obvious and real drawbacks associated with proposal B;

(3)   describe a comprehensive listing of the deficiencies of proposal A;

(4)   indicate the most pertinent positive features of proposal A.

Following this presentation of the positive and negative features of the alternate proposals, the manager or the consultant should then draw conclusions as to why the favoured proposal (B) should be employed by listing the benefits to be accrued (i.e. service provided), the effectiveness of the new proposal (i.e. technical and economic superiority) and, if applicable, instances where such a proposal has been successfully employed.

Personality composition of the audience

To maintain control when dealing with a gathering or crowd of people is difficult at the best of times. When dealing with individuals or small groups, there are sometimes opportunities to use group members as enhancers of the change process.

Individuals who are poised, confident and have a certain amount of self-esteem appear to be able to influence others who lack these characteristics. In turn, these individuals with relatively high self-esteem appear to be more influenced by information containing optimistic rather than pessimistic or negative connotations.

The consultant should use opportunities to enlist support for the change process from persons who possess such traits of high self-esteem by drawing attention to likely optimistic results. These persons are then in a position to support the consultant's proposals before the group.

The informal communication network

Communications on a highly topical issue appear to produce a greater and more rapid attitude change in an audience when the information is "accidently overheard", or leaked through informal communication networks, than when delivered through formal channels. Rumours, which flourish in the absence of formal communications, are usually confined to informal channels and can often be countered by appropriate use of the same network. Even a fundamental piece of information, such as one stating that the future of a particular programme or unit is highly uncertain, may affect people's attitudes more strongly if spread informally than if officially issued by management. Occasionally, both formal and informal channels should be used to reinforce the message.

Handling objections to change

An essential skill for managing and assisting change is the ability to handle objections. Broadly speaking, objectors can be classified as "sharpeners" or "levellers". *Sharpeners* include those people who ask specific, detailed questions concerning the change process. They tend to be genuine objectors who want to be convinced that the change proposal is justified and are accessible to logical argument. *Levellers* are those who generalise and broaden the issue under review. They are usually quite difficult to convince as they are often more interested in the form of their objections than in the content.

Objections and resistance to change can be expressed in many different ways. Non-verbal messages, such as gestures, facial expressions, or repeated attempts to avoid discussing the issue with the manager or the consultant, may be very important and tell more than words.

In general, experience suggests that whenever a manager or a consultant senses that people may object to the change proposed, he should help those concerned to express their doubts or apprehensions by formulating objections. The objections made have to be analysed: they may point to weaknesses of the proposed scheme, show that not enough information was given to people affected by a change, reflect aversion to the manager's or the consultant's behaviour, or express resistance that will need to be dealt with.

When the consultant has to handle *specific objections*, it is more useful to repeat the objection, put it in writing if appropriate, break it down into component parts and treat each component as a separate entity, rather than attempt to deal with the problem as a whole. It is recommended to commence with those items on which agreement is most likely to be reached and move later to those items causing most disagreement. Should a total impasse be reached on an issue, it is better to reword the disagreement in objective terms relating to the new proposal rather than continue arguing in the often coloured and emotional words originally proposed by the objector. The consultant should frequently take the opportunity to recapitulate, and to refer to parts of the original objection on which agreement has already been reached, before continuing with new points.

If a point is reached when the consultant does not have the appropriate information to hand, this fact should be readily admitted and the objector advised that the information will be obtained and transmitted to him at a later date. The consultant should not fail to carry out this promise.

When objections to change become a matter of *inter-group conflict*, different problems requiring special treatment may arise. For example, this may happen if a group is to give up its work method to adopt one practised by another group. If a group sees itself threatened, there will be a closing of the ranks and more cohesive action, and the group will become more tolerant of authoritative rule by its chosen leaders. Hostility to other groups is likely to arise, especially if the situation is perceived as a "win-lose" encounter. Communication will become distorted and difficult, as each group will be prepared to admit only the positive aspects of its own argument and the negative aspects of the "enemy's".

Basic strategies to reduce inter-group conflict require the establishment of goals upon which both groups can agree in order to restore valid inter-group communication. If possible a common "enemy" should be identified, thus setting a superordinate goal. Emphasis should be placed on common needs and goals of different groups rather than on partial goals. If possible, a reward system which encourages effective communication should be introduced. Groups should be exposed to numerous activities likely to enhance empathy and mutual understanding.[7]

4.5 Interventions for assisting change

Managers and consultants have access to a wide range of intervention techniques, by which they are able to facilitate growth and change in individuals, groups and organisations. This section will review some commonly used techniques. These techniques can be applied for various purposes and at various stages of the change process: to demonstrate the need for change, develop an action programme, reduce resistance, help people to cope with new tasks and conditions, generate commitment, accelerate implementation, gear initiative and creativity towards priority goals, and so on. It is knowledge and practice of skills in choosing an appropriate technique and employing it in a life situation that set the consultant apart from the academic theoretician. The techniques may be acquired in part by studying research findings and publications, but, more particularly, they will be developed by experience.

Many of the techniques for assisting change are behavioural-science based, and emphasise change in attitudes, values and relationships. However, as Beckhard and Harris rightly pointed out,[8] over the last 15 years we have witnessed a shift in the technology of planned change. This technology has moved from an emphasis on team building, inter-group relations and the like to an emphasis on action-planning processes for coping with the total organisation and its environment, designing methods for organisational diagnosis, and applying comprehensive programmes for improving organisational performance. Essentially, there has been a growing understanding of the fact that a one-sided approach, as fostered by some behavioural scientists in the past, should give way to a comprehensive view of the organisation, embracing all organisational factors and sub-systems as well as their interaction with the environment.

Training and development

Reflecting on their experience with poorly designed and delivered seminars or courses, many consultants and managers do not believe that training and development can assist organisational change. Nevertheless, if properly used, training can be a powerful technique for change:

● management workshops, both external and in-company, can be used to sensitise managers and staff to the need for change, to environmental constraints and opportunities, to various options available to their organisations and to them as individuals, and to performance and other standards already reached elsewhere; experience has shown that managers can learn a great deal at workshops where other managers describe and analyse specific examples of organisational change;

- training can help people to develop the skills and abilities that are needed for coping with change effectively, such as diagnostic and problem-solving techniques, planning and evaluation techniques, or communication skills;
- tailor-made and paced training can assist the change process at its various stages by providing missing technical information and skills, thus helping staff to proceed to the next step and overcoming resistance caused by ignorance or lack of self-confidence;
- training of "internal" change agents increases the pool of those on whom management can rely in planning and assisting programmes of organisational change.

Organisational diagnosis and problem-solving techniques

There is a wide range of such techniques; many of them have special names given to them by their authors. Their main advantage is that they help to apply a systematic and methodical approach, making sure that important factors, relationships, or steps are not omitted and symptoms not mistaken for their causes. In a consulting project, the diagnostic phase and the action-planning phase can also serve as an intervention for making people aware of the need to change and mobilising their support for change. More detailed advice will be found in chapters 7-11 of this book.

Action learning

Action learning, pioneered by Reg Revans, is based on the assumption that managers learn best by solving real problems either in their own or in other organisations, and by exchanging relevant experience with other managers. The problems tackled must be important enough to the organisation concerned, and should involve both technical and human aspects. Emphasis is placed on implementation — that is, on the most difficult part of the change process. Exchange of experience with other managers involved in action learning is organised as a regular part of the programme. If necessary, the participants also receive technical assistance — missing information is supplied or expert advice is given on the approach taken. The ultimate objective is to achieve change both in individual skills and attitudes, and in organisational practices and performance.

Planning for improved enterprise performance (PIP)

The ILO and other international agencies have developed this technique and applied it over the years in a number of public enterprises in developing countries. PIP is a structured method, combining systematic problem identification and problem solving with organisational development approaches, and emphasising the involvement of total management teams in preparing and implementing action programmes for organisational change.[9] There are other methods similar to PIP.

Campaign-type, action-oriented programmes

A campaign-type, action-oriented programme is one that makes a special effort over a defined period of time to tackle a significant practical problem, mobilising fairly large teams and often requiring considerable resources. The intervention has to be extended long enough for bottom-line results to become visible or striking. Feedback on results achieved has to be provided with a view to maintaining interest in the programmes and adjusting the approach as appropriate. Also, missing information, skills, equipment and materials have to be made available when necessary. Examples of problems tackled include labour productivity, product and service quality, maintenance of equipment, energy consumption, waste, accident prevention and so on.[10]

Meetings

Meetings, which are used for many purposes, can also be designed to bring about and plan change. The focus of the meeting, as an intervention, is to enable various individuals to work on the problem face-to-face. It is important that the consultant involved should establish the appropriate climate. This may mean that the meeting may have to be held on "neutral ground", where none of the parties has any territorial advantage. The role that the consultant will play during the meeting should be clarified as early as possible. That role, essentially, is that of facilitator and process observer.

It is also possible to use meetings as an intervention without the consultant. When this is to be done, it is even more important that the relative roles and expectations of all those attending should be made clear prior to the meeting.

Temporary groups

Temporary groups, described above as one of the structural arrangements for managing change, can also be used as an intervention. Membership of a group to which a special task was assigned, coupled with appropriate motivation and leadership of the group, can have a strong stimulating effect and help to generate change.

Team building

This intervention is used frequently. Indeed, there are those who contend that it has been overused and abused. In part, the tendency to use this intervention is rooted in the early days of process consultation. Coming from group dynamics, the T-group approach, and the sensitivity movement, there was an assumption that the basic factor in improving individual and organisational behaviour resided in people working together in groups. Although this is important, it is by no means the only nor the chief type of intervention that should be considered. As with any other intervention, it should be based on the diagnosed need.

Although there are many variations, the team building approach focuses on how the team functions, rather than on the content area of the team. Slowly and carefully, the problem or task can be introduced into the situation, after work on interpersonal relationships has indicated that the climate is appropriate for moving into the real world.

Team building is not a one-off activity, although some consultants treat it that way. In many organisations, there is a recurring need to engage in team building activities.

Quality circles

Following the successful experience of Japanese industry, quality circles have been used in many countries for improving product quality, productivity, maintenance, working conditions, and so on. A quality circle is a small group established on a voluntary basis (as a rule within the same work area) and involving the full participation of all members. In addition to collectively seeking solutions to work-related technical problems, the circles focus on the mutual development of their members and on the improvement of communication and the human climate.

Because quality circles are autonomous in nature, they cannot be established or directly controlled by management. However, managers and consultants can encourage their creation and provide conditions under which quality circles can contribute to desirable organisational changes.

Goal setting

This type of intervention utilises many approaches. The focus is on having selected members of the organisation become involved in setting goals for themselves and for their parts of the organisation. In some situations, it is coupled with *management by objectives* (MBO), although this is not absolutely necessary.

During the process of goal setting, various problems will arise, such as competition for limited resources, or disagreement about the goals of the organisation. At that point, the consultant will introduce some of the other intervention techniques.

Confrontation

Within most organisations, there is generally competition for limited resources. There are times when an organisation appears to have unlimited access to resources, but these periods do not usually last too long. External influences impose limitations and restrictions. One way of dealing with internal competition for limited resources is to ignore it, but this merely forces various organisational members and units to devise ways to defeat other elements of the organisation.

This brings about the need for some kind of confrontation. This is a situation where individuals must confront each other and take action. It can result either in compromise (win-win), or in a situation where one unit or individual wins points at the expense of the other (win-lose). Confrontation is not necessarily negative — rather, it depends on how individuals deal with the confrontation.

Confrontation meetings normally employ a structured approach in which selected staff are exposed to (1) historical and conceptual ideas about organisations; (2) preparation of a list of significant problem-areas in their own organisation or unit; (3) classification of stated problems into categories; (4) development of plans of action to remedy problems; (5) comparison of the action proposals developed; and (6) planning for implementation.

There are cultures where confrontation is seen as negative behaviour. In these it is considered impolite and counter-cultural to force an individual into decision making. This does not mean that decisions are not made, but rather that they are not made through confrontation. The state of economic development has little to do with this aspect of cultural behaviour. It can be found in places as divergent as Japan and Malaysia. The consultant must also determine in which areas confrontation is inadvisable, as such cultural behaviour may only be appropriate for certain situations or between certain people.

When the need for a decision exists in a non-confronting culture, the consultant can bring about the needed confrontation as an intervention. He must do this very cautiously. One approach is to use a third party — that is, the confronting groups or individuals in the organisation do not meet face-to-face. Instead, the consultant engages in what is sometimes called "shuttle diplomacy". This can work effectively as the entering phase of a confrontation intervention, with the plan that, at a later phase, the parties will actually meet. In other situations, the entire confrontation may be dealt with indirectly.

Feedback

Feeding back data on individual, group and organisational performance can help to bring about some change in individual or group behaviour.

It is very important to provide feedback. Research and experience tell us that without feedback, data may be meaningless. Particularly when an attitude survey is used, it is important that the participants in the survey receive an analysis of the data that they have provided.

The process of feedback must be handled very cautiously, because raw data are frequently misunderstood. The analysis may prove critical or damaging to some individuals, and in such a situation the results can be anticipated. Obviously, those individuals will attempt to block any movement towards change.

On a positive note, feedback can be extremely helpful. Many people in an organisation do not receive sufficient feedback to enable them to assess their own performance or the performance of the organisation as a whole. The consultant should plan carefully, so that there will not be an information overload. Care should be taken with both the process and the content of the feedback.

Coaching and counselling

Commonly used change-assisting interventions are coaching and counselling. They are often used in process consultation where the client seeks help in improving his own performance or interpersonal relationships. The basic method is for the consultant to observe and review individual performance, provide feedback on problems or behavioural patterns that hinder operating effectiveness and inhibit change, and help the individual to acquire new knowledge and skills required by the changing nature of the job.

Choosing an intervention technique

In our discussion, intervention techniques were described independently. However, only rarely will one particular technique or approach lead to a successful implementation of change. In many situations, consultants have to use a variety of interventions.

A fully competent consultant is flexible in choosing intervention and change-assisting techniques, and combining several interventions as appropriate. As a rule, this choice is more effective if treated as one of the later areas of selection rather than being the subject of an early decision.[11] A trap to be avoided is choosing a wrong technique at the outset of the change process, and so rapidly creating a great deal of disenchantment, but obstinately continuing to use the technique although it is obviously leading nowhere.

In choosing an approach to problem solving and organisational change, some consultants stress the difference between closed-ended and open-ended problems experienced by client organisations.[12]

A closed-ended problem has a unique solution, which can be found by applying logical problem-analysis and problem-solving techniques, such as cost/benefit analysis or calculation of the break-even point. The problem is not affected by the people in the organisational unit concerned, and the commitment required for its solution is within the direct control of the problem solver. For example, a manager or a consultant can determine with considerable precision whether a machine tool ought to be replaced by a more productive, though a more sophisticated and expensive, one. Once the solution is found and implemented it is usually the end of the problem.

An open-ended problem has more possible solutions and no clear-cut answer. For example, product quality may continue to be a problem even though all technical aspects appear to be correct. Causes are not clear and the problem is affected both by the people working in the unit experiencing quality problems, and by the problem solver himself. The problem is vast, multifaceted, and essentially attitudinal. It is necessary to find and implement a solution which is both technically correct and likely to be understood and supported by the people who have to produce the desired result. This can be done only through their genuine involvement and commitment. The approach to adopt consists in *starting a process* of problem solving (change), involving those who "own" the problem, and using a change-assisting technique that will make this involvement possible. It can be one of the techniques reviewed above, or another technique. A longer time and a step-by-step approach will usually be required. Management will have to demonstrate a genuine interest in tackling all causes of the problem, even if the causes turn out to be mistakes of its own.

However, the consultant should be very cautious in assessing whether a management problem is to be approached as a closed-ended or open-ended one. A seemingly closed-ended problem may in fact be open-ended. A solution that looks technically simple and justified may affect the interests of the people involved in a way that was not foreseen and the problem then becomes open-ended.

Many consultants have specific variants of the "classical" intervention techniques: often these variants are not described in literature and are available only to clients. If a consultant proposes to use such a specific and not very well known technique, the client should ask him to explain what is unique in his technique and how it relates to the basic techniques. In fact, the consultant should take the initiative and give such an explanation when proposing his technique to the client.

4.6 Organisational culture supportive to change

A number of principles and techniques for managing and assisting change have been reviewed in this chapter. In the concluding section we want to stress some significant characteristics of organisations that have been successful in coping with change. Such organisations demonstrate that it is easier to keep pace with environmental change and generate effective changes from within if change has a prominent place in organisational culture (or climate), and if it is not handled as something exceptional, requiring a special campaign and ad hoc arrangements in every single case.

The following characteristics of organisational culture set favourable conditions for planned change.

Accepting the necessary pace of change

High-technology companies in electronics and other fields now operate in an atmosphere of constant change. Yet people understand that this is a salient characteristic of the sector with which they have to live. The required pace of change in many other organisations is not as high. Every organisation should define what is the optimum pace of change in its sector, and try to adopt it as a basic value shared by the staff. This includes balancing change and stability, and avoiding change for its own sake, as discussed in section 4.1.

Basing change on people's creativity

This requirement concerns all levels of management and all categories of employee. Where this principle is applied, every member of the organisation feels that his suggestions for changes are welcomed and will be dealt with in a competent manner. Suggesting and planning changes is not a guarded domain of senior management, and there is a scheme for collecting and examining change suggestions from managers, technicians and workers. This includes an operational workers' suggestion scheme. Management is obliged to follow up ideas received.

Orienting change efforts towards priority goals

People should know what preoccupies management and where they should focus individual and group performance improvement efforts to avoid dispersion of resources and help the company where it needs help most. However, every interesting idea should be examined, even if it is not in an area defined as priority.

Putting a high premium on innovation and change

Individuals and collectives must know that it pays to have a positive attitude to change and constantly to look for changes from which the organisation can benefit. Innovation and creativity can be stimulated by financial rewards, public recognition, promotions, making the job content more interesting, offering training and self-development opportunities, and so on. On the other hand, people must be able to see that it does not pay to be conservative and resist innovation and change.

As will be discussed in greater detail in chapter 5, values, attitudes and collectively held norms that make up organisational culture, develop over a number of years and, once established, they are not easy to change. But it is not impossible to influence and eventually to change them. Therefore if organisational culture constitutes the main obstacle to change, or if it does not stimulate change in an environment that is rapidly changing, the managers' and consultants' efforts may need to focus on organisational culture first of all.

---

[1] Whatever his field of speciality, a management consultant will be well advised to follow important works and articles on significant environmental developments world-wide, and in his own country and region. See, for example, A. Toffler: *The third wave* (London, Collins, 1980); J. Naisbitt: *Megatrends: Ten new directions transforming our lives* (New York, Warner Books, 1982); J. Diebold: *Making the future work: Unleashing our powers of innovation for the decades ahead* (New York, Simon and Schuster, 1984); or G. A. Steiner: *The new CEO* (New York, Macmillan, 1983).

[2] A similar conclusion was reached in several meetings of management consultants in the United States and in Europe. See, for example, comments made by J. Kennedy in *Consultants News*, July/Aug. 1983, and March 1985. See also further comments in chapters 12 and 21 of the present book.

[3] An American social psychologist, whose main writings on change date from the 1940s and 1950s. See, for example, K. Lewin: *Field theory in social science* (New York, Harper, 1951). Further contributions were made by G. W. Dalton and others. See also G. W. Dalton, P. R. Lawrence, L. E. Greiner: *Organisational change and development* (Homewood, IL, Irwin, 1970).

[4] The reader may be interested to note that not all psychologists subscribe to the sequence of these change levels. "Trying to change behaviour by changing values and attitudes is unnecessarily indirect ... while attitudes influence behaviour, behaviour

influences attitudes" (W. Fonviella: "Behaviour vs. attitude: Which comes first in organisational change?" in *Management Review*, Aug. 1984; p.14).

⁵ From P. Hearsey and K. H. Blanchard: *Management of organisational behavior* (Englewood Cliffs, NJ, Prentice-Hall, 1972); p. 160.

⁶ See also R. Bennett: *Management research: Guide for institutions and professionals* (Geneva, International Labour Office, 1983), chapter 4.

⁷ Further useful suggestions on how to deal with various expressions of resistance to change can be found in P. Block: *Flawless consulting: A guide to getting your expertise used* (Austin, TX, Learning Concepts, 1981), chapters 8 and 9.

⁸ R. Beckhard and R. T. Harris: *Organisational transitions: Managing complex change* (Reading, MA, Addison-Wesley, 1977), p. 5.

⁹ A detailed description of the PIP methodology is in R. Abramson and W. Halset: *Planning for improved enterprise performance: A guide for managers and consultants* (Geneva, International Labour Office, 1979).

¹⁰ ILO has assisted several countries and groups of enterprises in developing campaign-type programmes in areas such as productivity improvement, or raising the quality of maintenance in industry. See M. Kubr and J. Wallace: *Successes and failures in meeting the management challenge: Strategies and their implementation*, Staff working paper 585 (Washington, DC, World Bank, 1983).

¹¹ R. Beckhard and R. T. Harris: *Organisational transitions: Managing complex change* (Reading, MA, Addison-Wesley, 1977), p.44.

¹² The discussion of closed-ended and open-ended problems is taken and adapted, with acknowledgement of the origin, from a technical paper prepared for the ILO by George Boulden.

CONSULTING AND CULTURE 5

In helping clients to plan and implement change, the consultant may find that certain attitudes and beliefs are shared by many if not all people in a client organisation or in a whole community. He is looking for a rational explanation but does not find one. Yet he senses that he is facing a silent power which permeates people's behaviour and influences their stance on many issues much more strongly than any logical argument. If this is the case, it is most probable that the behaviour observed reflects the power of *culture*.

Culture is normally defined as a system of collectively shared values, beliefs, traditions and behavioural norms unique to a particular group of people. "Culture is the collective programming of human mind that distinguishes the members of one human group from those of another group. Culture, in this sense, is a system of collectively held values." [1] Or, in the words of the French mathematician and philosopher Blaise Pascal, "there are truths on this side of the Pyrenees that are falsehoods on the other".

Culture has its roots in basic conditions of human life, including material conditions, the natural environment, climate, and ways in which people earn their living, and in the historical experience of human communities which includes interaction with other countries and cultures. People create culture as a mechanism that helps them to cope with their environment and maintain the cohesion and identity of the community in interacting with other communities. In developing countries, in rural areas in particular, traditional cultures reflect the people's poverty and helplessness before the forces of nature. Culture tends to be deeply rooted and therefore cannot be easily changed. Some governments have learned about the power of their own country's culture only after having tried to impose changes that this culture did not tolerate.

5.1 Understanding and respecting culture

The problem with culture is that, although it is omnipresent and its influence on the functioning of organisations and whole societies is strong, it is difficult to identify and grasp. Definitions of it tend to be vague. Culture is nowhere precisely described, and it also includes taboos: values that people respect, but about which they do not normally talk and sometimes resent talking. Individuals and whole communities may be unaware of their culture because they have not learned it as a structured subject or a technical skill. Values and beliefs that make up culture evolve over generations, are transmitted from generation to generation, and are normally acquired unconsciously, early in people's lives — in the family, at school, through religious education, at work, and by socialising with other members of the community.

A management consultant faces the same problem. His personality and value system have been moulded by the culture in which he has grown up, worked and socialised with other people. Yet he may be unaware of it. For as "the last thing that a fish will discover is water", often culture will be the last thing that a management consultant, otherwise an outstanding expert in his technical field, will discover.

Being culture-conscious

In management consulting, a concern for culture is as important as a concern for the specific technical problem for which the consultant was brought in. But what can he do to be sure that he is culture-conscious and that neither his behaviour nor his suggestions clash with culture?

To be culture-sensitive, a management consultant does not have to convert himself into a sociologist or anthropologist. Some knowledge of culture can be gained by self-development and training. Reading about culture and discussing cultural issues with other people helps a great deal. Genuine interest in the meaning of culture and in different cultures provides a good background for understanding and correctly interpreting a particular cultural context.

However, this is only the first step. Like any other person, a consultant who has never lived and operated in a culture different from his own will find it difficult to perceive and understand the full meaning and power of another culture, and the role of various factors that may be unknown in his own culture. Experience has shown that only people who have been in contact with a different culture for some time start understanding not only that culture but also their own culture. Social and working contacts with other cultures provide us with a mirror in which to see our own culture.

Being culture-tolerant

Culture is very important to people. Their preference for fundamental cultural values is not rational, but emotional. They may even regard certain social norms and traditions as eternal and sacrosanct. In contrast, a management consultant may regard them as anachronistic and irrational. There may be a grain of truth in the consultant's view, since not everything is constructive and progressive in cultures: they often include values that inhibit development and progress. Nevertheless, cultures reflect centuries of society's experience and help people to cope with life. Respect for different cultures and tolerance for values and beliefs alien to his own culture, but dear to other people, are therefore essential qualities of a good consultant.

In his attitude to other cultures, a consultant is strongly influenced by his own culture. Tolerance towards other cultures is a cultural characteristic, too: some cultures are highly tolerant of different cultural values, while others are not. A consultant who has been moulded by a less tolerant cultural environment should be particularly cautious when dealing with delicate organisational and human problems in other cultures.

5.2 Levels of culture

National culture

The term "national culture" is used to define the values, beliefs, behavioural norms, habits and traditions that characterise human society in a particular country. There can be one national culture in an ethnically and linguistically homogeneous country, but in many countries there are several distinct cultures and the country may appear to be a mosaic of cultures. The question is, do these cultures mix with each other, cohabit and, especially, tolerate each other, or do they make the functioning of the state and of the economy difficult?

An important cultural phenomenon is the existence of minorities and their relationship to other ethnic groups within society. Often minorities make a special effort to preserve their particular culture in order to protect their identity and ensure survival within an environment where a majority culture prevails and tends to influence or even oppress minority cultures. Certain minorities possess attitudes, skills, historical experience and material means, thanks to which they have been extremely successful in business. The implications of this are well known in many countries. Thus, while sensitivity to cultural differences is essential in international consulting, a consultant operating within his own country also needs to be aware of culture.

It would be impossible to review here all the factors embraced by the concept of national (or local) culture. It would be even more difficult to point to all the differences between cultures which a consultant needs to be aware of because they may be related to his work in some way. The spectrum of cultural values and related norms and rituals can be extremely wide and can concern any aspect of human, economic and social life. Of particular importance to management are values concerning issues such as:

- the distribution of social roles and the status assigned to them;
- the criteria of success and achievement in economic and social life;
- respect for age and seniority;
- the role of traditional authorities and community leaders;
- democratic versus autocratic traditions;

- individualism versus collectivism;
- spiritual versus material values;
- responsibility and loyalty to family, community and ethnic group;
- socialisation and communication patterns;
- the acceptability and the form of feedback, appraisal and criticism;
- religion, its importance in social life and its impact on economic activity;
- attitudes to other cultures, religions, ethnic groups, minorities;
- attitudes to social, technological and other changes;
- the conception of time.

Language plays a prominent role in culture. Cultural concepts are described in words, the meaning of many words is culture-bound and language is a vehicle for the interaction of cultures. Non-verbal expressions and gestures are also culture-bound and may be very important. Non-verbal communication is more difficult to control consciously than verbal communication and tends therefore to be more trustworthy. Some cultures (e.g. North American) attach importance to what is said, while in other cultures (e.g. Asian) it is essential to understand non-verbal messages.

National cultures are unique, but they are not closed systems. There are similarities between cultures for many reasons, such as common language or religion. Long-term interaction of cultures (e.g. during domination of one country by another) also influences culture. In some developing countries, the social groups most exposed to the culture of the former colonial power (e.g. administrators, intellectuals and businessmen) tended to adopt some of its values and behavioural patterns. Cultural changes occur in many countries under the influence of an increase in material wealth, better general education, a massive expansion of contacts among cultures and other factors.

There is a growing interest in exploring the role played by national culture in the economic performance and development of particular countries. For many decades, North American culture has been widely regarded as a major factor in the dynamism, competitiveness and achievement of American businesses. At the present time, managers all over the world are keen to get a deeper insight into Japanese national culture, hoping that this will give them inspiration for improving management style and performance in their own organisations.

The term culture is also applied to values and behaviours that characterise other social groups: professions, trade groups, organisations, clubs and associations. Even small social units, such as families, may have their specific cultures. All of these are sometimes called micro-cultures.

Professional culture

Professional culture is one shared by individuals who belong to the same profession, e.g. by lawyers, medical doctors, civil engineers, or accountants. It is very much related to job content and to the role played in society by the members of the profession. It is influenced by professional education and training and tends to exhibit common characteristics across organisational and national boundaries. One of the objectives of professional associations and societies is to preserve and develop professional culture. Ethical values promoted by professional associations tend to become a part of this culture.

As will be discussed in more detail in chapter 6, managers, administrators and management consultants also share certain characteristics of a profession. A common cross-cultural characteristic of experienced managers is their pragmatism: they are keen to find solutions that will work rather than obstinately to insist on norms and rules that have proved to be unpractical. Managers in developing countries often face a real dilemma: how to reconcile the professional culture to which they tend to adhere with the local culture in which they grew up and which surrounds and permeates their organisation.

The understanding of professional culture may help a management consultant in establishing constructive relations with clients in foreign countries. It is useful to be informed about the background of managers and staff in a client organisation and know, for example, from which universities they graduated. Some members of a client organisation may share common professional values with the consultant: this may be of particular help in penetrating problems of local culture and working out practical measures likely to be accepted.

Organisational culture

Organisations, too, tend to have their specific culture: a peculiar mix of values, attitudes, norms, habits, traditions, behaviours and rituals that, in their totality, are unique to the given organisation. Some organisations are well aware of their culture and regard it as a powerful strategic tool, used to orient all units and individuals towards common goals, mobilise employee initiative, ensure loyalty, and facilitate communication. They aim at creating a culture of their own and making sure that all employees understand it and adhere to it.

Organisational cultures, or micro-cultures, reflect national cultures first of all. But they also include other values and norms. Recent research has provided some insight into organisational cultures of leading corporations in the United States, Japan and other countries. It has shown that many companies which have been outstanding performers over a long time exhibit a strong corporate culture.[2]

Many multinational corporations possess certain cultural characteristics world-wide, and the parent company's culture has considerable bearing on the cultural norms and behaviour of subsidiaries in other countries. The strong personalities of the founders and of certain top managers also influence organisational culture even in very large and complex corporations. This leads to an interesting mix of cultures in the case of foreign subsidiaries, where the influence of local national culture is combined with that of the parent company's culture.

The hidden dimensions of organisational culture tend to surface during company mergers and takeovers, which in many cases fail to produce expected results mainly because management is unable to harmonise different cultures.

The specific cultural values of an organisation may concern, for example:

- the organisation's mission and image (high technology; superior quality; pride in being a sector leader; dedication to the service ethos; innovative spirit; entrepreneurial drive);

- seniority and authority (authority inherent in position or person; respect for seniority and authority; seniority as a criterion of authority);

- the importance of different management positions and functions (authority of personnel department; importance of different vice-presidents' positions; respective roles and authority of research and development (R and D), production and marketing);

- the treatment of people (concern for people and their needs; equitable treatment or favouritism; privileges; respect for individual rights; training and development opportunities; lifetime careers; fairness in remuneration; how people are motivated);

- the role of women in management and other jobs (acceptance of women for positions of authority; jobs either unavailable or reserved for women; respect for women managers; equal treatment; special facilities);

- selection criteria for managerial and supervisory positions (seniority versus performance; priority for selection from within; political, ethnic, nationality and other criteria; influence of informal relations and cliques);

- work organisation and discipline (voluntary versus imposed discipline; punctuality; use of time clocks; flexibility in changing roles at work; use of new forms of work organisation);

- management and leadership style (paternalism; authoritative, consultative or participative style; use of committees and task forces; providing personal example; style flexibility and adaptability);

- decision-making processes (who decides; who has to be consulted; individual or collective decision making; need to reach consensus);

- circulation and sharing of information (employees amply or poorly informed; information readily shared or not);

- communication patterns (preference for oral or written communication; rigidity or flexibility in using established channels; importance attached to formal aspects; accessibility of higher management; use of meetings; who is invited to what meetings; established behaviours in the conduct of meetings);

- socialisation patterns (who socialises with whom during and after work; existing barriers and inhibitions; special facilities such as separate dining rooms or reserved clubs);

- ways of handling conflict (desire to avoid conflict and to compromise; preference for informal or formal ways; involvement of higher management);
- performance evaluation (substantive or formal; confidential or public; by whom carried out; how results are used);
- identification with the organisation (manager and staff adherence to company objectives and policies; loyalty and integrity; *esprit de corps*; enjoying working with the organisation).

Furthermore, many organisational cultures develop a specialised vocabulary and a wide range of symbols and rituals that staff members have to use and respect if they do not want to be regarded as outsiders by their colleagues.

A management consultant needs to learn about organisational culture as early as possible in his assignment if he does not want to be perceived as a stranger who does not know how things are normally done and how people behave in the client organisation, and whose presence therefore is an irritation. But there is another much more important reason for this: the client organisation's culture may be one of the causes, or the cause, of the problems over which the consultant was brought in. Even if changes in organisational culture are not explicitly stated among the objectives of his assignment, the consultant may have to deal with them and recommend what in his opinion needs to be changed. Such changes may be particularly painful: they may include important personnel changes and patient educational efforts. Yet they may be inevitable. We shall return to this question in chapter 12.

5.3 Facing culture in consulting assignments

The consultant's behaviour

A great deal of useful guidance is available on how consultants should behave when operating in other cultures. Most of it concerns interpersonal relations and manners. For example, it is good to get advice on:

- how to dress;
- how to deal with people;
- punctuality;
- when and how to start discussing business;
- written and oral communication with the client;
- formal and informal interpersonal relations;
- the use of go-betweens;
- display or restraint of emotions;
- what language and terms to use;
- taboos to avoid.

Such things are relatively easy to learn and remember. These days it is helpful that cultural tolerance is also likely to be observed by the client. An American consultant may be unable to resist the temptation to address people by their first names after having known them for five minutes, but today he would rarely be rejected for it, since this peculiar behavioural characteristic is well known and tends to be tolerated (though not always liked) by people who have been exposed to North American culture.

However important, questions such as whether to use first names and what topics should not be openly discussed represent only the tip of the iceberg in the cross-cultural consultant-client relationship. The less visible and more profound aspects of this relationship concern such issues as power and role distribution, decision-making processes, confrontation and consensus in problem solving, use of team work, consultation with employees, deep religious beliefs, and any criteria whereby management will judge the consultant's suggestions.

Some consultants feel that they must try to identify themselves with a foreign culture, behaving as the client behaves ("when in Rome do as the Romans do!"), and sharing the client's values and beliefs in order fully to understand his environment and render an effective service. This may be impossible, even undesirable, to achieve. It implies no longer being authentic and genuine, thus abandoning key behavioural characteristics of a professional consultant. Understanding and respecting other people's culture does not imply giving up one's own!

How to find out

, The consultant has to use all his experience and talent to learn enough about the cultural factors which may be relevant to his assignment.[3] In some cases, direct questions on how things are normally done in the client organisation and what pitfalls to avoid will be perfectly acceptable, in particular if the client is keen to get a technically valid solution and is himself aware of the power of culture. In other cases, tactful and patient observation of the client's behaviour may produce an answer. A great deal can be learned by mixing with people and observing how they act and socialise, what symbols they use and what rituals they observe. Discussions of cultural issues should be informal; formal and structured interviews are not well suited for dealing with culture. Judgement should be suspended until the consultant has learned more. Also, the consultant should try not to be nervous and uneasy in a new situation that appears ambiguous. To detect and overcome cultural barriers, it is useful to team up with an internal consultant or another member of the client organisation who is prepared to help.

A study of the client company's history can be revealing. The roots of present corporate culture may be far back in the past: in the personality of the founder, in past successes or failures, in the growth pattern (e.g. many acquisitions or frequent changes of owners), and the like. For example, the present organisational culture of some public enterprises in various countries continues to reflect the strong culture of private corporations from which they were established following nationalisation. While nationalisation has brought about great changes, deeply rooted organisational values and norms have survived.

We have already emphasised that it is important to establish as early as possible a climate of trust among all the parties in the consultant-client relationship. This can be difficult since not all cultures agree that trust of an outsider is desirable. One way of looking at these relations is by comparing high-context and low-context societies.

In *a high-context society*, relationships are based on friendship, family ties and knowing each other well. The context, the total situation, is essential to building relationships. The formation of these relationships is paced quite slowly and includes many rituals or rites of passage. This can include eating certain kinds of food, or engaging in various social activities unrelated to work.

In *a low-context society*, the relationship generally is spelled out in a written contract. The client is keen to obtain a precisely defined piece of technical work and may not care all that much about the total relationship with the consultant. What is not in the contract is not part of the relationship. Of course, there are subtle forms of interaction even in a low- context society. Generally, however, the relationship is built first on the written document; the building of trust follows.

In some cultures, developing trust takes time, but it is possible in most cultures. This need for time should be recognised and built into the plan of the assignment. Also, the concept of high- and low-context societies is a developing one. The consultant should be careful about applying it to an entire country or an entire people, since there are individual variations.

Criteria of rationality

In working for a client, a management consultant aims to find and recommend solutions which are in the client's interest. To justify the proposed measures to himself and to the client, a consultant applies as criteria what he regards as rationality. For example, he may apply economic effectiveness as a criterion and judge various alternatives by their impact on the productivity and financial performance of the organisation. He may use cost/benefit analysis as the main assessment technique.

However, the conception of rationality is culture-bound. Even in western industrial economies, where the notions of efficiency, competitiveness and profitability have not only an economic but also a strong cultural connotation, economic rationality is not always the main criterion applied by top management in evaluating alternative decisions. Personal, cultural and political preferences may prevail. The desire to maintain the status quo, fear of the unknown, or reluctance to make changes affecting collectively shared values, may eventually determine top management's choice even in a European or North American enterprise. In several Asian countries, certain cultural values tend to be applied as criteria of rationality: to preserve harmony, to avoid dismissing employees, to maintain status differences and respect feelings about ethnic groups may be seen as more effective and more rational than to optimise performance in strictly economic and financial terms.

Transferring management practices

Management consultants use their past experience in working with present clients. This involves transferring management practices from one organisation or country to another organisational or national environment. Other items could be substituted for "management practices". We could also speak about management techniques, technologies, methods, expertise, systems, concepts, patterns, approaches, and the like, but the question remains the same: to what extent and under what circumstances are management practices transferrable?

There are factors whose influence on the choice of management techniques is evident — for example, the nature of the product, the technology used, or the size of the organisation. The influence of culture is more subtle and not so easy to perceive, but experience has shown that it tends to be very strong.

Some management techniques are *value-laden*. They were developed for use in a particular culture and reflect its value systems and behavioural norms. They concern the human side of organisations: individual and group interests, interpersonal and inter-group relations, motivation and control of human behaviour. The possibility of transferring these techniques has to be carefully examined in each case. A value-laden technique may be difficult or impossible to transfer. Remuneration techniques stimulating individual performance rather than collective solidarity fail in collectivist societies; high wage differentials may not be acceptable in an egalitarian society; organisation development methods based on confrontation cannot be used where harmony and conflict avoidance are strongly valued; problem-solving approaches built on democratic values are difficult to apply in a traditionally autocratic culture; matrix organisation does not work effectively in cultures where people attach great value to the unity of command and prefer to receive orders from one single higher authority. Examples of failures caused by a mechanistic transfer of value-laden techniques are abundant.

Some other techniques were developed in response to organisational characteristics such as the nature and complexity of the production process, or the amount of data to be recorded and analysed; that is to say, they concern the technological, economic and financial side of organisations. Such techniques are relatively *value-neutral* and their transfer across cultures is a simpler matter. However, while a technique may appear value-neutral, its application creates a new situation that may be value-laden. For example, a production control or maintenance scheduling technique required by the technology used may conflict with the workers' beliefs and habits concerning punctuality, work organisation and discipline, justified absence from work, accuracy and reliability of records, and the like.

Culture and change

Values and beliefs concerning change have a prominent place in culture. Generally speaking, modernistic and optimistic cultures regard change as healthy; without it, business cannot flourish or society prosper. Cultures dominated by traditionalism value the status quo, stability and reverence for the past. They are suspicious about change and may perceive it as disturbing and subversive even if, in the consultant's view, the need for change is self-evident. To realise and appreciate this may be particularly difficult for a consultant who has been used to working with dynamic clients, keen to apply quickly any changes from which the company can derive benefits.

The presence of cultural factors impeding or retarding change does not imply that change is not possible. Even the most conservative individuals and groups are able to reconcile themselves to change if they realise its necessity, in particular if change is imposed by strong external influences, such as the deterioration of material conditions of living. Better information, education, contacts with more dynamic cultures and new technology also affect the traditionalist societies' attitude to change. However, the process of change may be slow and difficult.

When operating in an environment where resistance to change is significant, a consultant will be well advised to bear in mind:

- the sort of change that is acceptable (refraining from proposals that the client will judge to be culturally undesirable or unfeasible);

- the pace of change (deciding whether to plan for a fundamental one-off change, or for gradual changes in a number of small steps; assessing "acceptance time" needed by the client and his staff to convince themselves about the desirability of proposed changes);

- the client's readiness for change (it is unreasonable to press for change if the client is not ready to face the cultural problems that change may cause him);

- the level of management and the particular person (authority) by whom change has to be proposed and promoted in order to be accepted and implemented;

- the persuasion and educational effort needed to convince people that maintaining the status quo is not in their interest.

Consulting in social development

At the present time more and more management consulting is done for social development programmes and projects in sectors such as health, nutrition, basic education, drinking water supply, sanitation, community development, or population control. Many of these programmes requiring consulting interventions are in rural areas of developing countries. Management consultants, including consultants who have worked in developing countries and are aware of their cultural characteristics, are as a rule familiar with the cultural setting encountered in industry and central government administration, but rural and social development are new worlds to them.

In social development, the consultant's clients are not managers operating modern enterprises or well-established administrative structures, but managers, social workers and organisers working with local communities, groups of farmers, or even individual families and persons. The technology used is simple and may be outdated. The concepts of "professional culture" or "organisational culture" do not apply. In contrast, the impact of traditional social culture is extremely strong. Human behaviour, essentially fatalistic and conservative, is governed by deeply-rooted beliefs and prejudices. Cultural characteristics reflect difficult living conditions, poverty and poor education. Passivity, resignation, lack of personal drive, fear of change and uncritical respect for traditional authorities may prevail.

In consulting, knowledge of these factors is essential, but it is not all that is needed. A consultant needs to possess *cultural and social work skills* rather than knowledge of refined management techniques. He needs to be patient, to be able to live and operate under conditions of imperfection and uncertainty, to know how to improvise using limited local resources, and to apply a great deal of imagination in devising solutions which cannot be found in any management handbook. Personal commitment and empathy for the underpriviledged are qualities without which it is hard to succeed.

---

[1] G. Hofstede: "Culture and organisations" in *International Studies of Management and Organisation,* No. 4, 1981. The word culture, in English and some other languages, also has another meaning. It is used when referring to the arts, literature, and so on. Obviously, that is not the meaning intended here.

[2] See T. E. Deal and A. A. Kennedy: *Corporate cultures: The rites and rituals of corporate life* (Reading, MA, Addison-Wesley, 1982); R. T. Pascale and A. G. Athos: *The art of Japanese management: Applications for American executives* (New York, Warner Books, 1981); and T. J. Peters and R. H. Waterman: *In search of excellence: Lessons from America's best-run companies* (New York, Harper and Row, 1982).

[3] See, for example, G. Hofstede: *Cultural pitfalls for Dutch expatriates in Indonesia* (Deventer, Netherlands, Twijnstra Gudde International, 1982); G. L. Lippitt and D. S. Hoopes (eds.): *Helping across cultures* (Washington, DC, International Consultants Foundation, 1978); P. R. Harris and R. T. Moran: *Managing cultural differences* (Houston, TX, Gulf Publishing Co., 1979); and R. T. Moran and P. R. Harris: *Managing cultural synergy* (Houston, TX, Gulf Publishing Co., 1982).

PROFESSIONALISM IN CONSULTING

6

The growth of management consulting has given ample evidence that at one time almost anyone could call himself a consultant and set up in practice. In its early years the business attracted the good, the bad and the indifferent. The word "business" is used deliberately: "professions" seldom start as such. Professional awareness and behaviour come when the early juggling with a little knowledge gives way to skilled application of a generally accepted body of knowledge according to accepted standards of integrity. The professions of medicine, the law and the applied sciences all followed this path, and management consulting is proceeding in the same direction.

The development of management consulting towards professionalism is part of a wider movement which aims at developing management into a profession. As advisers to managers on the application of the science and art of managing, consultants follow the major trends that affect management practice and theory. In many respects, consulting can advance and become more professional only if the whole field of management is moving in the direction of professionalism. At the same time consultants constitute a specialised group, with its own way of operating and with its own set of behavioural rules and working procedures. The problem of professionalising management consultancy is therefore not completely identical with professionalising management as such. It is even necessary to stress that management consultants are aiming at professionalism with more vigour than practising managers, and that they play a pioneering role in professionalising management at large.

6.1 Defining a profession

Before discussing in detail how a consultant can enhance his professional approach and make a personal contribution to the professionalisation of consulting, we should mention the criteria normally used to define a profession. These criteria, about which much has been said and written, can be summarised under five headings.[1]

Knowledge and skills

There is a defined body of knowledge proper to the profession which can be acquired through a system of professional education and training. The necessary level of professional expertise is not reached without a certain number of years of practical experience, preferably under the guidance of senior members of the profession. In addition, the practising professional keeps continuously abreast of relevant developments in theory and practice.

The concept of service and social interest

The professional puts his knowledge and experience at the disposal of clients as a service against appropriate remuneration. He serves his client's interests, to which he subordinates his self-interest. However, he views client interest from a wider social perspective, and keeps wider social needs and interests in mind when serving individual clients.

Ethical norms

There is a set of recognised ethical norms, shared and consistently applied by the members of the profession. These norms define what is proper and what is improper behaviour in providing a professional service.

Community sanction and enforcement

The society in which the profession operates and the clientele which is served recognise the social role, the status and the behavioural norms of the profession. There may be explicit recognition (e.g. by means of a legal text governing and protecting professional practice). This may include definitions of educational standards required, as well as of behaviours considered as unprofessional and illegal, and of corresponding sanctions.

Self-discipline and self-control

A member of the profession applies self-discipline and self-control in observing the profession's behavioural norms while serving his clients. In addition, the profession organises itself in a voluntary membership institution, thus exercising collective self-regulation and self-control over the application of an accepted code of professional conduct.

6.2 The professional approach

What then are the salient characteristics of a truly professional approach in management consulting? Some of them can be found, in succinct form, in the codes of ethics adopted by the membership organisations of management consultants; others are set out in information pamphlets issued by some consulting firms. These are the norms held collectively, i.e. by the members of a consultants' association or of a consulting firm that has declared what its ethical rules are. However, in many countries and situations it is not possible to refer to a more or less formal declaration of norms defining truly professional and ethical behaviour. In such cases the consultant will be guided by his personal ethics — his own conception of what is proper and improper practice, and what is beneficial to the client and to society and what is not.

Every consultant, including those who have officially adhered to collectively-held behavioural norms, has to make many personal choices and decisions on what norms to respect and how to behave in particular situations. No one will make these value judgements for him, since they are inherent in the very concept of providing advice to clients in situations where multiple choices apply and conflicting interests have to be faced.

It should be stressed that the consultant is in a position of trust; the client believes that certain behavioural norms will be respected without their even being mentioned. For example, many clients believe that consultants would never use false credentials, and some clients are even unable to evaluate the consultant's technical competence. The consultant may be in a position of technical superiority and possess knowledge and information denied to the client. The client, on the other hand, may be in a position of weakness, uncertainty, and even distress.

Nevertheless, in many cases the "technical superiority" of the management consultant, and his "exclusive power" over the client, are quite different from what can be observed in some other professions, e.g. in medicine. There are two main reasons for this. First, if there is a knowledge and experience gap between management consultants and their clients, this gap can be quite small. To many clients management consulting is not a "black box". Both the consultant and the client may have the same educational background and similar practical experience. Hence the client may be quite well prepared for deciding to accept or reject the consultant's advice, and for controlling the consultant's work during an assignment. Clearly, this is not the normal position of a patient who turns to his physician, or of a layman (e.g. a farmer) who seeks legal counsel. Secondly, management consulting is not a closed and highly protected profession. We will see that in most countries there are no barriers or only minimal barriers to entering the profession. There are no jobs that would be reserved to management consultants. Thus, the consultant's and the client's roles can even be interchangeable. He who is client today can be consultant tomorrow. And vice versa.

Any consultant whose ambition is to become a real professional must clarify for himself his own conception of ethics and the norms he will consistently observe in working for clients. This applies equally to external and internal consultants, as well as to persons who intervene in a consulting capacity although they are not full-time consultants.

Some of the characteristics of a professional approach have already been mentioned in previous chapters, but they are worth repeating.

Technical competence

The consultant's technical competence is the basis of his professional approach. Above all, he must possess the sort of knowledge and skills needed by a particular client. This knowledge and these skills have several important facets, as will be discussed in detail in chapter 27.

Professional associations of management consultants in various countries have attempted to define *a common body of knowledge* that every member of the association must possess. They have also defined *the type and minimum duration of experience* which is a condition of membership — for example, 3-5 years in consulting, including a period of 1-2 years of responsibility for client projects.

These, however, are basic criteria of admission; they do not show whether a consultant is fully competent for a particular assignment. To determine this competence is a matter for the consultant's and the client's judgement; this judgement should be formulated after a more profound and more serious discussion than is often the case.

As a general rule, and this is a key feature of professionalism, the consultant must be able and willing to critically assess his own knowledge and skills when considering a new assignment. He will never misrepresent himself. If he wants to try to tackle a new sort of problem (experience cannot be increased except by trying out something new), he will tell his client about it.

Accordingly, a professional consultant refrains from assignments that are outside his field of competence. He may decline the assignment, suggest the use of specialists for some part of the job, or propose another arrangement convenient to the client.

The client's interest

During an assignment, the consultant makes his competence fully available to the client and his objective is to find the best possible solution in the client's interest. It is not always obvious what "client's interest" means and what the client really expects from the assignment. There is often a conflict between short-term and long-term interests, but the client may not see this until the consultant explains it to him.

In agreeing to serve a client, the consultant must be sure that his and the client's interests do not conflict. This can happen if the consultant also pursues objectives that have little in common with the client's objectives. For example, much consulting is done in connection with investment and systems design projects by consulting units linked in some way with engineering firms or manufacturers of computing hardware. The consultant's project can be oriented in a way that will influence the client to select one particular type of equipment. In such a situation the consultant's advice may be technically perfect and may even represent the best possible alternative. But the client should know right from the outset that he will not receive unbiased advice, but rather a "package deal" including both professional advice and a recommendation concerning the purchase of equipment. It is for him to choose what he prefers.

General and financial management consultants often participate in preparing decisions on mergers, acquisitions, divestment, turnarounds, and similar major changes that will affect the market value of stocks. Reliable inside information on imminent decisions may be worth a fortune, and certain individuals may be very tempted to make use of it in their personal interest. This is perhaps the most obvious instance of conflict of interests in working in a professional advisory capacity. Not only is such an abuse banned by the consultants' professional codes of conduct, but it is considered to be illegal in all countries where fair business practices are protected by law.

During assignments consultants meet, and see at work, many bright people in client firms. Frequently, they are tempted to recruit such people from the client. This may be another instance of conflicting interests. Offering a job to a client's employee, even after the completion of the assignment, is professionally admissible only if the client is informed beforehand and does not object to it.

Another aspect is the chance of success of an assignment. A client may want to take measures that come too late and cannot stop the overall deterioration of the firm's condition. Or improvements are possible, but would require drastic action as regards personnel or other measures that the client is unable to consider. If a professional consultant discovers such a situation in preparing the assignment, or even after he has started work, he informs the client candidly and suggests cancelling the contract.

There are urgent assignments in which advice and action are required very quickly so that a bankruptcy, a strike, or other very serious difficulties are avoided. A consultant must never take longer than the problem warrants and must make sure that his work is organised and implemented in accordance with the urgency of the situation.

Consulting services are not inexpensive, therefore it is not in the client's interest to extend an assignment beyond necessary time limits. The purpose is to help the client, not to milk his cash-box. For example, the consultant's presence during implementation is superfluous if the client's staff can be trained to do the job without any external help.

This leads us to a wider issue — that of a potential conflict of interest in deciding whether and how to train the client. It should be clear from what was said in the previous chapters that a truly professional consulting approach, as currently viewed by the overwhelming majority of consultants, has a strong learning dimension. To "help the client to learn how he can help himself" is a fundamental objective to which consultants adhere whole-heartedly. However, a general declaration of a noble principle is not enough. The consultant must be sure that the assignment is so designed, and the client so involved, that the consultant will not retain for himself the knowledge and expertise that should be passed on to the client. Consultants who are looking to the future do not see teaching and training clients as a threat. Clients will have new sorts of problems, and a consultant from whom the client has learned a great deal may be called on again. He will gladly recommend the consultant to business colleagues. Other clients will come, and so on.

Impartiality and objectivity

In addition to the instances of conflicting interests mentioned above, there are other factors that may affect the consultant's impartiality and objectivity. In particular, the consultant is influenced by his whole value system, which is culture-bound, and in addition includes certain personal values that are not necessarily determined by the cultural environment.

Consciously or unconsciously, over the years consultants develop not only their own work patterns, but also beliefs in the efficiency of certain types of methods and approaches that have been successful in previous cases. Some consultants clearly favour one methodological approach which they consider as the most powerful tool for dealing with management problems. The same situation might be viewed by one consultant as a matter of diagnosing future business prospects and developing new corporate strategy, by another as an organisation-development, team-building exercise, and by a third as a typical case for the introduction of management by objectives throughout the organisation. Some consultants are strong believers in the behavioural sciences and pay great attention to the psycho-sociological aspects of change, while others prefer the traditional approach including the analysis and redesign of jobs, structures and systems.

By emphasising that consultants may apply different personalised approaches to the same problems, we do not want to devalue their advice. But the word "objective" is to be used with extreme caution. If a consultant decides to approach his client's business and organisational problems in one particular way, although there may be other options, he should in any event inform his client about such a choice and give his reasons.

But more than that. The consultant's stance may be influenced by political, racial, religious, or other beliefs and prejudices. An experienced professional may be able to control his beliefs and prejudices, thus making sure that he remains objective. He should decline an assignment if he cannot be objective for emotional reasons.

Internal consultants should be particularly aware of their dependence on their own organisation and of the factors which might make them less impartial than an external adviser. As explained in chapter 2, they should not be put in situations where they clearly cannot be impartial.

Confidentiality

Confidentiality is a generally accepted principle of all work done by independent professionals. Management consultants engage themselves neither to disclose any confidential information about clients, nor to make any use of this information to obtain benefits or advantages. The clients must be convinced that they can trust consultants, otherwise consulting cannot get off the ground.

In internal consulting, the situation with regard to confidentiality can be complicated. In certain cases consultants have an obligation to (or there is a possibility that they may) disclose information on the client to a common superior (minister, director-general or other person). Under such circumstances, managers regard internal consultants as central management's spies and are reluctant to use them. To counter this, many business corporations have declared confidentiality as a principle that will be respected in using internal consultants as well as external ones. A similar approach tends to be increasingly taken within the public sector. For example, in organising its Bureau of Management Consulting, the Canadian Government has adopted the following principles:

— studies are undertaken only upon the request of the client department or agency;

— services are advisory in nature;

— services are confidential, and reports resulting from the assignment are made available only to the client.

Confidentiality is still an issue in some developing countries, where local businessmen do not feel sure that information given to consultants coming from management or productivity centres will not be passed on to government departments or tax collectors.

Confidentiality can also be violated unintentionally — for example, by carelessness in handling documentation and naïvety in discussing work-related issues in social contexts.

Value for money

The fees charged to clients raise several ethical questions. Professionals are concerned about the relationship between the benefits drawn by the client and the cost of the assignment. If they feel that the outcome does not justify the price, that the benefit will be none or too small, they warn the client before the job starts.

Here again, the client may be uninformed about the cost and price structure in a professional firm, and may trust the consultant blindly. Without going into details that will be the subject of chapter 23, we should like to stress that a normal fee structure reflects the costs incurred by the consultant on the one hand and the market price paid for professional services in a particular country on the other. Charging excessive fees to uninformed clients is unprofessional. Undercutting fees and working at a loss in the hope that this will eliminate competition is unprofessional too, in particular if the consultant does this with a new client, knowing that he will soon have to readjust his fee to the normal level.

Contingency fees (fees determined as a proportion of savings or gains achieved by the client thanks to the consultant) are one of the traditionally controversial issues in management consulting. They have been banned as unprofessional by some consultants' associations and individual firms, for several reasons. In particular, they force consultants to achieve and demonstrate measurable results in the short term, which can often be done relatively easily to the detriment of longer-term interests of the client organisation. In addition, they carry with them other risks which will be reviewed in chapter 23. Yet it appears that there is a tendency to make greater use of contingency fees, in particular in the United States, in situations that are considered to be sufficiently under both the consultant's and the client's control. Thus a formal ban against contingency fees, included in the 1972 edition of the code of conduct of the Association of

Management Consulting Firms (ACME) in the United States, disappeared from the 1981 edition of the code.[2]

Ethics in marketing

Marketing of consulting services will be the subject of chapter 22. At this point we shall limit ourselves to comments on recent trends in the ethical aspects of marketing.

Whether and how professionals should market their services is a controversial issue of long standing. For many years *advertising* was formally banned by professional associations for management consulting and other professional services alike. In 1961, an accountant sued the Institute of Chartered Accountants in England and Wales which "alleged that he had been guilty of professional misconduct by being employed by an organisation which offered its services by advertising".[3] He lost the case. In 1979 the ban against advertising was dropped by the American Institute of Chartered Public Accountants. In the same year, the American Medical Association received an order from the Federal Trade Commission to lift its ban against physician advertising. As from October 1981, a member firm of the Management Consultants Association in the United Kingdom "may advertise or promote its services through the media or in other ways, provided that the method and material used are compatible with professional good taste and do not impair the standing and dignity of the management consultancy profession".[4] The Association's by-laws then specify what types of promotional materials and techniques are acceptable and unacceptable. In particular, derogatory comments on other consultants and materials giving the public a false impression of the firm's capabilities are regarded as unprofessional. Thus, the changed attitude to advertising is of very recent date, and reflects a trend that is common to various professional services.

Cold contacts (unsolicited personal visits, telephone calls, or letters to new potential clients) are more and more admitted, again on the condition that professional and ethical viewpoints are observed.

Corruption is a topic which, in theory, should not have to be mentioned in a book on professional consulting. Yet it does occasionally happen (in the climate of cut-throat competition found in today's economy probably more often than previously) that a consultant seeks preferential treatment by bribing the persons in the client organisation who play a key role in choosing consultants or in approving the level of fees and the budgets for consulting projects. This may bring in more business and other advantages in the short term, but the long-term consequences for the credibility of the consulting firm and the whole profession can be disastrous.

Wider social concerns

Assignments undertaken by management consultants often involve issues where the client's interest may be in real or potential conflict with wider social interests. Or the consultant may uncover practices that, according to prevailing social norms, or in his personal opinion, are socially harmful and undesirable. The consultant may face a real ethical conflict. He may have an opportunity to seek advice from senior colleagues and friends, but eventually he must himself resolve such a dilemma.

The current trend is towards increased awareness of the social consequences of managerial decisions and the enhanced social responsibility of business managers and firms. Management consultants cannot stand aside. They have to make clients sensitive to the social consequences of various decisions that may be taken as a result of consulting assignments. It is fully justified to request consultants to warn managers strongly before proposing practices whose social and environmental implications are or could be negative. This may have a positive educational effect on the client. If the consultant feels that his personal ethics do not permit him to tolerate the client's behaviour, he should not hesitate to decline or interrupt the assignment.

6.3 Professional associations and codes of conduct

Professional associations

In a number of countries management consultants have established voluntary professional associations to represent their interests and regulate the activities of both individual consultants and consulting firms.[5] These associations have played a leading role in promoting professional standards of consulting and helping this young profession to gain the confidence of management circles and a good reputation in society.

By and large, associations of management consultants contribute to the development of the profession by:

- developing and up-dating the common body of knowledge;
- determining minimum qualification criteria for new entrants to the profession (education, type and length of experience);
- defining and adopting a code of professional conduct and practice for their members;
- investigating complaints of violations of the code of conduct and taking disciplinary action;
- examining various aspects of management consulting, organising an exchange of experience and making recommendations to members on improvements in consulting methods, organisation of units, selection, training and remuneration of consultants, etc.;
- providing information on services available from members.

In some countries, there are two types of consultants' organisations: associations of firms, and institutes or associations of individual consultants. This reflects the different perceptions of what consulting firms need as distinct from individual persons employed in management consulting. This dichotomy is quite deeply rooted in countries such as the United States and the United Kingdom, although some consideration has already been given to merging the two sorts of organisations into one authoritative and fully representative national professional body. The dichotomy has historical roots and does not represent a model that other countries would have to follow. Where the two types of membership organisations exist, dual and overlapping membership is quite common: a consulting firm is member of an association, while some or all of the consultants it employs are members of an institute where membership is individual.

Membership of a professional association is voluntary, but is governed by several conditions defining the member's profile and commitment to a collectively endorsed moral obligation.[6] Consequently, not all consultants are members. There have been cases of important consulting firms which do not subscribe to all conditions of membership, or whose management has taken an elitist approach, feeling that a well-established firm can define its own professional standards and does not need any guidance or supervision by a professional association. There are quite a few individual management consultants, too, who are not members because they do not meet some criterion, or do not see what benefits they could draw from membership.

Codes of conduct

Professional associations of management consultants attach great importance to the codes of professional conduct (ethics, professional practice), which they use as basic instruments to establish the profession and protect its integrity, and to inform clients about behavioural rules observed by the consultants. As indicated in the code of the oldest association — ACME, established in the United States in 1929 — the codes "signify voluntary assumption by members of the obligation of self-discipline above and beyond the requirements of the law".

Appendix 3 reproduces the full text of two codes: the fairly detailed ACME code, in which the "code of ethics" is separated from the "standards of professional practice", and a very brief, internationally applied, code of the European Federation of Associations of Management Consultants (FEACO). The perusal of these codes will show the reader that they try to define in general terms the various aspects of professional behaviour as discussed in section 6.2 above, as well as some further aspects.

First, there is a definition of professional ethics, which is mandatory and serves as a basis for disciplinary action if a member infringes the agreed standards.

Secondly, as in the ACME code, there is a tendency for some codes to include a set of rules that describe standards of good professional practice and provide broad methodological guidance to the members of the association. As distinct from a code of ethics, standards of practice are "largely aspirational in character"; they normally would not be enforced by disciplinary action. For example, the code of the Smaller Enterprise Consultants' Association of Japan defines a number of principles to be observed in consulting assignments. These principles emphasise, among others, the need to use the total approach to the client's problems, to examine each enterprise in a dynamic way, including its past history and future development prospects, to pay full attention to the individuality of the enterprise and to present proposals with their financial and other implications in a practical manner which will be easily understood by the client.

It is, of course, not the code of conduct itself, but its rigorous and intelligent application by all members of the association which determines the real professional value and integrity of consulting services. Some codes even have a clause by which the consultants engage themselves to do nothing likely to lower the status of management consulting as a profession. This leaves much to the discretion of the consultants themselves.

This is quite understandable. A code cannot be excessively detailed and specific, since it would not be applicable to all members and all situations in which they intervene. Furthermore, a code cannot anticipate new problems and future situations in which consultants may have to weigh what is professional and what is not. "The process of continually evaluating one's code of ethics and the application of those ethics must continue throughout one's professional life, with the use of trusted colleagues as testers and clarifiers. The acquisition of ethical competence reduces anxiety and increases effectiveness in the situational decision making that is a constant in the consulting process." [7]

Assisting professional development

Some consultants' associations have had a limited scope of activity; their principal aim is to define professional standards and supervise their application. This may be regarded as sufficient by well-established consulting organisations in countries with some tradition of consulting, and of professional services more generally. However, new firms, and especially single practitioners who are new to the business, need much more help and guidance. To provide it is in the interest, not only of the consultants themselves, but of all users of consulting services.

Consultants' associations can help their members to raise the standards of professional service in many ways. These can include training courses for new consultants, refresher training and workshops for experienced practitioners, conferences aimed at broad information and experience exchange, research into new consulting approaches and methods, information on useful literature, information on what goes on in other professions, examining new trends in management and business and their implications for consulting, and so on.

As the consulting profession is a young one, all these activities should have a strong educational dimension, by which we mean they should help members to adhere fully to professional ethics as defined by the association, and to be able to interpret them correctly in concrete situations.

Finally, management consultants' associations could be more active as platforms where experienced consultants speak on topics of concern to both private and public managers, thus generalising the rich consulting experience and sharing new findings with the management public.

6.4 Certification and licensing

Whether and how to apply certification or licensing to management consultants is another notoriously controversial subject, debated not only in consulting firms and associations but also in users' circles. This debate is indicative both of the professional aspirations and the growing sense of social responsibility of consultants, and of the various factors that slow down professionalisation.

Certification, it is felt, would be a step towards a wide recognition of management consulting as a true profession. Business, governments and the public at large want to have a guarantee that management consultants associated with important decisions in the private and public sectors are proven professionals. Certification should help to put more order into the consulting business and to eliminate those who sell their services as consultants although they do not meet the standards. On the other hand, various objections are raised: that certification cannot really guarantee anything more than the application of a few general and rather elementary criteria of admission to the profession; that it cannot show whether a consultant is actually suitable for a complex job; and that, after all, consulting to businesses is itself a business and if a consultant passes the market test by finding enough clients, his service is regarded as technically valid by those clients.

Developments towards certification

Facts show that certification is making headway. If a consultants' institute or association establishes and applies admission criteria indicative of the new member's competence, this is a step towards certification even if it is not so called. There may even be an examination on entry.

For example, in 1980 the Institute of Management Consultants in the United Kingdom started using written *entrance examinations*.[8] The papers cover the practice of management consulting; business appraisal and the implementation of change; and the application of specialist skills. There are three grades of membership: *associates*, *members* and *fellows*. All new admissions to the Institute are to the associate grade. After three years, at a minimum age of 30 and on evidence of a satisfactory standard of practice, an associate can become a full member. The grade of fellowship is available after a minimum of seven years of membership and distinguished services to the profession. Those who have attained the grade of fellow or member are listed in a *professional register* maintained by the Institute; the register, which is available to potential clients, also records the members' special skills and experience.

In the United States, the Institute of Management Consultants, founded in 1968, applies a certification procedure and authorises its members to use the title *certified management consultant* (CMC). A CMC must have a bachelor's degree or equivalent experience and five years of consulting experience, provide six client references, submit written summaries of five assignments, and pass a qualifying oral interview where he is thoroughly questioned by a panel of senior members. Consultants with ten years of consulting experience are exempt from the interview and from submitting assignment summaries. The Institute also admits (without examination) new consultants with little or no consulting experience as associate members, and helps them through a "CMC candidate study programme". Successful completion of this programme qualifies the young consultants for certification after three years of consulting experience. By the end of 1984 the Institute had some 1,700 regular members authorised to use the CMC title.

Licensing

Certification and similar procedures are voluntary, and fully in the hands of a private membership organisation. *Licensing* or *official registration* can be made compulsory. This means that, to be authorised to practise, a professional (firm or individual person) must request and obtain an official licence, which is granted if the professional meets certain criteria. The licence can be withdrawn in instances of malpractice. Licensing can be directly by a government authority, or delegated to a membership association, which carries it out under government guidance and surveillance.

Licensing is common in several professions, although national practices vary considerably. In France, for example, the public accounting practice is regulated by legal texts in considerable detail. The *experts comptables* (accounting experts) have to be registered members of the national *Ordre des experts comptables et des comptables agréés* (Order of accounting experts and certified accountants), which administers and supervises the profession within a framework stipulated by law. The government can overrule the decisions of the superior council of the Order and the national disciplinary commission of the profession includes three government representatives and two elected members.

An interesting initiative has been taken in Canada through the efforts of the Institute of Management Consultants of Ontario. In 1984, the Ontario provincial legislature recognised management consulting as a self-regulating profession. The designation CMC is recognised by law as certifying the competence and professionalism of a management consultant, and the Institute is authorised to prescribe conditions of membership and enforce the code of ethics. However, compulsory licensing was not introduced, so consultants can practise in Ontario even if they are not recognised as CMC.[9]

In contrast, in Austria, to be authorised to practise, management consultants have to become members of the *Bundeswirtschaftskammer* (Federal Chamber of Economy) and obtain a licence, which is granted if the candidate meets certain requirements concerning education and experience, and succeeds in a written and oral examination. However, Austrian consultants have doubts about the actual impact of the procedure on the enhancement of professional standards in consulting.[10]

By and large, management consultants have little experience of licensing; their views on this practice reflect mainly their general attitudes to business and to government intervention. Some consultants are strongly opposed to the idea of licensing, which they regard as an unnecessary infringement of their freedom.[11] Others tend to recognise that progression towards professionalism may require some form of flexible and non-political licensing, with a key role being played by a professional membership organisation enjoying a high reputation and the full confidence, not only of the consultants, but also of clients, government authorities and the general public.

---

[1] Readers who want to learn more about various views on professionalism in management are referred to P. Donham: "Is management a profession?" in *Harvard Business Review*, Sep.-Oct. 1962; K. R. Andrews: "Towards professionalism in business management" in *Harvard Business Review*, Mar.-Apr. 1969; G. Kanawaty: "Turning the management occupation into a profession" in *International Labour Review*, Vol. 115, No. 3, May-June 1977; and L. Benson: "The profession and the community" in *Journal of Accountancy*, Apr. 1983.

[2] The complete text of this code is reproduced in appendix 2.

[3] Quoted from P. Tisdall: *Agents of change: The development and practice of management consultancy* (London, Heinemann, 1982). The case is described on pp. 64-65.

[4] Section 203 of the by-laws of the Management Consultants Association.

[5] Appendix 2 gives a list of associations of management consultants in various countries and of international associations of management and engineering consultants.

[6] For example, the Management Consultants Association (MCA) in the United Kingdom requires member firms to have at least five consultants and be in practice for five years, and 80 per cent of the consulting staff must hold degrees of recognised universities or equivalent qualifications. The by-laws of the MCA stipulate in detail a number of further conditions of membership.

[7] G. Lippitt and R. Lippitt: *The consulting process in action* (La Jolla, CA, University Associates, 1978); p. 74.

[8] The history of the Institute, including the work which preceded the introduction of entrance examinations, is described in P. Tisdall: *Agents of change: The development and practice of management consultancy* (London, Heinemann, 1982); chapter 6.

[9] Cf. R. B. Robinson: "Building professionalism in Canada" in *Journal of Management Consulting*, Vol. 1, No.4, Fall 1984.

[10] Information provided by the Vienna-based "Consulting Studien Gruppe".

[11] See. H. J. Klein: *Other people's business* (New York, Mason-Charter, 1977); chapter 13.

PART II

THE CONSULTING PROCESS

ENTRY

7

Entry is the initial phase in any consulting process. During entry, the consultant and the client get together, try to learn as much as possible about each other, discuss and define the problem for which the consultant has been brought in, and on this basis agree on the scope of the assignment and the approach to be taken. The results of these first contacts, discussions, examinations and planning exercises are then reflected in the consulting contract, the signature of which can be regarded as the conclusion of this initial phase.

Entry is very much a matching exercise. The client wants to be sure that he is dealing with the right consultant, and the consultant needs to be convinced that he is the right person, or that his unit is the right consulting organisation, to address the problems of this particular client. Such a matching exercise can be difficult technically, but there may be other even more difficult psychological problems. True, it is the client who has invited the consultant, or agreed to consider his offer, and when doing so he certainly has had some purpose in mind. It may be that he has turned to the consultant with great hopes, or regards him as a last-resort solution in a crisis. Nevertheless, the consultant is a stranger to the client organisation. There may be mistrust, uncertainty, anxiety. The consultant has probably been in similar situations before. He knows, however, that every organisation is unique and that while his past successes with other clients are very useful experiences for dealing with a new client, they are by no means an absolute guarantee of repeated success.

Thus the contacts and activities that constitute the initial phase of the consulting process have to achieve considerably more than the definition of terms of reference and the signature of a contract. Experience shows that the foundations of successful assignments are laid down at this very early stage by establishing mutual trust and empathy, fully agreeing on the "rules of the game", and starting the assignment with shared optimism and a vision of what can be achieved.

Obviously, the full range of initial contact activities described in this chapter concern *new* assignments with *new* clients. If a consultant returns to a familiar client organisation in repeat business, entry will be simplified. But even in such cases it must not be forgotten that a new assignment with a previous client may involve making new relationships between persons. Even if organisations have co-operated successfully in the past, individuals on both sides must be sure that they will be able to co-operate in the same spirit in a new assignment.

7.1 Initial contacts

The consultant makes the contact

Contacting potential clients without being solicited by them is one of the ways of marketing consulting services (this will be discussed in detail in chapter 22). A cold call can arouse the interest of the client, who may decide to keep the consultant's name in mind for the future. Only rarely would a cold contact lead immediately to an assignment. This does occur from time to time, however − e.g. if the consultant happens to appear just when the client himself starts feeling that he may need the help of a consultant.

If the consultant contacts a client about whom he has enough information, and can show that he knows about that client's problems and has something very relevant to offer, the chances that such an initiative will produce an assignment are considerably increased. This can also happen if the consultant is introduced by another client for whom he has worked in the past.

A special case is when public authorities or other organisations publicly announce their intention to carry out a consulting project, and invite consultants to manifest their interest. In such a situation, the consultant will probably not be the only one who offers his services.

The client makes the contact

In most cases it will be the client who makes the first contact. This implies that he senses some performance and management problems in his organisation and for some reason decides to bring in a management consultant. In addition, he must have a reason for turning to a particular consultant:

- he has heard about the consultant's professional reputation;
- a business friend was satisfied by the consultant's services and recommends him (very frequent);
- the client found the consultant in a register or directory (less frequent);
- the consultant's publications or interventions at management conferences have impressed the client;
- the client may remember having been contacted by the consultant previously;
- the client likes to return to a consultant who satisfied him fully in the past (as we know, repeat business can be very important).

In any event, the consultant will want to find out *why* the client selected *him*. This will not be difficult.

First meetings

The importance of the consultant's behaviour and performance during the first meetings with the client cannot be over-emphasised. In fact, while meeting a client to negotiate a specific assignment the consultant is still in the process of marketing his services, and it is not certain whether a contract will be concluded. The first meeting should therefore be regarded as a short opportunity to gain the client's confidence and make a favourable impression on him. The consultant wants to make sure that he will meet the decision maker — the person who is not only technically interested in the assignment but also able to authorise a preliminary diagnostic survey, and who will make sure that resources required by an assignment will be available. If a top executive (managing director, senior administrator) of an important organisation agrees to meet the consultant, the consulting organisation should send a representative who is at an equally high level.

The question of who should go to the first meeting with the client may present a problem if a consulting organisation uses one group of consultants (as a rule very senior ones) for negotiating assignments, and another group (including both senior and junior staff) for executing them. Some clients know about this pattern of organising services and do not object to it. Many clients do not like it. They emphasise, rightly, that a productive consultant-client relationship starts with the first meetings and preliminary surveys and that it is at this moment that they decide whether they like to work, not only with a consulting organisation, but with particular persons in it. Also they resent an approach whereby the best people represent the consulting organisation at the beginning in order to impress clients, but execution is in the hands of lower-calibre staff.

Initial meetings require thorough preparation by the consultant. Without going into much detail, he collects essential *orientation facts* about the client, his environment, and the characteristic problems of his sector of activity. The client does not want the consultant to come with ready-made solutions, but expects someone who is very familiar with the kinds of problems that may be found in his organisation. The consultant should find some subtle way of demonstrating this.

In collecting orientation facts, the consultant starts by finding out which products or services his client provides. This information is easily obtained during the very first contact with the client, or by asking him to supply sales literature. The nature of the products or services will place the client within a specific sector or trade, and the consultant will want to know its main characteristics and practices. Usually he will gather information on:

— terminology commonly used;
— nature and location of markets;
— names and location of main producers;
— types and sources of raw materials;
— weights and measures used in the industry;
— processes and equipment;
— business methods and practices peculiar to the industry;

—   laws, rules and customs governing the industry;

—   history and growth;

—   present economic climate and main problems of the industry.

Trade journals and government publications will provide much of the information, especially on economic trends. To gain a quick understanding of an unfamiliar manufacturing process, the consultant can look at flow sheets of industrial processes, which summarise on one page a production process and its technical terms.

As regards the position of the client's business, the consultant needs little information before he meets the client. He may be able to learn the client's financial position, recent operating results and immediate expectations and problems from published annual reports or returns filed in a public registry or credit service. He can also scan brief biographies of the top managers in a publication of the *Who's Who* type (if one exists in the client's country).

The meeting is a form of investigational interview in which each party seeks to learn about the other. The consultant should encourage the client to do most of the talking: he wants the client to speak about his problem, his difficulties, hopes, and expectations. It is as well for the discussion to develop from the general situation to the particular and to focus eventually on the real issue.

When listening and when putting his own questions, the consultant assesses the client's needs in terms of sound management practice, his perception of consulting, and his readiness to work with consultants assuming different types of roles. The consultant decides how best to describe the nature and method of consulting as it applies to the client's problem. He must be sure that the client understands what his own role and responsibility will be.

The individual who invited the consultant into the organisation may not be *the* client as described in section 3.3, i.e. the person who "owns the problem" and will play the main role in solving it. All too often the consultant is invited in by top management to act as an adviser to somebody lower in the hierarchy of the organisation. This "client" may not feel a need, or may even resent being forced into a consulting assignment by his superiors. The consultant may have to spend some time clarifying these relations. Clearly, the client who will work with the consultant should be specifically identified and should agree to this relationship.

The client may wish to discuss the proposed work with other clients of the consultant and may ask for references. This may happen at any moment during the entry phase. In giving names, the consultant must remember confidentiality and cite only those clients who have agreed to provide references.

As regards fees, the client may know how consultants charge for their interventions and be aware of the rates applied. If not, the consultant will have to consider at what stage of the entry phase he should give this information to the client. Some clients prefer to ask about standard fees and other costs right at the outset; others wait with these questions until the consultant has formulated his proposal and made his offer to the client (see section 23.3 for a detailed discussion of principles and methods of fee setting).

The client may be eager to proceed without any preliminary diagnosis and planning, or, on the contrary, may be hesitant in making up his mind, even though he obviously has problems with which the consultant can help. The consultant should use care and patience in explaining and persuading, and keep mainly to the potential benefits to the client. Pressing for an immediate decision is not a good tactic; it can spoil everything. It is no good, either, if the client gets the impression that the consultant badly needs the assignment because he does not have enough work.

The consultant should not be insistent if he is clearly not on the same wave-length as the client. If the client has firm ideas on how the consultant must proceed, and the consultant does not subscribe to them, it is better to drop the assignment. This could be suggested either by the consultant or the client.

Agreement on how to proceed

If the consultant and the client conclude that they are interested in principle in working together, several further questions must be answered. With the exception of straightforward cases, which are often an extension of past work, it is not possible to start an assignment immediately without some preliminary problem analysis and work planning. The terms of business must be discussed and agreed. These are the activities that follow the first meeting.

If the client is ready to agree to a preliminary problem diagnosis,[1] the discussion can move on to the arrangements for it, and cover:

- terms of reference for a preliminary diagnosis;
- records and information to be made available;
- who should be seen and when;
- how to introduce the consultant;
- attitudes of staff to the matters to be surveyed;
- when to conclude the preliminary diagnosis and how to present proposals to the client;
- payment for the diagnosis.

In addition, the consultant wants to be informed about the selection procedure. The client may have contacted several consultants in order to be able to choose from alternative proposals. He should, in principle, tell the consultant about it. In some cases a formal selection procedure is applied: the consultant's proposals have to be presented in a predetermined format by a given date. The client will then allow a period of time (say 45 days) for comparing the proposals received and making a choice.

As regards charging for a preliminary diagnosis or survey, the prevailing practice is that a very short diagnosis (say 1-2 days), which the consultant needs to do in order to prepare a proposal for the client, is not charged for. However, if the contract is awarded, the consultant will bill the client for the time spent on this preliminary diagnosis. In contrast, if the preliminary diagnosis is needed to prepare for a complex assignment, and requires a longer time, the opinion prevailing in consultancy circles is that the client should pay for it. This helps to avoid two practices that are increasingly considered as undesirable:

— some consultants' practice of using free diagnostic surveys as a marketing tool (since the consultant cannot really work for nothing, another client will then pay for this "free" survey); and

— some clients' practice of collecting a considerable amount of information and ideas for action from several consultants (who are all invited to make the same survey), without paying anything for this professional service.

The practice of free diagnostic surveys used to be quite common in some countries in the past, but recently has tended to disappear.

7.2 Preliminary problem diagnosis

To be able to start an assignment, the consultant must know exactly what the client expects from him. That is why, during the initial meetings, the consultant encourages the client to say as much as he can about his personal perception of the problem that needs to be resolved. As we already know, many organisations insist on doing a thorough internal examination of the problem before deciding to contact a consultant. The client may even have drafted terms of reference outlining what he wants the consultant to do.

Yet there is no guarantee that the client's perception and description of the problem is correct and that the consultant receives complete and unbiased information. Before starting to plan the assignment and proposing a specific job to the client, the consultant should undertake his own independent problem diagnosis. In fact, an experienced consultant starts such a diagnosis right from the very first moment he is in touch with the client. Everything interests him: who contacted him and how; how he is received at the first meeting; what sort of questions the client asks; if there are any undertones in those questions; what the client says about his competitors; if he is relaxed or tense; and so on. There comes a moment, however, when the consultant has to sort out this information, get some hard data, and complete the picture he already has by looking at the problem from new angles — for example, by talking to people other than those who were involved in the first meetings.

Scope of the diagnosis

The purpose of the preliminary problem diagnosis is not to propose measures for solving the problem, but to define and plan a consulting assignment or project which will have this effect. The preliminary diagnosis limits its scope to a quick gathering and analysis of essential information which, according to the consultant's experience and judgement, is needed to understand the problem correctly, to see it in the wider context of the client's activities, achievements and other existing or potential business and management problems, and realistically to assess opportunities for helping the client.

The scale of this preliminary diagnosis depends very much on the nature of the problem. Very specific and rather technical problems do not normally require a comprehensive survey of the whole client organisation. On the other hand, an experienced consultant knows that he must avoid the trap of accepting a client's narrow definition of a technical problem without himself looking into constraints and tendencies that may make the solution of that problem an impossible task, or may show that the problem is much more or much less serious than the client assumes. Therefore even if the problem lies in one functional area only, or concerns the application of some specific techniques, a truly professional management consultant will always be interested in the more general and global characteristics of the client organisation.

If the consultant is brought in to deal with a general problem, such as deteriorating financial results, or inability to maintain the same pace of innovation as competitors, a general and comprehensive diagnosis or management survey of the client organisation is essential.

The time allocated to preliminary problem diagnosis is relatively short. As a rule, 1-4 days would be required. In the case of more complex assignments concerning several aspects of the client's business, 5-10 days may be needed. If an extensive diagnostic survey is required (e.g. in preparing company turnarounds, major reorganisations, buy-outs or mergers, or for any other reason), this is no longer a *preliminary* diagnosis, but an *in-depth* diagnostic survey, which will be described in chapter 12.

An outline of a management survey, including checklists of topics to be examined in various areas of management, is reproduced in appendix 4.

Issues in problem identification

Before outlining the methodology used in preliminary problem diagnosis it is useful to recall briefly some common mistakes made not only by clients in defining their problems, but also by some consultants. "The way I define problems limits my ability to solve them." [2]

Mistaking symptoms for problems. This is the most common error. Some very obvious issues which worry management (e.g. dropping sales, shortage of innovative ideas in the R and D department, absenteeism) are looked upon as problems, although they may be only symptoms of more profound difficulties.

Preconceived ideas about the causes of problems. Some managers and consultants "know" what the causes "must" be without bothering to gather and analyse facts.

Looking at problems from one technical viewpoint only. This happens frequently if the diagnosis is made by a manager or a consultant with a strong background and bias in one technical area (engineering, accounting, psychology) and if the multidisciplinary nature of management problems is disregarded.

Ignoring how the problem is perceived in various parts of the organisation. For example, the consultant may accept the definition made by top management, without finding out how the problem is seen by the lower management echelons.

Unfinished problem diagnosis. Since the preliminary problem diagnosis has to be done quickly, the consultant may be tempted to conclude his diagnostic work prematurely. He will not find out about further problems that may be directly related to the original issue presented to him by the client.

Some methodological guidelines

Preliminary problem diagnosis follows the same basic rules and procedures and uses the same analytical techniques as any problem diagnosis. These will be reviewed in detail in chapter 8. In addition, management consultants have developed certain approaches that are particularly useful at this initial stage.

The diagnosis includes the gathering and analysis of information on the client's activities and performance. It also includes discussions with selected managers and other key people, and in certain cases also with people outside the client organisation. Basically, the consultant is not interested in details, but is looking for principal trends, relationships and proportions. However, an experienced consultant keeps his eyes open and can sense potential problems behind apparent details that may escape another observer: the way people talk to each other and speak about each other, the respect for hierarchical relations, the cleanliness of workshops and offices, the handling of confidential information, the courtesy of the receptionist, and so on.

It is essential to take a dynamic and comprehensive view of the organisation, its environment, resources, goals, activities and achievements.

Dynamism in this context means examining *key achievements and events in the life of the organisation*, and *probable future trends* as reflected in existing plans and assessed by the consultant himself. The client's strengths and weaknesses ought to be viewed in a time perspective — a present strength may be merely short-term, while a new weakness, hidden at the present time, may become a threat to the client's organisation in the long term. The consultant is particularly interested in future opportunities — indeed, the detailed diagnosis and further work to be proposed to the client should be oriented towards these opportunities above all. This approach is summarised in figure 7.1.

As already mentioned, even if the problem is, or is likely to be, in a single functional area, the consultant will take *a comprehensive view of the organisation.* How far and how comprehensive is a matter of experience and judgement, and no universal recipe can be given. As the purpose is to determine what to do about a problem in the course of a consulting assignment of a certain size and duration, most management consultants emphasise the need for some wider appraisal of the organisation before confirming the existence even of a fairly limited problem, and the feasibility of handling it within certain terms of reference.

It can be recommended that the consultant should proceed *from the general to the particular*: from overall objectives and global performance indicators to the reasons for sub-standard performance, and then to an examination in some detail

Figure 7.1   The consultant's approach to a management survey

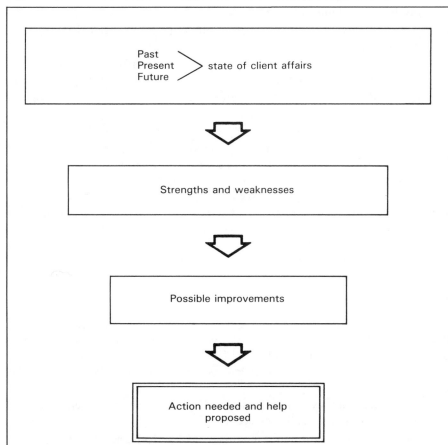

of selected areas of the organisation's activities. An approach which starts the other way round, by examining each management function (production, purchasing, marketing, etc.) in turn and hoping for a balanced synthesis at the end, will entail much unnecessary work and might well prove misdirected. The movement from the general to the particular helps the consultant to limit the preliminary diagnostic survey to matters of critical concern to the client organisation, or conversely may persuade him that, to stand the best chance of achieving the results expected, the enquiry must take into account every aspect of the enterprise's operation.

Such an approach implies that the consultant's analysis will pay considerable attention to *basic relationships and proportions* in the client organisation, such as the following:

—   proportions between major functions and activity areas (e.g. allocation of

117

      human and financial resources to marketing, research and development, production, administration);

—   relations between main inputs and outputs (e.g. sales related to materials consumed, the wage bill and the total work force);

—   relationships between the principal indicators of performance, effectiveness and efficiency (e.g. productivity, profitability, resource utilisation, growth);

—   relationships between global performance indicators and main factors affecting their magnitude in a positive or negative way (e.g. influence of the volume of work in progress on working capital and profitability).

    The comprehensive, overall approach is combined with a *functional approach* as necessary. For example, the precarious financial situation of a company may be caused by problems in any functional area: by badly organised production, by costly or ineffective marketing, by excessive spending on research, by the shortage or high cost of capital, or something else. As already mentioned, if an assignment is likely to be exclusively or mainly in one technical area, this area will need to be examined in greater depth than other areas, and the examination of the organisation as a whole will be limited to what is necessary.

Using comparison

    An essential technique for preliminary problem diagnosis is *comparison*. In the absence of an exhaustive detailed analysis of data the consultant needs reference points which could guide him in his preliminary assessment of strengths, weaknesses, and desirable improvements. He will find them by making comparisons with:

—   past achievements (if the organisation's performance has deteriorated and the problem is essentially corrective);

—   the client's own plans and standards (if real performance does not measure up to them);

—   other comparable organisations (to assess what has been achieved elsewhere and whether the same thing would be possible in the client organisation);

—   standards available in the consulting unit or another source of data for interfirm comparison.

    A comparison of well-selected data with sectoral standards or with data from specific similar organisations is a very powerful diagnostic tool. It helps not only in quick orientation, but also in making the client aware of his real situation, which may often be quite different from what he believes.

    The consultant would make extensive comparisons not only when he works with figures, but also in assessing qualitative information (e.g. the organisational structure, the computer applications, or the forecasting techniques used). In other words, the consultant's work is greatly facilitated if he can ask himself what levels of performance and what sorts of problems he would normally expect to find in that type of organisation to which the client enterprise belongs.

Such a question is meaningful if the consultant has some method of classifying organisations (e.g. by sector, product type, size, ownership, market served and the like). For each class there would be a list of various attributes that are characteristic of it. Well-established consulting firms try to provide their consultants with such data and guide them by means of manuals and checklists for management surveys and company appraisals. It is in the interest of the younger units in the profession to acquire or develop such documentation and use it in preparing and executing assignments.[3]

Notwithstanding certain general rules, senior consultants undertaking diagnostic surveys tend to have their *personal priorities* and *specific approaches*. Many of them start by looking at principal financial data, since these reflect the level and results of the activities of the enterprise in a way which best lends itself to synthesis. Others emphasise production: they believe that a simple factory tour is most revealing and tells an experienced observer a great deal about the quality of management. Still others prefer to examine markets, products and services before turning to a financial appraisal and further investigations. These are just different starting points reflecting personal experience and preferences: eventually the consultant has to study all areas and questions needed for a global diagnosis in order to see the problem in the right context and perspective.

The client's involvement

It would be an error to think that while the first contact meetings involved intensive and direct interaction between the consultant and the client, the consultant then does his preliminary problem diagnosis by himself, confining his contacts with the client to interviewing certain people and requesting information. The dialogue with the client is pursued during problem diagnosis. This will show how the client feels about various aspects of his business: what his technical and human capabilities are, what his potential is for making changes, and the style of consulting that should be applied in his case. The client, on the other hand, learns to know the consultant better and has an opportunity to appreciate his professional way of obtaining information, establishing contacts with people, grasping the overall situation, and distilling essential facts from the vast amount of data that can be found in any organisation. The consultant's knowledge and method may impress the client so much that he readily agrees to the proposed assignment.

Sources of information

A successful diagnostic survey is based on the rapid collection of information that reveals the type and extent of help that the consultant can give to the client. This information has to be selective (the reader already knows why).

Diagnostic data tend to be global in nature. As already mentioned, the consultant is interested in details only if they are indicative of some major problems and help to elucidate the problems for which he has been brought in. For example, some detailed insights into the work style of top management may help to diagnose overall management patterns and practices that determine the working atmosphere in the whole organisation.

The main sources of information for a preliminary diagnostic survey are published material, the client's internal records and reports, documentation files of the consulting unit, observation and interviewing by the consultant, and contacts outside the client organisation.

Published material may be issued by the client, or by other interested organisations. The client's publications usually include:

- annual financial and operating reports;
- financial, statistical, trade and customs returns to government, trade associations and credit organisations, and economic surveys;
- sales promotion material such as catalogues and advertising brochures;
- press releases.

Other published sources may provide information on:

- conditions and trends in the client's economic sector, including technological developments;
- trade statistics and reports;
- regulations which the client must observe;
- management practices;
- labour-management relations.

The client's internal records and reports will provide information on his resources, objectives, plans and performance, including:

- information on plant and equipment;
- reports to management on financial results and costs of activities, services and products;
- sales statistics;
- production performances;
- movement of material;
- personnel appraisal.

The documentation files of the consulting unit will contain information on the client if he is not a new one, and may also supply information on similar organisations.

Observing activities and interviewing key people is vital to information gathering. Tours of the client's premises, seeing people in action and hearing their views, worries and suggestions, give first-hand knowledge of how the organisation works in practice, how it lives, the pace it sets and the relationships between its workers. These are invaluable insights which records cannot convey, but extensive interviewing and observation of activities are beyond the possibilities of preliminary surveys.

Contacts with other organisations associated with the client may be made either by the consultant, or by the client himself.

During their work, consultants make contact with many organisations apart from those of their clients. These contacts not only assist the current assignment but also establish a relationship which can be used in future work. For example, contacts may be established with trade unions, employers' associations, sectoral research and training institutions, or management associations.

The consultant informs his client of the purpose and nature of any contact made. The client himself may contact some outside bodies (e.g. employers' associations), and should know of any consultant contact.

Alternative approaches

The approach described in the previous paragraphs is the classical consultant's approach: it is the consultant who performs the diagnosis as an expert, using data collection and analytical techniques of his choice, with smaller or greater participation on the part of the client. Moving closer to the process function along the continuum of consulting roles, the client and his staff become more active and the consultant focuses on providing effective diagnostic methods instead of doing the diagnosis himself.

For example, some organisations have used *problem-identification workshops*, which can be run as part of a problem-oriented management development programme, or used directly as a technique for identifying problems on which the organisation will have to act. In this workshop or group approach, the members of the group develop their own lists of problems requiring action, compare and discuss their lists, and agree on a joint list. They then work separately on a more detailed definition and analysis of the principal problem(s) from each list, paying attention to relations between various problems. This is followed by another meeting, where individual analyses are compared, a collectively agreed analysis is made and action proposals are developed.

This exercise can be organised in one group, or as a system of groups. The initial groups can be heterogeneous (from various levels and functions of management), thus examining one problem from several angles. Alternatively, technically homogeneous, functional or departmental groups can first look at one problem from their specific technical angles (financial, organisational, production, staffing, etc.), followed by workshops involving representatives of the groups, who meet to compare and harmonise the different viewpoints and develop a problem definition that is endorsed by all groups.

Management can decide to involve an external or internal consultant in these group exercises. The consultant's approach may be low key, reminding the group of the appropriate procedure, of criteria that may have been overlooked, and of methodological errors that might lead to false conclusions.

The use of the group approach is often preceded by a thorough explanation of diagnostic and problem-solving methods. If appropriate, the consultant also provides technical information on the problem under discussion (e.g. data from similar organisations for comparison), or helps to collect input data on which the groups can start to work.

121

Self-diagnosis by individual businessmen or managers is another approach which has been used in assisting small firms in various countries. The consultant meets with a group of owners or managers of small firms, provides them with a self-diagnostic instrument adapted to their needs, and explains the method to be used. He is then available to review the results of the diagnosis and proposals for action with each individual. Alternatively, the businessmen may agree to meet again and compare the ratios and other indicators characteristic of their firms, and exchange views on factors explaining differences in performance. They will then decide individually or as a group on the courses of action to follow in each firm.

Further approaches are described in section 4.5.

7.3 Assignment plan

During his initial contacts with the client and the subsequent preliminary problem diagnosis the consultant should have collected and evaluated enough information to be able to plan the assignment. This is what the client expects at this stage: he will want to receive not only the consultant's findings on the problem to be tackled, but also a proposal describing what the consultant suggests doing and under what terms he is able to offer his help.

In fact, right from his first contact with the client the consultant has been thinking of the approach to take, but he has suspended judgement until after he has become better acquainted with the situation. For example, the co-operation of the client's staff during preliminary problem diagnosis shows what consulting mode may be most appropriate (see sections 3.4 and 3.5) and the quality of the data found during this activity suggests how much time will be needed for detailed fact finding and analysis.

A fundamental aspect of designing and planning a consulting assignment is the choice of *assignment strategy*. By this we mean the respective roles to be played by the consultant and the client, and the way (and the time sequence) in which they will apply and harmonise their interventions and the resources allocated to the assignment.

The assignment plan, including the strategy that will be followed, is formally presented to the client as a proposal, as described in section 7.4 below. Assignment planning and drafting of a proposal is not normally finalised at the client's premises. Unless it has been otherwise agreed, the consultant returns to his office with the data collected during preliminary problem diagnosis and works on the proposal, often in collaboration with other senior members of the consulting organisation. He should never take more time than the client expects. Momentum can be lost and relations can cool down if the client feels that his problem is not receiving enough attention.

The main elements of assignment planning are given below.

Summary of problem identification

The conclusions from preliminary problem diagnosis are summarised and the consultant presents his description of the problem. This may include a comparison with the original problem definition presented to him by the client: the consultant may suggest widening or narrowing down this definition, or refer to other problems he discovered and to possible developments (e.g. the effects of recession, or tensions in labour relations) that may take place during the assignment. As appropriate, the problem will be set in the wider context of the client's activities, achievements and resources.

Objectives to achieve and action to take

The assignment plan then outlines the objectives to be achieved and the kind of technical activities which the assignment will consist of (redesigning an information system, reorganising distribution networks, introducing a new staff training programme, and the like).

Whenever possible, the objectives should be presented as *performance measures in quantified terms*, describing benefits that will accrue to the client if the assignment is successfully completed. Global financial benefits are commented on to ensure that the client understands the implications. For example, savings from a reduced inventory of finished goods would only be achieved when stocks had been run down, and this may require production to be cut back for some time. Benefits in other terms are stated as appropriate, e.g. output would increase from one level to a new level (in this case the client would be warned of the need for orders to keep the factory occupied).

Social and qualitative benefits may be difficult to express in figures. They are described as precisely and clearly as possible and carefully explained. Vague notions that lend themselves to many different interpretations should be avoided.

However, at this early planning stage, before a detailed investigation has been carried out and some work on alternative proposals done, it may be impossible to indicate all benefits with absolute precision. If this is the case, it is preferable to indicate the order of magnitude of the benefits to be achieved (e.g. sales increased by 20 to 30 per cent). Also, if the consultant regards certain objectives as feasible *on condition* that the client takes certain measures (which may include difficult restructuring, organisational or personnel decisions), these measures should be specified as clearly as possible.

Phases of the assignment and time-table

The steps in which the assignment will be undertaken have to be programmed in some detail. Basically, the consultant will follow the phases of the problem-solving or consulting process, as outlined in section 1.4 (figure 1.1) and described in detail in chapters 8-11. This is essential, not only for work scheduling, but for several other reasons.

The nature of the consultant's and the client's activities changes from phase to phase. Both parties must know exactly what the other party expects at each phase. In particular, the client will want to know whether the assignment is making headway towards its final objectives. To make control possible, the assignment plan will describe the outcome of each phase and define what *reports to the client* will be submitted at what points during the assignment. Each major phase will require an end-of-phase report, but in long and complex assignments short interim reports may be required at the end of each sub-phase or periodically (monthly, quarterly), for monitoring progress and allowing regular payments to be made to the consultant.

The time dimension of the assignment plan is a key element of strategy. What *pace of work* should be adopted? The urgency of the client's needs is the main determinant. But there are other considerations, such as:

● the client's and the consultant's technical, manpower and financial capacities;

● the feasible and optimum pace of change (as discussed in chapter 4 and chapter 5);

● the desirability of a phased approach to implementation (starting in a unit that is best prepared for change and willing to co-operate, introducing the new scheme on an experimental basis first, etc.).

Role definition

This is another strategic dimension of assignment planning. The consultant will suggest the style or mode of consulting (see sections 3.4 and 3.5) that he considers most appropriate with regard to the nature of the problem and the motivation and capabilities of the client's staff. A general definition of the mode to be used is not enough. Precise arrangements have to be proposed. They should specify:

— what activities will be carried out by the client or by the consultant;

— what data and documents will be prepared by whom;

— what meetings, working parties, project groups and other forms of group work will be used and who will be involved;

— what special training and information activities will be undertaken.

It may be both possible and desirable to foresee a shift in roles during the assignment. For example, intensive training of the client's staff in the subject area covered and in problem-solving and change methodologies, carried out during the first stage of the assignment, may enable the consultant to suggest reducing his presence and changing his role during subsequent phases.

Lack of precision in defining role expectations for each phase of the assignment causes much misunderstanding. As already mentioned, this happens frequently in connection with implementation. Is the consultant's objective to design a new scheme and submit it in a report, or to help the client to implement the scheme? Who is responsible for what? Where does the consultant's responsibility end? What does the client actually want? Does he want another report, or is he really keen to make a change? In designing an effective assignment these questions must not remain unanswered.

Resource planning

Following a detailed role definition the consultant can determine the resources required by the assignment in each phase. This includes:

- resources to be made available by the consultant (consultant time, material, clerical support, special computing, research, legal advice, and other services), including their cost; and
- resources to be made available by the client (management and staff time, liaison arrangements, administrative support, office facilities, resources for testing, experimental work, computing, and so on).

Obviously, the client will want to know what resources provided by the consultant will have to be used, and paid for, during the assignment. But more than that: the client will participate, too, and the inputs required from his organisation may be high. The failure to figure them out as precisely as possible may cause considerable difficulties once work has started and the client learns, to his great astonishment, that he is supposed to do something which he has not counted on doing at all.

It may be difficult to tell the client at this stage how much *implementation* will cost: it is the action planning phase (chapter 9) that will generate precise figures. None the less, a preliminary assessment ought to be made in all assignments that are likely to propose costly changes (e.g. new investment or compensation to staff whose employment will be terminated). The client should have the opportunity to look into these probable financial implications before deciding whether to embark on such an assignment.

The costing and pricing of an assignment is discussed in detail in section 23.4.

7.4 Proposal to the client

As a rule, the assignment proposed will be described in a document presented to the client for approval and decision. It may be given different names: survey report, technical proposal, project document, project plan, contract proposal, and the like. Some clients require the consultant to present the proposals in a predetermined format. This facilitates study by the client and his evaluation of alternative proposals received from several consultants.

A proposal submitted to the client is an important selling document. It is not enough for the consultant to have a clear vision of how to execute the assignment to make it a total success: he must be able to describe his vision on paper in a way that will make this clear to other people. This may include individuals who did not meet him when he first came to the client organisation, and will be formulating their opinions of him solely on the basis of the written proposal.

The client should be impressed by the technical quality of the proposal and pleased by its business-like presentation. Writing "winning" proposals is an art that no consultant can afford to ignore.[4]

Sections of the proposal

In most cases the following four sections are included in the proposal to the client:

(1)   technical section;
(2)   staffing section;
(3)   consultant background section;
(4)   financial section.

The technical section describes the consultant's preliminary findings, his assessment of the problem, the approach he wants to take, and the work programme that he proposes to follow. These topics were reviewed in sections 7.2 and 7.3.

One caveat has to be made: the consultant and the client may have a different conception of how detailed and specific this technical section should be. If it is too global, the client may feel that the consultant is not really telling him what he proposes to do. In contrast, if it is too detailed and specific, the consultant may have gone beyond assignment planning − he may already have embarked on executing the assignment without having obtained the client's agreement. This may present no problem if a co-operative relationship has already been established and the consultant knows that he will get the assignment. However, if it is not clear who will be chosen (e.g. if several consultants were invited to submit proposals) this may prove to be a reckless approach: giving away free expertise before the assignment has been approved.

The staffing section gives the names and profiles of the consultant's staff who will be executing the assignment. This also includes the senior consultants who will be responsible for guiding and supervising the team working at the client's organisation. As a rule, the proposal guarantees the availability of particular persons for a limited period of time, say 6-8 weeks. If the client delays his response, or decides to postpone the assignment, he knows that he will have to accept other consultants of a comparable profile, or renegotiate the assignment.

The consultant background section describes the experience and competence of the consulting organisation as it relates to the needs of the particular client. There may be a general sub-section with standard information given to all clients (including a section on ethical standards and professional practice adhered to by the consultant) and a specific sub-section referring to similar work done and providing evidence that the consulting unit will be the right partner to choose. References concerning former clients can be u43sed only with these clients' prior agreement.

The financial section indicates the cost of the services, provisions for cost increases and contingencies, and the schedule and other indications for paying fees and reimbursing expenses. If the client applies a selection procedure, the financial section may have to be submitted separately.

The consultant may have a standard description of his *terms of business* (appendix 5) and attach it to the proposal.

Presenting the proposal

Most consultants prefer not just to mail the proposal, but to hand it over to the client in a meeting which starts with a short oral (and visual, if appropriate) introduction of the report's summary.

The consultant is ready to answer questions about the start of the proposed assignment. If the client is keen and ready to start, there are obvious advantages in doing so while the enthusiasm is there and the contacts established are fresh in people's minds. But an early date may not be easy to meet because of existing commitments.

Though the consultant would obviously like to have a decision before the end of the meeting, the client may have good reasons for not wanting to give one. He should not be pressed. A professional consultant knows whether his performance was good enough and he can only exercise patience over the outcome.

If the client wants to read the proposal prior to the oral presentation, or if he wants no oral presentation, the consultant should hand the report over without insisting on a meeting.

The client's reaction

A public-sector client is usually bound by rules which specify a minimum number of tenders and an internal evaluation procedure before awarding a contract. But private-sector clients may also use a selection procedure based on the evaluation of alternative proposals, in particular for large and complex assignments. In such cases it may take several weeks or months before the client will be in a position to communicate his decision.

If a selection procedure is applied, the consultant wants to know by what criteria he will be judged. As a rule, the client will inform him about these criteria in the original invitation to submitting proposals. In most cases, the client will also give the names of the competitors.

The consultant should be aware of the relative weight that will be assigned to the various aspects of his proposal in the selection procedure. For example, the World Bank recommends its borrowers to give a weight of 10-20 per cent to the consulting firm's general experience, 25-40 per cent to the work plan, and 40-60 per cent to key personnel proposed for the assignment.[5] Thus, even a highly competent consulting firm stands little chance in a selection procedure if it does not propose consultants of the right calibre.

Negotiating the proposal

The client may be keen to use the consultant's services, but he may not be happy with some aspects of the proposal. For example, he feels that he can play a more active role than foreseen by the consultant and himself undertake various tasks not requiring costly external expertise, or he wishes to suggest a different timetable. It is normal to review these and similar technical aspects of the proposal and to make changes if the consultant is able to modify his approach. After all, the two parties have to be in full agreement on how to proceed.

Table 7.1   Confidential information on the client organisation

1. Names of managers met and information collected on them.
2. Comments on organisational relationships, management style and cultural values and norms.
3. Attitudes of various people in the client organisation to consultants and likely reactions to the assignment.
4. Best sources of internal information.
5. Additional comments and data on the problem for which the assignment is proposed.
6. Other problems identified, potential problems, or areas of further work not tackled in the proposed assignment and not discussed with the client.
7. Useful background information collected and not used in the proposal to the client.
8. Any other suggestions to the operating team that will execute the assignment.

As regards fees, in many countries consultants emphasise that their fees represent a fair charge for a high-quality professional service and hence are not negotiable. A minor provision for negotiation is sometimes made in countries where this is the customary way of doing business (see section 23.4).

What is not included in the proposal

In parallel with drafting his proposal to the client, the consultant is preparing *internal confidential notes on the client organisation* and *ideas for the approach to take* (table 7.1). These notes (sometimes called "survey notes") are particularly important in a larger consulting organisation if different professionals are used for planning and for executing assignments.

7.5 Consulting contract

The entry phase of the consulting process can be regarded as successfully completed if the consultant and the client conclude a contract whereby they agree to work together on an assignment or project. What is the usual form of such a contract? What can we recommend to our readers?

We have to stress at the outset that the contracting practices regarded as normal and advisable depend very much on each country's legal system and customary ways of doing business. A new consultant has to seek legal advice on the form of contracting authorised by local legislation and preferred by business and government organisations. In addition, he can get advice from the local consultants' association and from professional colleagues. Where alternative forms of contracts are admitted, choosing one or more will be a matter of the consulting organisation's policy and judgement on what is most effective in dealing with particular clients. The form chosen must ensure that mutual commitments will be understood and respected and misunderstanding avoided on either side.

In some countries, such as the United States, the contracting practices in professional services are quite well defined and enough literature is available.[6] In

Table 7.2 What to cover in contracting

1. Contracting parties (the consultant and the client).
2. Scope of the assignment (as discussed in section 7.3: objectives, description of work, starting date, timetable, volume of work).
3. Work products and reports (documentation and reports to be handed over to the client).
4. Consultant and client inputs (expert and staff time and other inputs).
5. Fees and expenses (fees to be billed, expenses reimbursed to the consultant).
6. Billing and payment procedure.
7. Professional responsibilities (handling confidential information, avoiding conflict of interest, and other aspects as appropriate — see section 6.2).
8. Copyright (covering the products of the consultant's work during the assignment).
9. Liability (the consultant's liability for damages caused to the client, limitation of liability).
10. Use of subcontractors (by the consultant).
11. Termination or revision (when and how to be suggested by either party).
12. Arbitration (jurisdiction, procedure for handling disputes).
13. Signatures and dates.

many other countries this is not yet the case. Thus a consultant doing work abroad may have to compromise between what is customary in his home country and what the law and practice in the client's country demand.

The three main forms of contracting are verbal agreement, letter of agreement and written contract. Before reviewing them we will first list the aspects of consulting assignments that are normally dealt with in contracting (table 7.2). These aspects do not represent sections of a standard contract since various arrangements are possible.

Verbal agreement

A verbal agreement is one given by the client orally either after having reviewed the consultant's written proposal, or even without having reviewed a proposal if he feels that the consultant is the right one and will have the required professional approach. Verbal agreement was used extensively in the first decades of management consulting, but now the tendency is to use written contracts. Nevertheless, those who believe strongly in the power of the written word and legal texts would be surprised to find out that even nowadays a lot of consulting is undertaken on the basis of verbal agreements.

Verbal agreement may suffice if the following conditions exist:

- the consultant and the client are well versed in professional practice;
- they trust each other totally;
- they are familiar with each other's terms of business (the client knows the terms applied by the consultant and the consultant knows what he can expect from the client, e.g. if the client is able to make any advance payment, if he can accept monthly billing, how long it takes him to approve a payment, etc.);

- the assignment is not too big and complex (if this is the case, it may be difficult to manage the relationship from both sides without any formal document).

Verbal agreement would be used more frequently in repeat business than with new clients.

Letter of agreement

A letter of agreement is the prevailing way of contracting professional services in many countries. Having received the consultant's proposal, the client sends him a letter of agreement, or of intent, confirming that he accepts the proposal and the suggested terms of reference. The letter may set out new conditions which modify or supplement the consultant's proposal. In this case it is the consultant who in turn replies as to whether or not he accepts these new conditions. Or all this can be negotiated orally and then reduced to a written agreement.

Alternatively, it is the client who drafts the letter describing the work required and the proposed terms of reference, and the consultant who gives his written agreement.

Written contract

The use of a written consulting contract duly signed by the parties involved may be required for various reasons. It may be imposed by law or by the client's own regulations on the use of external services (this is the case in nearly all public organisations and international agencies, and many private businesses). It is often the best form to choose if the consultant and the client come from different business and legal environments and would easily misinterpret each other's intentions and attitudes. It is advisable, albeit not absolutely necessary, in the case of large and complex assignments involving many different people on both the client's and the consultant's side.

It may be the client's practice to use a *standard form of contract*. Most management consultants are quite flexible and accept various forms of contract. However, they should not underestimate the need for consulting their lawyer if a new and unusual form of contract is proposed to them by a client.

As a rule, the consultant will know in advance that he will have to sign a formal contract. He should obtain the standard form from the client, show it to his lawyer, and keep it in mind in preparing his proposals for the assignment. Thus he will be able to formulate the proposals so that they could be directly included in the body of the contract, or attached to it without making any substantial modifications.

A consulting firm should also have its own standard form of contract. It will be used with clients who do not have a standard form of their own and expect the consultant to propose one.

Built-in flexibility

The purpose of contracting is to provide a clear orientation for joint work and to protect the interests of both parties. This implies a certain degree of flexibility.

At any stage of the assignment, the nature and the magnitude of the problem may change and other priorities may become more urgent. The consultant's and the client's capabilities and perceptions of what approach will be effective are also evolving. Obviously, a professional consultant will not insist on continuing with a job because it is stipulated in a contract if that job is no longer required and causes unnecessary expense to the client.

Whatever form of contract is used, it should be agreed under what conditions and in what way either the consultant or the client can withdraw from the contract, or can suggest a revision. In some cases it may be better to contract only for one phase of the assignment (e.g. fact finding and detailed diagnosis) and delay a decision on the work to follow until enough information has been collected and examined.

Psychological contract

In an era in which more and more features of our lives are regulated and constrained by legislation, and formal contracts tend to become more and more common in professional sectors, it is useful to underline that the formal legal side of contracting is *not* the main one. We have explained why a well-drafted formal contract may be required. However, the reader should keep in mind that excellent consulting assignments are those where another type of "contract" exists, which is not codified in any document and is not easy to describe: *a psychological contract*, under which the consultant and the client co-operate in an atmosphere of trust and respect, believing that the approach taken by the other party is the best one to bring the assignment to a successful completion. Such a "contract" cannot be replaced by even the finest legal document.

---

[1] Various terms are used: preliminary problem diagnosis, diagnostic study, management survey, diagnostic survey, consulting survey, diagnostic evaluation, pilot study, company appraisal, management audit, etc.

[2] J. Selman and V. F. Dibianca: "Contextual management: Applying the art of dealing creatively with change" in *Management Review*, Sep. 1983; p. 15.

[3] Similar classifications, with empirical or recommended performance data, can be obtained from engineering consultants, suppliers of equipment, sectoral research institutes, centres of inter-firm comparison and other sources.

[4] Suggestions for consultant report writing can be found in appendix 9. J. Kennedy has compiled a number of sample proposals and published them in *25 "best" proposals by management consulting firms* (Fitzwilliam, NH, Consultants News, 1984). A useful section on report writing is in H. Holtz: *How to succeed as an independent consultant* (New York, Wiley, 1983).

Management consulting

[5] *Guidelines for the use of consultants by World Bank borrowers and by the World Bank as executing agency* (Washington, DC, World Bank, 1981); p. 14.

[6] Detailed guidance on contracting in the United States can be found in J. J. Gonagle: *Managing the consultant: A corporate guide* (Radnor, Pennsylvania, Chilton Book Co., 1981); H. L. Shenson: *How to strategically negotiate the consulting contract* (Washington, DC, Bermont Books, 1980); and N. Pyeatt: *The consultant's legal guide* (Washington, DC, Bermont Books, 1980).

DIAGNOSIS 8

Diagnosis, the second phase of the consulting process, is the first fully operational phase. The purpose of diagnosis is to examine the problem faced by the client in detail and in depth, identify the factors and forces that are causing the problem, and prepare all information needed for deciding how to orient work on the solution to the problem. An additional purpose is to examine thoroughly significant relationships between the problem in question and the global objectives and performance results achieved by the client organisation, and to ascertain the client's potential to make changes and resolve the problem effectively.

In principle, problem diagnosis does not include work on problem solutions. This will be done in the next, action-planning phase. Diagnosis may even lead to the conclusion that the problem cannot be resolved, or is not worth the effort of resolution.

However, in practice it is often difficult or inappropriate to make a strict distinction and draw a line between the diagnostic and the action-planning phases of the consulting process. It is not only that diagnosis lays down the bases for the work to follow. Frequently diagnostic work will already identify and explore possible solutions. In interviewing people it may be impracticable and even impossible to confine the discussion to problems and their causes, carefully avoiding touching upon possible solutions. Thus operations that are clearly separated in our text for methodological reasons will have to be organised by the practitioner in a pragmatic way, likely to be effective in his client's particular case.

There is another significant phenomenon. As already mentioned, the very fact that a management consultant is present in the organisation and starts asking questions puts the change process into motion. There may be an immediate impact on the organisation. Many of us do not have to be told what to do; it may be enough if someone asks us a question which implies that there might be an alternative way of doing the job. Sometimes an employee is heard to say, "I didn't know they wanted me to do the job that way. Had they spoken to me about it, I would have done it!"

This is what often happens in consulting assignments. By diagnosing problems, and closely co-operating with the client in this exercise, consultants already influence attitudes to change and may bring about a number of specific changes.

This can have very positive effects. By gradually developing a complete picture of the situation, based on hard data, diagnosis increases awareness of the need to change, and indicates more specifically the sorts of changes that will be required. If well managed, an extensive data collection and analysis exercise can involve the client's staff more and more in the assignment, thus enhancing their sense of "ownership of the problem". As a result, at the end of the diagnosis the client organisation will be better prepared to cope with the necessary changes than at its beginning.

There can be a useful learning effect, too. The client and his staff should not only feel that they are themselves discovering the full truth about their organisation or unit, but also gain a conviction that the consultant is sharing his diagnostic method with them so that they learn how to diagnose problems by themselves. The client's problem-solving potential can be considerably enhanced during diagnosis. If this opportunity is missed it may be too late to start soliciting people's involvement at the action-planning stage.

However, certain negative effects may also occur. Some clients try to maintain secrecy within the organisation about using a consultant. It is doubtful whether such a secret can be kept, but, even more important, an attempt to do so can cast doubt upon the consultant and on the entire process. The informal communication network in an organisation (all organisations have their "grapevines"!) will quickly disseminate the information. In the absence of a formal communication from the client to the system, the informal communication system will tend to generate negative data. This will seriously inhibit the ability of the consultant to perform effectively.

Think back to the discussion of change and organisational culture. Introducing a consultant into the organisation, without sufficient preparation by the client, produces a need for the people in the organisation to cope with that situation. New cultural behaviour will emerge. In essence, the consultant has already caused a change in the organisation — without lifting a finger! Premature change will have taken place and could confuse the initial problem, or mask the real reason for the consultation. During the entry phase, this may not be too difficult to deal with, as the consultant will be relating essentially only to the manager who recruited him and perhaps to a few others. During diagnosis, the consultant must move through many levels of the organisation, so many more people will be involved. If the purpose of the consultation has not been disclosed, the consultant can expect to encounter only limited cooperation from some members of the organisation. Certain high level managers may think that the situation can be handled by merely sending out a memo, telling people to co-operate. It will take more than that.

Unless the client system is prepared to accept the consultant, the entire relationship can be doomed to failure from the outset. Therefore, if possible, the client should prepare the organisation for the introduction of the consultant. As clients are not always aware of this need, it may become necessary for the consultant to plan a course of action during the entry phase. Obviously, such preparation is in itself an intervention into the organisation. It must be handled with extreme care, with all the competence required of the consultant from the outset.

The consultant must use a variety of approaches to dispel any fear or misinformation. One way to do this is by being readily available to all those in the organisation who would like to meet him. Particularly when consulting on human resources and organisational development, the consultant should be generally visible and very accessible.

Diagnosis can be a painful exercise in an organisation in difficulties. But in any organisation diagnosis may uncover situations and relationships of which the client is not proud, which he is unable to handle, and which he would have preferred to hide from anybody coming from outside. The consultant, however, may badly need this sort of information to be able to do anything useful for the client. Diagnosing delicate situations requires a great deal of tact. An aggressive diagnostic attitude (e.g. if people can deduce from the consultant's questions that he is looking for errors in their work and is going to criticise them) will invariably generate resistance.

Another type of potentially negative effect is spontaneous change of work methods before a new method has been properly developed, tested and adopted for general use. Often such changes are not real improvements even if they are well intentioned. Energy may be wasted if there is a misunderstanding about the likely direction of the change effort and about the sequence of steps in which the consultancy is being carried out. Some people may be disoriented — they change their method of work in good faith, but this is not appreciated by the consultant and by the managers.

These and similar misunderstandings can be prevented by giving *frequent feedback* from data collection and analysis. The client and his staff need to know how the assignment has progressed, what facts have been established, and what findings are preliminary, requiring further fact finding and verification, or final, capable of serving as a basis for action. There should be no ambiguity and no suspicion about the type of action that diagnosis is likely to recommend and about the moment at which action can start. On the other hand, getting the client's reaction to the feedback given to him is feedback to the consultant. The consultant should seek this feedback as much as possible during the whole diagnostic phase.

8.1 Conceptual framework of diagnosis

Restating the problem

The assignment plan prepared following the preliminary problem diagnosis (see sections 7.2 and 7.3) has provided guidelines and a basic time-schedule for the diagnostic phase. It may, however, require revision and adjustment before detailed investigations are started. There may be a time-lag of several months between the end of the entry phase and the start of the diagnostic phase. The consultant wants to be sure that the original problem definition is still valid and can direct the diagnostic work. It is useful to restate the problem and make sure that the client has not changed his mind and does not want the consultant to do something else. A special meeting with the client may be arranged to this effect shortly before starting diagnosis.

Conceptual framework

The diagnostic work should start with a clear conceptual framework in mind. To embark on extensive and costly investigations without such a framework could be a hazardous undertaking. In any organisation the consultant encounters a host of problems varying in nature: technical and human, apparent and hidden, major and minor, real and potential. He will hear many critical opinions as to what the main problems are and what should have been done about them. In diagnosing the problem, the consultant will be constantly exposed to the risk of taking a wrong direction, getting unduly influenced by the views expressed to him, and collecting interesting but unnecessary facts while omitting essential facts and ignoring some important dimensions of a complex problem. The dangers of diagnostic flaws already mentioned in section 7.2 are to be kept in mind and the consultant will need to make a great effort to avoid them.

It would therefore be wrong to view fact gathering and fact analysis as the kind of meticulous but routine work that a junior assistant can do if given some guidelines, while the really experienced man can come in at a later stage, when creative input will be needed in order to devise effective solutions to the problem. Diagnosis, too, requires a great deal of imagination and creativity in addition to experience in analysing business, management and human problems.

What is to be established

First, the consultant must keep in mind what is to be established, proved, tested and justified during diagnosis. He must consider what the end result of this phase should be, on the basis of which the assignment will be able to move to the next phase. This includes the definition of:

● the problem;
● the causes of the problem;
● other significant relationships;
● the client's potential to solve the problem;
● possible direction of further action.

The problem

It may be useful to recollect what was said about business and management problems in section 1.3. A consultant may be asked to help rectify a deteriorating situation, improve an existing one (even if it cannot be described as deteriorating), or create a totally new situation (identifying and taking new opportunities). There are therefore three basic categories of problem: *corrective, progressive* and *creative* problems. Yet they have one common characteristic: in each case, there is a *difference between what is (or will be) actually happening and what should (or might) be happening.* This difference defines the problem with which the consultant is supposed to deal.

To establish this difference or discrepancy we have to compare two situations. It is not so difficult to find out *what is actually happening,* i.e. *the actual situation.* In this chapter we will describe a number of fact-finding and analytical techniques whose mastery helps the consultant to identify the actual situation. To determine *what should be happening,* i.e. *the ideal or desired situation,* is infinitely more complex, but it is an essential part of problem diagnosis. For it is only in this way that the problem can be described and analysed, be it a corrective, progressive or creative one.

Let us take as an example growing production costs. The costs of a particular product have increased from 10 to say, 10.80, i.e. by 8 per cent, over the last two years. But the market price is not growing and the distribution agents cannot reduce their margin. There is a suspicion (or it has been established) that some competitors offering the same product have maintained the same level of production costs, and others have even been able to reduce them. Technologies making production considerably cheaper are known, but, as usual, can be efficient only under certain conditions. What then is the problem? The actual level of production costs is known, but how can the desired level be determined? This may be a complex business decision. The diagnostic phase starts with some assessment of what is desirable (actually this was provided by the preliminary problem diagnosis made during the entry phase), an assessment which will be further specified, deepened and adjusted during diagnosis, based on new data that will be collected and new relationships that will be discovered. Only then will it be possible to determine the real magnitude of the problem and all its important aspects and suggest ways of searching for a solution.

The problem will be identified by the following five principal dimensions or characteristics:

(1) *Substance or identity.* The substance or identity of the problem has to be described (low performance; growing production costs; shortage of competent staff; lack of ideas on how to invest idle capital). It has to be established what basis of comparison is used and how it is justified. (Why do we say that performance is low? Low in comparison with what standard?) The various symptoms of the problem have to be described as well.

(2) *Organisational and physical location.* In what organisational units (divisions, departments, subsidiaries) and physical units (plants, buildings, stores, offices) has the problem been observed? What other units are or might be affected? How wide-spread is the problem within the organisation?

(3) *Problem "ownership".* Which people (managers, staff specialists, clerks, workers) are affected by the existence of the problem and primarily interested in resolving it? Is the problem closed-ended or open-ended? (This, as we know, is essential for defining the "real clients" and working with them throughout the problem-solving process.)

(4) *Absolute and relative magnitude.* How important is the problem in absolute terms (e.g. amount of working time or money lost, volume of

under-utilised productive capacity, potential savings)? How important is it in relative terms? How does it affect the unit where it has been observed, and the people who "own the problem"? How important is it to the organisation as a whole? What will the organisation actually gain if the problem is resolved?

(5) *Time perspective.* Since when has the problem existed? Has it been observed once, or several times, or is it recurrent? How frequently does it appear? What is its tendency: has the problem been stabilised, or is it increasing or decreasing? What forecasts can be made about the future evolution of the problem?

The causes of the problem

The fundamental task in diagnosis is to identify the forces and factors which are causing the problem. The exercise will start with some preliminary knowledge or assumptions about what these causes might be. This will help to establish hypotheses on possible causes. It is useful to form as many hypotheses as possible, without, however, embarking on superficial speculation. This will provide a starting point for the investigation. Data gathering and analysis will then focus mainly on the hypothetical causes, eliminating hypotheses that cannot be justified by facts, and adding new hypotheses which will emerge from interviews with the client or from other sources. A rigorous scientific approach should be applied. For example, the fact that it is difficult to find data in support of a hypothesis does not mean that the hypothesis should be dropped. Eventually the consultant should be able to identify the real cause(s) amongst the many factors which are in some way related to the problem.

Further comments on causal analysis are made in section 8.4 below.

Other significant relationships

Any business and management problem is interwoven with other problems; and there are other relationships in addition to that which can be established between a problem and its cause or causes. For example, there are factors which aggravate or alleviate the problem without being its direct cause. They can make the solution of the problem more or less difficult. In solving one problem, new problems may be discovered. Often a new bottleneck is created by removing an existing one, and so on. These relationships and potential problems have to be investigated and identified.

The client's potential to solve the problem

The client's potential has several dimensions. It is necessary to find out whether he possesses the material and financial resources and the technical expertise required for solving the problem. The time perspective is important. What has been the client's experience in solving other problems and making organisational changes of varying nature and magnitude? What is the client organisation's culture as regards change? What will be the likely future development of the client's resources in relation to the problem to be solved? Can he mobilise other resources? What attempts have been made to solve the given problem? Have past attempts failed? Why have they failed?

Considerable attention will be paid to the client's attitudes to the given problem. How do people (at various levels and in various categories) perceive the problem? Are they aware of it and keen to make a change? Have they experienced the problem for so long that they have accommodated themselves to living with it?

Possible directions of further action

The purpose of diagnosis is preparation for action. Throughout the investigation, information and ideas on how the problem could be resolved will be collected, recorded and analysed with the same care and determination as data on the nature and the causes of the problem. This will provide a link to the next, action-planning phase. Action proposals should emerge logically from diagnosis. However, the consultant will keep in mind the pitfalls of premature changes started before the facts have been established, causes identified and conclusions drawn from diagnosis.

Main steps in diagnosis

The general framework provided above can be used by the consultant when making a detailed plan for diagnostic work, bearing in mind that the scope and methodology of the exercise will have to be adapted to the nature and complexity of the problem, and to the profile and the attitude of the client. Diagnosis consists in seeking answers to the questions in the five areas reviewed above: the problem; the causes of the problem; other significant relationships; the client's potential to solve the problem; and possible directions of further action. The exercise starts with some information obtained through preliminary problem diagnosis during the entry phase, and with assumptions and hypotheses which the consultant, as an experienced analyst, will be able to make at the beginning in collaboration with the client. Hypotheses and tentative answers will be replaced by definite answers, and missing data will be provided.

In planning the diagnostic phase it is essential to determine the degree and form of the client's involvement in each step of the phase. If the process-consulting mode is chosen, the client and his team will accept the main responsibility for collecting and analysing data, and the consultant will act mainly as a catalyst, making the client aware of the approach taken and drawing his attention to questions and to facts that should not escape his attention. In other instances, however, the consultant will carry out the bulk of the diagnostic work. Or, it will be possible to plan for gradually increasing the involvement of the client and his staff in the course of the diagnostic phase.

Basically, diagnostic work will be carried out in four principal steps. The definition of the framework as described in this section, and the decision on the data to collect (section 8.2), is the first step. Fact finding or data gathering is the second step (section 8.3). Fact analysis constitutes the third step (section 8.4). Feedback to the client, including reporting and conclusions on diagnosis, is the fourth and final step (section 8.5). This logic will be followed in our explanation. However, this logic may not fit every situation and every consultant's personality. If the consultant finds it more productive to organise his diagnostic work in a different way, he should feel free to do so.

Let us quote an experienced practitioner: "My personal approach involves techniques which I find most useful. I do not attempt to analyse or compartmentalise data into fact finding, analysis and synthesis, but let it flow as it begins to come in. I let it overlap to a certain extent in each of these stages until a pattern begins to develop. Only then do I begin to weave raw factual material into the analytical phase. When my facts are complete I want them to be so clear that they mirror what the ultimate conclusion of the study will be." [1] The reader may also look at appendix 6, which describes the sequence of diagnostic operations in a particular consulting assignment in production management.

8.2 Defining necessary facts

Facts are the building blocks of any consulting work. Operating consultants need a considerable number of facts to get a clear picture of the situation, arrive at a precise definition of the problem and relate their proposals to reality. Facts are also needed for assignments that deal with creative problems, where the consultant is trying to develop something very new and using a great deal of imagination and creative thinking. Collecting facts may be the most tiring and painful phase of the consultant's work, but there is no alternative.

When diagnosis starts, a certain amount of data will be handed over to the operating consultants by their colleagues who did the preliminary problem diagnosis during the entry phase. The diagnostic phase will go much further, and will define issues and collect facts in considerably greater detail.

The kinds of facts collected will depend on the area in which the assignment takes place, and on the definition of the problem and the assignment objectives. Facts should enable the examination of processes, relations, causes and mutual influences, with special regard to under-utilised opportunities and possible improvements. The conceptual framework reviewed in section 8.1 indicates the main areas in which facts are normally collected.

Plan for collecting data

Fact collecting has to be prepared for by thoroughly defining what facts are wanted. Experienced consultants will continue to apply the principle of selectivity, although they know that they need more detailed and precise facts than their colleagues who did the preliminary diagnosis. They appreciate that virtually unlimited amounts of factual information are available in any organisation, but that an excessive amount of such information easily becomes unmanageable and cannot be fully utilised in the assignments. The cost of fact gathering cannot be ignored, especially if some data are not readily available and special schemes (observations, special record keeping) have to be established to obtain them.

But the definition of facts and their sources must not be too restrictive. If it is, this might exclude facts from which significant information on causes, effects or relationships might be drawn, and these facts are often found in unexpected places. At the beginning of the assignment, the consultant may well cast his net fairly widely, rejecting some data after preliminary examination, but adding other data, and so on.

In defining the scope of data the management consultant keeps in mind that "the purpose is not research. The purpose of diagnosis is to mobilise action on a problem. Action that will improve the organisation's functioning".[2]

The facts to be collected and investigated have to be defined in closest collaboration with the client, especially with those members of the client organisation who know what records are kept, how reliable they are, and what data will have to be sought from other sources. This includes the definition of the content of data, degree of their detail, time period, extent of coverage, and classification and tabulation criteria, as described below.

Data gathering may be a lengthy process and in a complex case some logic should be followed, e.g. by making sure that each step (finding data on marketing and sales) provides information for the next step (data on production) and so on. This should be reflected in a work plan to be agreed on with the client.

Planning for data gathering also includes deciding what aspects of the problem and what relationships do not require detailed data. This concerns cases when the consultant, thanks to his experience, can arrive at reliable conclusions on the basis of global data and through comparison with similar situations in other organisations.

The client may not understand why the consultant insists on finding certain sorts of information. This often happens if, in the client's opinion, the assignment should be kept within a limited technical area and the consultant should not become involved in other areas. The consultant has to explain why he wants to obtain certain data on events, situations and problems that may be somehow related to the problem with which he is dealing. This may make the client aware of relations to which he was paying no attention, and provide further evidence of the consultant's methodical approach.

Content of data

Every experienced consultant knows well that apparently identical types of data may have *a different meaning or content* in different organisations. For example "work in progress" may be defined in a number of different ways; it may or may not include certain items, and its financial value may be determined by various methods. The definition of categories of employees (technicians, middle managers, administrative personnel, production and other workers, etc.) is also subject to many variations. In old firms with established traditions definition is complicated by the existence of their own terminology, which may differ from terminology prevailing in the industry to which they belong. The uniformity of data used in the management of various organisations will be higher in countries where some central planning and control exists, and where financial and statistical reports have to observe government regulations. But even in these cases many differences will be found, especially in the production area.

For *quantities*, the consultant specifies the units of measure, e.g. the number of products, or their weight or volume, and sets the limits of accuracy, e.g. to the nearest 100 or to the last unit. Accuracy depends upon the purpose for which the data are to be used. Work study to set standard operating times may require accuracy to the nearest second with an error allowance of 5 per cent. By contrast, a forecast of total volume of production per year may approximate to the nearest thousand with an error allowance of 10 per cent. If the consultant fails to set the limits of accuracy before data are collected, he may not obtain what he requires and have to repeat the recording process, e.g. operating times may be recorded in minutes or tenths or hundredths of minutes, when seconds are required.

Degree of detail

The degree of detail required for facts will generally be higher than that needed for data used in preliminary diagnostic surveys. While general diagnosis stems from aggregate figures, e.g. total time spent by machines on productive work, change rests upon more detailed data, e.g. machining time for each operation, or time spent on productive work by certain types of machines, or in certain shops. Information on individual persons and their attitudes to the problem concerned may be needed. The more detailed the facts, the more time they will take to collect. At the start of an assignment the consultant may have difficulty in evaluating the advantages which detailed facts will yield. Before he collects the data he cannot know what weaknesses or opportunities for improvement they will reveal. He will probably point out problems that deserve close examination. Otherwise the consultant may first collect data in broad categories, e.g. total number of days of sick leave taken by all workers. Analysis of these data will suggest more detail for certain categories, e.g. number of days of sick leave taken by each age group during the winter months. Data may thus be gathered in several stages before the consultant has a sufficiently detailed picture of the present situation to suggest ways of improving it.

Period of time

Defining the period of time is equally important. For example, to design an inventory management system for finished ceramic products, the consultant must know the number of products sold. For how many years must he calculate the sales and at what intervals? The answer might be for each month over the last three years. The period of time should be long enough to set a firm pattern of activity, indicate rates of growth or decline, and reveal fluctuation in activity due to seasonal variations or economic cycles. A longer period will be chosen in enterprises producing large capital goods, with a lead time of several years in product design, manufacturing and installation, than in enterprises producing current consumer goods.

Periods of time need to be comparable: months or weeks have to include the same number of working days and so on. Periods when exceptional events occurred should be excluded, but recognised and accommodated in the new situation. Periods preceding major changes in operations, e.g. introduction of new products and dropping of old ones, have to be examined separately from periods of normal operation.

The choice of a period close to the start of the assignment recognises that the mere presence of the consultant may affect the results. In a particular instance, material wastage dropped substantially from the moment the consultant began to ask questions about it and before he actually did anything.

Obviously the choice of the period of time takes account of the availability of past records, and of changes that the client may have introduced in recording procedures.

Coverage

When it comes to coverage, the consultant must decide whether to collect total information (on all products, all employees, whole units and processes), or a selection only. As a rule, information will be collected for the vital few items that account for the bulk of activity in the current period, and for such items as are likely to become vital in the future (prospective new products, etc.). If the productive capacity is clearly limited by one group of machines which have become *a bottleneck*, the solution of the problems of this group may be a key to the solution of most other problems of the given department. In other cases, data will be collected for representative samples.

Organisation and tabulation of data

Finally, the preparatory work for fact collecting includes decisions on organisation and tabulation of data, which are made in the light of the ultimate use of the data. Typical groupings are:

- *for events* — time, frequency, rate, trends, cause, effect (e.g. number of accidents resulting from specified causes that occurred each day of the week during the past year);
- *for people* — age, sex, nationality, family status, qualifications, occupation, length of service, earnings (e.g. average annual earnings of unmarried female employees with selected educational qualifications during each of the last five years);
- *for products and materials* — size, value, technical characteristics, source (e.g. value of materials by type and size in the inventory at the end of the last 12 calendar quarters);
- *for resources, inputs, outputs, processes and procedures* — rates of activity (sale, consumption, production), location, control centre, geographical distribution, use of equipment (e.g. numbers of specified parts produced by selected processes during each of the last 24 months).

To arrange facts in digestible form the consultant plans how to tabulate them. Descriptions and narratives may be noted under selected headings on a separate sheet of paper or card for each heading, e.g. responsibilities of each manager. Answers to a questionnaire can be tabulated on a "summary questionnaire", i.e. using the same form of questionnaire that will be distributed to the respondents. Processes and procedures may be represented by a chain of symbols, such as the activity symbols used by systems analysts or in work study. Shapes are best shown on drawings. Figures are usually set out in tables.[3]

It may be useful to anticipate data processing by a computer. This will involve the selection of a suitable model and programme, or the elaboration of a new one if none is available for the particular analytical purpose. This, however, will require some time which should be allowed for in the scheduling of diagnostic work.

The consultant's preliminary notes will tend to be wordy and speculative while he is feeling his way and getting the situation into focus. As the course of the investigation becomes clearer, recording of the facts becomes more systematic. General note-taking may give way to charting and other analytical methods. The original decisions on tabulating and classifying data are verified and amended.

The orderly way the operating consultant keeps his papers, and how he files them for retrieval of information, will help him to keep on course and allow for easy reference by the supervisor. The meaning of notes should be as clear months after the event as when they were written. No figure should be recorded without being qualified by its terms.

8.3 Sources and ways of obtaining facts

Sources of facts

By and large, facts are available to consultants in three forms:

- records,
- events and conditions,
- memories.

Any of these sources may be internal (within the given organisation), or external (official publications, statistical reports, opinions of people outside the organisation).

Records are facts stored in forms that are readable or can be transcribed. They include documents (files, reports, publications), computer files, films, microfilms, tapes, drawings, pictures, charts, etc. Facts from records are obtained by retrieval and study.

Events and conditions are actions, and the circumstances surrounding them, which can be observed. Hence facts of this kind are obtained by observing, and recording the results of observations.

Memories are all the information stored in the minds of people who work in the client's organisation, are associated with it, or simply are able to provide information of use to the consultant (e.g. for comparison). This encyclopaedia of knowledge embraces hard proven facts, experiences, opinions, beliefs, impressions, prejudices and insights. The mind stores all this data in the form of words, numbers and pictures which the consultant cannot see, but can obtain from people by means of interviews, questionnaires, special reports, and so on.

A skilful consultant will avoid having recourse to indirect and time-consuming ways of collecting information if the same information can be obtained directly and simply. In many cases this means — go and ask people. People at all levels in industrial firms and other organisations possess an unbelievable amount of knowledge about their organisation, and nearly everybody has some ideas on needed and possible improvements. But they do not divulge this information if they are not asked.

Retrieval of recorded data

Records are a prolific source of information, and some records will be examined and studied in any management consulting assignment. Clearly, consultants will give preference to the use of information which is already available in records before looking to other ways of data collecting. There are, however, certain pitfalls to be avoided in retrieving recorded data.

- Many records are not reliable and give a distorted picture of reality. This is common in such cases as records on machine breakdowns and stoppages, or waste. Materials may be charged to products for which they were not used. Factory plans and layouts may be claimed to be up to date but seldom are. Organisational and operational manuals may include detailed descriptions of procedures which were abandoned long ago. If the consultant or the client himself has doubts, the validity of existing records should be verified before they are used.

- It is common in organisations, both business and government, to find that various departments have different records on the same activities, inputs or outputs. These records may differ both in the criteria used and in the magnitude of the recorded data.

- Criteria and values used in recording are modified from time to time and the consultant must find out about all such modifications.

Special recording

Special recording can be arranged if information is not readily available in existing records, or cannot be relied upon. It may be established for a limited period, say a month or two, according to criteria proposed by the consultant. As a rule, the client's employees working in a given area will be asked to record data and pass them to the consultant. For economy reasons such recording should be kept simple and last no longer than necessary for reliability. Everyone should know at the start how long the period will be, and why special recording has to be introduced.

Observing

Observing is the method the consultant uses to obtain information which is not readily recorded. He is present while an event occurs, e.g. while a manager instructs his subordinates, or while a worker performs a task, and uses his faculties of sight and hearing to note how the event occurs, so that he will be able to suggest an improved practice at a later date.

In process consulting, the consultant can observe staff meetings during which it is possible to identify group processes and behaviours that are related to the problem. Usually, the observation will be of groups, rather than individuals. If, however, the purpose of the consultation is to help an individual improve performance, then the observation can focus essentially on that individual. This would be the case where a high-level employee in the organisation has been experiencing interpersonal problems. This client may seek an external consultant who could observe him in action in a variety of situations, and provide help in improving the interpersonal aspect of his management performance.

Or the consultant can observe socialising patterns. Where do people gather to talk and exchange information? Who has frequent working or informal contacts with whom? What pattern emerges from these contacts?

Information which the consultant usually obtains by observation includes:

- layout of factory, warehouses and offices;
- flow of operations, materials and people;
- work methods;
- work pace and discipline;
- working conditions (noise, light, temperature, ventilation, orderliness and cleanliness);
- attitudes and behaviour of higher and middle managers, supervisors, staff specialists and workers;
- interpersonal and intergroup relations.

Because most people feel uncomfortable under scrutiny, the consultant must take special care to put them at their ease before starting to observe their activities. First he should tell them what he is going to do. He should never start watching workers without warning. He should explain the purpose of his survey and make it clear that it is in no way critical but simply aimed at obtaining reliable information on how the activity is performed. An exchange of views with those under observation, allowing them an opportunity to point out all the factors influencing the activity and inviting their suggestions for improvement, will probably enlist their co-operation. As far as possible they should behave normally under observation and make no attempt to give a better or faster, or worse or slower, performance than usual. If there is any unusual occurrence, the observation should be disregarded and repeated when conditions return to normal.

If procedures, operations and processes are observed, the consultant would choose one of the many methods that have been developed for that purpose and whose description is available in the literature.[3]

Where the assignment deals primarily with human problems and relations between individuals and groups, the consultant may have to explore the attitudes and behaviour of the client's staff in depth. In other assignments he probes less deeply into these aspects. Nevertheless, he observes the inclinations, preferences and prejudices of staff to the extent necessary to understand how these affect the problems he is concerned with, and to enlist co-operation. Such observation continues throughout the assignment. It starts during the introductory meetings when he gains his first impressions. These he will verify during later encounters. To a considerable extent the consultant gathers information on attitudes and behaviour as a by-product of interviews to question memories, exchange ideas, or develop improvements. However, during interviews not directly concerned with personal traits, the consultant would distract both himself and his client by writing down his impressions. He should therefore make mental notes and only afterwards put them into writing and classify them.

In doing this, the consultant will be interested in information such as:

— experience;
— beliefs;
— degree of self-confidence;
— likes and dislikes;
— special interests or motives;
— people the interviewee respects and those he doesn't;
— sociability;
— willingness to co-operate;
— management style (autocratic, consultative, permissive);
— extent of original thinking and innovation;
— receptivity to new ideas.

By taking such personal traits and attitudes into account the consultant will increase his chances of understanding factors that affect change in the client organisation.

Special reports

Individuals or teams in the client organisation may be requested to help in the assignment by giving thought to particular aspects of the problem and putting suggestions on paper in the form of a special report. This would include any supporting information that the author might be able to supply. This method is selective — in co-operation with the client, the consultant would choose those employees who are likely to have specific views on the problem in question, who are aware of various pitfalls, and who know about past attempts to solve the problem. If, however, anybody in the client organisation offers to prepare a special report on his own initiative, this should be welcomed, although treated with some caution. The impact of special reports will be increased by defining in advance a desirable structure for them.

Questionnaires

In management consulting a questionnaire is useful for obtaining a limited number of straightforward facts from a large number of people (e.g. in a market survey), or from people widely separated from each other (e.g. reasons for equipment failure from users throughout a whole region). They are generally unsatisfactory for gathering all but simple facts.

The questionnaire may be distributed to correspondents with an explanatory note asking them to complete and return it, or canvassers may question people and note their answers on the questionnaire. Either case calls for a full explanation, telling the respondent:

- why he is being asked the questions;
- who is asking them;
- what the questioner will do with the replies;
- who else is being asked.

Before drawing up the questionnaire the consultant decides exactly what information is wanted, how it will be used, and how the answers will be summarised and classified. Then precise, simple questions free from ambiguity are framed. As far as possible, "yes" or "no" or numerical answers should be invited. Where longer answers are required, it may be useful to provide a list of possible answers and ask for the right one to be marked. Questions should be arranged in logical order so that each answer leads to the next. It is advisable to group questions and lay out the questionnaire so as to facilitate summarising and tabulating answers, particularly where mechanical or electronic sorters and tabulators will record them.

If there are some doubts about the respondents' ability to understand the questions and give clear answers, the questionnaire should be subjected to preliminary tests.

Interviewing

In management consulting, interviewing is certainly the most widely used technique of data gathering, together with the retrieval of recorded data.

One advantage that questioning during an interview has over the use of questionnaires is that every answer can be tested and elaborated. Questions supplement and support each other, confirming, correcting, or contradicting previous replies. They also lead to related facts, often revealing unexpected relationships, influences and constraints. The interview is adaptable. If one line of questioning fails to produce required data, another can be tried. This may be suggested by the interviewee's answers. The consultant learns not only from the direct replies he receives but also from the inferences, comments, asides, opinions, anecdotes, attitudes and gestures that accompany them — provided he is alert and attentive. As we know, non-verbal messages can be very significant!

In interviewing people the consultant is guided by general rules of effective interviewing, which have been described in various texts.[4] Some more specific experiences and suggestions concerning the use of interviews in management consulting are given below.

In planning the interviews, the consultant determines *what facts* he wants to obtain, from *whom, when, where* and *how*.

What facts. In setting down the facts he needs the consultant takes account of the knowledge he can expect the interviewee to have — for example, a production manager is unlikely to know precisely what terms of credit are extended to customers, while a district sales manager is probably not informed about the planned maintenance of machines. For background information, a general discussion may suffice. On the other hand, information that will help to solve problems or develop improvements needs to be thoroughly examined, probed and understood (e.g. workers' attitudes to simplifying working procedure in order to raise output).

Who should be interviewed. Obviously interviewees should be those dealing with the activities under study — for example, for billing procedures, the invoice clerk should be the best source of information. To obtain full co-operation and avoid slighting anyone, however, the consultant should first approach the manager responsible and allow him to designate informants. Later he may refer to others to complement or confirm information. During initial interviews he can ask who will have supporting information.

When to interview. Information gathered from interviews makes more sense if it comes in logical order — for example, if products are known it is easier to follow the operations for manufacturing them. Interviews should therefore follow a sequence so that each builds on information derived from those preceding it. They should be preceded by a careful study of records, so that time-consuming interviews are not used to collect data available in another form. The amount of time an interviewee can make available for the interview and his state of mind cannot be ignored.

Where to meet. Selection of a meeting place takes into account the following:

— proximity to the activity under study;
— the convenience of the interviewee;
— avoidance of noise and interruption.

Generally people are more relaxed and communicative in their own surroundings. They also have all information to hand there. Only if the interviewee's workplace has serious drawbacks, such as noise, cramped space, or frequent interruptions, should the consultant invite him to meet elsewhere (perhaps in the consultant's own office).

How to proceed. Although the conduct of an interview varies according to the characters of the interviewee and the consultant, their relationship, and the circumstances under which they meet, the following guidelines usually apply:

(1) *Before the interview.* The consultant prepares questions likely to reveal the required facts. The list will merely serve as a guide and a check that the interview covers all the necessary ground, and will not prevent the exploration of related topics. The consultant also informs himself about the interviewee's job and

personality. When making an appointment, he informs the interviewee of the purpose of discussion.

(2) *During the interview.* Further detailed explanations are given to the interviewee at the beginning of the meeting. He is requested to help in solving the problem, encouraged to talk in an informal way and asked for agreement to note-taking. The questions asked should lead towards the required information. Nevertheless, they should allow the informant to follow his own line of thought so long as it does not stray too far from the subject under review or become too trivial. He is likely to disclose more when free to express himself than when pinned down by insistent questions. Judicious comments supplementing his statements, or relating them to required facts, encourage communication and guide it. Except for such encouraging interjections, the consultant should not interrupt. Nor should he appear critical of the way things are done now, since this may antagonise the informant and he may dry up. Arguing, or jumping in with suggestions for improvement, is to be avoided. Rather the informant should be encouraged to point out possibilities for improvement. Taking careful notes of information and suggestions for improvement (but distinguishing between fact and opinion) ensures that the consultant forgets nothing, and also shows that views expressed are taken seriously. Suggestions for improvement are noted without commitment, but if they are used later this should be acknowledged. Before leaving, the consultant confirms what he has noted. He takes his leave pleasantly, thanking the informant for his help, thus leaving the way open for further interviews if necessary.

During the interview, the consultant may encounter unexpected resistance. This can be expressed in many different forms (see also section 4.4): questions are not answered, answers are evasive or too general, doubts are expressed about the usefulness of the exercise and the consultant's approach, and similar. If this happens, the consultant should quickly consider whether he is not provoking resistance himself by aggressive or tactless questioning, or by asking questions that the informant considers banal or superficial. It may be good tactics to ask the informant directly about his feelings concerning the interview: this may unblock the situation. There is, however, not much point in pursuing an interview in which the informant clearly refuses to co-operate.

(3) *After the interview.* The consultant reads over the notes of the interview, lists points to be checked and transcribes reliable information in the assignment's classified data record. In some cases it may be useful to send the interviewee a typed summary for verification. Information from one interview is used to prepare questions (e.g. cross-checking or tentative) for other interviews.

Data-gathering meetings

Another possibility in diagnosis is for the consultant to arrange a special meeting, the purpose of which is to generate data related to the problem under consideration. Caution must be exercised, for it is also possible for the meeting to move into discussing possible solutions in general and in detail before sufficient data have been gathered.

Data gathering should involve all those who are related to the problem in any way. Sometimes the consultant may suggest including others who are not directly related, but whose presence could be helpful for data gathering. However, a data-gathering meeting should not be too large; this can inhibit some of those present and prevent the sharing of needed information. It may be preferable to schedule several small meetings in order to offer the more intimate climate essential for data gathering, and to hold separate meetings with people who would not give their views openly in the presence of their superiors or other colleagues (e.g. supervisors may speak more openly in a meeting where the production manager and the personnel manager are not present).

Employee attitude surveys

Attitudes of people in the client organisation play some role in most consulting assignments. The consultant is alert to attitudes in observing operations and processes, in interviewing people, and in any other contacts with the client and his staff.

There are, then, assignments where a special employee attitude survey may be required. This may be necessary in assignments involving changes in employment and working conditions if the consultant needs to establish how people feel about present conditions and how they could react to the change likely to be proposed. As a rule, a survey is more likely to be needed in a larger organisation than in a small one if it is suspected that different opinions and attitudes exist but the number of people concerned makes it difficult to judge the relative importance of different attitudes without surveying them in a systematic manner.

The organisation and the techniques of attitude surveys are described in specialised publications.[5] If he is competent in this area, a management consultant may undertake such a survey himself. Alternatively, he can turn to a specialist in social and behavioural research. The main techniques used would be those described above, including observation, interviews and questionnaires. There are, too, special techniques, used for instance in sociometric studies or motivational research. Their effective use requires special training, but they would not be needed in most management consulting assignments.

Estimates

An estimate is makeshift and never fully replaces established data. Only when proven facts are not available, or for some reason are difficult to obtain, should the consultant consider estimates.

Estimates are best made by people performing the activity concerned, who have first-hand knowledge and who, in addition, will more readily accept proposals based on data they themselves have supplied. But wherever possible estimates should be obtained from more than one source and checked. If there are significant differences, the informants themselves should try to resolve them. If they cannot do so, a test may be applied, observations taken, or special recording installed.

The consultant may accept the client's estimates:

- in respect of facts familiar to the client (e.g. frequent machine operations, or regular patterns of work);

- on aspects of the present situation that need not be precise (e.g. percentage of total costs represented by administrative overheads, in order to decide whether to control these costs closely);

- to indicate whether further observation would be rewarding (e.g. incidence of machine breakdowns, or stock-outs of finished products);

- to ascertain whether benefits from improvements are worth more accurate measurement (e.g. savings from substitute materials or change of product design);

- where the estimate can be tested (e.g. if estimates of operating times to be used for production planning and control would result in a product cost permitting the client to sell at a fair profit).

The last example illustrates a sound use for estimates. For both control of production and control of costs it is necessary to know for each product the quantity of each material used in production, and each manufacturing operation and the time taken to perform it. Obtaining all this information by observation and measurement is a lengthy and painstaking task which would cause long delay in installing controls. Supervisors, technicians and workers, however, can provide close estimates because they are familiar with the materials and operations. From their estimates a product cost can be calculated. If this permits the client to sell the product at a fair profit, estimates can be used to start production control and cost control systems. Later, precise measurements can replace the estimates and improve controls.

Before using estimates the consultant *checks their validity* against proven experience. An effective way of doing this is to use a known total volume, quantity, or cost for a recent period or a known capacity. This is compared with the measurement or capacity that results from multiplying an estimate for a single item by the total number of items. For example, the estimated quantity of material required to manufacture a product is multiplied by actual numbers produced during a recent period. This is compared with the quantity of material actually issued from store to production.

Another means of checking estimates is to compare them with data recorded elsewhere. Such a comparison must be made with care and will only be valid if the data being compared relate to identical circumstances. Data for comparison may be found in trade publications, or in the files of the consulting organisation.

In addition to checking the validity of estimates the consultant needs to consider the *degree of error* they entail and decide whether this is tolerable. Where there is a strong probability that the error will remain within the limits of tolerance, the estimate will be used. For example, procedures can be installed to trigger remedial action by management when the limit is reached. In an opposite case the consultant has to devise ways of obtaining more precise and reliable data instead of using an estimate.

Estimates often concern data on developments and trends that are independent of the enterprise concerned — e.g. market prices, transportation tariffs, exchange rates, interest rates, inflation. Many of these estimates can be obtained from competent specialised sources, such as government agencies, banks, business research institutes, or financial and market analysts. The consultant should choose an external source of estimates with extreme caution, bearing in mind that not all sources are equally reliable. It is good to know how the estimate was made — is it a "best guess", a common opinion shared by many experts on the topic, or was a forecasting model used? On what concepts was that model built? In particular, the consultant should never blindly accept, and provide to the client, estimates on the basis of which the client will have to make important business decisions. This does not mean that all risks can be eliminated, but the use of false information must be avoided.

Cultural issues in data gathering

Sensitivity to cultural factors, a general characteristic of excellence in consulting (see chapter 5), is very important in data-gathering activities, in which the consultant interacts with many different individuals and groups in the client organisation. In this respect the consultant must keep in mind both the country's and the organisation's culture. There are many cultural factors to consider when conducting an interview. For example, in some countries, the interview cannot possibly start until the host (respondent or consultant) has first offered a beverage to the visitor.

There may be cultural biases that hamper the use of a data-gathering technique. In a country where English was not the first language, a consultant went through the usual steps in preparing a questionnaire to be administered to a large group of people. When the data were reviewed, the unanimity of responses was surprising. As the consultant pursued this with some members of the client system, he discovered that it was the custom in that country for those answering a questionnaire to provide the information that they thought was wanted by those administering the questionnaire. It would have been impolite to do otherwise! The respondents had all shrewdly determined the kind of answer the consultant would want — and had provided it.

In a Moslem country, a consultant was on an assignment that required gathering data from workers, some of whom were female. When the interview was held, the interviewer/consultant was surprised to find that the respondent brought along another woman, even though the consultant was herself a woman. Obviously, having another person present during the interview raised a question as to the validity of the data. After several interviews had been conducted, the consultant discussed this with the client. Only then did she learn that in that Moslem country (and there are differences among Moslem groups) a woman was not permitted to converse with a stranger, even another female, without an older female from her own household being present.

Even the particular microculture in different parts of an organisation can be expected to influence how an interview is conducted or whether the group can be observed during work. It may be difficult and time-consuming for the consultant to determine the cultural norms of different groups, but it is essential if the data are to be collected.

8.4 Fact analysis

Data cannot be used without analysis, whose purpose goes beyond research and appraisal. As already mentioned, the ultimate aim of the consulting process is to initiate change, and fact analysis should bring us closer to achieving this.

A correct description of reality, i.e. of conditions and events and their causes, is therefore only one aspect of analysis. The other, more important aspect is to establish what can be done, whether the client has the potential to do it, and how to orient the whole business of change.

There are, therefore, no clear-cut limits between *analysis* and *synthesis*. Synthesis, in the sense of building a whole from parts, drawing conclusions from fact analysis and developing action proposals, starts somewhere during fact analysis. Thus, fact-analysis evolves gradually to synthesis. Indeed, to an experienced consultant analysis and synthesis are two sides of one coin, and he applies them simultaneously. He does not have to discover new wholes by combining parts each time he undertakes an assignment — his theoretical knowledge and practical experience help him to synthesise while he is analysing. If the consultant knows a general rule and can establish that the problem observed falls under that rule, he will apply the deductive method. Instead of collecting and analysing a vast number of facts in order to establish what rule applies in any given case, he will proceed in the opposite direction, assuming that the relationships described by the rule also exist in the case he is dealing with.

But the consultant has to avoid the traps that data and his past experience may set for him, such as the temptation to draw hasty conclusions from superficially analysed facts and allow ideas to become fixed before examining facts in depth ("This is exactly the same case I have seen many times before!"). Put in other terms, it is not possible to use *deduction* where *induction* applies, and vice versa. In practical consulting work, then, the two methods are combined and complement each other as analysis and synthesis do.

A simplified example can show the consultant's way of proceeding when he is examining facts. In a manufacturing enterprise, production records and observations have indicated that an important share of productive capacity is wasted owing to machine breakdown and stoppages. Waiting for the arrival of qualified repairmen is given as a cause of the length of stoppages — in fact, the maintenance service is physically centralised in one place and organised in one unit reporting to the production manager, although the enterprise has a number of workshops located in various parts of a vast urban area. The consultant is tempted to suggest a decentralised organisation of maintenance (e.g. a repairman in every shop, or several centres each located close to a group of shops). In this connection consideration would be given, among other things, to repairmen's waiting time — decentralisation would increase their number and full use of their time could not be guaranteed. The next step reveals that the production manager is opposed to decentralisation of technical support services and generally prefers centralisation. For a while the consultant is tempted to see this fact as a major obstacle to solving the problem. But he hits on the idea of re-examining the technical causes of machine stoppages and the attitude of workers to machine breakdown. He collects more data and discovers that the wages of machine operators are not related to the effective working time of the machines. He also finds that most stoppages are caused by minor faults, and that the operators could easily be trained to remove certain defects themselves. In his proposals, the consultant finally concentrates on changes in the wage system in order to motivate workers to keep machine stoppages to a minimum, on training operatives in minor maintenance and repairs, and on some adjustments in the functions of the central maintenance service.

Editing the data

Before being subjected to the analytical operations described below, data need to be edited and screened. This includes checking their completeness, verifying clarity of recording and presentation, eliminating or correcting errors, and making sure that uniform criteria were applied in data gathering.

The most obvious case is that of recording a production operation: if 19 recordings show a duration of between 4 and 5 minutes, one recording indicating 12 minutes cannot be used for calculating an average figure. But this happens in quite different contexts – for example in accounting, where overhead costs may be inaccurately distributed among various products, or where one account may include items which should be put in a different account.

Cross-checking helps in some instances: for instance, in the case of information obtained in an interview, which can be verified by subsequent interviews. In other cases there is no possibility of cross-checking and it is the consultant's experience and judgement, together with advice sought from the client's staff, that help to "clean" the data prior to using them for analytical operations.

Classification

The classification of data was started before the beginning of fact finding by establishing criteria for the organisation and tabulation of data (section 8.2). Further classification, and adjustments in classification criteria, are made during fact finding (e.g. the consultant decides to use a more detailed breakdown of data than originally planned) and after it. If facts are recorded in a way which enables multiple classification (e.g. in a computer), the consultant can try several possible classifications before deciding which one is most relevant to the purpose of the assignment.

Both quantified and other information needs to be classified. For example, if complaints about the shortage of training opportunities come only from certain departments, or from people in certain age groups, the classification must reveal this.

The main classification criteria used by consultants are:

- time;
- place (unit);
- responsibility;
- structure;
- influencing factors.

Classification of data under *time* indicates trends, rates of change, random and periodic fluctuations.

Classification by *place or organisational unit* helps in examining problems of various parts of the organisation and devising solutions related to specific conditions of each unit.

Responsibility for facts and events is a different aspect — in many cases responsibility is not identical with the place (unit) where a fact has been identified.

Classification according to *the structure of entities and processes* is an essential one and uses a number of criteria. Employees, materials, products, or plant and equipment can be classified from many different points of view. An important objective in this case is to define how changes in components affect the magnitude of the whole entity, and to direct action towards those components which have major influence on total results. For example, the total lead time of a steam turbine may be determined by the machining and assembly time of one component — the rotor.

Operations in a production process can be classified according to their sequence in time and presented in a table or diagram, or on the plan of the workshop (which makes it possible to indicate the directions and distances of material movements in reduced proportions).

Organisational relations and informal relationships in organisations can be classified by means of charts, diagrams, matrix tables, and so on.

Classification by *influencing factors* is a preparatory step in functional and causal analysis. For example, machine stoppages may be classified by factors that cause them: lack of material, break in energy supply, absence of worker, delay in scheduling, lack of spare parts, and so on.

In many cases simple classification (by one criterion) does not suffice: *cross-classification* is used, which combines two or more variables (e.g. employees classified by age group, sex, and length of employment with the organisation).

Analysing organised data

Data that have been prepared and organised by classification are analysed in order to identify relationships, proportions and trends. Depending on the nature of the problem and the purpose of the consulting assignment, a variety of techniques can be used in data analysis. The use of statistical techniques is common (averages, dispersion, frequency distribution, correlation and regression), and various other techniques, including the use of mathematical modelling or graphical techniques, are often used. The reader is referred to specialised literature for detailed discussion of these.[6]

Statistical and other quantitative analysis is meaningful only where qualitative relations can be identified. For example, association between two variables can be measured by correlation, but correlation does not explain the nature and the causes of the relationship.

The main objective is to establish whether a specific relationship exists between various factors and events described by data and, if so, to examine its nature. If possible, the relationship is quantified and defined as a *function* (in the mathematical sense of the term), where one or more dependent variables are in a specific relationship to one or more independent variables. The purpose is to discover and define relationships which are substantive and not just accidental.

For example, the consultant may find out from data gathered in various firms that the cost of a major overhaul of machine tools is in some relationship to their purchase price. If such a relationship is defined as a function, the consultant can forecast the cost of overhaul and its influence on production costs in other firms using similar equipment.

A common way of expressing and measuring relationships is *ratios*. They may test whether inputs to an activity generate commensurate outputs, examine whether resources and commitments are properly balanced, or express the internal structure of a particular factor or resource.

Some comments on the use of ratios were made in section 7.2. In detailed analytical work the ratios of global aggregate data may be broken down into analytical ratios. For example, a series of ratios can be used to measure labour productivity:

$$\frac{V}{E} = \frac{V}{DH} \times \frac{DH}{PW} \times \frac{PW}{W} \times \frac{W}{E}$$

where V = value of production,
 E = total number of employees,
 DH = total direct labour hours,
 PW = total number of production workers,
 W = total number of workers.

There are no limits to the construction of detailed analytical ratios in any business and any functional area of management. Here again, working with a quantitative ratio makes sense if there is some qualitative relationship, and if using a ratio makes the analysis more meaningful by measuring this relationship and comparing it to a standard or another known case.[7]

Causal analysis

Causal analysis aims to discover causal relationships between conditions and events. It provides a key to planning change and improvements. If causes that have brought about certain situations, results, or problems are known, action can focus on these causes and try to change them (if they can be changed, of course).

But how does the consultant discover that there is a causal relationship? Remember that in most cases he would start the investigation with one or more hypotheses as to what the cause(s) of a problem may be. As he has studied and practised management, and has probably seen similar situations before, he approaches causal analysis with a certain amount of knowledge and experience. He has an idea about possible main causes — and to confirm this he needs to have a comprehensive, synthetic view of the total process or system he is examining, and of the whole organisational context. Only rarely would a consultant face situations in which unusual causal relationships would be discovered. But this happens as well; for example, a consultant from an industrial country working in a developing economy may discover causal relationships between certain cultural factors and the economic performance of an organisation which are unknown to him from his previous studies and work.

It is always necessary to proceed very methodically, examining in detail, on the basis of the information collected, whether a hypothetical cause could really have created the effect actually observed. An ideal situation is one in which the removal of one hypothetical cause does not result in the disappearance of the effect, indicating that we have not found the main cause. For example, in a workshop with bad working conditions workers get tired quickly and every day the output drops considerably after 3-4 hours of work. If these conditions (e.g. ventilation, lighting) are changed and output does not increase, or only very slightly, we have to look for a different cause. It may be malnutrition. Bad working conditions may aggravate the situation, but are not its main cause.

Unfortunately, to experiment by removing one or more hypothetical causes is not possible, or would be too lengthy and costly, in dealing with management and business problems. In most cases it is the quality of diagnostic work that has to eliminate some hypothetical causes and establish the real one.

Some difficulties and pitfalls of causal analysis have to be pointed out.

Cause and effect. Frequently conditions are observed that influence each other and there is a risk of mistaking an effect for its cause. A typical example is the relationship between poor staff morale and low performance of the organisation. Is poor staff morale a cause of low business results, or do low results depress the staff and lower morale? If a static view is taken, these conditions influence each other, and there may be a vicious circle; but which condition is the cause of the other?

Basic or primary cause. Suppose that the consultant establishes that dropping sales and profits are the cause of low staff morale. What then is the cause of poor business results? The consultant finds out that it is the loss of an important foreign market. But why was that market lost? It was lost owing to a serious mistake in pricing policy. Why was that mistake made? And the exercise goes on . . .

In diagnosing business and management problems, consultants face *chains of causes and effects*. The issue is how deep and how far to go in looking for basic (or primary) causes. Here again, it helps to keep the purpose in mind. It might be exciting, but not very helpful, to trace the causes back to the first sin! But this is not what consulting is about. The consultant will have to consider one cause as basic. It will be *relatively* basic. As a rule, it will be one upon which the client will be able to act. The consultant will thus be able to propose solutions that will address fundamental causes, without suggesting the impossible.

Multiple causes of one effect. A problem frequently has two or more causes, although one of the causes may be more important than the others. This is often observed in personnel problems (a manager's behaviour and performance are affected simultaneously by problems he encounters in the office or at home), or in organisational problems caused by parallel but independent events (e.g. changed foreign-exchange rate *and* death of an outstanding marketing manager).

Figure 8.1 Force-field analysis

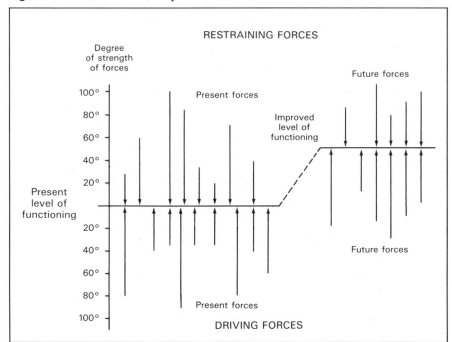

Multiple effects of one cause. The opposite also happens frequently: one condition is found to be the cause of a number of effects. For example, the existence of a political or ethnic clique in an enterprise can be the cause of numerous personnel, managerial and business problems.

Force-field analysis

A possible way of looking at relationships and factors affecting change is force-field analysis, developed by Kurt Lewin (figure 8.1). In this concept, the present state of affairs in an organisation is thought of as an equilibrium maintained by two sums of forces working in opposite directions: driving (impelling, helping) forces move towards change, while restraining (impeding, hindering) forces hamper change. In analytical work, these two sorts of forces have to be identified and the relative strength of each force assessed. Change occurs when imbalance is created between the two groups of forces, e.g. by adding one or more new forces, or increasing or decreasing the strength of an already existing force. When a new state of affairs is attained, a new balance between driving and restraining forces is established. And so on.

Comparison

Comparison is an essential analytical tool, closely interlinked with the methodological tools discussed above. The principal alternatives for comparison

Figure 8.2 Various bases for comparison

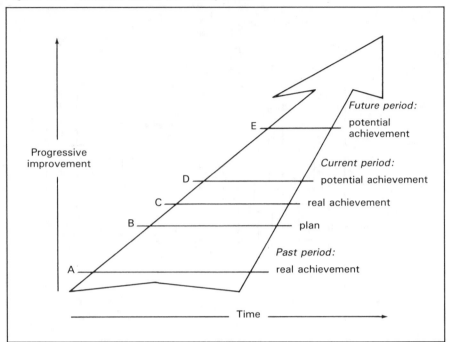

which are commonly used in preliminary diagnostic surveys were mentioned in section 7.2. In detailed diagnostic work the same alternatives apply, but in addition to global appraisal comparison is used to examine operating details and develop solutions. The various bases for comparisons made *within* the client organisation are represented in figure 8.2. The consultant can compare C with A, C with B, C with D, E with C and so on.

Of special interest to operating consultants is comparison, which helps to establish future standards (of potential achievement) and thus provides guidance for the development of proposals. It is particularly in this connection that comparison turns to examples, models and standards from outside the organisation and even outside the sector and country. The consultant considers whether the diversity of conditions permits such comparison, especially if this is to be used for more than general judgement — namely for specific suggestions to the client as to what he should do.

Analysing the future

Owing to its focus on action, all consulting work is essentially future-oriented. Whether the consultant deals with corrective, progressive or creative problems, the question always is: what should be done? This future orientation gives a particular slant to fact analysis. For consultants have to collect or establish data on a situation that does not yet exist in addition to collecting data on existing realities.

This statement is not exactly correct, since the future is related to the past and to the present. Many future events and relationships can be predicted. It is therefore essential to analyse trends in data describing the environment and the organisation concerned. All consultants are interested in trends, whether the assignment is a complex business strategy problem, or deals with a narrower problem such as simplifying production records.

Unfortunately, the most common approach to future-trend analysis is simple extrapolation. We tend to think of the future as a mere extension of past trends, because we are unable or unwilling to consider whether these trends will really continue and what new developments may alter them radically. In periods of rapid technological, social and other changes — and we are living in one such period — it is normal for past trends not to continue into the future without substantial alterations.

Data on future trends collected from various external sources of information have to be examined cautiously and their reliability needs to be assessed. For example, a consultant working for a client enterprise with highly energy-intensive production processes gets information on new power-generating capacities in construction, on their planned completion dates and on foreseen changes in the price of electricity. He should know that new power plants can be years behind schedule and that their actual cost tends to be higher than the original projected cost. How will this affect the future development structure of costs in a client organisation which is a major consumer of electricity? It may be necessary to develop alternative plans and estimate with what probability they are likely to become a reality.

Careful analysis is required when thinking of future developments within the client organisation. These developments will be affected by environmental changes. For example, in analysing the time dimension of a product-life cycle it is necessary to consider whether the curve which is usual in a given sector applies, or whether progress in technology imposes the use of a different curve.

The same applies to ratio analysis. Some ratios may lose their importance or even become meaningless. In retail selling the ratio of sales per employee maintained its meaning with the transition from small shops to department stores, supermarkets and self-service. However, it is losing its meaning with the advent of automatically-controlled sales surfaces if even the cashiers are replaced by electronic control and billing equipment. Ratios such as sales per square metre of selling surface, or sales per $1000 of invested capital, become more significant.

Synthesis

Remember, to a management consultant the analytic method and the synthetic method are two sides of one coin. As fact analysis is progressing the consultant's approach will increasingly involve synthesis — he will be identifying basic relationships, trends and causes, differentiating between fundamental and secondary events and factors, and defining factors and conditions that have to be changed if a whole process or organisation is to change. In particular, the consultant operates as a synthesist when looking ahead and helping the client to define an action programme for preparing the future of the organisation.

In management and consulting practice synthesis is considerably more difficult than purely analytical work. Many bulky analytical reports are difficult to use, although they are based on vast numbers of facts and define long lists of problems. But they lack synthesis and key measures are not identified. As all the measures proposed cannot be introduced at the same time or with the same vigour, action starts in a haphazard way or is soon abandoned.

The spirit to synthesise and skill in synthesis are not given to everybody. Using synthesis is probably one of the main things that a new management consultant has to learn.

Consultants are not the only people who may have problems with synthetic thinking and using the synthetic method effectively. Alvin Toffler points out that our civilisation "placed an extremely heavy emphasis on our ability to dismantle problems into their components: it rewarded us less often for the ability to put the pieces back together again. Most people are culturally more skilled as analysts than synthesists. This is one reason why our images of the future (and of ourselves in that future) are so fragmentary, haphazard and wrong . . . Today we stand on the edge of a new age of synthesis." [8]

Synthesis is the aspect of diagnostic work that provides a link with the next phase of the consulting process — the action-planning phase, which will be discussed in chapter 9.

8.5 Feedback to the client

Throughout this chapter we have been referring to the desirability of actively involving the client in data gathering and other diagnostic operations. The objective is to build a truly collaborative consultant-client relationship at an early stage of the assignment, and to prevent various negative attitudes and reactions on the part of the client, which are difficult to avoid if he is poorly informed about what is actually going on, and if the consultant's findings and conclusions come as a surprise. We have mentioned, too, the need to give feedback to the client during the diagnostic phase.

What is giving feedback?

Giving feedback provides the client with information that can:

● tell him something new and meaningful about his organisation;
● make him aware of the approach taken by the consultant and the progress made in the investigation;
● increase the client's active contribution to the assignment;
● help the consultant to stay on the right track, or reorient his investigation if necessary.

The notion of feedback implies that it concerns not just any useful information, but information collected, analysed and selected by the consultant while working with the client.

Feedback used during diagnosis is, in fact, itself a diagnostic method. The assumption is that properly selected and presented information will provoke some reaction on the part of the client, and so the consultant should keep firmly in mind what reaction he wants to generate. Does he want more information on the topic? Does he seek information on a new topic, about which the client was reluctant to speak? Should the client criticise data submitted by the consultant? Giving feedback to the client is simultaneously an intervention technique used to stir up change. Is this what is wanted? Does the consultant have enough reliable information to feed back to the client with the intention of stimulating change? If there is a risk of generating premature change, the client should be warned against it.

When to give feedback

Feedback is more than reporting on the work performed. Therefore it should be given at moments when it can serve a specific purpose. An example is when feedback shows the client that the data collected so far indicate the existence of some new problem, not foreseen in the negotiation and planning of the original assignment, or when the consultant feels that he has enough information to eliminate certain hypotheses formed at the beginning of the assignment, but prefers to discuss this with the client. A consultant who adopts the strategy of "many small steps" may give feedback each time he has enough information to decide on the next step to take.

To whom to give feedback

In principle, feedback should be given to those from whom the consultant expects further help, more information, or some action related to the problem concerned. It is often emphasised that if feedback is too restrictive (reserved to selected individuals or small groups of senior managers), it is unrealistic to expect that other people will maintain or even increase their interest in helping the consultant. Some authors regard this as a question of consulting ethics: if people readily provide information and demonstrate their interest in the assignment, they have the right to receive feedback on what has been done with their information.

In practice there are limits to this. Some information will clearly be confidential and cannot be divulged to a large number of employees. Deciding who should be informed on the consultant's findings, and at what stage, is also a question of consulting tactics. For example, individuals who originally refused to give information to the consultant may change their attitude if they see that the consultant is sharing information with them.

What feedback to give and how

The consultant wants to show that he has not been wasting his time and that he has meaningful information to share. But the purpose is not to impress people.

The consultant should be selective, sharing information about which the client is likely to be seriously concerned, to which he probably will react, and which will activate him.

Giving feedback is not telling the client what he already knows. This is a general rule, to be consistently observed in reporting and communicating with the client. But when the information collected contains factors that are genuinely news to the client, or shows unsuspected links between effect and cause or hidden strengths and weaknesses, it is useful to give feedback on these issues.

Giving feedback is not evaluating the client. Therefore, the consultant avoids value judgements; it is the client who should be able to draw such conclusions from information chosen and presented to him in an impartial manner. The purpose should always be kept in mind. For example, it is not good tactics to speak only about problems and difficulties, and more problems and more difficulties, encountered by the consultant. Feedback should also point to the client's problem-solving potential, and suggest directions in which he may start searching for feasible solutions. The need for careful preparation of the data and of the form of feedback to be used cannot be overemphasised.

Form of feedback

Individualised oral feedback to important members of the client organisation is used by many consultants. Another form is written information, e.g. interim reports or memos. A common form is feedback meetings with various groups in the client organisation. These meetings can provide valuable additional information and help the consultant to focus the investigation on key issues. They invariably reveal attitudes to the problem at hand and to the approach taken by the consultant.

Closing the diagnostic phase

The end of the diagnostic phase provides an important opportunity for feedback. Before submitting a diagnostic report, the consultant may find it useful to suggest one or more feedback meetings to review the main findings; this may help him to identify the last gaps in his analysis and also prepare the client for the conclusions to be formally presented to him.

Even if the assignment is to continue, i.e. if it is clear that there will be a smooth transition from the diagnostic phase to action planning and then to implementation, there is a good case for submitting a progress report at what is ostensibly the end of the fact-finding and diagnostic stage in an assignment. The period of obtaining and examining facts may have been lengthy, and costly to the client. Many managers may not have been involved very deeply, although they are interested in what the assignment will produce. A good progress report will certainly be welcomed.

There are, then, assignments that will have no further phase, such as management audits and comprehensive diagnostic studies of organisations, in which the consultant is required to establish and analyse facts, but for some reason the client does not want him to go beyond this point. In such cases the diagnostic report will also serve as an end-of-assignment report (see chapter 11).

If the assignment is to continue, obtaining the client's agreement before embarking on the action-planning phase (e.g. on detailed and extensive work on designing a new scheme and planning its application) is essential. Consulting contracts often specify in detail what exactly will happen at the end of the diagnostic phase, before deciding if and how to pursue the assignment.

---

[1] J. H. Fuchs addressing the Society of Professional Management Consultants in New York. See also appendix 6 which describes diagnostic work in the field of production management.

[2] P. Block: *Flawless consulting: A guide to getting your expertise used* (Austin, TX, Learning Concepts, 1981); p. 141.

[3] There are many books with detailed descriptions of various techniques of graphic representation of processes and relationships. See, for example, A. Daniels and D. Yeates (eds.): *Basic training in systems analysis* (London, Pitman, 1969); ILO: *Introduction to work study*, third (revised) edition (Geneva, International Labour Office, 1979); or H. B. Maynard (ed.): *Industrial engineering handbook* (New York, McGraw-Hill, 1971).

[4] See, for example, in H. and Z. Roodman: *Management by communication* (Toronto, Methuen Publications, 1973), chapter 5 "The effective interview"; or F. M. Lopez: *Personnel interviewing* (New York, McGraw-Hill, 1975).

[5] See e.g. T. K. Reeves and D. Harper: *Surveys at work: A practitioner's guide*, (London, McGraw-Hill, 1981).

[6] See e.g. V. T. Clover and H. T. Balsey: *Business research methods* (Columbus, OH, Grid Publishing Co., 1979).

[7] A detailed description of the use of ratios in various sectors and management functions is in C. A. Westwick: *How to use management ratios* (Epping, Gower Press, 1973). See also C. Guthrie: *Interfirm comparison and business clinics in road transport* (Geneva, International Labour Office, 1985, mimeographed).

[8] A. Toffler: *The third wave* (London, Pan Books, 1981); p. 141.

ACTION PLANNING

9

With action planning the consulting process enters its third phase. This phase includes developing one or more solutions to the problem diagnosed, choosing among alternative solutions, presenting proposals to the client, and preparing for the implementation of the solution accepted by the client.

The continuity between diagnosis and action planning cannot be overemphasised. The foundations of effective action planning are laid in excellent diagnostic work, i.e. by a detailed, precise and comprehensive analysis of the problem and its causes, as well as of the factors and forces that influence the change process in the client organisation. In addition, diagnosis provides basic orientation for action-planning efforts. If the problem has been defined as "low production capacity, which will make it impossible to meet the opportunities offered by growing demand", action planning will focus on elaborating alternative solutions such as reconstructing an existing plant, building a new plant, purchasing and adapting another plant, acquiring another company, making new subcontracting arrangements, and the like. If the problem is "low wage differentials" (highly skilled workers are underpaid while some categories of unskilled workers are overpaid), action planning involves a search for feasible ways of re-establishing economically and socially justified differentials, bearing in mind the existing wage regulations, collective agreements and other factors impossible to ignore. Diagnostic work should have identified and examined these factors, thus providing enough information for orienting work towards feasible solutions.

Despite this emphasis on continuity and on the need to base action planning on diagnosis, there are significant differences in approach and methodology. The emphasis is no longer on systematic and meticulous fact-finding and analytical work, but on innovation and creativity. The objective is not to find more data and further explanations for the existence of one problem or another, but to come up with something new. Obviously, not all solutions to clients' problems will involve totally fresh approaches. Often there is no need to develop new solutions from scratch because they already exist somewhere else; it is enough to find out about them and to transplant them. But even transfer and adaptation require imagination and creativity.

It is highly desirable that in action planning the client's involvement becomes even more active than in the diagnostic phase. There are several reasons for this:

- extensive conceptual, design and planning work on one or a small number of alternative solutions should not be undertaken if it is not certain that the client is fully familiar and in complete agreement with the approach taken and will be able to go along with the alternatives that are being pursued; this agreement can best be established by working jointly with people who are in a position to ascertain what the client organisation will accept and be able to implement;

- action planning requires mobilising the best talents and examining all good ideas; it is ineffective if the client organisation's talents do not contribute to this effort;

- as with diagnosis, the client's personnel can do a great deal of design and planning work under the consultant's technical guidance, thus reducing the cost of the project;

- participation in action planning generates commitment that will be badly needed at the implementation stage;

- lastly, action planning provides a new range of learning opportunities for the client; these opportunities will definitely be lost if the consultant is left to proceed by himself.

Once more, the reader should refer to section 4.5 describing various intervention techniques for assisting change. Some of these techniques can be used for working on action proposals in a team with the client and his staff.

Time may be a constraint: in many assignments the time spent on collecting and examining facts has been relatively long, and when it comes to the development of proposals there is a general desire to finish the project as soon as possible. The consultant is left with little time to prepare alternatives and develops only one solution. But even work on one proposal may have to be concluded somewhere short of perfection. As a professional the consultant may deplore this, and in many cases the difficulty can be avoided by properly scheduling the assignment and making sure that enough time is left for creative action planning. If, however, the time problem cannot be overcome, the consultant should consult the client and reach agreement on whether the time limit is to be maintained, or extended in order to arrive at a more effective solution.

9.1 Searching for ideas on possible solutions

The client expects that the consultant will find and recommend the best solution to the problem. However, when action planning starts, it is seldom possible immediately to point to an obvious best solution (although this can happen). Most business and management problems have more than one solution and in some cases the number of alternative solutions is high. The consultant may be aware of some possible solutions, but unaware of other alternatives. Often the complexity and the originality of the situation are such that no clear-cut solution

Table 9.1 Checklist of preliminary considerations

I.   What should the new arrangements achieve?
   • what level of performance?
   • what quality of output?
   • what new product, service or activity?

II. How will the new situation differ from the present?
   • different products, services or activities?
   • different method?
   • different equipment?
   • different location?

III. Are the effects likely to last?
   • is the clients's business and his market changing so rapidly that before long there may not be a need for the new product, service or activity?
   • is there a possibility that people will revert to present practices?

IV. What difficulties will arise?
   • employee resistance?
   • work hazards?
   • over-production?
   • shortage of materials?

V.   Who will be affected?
   • are employees receptive?
   • what should be done to prepare them?
   • do matching changes have to be made elsewhere?

VI. When is the best time to change?
   • at the end of a season?
   • during vacation time?
   • at the close of a financial period?
   • at the beginning of a new calendar year?
   • any time?

---

comes to anybody's mind immediately. New situations cannot be dealt with by old approaches, and management consultants operate in a field which is changing extremely rapidly.

The action-planning phase starts therefore by searching for ideas and information on possible solutions to the problem. The objective is to identify all interesting and feasible alternatives and subject them to preliminary evaluation before starting detailed design and planning work on one proposal. Thus the consultant will be sure that he gives his client the best he can. The client, on the other hand, will feel confident that he is not being forced into accepting one solution without being informed about other possibilities.

Orienting the search for solutions

The main factor to be considered is the nature of the problem, especially its technical characteristics (functional area; techniques or methods to be changed), complexity (technical, financial, human and other aspects of management involved; importance to the client organisation; need to respect sectoral technical standards), and degree of newness (whether the consultant and the client are familiar with the problem involved; whether a completely new solution has to be developed, or an established solution can be applied with or without adaptation).

The consultant, in collaboration with the client, will have to decide whether to direct the search towards solutions that may be available (e.g. purchasing a software package from a computer firm), or towards a new original solution (developing new software using the client's own resources, or commissioning such work from a specialist in software design). It is necessary to decide how far this search should reach. Should it be limited to the client organisation? Could possible solutions be found in other organisations, sectors, or countries? Is it necessary to screen technical literature?

Table 9.1 provides a checklist of some questions to consider in deciding how to focus the search for feasible solutions to the problem.

Using experience

In devising ways of improving the client's situation, the consultant often draws on experience. He considers methods successfully used elsewhere, on the basis of knowledge derived from a variety of sources:

— the consultant's previous assignments;
— the consultant organisation's files and documentation;
— colleagues in the consultant organisation who have worked in similar conditions;
— professional literature (including periodicals);
— makers of the machinery, who may have developed improvements;
— staff in other departments of the client organisation, who may have knowledge of the particular process;
— organisations which are prepared to communicate their experience.

All sources should be considered in the search for improvements. In simple cases, it may be possible to transfer a method used by another organisation, including forms, system of coding, and so on. (It may first be necessary to obtain permission to use such methods and systems.) This will be easier if the problem to be solved is essentially of a corrective or progressive nature. In solving creative problems which require innovative solutions, the sources listed above may fail to suggest any suitable course of action and the consultant, in co-operation with the client's staff, will have to think out his own. In this connection, it might be useful to review some principles and methods of creative thinking.

Creative thinking

Creative thinking has been defined as *the relating of things or ideas which were previously unrelated.* The purpose is, of course, to discover or develop something new. The history of science and business is full of examples of discovery based on creative thinking, and there is no reason why the consultant could not approach many practical industrial and management problems by the same method.

There are *five stages* in the creative thinking process, and all need to be practised consciously to get the best results:

(1) PREPARATION: Getting all the known facts; applying convergent (analytical) thinking as far as possible; getting the problem defined in different ways, i.e. restating the problem.

(2) EFFORT: Divergent thinking, which will lead either to possible solutions or to frustration. Frustration is an important feature in the effort stage and in the full creative thinking process. It is usually followed by the production of really good ideas.

(3) INCUBATION: Leaving the problem in one's subconscious mind while one gets on with other things. This also gives time for inhibitions and emotional blocks to new ideas to weaken, and gives opportunities to pick up additional ideas from what one sees or hears in the meantime.

(4) INSIGHT: The flash of illumination that gives an answer and leads to possible solutions of the problem.

(5) EVALUATION: Analysing all the ideas obtained in the last three stages so as to find possible solutions.

Two of the stages — preparation and evaluation — require analytical thinking. The three central stages — effort, incubation and insight — require suspended judgement and free-wheeling. Wild ideas are deliberately fostered, the aim being quantity, not quality. Large numbers of ideas are obtained, new ideas being sparked off by earlier ideas. The key to successful creative thinking is the conscious and deliberate separation of idea-production and idea-evaluation.

Techniques of creative thinking include, among others: [1]

Brainstorming. This is a means of getting a large number of ideas from a group of people in a short time. Typically a group of 8-12 people take a problem and produce ideas in a free-wheeling atmosphere. Judgement is suspended and all ideas, particularly wild ones, are encouraged. In fact the wildest ideas can often be stepping-stones to new and very practical ones. Ideas are displayed on sheets of newsprint and are produced very quickly; a session may produce over 200 ideas in about an hour. Brainstorming is the best known and most widely used of the techniques. Its main disadvantage lies in the fact that all ideas are evaluated. Many of them are foolish or totally irrelevant and have to be discarded to arrive at a few really good ideas.

Synectics. In this technique, which is similar to brainstorming, a group of about nine people take a problem. The "client", whose problem it is, explains it, and participants put forward a suggestion for solving it. After a few minutes the client analyses the suggestion, saying what he likes about it before touching on the drawbacks. Then new suggestions are put forward and analysed until possible solutions are found.

Attribute listing. This technique lists the main attributes of the idea or object, and examines each one to see how it can be changed. It is normally used on tangible rather than intangible things. For example, a screwdriver has the

Table 9.2   Variables for developing new forms of transport

Travelling in	air, water, space, land surface, underground
Travelling on	wheels, rollers, air cushion, magnetic cushion, skids, moving belt, aerial ropeway
Travel path	reserved, shared with other vehicles
Control	under operator's control, externally controlled
Energy provided by	electricity, petrol, gas, special fuel, atomic power, wind, water
Energy transmitted by	pulling, pushing, ejecting, own engine
Energy transmission	internal: to wheels, propeller (air), propeller (water), caterpillar tracks, ejection
	external: magnetic, hydraulic, pneumatic, mechanical, via cable, via moving belt, via screw transmission
Position of traveller	sitting, lying, standing, hanging

following attributes: round steel shank; wooden handle; flat wedge end; manual operation; torque by twist.

Each attribute is questioned and changes are suggested. Some modern screwdrivers, i.e. with ratchets or a cruciform head instead of the wedge end, are examples of improvement.

Forced relationships. This technique takes objects or ideas and asks the question, "In how many ways can these be combined to give a new object or idea?" For example, a manufacturer of furniture could take the items he makes and see if two or more could be combined to give a new piece of furniture.

Morphological analysis. This technique sets down all the variables in a matrix and tries to combine them in new ways. For example, if a new form of transport is required, the variables could be as shown in table 9.2. Although the matrix does not give all possible alternatives, the various combinations of the variables listed give an impressive number of forms of transport, many of which exist. Many alternatives will be discarded, but some are worth considering and may suggest new, practical, useful and feasible solutions.

Lateral thinking and PO. If a problem is tackled analytically, it is necessary to go into greater and greater depth and detail — this is vertical thinking. Creative thinking involves the examination of all options, including those that appear to be outside the given problem area — that is to say, lateral thinking. De Bono has recommended deferring judgement by prefacing an idea with the letters "PO", which stands for "give the idea a chance, don't kill it too quickly, it may lead to useful ideas." [2]

Checklists. These may be used as pointers to ideas. Lists may be particular to an area (e.g. marketing, design) or general. Osborn's generalised checklist [3] is well known; the main headings are: *Put to other uses?, Adapt?, Modify?, Minify?, Substitute?, Rearrange?, Reverse?, Combine?* Checklists need to be used with care, as they can inhibit creativity by limiting the areas of enquiry.

The search for new creativity techniques continues. *Daydreaming* has been suggested if long intensive work on a problem does not generate any innovative solution; in such a situation complete relaxation and virtual dreaming may bring about creative insight. *The "group-genius" technique* gathers in one group several individuals who normally use different ways of creative thinking, thus forming a team able to combine these techniques.[4]

In summary, no matter which technique is used, the following four guidelines apply:

SUSPEND JUDGEMENT — Rule out premature criticism of any idea.

FREE-WHEEL — The wilder the ideas the better the results.

QUANTITY — The more ideas the better.

CROSS-FERTILISE — Combine and improve on the ideas of others.

Barriers to creative thinking

In business and management practice, there is a need to struggle against barriers to creative thinking. Most people are educated and trained to think analytically, but only a few are trained to use their creative ability. Creative thinking is also restricted by:

- self-imposed barriers;
- belief that there is always one right answer;
- conformity or giving the expected answer;
- lack of effort in challenging the obvious;
- evaluating too quickly;
- fear of looking a fool.

Awareness of the barriers to creative thinking, and a conscious effort to break them down in a creative situation, open a vast area of new ideas, or ways of tackling problems. Suspending judgement is a particularly pertinent example of how a better understanding of the creative thinking process can help towards a fuller use of creative abilities in seeking solutions to difficult management problems.

Respect for authority is a major barrier, difficult to overcome. Even if a person perceived as an authority (a manager, a chief designer, a consultant, an older person) does not explicitly require conformity and uniformity, and encourages colleagues to look for new ideas, challenging his views may be difficult or even impossible in many organisational and national cultures. This is one more reason why managers should refrain from expressing preference for one solution if the search for the best solution is to continue!

Excessive individualism and the failure to use teamwork is another serious barrier. If people work in a team examining a complex problem from various angles, information on a new idea put forward by one team member usually helps other members to widen or correct their outlook and come up with other new ideas. Members of a team can not only help but also emulate each other.

Preselecting ideas to be pursued

As mentioned in the previous paragraphs, in the search for innovative ideas judgement has to be deferred to avoid blocking the process of creative thinking.

There comes a moment, however, when new ideas have to be sorted out, reviewed, discussed and assessed (e.g. very interesting; interesting; trivial; useless; not clear). Since it would be impossible to pursue a large number of ideas, a preselection is made. For example, only "very interesting" ideas will be followed up.

How many ideas should stay on a short list and what criteria to use in classifying certain ideas as "very interesting" is a matter for expert judgement. The selection should be made in close collaboration with the client. If the client decides that several ideas may lead to acceptable solutions, he should also realise that, while parallel work on several solutions may increase the chance of arriving at an ideal solution, the length and the cost of the assignment will probably have to be increased, too.

9.2 Developing and evaluating alternatives

Working on alternatives

If the preliminary screening of ideas has retained more than one alternative, the detailed design, systems development and planning work should in theory be started on all alternatives that were short-listed. In practice a pragmatic attitude is needed since the client and the consultant may be short of resources for working on a number of possibilities simultaneously, and detailed design and planning of several alternatives may be inefficient if only one is to be retained.

A phased approach may help. For example, work may be started on two or three alternatives, but carried only to a pre-project or sketch-plan level. This will make it possible to collect more factual data, including tentative figures on potential costs and benefits. An evaluation of alternative pre-projects can result in the conclusion that from that moment only one will be pursued, or, on the contrary, that the client wishes the design of two or more alternatives to be completed.

Another possibility is to start by developing the alternative that received the highest preliminary rating as an idea. This alternative may be pursued as long as facts show that it would provide a satisfying solution. It would be dropped, and work on a second alternative started, only if assessment reveals that the course of action taken was incorrect, or that cost/benefit analysis is not showing satisfactory results.

It could be objected that these (and similar) approaches do not give a 100 per cent guarantee that the ideal solution will be found and applied. True, but the solutions are being developed in real life, within given time, financial, human and other constraints. The ideal solution may be within the consultant's and the client's reach — but the time or cost required could be prohibitive.

Evaluating alternatives

It can be seen that evaluating alternatives is not a one-off action to be undertaken solely at a defined point in time in the assignment. When data are collected and analysed, this is being done with due regard to the forthcoming evaluation exercises. At the beginning of the assignment, the consultant pays great attention to the definition of the reference period during which data will be collected and used for comparing new solutions with the existing ones. When action planning has started, preliminary evaluation may be made in several steps to eliminate ideas and to reduce the number of alternatives on which the consultant and the client will start doing detailed work. A comprehensive evaluation is required when the client finally opts for one particular alternative.

Some comments on the evaluation criteria used may be useful. There are some comparatively easy cases, such as the choice between two or three machine tools (of different technical level, productivity, service and maintenance requirements, and price) for the same production operation. The number of criteria is limited and can be quantified, especially if production records are reasonably good. In contrast, there are complex cases (e.g. a major reorganisation in a manufacturing company — a frequent assignment in the general management field). There may be several alternatives, with varying degrees of decentralisation, different approaches to specialisation of major units within the company, and different channels and techniques of communication. Personnel and training measures will be involved and so on. In this case some criteria lend themselves to fairly exact calculation of costs (e.g. the cost of training needed). Others do not (e.g. the greater effectiveness of decision making obtained following decentralisation of authority and responsibility in marketing and product-policy matters).

In management consulting, the following situations prevail:

- ideal alternatives are rare, and in most cases there is a need to compare positive and negative consequences of several alternatives;
- the number of criteria is high: certain basic criteria are met by all alternatives and further criteria have to be examined;
- some important criteria (especially environmental, social, human and political criteria) are difficult, if not impossible, to quantify;
- the evaluation involves some assessment of criteria which are not directly comparable (e.g. financial and political criteria),
- this introduces a strong subjective element into evaluation: in the absence of hard data somebody has to decide how important various criteria are in the given case.

To overcome this last difficulty, and to increase the element of objectivity in subjective evaluations, various attempts have been made in recent years to associate numerical values with adjectival scales. The principle is to use a group of experts (from the client organisation or other) to assign point values to particular criteria. The values thus obtained are then used in an evaluation model, e.g. in decision analysis. The scale may be as follows:

Major improvement	=	10
Considerable improvement	=	7
Some improvement	=	4
No change	=	1
Some deterioration	=	-2
Considerable deterioration	=	-5

The evaluation technique used will be selected with regard to the nature and complexity of the particular case. It may be a simple break-even analysis, cost-benefit analysis, return on investment analysis, linear programming technique, decision analysis, or some other technique. Broader social and environmental consequences of managerial decisions will be, as mentioned, difficult to quantify and compare with economic and financial costs and benefits. Notwithstanding that, the number of techniques which attempt to account for these aspects in evaluation models and schemes is rapidly growing.

Two examples of evaluation are given below.

Example 1

The first example is a simple calculation of the benefits from an assignment whose main objective was to increase productivity in a factory. The client has decided that wages will remain the same, but that only the normal hours will be worked, overtime being stopped. Incentive bonus is not paid, although the maintenance of wage levels, with a fall in hours worked (resulting from no overtime), gives an increase in the hourly rate. The figures in one section are given in table 9.3.

Table 9.3   Data from one section

	Per week		
	Results during reference period	Results anticipated after change	Benefit from change (%)
Output of blanks (in thousands)	1,740	2,610	+50
Hours worked	450	410	−9
Wages paid in $	920	920	None

Using these figures, the results anticipated from implementing the change are as indicated in table 9.4.

Table 9.4   Benefits from change

	Results during reference period	Results anticipated after change	Benefit from change (%)
Productivity			
Blanks per hour (in thousands)	3.86	6.36	+65
Earnings			
$ per hour	2.04	2.24	+10
Labour cost			
$ per 1,000 blanks	0.529	0.352	−33

Table 9.5   Effect of alternative policies

POLICY	EFFECT ON		
To have the same —	Volume of work	Money spent	Labour required
Labour force	Up	Up	Same
Money spent	Up	Same	Down
Volume	Same	Down	Down

The reduction in labour cost from $0.529 to $0.352 per 1,000 blanks will result in financial benefits, at the anticipated output of:

(0.529 − 0.352) x 2,610 = $462 per week,
or $23,100 per annum (50 weeks).

It should be noted that the benefits are calculated on labour cost only. As output has increased substantially, other benefits may arise from overhead recovery. Offsetting these benefits are the costs of the changes − in this case, purchase of new machinery and re-layout. It should also be noted that two quite different costs are involved: capital (or one-off) costs of new equipment or re-layout in the section, and labour costs which continue.

In the figures quoted above output increased by 65 per cent. This is a large increase which must be pointed out to the client who has to act: he must sell more of his product, or tie up capital by storing it. The client may decide that the increase in output is too high, and that the increase is to be limited to, say, 30 per cent (i.e. to 1,158 instead of 2,500 blanks per hour). In addition to altering the benefits considerably, such a decision would change other figures, principally hours worked (and therefore the number of workpeople required).

The effect the consultant has to achieve depends on the policy that the client adopts. This is shown in table 9.5 which indicates how the three aspects interact. Reliable data from the reference period enables various possible solutions to be evaluated, not only as to the ultimate benefits, but also as to the effects of the client's policy, i.e. how much more money he has to find for wages, or how much more output he has to sell.

Example 2

The second example uses a variant of *decision analysis*.[5] The consultant has to evaluate two alternatives involved in erecting a new plant.

As a first step, the consultant examines whether both alternatives meet *essential needs* (table 9.6).

As both schemes meet essential needs, evaluation from the viewpoint of *desirable needs* will next be made.

The simplest way is to decide which alternative meets a higher number of desirable needs (table 9.7).

Table 9.6   Essential needs

Essential needs	Criterion	Alternative A	Alternative B
Capital available — maximum cost (US$)	2,500,000	2,400,000	2,100,000
Minimum area of building (m²)	3,000	3,000	3,000
Mains service	yes	yes	yes
Access to railway	yes	yes	yes
Maximum distance from existing works (km)	15	7	10
Latest occupation within (months)	12	8	10

Such a comparison may, however, be considered too primitive for a deep evaluation. Instead of marking alternatives by a positive $(+)$ or negative $(-)$ symbol, points may be assigned to them (e.g. from 1 to 9) and the alternative that has scored a higher total number of points will "win". A third possibility (shown in table 9.8) is to assign, first, a degree of importance (weight) (e.g. from 1 to 10) and, second, a number of points (e.g. from 0 to 10) to each desirable need. In table 9.8 the desirable needs are re-ordered in accordance with their weight.

The importance of the subjective element in such evaluation is high, although a quantitative method is used. First, both the weight and the points assigned to each desirable need depend on the sound and objective judgement of those who will be deciding on the respective importance of these criteria. For example, "space for further expansion" may be considered unimportant if no further expansion is foreseen and local labour resources will soon be exhausted. In another case, this criterion may be given the highest weight. Secondly, the higher total number of points assigned to one alternative (B) does not automatically imply that it must be adopted without further examination — this again will be based on the individual judgement of experienced people, and may also reflect personal preference and bias.

Table 9.7   Number of desirable needs met by each alternative

Desirable needs	Alternative A	Alternative B
1. Lowest possible running cost	+	+
2. Under 10 miles from shops	+	−
3. Served by public transport	+	+
4. Property appreciation prospects	+	+
5. Additional female labour available	−	+
6. Accessible to existing workforce	+	+
7. Maximum use of existing equipment	+	+
8. Lowest possible capital cost	+	+
9. Near low-priced housing	−	+
10. Space for further expansion	−	+
11. Park for 200-250 cars	+	+
Total	8+	10+

Table 9.8 Decision analysis

Essential needs	Alternative A	Alternative B
Capital available: $2,500,000	Cost: $2,400,000	Cost: $2,100,000
Minimum area of building: 3,000m²	3,000m²	3,000m²
Mains services	yes	yes
Within 15 km of existing works	7 km	10 km
Occupation within 12 months	8 months	10 months

Desirable needs	Weight	Detail	Points	Value	Detail	Points	Value
1. Lowest possible running costs	10	Est. $144,000 p.a.	9	90	Est. $132,000 p.a.	10	100
2. Additional female labour available	9	Few	2	18	Many	7	63
3. Accessible to existing workforce	8	7 km	9	72	10 km	6	48
4. Maximum use of existing workforce	8	Very good	10	80	Good	8	64
5. Lowest possible capital cost	7	$2,400,000	8	56	$2,100,000	10	70
6. Served by public transport	7	20 min. bus	7	49	15 min. bus	9	63
7. Park for 200–250 cars	6	210 cars	8	48	300 cars	10	60
8. Near low-priced housing	6	No	0	0	Two estates	10	60
9. Space for further expansion	5	Limited	5	25	Ample	9	45
10. Property appreciation prospects	4	Fair	5	20	Fair	5	20
11. Under 10 minutes from shops	3	8 minutes	10	30	15 minutes	0	0
Total value				488			593

9.3 Presenting action proposals to the client

When work on action proposals and the evaluation of alternatives has reached an advanced stage, the consultant has to consider the time and form for the presentation to the client. This will depend mainly on the type of project undertaken and the working relationships between the consultant and the client's managerial and specialist staff.

In long and complex assignments, involving strategic issues and costly investment or other measures, the client's staff is usually very much involved and keeps the senior management informed about progress. The consultant submits progress reports and seeks further guidance from the client at several points during the assignment, so the presentation of final proposals does not bring up anything completely new. Essentially, information that the client has had from previous reports and other contacts with the consultant is summarised, confirmed and put up for decision.

In many cases, however, the reporting which has preceded the presentation of proposals may have been limited. The scope of the assignment may not require reporting and discussions at each step; or, in assignments that will affect some vested interests (e.g. re-organisations), the client does not want to hold many meetings and have information circulated before the solutions have been defined and thoroughly examined by a restricted managerial group. Hence the need for a well-prepared presentation which, in the latter case, may convey completely new information to a number of people.

The presentation

Most consultants prefer to be able to make an oral presentation with the backing of all written evidence and any audio-visual aids needed to support the case. A combination of written and oral presentation is often required. The consultant can make an oral presentation, introducing documentation that will be left with the client, to be followed by another meeting once the client has examined the proposal in more detail. Alternatively, the client may prefer to receive the proposal in writing first and arrange a presentation meeting after having read the proposal.

The objective of the presentation is, of course, to obtain the client's acceptance of the recommendations. The degree of persuasion will depend on many factors and must be anticipated, prepared for and built into the presentation. The presentation meeting is held between the consulting team (including the supervisor), the client and those members of the staff chosen to attend. The client's liaison officer and other staff specialists may have an important role to play. Having taken part in the investigation they may be informed about many details and should be completely in favour of the recommendations.

The consultant's presentation works through a logical series of steps, building up the case for the recommendations in so effective a manner that the client should have little or no hesitation in accepting them. At least, that is the idea.

No presentation should be made unless the consultant believes that the probability of acceptance is high.

The presentation must never flood managers in the client organisation with analytical details, or try to impress them by techniques that are normally the specialist's domain. However, the techniques used in evaluation should be mentioned. A clear picture of all solutions that have been envisaged is given and the choice proposed by the consultant is justified. The consultant must be absolutely honest with the client, especially when he is explaining:

● *the risks involved* (the solution has never been used before; some employees will probably be against it; the real cost may be higher than foreseen);

● *the conditions that the client must create and maintain* (a high discipline in recording primary data is needed; some members of senior management must be transferred).

There may be circumstances known to both parties owing to which acceptance at this point may be in principle only. There may be an agreed intention, but a final decision may be contingent on a detailed study of written proposals by the client, or on the recommendations being explained to and accepted by employees' representatives.

Where there have to be further presentations to representatives of trade unions, staff associations, or other employee groups, the role of persuader and negotiator shifts to the client. Under no circumstances should the consultant take this on alone. He is, of course, ready to back up the client and help him to organise whatever explanatory campaign is necessary — and he should strongly advise against trying to get everything over at one mass meeting.

Plans for implementation

One section is often missing from action proposals presented to clients: a realistic and feasible plan for the implementation of the proposals. The client receives a static picture, describing the new project or scheme as it should look when implemented. Yet there may be a long way to go to achieve this desired condition, and several different paths may be available. Moreover, the planning of stages and activities to put the new scheme into effect can reveal further problems, allowing the proposal to be further improved before the final version is submitted to the client.

Thus an effective action proposal shows not only *what* to implement but also *how* to do it. A plan for implementation should be included in the proposal in any case. The client and the consultant can agree that this plan will be a global one, leaving the details to a later stage, immediately preceding each step towards implementation.

The decision

It is the client and not the consultant who should decide what solution will be chosen and applied. On no account should the client feel that the consultant has made his own choice which the client must follow in order not to upset the whole scheme. A client who feels that a solution was imposed on him will not be very active during the implementation phase, and will take the first opportunity to put the blame on the consultant if matters do not work out as suggested.

The client's decision on the consultant's proposal is subject to the same influences as any other management decision. The number of important decisions that are determined by emotional rather than rational criteria is surprisingly high. Furthermore, the client's conception of rationality may differ from the consultant's conception because their cultural background is not the same.

It is essential that the consultant is aware of the client's personal preferences, and of cultural and other factors affecting decision making in the client organisation. This awareness helps him to refrain from putting forward proposals which will not be accepted, and to recognise again that consulting is much more than presenting technically ideal solutions: it also involves patient persuasion and explanation to the client and his staff so that they will accept rational measures as their favourite personal choices.

The decision taken on the consultant's proposals may be the final point of an assignment if proposals are accepted for immediate or later implementation, and the client wants to undertake the work himself. It will act as an introduction to the next step in an assignment if the client prefers the consultant to assist with implementation.

---

[1] A more detailed description of most of the techniques is in J. G. Rawlinson: *Creative thinking and brainstorming* (Farnborough, Gower, 1981).

[2] E. de Bono: *Lateral thinking: A textbook of creativity* (Harmondsworth, Penguin Books, 1977).

[3] A. F. Osborn: *Applied imagination* (New York, Charles Scribner's Sons, 1957).

[4] These and other newer techniques are briefly described in R. L. Bencin: "How to keep creative juices flowing" in *International Management*, July 1983.

[5] See e.g. J. W. Ulvila and R. V. Brown: "Decision analysis comes of age" in *Harvard Business Review*, Sep.-Oct. 1982.

IMPLEMENTATION

10

Implementation, the fourth phase of the consulting process, is the culmination of the consultant's and the client's joint effort. To *implement* changes that are *real improvements* from the client's point of view is the basic purpose of any consulting assignment. The consultant, too, wants to see his proposals not only well received in meetings with the client, but put into effect with good results.

If there is no implementation, the consulting process cannot be regarded as completed. This is the position if the client does not accept the consultant's proposals presented at the end of the action-planning phase. It demonstrates that the assignment has been poorly managed by both parties. If the consultant and the client collaborate closely during the diagnostic and action-planning phases, the client cannot really reject proposals that are the product of joint work. If there is any doubt about the focus of the consultant's work during action planning, and about the feasibility of the proposals that will be forthcoming, corrective measures should be taken immediately, without waiting until the proposals have been finalised.

It may happen, too, that the consultant does not find any solution to his client's problem. Maybe the problem as formulated does not have a solution (e.g. the goal set was too ambitious and unrealistic). Such a situation should also be discovered and the work on proposals redirected at an earlier stage, so that action planning comes up with realistic proposals on how to deal with a re-defined problem.

10.1 The consultant's role in implementation

Why the consultant should be involved

In chapter 1 we gave some arguments justifying the consultant's involvement in the implementation phase of an assignment. The issue is important enough to be reviewed once more.

As we know, the ultimate responsibility for implementation is with the client. It is the client, not the consultant, who makes all the management decisions and sees to it that they are put into effect. This, of course, is more easily said than done. The more complex the assignment, the higher the probability that implementation will be an equally or more difficult matter than diagnosis and action planning. The plan or project presented by the consultant is a model of future conditions and relationships, assuming certain behaviours on the part of the client and his staff, as well as particular environmental and other conditions affecting the client organisation. The consultant can make mistakes in developing such a model. In addition, many of the conditions can change after the proposal has been presented and accepted. The consultant's co-responsibility for implementation helps to overcome these difficulties.

The issue of the consultant's participation in implementation should never be underestimated, but always thoroughly examined and discussed when designing a consulting project. Both the consultant and the client should give their arguments for and against this participation and consider various alternatives.

The consultant does not have to be involved in implementation:

- if the problem is relatively straightforward and no technical or other difficulties with implementation are anticipated;
- if joint work during the diagnostic and action-planning phases shows that the client has developed a very good understanding of the problem and a capability to deal with implementation without further assistance.

The client's reluctance may be motivated by financial reasons. By the end of the action-planning phase the cost of the assignment may already be high and the budget may be exhausted. Or the manager who has to approve the contract may feel that involving the consultant in implementation implies expenditures that can be avoided. Here again a frank discussion helps. The consultant can suggest a more economical design for diagnosis and action planning in order to free resources that will allow him to be involved in implementation.

Finding a suitable arrangement

The failure to involve the consultant in implementation often reflects a lack of imagination and flexibility on either the consultant's or the client's part. Of course the client worries about the cost of the assignment, and the more time the project takes, the stronger may be the feeling that the consultants are staying for too long.

The following arrangements can keep the consultant involved in implementation without imposing high charges on the client:

- the size of the consulting team present at the client's premises will be gradually reduced during the implementation phase;
- only one consultant will stay during the whole implementation phase, providing advice and bringing in additional expertise from the consulting unit if appropriate;
- the consultant will deal only with the more difficult tasks in implementation, leaving all other work to the client;

- the consultant will visit the client periodically, or at agreed points during implementation, to check progress and provide advice;
- the consultant will be available to intervene only at the client's special request.

Clearly, all these options will not be available to every consulting unit. Larger firms will be able to consider more options. An individual practitioner will be working with a new client when a former client calls for help in implementation. As a rule, it is possible to co-ordinate both interventions; however, the new client should know that the consultant has not fully completed a previous assignment, though he is phasing himself out of it.

10.2 Planning and monitoring implementation

A set of proposals for implementation should be part of the action plan presented to the client, for reasons explained in section 9.3. Before implementation starts, a detailed work programme will be prepared.

Steps to take

Planning a campaign to introduce a new method or system is another instance of the usefulness of network planning or bar-charting techniques. The day chosen as "implementation day" will be more definite if planned for in this way. The time needed to obtain equipment and to design detailed procedures may be relatively easy to estimate. When there is a major physical move, as required by, say, a new factory or general office layout, a scheduled sequence of individual moves is necessary. When there has to be "business as usual" during the move, the schedule recognises the need for the minimum of upset. Sometimes a short, sharp campaign can take place during an annual shutdown. When it does, all employees are briefed on what they will find when they return so as to avoid some days of chaos.

Defining responsibilities

Implementation will create new tasks and relationships, while abolishing old ones. People's commitment and participation cannot be solicited without specifying their contributions. Such a specification will be particularly helpful in drawing up a training programme and in establishing controls for monitoring implementation.

Pace and lead-time of implementation

Obviously, various technical and resource factors will have a bearing on the pace and lead-time of implementation. As a matter of principle, the consultant will aim to schedule implementation in the client's best interest (e.g. to make new production capacity operational as early as possible, or to avoid situations in which the client has to deal with several difficult projects simultaneously).

The feasible and desirable pace of change, as discussed in chapter 4, is a most important criterion. It may be necessary to gain the commitment and support of a number of individuals, who will constitute a kind of *critical mass*. Considerable time and persuasion may be needed to create this critical mass, but once attained its existence will accelerate the whole process. These are important aspects of the strategy of planned change.

Controls

The programme of implementation should define controllable, and, if possible, measurable results of individual tasks, operations and steps. This is essential for monitoring.

Built-in flexibility and contingency

The more complex and innovative the assignment, the greater the chance that the work programme will need to be adjusted several times during the implementation phase. Monitoring will show this need. However, adjustments are easier if some flexibility is built in. Completion of the assignment should not be scheduled for the very last moment (i.e. the time when the new scheme or plant *must* be in operation); some time should be kept in reserve for final adjustments. The same may apply to the allocation of resources and to provision for further help by the consultant during implementation.

Detailing procedures

When a good deal of new methodology is involved, it is usual to prepare a manual for guidance in the procedures to be followed. Virtually all forms of reorganisation, irrespective of their functional or inter-functional aspects, require simple instructions on how to operate them. New stationery has usually to be designed. The consultant may do this himself or may adopt part or all of some proprietary system.[1]

Monitoring implementation

When implementation is about to start, the consultant checks that all conditions have been fulfilled and all prerequisites are on hand.

At the commencement of the running of the new system and for a time after, the consultant is available to answer any queries and to help the client's staff to deal at once with any problem that may arise. This is as much a question of tactics as of techniques, since little deficiencies and misunderstandings at the moment when a new system is starting up have a tendency to grow and become major difficulties if not dealt with immediately. In this the consultant may have more experience than the client.

It is not uncommon for decision makers, including the consultant, to experience uncomfortable after-thoughts once a decision has finally been reached and implementation commences. This phenomenon is known as *cognitive dissonance*. Prior to reaching a decision, the decision makers usually spend an inordinate amount of time focusing on the benefits of the new scheme and the disadvantages of the present, or alternative, scheme. However, once a firm decision has been reached, the implementation process commences and the first problems inevitably appear, it seems that a good deal of time is now spent on reviewing the advantages of the previous, or displaced, scheme, while comments are voiced on the drawbacks of the new scheme currently being implemented.

It is readily conceded that it takes considerable talent to examine an existing scheme and, on the basis of investigations and results obtained, devise a new, more effective one, but it also takes considerable courage to proceed with the implementation of the new scheme when problems are met with in the early stages of the implementation phase (as is usually the case). When this happens the consultant would do well to take note of the maxim: "Take time to plan your work, then take time to work your plan."

Jointly with the client, the consultant makes a regular and frequent assessment of the progress of implementation. Attention is paid to the pace of implementation and its broader consequences — e.g. whether the changes in plant layout and organisation of the production department are proceeding according to schedule and the delivery of any new product will start as promised. Adjustments in the time schedule, the approach taken, or even the original design of the new scheme, are made as appropriate, but in an organised manner, avoiding ad hoc, blind panic decisions.

The consultant's poised behaviour during this phase of the work affects the attitudes of the client and his staff towards implementation. He must be seen as an enthusiastic senior colleague who feels fully involved and co-responsible, who has a vision of what should be achieved, and who is able to explain the roles and responsibilities of others engaged in the project.

10.3 Training and developing client staff

In chapter 1 we have shown that the link between consulting and training is logical and natural. Both have the same ultimate objective — to do things better — and they support each other. In most operating assignments some training and development of client staff is foreseen in the work programme. It may take a variety of forms and its volume will differ from case to case.

Developing the co-operating team

Perhaps the most interesting and efficient, although the least formalised, method is the development of client personnel through direct co-operation with the consultant on problem solving. In a smaller enterprise this may concern the owner-manager himself. In other organisations it will concern some managers, the liaison officer and other members of the team who are responsible for the project jointly with the consultant. If the consultant is a good one, he uses every opportunity not only to pass on routine jobs (such as data collection) to client staff, but increasingly to involve them in the more sophisticated operations demanding skills and experience and stimulating self-education. As this is an excellent learning opportunity, it is useful to assign to this job able people with good development potential, and not just those who can be spared from their normal duties for the period of the assignment.

Managers in senior positions will also learn from the assignment if the consultant knows how to communicate with them and if they are keen to find out what the consultant's work methods are. That is why it is more interesting for a senior manager, if he finds a really good consultant, to interact with him frequently instead of just reading his final report at the end of the assignment.

Training for new methods and techniques

A common element in assignments is the training of client staff in specific techniques. This concerns those staff members who are involved in the introduction and use of the technique (e.g. time measurement, statistical quality control, standard costing). A number of people may have to be trained; this may necessitate a precisely defined and scheduled training programme which precedes implementation and may continue during its first stages. A number of approaches are possible, such as:

- on-the-job training by the consultant;
- training of trainers by the consultant;
- training of experimental groups whose members will then train the remaining staff;
- formal in-company training courses (run by the consultant, by special trainers brought in for this purpose, or by the organisation's internal trainers);
- participation of selected staff in external training courses;
- appreciation programmes for those who are not directly involved, but should be informed.

Staff development in complex assignments

As the problems tackled by the consultant become increasingly sophisticated and complex, the related training and development of staff also becomes more difficult to design and organise. This is, for example, the case in assignments aimed at major changes, such as extensive reorganisations, important changes in product and market strategies, or the establishment of a new plant including the installation of a new management system. In addition to specific training in new techniques, which may be needed, there is a case for a collective development effort which should bring about more substantial changes in management concepts, strategies, communication and styles.

In these situations, training in particular work techniques may have to be supplemented by programmes aimed at behavioural change. These may include seminars, working groups, discussion groups, special project teams, individual project work, exchange of roles, counselling by the consultant and by in-plant trainers, and so on. Some of these intervention techniques were described in chapter 4.

In addition to practicality, another important feature of training in connection with consulting assignments is that it generates interest in further training and self-development. Sound management stimulates and nurtures this interest, which may actually be the most lasting contribution of many consulting assignments.

10.4 Some tactical guidelines for introducing changes in work methods

In this section we summarise a few practical guidelines on how to introduce new work methods and help people to master them without major difficulties. Here again, the purpose of the guidelines is to make the consultant alert to what might happen and suggest in what direction to search for a remedy, not to provide universal recipes for handling any situation. The guidelines that follow should be read in conjunction with chapter 4 which the reader may wish to review at this point.

Tactic 1 : The best method

It has been mentioned in chapter 4 that the process of change involves: (i) identification with the change, and (ii) internalisation of the change. Whether these phases are carried out in sequence or simultaneously is not very important. The essential point is that they require commitment, involvement, or participation by the person doing the changing. The change must be tested by the individual as he moves from the general (identification) to the specific (internalisation).

Therefore the people concerned in the change process should be involved as early as possible, so that these two vital elements can be comprehensively covered. However, a strong note of warning is offered as to how participation might be achieved. Apart from attending meetings or brainstorming sessions for specific purposes (such as to provide a data bank of ideas for the solution of creative problems), individuals should not start using their own new methods for performing tasks if the idea is to develop a best method for general use. Results of studies show that where individuals are encouraged to adopt their own approaches and the best method or approved solution is later imposed, those people will exhibit some conformity to the new proposal, but will still diverge significantly from the approved method in following their own.

However, where persons in groups are provided with a best method or approved approach in the first instance, it is found that subsequently individuals will vary only insignificantly from the set procedures. Diagrammatically, these results can be shown as in figure 10.1.

Figure 10.1 Comparison of two cases illustrating the effects on eventual performance when using individualised versus conformed initial approaches

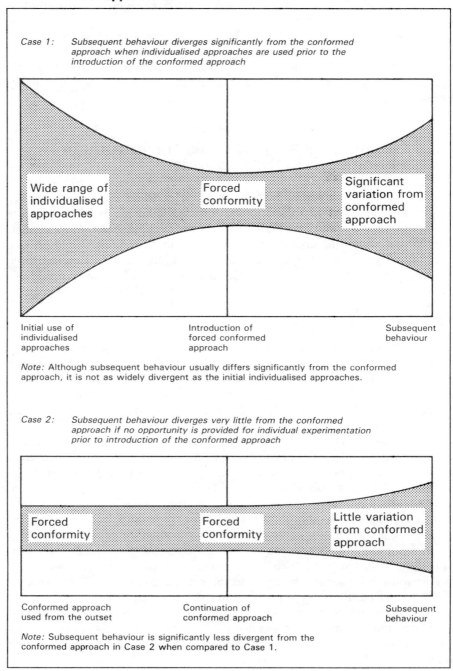

Case 1: *Subsequent behaviour diverges significantly from the conformed approach when individualised approaches are used prior to the introduction of the conformed approach*

Wide range of individualised approaches

Forced conformity

Significant variation from conformed approach

Initial use of individualised approaches

Introduction of forced conformed approach

Subsequent behaviour

Note: Although subsequent behaviour usually differs significantly from the conformed approach, it is not as widely divergent as the initial individualised approaches.

Case 2: *Subsequent behaviour diverges very little from the conformed approach if no opportunity is provided for individual experimentation prior to introduction of the conformed approach*

Forced conformity

Forced conformity

Little variation from conformed approach

Conformed approach used from the outset

Continuation of conformed approach

Subsequent behaviour

Note: Subsequent behaviour is significantly less divergent from the conformed approach in Case 2 when compared to Case 1.

Figure 10.2 Comparison of spaced practice with a continuous or massed practice approach in terms of performance

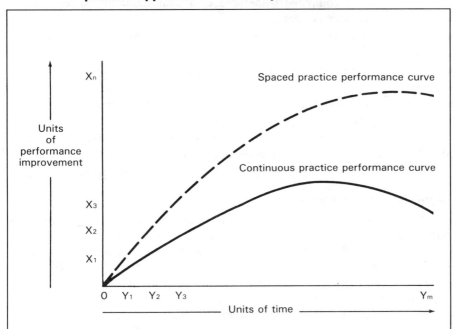

In case 1 the end result is that individuals perform in a manner significantly different from the approved method, although not quite as widely different as during their initial trials. There is some tendency towards the norm. In case 2 there is in subsequent performance much less divergence (significant in a statistical sense) from the approved norm because individuals have not had an opportunity to rehearse in any other manner than the approved one.

Thus, where feasible, the consultant should attempt to introduce the approved method as a scheme applying to the whole group where individual differences can be kept to a minimum (often as a result of normal group pressures, coupled with the fact that no opportunity to develop individual ad hoc approaches is provided).

Tactic 2: Spaced practice

Improvement in performance occurs more quickly, in greater depth, and lasts for a longer time (i.e. the decay or extinction curve is longer), if new approaches are introduced in relatively short periods with ample provision for rest periods than if continuous or massed practice periods are employed.

A generalised improvement in performance noted where the "quick and often" tactic is employed (compared to a continuous practice scheme) is shown in figure 10.2.

From the figure it can be seen that when a spaced practice approach is used and the results are compared with those of a continuous or massed practice approach for the same period:

- improvement using spaced practice is quicker, i.e. the performance curve is sharper;

- improvement using spaced practice is greater, i.e. the performance curve is higher;

- improvement lasts longer, i.e. the decay or extinction curve is shallower.

These performance curves will almost invariably be obtained where improvement in skill can be measured as a result of practice or rehearsal. Thus the consultant is well advised to consider introducing change gradually using relatively short practice sessions rather than relying on one great training input.

Tactic 3: Rehearsal

It is a proven fact that where skill is involved results constantly improve with spaced practice provided, of course, that the correct procedures are followed.

As shown in figure 10.2, performance constantly improves with continued practice until a ceiling or plateau of performance is reached. Continued practice is then required to maintain this level of performance.

Although there may be grounds for debate as to whether or not learning (i.e. the cerebral functioning involved) of a new technique takes place

- as a sequential process, i.e. a little-by-little approach,

- as an all-or-none process (e.g. the "Eureka — I've got it!" type of phenomenon),

- or by repetitive exposures of the same input in different settings,

the technique is not really relevant since the learning process cannot, as yet, be appropriately measured. However, there is no escaping the fact that performance, which can be measured, always improves with practice. Constant practice can eventually lead to a condition known as overlearning in which routine and procedures become virtually automatic reactions.

The consultant must therefore make provision for appropriate training and practice sessions (rehearsals) when introducing new approaches.

Tactic 4: Moving from the known to the unknown

There is considerable evidence that the knowledge of a prior skill can have either a positive or negative transfer effect on the acquisition of a new skill.

As mentioned earlier, the consultant is usually faced at the beginning with the need for an "unfreezing" phase, designed to break down old habits. Surprising as it may seem, in order to be able to facilitate new learning it is usually more effective to have the learner in an "anxious" rather than a "comfortable" state, because he is then more likely actively to seek information to reduce his level of anxiety. In a "comfortable" state, he is more likely to select information which will continue that state, to reinforce old habits rather than seek new approaches.

The consultant can use this attention-rousing device by showing that the "known" procedures are no longer suitable for present purposes. If he moves directly to the introduction of new methods without first breaking down established practices, there is a grave risk of negative transfer effects taking place.

When introducing a totally new approach, however, there may be some benefit in building it on an appropriate existing procedure. In short, when introducing change, move from the known to the unknown (new approach).

Tactic 5: Setting demanding but realistic goals

According to S. W. Gellerman, "stretching" is desirable when goals are being established.[2] By this he means that targets should be set a little higher than would normally be expected. D. C. McClelland supports this notion and adds that the goals should be realistic and neither "too easy" nor "impossible", but such that a feeling of achievement can be experienced when they are reached.[3]

There is ample evidence to show that high expectations coupled with genuine confidence in a prestigious person often result in a changee attaining higher performance and productivity. This effect can become cumulative — the improved performance encourages the individual to assume more responsibility and so creates in him greater opportunities for achievement, growth and development. Conversely, low expectations may lead to low performance which, in turn, leads to a situation in which credibility is lost and distrust and scepticism become the order of the day.

When introducing change, the consultant has to ensure that all those involved readily understand what this means in terms of goals. Such goals should be expressed in terms which are:

● quantitative (able to be measured in numerical terms);

● qualitative (able to be described specifically);

● time-phased (provision of commencement dates and expected duration before final attainment).

It is important to correctly determine *the time* by when a new goal has to be achieved. Because attitudes and work habits take a long time to form, time must be allowed for replacing them by new ones. Unless there is a perceived dramatic need to institute a change immediately, the process may take longer than originally expected.

Tactic 6: Respecting the absorptive capacity

People differ tremendously in their capacity to absorb new information and their ability to undertake new activities. Many writers have argued that there is a maximum number of "units of information" which an individual can absorb and process at any one time. In this connection G. W. Miller refers to the "magical number seven" (plus or minus two, to allow for variations in individual capacity).[4] By confining inputs to the lower end of the scale (namely five), the consultant can avoid overtaxing any of his audience, although he may cause some degree of impatience among the most gifted.

Figure 10.3   Generalised illustration of the high points in attention level of a captive audience

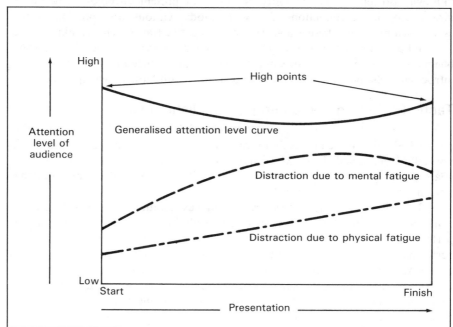

The information can first be presented as a single whole and then be broken down into sub-units for more detailed study, or it can be built up gradually by synthesis of the individual parts. The method chosen will depend on the nature of the problem, the composition of the audience and the consultant's personal preference.

During the introductory and concluding phases of an information session it is well to provide a summary of the complete presentation. There is support for the idea that the attention of an audience reaches its highest level shortly after the commencement of a session and again shortly before its conclusion. At the outset the exposition probably has a novelty value, which begins to be dissipated as physical and mental fatigue build up. Shortly before the conclusion is reached, however, the decrease in the level of attention accounted for by lack of concentration is usually removed as the audience begins to anticipate the end of this activity and the beginning of a new one. These high points in concentration are illustrated in figure 10.3.

Tactic 7: Providing evidence and feedback

Verbal persuasion is inherently unstable and requires support in terms of proven facts. Action speaks louder than words. The consultant must keep records of all performance improvements as support for the change process. For example, although daily output figures may decrease immediately following a change process, it is possible that errors or accident rates may decrease even more significantly at the same time.

Successful introduction of change requires presentation of appropriate feedback information to permit the necessary adjustments on the part of those undertaking the change process. The consultant must make provision for review and reporting sessions, not merely as morale-boosting devices, but as a requisite for control and correction.

10.5 Maintenance and control of the new practice

If a new scheme is to survive and yield more in benefits than it costs, it has to be protected against a number of more or less natural hazards. Standards, systems and procedures are as prone to deterioration through wear and tear and neglect as are machines. Like machines, their performance may be eventually reduced to zero.

Maintenance and control should start while the consultant is still with the client organisation, but must continue after his departure.

Backsliding

A maintenance and control system has to guard against simple backsliding, which is liable to occur as long as people remember what they used to do before the change. Backsliding is not always reactionary. If a new method breaks down through trouble with equipment, supplies, and so on, work can only continue by doing something else. The most natural thing is to revert to the old practice if that is still possible. While the consultant is well advised never to stop anyone working to the old method until it can be completely replaced, he should also make sure that after the new method has been proved it is impossible to revert to the old one.

The way this is done will depend, as always, on the function of the assignment and the nature of its problem. A few examples are given below.

Paperwork. When a new documentation procedure is installed, the stock of old forms is destroyed; so are the printing plates. Some official is made responsible for maintaining stocks of new forms and signing orders for reprints. The purchasing clerk does not pass on orders for printing signed by any other person.

Operating standards. The maintenance of factory work standards requires similar vigilance. Working to standards must be made easier than working to non-standards. Any work outside the specification of the product or method should not be feasible using the standard forms and documentation. This is not to say that departures from standard are never allowed, but when they are they are made self-evident.

Drawings. In an engineering drawing office it must not be easier to make a new drawing for a part than to find whether an existing part may be used. When a drawing is permanently changed, all old prints are tracked down and destroyed.

An adequate control system would prevent unauthorised prints being in circulation at any time.

All such measures are, of course, preventive. In their absence, the alternative is often not a cure but a temporary expedient with a strong likelihood of a recurrence of the problem.

Control procedures

A system of control does not necessarily stop at maintenance in the narrow sense of keeping a scheme in the same state. After a time, any piece of reorganisation will begin to suffer from old age, if nothing else. Other changing influences may render it less and less appropriate; the objective for which it was designed may no longer be there. Without a means of control, opportunities to modify and develop in line with changing circumstances may be lost.

It is, however, as easy to overdo control for its own sake as it is to become fascinated by any other technique. The consultant needs only to identify the key points at which significant departures will show up and choose the times at which they are to be checked. It is unnecessary to check everything every day: the criterion is usually how long it would take for anything serious to happen if it were not checked. More frequent checks are needed immediately after a change than later on, when stability at a new level has been reached.

In financial areas, checks are part of budgetary control and made as often as the sensitivity of the situation demands. Labour performance checks may be built into weekly payroll/production analyses. Inventory controls may be in accordance with the main categories of stores.

Business companies accept the annual audit of their books as a matter of course, but may forget that a periodic audit of their organisation and administrative methods is equally necessary. Apart from those detailed safeguards already mentioned, a periodic audit may be the only way of checking the whole system. Only an audit may reveal whether the total objectives are still being met, or are even still the same. Failure to make such a check allows the passage of time insidiously to erode the good work and its benefits.

Staff turnover is a common source of danger. If new staff members are not adequately briefed, they have little option but to act as they think fit. They may pursue surprisingly different objectives. The number of corrective problems the consultant has met in the client organisation may be an indicator of habitual neglect. If he does not change the client's basic attitudes to controls, his own work may get no better treatment.

---

[1] In the latter event it has to be remembered that suppliers of such systems have a vested interest in selling stationery and that "standard" packages may **not** fit the given situation very well.

[2] S. W. Gellerman: *Management by motivation* (New York, American Management Association, 1969).

[3] D. C. McClelland and D. G. Winter: *Motivating economic achievement* (New York, The Free Press, 1969).

[4] G. W. Miller: "The magical number seven, plus or minus two" in *Psychological Review*, Vol. 63, No.2, Mar. 1956.

TERMINATION

11

Termination is the fifth and final phase of the consulting process. Every assignment or project has to be brought to an end once its purpose has been achieved and the consultant's help is no longer needed.

It is not enough to execute the assignment in a professional manner. The disengagement also has to be fully professional: its timing and form have to be properly chosen and all commitments ought to be settled to the mutual satisfaction of the client and the consultant.

It is the consultant who has primary responsibility for suggesting at what point and in what way he would withdraw from the client organisation. He bears in mind that the client may feel uncertain about the right moment for terminating the project, in particular if the consultant's presence has clearly contributed to important improvements in management and the client has become used to seeking his advice on important items. The client may feel more secure if the consultant continues to be available to help with any new problems that may arise. This, however, could make the client excessively dependent on the consultant, who would, to use an analogy, function as a crutch needed by a permanently handicapped patient instead of an orthopaedist who helps his patient to recover all physical capabilities.

Termination concerns two equally important aspects of the consulting process: the job for which the consultant was brought in, and the consultant-client relationship.

First, the consultant's withdrawal means that the job in which he has participated:

● has been completed;
● will be discontinued;
● will be pursued, but without further help from the consultant.

In deciding to terminate the assignment, the consultant and the client should make it clear which of these three applies in their particular case. There should be no ambiguity about this. It is of no benefit to anybody if the consultant is convinced that he has done a good job while the client waits only for the consultant's departure in order to stop the project. Thus the consultant and the client should jointly establish whether the assignment can be qualified as a success, a failure, or something between these two extremes.

Secondly, the consultant's withdrawal terminates the consultant-client relationship. The atmosphere and the way in which this relationship is discontinued will influence the client's motivation to pursue the project, and his attitude to possible future use of the same consulting organisation. Here, too, the assignment should not be terminated with uncertain and mixed feelings. Ideally, there should be satisfaction on both sides about the relations that existed during the assignment. The client should be convinced that he has had a good consultant, to whom he would gladly turn again. The consultant should feel that he has been trusted and respected, and that working again for the same client would be another stimulating experience. The relationship has a financial dimension, too: both parties should feel that a proper price was paid for the professional service provided.

All in all, professional consultants attach great importance to the way in which they terminate assignments. The last impressions are very significant, and an excellent performance at the end of assignments leaves the door open for future work. We know how important repeat business is to management consultants. Repeat business, however, is available only to those whose performance remains flawless until the very end of every assignment.

11.1 Time for withdrawal

To choose the right moment for withdrawal is often difficult, but if a wrong decision is made a good relationship can be spoiled and the success of the project jeopardised.

Planning for withdrawal

Some assignments are terminated too early. This is the case if:

- the consultant's work on the project could not be completed;
- the client overestimated his capability to finish the project without having been sufficiently trained for it;
- the client's budget does not permit the job to be finished;
- the consultant is in a hurry to start another assignment.

Instances of assignments that finish later than necessary are also frequent. This happens if:

- the consultant embarks on a technically difficult project without making sure that the client is properly trained to take over from him;
- the job is vaguely defined, and new problems are discovered in the course of the assignment;
- the consultant tries to stay longer than necessary.

To avoid these situations, the question of timely withdrawal should be discussed right at the beginning of the consulting process, when the consultant presents the whole five-phase cycle to the client and explains what the normal course of an effective assignment is. The consulting contract should define when and under what circumstances the assignment will end. As already mentioned, the choices are numerous. The assignment can end after the diagnostic phase, after action planning, at some stage during implementation, or when implementation is completed.

It may be difficult to determine the right moment for withdrawal when signing the contract. At such an early stage it is often impossible to foresee how implementation will progress, how deeply the client's staff will be involved, and what new relations and problems will be discovered during the assignment.

That is why it is recommended that the assignment plan is reviewed at critical points during the assignment; at each review it should be asked how much longer the consultant should stay, and what remains to be done before the assignment could be terminated.

Gradual withdrawal

Gradual withdrawal has already been discussed in section 10.1. In many situations this can be the best arrangement from both the client's and the consultant's point of view.

Watching withdrawal signals

Withdrawal signals, as some consultants call them,[1] show the consultant that the client would like to terminate the assignment. They can be very overt, or indirect and hidden. For example, the client may start being less frequently available to meet the consultant, or may indicate in some other way that enough time has been spent on the project. It is essential to be alert to these signals. This does not necessarily mean that the consultant should immediately pack his effects and quit if he has valid professional reasons for staying, but the point should be frankly discussed with the client. If the client is convinced that he can proceed by himself, the consultant should never insist on staying longer even if he does not share his client's opinion. After all, he who pays the piper calls the tune. It is the client who is paying the consultant, not vice versa.

11.2 Evaluation

Evaluation is a most important part of the termination phase in any consulting process. Without evaluation, it is impossible to assess whether the assignment has met its objectives and whether the results obtained justify the resources used. Neither the client nor the consultant can draw useful lessons from the assignment if there is no evaluation.

Yet many assignments are never evaluated, or their evaluation is superficial and of marginal interest. This is due to certain difficulties inherent in the evaluation of change in organisations and human systems. The number of factors affecting such systems is considerable and to isolate factors changed following a discernable consulting intervention may be difficult. For example, if the purpose of the assignment was to increase output, evaluation cannot take for granted that any higher output achieved by the end of the assignment is due only to the intervention of the consultant. It may be that the increase is due to other factors and the assignment actually made no contribution. Some changes are difficult to identify, measure, describe and assess. In addition, evaluation can be the most delicate part of the consultant-client relationship and it may be more comfortable to avoid it, in particular if the client is not very happy with the consultant's performance. Financial reasons also play their role: even the simplest evaluation exercise will cost some money and the client may feel that this money can be saved, because it is not used for developing anything new.

Who should evaluate

As with the whole consulting process, effective evaluation is a joint exercise. Both the client and the consultant need to know whether the assignment has achieved its objectives and can be qualified as a success story.

The client has, of course, certain specific interests and viewpoints. He is evaluating not only the assignment but also the consultant and his performance. If the client is keen to perform better next time, he also makes a self-evaluation, assessing his own technical and managerial performance in co-operating with the consultant and monitoring the progress of the assignment. In the same way, the consultant will evaluate his own and the client's performance.

How much of this will be a joint exercise and what information will be shared is a matter of confidence and judgement. In an assignment that has been a true collaborative effort, evaluation is usually open and constructive. Yet no one can force the client and the consultant to share all conclusions from their evaluations.

In consulting, evaluation focuses on two basic aspects of the assignment: the benefits to the client and the consulting process.

Evaluating the benefits to the client

The reasons for evaluating the benefits of the assignment are self-evident. The benefits define the change achieved, a change that must be seen as an improvement.

Remember our discussion of assignment objectives in section 7.3. Basically, the benefits are evaluated by comparing two situations, one before and one after the assignment. This is possible if the evaluation was foreseen in designing the assignment, i.e. in defining criteria whereby the results achieved will be measured and assessed.

In typical consulting assignments there are three kinds of benefit:
● new capabilities;
● new systems and behaviour;
● new performance.

New capabilities. These are the new skills acquired by the client: diagnostic and other problem-solving skills, communication skills, as well as special technical or managerial skills in the particular areas affected by the assignment.

New systems and behaviour. Many assignments help introduce specific systems changes, such as new information systems, marketing systems, workshop organisation, personnel recruitment and appraisal systems, preventive maintenance, and so on. These systems can be considered as assignment outcomes if they are, or are likely to become, operational. Changed behaviour means doing things in a different way. This term is mainly applied to interpersonal relations, e.g. between managers and their subordinates, or between co-operating teams from two different departments. However, it also embraces individual behaviour in work situations, e.g. whether or not a worker uses a safety device preventing accidents.

New performance. New performance is achieved if changes in capabilities, systems and behaviour produce corresponding changes in economic, financial, social or other indicators used to measure performance. These changes can be observed at individual (workplace) unit (workshop, team, group, plant, department), or organisational (enterprise, agency, ministry) level.

Higher performance is an overriding goal and should be used for evaluating outcome and showing benefits whenever possible. Consulting which would improve capabilities without aiming at improved performance could be an academic exercise, and a luxury from the financial point of view. It does happen, however, that changed performance cannot be used to assess results (e.g. new capabilities have been developed, but the client has to postpone the measures that will bring about superior performance). Also, as already emphasised, the client's improved problem-solving and managerial capabilities are regarded by many observers of consulting as more important benefits, and of longer duration, than immediate measurable changes in economic and financial performance.

Evaluating the consulting process

The evaluation of the consulting process is based on the assumption that the effectiveness of the process strongly influences the results of the assignments.

This concerns assignments aimed at behavioural changes above all: if new sorts of behaviour and processes are to become established in the client organisation (result), the consultant must choose and propose to his client a consulting style and intervention methods (process) that can produce the desired outcome. For example, it is unlikely that a real change in the client's problem-solving capabilities will be achieved by giving a lecture or distributing a technical note on decision making.

The consultant-client relationships and the intervention methods used develop during the assignment. Different methods can be used, and the process can become more or less effective. The evaluation should reveal this.

The principal dimensions of the consulting process to be evaluated are as follows.

The design of the assignment (the contract). It is useful to start by examining the start of the relationship. The questions to be raised include these:

● Was the design of the assignment clear, realistic and appropriate with regard to the client's needs and particular set-up?

●. Did the original definition of objectives and inputs provide a good framework and guidance for the assignment plan? Were the objectives sufficiently demanding but not impossibly so?

● Was the consulting style to be used properly defined, discussed and understood? Were people briefed about their roles and responsibilities right at the outset?

The quantity and quality of inputs. In addition to assessing the original definition of required inputs made in the assignment plan, evaluation includes the examination of inputs that were provided by the consultant and the client. The main questions are:

— Did the consultant provide a team of the required size, structure and competence?

— Did the client provide the resources (human and other) needed for the assignment?

The consulting mode (style) used. In this section, the consultant and the client assess in retrospect the events that took place and the relationship that existed during the assignment. They ask in particular:

● What was the nature of the consultant-client relationship? Was there an atmosphere of mutual trust, understanding, respect and support?

● Was the right consulting mode (style) used? Was it adapted to the client's capabilities and adjusted to the task at hand? Was every opportunity taken to increase the client's involvement in the assignment? Was proper attention paid to the learning dimension of the assignment?

The management of the assignment by the consultant and the client. Gaps and errors in the orginal assignment plan can be corrected and modifications required by changed conditions can be made if the assignment is aptly managed by both partners. An evaluation addresses the following questions:

— Was the necessary flexibility built into the original design?

— How did the consultancy organisation manage and support the assignment?

— How did the client control and monitor the assignment?

— Was there an interim evaluation at key points in the assignment? What action was taken on the basis of it?

Evaluation tools

Priority is given to collecting and examining hard data permitting measurement and quantitative assessment. In addition, identifying and examining opinions is important, particularly for evaluating the consultant-client relationship and the consulting style. Classical techniques are used, including interviews, observations, questionnaires and discussions at meetings (see chapter 8).

A frank discussion between the client and the consultant is essential. Step by step, the discussion should try to review what happened in the client's and in the consultant's opinion, as well as the causes underlying particular attitudes and behaviours, achievements and failures.

Evaluation should be summarised in a short report, which can become a part of the final assignment report, or be presented separately, e.g. if the evaluation of results takes place several months after the completion of the assignment.

When to evaluate

There is a case for evaluation when the assignment is coming to an end. Some benefits to the client may already be identifiable and it is possible to evaluate the consulting process in retrospect. The end-of-assignment evaluation is certainly the most important one. But it should not be the only one.

In particular, evaluation following implementation comes too late for suggesting any improvements in the assignment strategy, methodology and management. It is of interest only for future assignments. That is why interim evaluations should be foreseen at the end of the diagnostic and the action-planning phases. They should be treated as a normal part of the joint control and monitoring of the assignment by the consultant and the client. If necessary, e.g. in long and complex assignments, even *within* diagnosis, action planning and implementation, there may be a need for several evaluation exercises to review progress and interim results, and, if necessary, to adjust the assignment plan and the work methods used.

On the other hand, it is often impossible to complete evaluation at the end of the assignment. If measurable results cannot be identified immediately, or if the projected performance cannot be achieved until some time later, there is a case for follow-up evaluation.

11.3 Follow-up

The client and the consultant often agree to terminate a particular assignment without completely discontinuing their working relationship. If further work done by the consultant is still related to the current assignment in some way, we call it follow-up. The desirability of some follow-up is often identified in evaluating the assignment. If the consultant is convinced that follow-up is in the client's interest and that he has something more to offer to the client, he suggests this in his final report.

The advantages to the consulting organisation are obvious. A follow-up service is an invaluable source of information on the real impact of operating assignments and on new problems which may have arisen in the client organisation. New assignments may develop from these visits, which may not cost the consulting organisation anything if the follow-up is provided on a paying basis.

Many client organisations may also find that follow-up services are a useful form of assistance through which new problems can be discovered and resolved before they become a headache. However, no client should be forced to accept a follow-up arrangement if he feels that he does not need it.

Follow-up evaluation

As mentioned above, an agreement may be made to undertake a follow-up evaluation 6-12 months, say, after the end of the assignment.

Follow-up of implementation

There are many options for the consultant's involvement in implementation. In addition new technical developments will take place in the area covered by the assignment and there may be other reasons why the client wishes the consultant to take a fresh look at the situation created by the implementation of his proposals.

Therefore the client may be interested in a follow-up arrangement. For example, the consultant will pay him a three-day visit every three months over a two-year period. The purpose will be to review progress on implementation, to help to take any necessary corrective measures, and to find out whether or not new problems have arisen. If a new intervention is required that exceeds the scope of these periodic visits, the client receives a separate proposal for this.

Retainer arrangements

Follow-up visits related to specific assignments are normally programmed for a limited period of time. The client may be interested in maintaining a more permanent working relationship with a consultant who gave him satisfaction. This can lead to a so-called "retainer arrangement", "retainer contract", or simply "retainer". Under this arrangement the consultant is available to the client for an agreed number of days every month or quarter. The job content is either defined in advance, or on each occasion the client tells the consultant what he wants, or the consultant acts as a kind of sounding board and general adviser, looking at various aspects of the client's business and suggesting where improvements might be possible.

Many retainer arrangements are the result of successfully implemented consulting projects. This is quite logical. Why should a client enter a permanent collaborative relationship with a consultant without having seen him at work?

There are various types of retainer arrangements, but from a technical viewpoint two types tend to prevail:

- *a generalist retainer*, under which the consultant follows global results and development of trends of the client's business, looking for improvement opportunities in various areas and feeding the client with new information and ideas;

● *a specialist retainer*, providing the client with a permanent flow of technical information and suggestions in an area where the consulting firm is particularly competent and advanced (e.g. computer applications, materials handling, purchasing, international financial operations, identification of new markets).

11.4 Final reporting

Before and during the assignment the client has received several consulting reports:

— the report in which the assignment was proposed, based on a quick diagnostic survey;

— progress reports, whose number and scope varies, and in which modifications in problem definition and assignment plans may have been proposed;

— reports and documentation linked with the submission of proposals for the client's decision prior to implementation.

Whatever the pattern of interim reporting, there is a final assignment report issued at the time the consultant withdraws from the client organisation. Furthermore, the consulting unit requires reports which will be of help, above all, to its members who may be called upon to undertake similar assignments.

Report to the client

For a relatively short assignment, this may be the only report and so has to be comprehensive. For longer assignments, the final report may make passing reference to previous reports and go into detail only on the events since the last report was written. In all cases, as a closing report, it tidies up all the loose ends and covers the essential end-of-assignment facts and confirmations. It should be known before it is written whether the consultant is to provide a follow-up service. If so, the report may not be quite as "final" as it otherwise would be.

In addition to a short comprehensive review of work performed, the final report should point out the real benefits obtained from implementation and make frank suggestions to the client on what he should undertake, or avoid, in the future.

Evaluation of benefits

An evaluation of benefits is included in the final report if this is practical, i.e. if the consultant is leaving the client after a period of implementation which lends itself to evaluation. In other cases, it may be submitted later as already discussed.

Through the evaluation of real benefits the consultant proves the correctness and accuracy of both the preliminary assessment (given when proposing the assignment to the client) and the evaluation of alternative solutions (presented to the client for decision prior to implementation).

Clearly, implementation must have progressed far enough, and the conditions of operating the new technique or system must have become normal and stabilised, if an evaluation of benefits is to give objective information. The consultant emphasises direct benefits obtained as a result of the assignment and leaves the consideration of indirect benefits (e.g. no increase in fixed costs) to the client.

In presenting the benefits the reports should focus on measurable economic, financial and social benefits that have been or will be drawn from superior performance. However, the report should also describe the new capabilities and new systems and behaviours created by the assignment and stress their impact on superior performance, as discussed in section 11.2.

It is not recommended practice in consulting to point out the savings/fee ratio. Such analysis is left entirely to the client, who appreciates that all benefits cannot be costed and that this ratio may be high in many simple, low-risk assignments, whose impact on overall business results is limited.

Evaluation of the consulting process

Whether to include the evaluation of the consulting process in the final report is a matter of judgement. There may be a strong case for doing so if the client can learn from it for the future, and if the client's behaviour during the assignment was the reason for some superior or sub-standard results achieved. The consultant and the client should agree on how detailed and open this section would be, and what matters would be discussed, but not included in the final report.

Suggestions to the client

Although his job is completed, the consultant shows that he sees the client organisation in perspective if he points out possible further improvements, bottlenecks, risks, necessary action, and so on. In any case he has to make suggestions on how the new system introduced with his help should be maintained, controlled and developed after his departure. An agreement reached on a follow-up service would also be confirmed in the final report.

A good consulting report should be capable of commanding the respect of the client, who will consider it a source of further guidance. He will also be pleased to show it to business friends and associates as the record of a worthwhile achievement.

Further suggestions on writing and presenting consulting reports can be found in appendix 10.

Assignment reference report
to the consulting organisation

In addition to the final report to the client, consultants compile an assignment reference report for their own organisation. This report is described in section 24.4.

The client's internal report

Some organisations using consultants prepare internal reports on completed assignments. In addition to summary information the report includes the client's assessment of the job done and of the consultant's approach and performance. Although this is a most useful practice, it is not very common.

---

[1] See e.g. D. Casey: "Some processes at the consultant/client interface in OD work" in *Leadership and Organisation Development Journal*, No. 1/1982.

PART III

CONSULTING IN VARIOUS AREAS OF MANAGEMENT

CONSULTING IN GENERAL MANAGEMENT

12

This chapter is the first of a series of eight, each dealing with consulting in a specific area of management. The authors' intention is not to provide an exhaustive analysis of management techniques, practices and problems of each area covered, but, in keeping with the spirit of the book, to show how management consultants can help clients and how they normally operate in these areas. This opening chapter, and the following seven chapters, can serve, therefore, as an introduction to a more detailed study of consulting in various areas of management. Appendix 11 provides selected lists of literature for all chapters in part III.

12.1 Nature and scope of general management consulting

A considerable amount of management consulting concerns the very existence, the basic goals, the business policy and strategy, or the overall planning, structuring and control, of an organisation. These problems are defined as general management problems, and management consultants who handle them are general management consultants as distinct from specialists who intervene in one functional area (finance), or deal with a particular technique (computerised production control, or employee incentive schemes).

But how do we find out if an enterprise requires the assistance of an all-round management consulting generalist? In some cases this is quite obvious from the state of the business: its deteriorating overall performance, the growing dissatisfaction of the staff, the generally bleak prospects of the industrial sector, and so on. The business may be in crisis, or very close to it, and it is not clear how to restore prosperity. In other cases, a problem that seems at the outset to be a special or functional one (inadequate marketing methods, say) has ramifications in other areas of management and eventually is found to be only a symptom of a much deeper general management problem affecting the whole organisation.

Multi-functional and inter-disciplinary problems

The most prominent characteristic of problems handled in general management consulting is, therefore, that they are:

- *multi-functional:* the consultant deals with several functions of the business (production, technology, organisation, marketing, etc.) and focuses on the interaction between these functions and on problems involving more than one function;

- *inter-disciplinary:* the consultant must be able to view business problems from several angles; typically, a business strategy problem may have technological, economic, financial, legal, psycho-sociological, motivational, political and other dimensions.

General managers, too, have been chosen for their ability (real or expected) to deal with multi-functional and inter-disciplinary problems. Experience shows that many of them find this difficult. There are cases of general managers, previously excellent plant managers, who continue to be plant managers in their new position! This is an area where a management consultant can be of great help to his client — the general manager who has to change his habits, learn how to deal with new functions, and look at the problems of the business from new angles.

In fact, a general management consultant is also a kind of specialist: his speciality lies in combining other specialities into a balanced and coherent multi-functional and inter-disciplinary approach. Like the general manager himself, however, the general management consultant turns to other specialists when appropriate. He must know how to *use* the specialist's skill and advice, and help the client to do the same, to prevent situations where specialists (e.g. market researchers or financial analysts) would dominate the business.

Paths to organisational excellence

In chapter 1, "organisational excellence" was shown to be a common "super-ordinate" goal of management consulting. Consultants help to nudge organisations towards excellence. They require therefore a validated vision of excellence in order to raise the expectations and ambitions of managers to the effort necessary to change organisations for the better. They need, furthermore, a conceptual framework for devising action objectives and programmes that lead to excellence, or at least bring organisations closer to it.

Interest in organisational excellence waxes and wanes; it is now higher than it has been for decades.[1] Research on excellent organisations shows that they mutate: excellent organisations today are not exactly like those of yesterday. They tend to share certain common features: for example, many of them exploit technological frontiers — the railroads of the 1860s, the motor companies of the first half of our century, and the electronics companies of today. Another common feature is that they are well adapted to the needs and aspirations of their work forces, and, paradoxically, this is where they can differ very considerably from one another, because of the differences in both work forces and cultures. Invariably, excellent organisations are more sensitive than other organisations to their environments, and to the needs, wishes and satisfaction of the clients in particular.

Thus there is no one single, simple path to excellence. The management of today's organisation requires a holistic and integrated approach in devising and implementing programmes for achieving excellence. The consultant should beware of simplistic solutions and explain to the client that there is no panacea, no "quick fix" for achieving high performance, effectiveness, or excellence.

Unfortunately, management theory does not provide the general management consultant with a research-based and generally accepted conceptual approach to designing and evaluating action programmes leading to excellence. What is available, and certainly of interest to the consultant-practitioner, is a range of pragmatic and experiential models describing organisations and analysing the causes of their successes or failures. For example, the so called seven-S framework examines high-performance organisations under the following main headings: strategy, structure, systems, style, shared values, staff (people) and skills, emphasising that these variables constitute an interdependent reinforcing network.[2] Another framework suggests the following five tracks: (1) culture; (2) management skills; (3) team-building; (4) strategy-structure; and (5) the reward system.[3] Research into factors affecting organisational excellence is likely to continue, and will no doubt pay increased attention to factors that are specific to various socio-economic and cultural settings, especially those which differ from the environments of the United States and Japan where most recent research into organisational excellence has been based.

Diagnosing organisations

As explained in detail in chapter 7, many consultants prefer to carry out a quick preliminary survey of the organisation before proposing a specific problem-solving assignment. Thus the first technical contact between the client and the consultant is often at the general management level, before the consultant moves into specific areas identified by the survey.

There are situations where a very thorough diagnostic survey (diagnosis, audit, etc.) of the whole organisation is required in preparation for important decisions on the future of the business. A comprehensive diagnostic survey may precede a major reorganisation, an acquisition, a merger, nationalisation or denationalisation, or a decision to close down a business. The consultant's mandate is to help the client to diagnose the organisation concerned; he may even be asked, as an independent expert, to examine the organisation in order to provide an objective and neutral report on the status, strengths, weaknesses and development prospects of the business. The assessment of the management systems used and of senior managerial personnel may be included. The assignment may end with the consultant submitting a report on the diagnosis. Diagnostic surveys of this type may be fairly extensive and difficult assignments. While a quick survey is a matter of a few days, comprehensive and in-depth surveys may take several months, depending, of course, on the size and complexity of the organisation and on the nature of its problems.

Some comprehensive diagnostic surveys intervene too late, when the company concerned is no longer susceptible of rescue, or when rescue would require resources that are not available. In certain cases such a crisis could have been prevented by undertaking a thorough diagnosis at an earlier date, and arranging for a periodic business diagnosis, or self-diagnosis, as a preventive measure. The consultant may have an opportunity to help a client to design and install a self-diagnostic scheme on a regular basis. This opportunity should not be missed!

Organisational level of interventions

In many cases the general management consultant intervenes at the highest level in the organisation: with the chief executive in person, or the top management team. Even leaders keen to introduce change often do not realise what will be involved, or see that they ought to start by changing themselves. They frequently have a particular self-image, though the consultant may find that this image is not shared by other people in the organisation. The consultant's problem then lies in persuading management of the need to change thinking and behaviour at the very top.

The possibility of working directly with the chief executive and his management team provides an excellent introduction to the organisation, rapid access to key data, a true picture of the operating style of top management, and usually strong support from the top for the consultant's work. Yet it is often risky to confine intervention to top management level. The general management consultant needs to find out how top management is perceived throughout the organisation, and how management policies influence the work style, performance and job satisfaction of employees. Furthermore, general management is also practised at intermediate and lower levels in the management hierarchy, and eventually affects every single worker. For example, supervisory management is often underestimated and constitutes one of the weakest links in the management hierarchy.

12.2 Corporate strategy

The concept of corporate strategy has made a significant contribution to the advancement of management practice and theory over the last 25 years. Consulting in corporate strategy (business strategy, strategic analysis, strategic planning, etc.) has become a rapidly growing area of management consulting. Some consultants have made corporate strategy their main or exclusive field of intervention ("the strategy boutiques"). Consulting in corporate strategy has been strongly influenced by the use of quantitative techniques and models, and by the profiles of consultants employed in this field. Strategic studies began to be dominated by young econometricians and operational researchers, with excellent education but often without business experience, and with no knowledge of people, or of social and other problems that determine strategy *in reality*. Quite a few business firms created strategic planning units, but these rarely commanded the attention or respect of top management.

Corporate strategy will continue to be an important field of consulting for many years to come. However, lessons are being drawn from the past, and a more comprehensive and realistic view of corporate strategy is being taken, going beyond the analytical studies and model building that flourished in the 1970s. Strategy is too important to be left in the hands of junior analysts and planners. It has to be handled as a priority by the management team of the company. The very word "strategy" tended to be interpreted in many different ways, and it became fashionable to call any studies and plans "strategic". It is therefore important that the consultant reaches an understanding with the client as to what strategy means and embraces in the context of a particular organisation whose future it should help to shape.

Strategic vision

Corporate strategy is usually defined as the organisation's response to environmental opportunities, challenges and threats, consistent with its competence and resources.[4] However, strategy is not an aim in itself but a set of paths and choices for achieving a basic organisational goal in the future. This is where a consultant can start helping his client. Many organisations practising strategic planning actually lack a vision of the future. To begin with, they have not asked the strategist's fundamental question about "the sort and purpose of business they are in." Furthermore, they have not tried to position the business in the context of the future, i.e. to define where they want it to go in relation to the environment, markets, competitors and technology.

A strategic vision should be as rational as possible and not a result of wishful thinking. However, total rationality is not achievable for one simple reason — the future is unknown and is being shaped by a myriad of independent actions all over the globe; the client's own actions will form only a tiny fragment of this future, however important his business is. Personal values and judgement of the key decision makers therefore play a vital role in positioning the organisation for the future (as they will strongly influence the implementation of *any* strategy!). That is why current thinking on corporate excellence and strategy puts so much emphasis on *organisational leadership*. A leader is an individual (or team) with a vision of the future position of the organisation. Furthermore, a leader is able to express his vision in goals understandable to people in the organisation, and influence and motivate people to achieve these goals. There is a unity of vision and a unity of actions guided by this vision.

Distinctive competitive advantage

A competitive advantage is a key dimension of organisational excellence in environments where organisations must compete with each other. This advantage is not a trick that can last a few months (e.g. a smart advertising campaign), but an inherent capacity to sustain superior performance on a long-term basis.

The consultant can be most helpful in examining whether the client business enjoys any competitive advantage, and in developing a strategy for achieving one. He can draw the client's attention to the ways in which organisations regarded as excellent achieved their competitive advantage. He can point out certain factors that tend to be characteristic of all firms that possess such an advantage (for example, priority attention paid to the clients' needs and satisfaction, and to the quality of products and services). Furthermore, the consultant can help the client in choosing from alternatives that are available to him, and which reflect the real possibilities of his technical and production staff, production facilities, marketing networks, business experience and the like. Examples of choices to be made are:

● offering state-of-the-art technologically advanced products not available from other firms or available from very few; abandoning these products when the technology becomes common and prices start dropping;

● providing service to clients with speed and reliability superior to that offered by competitors;

● selling high-quality and particularly reliable products for relatively high prices;

● selling special-design products to clients who prefer to avoid standard products;

● selling standard products of acceptable but not particularly high quality for very competitive prices (cost and price-cutting strategy).

In defining a competitive advantage emphasis is put on the adjective "sustainable".[5] This stresses the fact that the client will have to evaluate, and enhance as appropriate, his ability to adapt to changed conditions, and to innovate. For example, only organisations that are closely linked to technological research and where the flow of technological innovation has become a permanent internal process can choose the provision of state-of-the-art technology as their business strategy.

Technology in corporate strategy

The role of technology in developing and implementing "winning" corporate strategy is another area where management consultants can be extremely useful to their business clients. There are several reasons for this. "A company that integrates technology into its strategy significantly improves its chances of reaping benefits from technological changes. Whether it decides to be a technological leader or not, the results of integrating technology into strategy can improve a company's determination of priorities among technology options, identify the technical resources needed to achieve business goals and speed up the movement of ideas into production."[6] However, technological developments occur simultaneously in so many areas, and so rapidly, that even large companies with well-staffed R and D departments and information services find it increasingly difficult to keep abreast of developments, and think of possibilities offered by technologies and materials created in other sectors and countries.

Increased emphasis on technology strategy and its impact on manufacturing, marketing and other strategies is a new challenge to most management consultants, who often used to handle strategy as a problem of marketing and finance. Some consultants have already responded by establishing R and D departments which can both participate in consulting assignments in corporate strategy and undertake specific R and D tasks for the clients. Providing technological information analysed from the viewpoint of its potential business applications has become a rapidly growing service. Several important consulting firms already offer such a service to their clients. Consultants advising on business development opportunities and projects in developing countries are increasingly involved in questions of technology transfer, helping to choose both the appropriate technology to be used and the terms under which such a transfer can be effectively implemented.

This trend is likely to continue and management consultants who devise new services in response to clients' pressing needs will themselves gain a distinct competitive advantage.

The environment of business

The whole environment in which organisations operate is becoming so complex, variable and even confused that managers find it more and more difficult to identify significant information and monitor changes that should be reflected in corporate strategy. Here again, management consultants can be of great help. Some clients may need guidance in order to become more aware of the environment and so realise that on-going or forecasted environmental changes can have far-reaching consequences for their businesses. Other clients may be aware of the scope and depth of environmental changes, but are short of the skills and resources needed to collect necessary information and draw the right conclusions from its analysis. They find it difficult to consider what information is relevant, or may be relevant in the future.

As a result, many consulting firms provide services to clients in matters of corporate strategy which focus increasingly on environmental information and analysis. In addition, these firms help clients to devise systems and procedures in which environmental analysis is not undertaken as a special study, but is internalised to become a standard part of the strategic management system in the client organisation. In some cases (e.g. in small and medium firms in rapidly changing industrial and service sectors), the clients may require long-term support from a competent information agency, which would screen and monitor the environment, or some aspects of it, on their behalf. Some consultants have already decided to build up a new client service for this purpose.

Environmental analysis tends to embrace new issues in addition to classic marketing, economic, demographic and financial information. For example, new regulations concerning product quality, safety, or the protection of the natural and living environment, can determine the life or death of firms whose products or technologies are affected. Some of these regulations have a long gestation period, while others become adopted very quickly. Political and social interests as well as organisations are involved in the promotion of new regulations. Seen from another angle, new regulations also offer new opportunities to firms which adapt their products faster than their competitors, or which come up with new products that specifically serve the purpose of increased safety or reduced pollution.

As regards the legal environment of business in general, many companies find it impossible to keep track of all strategically significant changes in their home country, let alone changes having impact on foreign operations. Management consultants can respond (in collaboration with law firms if appropriate) by helping the clients with this task.

Implementing strategy

Strategy that remains on paper is of little use. It is essential to help the client to develop operating systems, procedures and technical capabilities for putting the strategy into effect. This raises, among other questions, that of communications. While certain strategic choices may have to be kept strictly confidential for obvious reasons, the failure to communicate important choices to staff will mean that no one in the organisation (with the exception of the planners and top managers) will adhere to the strategy chosen. Activities such as production planning and control, inventory management, quality improvement and staff development, as well as leadership and management style, become critical to the successful implementation of strategy.

The consultant can help the client, too, in developing competence for *adapting strategy* to new opportunities and constraints. There may be a need for a monitoring, or "early warning", system for detecting trends, events and ideas that may lead to a change in corporate strategy. The company's management system, including procedures for auditing and redefining strategy, should be flexible enough to make adaptation possible. This means, in particular, encouraging people in marketing, production, R and D and other departments to "keep their eyes and ears constantly open" for signals and ideas that may have a bearing on strategy and should lead to its modification sooner or later.

Consistency with internal capabilities

Emphasis on implementation and adaptability to new conditions underlines the principle whereby consistency with the internal capabilities of a company is as important in consulting on strategy as the alignment of the firm with the business environment. Every pattern of corporate strategy has its own requirements as regards the technical profile and capabilities of the staff, as well as managerial and work style and employee motivation. Clearly, an ambitious strategy intended to maintain the company at the cutting edge of technological innovation, without much concern for costs and prices, requires a different style and working climate to a strategy which is not too demanding as regards technology but extremely rigorous as regards execution and costs of standardised work operations.

Ideally, not only management but also other staff members should be associated with strategy formulation as much as possible. The *process* of defining strategy is even more important than the *content* for achieving staff commitment and a shared belief that the strategy chosen is a way to success.

Some special strategic patterns

Management consultants are often called in when the development pattern of a company deviates substantially from the normal pattern. These tend to be difficult assignments, uncertain as to the chances of success, often carried out under severe time pressure if the client organisation is in financial difficulties, or, on the contrary, feels that it would miss an exceptional opportunity if the consultant takes too much time over his analysis.

How to cope with an excessively high *rate of growth* has been a problem faced by companies wanting to take the maximum opportunities offered by a favourable business climate. In such cases the consultant can point out the possible negative impact of rapid growth on liquidity and on the capability to sustain operations if growth suddenly slows down. In trying to maximise sales, a company is often tempted to expand production capacity and increase inventories beyond reasonable limits, instead of looking for better utilisation, modernisation and maintenance of existing capacity or product and service quality. In the expansion new staff are recruited, but training is inadequate. All this can be a serious threat to long-term survival, and adaptation to new conditions may be very painful.

Advising clients on *mergers* and *acquisitions* has become an "elitist" area of consulting. This is not totally unjustified as wide business experience and sound judgement are required in these cases. The financial side of the scheme has to be examined carefully (see chapter 13). However, the consultant should not confine himself to finance. A scheme which is perfectly feasible from the financial point of view may involve unrealistic strategic choices as regards marketing, production capacity, staff capabilities, or compatibility of organisational cultures.

Company turnarounds

A general management consultant may be asked to assist with a *turnaround* of a company that is in trouble. A turnaround strategy involves total restructuring and reorganisation and usually affects all functions and activities of a company. This is a particularly difficult kind of strategic assignment. Probably the consultant will be brought in at a very late stage, when the threat of bankruptcy is imminent. He may be regarded as a saviour. The management of the company is often paralysed and starts panicking under extreme pressure from creditors, banks, trade unions, tax collectors and others.

The consultant should consider whether his experience is adequate for an assignment involving so much risk and responsibility. If he accepts the assignment, he should make sure that his and the management's roles are clearly defined and understood, since there will be no time for lengthy discussions and negotiations and some measures will need to be approved and executed immediately. If the consultant feels that senior management itself is the cause of trouble, or one of the major causes, he should make it clear that personnel changes may be necessary before committing himself to the assignment.

A quick preliminary diagnosis will help the consultant to evaluate the overall situation. In particular, he has to assess whether the company can still be rescued, and if so, how much this is likely to cost and whether the task is beyond the management's capabilities or not. If it is too late, or the cost of a turnaround operation would be prohibitive, there may be no solution other than to sell or liquidate the company.

Following this preliminary assessment, it is not advisable, and often not possible, to start a turnaround by lengthy in-depth diagnostic studies. There is a crisis situation; some creditors have to be paid today, others tomorrow, and the most competent people may be thinking of leaving the sinking ship. Emergency measures have to be given priority: for example, a dialogue with the creditors is essential, and resources ought to be concentrated in order to make those payments that cannot be postponed in any way. Emergency measures also involve decisions that produce immediate savings, or stop a further deterioration in the company's financial condition (e.g. recruitment freeze, restrictions on foreign travel, termination of temporary help, increased emphasis on time-keeping and work discipline, cuts in entertainment costs). Though spectacular, some of these measures do not produce major savings, but rather help to create a new atmosphere, in which people start realising how serious the situation is. At this point the consultant should make sure that employees are invited to contribute to the turnaround in every possible way. This may involve the establishment of various means of making such participation possible, without, however, divulging information that has to be kept confidential.

Stock should be taken as quickly as possible of existing resources and financial and other commitments since the company will have to avoid further crises, pay interest and settle certain liabilities, while progressing with the turnaround. Step by step, the consultant will be able to complete his picture of the client company's condition. It is essential to identify the real causes of trouble. They may be external (depression in the whole sector, prices of raw materials too high, important markets lost for political reasons), or internal (incompetent management, antagonistic conflict between management and trade unions). In many cases, external and internal causes are combined (external factors cause serious trouble because management did not spot them early enough, or management gradually became depressed and paralysed under the influence of adverse external conditions). Financial and other controls have to be tightened in all departments.

The external partners in the game, in particular the creditors, must see that a serious turnaround exercise has been started and is producing results. In some countries (e.g. in the United States under Chapter 11 of the Bankruptcy Code) a company can obtain temporary protection from creditors' claims while it is restructuring its finances and reorganising operations in order to become solvent again.

Following the inevitable emergency measures, the turnaround programme should turn to strategic measures needed to recover financial health and viability in the long term. Time continues to be short, therefore every change planned has to be carefully programmed and the timetable controlled. Also, responsibilities of all managers and departments must be clearly defined, and their contribution to the total programme specified to permit evaluation and rewards corresponding to real results.

It sometimes happens that, when helping with a turnaround, the management consultant, with the client's formal or tacit agreement, steps out of his strictly advisory position to tell the client what he must do, or even to give direct instructions to the client's employees. No general rule can tell how far such behaviour can go, in particular if it helps avoid a crisis. Then, there have been cases of consultants recruited to assist in a major turnaround who have accepted managerial positions with the client company in order to bring the whole programme to successful completion.

A case history of a successful company turnaround in which management consultants were involved is reproduced in appendix 8.

12.3 Structures and systems

The structuring of an organisation concerns the division of tasks and responsibilities among people, the grouping of tasks and people in units, the definition of vertical and horizontal information flows and collaborative relations, and arrangements for co-ordination. The purpose of structuring is to provide a more or less fixed and stable framework for an effective functioning of the total organisation, i.e. of all its members, resources and units, in achieving organisational goals. The products of structuring are various systems and sub-systems — organisation systems, management information systems, decision making systems, control and evaluation systems, systems for handling emergencies and crises, and so on. Any complex organisation is operated through and with the help of these systems. However, experience shows that structures and systems can easily become a straightjacket, e.g. if they try to standardise and prescribe behaviour for situations that are very specific and where standardisation does more harm than good. The design and maintenance of systems is a costly affair; some kind of cost/benefit analysis is therefore required in starting a project to design or revise a system. Many organisations need help to prevent proliferation and overlapping of systems, as well as to avoid lack of co-ordination and conflicting requirements of various systems for supplying and interpreting information.

Organisation structure

To examine and redesign the organisational structure used to be the "classical" intervention of many general management consultants. When the basic structure was agreed, the consultant continued his work by producing detailed diagrams and charts, as well as job descriptions for each unit and position within the client organisation. The end-product was often a set of organisational charts and instructions but, in fact, the principal benefit to the client was the effort and analysis that went into this job. Forgotten and "orphan" activities were rediscovered, activities for which nobody seemed to be responsible were defined, and overlapping activities were reassigned or done away with.

Today's management consulting has overcome the rather narrow approach taken by the "re-organisation experts" in the past. As mentioned above, structure is treated as one of the factors of excellence, which is linked in many ways with strategy, organisational culture, the competence and motivation of employees, new technology and other factors. Competent and committed staff working in a loosely organised framework will produce better results than incompetent people inserted in a "perfect" structure! In any event, every consultant must realise that formal organisation reflects only a small part of the very complex network of relations existing in an organisation.

Reorganisations destroy existing work relations, collaboration patterns and socialisation habits. Unjustified and frequent reorganisations paralyse enterprises and institutions and generate lethargy instead of enhancing innovation and efficiency. A decision to reorganise often reflects management's failure to identify and tackle the *real* issue. Therefore consultants are more and more cautious, and tend to prescribe reorganisation only if there are very valid reasons for it (e.g. a new division must be established because the existing structure is clearly not willing and able to maximise efforts and resources to put a new product on the market in the shortest possible time).

Decision-making systems

In many organisations it may be the method and organisation of decision making (for both key and routine matters) which cause trouble. Excessive centralisation of operational decisions may deprive the organisation of the flexibility needed to react to new market opportunities. In another case, an autocratic owner may be taking decisions without conferring with professional experts on his own staff, who could easily prove that many of his decisions were based on wishful thinking rather than rational analysis.

The need to examine and reform the decision-making system may be the very reason why the consultant has been brought in; it may concern:

- the classification of decisions in groups by their nature, urgency, financial implications, degree of complexity, etc.;
- the ways in which typical decisions are taken (this may be quite difficult to find out);
- the respective decision-making roles played by staff specialists and line managers;
- the role of collective bodies in preparing and adopting decisions;
- the participation of employee representatives in decision making;
- the decision-making and advisory roles of individuals in informal positions of influence;
- the responsibility for decisions, their implementation, and control of implementation;

- the use of decision-making techniques, models, or formalised procedures.

The possibilities of improvement in this area are tremendous and general management consultants are well advised to pay close attention to them.

Management information systems

Most managers do not ignore the fact that information is becoming a strategic asset of business and that the whole world is facing a real "information revolution". However, it is a long way from recognising this new role of information to actually developing and implementing an effective management information system.

Many general management consultants focus on this area and offer services such as analysing the existing information system; defining information required for strategic management and operational control; harmonising and integrating systems used in various departments; and choosing and introducing appropriate information processing technology. This work concerns both *external* information (on the environment, including the enterprise's relations to this environment) and *internal* information (on resources, processes and results achieved). The purpose is to make sure that the client does not ignore information essential to strategic and operational decisions, but at the same time avoids collecting and developing information that is of no direct use to him. To decide where the limits are is difficult and it may be advisable to cast the "information net" more widely rather than to save money at the risk of missing some essential information.

In today's consulting, management information systems are often handled as a problem of information technology, including the choice, installation and effective use of appropriate hardware and software. Yet this is only one side of the problem. Information technology is a key factor determining what sort of information and how much of it a company will be able to collect, process and analyse. However, choosing information that is *needed* for preparing and making decisions is not a computer specialist's problem but an information user's (and his management consultant's) problem. Close collaboration between the two has to be established and maintained in developing effective information systems, as will be discussed in chapter 19.

12.4 Corporate culture and management style

Finally we have to turn to the "soft" and "intangible" side of organisations. The meaning of culture was explained in chapter 5. We emphasised that, when entering a new organisation, the consultant has to find out as much as possible about its specific culture. He does this in order to develop a full understanding of values and motives underlying managerial and employee behaviour, and so assess the organisation's potential for making improvements. Organisational culture may be found to be one of the causes, or even the main cause, of the difficulties experienced (e.g. due to the conservatism of senior management and the impossibility of submitting new ideas). In such a case, culture may even become the central theme on which the assignment would focus.

Consulting in corporate culture became extremely popular at the beginning of the 1980s, in the United States in particular. Some consultants have not escaped the danger of regarding and prescribing cultural change as a panacea: "Corporate culture is the magic phrase that management consultants are breathing into the ears of American executives." [7] Nevertheless, in warning against the corporate culture fad we must not throw out the baby with the bathwater. The current interest in corporate culture and in the impact of culture on long-term organisational performance is basically a positive phenomenon, needed to reinstate a balanced approach to organisational problems. If organisational culture is ignored, a sophisticated planning or management information system is unlikely to lead to any improvements in performance.

When to focus on culture

A change in corporate culture will rarely be an explicitly stated task in a consulting assignment.[8] Yet in some situations corporate culture requires the consultant's special attention:

- When a company is in difficulties. A strong traditional and intransigent culture may prevent the company from assessing its condition realistically and proceeding with changes that have become inevitable.
- When a company has grown very rapidly. There may be various problems. The original culture of a small family company may no longer be suitable. There are many new managers and workers, coming from different cultures. Growth by acquisitions may lead to serious cultural clashes.
- When major technological and structural change is planned. Revolutionary changes in products, technologies, markets, and so on have strong cultural implications.
- When there seems to be a conflict between the company's culture and values that prevail in the environment — for example, if the public increasingly requires a company to behave in ways that are contrary to its culture.
- When the company's operations are internationalised and the problem is how to adapt to foreign cultures.

What to recommend

The consultant will try to "separate wheat from chaff", and ascertain what in corporate culture stimulates and what inhibits further growth and performance improvement. He will point to values and norms that need to be discarded or changed, and to those that should be preserved and even reinforced. If he has had enough experience with corporate culture issues, he may be able to be more specific in suggesting what to do (e.g. in defining corporate mission and objectives, explicitly affirming the value system, enhancing consultation and participation, modifying symbols used to obtain cultural cohesion, changing established role models, reorienting the rewards system, providing training and information needed to support new cultural values and norms, and similar.[9] If the consultant finds out that the client organisation's culture is hardly noticeable, he may be able to suggest how to create a stronger culture, congruent with the goals, resources and external environment of the organisation.

Leadership and management style

Leadership and management style are closely related to corporate culture, and certain aspects of style can become part of the organisation's culture. Managers in organisations tend to behave in coherence with the culture, in ways in which the owners, other managers and employees expect them to behave. At the same time, the style of an individual manager is co-determined by his personality, which may be in harmony or in conflict with existing corporate culture. If there is a conflict, it is usually resolved in one of two ways: either the style of a strong personality at the top will affect corporate culture, and be accepted as a feature of a new culture, or the existing strong culture will reject the person's style and he will have to alter it, or leave the organisation.

Here again the consultant may face a wide range of different situations in which, even if he has no explicit mandate to make proposals in respect of leadership and management style, he might have to find a tactful way of making the client aware of the problems, and help to resolve them by coming up with a feasible solution.

The following situations and problems are quite common in organisations:

(1) People would like to support the manager, but they do not really know what he wants and they do not understand his priorities; there is a problem of formulating ideas and goals clearly enough, and of communicating them to people.

(2) The manager uses an authoritarian style although he should be consulting people, discussing problems and priorities with them, and explaining his decisions.

(3) People are puzzled by the way in which the manager allocates his time: he speaks about priorities, but spends his time in dealing with issues that command no priority.

(4) Innovation is encouraged on paper, but the manager does not give it any overt support in planning and distributing work, neither does he show personal interest in innovative projects, praise and reward innovators for their achievements, etc.

(5) Although the situations with which the manager deals are different, he consistently treats them in the same way; this rigidity means that the style used is adequate in one situation and inadequate in another.

(6)   Because a strong personality at the top exhibits a strong style (which can have either positive or negative characteristics), and favours people who use a similar style, managers throughout the organisation try to copy this style even if it does not fit their own personality.

The consultant can achieve a great deal by making a manager aware of the strong and the weak sides of his style. Awareness of one's style is a first step towards its improvement! Even a manager who is not able to change his style completely can mitigate his weaknesses and compensate for them if he is aware of them.

12.5 Innovation and entrepreneurship

Whether a consulting assignment deals with strategy, structure, systems, culture, staff development, motivation or any other aspect of managing a company, (including aspects and functions that will be discussed in the following chapters), there is an overriding theme: the client wants his organisation to become more innovative, and hopes that the consultant can help. Typically this is a problem of established companies which have performed well for years, but eventually find out, at a moment when new, aggressive competitors enter the market, that their ability to innovate is no longer what it used to be. When faced with this problem the consultant tries to find out whether the client lacks technical know-how, or whether his management system or corporate culture inhibits innovation.

If lack of technical expertise is the reason, solutions may be costly but quite straightforward. Either the client company will be able to strengthen R and D and accelerate the transfer of new ideas from research into production, or it will have to look for know-how outside, e.g. by purchasing a patent or license, or establishing a joint venture with another company.

The task is more difficult if innovation is inhibited owing to systems and cultural barriers. A thorough diagnosis will be required, and the consultant will try to learn as much as possible from managers who head units with direct responsibilities for innovation (technological information, new product design, testing, production engineering, quality control, technical marketing).

The main sources of information will be the doers — professional researchers, design engineers, salesmen, as well as shop-floor supervisors and experienced workers. The consultant will probably come to the conclusion that the company could recover its innovative capability if it removed red tape, reduced centralisation of decisions and controls, encouraged experiments, appointed managers who understood what innovation meant, used financial and other rewards to show how innovation was valued by the company, and fostered a climate favourable to innovation.

The current attempts to develop formulae and incentives that encourage *entrepreneurship within corporations* are certainly of some interest to management consultants. The term "intrapreneurship" has been coined for these formulas. The object is to tap valuable innovative talent existing within the company and create conditions under which talented and dynamic people will not only stay with the company but be able to act with considerable freedom, as if they were running their own "business within a business".[10] Various formulae are being tested in business companies. Under these formulae, the intrapreneurs (individuals or teams) have broad authority to gather and organise resources and decide what to do to achieve the object of their venture. This includes responsibility for profits and losses.[11]

The search for new approaches and methods that stimulate innovation in business and other organisations is likely to continue. The management consultant will be well advised to be at the forefront of this effort.

[1] See, for example, R. T. Pascale and A. G. Athos: *The art of Japanese management: Applications for American executives* (New York, Warner Books, 1981); T. Peters and R. H. Waterman: *In search of excellence: Lessons from America's best-run companies* (New York, Harper and Row, 1982); and T. Peters and N. Austin: *A passion for excellence: The leadership difference* (New York, Random House, 1985).

[2] ibid.

[3] R. H. Kilmann: *Beyond the quick fix: Managing five tracks to organisational success* (San Francisco, CA, Jossey-Bass, 1984).

[4] Cf K. R. Andrews: *The concept of corporate strategy* (Homewood, IL, Irwin, 1980).

[5] T. Peters: "Strategy follows structure: Developing distinctive skills" in *California Management Review*, Vol. XXVI, No. 3, Spring 1984, p. 120.

[6] A. L. Frohman: "Putting technology into strategic planning" in *California Management Review*, Vol. XXVII, No. 2, Winter 1985, p. 48.

[7] S. Salmans: "New vogue: Corporate culture" in *New York Times*, 7 Jan. 1983. See also B. Uttal "The corporate culture vultures" in *Fortune*, 17 Oct. 1983; and D. Berry: "The perils of trying to change corporate culture" in *Financial Times*, 14 Dec. 1983.

[8] For a more detailed discussion of corporate culture, see T. E. Deal and A. A. Kennedy: *Corporate cultures: The rites and rituals of corporate life* (Reading, MA, Addison-Wesley, 1982); and E. H. Schein: *Organisational culture and leadership* (San Francisco, CA, Jossey-Bass, 1985).

[9] See, for example W. Brooke-Tunstall: "Cultural transition at AT and T" in *Sloan Management Review*, Fall 1983; H. Gorlin and L. Schein: *Innovations in managing human resources* (New York, The Conference Board, 1984); or "Changing a corporate culture" in *Business Week*, 14 May 1984.

[10] The term "intrapreneur" was coined by Gilford Pinchot, author of *Intrapreneurship: Why you don't have to leave the corporation to become an entrepreneur* (New York, Harper and Row, 1985). See also N. Macrae: "Intrapreneurial now" in *The Economist* 17 Apr. 1982; and E. M. Shays and F. de Chambeau: "Harnessing entrepreneurial energy within the corporation" in *Management review*, Sep. 1984.

[11] See R. A. Burgelman: "Designs for corporate entrepreneurship" in *California Management Review*, Vol. XXVI, No. 3, Spring 1984.

CONSULTING IN FINANCIAL MANAGEMENT

13

All consulting projects and assignments involve the use of financial and accounting data, and all management consultants, whatever their particular field of specialisation, inevitably find themselves concerned with financial issues and practices. There are two reasons for this. The first is quite simply that finance and accounting provide the working language of business, and it is virtually impossible to analyse the operations or results of any complex organisation except in financial terms. The second reason is that there are close and complex linkages between the finance function and all other functional areas. Decisions made in any area of line operations (such as an increase in the social benefits provided to workers) will have an impact on the organisation's overall financial position, and may call for a revision in existing financial plans and budgets. Equally, a decision which appears to be entirely financial in nature, such as a reduction in short-term bank borrowing, may lead to a shortage of working capital that imposes a real constraint on other operating areas, particularly marketing and production. Virtually all consulting assignments uncover such linkages.

The purpose of the present chapter is to focus upon the special problems of consulting in decision areas that are specifically financial in nature, such as the financial structure of the company and the analysis of capital investment projects, rather than the use of financial information in general. Even here, however, the impact of financial decisions and policies on other areas of activity cannot be overlooked, and such issues will be examined as they arise in the course of the chapter.

It remains to ask whether the management consultant is the person best qualified to assist his clients in this complex area. After all, there are other professionals who work in the financial area: bankers and accountants. Are they not the obvious source of such advice? Both groups are specialists, however, whose competence covers only a part of the financial area.

The company's commercial bank will provide sound (though probably highly conservative) advice on short-term funds management, but the bank officer will have little knowledge of company valuation or project analysis techniques. The merchant banker (investment banker in North American terminology) is an expert in the raising of funds in long-term capital markets, but not in corporate operations or liquidity management.

The accountant, who is sometimes viewed as a "full range" financial adviser, is often nothing of the sort. No-one is better qualified to advise on the setting-up of a budgeting system, but the emphasis upon standard accounting practice that dominates the accountant's own training makes it particularly difficult for him to recognise the limitations in accounting data and to think in cash flows or in probabilistic terms (clearly, this comment is aimed at accountants in general accounting and auditing practice, and not at the highly competent consulting divisions which exist within many large public accounting firms).

The consultant who takes on none of these specialised professional roles can adopt a viewpoint spanning all the financial decision areas. If he is willing to make the considerable investment of time needed to familiarise himself with all of them, he can indeed perform valuable services in an area that is very important for his clients.

13.1 Financial appraisal

It will be difficult for the consultant to assist his client in the finance area unless the client is himself "financially literate": that is, possesses some basic understanding of accounting and financial terms and procedures, and is able to use them in a simple financial analysis. Bringing the client "up to speed" in financial appraisal is therefore a prerequisite for further consulting work in finance.

This book is not the place to set forth the basic principles of accounting or of financial analysis. We assume that a professional consultant has already mastered some basic financial skills. It may still be in order, however, to offer some advice as to how he should go about educating those of his clients who do not yet possess such skills. A wealth of instructional material on financial analysis and appraisal is now available. So much material is offered, in fact, that the consultant can play a useful role by reviewing as much as possible of it and selecting an appropriate combination for his client's needs.

Whatever medium is selected to provide instruction for the client, however, there are certain essential elements that need to be covered, and which therefore form the basic criteria that the consultant will bear in mind in putting together a training package.

Bookkeeping

The conventional approach to the teaching of accounting invariably started with bookkeeping. We believe that for managers this is time-consuming and unnecessary. The concepts of "credits" and "debits" can also be dispensed with. The emphasis should not be upon how financial information is collected, but upon how it is *used* in managerial decisions.

Accounting principles

There are some basic accounting principles which clients must understand because financial statements will otherwise be meaningless. The essential items here are:

- the accrual concept, and the resulting differences between "accounting" and "cash-flow" figures;
- conservatism, and the "lower of cost or market" rule;
- the concept of non-cash charges (depreciation and amortisation);
- the distinction between the company (corporation) as a "legal entity" and its owners.

Financial statements

Clearly, the client must be familiar with the basic components of a financial report. Understanding the balance sheet is important. Some trainers and consultants, however, give undue emphasis to the balance sheet and largely ignore the income statement. The consultant should seek out material which not only gives "equal time" to the analysis of the income statement, but then brings together information from both documents to produce a "sources and uses of funds" analysis.

Ratio analysis

Virtually all financial analysis involves the calculation and use of ratios. Here the problem is that there are so many ratios, and so many variations on them, that the client is likely to become thoroughly confused. Fortunately, nobody needs to be familiar with scores of different ratios. It is much better to select a dozen or so, and then become thoroughly proficient in their use. But although a very few ratios will suffice, the short list must include representatives of four quite different areas. They are:

- Ratios concerning *liquidity*, or the ability of the company to pay its bills as they become due. The "quick ratio", or "acid test", is clearly the most important ratio in this respect. For companies making significant use of debt financing, the "times interest earned" or "interest coverage" ratio is equally important.
- Ratios concerning managerial efficiency, as expressed in *turnover* figures. The most important ratios here are accounts receivable expressed in average daily sales, and inventories expressed in average daily cost-of-goods sold.
- Ratios concerning *capital structure*: the relative proportions of debt and equity funds. The actual ratio used may be long-term debt to equity, total debt to equity, total debt to total capital, or one of many other possible formulations. It is important to choose one of these ratios and to use it *consistently*.

● Lastly, but most important of all, ratios which measure *profitability*. These include return on total assets, return on equity funds, and many possible variations thereon. While all of these are acceptable, it is important to supplement them with the one ratio which removes the influence of existing financial structure on profitability: "earnings before interest and taxes as a percentage return on total assets".

Equipped with these basic tools and concepts, the client will now be better able to explain his requirements and to understand the consultant's analysis and recommendations. There are, of course, instances in which the client will prefer the consultant to do the financial appraisal, or comment on the financial appraisal done by the client himself. Here again, the consultant should use these opportunities for developing the client's competence in basic financial analysis.

13.2 Working capital and liquidity management

It should be asked at this point what financial management seeks to achieve. Most current financial theory is based upon the assumption that the underlying objective of all financial decisions should be the maximisation of long-term stockholder (shareholder) wealth: a viewpoint that has led to the preoccupation with the formulation of models to determine the value of financial securities under "efficient market" conditions that now dominate financial literature. Some commentators reject this view, and argue that the organisation's responsibilities are to all its "stakeholders": creditors, employees, and society in general as well as to the stockholder group. It is certain, however, that the organisation cannot benefit anybody unless it continues to exist, and that in order to survive it must be able to meet all its commitments as they fall due. In everyday language, it must be able to pay its bills on time.

Working capital definitions

Accountants define working capital in accounting terms as the difference between current assets and current liabilities. This is a static approach, and not a very useful one. Liquidity — the ability to meet commitments and to pay bills — comes from the availability of cash. A company could have considerable working capital in the accounting sense (because of very large inventories) but no cash at all, and thus be on the point of insolvency. The approach taken here will be based upon *cash flows* rather than upon accounting concepts, and one of the most useful services that the consultant can perform is to educate his client to think, and to plan, in cash-flow terms.

Working capital and the operating cycle

Every manufacturing business has an intrinsic "operating cycle", in which materials are purchased, stocked, converted into finished products and finally sold. Even service industries have such a cycle, though its duration is shorter. Cash flows out of the organisation when purchases are made, and returns when accounts receivable are collected. The task of the consultant is to help his client to understand his organisation's own unique operating cycle, and then to find ways of increasing operating efficiency so that the cycle is shortened and cash is conserved. Experience has shown that in most organisations improvements of 25 to 40 per cent in cash utilisation may often be made simply by careful analysis and the use of common sense.

One of the factors that the consultant should remember here (and one of the advantages he has over the banker or the accountant in this area) is that the changes leading to these improvements in cash utilisation are as likely to be in production or other operating areas as in purely "financial" ones. Improvements in inventory control leading to a reduction in average stock levels, and improvements in quality control that produce a fall in wastage and scrap, will reduce the cash tied up in the operating cycle just as effectively as an improvement in collection of accounts receivable, or an acceleration in the transfer of funds from remote locations to a central concentration account. The very fact that most managers working in these non-financial areas do *not* fully understand the cash-flow consequences of their activities makes this a field in which the consultant has a particularly valuable contribution to offer.

Managing cash

Even though the entire operating cycle has cash-flow implications, the management of cash itself should not be overlooked. Here, the banks are indeed the experts, and most major banks have actively developed and marketed cash management systems in recent years. The consultant can play a useful role even here, however, by assisting his client in evaluating the bewildering array of different "packages" in which the banks offer him combinations of concentration banking, lock-box collection systems, remote disbursement, zero-balance accounts, intra-group payments netting and so forth, and in finding a solution appropriate to his needs.

13.3 Capital structure and the financial markets

Every business organisation needs an adequate capital base to support its operations. It has been repeatedly demonstrated that operating a business with inadequate capital — which in British financial circles is called "overtrading" — is one of the most widespread causes of business failure. In addition to having adequate capital, the business must have an appropriate capital structure: the right mix of equity funds and debt. All of this is easily said, but difficult to achieve in practice.

Determining an effective capital structure

A major portion of current financial theory is concerned with the capital structure of companies and with the effect of long-term financing decisions on the organisation's cost of capital. Most of the theory is based upon assumptions that do not reflect reality, however. In addition, such theory is usually expressed in a highly quantitative form. Once again, a consultant who is conversant with the current financial literature can play an invaluable role in helping his clients to identify the usable and useful concepts which are now beginning to emerge from this mass of theory.

The management of an organisation's capital structure actually involves a two-stage decision process. The first task, when any new financing operation is proposed, is to review the organisation's current capital structure in the light of management's policies, accepted debt/equity ratios, market conditions and, most important of all, expected cash generation and use over a period of some years. On the basis of this analysis a decision can be made whether to seek new equity funds or additional debt. Once this is complete, the second stage involves the determination of the exact type of security to be issued, the selection of underwriters, the pricing and timing of the issue, and so forth. These second-stage decision areas are the distinct professional field of the investment banker (merchant banker in British terminology), and the general consultant should ensure that his client seeks such specialist services at the appropriate time. But in the first stage of the process — reviewing the overall financial position to decide what kind of funds should be sought — the consultant's help can be invaluable.

Using debt funds

The advantages of using debt funds are very great: judicious amounts of debt increase the earnings per common (ordinary) share through the leverage effect, and the fact that interest charges are tax-deductible makes the net cost of borrowed funds relatively low. In general, debt financing will be the first choice if the company can safely add the proposed new borrowing to its existing debt. The key task in capital structure management, then, is to determine the company's *debt capacity*. There are many possible approaches to this question, but few of them are satisfactory. Policies which allow some external standard or institution to determine the decision (for example, keeping a debt/equity ratio more or less equal to the average for the industry, or limiting borrowing to what can be done without lowering the "rating" of the company's debt securities by the rating agencies) are unlikely to produce optimal results.

In most cases, the consultant will face a difficult task in this area. He will have to "re-educate" his clients away from rules of thumb, and convince them that nothing can replace a systematic analysis. The ability of a company to use debt depends upon its ability to *service* that debt: to meet all interest charges and repayments of principal as they fall due. This in turn depends upon cash flows. The consultant's task, then, is to persuade the client company to undertake a long-term projection of the cash likely to be generated by its operations, not only under "normal" economic conditions, but also during periods of economic uncertainty and recession. This is likely to require the use of simulation techniques, and the development of a computer-based model of the company's financial dynamics.

Few companies can undertake such projects without outside assistance. Effective consulting work in this area depends upon the availability of a consulting team which combines financial expertise with EDP systems analysis and programming skills. Consulting organisations that are willing to develop such teams can expect growing needs for their services as more and more companies realise the fundamental importance of such an analytical approach to financial decisions.

13.4 Mergers and acquisitions

Mergers between companies or the acquisition of one company by another provide many opportunities for consulting work. Most of these opportunities come in the post-merger phase, when work begins on the rationalisation of the production and marketing activities, and the task of reconciling the different budgeting systems, personnel policies and a host of other procedures. There is, however, one key financial task that must be undertaken before the merger, and in which consultants are very often needed: the determination of the *fair value* of one or both of the companies involved. The consultant may also be called upon to advise as to the method of payment to be used. He will normally have either the acquiring company or the one to be acquired as his client, but in some cases of "friendly merger" he may be advising both organisations.

Valuation of a company

There are essentially four approaches to the valuation of a going-concern company. Value can be based upon:

● the current market price of the company's common stock (if the stock is listed and actively traded);

● the market value of the assets;

● capitalised future earnings; and

● "replacement" or "duplication" value which involves an attempt to estimate the cost of building up a similar organisation from scratch instead of making the acquisition.

The first of these, the current market approach, is widely used. It does not in fact give the fair value of the company, but provides a "floor price" below which negotiations cannot go: if the common shares have recently been changing hands at, say, $50, then any offer price that values the total company at less than $50 per share is unlikely to be acceptable. The other three approaches do try to establish a real fair value. The consultant may be called upon both to advise upon the method to be used and to assist in its implementation.

In recommending a basis for valuation, the consultant will obviously pay close attention to his client's particular situation and needs. If his client is the company which is receiving the offer, then the appropriate method will be whichever yields the highest value: the consultant will not suggest a price based upon current earnings if he estimates that the realisable value of the physical and financial assets of the company might be higher. But when his client is the acquiring company (that is, the company *making* the offer) the situation is more complicated. The appropriate valuation method now depends upon the company's motives for making the acquisition, and these motives in turn are vested in its corporate strategy and long-term plans. If the acquisition is being made simply as part of a diversification strategy and the company that is being purchased will be allowed to continue its operations largely independently, then a figure based upon capitalised earnings will be appropriate, and the main task of the consultant will be to scrutinise the current and forecast earnings to ensure that they are credible and based upon sound accounting practices, and that no special "window dressing" has taken place to increase reported earnings at the expense of long-term financial health.

The consultant is likely to be most deeply involved in those cases in which the client organisation is making an acquisition for operating reasons rather than pure diversification: in order to gain additional production capacity, for example, or to acquire new products that will complement its own existing product range. In such a situation it will be necessary both to establish asset values and to adopt the "replacement" approach. Some consultants have developed particular expertise in asset valuation and have become known specialists in this area.

Method of payment

The selection of the method of payment to be used in making the acquisition is a highly complex question which requires both expert knowledge of the financial markets and special skills in determining the tax consequences of the method used. The choice of possible methods includes a simple cash payment for the shares of the other company, a cash payment for assets, a "stock for stock" exchange, and the use of bonds or notes, preferred stock, convertible bonds, convertible preferred stock, or any combination of these. The transaction may be at a fixed price, or may use a sliding-scale payment contingent upon future performance. The complexity of the matter is such that the consultant is urged to recommend to his client the use of an appropriate team of specialists, which will include investment bankers, tax specialists and legal advisers.

13.5 Finance and operations: capital investment analysis

Most business organisations tend to generate more investment proposals than they can immediately finance. They therefore require a systematic method of calculating the economic attractions of such investment proposals, and of ranking them in order of preference so that the limited funds available go to the most productive investments. In a majority of companies the analysis of capital investment proposals is still done partly or wholly on the basis of "rules of thumb" or personal preference, so yet again the consultant has a useful task to perform.

Choosing among analytical methods

The consultant's first task in this area is to persuade his client that outdated and simplistic methods of investment appraisal, such as a simple rate-of-return analysis or the "years to payback" principle, are unsatisfactory and yield misleading results. He should instead encourage the use of one of the techniques based upon the time value of money. The general term used for this approach is *discounted cash flow* (DCF) analysis. There are, however, two different methods of implementing this approach. Most textbooks advocate the calculation of *net present value* (NPV) and the use of net present value per dollar invested as the decision criteria. The consultant should note, however, that this method requires the company to calculate its overall average cost of capital, which is then used as the discounting rate, and that this figure is difficult to develop and often unstable. The alternative approach, the *internal rate of return* (IRR), has some theoretical disadvantages but also enjoys the practical advantage of not requiring a cost-of-capital calculation. It is much more widely used than the NPV approach and should be the consultant's first choice.

The selection of an analytical method and a decision criterion, however, by no means solves all the problems in this area. The various investment proposals facing a company are likely to be very different in nature. In particular, some of them, such as proposals to replace old machinery which is giving rise to high maintenance costs with new but similar equipment, involve neither risk nor uncertainty. Other projects, such as the replacement of a known but outdated technology with an advanced but unfamiliar one, clearly involve both uncertainty and risk. It becomes very difficult to rank one project against the other unless some adjustment is made for the differing degrees of risk.

Sensitivity analysis

In order to arrive at a ranking for proposed projects, many companies will need outside assistance. The most satisfactory solution is to adopt a "sensitivity analysis" approach. Those projects that are seen as important but also as involving a high degree of uncertainty should be modelled (simulated), so that the model can be run many times with different values for key variables. A project to build a plant for the production of a radically new product, for example, may involve considerable uncertainty both about the time needed to bring the new product into production and about its market acceptance. The model would therefore require numerous reruns ("iterations") with different assumptions about the time needed to bring the plant on-stream and about the likely sales volumes, and a probability distribution of expected net cash flows will be developed from the results.

It will be obvious from the above paragraph that this is yet another area in which the consulting organisation will best be able to help its clients if it can offer the services of specialist teams in which financial consultants work closely with computer experts.

Follow-up of project effectiveness

There is yet another valuable service that the consultant can provide in this area. Many companies, even those that have adopted relatively sophisticated procedures for the evaluation of project proposals, overlook the need for systematic follow-up and monitoring of subsequent project performance. A project is adopted because it appears to promise a very high discount-adjusted rate of return. If it fails to perform as well as the project proposal promised, it is important to find out *why*. Was there an unexpected downturn in the economic environment? Did the project encounter technical problems that were not foreseen? Was the marketing staff unduly optimistic in predicting sales? Or were the forecasts of sales and earnings consciously inflated for political purposes by an "empire-building" divisional head? The development and installation of a follow-up system to answer such questions will rapidly pay off in improvements in project selection, and is one of the most useful tools that the consultant can provide.

13.6 Accounting systems and budgetary control

Financial consultants may be invited to assist their clients in the development of accounting systems by means of which various transactions are recorded, collected and classified, entered into the various ledgers and books of account, and finally used to prepare the organisation's formal financial statements. This, however, is properly the work of qualified accountants, and consultants who are not themselves also accountants will recommend their clients to obtain proper professional assistance in this area.

Budgetary versus accounting systems

Consultants participating in general "management services" activities are very likely to find themselves called upon to assist in the design of budgetary systems rather than formal accounting systems. The emphasis here will be upon "management accounting": methods of collecting and analysing data to support internal decision making rather than formal financial reporting. Both the objectives and the methods of management accounting are different from those of financial accounting, and the difference is essentially one of timeliness versus accuracy. Financial accounting emphasises accuracy and detail, but produces reports that are historic. If decisions are not made until formal financial accounts are available, it is likely to be too late for those decisions to be effective. The consultant realises that his clients need information quickly to support their decision making, and that information which is approximate but timely is of far more value than that which is accurate but three or more months late.

The budgetary and control system should be developed for an individual organisation rather than bought "off the shelf", and will therefore differ from company to company. For most manufacturing companies, the component parts will include:

- a profit plan;
- the capital investment budget;
- wage and salary budgets;
- purchasing budgets and inventory control procedures;
- manufacturing direct cost budgets;
- general overhead budgets;
- sales, marketing and promotion budgets;
- recruitment and training budgets;
- the overall cash budget.

Most of these budgets will be further broken down by division and by department, reflecting the structure of the company.

Budgetary control

The consultant needs to keep in mind the multiple objectives that underlie any system of budgetary control. They are:

- that expenditures of funds and commitments of resources resulting from decisions in the various operating areas do not reach an overall aggregate that places an unacceptable strain on the company's financial structure and resources;
- that all revenue and cost items be planned and co-ordinated in order to ensure a positive stream of earnings and cash flows and to guarantee the organisation's liquidity;
- that all actual revenue, cost and expense items can be monitored and compared with budgeted levels, and the variances understood and corrected.

The consultant must be acutely aware of the fact that designing a budgetary control and management information system involves much more than itemising what budgets are needed and how often they should be prepared. Attention will have to be given to the company's organisational structure and existing procedures. In a large company it may be necessary to create a number of "profit centres" or "investment centres", or even to designate some divisions as near-autonomous "strategic business units". In smaller organisations, a simple "cost centre" approach is likely to be used.

Once the organisational structure is agreed, it will be necessary to design procedures for the collection and submission of data for the development and review of budgets by higher authorities and for the determination of corrective action. Paper forms and/or EDP programmes and documentation must be selected. In this, as in most other areas, the development of the new procedures will involve a partnership between the consultants and key company people from the finance, organisation development, EDP and personnel departments, while line management must be consulted at all stages to ensure that the completed system meets all its needs. Finally, the consultants will be actively involved in training company staff to operate the new procedures and will probably remain on call until the system has successfully been implemented.

13.7 Financial management under inflation

During recent years, businesses in many countries have had to operate under high rates of inflation. When inflation rates average between 2 and 5 per cent, as they did in most OECD countries during the 1960s, inflation can usually be ignored in business decision making without disastrous consequences. When inflation reaches or even exceeds the 15 to 20 per cent level, as it did in some countries in the late 1970s, and in certain countries continues to do so at the present time, it can no longer be ignored. Few managers, however, even though they realise the importance and the consequences of inflation, know how to predict it or how to take it into consideration in their forecasting, planning and budgeting. Here again the financial management consultant can provide guidance that will be valuable to various areas of the client's business.

Inflation accounting

The aspect of inflation that has been most widely discussed in business circles is its impact on reported earnings. Conventional accounting permits only the original purchase value of capital goods and of inventory items to be used in calculating operating earnings. The resultant profits figure is therefore seriously overstated because the calculation of profit has not made proper provision for the replenishment of inventory or for the replacement of capital assets as they wear out. There has been very widespread debate concerning the introduction of new accounting rules that would provide for "inflation adjustment" and thus generate a lower but more realistic earnings figure.

Much of the "inflation accounting" debate has hinged upon the method of adjustment to be used. All the proposed systems seek to establish the use of more realistic current values of assets rather than using the historic (original) ones, but differ in their methods.

One approach, the "replacement cost" or "current cost" method, necessitates finding the current price in the market of equipment similar to that being used, and using this current market price as the basis for depreciation.

The alternative method, "index adjustment" or "current purchasing power", retains the historic purchase price as its basis but multiplies this historic price each year by a factor obtained from an inflation index to give a new depreciation base.

The first method is clearly more accurate but administratively tedious and costly; the second method is more approximate but much easier to apply.

Up to the present time, the "inflation accounting" debate has been sterile for three reasons:

(1) accountants have been unable to agree as to which adjustment method should be used;

(2) some accountants do not accept any form of inflation adjustment, believing that any such system would turn accounting into a highly arbitrary and inexact process;

(3) most serious of all, very few tax authorities will accept inflation-adjustment accounts for the determination of corporate tax liabilities, and until such accounts are acceptable for tax reporting purposes it is unlikely that many companies will be willing to adopt them as the primary reporting vehicle.

Financial operations under inflation

Successful management under high inflation is not simply a matter of changing accounting procedures. There are practical operating steps to be taken. The consultancy can provide services to its clients in many areas, primarily the following:

- the development of inflation rate forecasts, either by primary analysis on the basis of monetary aggregates or by combining the forecasts readily available from official bodies and financial institutions;

- the incorporation of inflation expectations in the company's strategic planning procedures;

- the modification of capital investment analysis procedures to take explicit and systematic account of inflation expectations, particularly inflation differentials where wage costs, for example, are expected to rise more quickly than selling prices;

- the review of working capital management procedures, in recognition of the increased need to speed up the conversion of financial assets and to minimise unproductive cash balances under inflationary conditions;

- the recognition of the close relationship between inflation rates and interest rates, and the anticipation of likely interest rate changes in planning the company's capital structure;

- continuing emphasis upon the close relationship between inflation rates and changes in the value of currencies in the foreign exchange markets, leading to an increase in the importance of foreign currency exposure management.

Although at the time of writing inflation rates have fallen below their peaks in most OECD countries, this area is likely to be one of uncertainty and concern for many years to come. Yet many executives still find it difficult to think logically about inflation or its effects and attempt to ignore it — with grave results. The educational requirement in this area is one of the greatest challenges facing the financial consultant at this time.

13.8 Cross-border operations and the use of external financial markets

Where the client company is engaged in any form of cross-border operation, either selling its products and services in foreign countries or purchasing some of its own materials from foreign suppliers, a number of important additional complications arise. Many of the issues involved are unfamiliar to corporate executives. The field of international finance is, then, a fruitful one for the consultant who develops the requisite expertise.

The most important issues arising in this area can be grouped under three subheadings, as follows:

— determining foreign exchange exposure;

— hedging techniques and decisions;

— using external money and capital markets.

Determining foreign exchange exposure

Very few companies engaged in cross-border trading are able to invoice their products and purchase their imported supplies entirely in their own domestic currency. As soon as sales are invoiced in a foreign currency, or the company contracts to purchase items priced in a foreign currency, a foreign exchange exposure exists. Many companies are unable to identify the exact extent of their exposure, and the consultant may be of considerable assistance here. The confusion which exists in many companies arises from the fact that there are three distinct kinds of foreign exchange exposure. The consultant needs to understand them all and to be able to assist his client in recognising them, determining their relative importance and deciding what to do about them.

Many multinational companies, especially those whose headquarters are located in the United States, are much concerned with *translation exposure*: the risk of gain or loss when the assets, liabilities and earnings of a subsidiary are "translated" from the foreign currency in which the subsidiary's books are kept into the parent currency (US dollars). Such losses are "real" in so far as they influence the parent's overall reported profit and loss and taxes on income. In another sense, however, they are "unreal" in that they arise from a particular accounting convention, and that a change to a different accounting basis may change a translation "loss" into a translation "gain". The consultant must be familiar with the current rulings of the client's national taxation authorities and the degree of freedom permitted under those rulings. Where there is no freedom of manoeuvre under the regulations, it may be necessary to advise the client to change the currency denomination of his liabilities to minimise the translation exposure.

Transaction exposure is simpler to understand and affects all companies which engage in international trade. Whenever a company commits itself to a transaction — whether a sale or a purchase — denominated in a foreign currency, there exists the risk of gain or loss if the value of that foreign currency changes in relation to the company's own domestic currency. If a Swiss company supplies pharmaceutical drugs to a British buyer, giving 90 days credit and invoicing in pounds sterling, then that Swiss exporter will make a loss if the value of the pound falls relative to the Swiss franc during 90 days: the seller will receive only the agreed number of pounds, and those pounds will now buy fewer francs. The exporter's home currency cash flow is reduced, and the loss in this case is very clearly a real one. The consultant will probably not need to involve himself much in the determination of exposures of this type: most companies are aware of their transaction exposures. They may still, however, be very unsure what to do about them.

The third type of exposure, which is now increasingly referred to as *economic exposure*, is more complex. It deals with the impact of an exchange rate change upon the organisation's overall long-term profitability, rather than simply its effect upon currently outstanding transactions. Assume, for example, that a Swiss exporter sells watches to a distributor in the United States, and that the value of the dollar now falls abruptly against the Swiss franc. The immediate effect may be a transaction loss if a recent shipment of watches, invoiced in dollars, has not yet been paid for. The longer-term effect is much more serious: the Swiss manufacturer must choose between keeping the same dollar price, which will now yield fewer francs for every watch sold, or, alternatively, holding his price in Swiss francs constant, which means increasing the dollar selling price, probably losing sales and market share, and handing his customers over to competitors from Japan and other lower-cost countries. The need for professional advice in this area is clear.

Hedging techniques and decisions

Once the foreign exchange exposures have been determined, the next step is to decide whether they should be "hedged" or "covered"; and if so, how? Many companies turn to their commercial banks for advice. The local bank manager, however, probably has no experience of, or special training in, foreign exchange management. Consequently, his advice is likely to be highly conservative. Many bankers tell their clients: "You are in the business of making and selling products, not speculating in the foreign exchange markets. You should therefore cover all outstanding exposures by buying or selling the foreign currency in the forward market."

Any consultant working in this area should realise that this advice is an oversimplified answer to a very complex problem. A policy of 100 per cent cover by using the forward market does at least lock-in a known rate of exchange, but not necessarily an advantageous one. Using the forward market can in fact be considered just as much a speculation as holding an open (uncovered) foreign exchange position: both policies will ultimately provide either a gain or a loss, depending upon the relation between the forward price when the transaction was generated and the spot price on the day the transaction matures. Beware of textbooks offering nonsensical formulae which claim to calculate the "cost" of hedging at the time the transaction is undertaken: the cost can *only* be calculated retrospectively when the final spot price is known.

The most important service that the consultant can provide in this area is to show his client that there are no simple golden rules or magic formulae available, and that foreign exchange operations require a systematic step-by-step analysis and decision process. The required steps are as follows:

(1) Determine overall foreign exchange exposures and distinguish between the different types of exposure as described above.

(2) Evaluate these exposure positions in the light of the best available forecasts and expectations concerning foreign exchange price movements, and decide if there are serious exposures that may produce foreign exchange losses. If so, hedging will have to be considered. For most companies, it will only be practical to cover transaction exposures on a continuing basis.

(3) Consider the possibility of hedging the exposures by operational means, rather than purely financial ones. A company which is regularly exporting goods to Italy and invoicing those sales in lire, for example, may be able to offset this exposure by purchasing some of its own raw materials and supplies from Italian companies. Another method, particularly useful for large transnational companies with a high level of intra-group transactions, is "leading and lagging": a deliberate acceleration of some payments and delay of others in order to take advantage of expected exchange-rate movements.

(4) If operational hedging is not possible and some form of financial operation is to be used, the next question is whether the risk is so serious as to require 100 per cent cover, or whether partial hedging is acceptable. The specialised services which supply foreign exchange forecasts will usually also advise upon this point.

(5) The next step is to obtain from the banks the best available quotation for a "forward" transaction, and to compare this with management's expectations about what might happen to the spot rate. A British company has, for example, an exposure in French francs, and the exposed position is expected to continue for 90 days. The spot rate is £1 = 10.55 French francs, but the banks quote a 90-day forward outright bid rate as £1 = 10.95 French francs, a significant "forward discount" on the franc. The question now is not whether the French franc will fall, but whether the spot price in 90 days' time will fall below 10.95. If it is expected to fall to a price below this, then the transaction should be covered. If it is expected to fall, but only to, say, 10.85, then it will be cheaper *not* to cover the transaction.

(6) The consultant will find that many client companies, including some that have been making regular use of the forward markets for hedging purposes and consider themselves quite sophisticated in this area, do not realise that it is possible to achieve the same result by using the money markets. For example, a company which is based in Switzerland, but sells regularly to the United Kingdom and invoices in sterling, will have regular "long" sterling exposure. Rather than hedge such exposures by selling the pounds forward,

the company could borrow pounds in the London money market, use those pounds to buy Swiss francs, and use the francs for working capital purposes. The pound borrowing creates a sterling liability which offsets the long sterling position arising from the exports. The consultant should be able to show his client how to compare the cost of such an operation with conventional hedging, and to explain that when the local currency generated (Swiss francs in this example) can be used to repay an existing overdraft or credit line, the interest saving may be enough to make this the least-cost form of covering.

(7)   The period since 1982 has seen the development of another and quite different approach to foreign exchange hedging in the form of the currency option. Active trading in such options started in the Philadelphia stock exchange, but is now spreading rapidly. Other exchanges (Chicago, London) are offering similar facilities and, even more significantly, major banks are selling such options on a "custom-tailored" basis. The option is essentially different from any other form of hedging in that its use is indeed "optional": the right to buy or sell currency at a stated price if the option-holder chooses. There is no obligation to exercise the option if it is not advantageous to do so. This approach therefore offers a degree of downside protection if the currency movement is adverse coupled with the possibility of still making a profit if the movement is in a favourable direction. The pricing of options is very complex, and the markets have unique procedures and jargon. This is yet another area in which the client company is much in need of guidance.

Using external money and capital markets

Smaller companies in most countries automatically and quite logically look to commercial banks in their own country as the normal source of external funds. As companies grow in size and sophistication, however, the possibility of using external financial markets presents itself. Corporate management will initially have little knowledge about such markets, and probably believe them to be very exotic, perhaps dangerous or open only to the multinational giants. This is a further area, therefore, in which the management consultant's role is primarily an educational one.

The consultant will point out to his client that a number of international financial markets exist: the Eurocurrency market (sometimes called the Eurodollar market, although the dollar segment is only a part of it), the Eurobond market, and several "foreign bond markets" existing in various centres, particularly New York, London, the Swiss and West German financial centres, and Tokyo. The various international bond markets cater primarily to the "high quality" borrower and a relatively small company may find access difficult. The Eurocurrency markets, however, despite their ability to accommodate single transactions of US$5 billion or more on a "syndicated" basis, are readily accessible to the medium-sized company, both as a source of loan funds and as a temporary investment medium for corporate cash that will later be needed for working capital purposes.

Management consulting

Corporate management will probably be surprised that banks operating in the "Euro" market can often pay a slightly higher interest rate on funds deposited than can the domestic banks, but at the same time can charge a slightly lower rate on the loans they make. The consultant will point out that this is a perfectly logical outcome of the fact that the Eurobanks have cost structures that are significantly different from those of domestic banks, the most important difference being the absence of any reserve requirements against their deposits. The lower operating costs allow them to work on a smaller "spread" between their borrowing and lending costs than can domestic banks, and their customers benefit accordingly.

Nevertheless, the area is a complex one, and the consultant will have to guide his client through a mass of new terms and procedures. In Eurocurrency lending virtually all loans are "floating rate", and are priced not at a stated per cent of interest rate but at a "spread" or "mark-up" over a base rate such as LIBOR (the London Interbank Offered Rate), this latter being the wholesale cost of money in the interbank market. The procedures for determining "value dates" for repayment are complex, and these in turn can affect the overall interest cost. Lastly, although most financial institutions active in these markets are of undoubted superiority and creditworthiness, a few are of distinctly lower quality. There is much for the consultant to learn here. It can be a rapidly developing field for his professional services once he has made himself familiar with these fascinating markets.

CONSULTING IN MARKETING AND DISTRIBUTION MANAGEMENT

14

Consulting work involving the client's marketing activities differs in several ways from that dealing with other functions. It is in its marketing that the firm finds itself in contact with external entities (competitors and clients) having an independent existence. The firm's very survival depends upon how well it manages to adapt to the market conditions influenced by the activities of these entities.

One of the paradoxes of the marketing function is that when it is looked at closely it tends to disappear, like a stream going underground. It is first found at the very highest level of the firm, in its overall strategy formulation. It then resurfaces in the organisation and management of the various market-related activities: sales, advertising, market research, etc. This leaves a definite gap in the organisation chart. Matters concerning the firm's overall strategy, of which marketing strategy is an important part, can only be decided at the topmost level of the organisation, while running the various activities is predominantly a middle-management function. As compared with his counterparts in the other management functions (production, finance, and so on) this leaves the senior marketing manager in a somewhat ambiguous position, and the same necessarily applies to a management consultant working with this manager.

Thus a consulting assignment that embraces the marketing function will usually develop into two quite separate tasks, one at the *strategy-formulation level* and one at the *activities level*. These two tasks are treated separately below. It is convenient here, however, to note briefly a third type of consulting activity.

This third type is *marketing research*, the study of the prospects and performance of a firm's products in the market. Marketing research consultants do not carry out marketing management consultancy. However, marketing management consulting assignments may involve some marketing research, to verify the client's assumptions about his corporate image, the nature of his customers, and so on. Since this work is often very specialised, and may require the availability of substantial numbers of trained interviewers, the consultant, unless he belongs to an organisation with its own marketing research division, will find it cheaper and less time-consuming to sub-contract it to a specialist rather than to undertake it himself. He should therefore keep himself informed of marketing research organisations, the areas they specialise in and the quality of their work. He should also keep up to date on developments in this field.

Information technology (IT), based on microprocessors linked together by the telephone network or other means, is now firmly established in many areas of marketing and distribution. Its growth is likely to be explosive. Applications, for the next few years at least, will be limited more by the ingenuity of the users than by the capabilities of the technology. Its effects will be profound, and the marketing consultancy which does not keep in touch with developments in this field will rapidly be rendered obsolete. Some newer developments that are of interest to consultants will be reviewed in chapter 19.

14.1 The marketing strategy level

Strategic decisions in marketing have far-reaching implications for the enterprise as a whole and for the management of particular functions, such as production, product development, or financial control. It is no wonder, therefore, that even minor proposals may meet with strong objections from senior management of other departments. Major changes, such as dropping or adding product lines, or changing overall pricing policies, are clearly general management decisions to be taken at top level.

A useful starting point is to classify the client's orientation towards the market. Three classifications are recognised: *product-oriented*, *production-oriented*, and *market-oriented*. In a product-oriented firm the emphasis is on the product itself, while in the production-oriented firm the dominant considerations in product design or modification are those of ease or cheapness of production. In either case market considerations are ignored or suppressed. In a market-oriented firm the decisions are based upon the analysis of market needs and demands. The object is to take the opportunities the market offers. This approach can produce any of the good effects of the other two orientations, and avoids their drawbacks. More importantly, it can identify new opportunities. Figuratively speaking, the management of the firm asks itself the following questions:

- What are the problems of our customers that our products (or services) can solve more cheaply or better than products from other suppliers?
- Who has these problems (in addition to our present customers)?
- What are the particular circumstances of our customers, actual or potential, which would suggest modifications in our products, conditions of delivery, after-sales servicing, etc.?

The idea of thinking in terms of providing solutions to problems is a very useful one in marketing. It helps considerably in identifying new markets, finding new products for existing customers, finding new customers for existing products, and, most importantly, discovering potential and possibly unsuspected competition.

As a very simple case, consider a manufacturer of nuts and bolts. This enterprise probably thinks of itself as being in the metal-working business, and looks for new business on this basis. But what about its customers? Their problem is joining things together. So the firm could meet competition from firms making welding equipment, rivets, cotter pins, or glues. This threat is also an opportunity, since the firm's sales force and distributors are already in touch with people who form a potential market for these items, which suggests that they could profitably be added to the firm's product line. The costs of marketing are high, so that anything that can add to the effectiveness of the various marketing functions (i.e. reduce the unit costs of marketing activities) can be surprisingly profitable. Such help can come from selling more items per sales visit, sending out shipments with more items, and turning small, unprofitable accounts into at least medium-sized ones.

It should be noted, however, that in the early 1980s some articles were published which queried the validity of the "marketing concept".[1] It remains to be seen whether these were based on a genuine analytical approach and so represent a movement likely to gather strength, whether they were a reaction against some marketing excesses of the previous, easier years, or whether they were a reaction to hard times, a return to the illusory protection of "doing what we know we can do" rather than running the risks involved in adopting market-oriented strategies.

Another theme emerging is that of the "global market". The thesis here is based on the observation that a very wide range of branded goods, from jet aircraft to cars, hi-fi and jeans to hamburgers, are being sold world-wide with little or no adaptation to local conditions. Production for a global market gives substantial economies of scale compared with production for a national market, and even compared with multinational firms which adapt their products to what they believe are local national preferences. Thus national and multinational firms are vulnerable in the face of firms which adopt a global strategy.

Stated in this way, this thesis appears to advocate a product-orientation rather than a market-orientation, and it is ironic that the chief proponent of the global market strategy is Theodore Levitt, whose 1960 article was such a devastating attack on those firms obsessed with their products.[1] It can also, however, be interpreted as an assault on the marketing excesses of the boom years when marketers became hypnotised with their own jargon, marketing departments were swollen beyond all reason, markets were segmented for segmentation's sake, and so forth.

The global market concept is still a controversial subject, but it appears to be widely accepted that the firms which most successfully weathered the recent hard years were those which had adopted and which *understood* the marketing concept, and applied it in pursuit of clear objectives. Marketing has emerged leaner and fitter. An important product of this period is a proprietary service called PIMS (Profit Impact of Marketing Strategy). Based on a sample of several thousand firms, orginally all American, but now including European ones, this service correlates return on investment and other profitability measures with the various factors of the firm's marketing strategies. Marketing consultants should be familiar with this service.

Marketing strategy analysis

Since the firm's products are the hub of its whole marketing strategy, the first step in a marketing assignment should be to analyse the client's whole product line in the way described above, checking whether the products (1) provide answers to consumers' problems, and (2) are mutually supportive. Ideally, all the products in the line should be of interest to every customer, and should fit in well with the production facilities. This ideal is unlikely to arise in practice, of course, and a certain amount of departure from it must be tolerated. Consultants should pay attention, however, to the "odd" product, which is in the line because it fits the production facilities but requires a different set of customers and thus involves undue dispersion of selling efforts. Such spare production capacity might be better used in producing for other firms under contract or sub-contract. Also, a check needs to be made for gaps in the product line which could be filled by buying-in, in order to make full use of the available sales efforts.

Next, the product line may be reviewed according to the criteria set out by Drucker, especially from the viewpoint of future opportunities offered by various products, and the costs related to the use of these opportunities.[2]

Such an analysis should provide a sound basis for the consultant's recommendations for product additions or deletions. Sometimes it will indicate areas that need further investigation. For example, the marketing manager might insist that some sizes in a product line, although very small sellers, are necessary because the firm's distributors demand a "full" line from their suppliers. This should be investigated (sometimes "demand" means simply a mild preference), as should the possibility of "buying-in" the more extreme sizes. The analysis is also, of course, a pre-requisite for a review of the client's new product development programme.

One of the interesting points noted by various studies during the depression of the early 1980s (and depressions are widely believed, probably correctly, to bring managers back in touch with business basics that are too easily forgotten in boom times) was that quality of goods and reliability of delivery (supply) were generally perceived as more important than price, especially by industrial purchasers. The implications of this for marketing strategy are clear.

In many enterprises pricing is regarded as the special province of accountants, who determine at what prices the marketing staff must sell. Yet this is an area in which both marketing considerations and cost criteria apply. If a marketing consultant finds that prices are set by unilateral decisions of accountants, he will be interested in reviewing how this affects marketing and the volume of sales. This may lead to a revision of pricing policy, including the establishment of new procedures for price-setting in the client organisation. The ultimate objective would be to make better use of prices as a marketing tool, but without running the risk that an increased volume of sales of underpriced products would cause a financial loss.[3] It should be noted that absorption costing and other cost-accounting methods can give rise to misleading ideas about the profitability of different items in the product line.

Credit to customers can be another common source of conflict between the marketing manager and the finance manager, especially in times of tight money. It is probably the case that, more often than not, the marketing manager attaches too much importance to the use of credit. This is understandable, because his information on this matter comes from the salesmen, who like to have such a tool in their selling kit. When this conflict is encountered it is advisable to undertake some market research in order to find out what the situation really is.

Another problem area for consideration by top management is the firm's public image — the opinion that customers, actual and, more importantly, potential, have of the firm. This should be broadly consistent with the image the firm has of itself, and which its product line, advertising, public relations and salesmen are expected to create.

This problem can be illustrated by the results of research into the public image of three department stores in a North American city, carried out by the local business school. When the students interviewed the store managers, one manager said his store's image was built on quality, the second said his was built on prices, and the third said his store's strength lay in service. The research on consumer attitudes revealed that the same three images, of price, quality and service, indeed existed, but that each of the three managers was wrong about the image attributed to his own store. Thus each manager was, and for some years had been (1) wasting most of his advertising expenditure; (2) wasting most of the effort expended in training his salespeople; and (3) failing to give his customers the type of treatment they expected from his store. It was extremely fortunate for each of these managers that the other two had misread the market as badly as he had himself. In the meantime the smaller stores in town were profiting from the way the three big ones were failing to cash in on their advantages.

When the consultant suspects that such a clash between his client's internal and external images exists, he should investigate this possibility thoroughly. How to approach it is a question of consulting strategy. To change the firm's image is a difficult decision to take; the case for change must therefore be very strong. For example, the marketing consultant may call for the help of an independent market research consultant of good reputation, familiar with attitude research techniques. In any case, the relevant evidence should be collected and presented by a disinterested party, so that the client is assured of the objectivity of the recommendation.

Concentration in retailing

The trend towards concentration, apparent for many years in food retailing, is if anything intensifying and extending into other goods. For example, hardware is being sold increasingly through chains of do-it-yourself outlets, themselves often subsidiaries of other retailers. This trend will have increasingly profound effects on the marketing of such goods:

(1) The major firms will obviously use their purchasing power leverage to get the greatest possible discounts; this drive will be strengthened as the chains fight for market share.

(2) The major retailers will try to influence and to participate in the manufacturer's advertising.

(3) Selling techniques will be changed. A great part of the role of salesmen dealing with independent firms and small chains is to function as "order-takers", and the actual selling function is relatively limited. With re-ordering being increasingly automated through the use of EPOS (electronic point of sale), the order-taking function is being reduced, and centralised purchasing means that salesmen deal with buyers who are sophisticated negotiators. This will entail corresponding training for salesmen if they are to hold their own in these negotiations.

(4) The spread of "own-brands" and "generics" means that in many lines of goods major retailers are in effect competing directly with manufacturers on ground of their own choosing.

At the other end of the scale, many small food retailers are being forced to find a niche for survival by becoming convenience stores. The different mix of goods sold by such stores is reflected in changed stocking and purchasing patterns by their wholesalers; this may work back in due course to different assemblages of manufacturing facilities.

These trends are affecting, and will continue to affect, the overall and marketing strategies of all the firms involved, and the marketing consultant must ensure that he is aware of them and of the effect they will have if he is to provide sound advice to his clients.

What the advice is will depend on various factors, such as the strength of the client's brand name, the technology behind his products (a new product which can be copied in a matter of months has no market strength), the negotiating skills of his salesmen, and so on. One practice that must be looked at with concern is that of recouping the discounts exacted by large customers by charging high prices to small customers. This hastens their demise and makes the manufacturer even more dependent on a few large customers, any one of whom could de-list his products and bankrupt him in a matter of months.

There would seem to be very good prospects for the consultant who knows how to show groups of (non-competing) manufacturers how to provide low-cost support to corresponding groups of wholesalers and retailers. It must surely be safer for a manufacturer to have a hundred healthy customers than four or five overgrown ones. Whether the client has the vision to perceive this is a matter for question.

14.2 Marketing operations

Different firms have different ideas about which operations are part of the marketing function and which are not. Selling, advertising, promotion, dealing with distributors and market research are considered by almost all enterprises to be the responsibility of the marketing manager, but the responsibility for new-product development, package design, or transportation and storage of finished goods (physical distribution) is usually less clear.

For example, the case has been reported of a Canadian firm that for over two years deferred action on a consultant's report which recommended building an intermediate storage and distribution warehouse, with expected savings to the firm of about two million dollars a year. The simple reason was that no one could decide which department was to operate the proposed warehouse. While this degree of organisational futility is rare, the case nevertheless shows that top managements may have difficulty in making positive decisions concerning the administration of activities that cross departmental boundaries.

Such situations should be detected at the diagnostic stage and the assignment formulated so as to include the appropriate recommendations. If the operating marketing consultant detects such a case, he would be well advised to consult his supervisor, because organisational fuzziness in these areas could slow the progress of the assignment very substantially.

Sales management

The consulting activities in this field are straightforward. Proper training and motivation of salesmen are key items to be checked, as is the way that salesmen share their effective selling time between existing and potential customers, and among large, medium and small accounts. Another point to check is whether the client's advertising is being used to increase salesmen's effectiveness by generating curiosity and interest in the minds of customers. Such interest makes it easier to obtain appointments and helps interviews get off to a good start. This aspect of advertising is particularly important in marketing industrial goods.

Motivation of salesmen is a complex matter, given the conditions under which they work. A wide variety of incentive schemes is in use. The primary motivator, of course, is the payments system which usually has a large commission and bonuses component. The consultant should check that the incentive scheme is at the same time fair to the salesmen and designed to obtain the results desired by the enterprise (to encourage the selling of profitable items in preference to less profitable ones).

Application of information technology can do a great deal to increase salesmen's effectiveness. It can save much time spent in making reports, preparing orders, and so on, and leave more time for active selling, and it can promote more effective selling by making up-to-the-minute information on stock position and other relevant matters available during the interview.

Advertising and promotion

Usually the consultant's client can obtain good advice on these activities from an advertising agency, but occasionally a situation can arise in which those responsible for advertising and promotion are rather uninspired, both at the client's end and at the agency's. The consultant should check that the role of advertising and promotion in the client's marketing mix has been fully thought out, and is consistent with the type of product being sold: for example, "push-pull" advertising for fast moving consumer goods (FMCG), producing leads for salesmen of industrial goods, or image-building for prestige goods; next, he should check that this role has been properly communicated in the brief given to the advertising agency; finally, he should ensure that the agency has correctly interpreted the brief in terms of the advertising message and choice of media.

A common but undesirable practice is that of setting advertising expenditures purely as an arbitrary percentage of sales, either past sales or forecast sales. It is much sounder to plan advertising campaigns in terms of objectives and then calculate the money needed to attain these objectives. This amount may be quite out of line with the resources available, in which case the objectives will have to be redefined on a more modest scale. This method has the advantage of giving the client some idea of what he can expect to achieve with his advertising expenditure.

Recent advances in information technology, allowing the use of large demographic data bases, are leading to changes in advertising practices and the way campaigns are planned and managed. We might expect, for example, that television advertising would concentrate on house image building, with emphasis on sponsoring programmes and such things as sporting events rather than on 15-second and 30-second spots, while the actual selling advertising would be done more by direct mail.

Distribution channels

The trend towards concentration in the retailing of consumer goods is bringing with it corresponding changes in the channel structures for these goods, the manufacturer being increasingly replaced by the retailer as the "channel captain". The reduction in numbers of independent retailers, and their share of trade, is also reducing the importance of the wholesaler, and this trend is being reinforced by the increasing sophistication of the physical distribution process, which reduces the need for the intermediate storage function performed by wholesalers. High interest rates, increasing the costs of holding stock, also contribute to the weakening of the wholesaler. This reduction in available options will mean that the marketing consultant will be less involved than previously in assignments involving channel policies. These will be replaced to some extent by assignments concerning physical distribution.

In developing countries this increase in retail concentration is also present, although so far it is not as advanced as in the developed countries. In the developing countries the wholesaler is still an important factor in the distribution channel. However, the consultant should be aware that many manufacturers, particularly the larger ones, have a tendency to maintain large sales forces who visit retailers directly, bypassing the wholesalers. This may be due to a desire by marketing managers to keep tighter control, but unless the manufacturer has a wide product range it is likely to be excessively costly. The consultant should be able to evaluate the costs of these alternatives.

Franchising is a form of distribution channel which has been widespread in the United States for many years, and is now increasingly being found elsewhere. Marketing consultants have seldom had much work with franchises, but this will probably change as an ever wider variety of goods and services are marketed through this type of structure.

New product development

This is very much an inter-departmental process, involving overall strategy, R and D, engineering, production, finance, and so on. The usual difficulty here is that the marketing department is brought into the process too late. Information about the size of the potential market, competing products, competitors' possible reactions, prices, the way customers will use the product, even the levels of skill that the distributors' staff will be able to devote to servicing and repairing it, ought to be available right from the inception of the product, if the design work is to start off in the right direction. The marketing department's involvement should, if anything, increase as the development progresses.

The consultant's role in this function is twofold. In the first place, he should verify that the marketing department can supply reliable information of the type described (too often marketing departments are only sales departments with a fancy name) and, if not, advise on how to develop this capability. Secondly, he has to ensure that organisational arrangements exist allowing the marketing department to be involved at a suitably early stage. If such arrangements do not exist, then he will have to advise on their creation and operation.

New product development is a vital function, because the firm's future lies in these new products or services. Yet the process of new product development is very often a hit-and-miss affair, which attracts little top-management attention (unless a top manager has suddenly had a "brilliant idea", usually with disastrous consequences).

Packaging

Package design is an intrinsic part of new product design (and is often the major component in refurbishing existing products) and its importance, particularly in the case of fast-moving consumer goods, is often under-rated. The package can be used, as in the case of window-cleaners in spray containers, to enhance convenience in use (or even in after-use, as when honey manufacturers package their products in coffee mugs or beer mugs), and thus give otherwise indistinguishable products a competitive edge. It is an indispensible way of attracting the customers' attention on crowded supermarket shelves, particularly in health and beauty aids, which also offers the talented designer the opportunity of creating a coherent brand image by developing a "matched set" of containers for a range of products. At the same time the package must satisfy the retailers' requirements for stackability (there was a recent case of an otherwise excellent product which flopped because it was in a wedge-shaped package which could not be stacked on a shelf), and protection against pilferage and damage in transit and storage. At the wholesaler and bulk transport level the package has to adapt to the dimensional requirements of palletisation and containerisation, without excessive waste of space.

In the industrial goods field as well, packaging primarily has to take into account the requirements of palletisation and containerisation. But even here the "value added in packaging" concept can be used constructively. For example, diesel-generator sets could be shipped in standardised containers which could be reassembled on site to form sheds for the equipment.

Modern materials and techniques are making packaging a rapidly-developing area. The consultant who expects to undertake marketing assignments should keep abreast of these developments. Subscriptions to one or two of the relevant trade journals and visits to exhibitions would be good professional investments.

14.3 Consulting in commercial enterprises

In this sector stock turnover (stock rotation) is one of the key issues. In a well-run firm this forms the focal point of all activities; purchasing and stock level planning are based on target stock rotation objectives. The consultant's first task in such enterprises is to check the *stock-control procedures*. Often these will be found to be unsatisfactory and suitable procedures will have to be established. Different types of goods need different stock-control systems. There are four main systems, suitable for groceries, general merchandise, fashion goods, and "big-ticket" goods (i.e. furniture, "white goods", expensive cameras) respectively. Many enterprises will need to use two or more of these systems, depending on the variety of goods carried.

The establishment of stock-control procedures comes first, because further work will need the data such procedures will produce. Indeed, very often the assignment need consists of no more than installing good stock-control procedures and training management in using stock-control data in planning and administration.

Some assignments, however, will also have various general management aspects (for example, setting up management-by-objectives schemes in multi-department firms), and sometimes training in specialised techniques will have to be arranged.

The above account for the bulk of what might be called corrective or remedial consulting activities in commercial enterprises. But there are firms that get themselves into more serious trouble through unsound policies. In these cases the remedies are usually obvious, if drastic, and the consultant's main function is to provide management with the moral support needed to make disagreeable or unpalatable decisions.

For example, a retailer of luxury goods (watches, sports goods, and so on) might have been seduced into giving extended credit terms because it is so much easier to sell such goods in this way (especially to irresponsible consumers), only to find himself with accounts receivable equal to six-months' sales or more, largely uncollectable.

Quite often retailers will pick store locations unsuitable for the goods they handle, trying to sell shopping goods in a convenience store site or vice versa. A variation of this situation is the case of the real-estate developer, innocent of all knowledge of retailing or consumer behaviour, who builds a shopping centre and then leases space to retailers of inappropriate type. Problems of this kind appear, and consultants are called to deal with them, soon after the shopping centre "boom" starts in any area. They are quite common in many developing countries.

14.4 International marketing

There was a time when international trade meant that developing countries exported raw materials to, and imported manufactured goods from, developed countries. This simple dichotomy is no longer valid. A rapidly growing variation on this theme (which will probably become dominant in the not-too-distant future) is that developed countries export manufacturing technologies to developing countries, with manufactured goods flowing in the other direction. This leads to corresponding changes in marketing consultancy, with developed-country consultants being asked to evaluate prospective host-country markets in connection with proposed technology-transfer activities through joint ventures or other arrangements, and developing-country consultants having to evaluate developed-country markets for manufactured goods and set up suitable marketing channels. Consultants in both developed and developing countries will have to polish up their knowledge of export credit guarantee (ECG) systems, preferential tariff systems, "most-favoured-nation" and GATT agreements, and other arrangements that influence international trading. They will also, of course, have to find out how much of their marketing experience is culture-specific, and so not transferable to other countries.

In addition to this new trend in international marketing, the consultant may also be asked to advise on the more traditional form of export marketing. This differs from international marketing in degree rather than kind, the principal differences being the complications of the required paperwork (shipping firms will usually take the responsibility for executing this) and the additional difficulties of working with distributors in a remote country (language, distance, product training and support, etc.). Bankers, with their international contacts, can be helpful in checking references and credit ratings, and the exporter and his consultant can call upon the services of the commercial attaché of the national embassy in the destination country.[4]

The main point to keep in mind about going into exporting is that it is *not* a quick fix for getting rid of surplus goods or finding an outlet for spare production capacity. Developing an effective international distribution network requires time and effort, and must be taken very seriously if any success is to be obtained. There must be a definite commitment of financial and human resources to a planned programme with a specific objective.

14.5 Physical distribution

At long last physical distribution is coming to be regarded as a distinct (and serious) activity, accounting for a substantial part of the total costs of an enterprise. Consultants will find themselves increasingly being asked for advice in this area.

Complications arising in such assignments will have three sources. First, there is the problem of arriving at a clear definition of the authority and responsibilities of the distribution manager, as the physical distribution function is affected by decisions made in all departments, from purchasing through to sales, and procedures that minimise costs within each department will not necessarily result in the lowest overall cost. This can result in difficulties in reconciling conflicting objectives. Secondly, very few firms have cost-accounting systems geared to reporting physical distribution costs, so the assignment will usually have to be extended to include changes in cost accounting. Thirdly, although a substantial amount of operations research work has been done in this area and some useful results obtained on some topics (for example, vehicle scheduling), there are still no algorithms which can conveniently be used in physical distribution planning, for calculating how to arrive at overall lowest costs. Trial-and-error methods are too time consuming to be practicable in a system of any complexity. Computer-based simulation programmes ease this problem, and the advent of decentralised computer availability can make such programmes part of the regular tool-kit of physical distribution management.

14.6 Public relations

This is an area which is both a part of marketing, in that it is a component of the marketing mix, and at the same time transcends marketing in that it addresses a much wider audience than simply the firm's customers. This audience includes the general public, government regulating agencies, shareholders, and the firm's employees themselves. However, it is in the nature of public relations (PR) that the corporate image which PR seeks to create in the minds of these various sub-audiences will inevitably feed back into and affect the image held by the firm's customers — a presentation given to stock market analysts and reported in the financial pages of the newspapers cannot be kept secret from customers — so it is important for the marketing department to be involved in the design of all PR campaigns. If not, conflicting images may be created.

Expenditure on PR has increased dramatically in recent years, as companies have started to use it pro-actively rather than simply reactively. Press conferences are tending to replace (at much greater expense) press releases, PR consultants are being brought in, some to train executives how to handle media interviews, and others to advise on corporate image creation. It is likely that this trend will continue, in accordance with the trend noted earlier for broadcast advertising to focus on image building while the actual "selling proposition" communications rely more on direct mail shots and developments in information technology.

As far as the consultant is concerned, this tendency means that he should check that the images which the client's advertising and PR efforts seek to create are consistent with each other, and that the client's internal organisation is such that there is close liaison between the marketing and PR functions. He may also recommend training in how to handle media interviews for a selection of the client's senior managers. Statements made by named officers of the firm carry much more conviction than those made by an anonymous spokesman, but this is a two-edged weapon, and a clumsily handled interview can generate undesirable publicity even if the underlying situation is favourable to the firm.

---

[1] T. Levitt: "Marketing myopia" in *Harvard Business Review*, July-Aug. 1960. See also T. Levitt: *The marketing imagination* (New York, The Free Press, 1983).

[2] P. Drucker: *Managing for results* (New York, Harper and Row, 1964).

[3] See R. A. Garda: "The successful marketing managers gain the decisive pricing edge" in *Management Review*, Nov. 1983 pp. 19-22.

[4] A very useful series of publications on export marketing, covering market studies, use of trade fairs, packaging, and general advice, is available from the International Trade Centre (ITC) in Geneva.

CONSULTING IN PRODUCTION MANAGEMENT

15

Production is essentially a process of transforming certain inputs into some required outputs in the form of goods or services. As such, a production function does not apply exclusively to manufacturing operations but also to other activities, such as construction and transport operations, health or even office services.

This process of transformation requires decision making on the part of the production manager with a view to getting an output of the desired quantity and quality delivered by the required date and at a minimum cost. The consultant's task is to advise management, whenever necessary, on the best means of achieving such an objective. In most cases, a production management consultant is able, in the performance of his functions, to measure and assess the fruits of his work quite tangibly. In this sense, he is probably in a more fortunate situation than his colleagues in other areas, such as general or personnel management.

In the production area, problems submitted to the consultant may have very different degrees of importance to the client organisation.

At one end of the scale there are problems which belong to the group of "basic choices". A production consultant may have an important say in a team which is examining the client's total strategy: for example, problems involving the adoption of a business strategy that aims at a high-quality product, or problems dealing with seasonal or low capacity utilisation. In this case, the production consultant forms part of a team that usually includes consultants in other areas (such as marketing and finance).

At the opposite end of the scale there are myriad problems whose common denominator is the need to meet certain criteria with regard to productivity, cost, or job satisfaction in the performance of specific production tasks. Such problems tend to be operational in nature. But the consultant will be well advised not to lose sight of the broader needs of the client organisation, as it is not unusual for assignments in very specific production fields to disclose problems that are much more profound and lie outside the scope of the production area itself.

More recently, rapid advances in technology, in particular the increased use of computers in manufacturing operations, have put pressure on many organisations to introduce what may be generally known as computer integrated manufacturing. In several cases, this introduction has been made or is being sought to "keep up with the others", and without the necessary preparatory work being thoroughly done. Computer applications have found their way into production through computer assisted design (CAD) and computer assisted manufacturing (CAM). There have been several developments in CAM, as well as the introduction of flexible manufacturing systems (FMS), which will be referred to later in this chapter, and in chapter 19. The production consultant would do well to remind his client organisation that if the layout is poor, the product design old, production planning and control not the best, and standards loose, transferring these ills to a computerised manufacturing system is not going to help much.

Furthermore, it is the rule rather than the exception that new technology is introduced side by side with traditional technology. This may be a permanent feature of a transition phase, and the consultant must be able to diagnose the problems and improve the efficiency, particularly of traditional technology, either for increasing productivity and cutting costs, or as a prelude to the introduction of advanced technology.

In performing this task, the consultant can approach it systematically, keeping in mind three major aspects:

● the product or products;
● the methods and organisation of work;
● the people involved.

The consultant can concentrate on any of these areas in line with the agreement reached with the client. In many cases, however, this classification is somewhat artificial — problems to do with product quality, for example, may be due to poor methods of work, or poor training of workers, and so on. Nevertheless, for the purpose of structuring his thoughts the consultant will find this approach helpful.

Within each area, the consultant has at his disposal a variety of production and management techniques ranging from the simple to the more complex. In the production planning area, for example, techniques used in solving planning problems can range from simple bar charts to network planning to more advanced operation research tools such as waiting line models. The choice invariably depends on the situation faced and the degree of sophistication of the industry concerned. No attempt will be made in this chapter to describe these techniques. They can be referred to in various publications dealing with production management and operations research. Instead, we will concentrate on the systematic approach to identifying and prescribing methods for improving productivity, reducing production costs, and improving quality, so that the consultant develops an approach to problem-solving which is problem-oriented rather than technique-oriented.

15.1 The product

A product starts as a single substance or a multitude of raw materials, processed so as to give quality characteristics that match a pre-determined standard. It is rare, however, to find enterprises that produce only one product. What we usually have is a "product line", or a composite of many products, which are sometimes produced to order or produced for stock or both. In the majority of cases, only a few products will form either the bulk of items produced or represent the most expensive (and presumably yield the highest rate of return). The consultant would then be well advised to start the assignment by analysing this product line to identify the one or more products representing the bulk of production, or the highest value, and to focus his attention on certain major areas in respect of this particular product or products. At the same time, this analysis may help to bring another question to the fore: is there a need for all these product variations, or can some products be eliminated or standardised? Obviously the answer to such a question needs to be taken in consultation with the marketing specialists and the management of the enterprise. The production areas that need to be looked into with respect to the products concerned are:

- product design;
- raw or semi-finished materials utilisation;
- control of inventory (stock);
- control of quality.

Product design

It may come as a surprise to the consultant who is starting his career to find that this area rarely receives the attention it deserves. In many cases, a traditional or a successful product will continue to be produced for years without enough thought being given to its design features. In other cases, product design is considered to fall solely within the domain of the marketing staff, and it is left to them to make all decisions in this area. Development work leading to a design involves more than just producing an appealing product. It should be based on the full co-operation of several enterprise functions, particularly marketing, production and costing.

On the production side, the consultant is concerned with the fact that a design will normally predetermine the process and method of work, the type of raw materials, jigs or fixtures, or materials-handling equipment that will be used. This is true of the product as well as of its constituent parts. The most frequent questions that the consultant needs to ask are:

- How many parts is the product composed of — can some parts be eliminated through better design, and have any unnecessary features been removed?
- Can certain component parts be standardised to match parts of other products and so enable the use of the same machines, tools, jigs and fixtures?

- Can some components be replaced by cheaper ones which would perform the same function? (For example, in the chemical or cosmetic industries some fillers can easily be replaced by others.)
- Does the design lend itself to easy handling?
- Can a change in the design eliminate one or more processes? (For example, a process of stamping a metal product may eliminate one or more processes of assembly, though it could also alter the appearance of the product.)
- Can some component parts be standardised and yet by using them in different combinations variety in the product line still be obtained? (An example is standardising length, width and depth (LxWxD) in cabinet making. By having no more than two different measurements for each of the LxWxD, it is possible to have eight different sizes of cupboards or sideboards, and such a standardisation would enable longer production runs for the component parts.)

The consultant knows that products have to be matched with the equipment on which they are manufactured (e.g. with its dimensions, precision, productivity and cost), and vice versa. In a number of cases, he may have to examine this relationship and make recommendations to the client concerning either the product, or the equipment used, or both. As mentioned earlier, any proposed modifications in product design should be checked with the marketing specialists for their marketing penetration potential.

Utilisation of materials

While the focus of attention here is on the raw materials which go to shaping the final product, the assignment can be extended to cover other materials used in the production process, such as packaging material, fuel and even paints and lubricants. This is an area where substantial savings can be achieved without too much effort, particularly in certain industries such as garment making, furniture, metallic products and the like. It stands to reason that the higher the percentage of material cost, the more there is a need for a proper investigation of this area. There are three approaches to reducing the waste of material:

- design changes, with a view to reducing waste of raw material;
- if the design cannot be changed, then efforts may be undertaken to improve the yield, by changing the method that is used in cutting garments, metal, or wood so as to reduce waste to a minimum, or by changing the original size of the raw material used;
- inevitably some waste will result during the various sequences of production. Two questions should come to mind: can this waste be reworked to yield another by-product or component, or can it be sold? For example, the process of wine making produces a residue which is mainly sodium potassium tartrate. This is sometimes treated as waste that needs to be disposed of. In fact, it can be converted into tartaric acid, an expensive product used as a preservative in the confectionery industry.

It should also be borne in mind that a certain percentage of waste invariably results during the various sequences of a production operation. Some operations generate more waste than others, and therefore the analysis of the problem needs to concentrate on operations producing the most waste or by-products.

Inventory control

The consultant needs to keep in mind three types of inventory: *raw materials, work-in-progress* and *finished products.* One general principle should govern all these: the need to keep them at a minimum but safe level. For raw materials and finished products, a safe level is one that allows for uncertainty of delivery or avoids opportunity costs resulting from lost sales. This "safety stock" usually known as "buffer stock", is not a justification for having a high stock level, nor is it to be used indiscriminately to take advantage of quantity discounts or special deals.

For finished products, the desired level of stock needs to be determined in close consultation with the marketing and finance specialists in an effort to balance opportunity costs (the probability of lost sales if one runs out of stock) against carrying charges (the cost of carrying the inventory).

Great savings in carrying charges can be made if the work-in-progress inventory is kept at a minimum. This system has been cited as one of the main features of Japanese industry.[1] To achieve it, however, the consultant may have to look at the balance of operations, remove or reduce bottlenecks, and propagate the virtues of a system whereby no or very little inventory is allowed to accumulate beside each machine.

Most consultants approach the problem of the raw materials inventory by analysing the values of the various items to distinguish the "A" items (which are few in number but very costly) from "B" and "C" (the latter being the great multitude of relatively cheap items that are carried in stock).

An ordering strategy is then developed for the "A" items resting on the use of inventory models to determine the economic order quantity by balancing ordering costs against carrying charges. Quantity discounts can also be evaluated against incremental carrying charges, and a decision can then be reached as to when a quantity discount offer can be attractive. The problem, however, lies in the determination of the buffer stock level. Under normal circumstances, this is calculated by balancing opportunity costs against carrying charges. For the "B" items, ordering is carried out through regular review of stock, or whenever a minimum level is reached. For "C" items, mass orders may be placed at certain points in time.

This is the ideal situation, but in actual practice the skill of the consultant lies in his ability to move from the ideal to the practical. For example, in the case of a wholesaler of various widths and varieties of lumber, a comparatively arbitrary choice must be made for the classification of "A" items. In addition, the economic order quantity may prove impractical for various reasons. If the lumber wholesaler imports certain varieties from, say, the USSR or Canada, shipping from certain ports is not always possible during the winter months, and there is a need to readjust ordering points. Apart from that, an order quantity may prove too small to be shipped to a distant area. The question of buffer stock also needs careful consideration. In many cases, uncertainty of sources of supply or of transportation, the availability of foreign exchange, or the anticipation of inflationary trends, necessitate a re-assessment of the level of the buffer stock to be carried with a view to adjusting it from the rational to the practical.

The object of the above discussion is not to dissuade a consultant from applying scientific methods to inventory control, but to impress upon him that once such inventory strategies have been devised, they should be discussed with management and re-adjusted as needed.

The organisation of stock records is another area for intervention. In some cases, the feasibility of introducing computerised inventory systems (if these do not already exist) should be investigated. In other cases, it might even be possible to do away with record-keeping and depend on physical control for the sake of simplicity. For example, for an item like ribbons (a "C" item), a retail outlet keeping several "in-out" stock records depending on width, colour and material may well be advised to discard such entries in favour of a simple visual method such as the "two-bin" system.[2]

Quality control

It would be worth while to distinguish between acceptable quality standards for raw materials and those for finished products. For the former, a consultant should enquire whether or not the established standards for acceptability are too high, making these materials more expensive than is warranted, or too loose, resulting in a larger percentage of defects and rejects during the production operation.

During processing, each machine or operation produces its own variation from the established standard. These variations from the standard can be determined and a quality control chart is then drawn up setting upper and lower limits of tolerance. Falling outside these limits justifies rejection of the project. A consultant can be called upon to set up such tolerance limits, decide on inspection points within the operations and the sampling frequency and method to be used. In several cases, however, variations from the standard are automatically recorded avoiding the use of traditional quality controllers.

Of more interest, however, is the effort a consultant can undertake to decrease the fluctuations of quality with respect to the standard. The spectacular improvement in the quality of Japanese products over the last twenty years is credited to the fact that quality and dependability have become a goal that needs to be pursued by various personnel alongside cost reduction and not as a dimension that can be relaxed to reduce cost.[3] In other words, quality need not be at odds with costs. Here is where a consultant can make a useful contribution in the form of proposals for better training and involvement of the personnel (this latter aspect will be further examined), as well as proposals to up-date or improve methods of work.

15.2 Methods and organisation of production

Under this major heading, attention should be given to the following areas:
- flow of work and layout;
- materials handling;
- production planning;
- job and work methods;
- setting performance standards;
- maintenance operations;
- energy savings.

Flow of work and layout

The organisation's production operations normally fall under three major descriptions. First, *production by fixed position*, in which case the product is stationary and the workers and equipment move, as in building aeroplanes, heavy generators, or ships. Improvement in layout can sometimes be brought about by attempting to shorten the distances travelled by men, materials and equipment. However, the margin of manoeuvrability is rather limited.

Secondly, *line production*, where the equipment and machinery are arranged according to the sequence of operations, as in bottling plants, car assembly, and food canning operations. In these cases, the layout is more or less inherent in the sequence of operations which determines how the machinery is placed. Nevertheless, two sorts of issue can be examined by the consultant: the original balance of operations, and the problems which result from the fact that, in many cases, as the enterprise develops and the product line expands, or demand for the product changes, additional lines may be added which do not often work in harmony with the original line. The operations can therefore become unbalanced with certain stages producing at a faster rate than subsequent or preceding stages. A schematic diagram showing the sequence of operations and the time it takes to perform each one can be quite helpful. Depending on the type of problem faced and the complexity of the situation, correcting for balance can range from simple proposals, e.g. increasing work stations on parts of the line, additional machines, improvement in the method of work, to more sophisticated heuristic methods.[4]

The third type of organisation is that of *functional arrangement*, where all identical machinery is grouped together and the products move between these machines, depending on the sequence required for each. This is the case in many woodworking workshops and in the textile industry. This type of arrangement allows the consultant to do more to improve productivity through a better layout and organisation of operations. The key is to identify whether among the many finished products there is one or more constituting a sufficiently high percentage in terms of volume. The machinery needed to produce such items is then detached from a functional layout and arranged along a line layout flow. The gains in productivity in this case can be substantial.

The consultant could arrive at improvements, both for a functional and a line type of layout, by looking for the following:

- bulky or heavy material that is moved further than smaller or lighter material;
- a workplace that is either too congested (making access to machinery or equipment difficult) or too large for requirements;
- backtracking of work in progress or cross flow with other products;
- unused space overhead, particularly in stores;
- aisles that are not free or marked, materials lying about, and untidy working conditions.

Line operations require substantial production runs to render them economical. They also suffer from inherent inflexibility. Recently, the introduction of flexible manufacturing systems (FMS) has alleviated this problem. FMS consists of a series of numerically controlled machines, automated materials handling systems, and software for production planning and control. This integrated system makes it possible for a production line to turn out tens of products in tiny batches as quickly as in typical mass production. In some countries and some processes of manufacturing, such a system is as economical as traditional assembly line operations.

Once the need for tackling a layout assignment becomes apparent, a consultant must collect information on the space requirements for machinery, storage, work in progress, and auxiliary services (canteens, washrooms, telephone installations, etc.), calculate the space required, determine and plot the flow of work, and then integrate the space needs with the plotted flow.[5] An important consideration is that of making cost estimates of the proposed layout by comparing savings in space, equipment and labour costs with the cost of additional space, handling or storage equipment.

Materials handling

Most materials and products are moved from one place to another during a production operation. This movement is normally carried out manually, by using gravity (chutes), by the use of conveyors, cranes, or different types of truck such as fork-lift trucks, or robots. Within each of these broad categories there is a multitude of variations. Trucks can be electric or petrol driven, and have varying capacities for handling weights and many accessories and attachments to cope with a multitude of dimensions and shapes. Computer-assisted materials handling and retrieval equipment are also gaining increased acceptance. Catalogues of manufacturers, as well as materials-handling associations' literature, can be consulted on the choice of equipment, for cost estimates, speed, load, flexibility and maintenance needs.

The consultant should bear in mind three important issues. First, economy in handling can be achieved as the size of the unit and speed of transportation are increased. Secondly, versatile equipment and methods which can be used for several products are to be preferred to those that are mainly designed for a single product. Thirdly, gravity should be used as much as possible.

Production planning

The choice of the planning method to be used depends on the nature of the operation. In normal functional (also known as process) or line production operations, as mentioned earlier, various methods of planning can be applied, ranging from the sophisticated use of mathematical models for queuing or waiting line models to normal scheduling and charting. However, special projects, such as the construction of a plant or building of a ship, necessitate the use of network planning methods such as CPM or PERT [6] which allow a more rational allocation of resources.

In the case of production that is geared for distribution (as distinct from made-to-order or special projects), the starting point for a planning process is the forecast of demand which is worked out with the marketing specialists. A consultant should check the reliability of such a forecast before going into production planning itself. A discrepancy between sales forecasting and production planning can result in either lost orders or carrying excess inventory, and is often a subject of contention between the marketing and production departments. In addition to the forecast, which is translated into an aggregate of operations for various products in the product mix, the consultant has to calculate the machine hours required for each product component, determine the total working time, and introduce a certain flexibility in his planning system to allow for emergency situations.

The difficulty lies in the fact that invariably there are *bottleneck operations*, but instead of concentrating on them, many consultants gear their planning and scheduling to all operations. An effective analytical and planning exercise should indicate shortages of machines or operators' hours in certain work centres and present to management proposals to relieve these difficulties.

Production planning, particularly with a large product mix, or where hundreds of components are involved, becomes far more manageable if a computer is used. This is also true of network planning involving more than 200 activities. Finally, a control system must also be established with a feedback mechanism to check progress and adjust plans accordingly.

Job and work methods

Traditionally this has been an area where much of a production consultant's time is spent. But as production operations become highly mechanised, automated, or robotised, the scope for work in this area becomes increasingly limited.

A consultant working in this field examines the way a certain operation is being performed and attempts to develop an easier and more effective method. He utilises a number of well-known charts such as the operation chart, the flow chart, and man/machine and activity charts. He should also understand ergonomics, an essential element of job design.

While numerous jobs lend themselves to methods improvement, a consultant should give priority to those that are critical, because they either constitute a bottleneck or are repeated by a number of operators.

A consultant will find it most useful to invite workers', foremen's and managers' suggestions, to involve them in the working out of a new method. In many cases, production workers and technicians will be able to point to improvements that can well escape the consultant.

Setting performance standards [7]

This is probably one of the most intricate problems that faces a production consultant. Performance standards are needed for a variety of reasons, including the determination of labour costs, and hence the ability to decide on matters of pricing and bidding; in "make or buy" decisions; in machine replacement problems, and so on. Such standards are essential for production planning, wages and incentive schemes. Invariably a certain standard exists for every piece of work performed, either a formal recorded standard, or a perceived informal standard which a foreman or a worker estimates for a given job. The consultant is called upon either to review a formal standard or to establish one. A crucial point is the need to perform the assignment with the knowledge and approval of the persons whose performance is to be assessed, and of the trade unions.

Generally speaking, a consultant can use one of three methods: work sampling, a stop-watch time study, or predetermined time standards. Alternatively he may opt for a combination of two or all of these methods at a given working place. For example, he may use work sampling to determine the allowances to be included in a "standard time" based on stop-watch observations.

Work sampling is probably the easiest method of assessing the percentage of time worked and the distribution and causes of idle time. Since it is based on random observations, its reliability depends on sampling and sample size that can give a certain degree of confidence. Hence, if work sampling is to be attempted, a consultant should first determine what sort of confidence level is needed. The answer will depend on the intended use of his data. If he is interested merely in a quick estimation of the percentage of effective working time, the confidence level may be relaxed and sample size can be smaller.

Stop-watch time study is probably the most widely used method of measuring performance. Through sampling and timing, a consultant arrives at a certain "observed time for a given job". This has to be converted into "normal time" by a process of performance rating in which he rates a certain pace of performance as "standard". If he has been timing an operation which he rates as 80 per cent of this standard, then he has to adjust his "observed time" accordingly. However, performance rating is based on personal judgement and as such is a subject of controversy. Various suggestions have been made to cope with this problem, but rating is still based on the judgement of the observer to a great extent. Achieving

272

a certain consistency can be enhanced both by experience and by cross-checking with other observers.

The transformation of a "normal time" into a "standard time" requires the addition of allowances for delays normal to the job, allowances for personal needs, and fatigue allowances. The latter two, sometimes grouped together under the title of relaxation allowances, again raise controversy. Some research has been undertaken to determine what the fatigue allowance should be for a given job content and working conditions. It is difficult, however, to imagine an answer that can cater for all possible work situations. It is also uncertain whether or not research applicable to certain ethnic, climatic and other very specific conditions can be extrapolated to apply to other conditions. In making his assessment of allowances, a consultant should discuss them freely in order to achieve an agreement with both workers and management.

Predetermined time standards (PTS) offer certain advantages. They permit a quantitative means of comparing alternative methods of work without disturbing the existing methods, and can be used even before an operation has been established. They also avoid the rating problem and hence help to develop more consistent standards. They do, however, suffer from several weaknesses. They are generally designed for mass production and can become expensive for individual jobs; they also have limitations in machine-controlled operations, and the basic idea on which they are based, that motions can be added and subtracted, has been challenged.

Another issue is that over 200 different systems of PTS exist at present and are known by trade names, such as MTM, WF, DMT,[8] and so on, and a consultant has to decide which one is most appropriate for his purposes. He may, in this case, rely also on assistance not only from the literature but from associations such as the MTM Associations which exist in certain countries.

It may be useful to summarise the approach a consultant can follow to determine the standards of performance, and to ensure as much consistency as possible. The main steps can be as follows:

(1) identify the jobs or the activities for which standards are desirable, taking into consideration the cost and practicality of developing and applying such standards;

(2) on that basis determine the degree of coverage needed (standards to be established for all or certain jobs, departments and/or products);

(3) break the jobs into elements and attempt to have as many common elements as possible;

(4) decide whether to use macroscopic systems (e.g. stop-watch time study), or microscopic systems (predetermined time standards), or a combination of both, in which case decide what parts of the job will be measured by what system (the nature of the job and costs being a determining factor);

(5) if stop-watch time study is used, check for consistency among common elements performed in various areas of the workplace, and make sure

there are enough data to permit an estimation of observed time with a required degree of confidence;

(6) if PTS is used, make sure that the elements of the job can be readily deduced from the system of PTS that was chosen; it is also preferable to make spot checks with a stop-watch to verify whether PTS timetables need readjustment (this may become necessary when using a PTS table in another culture).

Needless to say, the development of performance standards assumes that the method of work has already been improved or cannot be varied, since any change in the working method would necessitate setting another standard.

Maintenance

The consultant should enquire about the methods used for maintaining and repairing equipment and machinery. In particular, he should find out:

- how normal greasing and lubrication is done and whose responsibility it is to do it;
- if a preventive maintenance scheme exists, whether it is justified, and how it is implemented;
- whether a proper inspection schedule exists;
- if a cost estimate of repairs is made and kept for each machine.

He should also enquire about emergency repairs and consider whether increasing the size of the maintenance crew could reduce the length of time machines are down. In addition, a consultant can examine whether the life of certain individual components of equipment or machines could be prolonged through either redesign or change of lubricant. Finally, he should study machine replacement problems in relation to maintenance costs.

If major equipment is to be overhauled, especially in process industries, the consultant can help the client to achieve considerable savings by introducing scheduling for such operations (applying network planning techniques if necessary).

Because disruption of production due to machine breakdowns can be very costly, there is a growing trend towards making production staff more maintenance-conscious. Seminars on proper identification of causes of breakdowns, and on the training of both production operators and maintenance crew (which may suggest assigning a certain responsibility to operators for simple oiling and lubrication), could be followed up with performance review seminars at a later stage. Approaches involving all personnel, not only maintenance specialists, can pay handsome dividends.[9]

Energy savings

With the steep rise in energy costs, there is a need to achieve substantial savings in the use of energy. These can result from simple good housekeeping (such as checking that thermostats are functioning and properly set, steam and air leaks repaired, and so on) through minor investments in additional insulation, heat recuperators, power-factor correction and the like, up to major investment decisions about changing over to low waste, low energy processes. Many of these issues can be highly technical in nature and would require the intervention of specialists. Nevertheless, the production consultant's contribution lies essentially in examining whether a potential saving in energy costs can be achieved, bringing this to the attention of his client organisation, and assisting management in deciding how to set up and implement an energy-conservation programme.

15.3 The human aspects of production

The human element is the determining factor in any operation. It would be naive to propose, let alone implement, any recommendation without the involvement of the employees concerned and without examining its impact on people. There are two major areas in production management consultations to be considered in this respect: physical working conditions and safety considerations; and job enrichment and group work.

Physical working conditions and safety [10]

The consultant needs to pay attention to measures at the place of work to protect the worker from adverse conditions of temperature, humidity, light and noise levels, as well as air contaminants, dust and radiation, exposure to which may cause poisoning or occupational diseases.

The ideal situation exists if hazards can be either eliminated altogether, or the workers removed from direct contact with hazardous situations. If this proves not to be feasible, then either the source of hazard should be isolated or the worker provided with protective equipment and clothing.

A common misconception is to concentrate on the so-called technical aspects of accident prevention — the provision of protective gloves, boots or goggles, and guards for machinery. In most plants, however, over half of the accidents are caused more through human misjudgement and negligence than through the absence of guards or protective equipment.

The consultant can discover much revealing information by analysing, from past accident records, the causes of accidents, the department, hour of the day, and day of the week in which they most frequently occur, and even the person injured. This information can prove invaluable for a concerted plan of action to introduce a scheme of safety which should invariably include training.

Since accidents can happen despite all precautions, it is appropriate to check on the availability and adequacy of health care, first aid, emergency and sanitation facilities, as well as fire protection systems.

Job enrichment and group work

Most production consultants are productivity conscious and underestimate the need for job satisfaction. In a production environment, the process design, the method of work, the arrangement of work assignments and physical working conditions greatly affect the worker's satisfaction. So a consultant would do well to examine the implications his proposed changes could have not only on productivity but also on job satisfaction.

There are several ways that job satisfaction may be increased, including the possibility of both job enlargement and job enrichment. Task time cycles can be lengthened, particularly in the case of tedious monotonous jobs; work can be made more varied by adding other tasks to the original one, or more authority may be delegated to a worker who can then take his own decisions on certain work-related matters.

In the last twenty years considerable research has been done on group work under various names: new forms of work organisation, socio-technical systems, industrial democracy and semi-autonomous groups. Whole factories (for example, the Volvo plant in Kalmar, Sweden) have been designed around these concepts, and many industries in Japan, Europe, North America, Australia, and some developing countries, have introduced such systems with a reasonable degree of success. These systems rest on two fundamental concepts. First, in designing and modifying work, it is necessary to consider the technical and social issues together. Thus improved methods of work have to be reconciled with the social needs of the working group in terms of factors such as the variety and the degree of challenge the job offers, the opportunities of learning and advancement and so on. Secondly, people performing a certain task should participate in redesigning their own job.[11]

Over twenty years ago, a movement started in Japan aimed initially at organising workers in small groups whose task was to propose improvements in quality. These so-called "quality circles" have over the years extended their scope of activities to cost reduction and productivity improvement.[12] The success of the quality circles idea prompted many companies in developed and developing countries alike to follow the Japanese model, adapting several of its features, with varying degrees of success. It is clear that the participation of production workers and supervisors in issues relating to their work is gaining wider acceptance.

Involvement and participation may sound at odds with a production consultant's job. This is not the case; all depends on his own attitude. A consultant who approaches his assignment believing that he knows all the answers and wanting to impose his views will invariably fail. There are many technical and human aspects of each job that have to be taken into consideration when designing or modifying an operation, and a consultant cannot be expected to know every detail. He may be surprised to find how readily people will respond to his enquiries (and offer helpful suggestions or improvements) if they feel he is sincere, appreciates their views and has their needs and interests at heart. A consultant who develops such an attitude will soon find out that involvement and participation, far from being obstacles are key factors in the success of his assignment.

¹ R. Hayes: "Why Japanese factories work" in *Havard Business Review*, July-Aug. 1981, p. 59.

² A system whereby an item in stock is divided and placed in two boxes; when the first box is empty, this constitutes a signal for reordering.

³ S. Wheelwright: "Japan — Where operations really are strategic" in *Harvard Business Review*, July-Aug. 1981, p. 71.

⁴ See E. S. Buffa: *Operating management: The management of production systems* (New York, Wiley, 1976).

⁵ See for example, ILO: *Introduction to work study*, Third (revised) edition (Geneva, International Labour Office, 1979), pp. 107-111.

⁶ CPM = Critical Path Method; PERT = Programme Evaluation and Review Technique.

⁷ For a more detailed discussion of how to achieve improvement in working methods and in setting performance standards refer to ILO: *Introduction to work study* (Geneva, 1979), parts 2 and 3.

⁸ MTM = Methods-Time Measurement; WF = Work Factor; DMT = Dimensional Motion Times.

⁹ See for example ILO: *Results-oriented maintenance management programme: A preliminary report*, Man. Dev./27, (Geneva, International Labour Office, 1982, mimeographed), a report which describes the work done by the ILO team in this field in collaboration with the Ethiopian Management Institute.

¹⁰ For more information, refer to ILO: *Introduction to work study* (Geneva, 1979), chapter 6.

¹¹ For more information on new forms of work organisation and how to introduce them, see G. Kanawaty: *Managing and developing new forms of work organisation*, Second (revised) edition, (Geneva, International Labour Office, 1981).

¹² See *Productivity and quality control: The Japanese experience* (Tokyo, Japan External Trade Organisation, 1981); and *Quality circles: New approach to productivity* (New York, Alexander Hamilton Institute, 1981).

CONSULTING IN HUMAN RESOURCE MANAGEMENT AND DEVELOPMENT 16

16.1 The changing nature of the personnel function

Personnel management, one of the traditional areas of management consulting, has undergone many changes over the last 20 to 30 years and has to be looked at from a historical perspective.

When consultants started dealing with the "people" side of business organisations, most of them tended to confine their interventions to problems grouped under the term "personnel administration". In French-speaking countries, for example, personnel problems were included in the so-called *gestion administrative* (administrative management). In typical cases, a personnel administration specialist dealt mainly with personnel records, regulations and procedures, and with questions of job evaluation and remuneration.

The main changes that currently affect the nature and role of the personnel function occur in the following areas.

First, the subjects of personnel management — people working in organisations — have changed in very many respects. People have become better educated and prepared for their jobs, more aware of their rights, better informed and more interested in many issues that used to be the exclusive domain of politicians or government officials. Their value systems have changed; their employment and life aspirations have increased. Human relations within organisations have become quite complex, diversified and difficult to handle. These changes in organisations reflect not only technological changes but also the significant trends of social change, such as the democratisation of political and social life in more and more countries, or the emergence of new social organisations and pressure groups (e.g. the environmentalists, or the consumerists).

Secondly, an increased number of personnel issues, including conditions of employment, work and remuneration, is regulated by legislation, or has become the subject of collective agreements between workers' and employers' organisations. When dealing with these questions the personnel consultant must be fully aware of the existing legal and labour-relations frameworks, of the role

279

of the trade unions, and of the need to inform or consult them (in conformity with local practice).

Thirdly, many new approaches to the "human element" in organisations have emerged. People began to be viewed as the most valuable resource of an organisation, and a number of conclusions were drawn from this basic premise as to ways of treating people and motivating them for higher performance, the role of leadership, the investment in training and development, or the choice of staff development systems. This has been linked with advances in the behavioural sciences, in particular in psychology and sociology applied to the functioning of organisations and to the relations between individuals and groups within organisations. A wide range of "organisational development" theories and concepts emerged, and began to be applied to the analysis of human problems in organisations, and to methods likely to increase the effectiveness of individuals and groups in achieving organisational goals.

These new approaches gave birth to the global concept of "human resource management and development", as distinct from the more narrow concept of "personnel administration or management". This, of course, is only a tendency. It would be an error to think that any "human resource manager" will by definition apply a more scientific and more comprehensive approach to managing people than his predecessor — the "personnel manager". Yet the understanding of human aspirations and motives and of interpersonal processes has increased quite considerably, and a growing number of personnel specialists, as well as general managers, make use of this knowledge in their work.

Fourthly, it has been increasingly recognised that the management of people is more culture-bound and value-laden than any other area of management. Practices regarded as standard in one country or organisation may be unthinkable in another environment (e.g. flexible working hours, open-plan offices, dining-rooms common to all staff irrespective of position and grade, direct access to top managers, or the use of confidential personnel files). Both personnel practitioners and management consultants have become more cautious and more selective in transferring personnel practices from one environment to another when dealing with people of different ethnic, social, cultural, religious and educational backgrounds. Sensitivity to these differences has increased with the growth of international business, the advent of modern enterprises and organisations in developing countries, the expanding employment of foreign workers and managers, and the improvements in management education.

Thus, after a period of moderate and even diminishing interest in such issues, we find ourselves living in an area when the role of personnel management is being reassessed and enhanced, new demands formulated, and new approaches developed. This creates many fresh opportunities for consultants in human resource management and development (the term used in this chapter). Both the personnel specialists and the general managers face increasingly complex human problems and find it difficult to keep informed about all conditions and factors to be considered in personnel decisions. In many cases they will appreciate help from an independent and objective human resource professional.

16.2 Policies, practices and the human resource audit

In the early stages of an assignment the consultant and the client may agree that a thorough diagnosis of the human resource management function is a desirable starting point and should be undertaken before deciding how to focus the consultant's intervention. Often the consultant will be told that there are organisational policies for dealing with the major elements of the personnel function — for example, recruitment, staff development, promotion and transfer, salary increments, labour-management relations, etc. The consultant may first attempt to conduct an appraisal of existing personnel policies and procedures by investigating, analysing and comparing policies with actual results obtained over a set period, by means of a systematic, in-depth audit.

Before starting to prepare a research design to uncover the necessary hard data, the consultant is likely to find that the alleged "policies" are often only pious hopes and good intentions. For a personnel policy to be worthy of the name it should fulfil several criteria:

(1) policy should be written, understandable, and present a comprehensive coverage of the function;

(2) provision should be made for ensuring dissemination and comprehension of stated policy throughout the organisation;

(3) policy should be soundly based, consistent with public policy and that of comparable organisations;

(4) policy should be internally consistent with the organisation's stated general objectives and policies;

(5) specific personnel policies (e.g. staffing, development and administration) should be mutually supportive;

(6) policy should be established as a result of multi-level discussion and consultation throughout the organisation, including consultations with employees' representatives as appropriate.

The major purpose of the audit is to provide information on and explanation of human resource management and development practices. To achieve this, information should be sought both vertically through the personnel department and horizontally across other departments. In other words, the audit is conducted throughout the organisation.

The procedures for conducting the audit may vary considerably. Basically, they consist of obtaining information of a quantitative and qualitative nature from various records and reports, supplemented by interviews, questionnaires, surveys, discussions, and so on. Information may be obtained by means of a latitudinal study (e.g. a department-by-department assessment of safety records or absenteeism) in which the percentage of lost time and other ratios are calculated on a comparative basis. Alternatively, a longitudinal study may be used in which a sample of individuals is examined in depth over time, in the light of the effects of the organisation's policies on their performance. Hard data should be sought.

Table 16.1   The human resource audit (data for the last 12 months)

Stated policies	Regular practices	Findings of audit
1. RECRUITMENT To promote, where possible, from within the organisation.	Recruitment from external sources is an on-going and continual procedure.	95% appointments made from external sources. High staff turnover of 40% per annum.
2. TRAINING No stated policy.	Organisation sends two senior members to courses conducted by professional associations at request of individuals concerned.	Staff claim only limited opportunities for promotion and development, feel they have to go elsewhere to "get on".
3. ... etc.	...	...

If possible, data should be compared to those available from other organisations (e.g. data on turnover, absenteeism, grievances, accidents, and similar).

A recommended method for setting out a human resource audit is to list the organisation's policies in sequence, to write down the practices regularly employed by the organisation and the results obtained from the study and then to draw the appropriate conclusions and recommendations. An example is given in table 16.1. A list of personnel policies for audit purposes would include references to organisation; manpower planning; recruitment; selection; induction; transfers and promotions; assessment; training and development; communications; remuneration and allowances; job evaluation; fringe benefits; social and welfare benefits; safety and health; industrial relations; discipline; motivation; and administration.

A commonly used method to find information required by the audit, or by any other interventions in human resource management and development, is *the interview*. General principles of interviewing were discussed in chapter 8 and there is no need to repeat them here. However, for the consultant working in human resource development (HRD) there is another and very significant element — *confidentiality*.

The consultant can expect to receive a good deal of information that must be held in confidence. The higher the level of trust engendered by the consultant, the more he can expect to receive data that are confidential or private — and, in addition, not all of the data may be related to the identified problem. New problems may surface that had not been anticipated during the entry phase. The consultant may have to go back to the client to renegotiate the problem and the focus of the consultation.

If the interviews are to be effective and are to produce the data needed, the consultant must work at a very high ethical level. If the respondent requests that the material gathered during the interview be regarded as confidential, the consultant has some choices and decisions to make. He can establish the ground rule that all data gathered will be merged and individual sources will not be revealed. This must be approved by the client, who may have other expectations. If the client agrees, then the consultant can indicate this to the individual respondent when arranging for the interview. If a respondent is still hesitant, this may indicate a low level of trust in the organisation and the consultant will have to drop that person from the list of those to be interviewed.

This procedure allows the consultant to use the interview without disclosing the source. It does not avoid the "guessing game" — that is, people trying to guess who provided what kinds of data during the interviews.

The results of the human resource audit should, if necessary, point out the need for definition, refinement, or rewriting of organisational policies. Similarly, a review of the organisation's regular practices may suggest improvements to facilitate conversion of policies to procedures. Inadequacy or total absence of data indicates that urgent attention is required in the field of personnel administration. The principal result of an effective audit is a set of conclusions as to what needs to be improved in one or more of the areas of human resource management and development to be reviewed in the following sections. Here again, the client should feel free to decide how to proceed. He may be satisfied by the audit and convinced that he has received enough guidance to implement the conclusions without further help from the consultant. He may agree to the consultant's suggestions in principle, but decide not to put them into effect because they would cause difficulties among his personnel. Or he may want the consultant to assist in planning and implementing the changes that are required.

16.3 Human resource planning

The purpose of human resource planning is to make sure that the organisation has the right number of people of the right profile at the right time. Many organisations do not discover this elementary truth until they face a major disproportion — either the shortage of competent people becomes an obstacle to further expansion or technological change, or the organisation employs more people than it can afford and has to prepare itself for staff retrenchment.

In most cases a management consultant will not be called in to install a manpower planning system as a regular management activity, but to help identify emergency measures to be taken if there is an acute shortage of competent staff, or if important redundancies are anticipated. However, an emergency situation provides an opportunity to demonstrate the advantages of human resource planning treated as part of, and coherent with, strategic corporate planning. This is particularly relevant in developing countries where many important projects have been considerably delayed, and newly installed capacities underutilised for long periods, owing to staff shortages. In many of these cases there was no manpower plan, or, if there was one when the project was approved, it was not used as a project management tool.

The consultant will be able to help the client in combining various human resource planning techniques, either global or analytical. If enough detailed information is available on the structure of production and other processes, it may be possible to define and describe all necessary job positions. This implies that a detailed job description is worked out for every job. In contrast, if detailed lists of jobs cannot be established with accuracy, or if manpower is to be planned for units with changing functions and a need to adapt easily to new conditions, it may be preferable to define broader technical profiles of the kinds of people who will be needed, describing their educational background and experience, rather than to produce a detailed list of tasks to be done.

Here again, interfirm comparison techniques may be of help if not used mechanically: the consultant may be able to show his client with what numbers and profiles of staff comparable organisations achieve the same or similar output. This underlines the relationship between the planning of human resources and of productivity and performance improvement.

Some authors advocate the consistent use of *job descriptions* in manpower planning and recruitment processes in all types of organisations and for all employees. There are valid reasons for this in many organisations, where detailed job descriptions are needed for recruitment, planning training, evaluating performance, deciding on promotions and transfers, and handling organisational conflicts. However, it appears that the role of job descriptions tends to diminish with the increase in knowledge content of the jobs (e.g. in research, professional services, or high-technology industries), and with increasing emphasis on creativity, flexibility and adaptibility to change.

16.4 Recruitment and selection

The consultant may be asked to provide advice on how to improve the recruitment and selection of various categories of personnel, including management personnel.

Both the *selection procedure* and the *criteria applied* reflect factors such as:

- the importance of the given positions in the organisational structure (job content, authority and responsibility, the possibility of correcting errors, etc.);
- the terms of employment that are to be offered (selection for long-term or short-term employment) and the possibility of terminating employment contracts;
- the normal career path of the employees concerned (likely promotions, assignments abroad, job relations);
- the legislation to be observed;
- the formally or informally agreed practices as regards the participation of employees' representatives, and of trade unions more generally, in staff recruitment and selection (joint selection committees, need to obtain the trade union's agreement).

In many instances the solutions to the problems identified are straightforward. Often the selection is not well done: an insufficient number of candidates is considered, references are not checked, and recruitment interviews are superficial and conducted by personnel officers who may know little about the job. In some organisations the problems faced are delicate. Political, ethnic, or other criteria may prevail strongly over technical competence, or trade union membership may be required as a condition of recruitment.

The consultant's professional responsibility requires him to tell the client what should be changed in the best interests of the organisation. But the client will be unlikely to follow advice that he deems unrealistic owing to political or other constraints that are not under his control.

In most instances, however, improvements in selection and recruitment will be feasible. The consultant may come up with a more objective procedure and more precisely defined criteria, or may suggest and carry out a training programme for staff responsible for selection. Particular attention will be paid to the selection of staff who will be offered permanent employment contracts in technical and managerial positions, with a view to minimising the risk of selection errors (which are costly and difficult to correct).

Some consultants assist clients with testing and assessing candidates for managerial or technical jobs. This is done through interviews, multiple tests, special tasks and exercises, very careful checking of references and in various other ways. For example, this kind of assistance has been found useful by enterprises recruiting managerial and marketing staff for work abroad, yet lacking experience of management patterns and living conditions in foreign countries.

Executive search

Executive search ("head-hunting") is a special service offered by some larger management consulting firms, or by consultants who are fully specialised in this function. It is increasingly used by business and other organisations to fill important managerial or specialist positions. The advantage of using an executive search specialist is that he can develop information on potential sources of recruitment and undertake a systematic search and objective selection in a way that is usually outside the normal capabilities of a line or personnel manager. Business firms turn to executive search specialists if they do not want to advertise a job publicly, or if they seek candidates in areas where advertising does not work. Most candidates also find executive search useful, for various reasons. Some of them are glad to learn that they could have a more challenging career with another employer, while others appreciate a confidential discussion on alternative job opportunities, since their current position does not permit them to make the first contact or show interest in another job.

The executive search function involves: the building up of files and contacts needed to identify potential candidates and recruitment sources (an international search firm may have from 5,000 to 10,000 names of potential candidates in its computerised files); assistance to clients in analysing the job to be filled and defining the ideal candidate; active and methodical search for candidates (by direct approach, search through various business contacts, in some cases advertising, etc.); contacts with candidates for the purpose of interviewing them and interesting them in the job; evaluation and preliminary selection of candidates; arranging the client's interviews with pre-selected candidates; and follow-up contacts with the selected candidate and the client.

Executive search consultants form their own professional associations (e.g. in the United States), or are members of national associations of management consultants. Codes of ethics for executive search have been adopted in several countries. For example, such codes forbid charging fees to the candidates and accepting any payment from them; the cost of the search operation is charged to the client according to an agreed scheme (as a rule, 30 per cent of the annual salary of the candidate recruited). Several specialised publications on executive search are listed in appendix 11.

16.5 Motivation and remuneration

Motivation

Every organisation whose purpose is to achieve certain economic and social objectives, but which has limited resources at its disposal, tries to motivate its personnel towards the achievement of a range of goals. These may include societal, organisational, group and individual goals.

A human resource management consultant may be requested to assist in determining what motivational tools and strategies should be used. This may concern, for example:

- the improvement of the overall *organisational climate* (the psychological and motivational environment of the organisation), the underlying assumption being that this climate, which is determined primarily by the people management practices of top and senior managerial staff, by the employment and working conditions, and by the encouragement given to individual and group initiative, innovation, creativity and self-development, strongly affects the motivation of people at every level in the organisation to work and to achieve;

- the enrichment of *job content*, where, by changing the structure of the work to be performed, the consultant endeavours to assist in creating intrinsic job interest and increasing job satisfaction;

- *reward systems*, where the appropriate behaviour is shaped as a result of certain rewards, in particular financial and material ones; there should therefore be a feedback system, so that the incentive used (e.g. pay) is tied as directly as possible to actual performance. However, the role of *non-financial rewards or incentives* can be quite important and must not be underestimated when trying to enhance staff motivation.

These methods do not operate independently, but affect separate components of the motivational process and call for different levels of intervention on the part of the organisation and of the consultant. A common problem faced by consultants is complaints made by clients about the lack of motivation of the managers or their staff for achieving higher performances in organisations where people are relatively well paid. A thorough study has to be prepared to determine the weight of various factors affecting staff motivation. The study may reveal that the client assumes that a good salary is a stronger motivational factor than it really is. It may be that the salary level is taken for granted by the employees concerned, that the client and the employees differ in their views on what salary level is adequate, or that certain adverse factors in the working environment negate the effect of good salaries. For example, young employees often regard interesting job content and real prospects for future careers as more important for job satisfaction than the level of the starting salary.

Wages and salaries

In some assignments, however, the consultant will be requested to assist above all in the examination and reorganisation of the wage and salary system. Logically, the consultant approaches such a problem by conducting a job analysis, followed by job evaluation and the building of job structure so as to develop an equitable salary structure and plan which will accommodate periodic reviews, supplementary remuneration and appropriate fringe benefits. Obviously, the consultant cannot see wage and salary problems as purely technical ones and has to be well informed on legislation and industrial relations practices related to wages, especially on collective bargaining.

The problems most frequently met in this area include:
— distorted salary systems (e.g. the wage differentials do not reflect the relative difficulty and importance of particular categories of jobs);
— no relationship, or a very weak one, between salary and real performance at work;
— wage and salary differentials that do not motivate employees towards training and self-development and to seek promotion to more responsible and more rewarding jobs;
— obsolete salary and pay structures, which have not been adapted to the requirements of new technologies and to the changing structure of jobs;
— the absence of flexibility in using bonuses and special rewards for encouraging high performance and in demonstrating that such performance is important to the organisation and is therefore properly remunerated by management;
— excessive secrecy in matters of salaries and other rewards, giving rise to various suspicions about the actual pay levels of certain individuals, and reducing confidence in the objectivity and fairness of management over questions of pay.

None of these problems is easy to handle, although from a strictly technical viewpoint the solution may be straightforward. The consultant should be cautious in establishing, and assessing with the client, the feasibility of changes, and the way in which the necessary changes are to be introduced, announced and maintained.

Job analysis, evaluation and classification

Job analysis includes the collection, organisation and examination of information on what people do in a particular job. Job analysis is used not only to produce job descriptions for recruitment and other purposes as discussed above, but also for *job evaluation*, that is determining job worth. Depending on the job in hand, the order of complexity of the job evaluation system employed usually moves from (1) job ranking schemes through (2) job classification to (3) point evaluation systems and to (4) factor comparison methods. The point evaluation system appears to be the most frequently used. *Job classification* involves the setting of wage and salary levels by classifying jobs within the organisation and comparing the levels of pay to those of competitive firms or other firms with a comparable job structure and conditions of business. The "market value" of individual jobs is given consideration, using various sources of information such as surveys and reports published by management associations, government departments, or independent business information services.

In practice, however, many jobs are not evaluated, or, if they are, their evaluation is only one of the factors determining the pay rate.

"While many employers believe that employees' pay should be differentiated on the basis of current performance, many others (perhaps a majority) believe that seniority, age and past performance and loyalty should have equal or greater weight in individual pay determination. Managers may claim that they have merit or performance-based pay systems, but many studies indicate that they are more accurately based on current performance plus seniority, or seniority alone."[1]

A recent survey concluded that the changes in the way work is done (e.g. due to new technologies and new forms of work organisation) have radically altered the kinds of job people do . . . it is clear that the key personnel functions of job analysis, job evaluation and job classification are becoming more and more complex and thus are getting more attention and "scientific scrutiny".[2] Thus, while some consultants started believing that in this traditional area of personnel management no further challenging assignments could be expected, the dramatic changes in technologies, job structures and staff competence requirements are generating new demands for advice and assistance. The human resource consultant should be ready to help.

16.6 Human resource development

In the last 10-15 years HRD has become the most popular and fastest growing area of consulting in personnel and human resources management. There are consultants who specialise fully in this area, while many other consulting firms have established important HRD divisions and trained most of their staff members in various aspects and technologies of HRD. At the same time, quite a few charlatans tried to take advantage of the "HRD boom" by selling package deals to clients who hoped for spectacular improvements by putting employees through crash programmes on how to improve communication, or how to increase productivity by team building. Fortunately, in most countries the situation is now becoming clearer; clients tend to be better informed about HRD, and hence more cautious and selective.[3]

The main purpose of HRD is to help people in organisations to face the challenges created by technological and other changes, to adapt to new requirements and achieve levels of performance needed for survival and staying competitive. A true HRD professional does not promise spectacular changes as a result of a few workshop sessions. He makes the client aware of the complexity of the human side of the enterprise, and of the need to consider all factors affecting motivation, behaviour, interpersonal relations and performance of people in organisations. He warns the client against inconsistencies in personnel and HRD practices, as these can devalue the impact of many well intentioned but partial and isolated measures in this field. He informs the client about the availability of a wide range of techniques for human resource and organisation development (OD), but points out the cultural bias of certain techniques and the need to avoid a mechanistic transfer which disregards differences in local cultural values and social systems.

HRD is an extremely broad topic and this section cannot review all the approaches and techniques used. Rather it will point to the main management concerns that may call for a consultant's intervention. The reader should also refer to chapter 4 on consulting and change, where several HRD and OD techniques are discussed in some detail.

Staff training and development

An HRD consultant can act as an adviser on how to increase the effectiveness of staff training and development, or can himself be directly involved in preparing and delivering in-company training. Typically, assignments in this area aim to answer such questions as:

- How can staff training and development be related to the goals and problems of the organisation and make it performance-oriented?

- How can training needs of various categories of personnel be identified?

- What should the content, methodology and organisation of staff development programmes be?

- How can the real impact of staff development on organisational performance be evaluated and the level of investment in human resources development determined?

- How can the training unit be organised and the competence of the training director and in-company trainers increased?

- What benefits can be drawn from sending managers and staff specialists to external courses at business schools, management institutes, consulting firms, productivity centres, and elsewhere? What sort of relationship should be established with external units offering training programmes, and should these units be used for mounting tailor-made in-plant programmes?

- How can employees be motivated for training and self-development and for using the results of training in their work? What obstacles are to be removed if training is to have the desired impact on both individual and organisational performance?

The last question, namely the real motivation for training and applying the results of training, is a crucial point on which the consultant can help.

Career development

Career development is a significant aspect of human resource development, although its importance may not be the same in all cultures. The consultant should be able to explain the consequences of the absence of career planning to the client. Although in many organisations a detailed plan of the career path of every individual may be impossible, or undesirable, it should be possible to establish a career development policy as guidance for staff development and for motivating individual performance. Without constituting a legal commitment to every individual concerned, such a policy provides a clear model to which employees can compare their individual expectations and gear their self-development and work improvement efforts.

Performance appraisal

Performance appraisal has been one of the weakest links in personnel management systems. Many small organisations do not practise any performance appraisal on a regular basis. Medium-sized and large organisations have introduced structured performance appraisal schemes in most cases, but the reality tends to be very different from declared objectives and policies. The consultant is likely to find that regular performance appraisals do take place and performance reports are duly produced and signed, but no conclusions are drawn and no use is made of the appraisals in deciding on staff development, promotions, transfers, merit increments and so on. In some organisations no conclusion can be drawn because annual appraisals have become formalities that must be carried out but do not reflect real performance. In other cases the appraisal reflects only the subjective views and preferences of direct supervisors. While it is not hard to find out about the formalism and other weaknesses of performance appraisals, it is much more difficult to change a deeply rooted practice. The consultant can help the client to realise that appraisal ought to be concerned with actual performance rating, that appraisers require training in performance assessment techniques, and that sensible performance appraisal commences with well-established organisational, group and individual goals. Whatever organisation and techniques of appraisal are chosen, the improved system will require the support of employees' representatives and strong management commitment.

Organisational development

Many consulting interventions in the HRD field are of the OD type. The original definitions of OD emphasised the application of behavioural sciences for assisting organisations in identifying, planning and implementing organisational changes. Interventions focused on organisational processes such as communication, sharing of information, interpersonal relations, team building, the use of meetings or the ways of resolving conflicts, rather than on providing solutions to substantive technical issues involved in the process. More recent approaches aim to combine "classical" OD with diagnosing and resolving specific (technological, organisational, financial) problems, using many other diagnostic and problem-solving techniques in addition to behavioural techniques regarded as the province of OD specialists. This requires that an OD consultant should become versed in a particular area of management and business problems, while consultants in various technical areas of management, as well as all-round generalists, can increase their effectiveness by mastering OD principles and some OD techniques in addition to the specific technical fields they cover (finance, business strategy, etc.).

16.7 Labour-management relations

We have already referred to the need for consultants to take into account industrial relations practices and implications generally, and particularly when dealing with responsibilities within the personnel management function. This section looks briefly at various points relevant to a labour-management relations consultancy.[4] In passing it might be mentioned that, while technical advice in this field may be provided by those who have specialised in labour-management relations, consultants in personnel management often possess or develop expertise and provide advice in this area. Needless to say, any consultant called upon should be well informed about the legal, political, social and economic circumstances of labour-management relations in a given country, sector and particular organisation.

The consultant may be called in because problems already exist in labour-management relations, because there are internal or external forces that are likely to lead to problems, or because advice is needed in the initial formulation or reformulation of labour-management relations policies. In each case a key issue will be the presence or absence of workers' representatives, in particular of a trade union in or for the enterprise, and, where trade union or another form of workers' representation does exist, the nature and role of that representation.

The essential questions in labour-management relations which the consultant may be called upon to deal with could include one or more of the following:

(1) Advice on dealing with workers' representatives on a day-to-day basis. These may be trade union representatives, or representatives directly elected by all the workers with no, or with only indirect, links with a trade union.

(2) The mechanics of handling workers' grievances, including advice on the setting up of grievance procedures, together with advice regarding other conflict resolution procedures.

(3) Collective bargaining and, in particular, management organisation for collective bargaining. The significance of this question will depend to some extent on the level at which bargaining takes place (for the industry as a whole; for the industry in a particular region or locality; for a group of enterprises; or at the enterprise level). But in most cases where there is a trade union presence in the workplace, a certain degree of collective bargaining, possibly of an informal character, will take place in the enterprise even if more formal or official bargaining takes place at a higher level. Consultants are sometimes called upon to participate in the management bargaining team or even to act as management spokesmen in negotiations.

(4) Machinery and procedures for management-worker consultation and co-operation on issues of common interest such as productivity, welfare facilities, etc. (as opposed to issues of an antagonistic nature such as grievances or bargaining demands).

(5) Dismissal and redundancy principles and procedures (whether within or outside the context of collective bargaining).

(6) The position to be taken by employers' associations in tripartite (government, employers, trade unions) or bipartite (either with government or with trade unions) consultation at the national level.

This is not necessarily an exhaustive list of possible areas with which the consultant may have to deal, but it covers the major areas in which advice will be sought.

Turning to factors to be considered in providing advice, one could mention in the first place the relevant legal framework of labour-management relations at the enterprise level. This framework, which is highly individual to particular countries, might reflect rules on: trade union recognition; workplace workers' representation; collective bargaining procedures; dispute settlement (including work stoppages); forms of workers' participation in decisions within the enterprise; the formation and content of individual contracts of employment, and so on. In charting courses of action to be recommended to clients, consultants must of necessity take account of existing legal rules. It is obvious that individual company rules on conditions of employment must also be taken into consideration. And where particularly complex legal problems have to be resolved with the aid of the consultant, he may have to suggest recourse to the services of a qualified lawyer specialising in labour law (if he himself does not have such training).

The consultant must also be fully aware of the relevant provisions of any existing collective agreement that applies to the enterprise concerned (whether such agreement be for the industry, the region, or the enterprise itself). He must be aware not only of the provisions of the agreements but also of possible interpretations of those provisions which may have been subject to scrutiny by labour courts, arbitrators, or other decision-making bodies.

But rules resulting from legislation or collective agreements are only two of the significant sets of norms to be considered by the consultant. In virtually all established enterprises, organisations or industries there will be labour-management relations customs, usages and practices which often demand the same respect that is accorded to legal regulations. At times these customs, usages and practices are common to a specific region or locality. It is essential that the consultant should be fully aware of them. This does not mean that he may not be in a position to influence changes in established industrial relations practices. Indeed this may be a crucial aspect of his assignment. However, he must recognise that in doing so extreme care should be taken and consideration given to possible unforeseen consequences of breaking with traditional practices.

It is also very important that the consultant should make himself familiar with the position, outlook and concerns of the workers' representatives who will be involved in any course of action that he might recommend, since possible reactions from the workers' side must be a determinant in such recommendations. However, before considering personal contacts with such representatives, the consultant should, in agreement with the client, consider what contacts would be appropriate before and during the framing of his recommendations. Dealings with workers' representatives can be very delicate, and the consultant should discuss with management just which areas he may touch on in such contacts as well as the limits of his authority to commit management should the contacts be of a nature where commitments may be made or inferred.

The consultant would be well advised to recommend that every opportunity for consultations between management and workers' representatives should be seized, particularly when new labour-management relations policies are being introduced. The co-operation or acquiescence of trade union or other workers' representatives can often be crucial to the success of the consultant's efforts.

This section is intended only to give an idea of what some of the more important preoccupations of the labour-management relations consultant should be. It must be recognised that the innumerable and complex factors impinging upon labour-management relations make for a situation where each consultancy is highly particular and individual and where pre-established formulae must yield in most cases to tailor-made specific approaches.

While typically it is management that recruits the consultant, there may be cases where specialists, particularly where very specific aspects of labour-management relations are concerned, are engaged jointly by management and the trade union and, sometimes, even by the trade union alone. In any of these latter cases the points made earlier would still warrant the attention of the labour-management relations consultant.

¹ W. F. Glueck: *Personnel: A diagnostic approach* (Plano, TX, Business Publications, 1982), p. 296. Quoted in H. C. Jain and V. V. Murray: "Why the human resources management function fails", in *California Management Review*, Vol. XXVI, No. 4, Summer 1984, p. 100.

² M. Lo Bosco: "Job analysis, job evaluation and job classification", in *Personnel* (USA), May 1985, p. 74.

³ See e.g. R. Sheldon: "Fraud in the training field", in *Education and Training* (UK), June 1985.

⁴ See also A. Gladstone: *The manager's guide to international labour standards* (Geneva, International Labour Office, 1986).

CONSULTING IN SMALL ENTERPRISE MANAGEMENT 17

The use of consultants by small enterprises is an emerging trend in business. As activities relating to the conduct of business become more complex, the need for outside assistance usually increases. Small enterprise managers who want to remain competitive need to consider using consultants as they would use other support services such as bankers, lawyers, accountants, and trade associations.

Consultants can play an important role in economic development by becoming more involved in assisting people to set up small enterprises. For new entrepreneurs, the start-up phase is the most difficult, yet few consultants focus on this important aspect of enterprise development. Consultants might consider training groups of entrepreneurs who intend initiating new enterprises.

Small enterprises use consultants mainly to solve specific operational problems. The duration of the consultancy will depend on the specific problem but most consultancies can be accomplished within six months. Longer consultancies may be required if the problem concerns expanding business operations. Expansion takes time and the consultant may be involved periodically for up to one or two years.

17.1 Characteristics of small enterprises

Definition of a small enterprise

The definition of a small enterprise tends to vary according to the nature of its activities, the purpose of the definition, and the level of development where the enterprise is located. The criteria for describing an enterprise as "small" might be the number of employees, money value of sales, capital investment, maximum energy requirements, or various combinations of these and other factors. In most discussions and writings on the subject by management consultants, it is conceded that a small enterprise is one in which the administrative and operational management are in the hands of one or two people who also make the important decisions in that enterprise. Such an operational definition has been found to include more than 85 per cent of all small enterprises no matter how defined.

The consultant should be aware of factors which usually distinguish the small from the larger enterprise. First, the small enterprise is primarily financed from personal or family savings with limited recourse to outside finance during the formative stages. Secondly, the manager has close personal contact with the whole workplace; and thirdly, the enterprise operates in a limited geographical area. These "smallness" factors greatly influence the consultative process.

The small enterprise possesses distinct advantages, including the ability to fill limited demands in specialised markets; a propensity for labour-intensity and low to medium skill level work; and flexibility to adapt rapidly to changing demands and conditions. Managerially speaking, there is an advantage in having a personal involvement in dealings which goes beyond price, product and delivery dates. The owner-manager is usually more highly motivated than a salaried manager - he works longer, harder, and provides greater incentive to workers by personal example.

Simple organisational structure means more direct and less complicated lines of communication inside and outside the business. The smallness of the firm assists in identifying and developing the capabilities of workers more quickly than happens in larger firms.

The small enterprise can also experiment with or enter new markets without attracting unwanted attention from large firms. It can cater for extremes in the market - either the right- or left-hand tails of an average distribution curve - since mass marketing for the average consumer is usually taken care of by big business. Similarly, the smaller firm can more quickly exploit changing market patterns and the "floater" consumer who drifts in the market place.

Special problems of small enterprises

Problems of small enterprises can be general or specific. Problems of a general nature involve legal aspects of business, access to credit and raw materials, and the lack of appropriate technical and managerial assistance.

Management consultants should be aware of problems at the enterprise level. These may appear more formidable to the manager of a small enterprise than problems in a large corporation might appear to its chairman. The following list demonstrates the range of difficulties which may be encountered:

- Whereas large, well-organised enterprises can usually afford both good line-management and specialist staff, the small enterprise manager is a relatively isolated individual dealing with policy and operational problems simultaneously despite personal biases and limitations.

- Small enterprise managers often operate with inadequate, or, at best, with minimum quantitative data. To save operating costs they are likely to dispense with information systems, a weakness which becomes glaringly apparent when the enterprise reaches a growth stage.

- Because the small enterprise can usually pay only minimum wages, has few fringe benefits, and offers low job security and few promotional opportunities, it is reasonable to expect difficulties in recruiting high calibre employees.

- Professional investors are seldom attracted to the new small enterprise, and the manager is severely limited in his ability to raise initial capital. This problem is compounded when, as is very often the case, the enterprise runs into growth problems, or operating difficulties, and the manager attempts to raise additional finance in order to cope with expansion or crisis situations.

- Because of this problem of limited reserves, coupled with low capacity to borrow, the small enterprise is particularly vulnerable to economic downturn and recessions.

- Although ability to change and adapt rapidly is a natural strength of a small enterprise, this quality may be nullified when an opportunity requiring rapid change suddenly appears. The manager may be too occupied with on-going operational problems to be able to think clearly about the future of the business.

- The hand-to-mouth financial existence of the enterprise does not encourage opportunities for staff training and development, with consequent loss in realisation of the full potential of the human resources within the enterprise.

- High productivity is difficult to achieve since the small enterprise does not enjoy the low costs of the large firm which can, for example, buy at a discount, achieve economies of scale, call on its sophisticated marketing and distribution system, and engage its own research and development and systems design teams.

- The small firm is usually limited to a single or small product or service range so that in times of trouble it cannot diversify activities as can large-scale enterprises.

- The manager is often not able to understand and interpret government regulations, actions, concessions and so on to best advantage.

The small enterprise is a relatively fragile structure with limited resources to overcome its problems. Even minor problems can be life-threatening to the enterprise. In one country it was estimated that the failure rate within the first two years of operation was as high as 50 per cent for new small enterprises.

Reluctance to use consultants

Many small enterprise managers are reluctant to use outside consultants for the following reasons:

- they believe that only large enterprises can afford the consulting fees charged;
- in many instances, consultants will not have practical experience in the type of business needing assistance;
- identification of a competent consultant is difficult and time-consuming, because most managers have little previous contact with consultants;
- managers are reluctant to provide outsiders with facts and figures relating to the business;

— using a consultant may be viewed by the manager as an admission of lack of competence.

To overcome the preconceptions of owner-managers, consultants need to provide facts and data which will indicate the value of their services, if possible referring to specific instances of other small companies where consultants have been used.

17.2 The role and profile of the consultant

The consultant dealing with small enterprises handles the whole spectrum of management and is required to be more of a generalist than a specialist. It can be taken for granted that consultants require professional training and considerable experience in management principles as applied to small enterprise development. Of prime importance is a knowledge of the interaction of functions of the small enterprise since change in one function usually has immediate repercussions in others. Furthermore, it is useful for the consultant to be at least familiar with the various entrepreneurial development approaches which provide a conceptual basis for current small enterprise development practices.

As with any combination of skill and art, mastery of business fundamentals is essential for a successful career in consulting with small enterprises. When assisting the manager of a small enterprise it is important to ensure that all managerial tasks are completed, even imperfectly, rather than having 75 per cent of the tasks completed to perfection while the remaining 25 per cent are neglected. The consultant must keep in mind the "total" picture of the business to see that functions of administration and operation are harmonised and integrated. Patience and dogged perseverance are required in encouraging the manager to complete managerial chores ranging from accounting to staff training, while preventing him from concentrating solely on preferred technical activities such as the actual production of goods and services.

The consultant's role becomes further complicated in that his main consulting duties lie in developing the manager and others contributing to managing the enterprise at the same time as he is expected to provide feasible practical solutions to a wide range of specific problems — for example, finance, sales, production and purchasing. Although the subject matter is specific, it generally exceeds the limits of a particular function or technique. The consulting technique is broad, including assistance with implementation where necessary, and informal training in many cases.

Routine consulting reports, usually submitted to larger organisations, do not apply to small enterprises. Written reports should be short, simple, limited to a minimum and often submitted only at the end of an assignment to explain what things were done and why, and what is required in the future.

The consultant should also appreciate that clients are not necessarily the best educated and skilled managers available. Moreover, there are often no training facilities readily available to help remedy obvious deficiencies. Thus, instead of adopting a professional air and emphasising his expertise to influence his clients, the consultant should use a simpler style. Coaxing, praising and reprimanding is likely to be more effective in obtaining the results he desires!

The client-manager of the small enterprise may suffer a severe sense of failure if forced to use a consultant. The consultant should, therefore, be alert to the possible need to restore a client's self-esteem in addition to providing technical assistance.

Unquestionably, lack of data is a major handicap in undertaking a consulting assignment with a small enterprise. Usually the sole source of information is the manager, who is often "too busy" to be interviewed. The consultant must use ingenuity, persistence and tenacity to extract the required information.

During the last thirty years many governments, employers' organisations, trade associations, chambers of commerce and similar bodies have established special services and facilities for small enterprises including:

- supply of credit (loans and guarantees);
- reduced tax rates (to enable accumulation of capital necessary for survival and growth);
- reserved and preferential markets for goods and services (special government set-asides, offsets and subcontracts);
- industrial estates or parks;
- product design and quality control services;
- advisory services on export possibilities;
- market and feasibility studies;
- reduced cost bulk purchase of raw materials, etc.

Although he is probably able to obtain advice directly from technicians in charge of particular services, a manager or owner of a small enterprise may find it difficult to decide when and how to use such services. The management consultant has to advise on the whole range of services and recommend priorities and acceptable costs of such services to the manager. This also includes advice on where to find relevant information. In developing countries, management consultants are increasingly involved in advising the local, small and medium-sized enterprises on technology transfer, joint ventures with enterprises from industrialised countries, subcontracting, or franchising.

Good health, persistence and stamina are the consultant's chief assets. Small enterprise managers have little respect for conventional working hours and, once preliminary fears are overcome, quickly learn to ask for help whenever and however they see fit. The consultant is very similar to the family doctor in that he is always on call - and some clients will, fortunately or unfortunately, take this for granted. Clients are often astonished to learn that consultants take time off for meals and may wish to be with their families on some weekends and evenings.

Responsibility is also disproportionate. In most conventional consulting assignments for large organisations, there is some tolerance for error as reports are checked by supervisors and very important reports are examined by a manager of the consulting unit. However, when dealing with small enterprises, mistakes by the consultant can be fatal to the organisation requesting assistance. Since such assistance tends to be direct and immediate, the consultant has limited time to check ideas and proposals with colleagues. Paraphrasing Reinhold Niebuhr's famous prayer, the Asian Productivity Organisation has set out the role of the small enterprise consultant in the form of a "Consultant's Prayer":

> God grant me
> COURAGE to change what I can,
> PATIENCE to accept what can't be changed, and
> WISDOM to know the difference.

Timing may be critical. The consultant usually works under extreme pressure since assistance is often not sought until after a crisis develops and the manager is personally unable to resolve the problem. By employing a judicious blend of "resource" and "process" forms of consulting, the consultant is expected to do whatever is necessary to assist the manager. In the final analysis, it must be remembered that the consultant's job is to consult and *not* to manage. In times when consultancy advice may not be accepted or followed by management, the consultant should be guided by the saying that "you can lead a horse to water, but you can't make it drink". Similarly the consultant should not be held responsible for the failure of a small firm, nor should the consultant claim responsibility for its success. The consultant should concentrate on the success of the assignment.

17.3 Consulting assignments in the life-cycle of an enterprise

The review in previous chapters of management situations and problems dealt with by consultants includes a number of concepts and experiences relevant to consulting in a small enterprise. However, certain situations are specific to small enterprise consulting.

Small enterprise consultants need to change as business activity changes. They must become more aware of information and how to gain access to it. It is essential for consultants to understand the uses of software packages and computers in relation to small enterprise operations, especially how to convert computer printouts into useful information for the small enterprise manager. An emerging area of concern for small enterprises appears to lie in the field of industrial relations in those countries where organised labour is making its claims heard and felt.

Communication skills are becoming increasingly important and may eventually overshadow even the technical knowledge and other skills of the consultant. The essential task is for consultants to use their communication skills to "pull out" problems and to "plug in" solutions. The consultant must have a good network of highly skilled technicians who can assist with specific problems.

Once a solution is determined, it is the communication skills of the consultant that will convince the manager that he should implement the solution.

The small enterprise owner is faced with a host of problems and the consultant should be prepared to meet these various needs. The consultant may be considered a "one-stop shop" where entrepreneurs can receive the necessary assistance. The following stages serve to illustrate the range of problems faced by consultants when dealing with an enterprise passing through a typical life-cycle.

Stage 1: At the very beginning

Biographical evidence suggests that successful small enterprise managers, sometimes referred to as entrepreneurs (a definition which has wider implications than for small enterprises only) commonly possess distinctive qualities. They are often the first-born of a family and have had to assume a more than average amount of responsibility at an early stage in life. In many cases they are the offspring of self-employed persons, but not necessarily in the same occupational grouping, trade or service. Such people have had a sound but not necessarily extended education and, as a rule, more than five years' experience of working in real-life conditions.

From a personality point of view they are inclined to be optimistic, moderate risk-takers as opposed to gamblers or non-risk-takers, and have a feeling that control over their own destiny rather than just making money is a key motivating factor in their life. Such people are usually married, with minimum distractions caused by family life - there is usually an understanding spouse who may not, in fact, care for the kind of life-style which results, but understands and appreciates the demands made on the marriage partner.

A key characteristic is that successful entrepreneurs are mentally and physically very active. They are usually very well organised and manage time efficiently. Success may result not so much from quality, but from the quantity of schemes prepared and developed. In short, the greater the effort, the greater the chances of success seem to be.

When dealing with a beginner, the consultant should take stock of the client's background and interests to ascertain whether he is dealing with a probable or a possible entrepreneur, and develop the assignment accordingly. The project in question should be closely examined, taking into account the strengths and weaknesses commonly found in small enterprises. A checklist of items to be reviewed should be worked out.

Stage 2: Starting up

Assuming that the client wishes to launch a new enterprise, the consultant should, after reviewing and discussing the proposal, prepare for at least three possibilities and develop appropriate contingency plans:
(1)   what is the best that might happen (the "blue skies" approach)?
(2)   what is likely to happen (the basis for the "business plan")?
(3)   what is the worst that can happen (realistically assess the "downside risk")?

The consultant should talk freely with his client about the first two possibilities, which are usually "creative" problems, whereas the third alternative, which is a "corrective" problem, should be reserved for the consultant's own counsel because (1) the client is unlikely to listen to or agree with the "worst possible", alternative, and (2) encouragement rather than discouragement should help attain the full potential of the proposal. The consultant must, however, draw up detailed contingency plans for all three alternatives if for no other reason than to make allowances for "Murphy's Law" ("If anything can possibly go wrong - it will!")

A good small enterprise manager can usually generate many ideas very rapidly. The consultant should encourage this and assist the client to obtain and record relevant quantitative data about these ideas for two reasons: first, to assist in making a logical choice between alternatives; and, secondly, to use as supporting evidence should the manager experience uncomfortable afterthoughts about a scheme once started.

Mistakes will happen, particularly in the early stages–it is part of the general learning process. The consultant's task is to minimise errors made by the manager in these stages. It is, however, better to ensure that an ineffective scheme never takes off than to attempt to salvage an impossible project at a later date, which gives rise to the consulting maxim: "Giving birth is a lot easier than resurrection." If necessary, allow the proposal to lapse and encourage the client to try afresh when more evidence and support is available. If it is decided to go ahead with the enterprise, full commitment should be encouraged. Effective decision making and prompt action are vital; there is little room for compromise or error in a new enterprise.

From a functional point of view the consultant should encourage clients to use the services of some specialists from the outset if they can possibly be afforded because, if the enterprise grows, the specialists will be familiar with its history, practice and results, and thus able to assist in a meaningful way. The specialists include:

- legal firm (of good repute and the best which can be afforded);
- accountant (possessing the same qualities as those required in the legal firm);
- banker (a person, not an institution, so that rapport and trust are established at a personal level);
- insurance agent (similar qualities as required in the banker);
- marketing representative (this clearly depends on the type of enterprise; where the enterprise is not intrinsically marketing-oriented, it is often sound practice to make links with experts or agents during the formative stages).

Small enterprise consultants require a wide range of functional expertise, with, perhaps most importantly, emphasis on financial matters. The finance field presents problems both in attracting formation capital and in controlling expenses and income; small enterprise management consultants not well versed in these fields are a danger to clients and cannot claim professional competence in the true sense of the word.

It is often only by thorough expert financial appraisal that the consultant is able to undertake the necessary though unpleasant task of recommending discontinuation of an enterprise rather than encouraging a holding operation which will eventually lead to insuperable problems for all involved.

This fear of tragedy deserves greater emphasis in the start-up stages of the enterprise than may seem warranted. Often family and friends' savings are used to finance the capital requirements of the new enterprise simply because "no one else will lend the money". This finding alone suggests that the scheme is probably not particularly sound. If no finance agency considers a proposal worthwhile (and they take into account an allowance for failure), why should a consultant recommend that family savings be jeopardised in a risky undertaking? There should always be proprietor equity in a venture, but not simply because no one else is prepared to support it. When preparing the third (worst-of-all) contingency plan, if project failure is likely to cause undue hardships the consultant is professionally obliged to dissuade the client from undertaking such a venture.

During the start-up phase the consultant might reflect on the following checkout routine which has been based on a considerable number of studies designed to pin-point potential problem areas in small enterprises. In order of importance for diagnosing trouble areas the consultant is likely to find deficiencies classified as the seven "M"s:

— managerial (lack of experience);
— monetary (lack of capital, poor cost control);
— material (poor location, too much stock);
— machines (excessive purchase of fixed assets);
— marketing (inappropriate granting of credit);
— mental (lack of planning for expansion);
— motivation (wrong attitudes to work and responsibility).

Stage 3: Getting bigger

Having weathered stages 1 and 2, the consultant may occasionally be rewarded with a brand new set of events which emerge as the enterprise matures and the consulting assignment takes on a progressive look. This is the right time to examine thoroughly the weaknesses to be overcome, opportunities to develop further, and alternative resource allocations to help the enterprise benefit from the most favourable opportunities. When assisting the manager to allocate resources, the consultant may care to refer to the "four to one principle" which can be set up as a rule of thumb:

● 20% of the customers account for 80% of the sales;
● 20% of the stocks result in 80% of movements;
● 20% of staff causes 80% of the problems;
● 20% of salesmen create 80% of the sales, and so on.

The consultant should encourage the manager to "play percentages" and concentrate on critical areas. During this maturation phase the manager, submerged in day-to-day operational problems, is usually not able to pay attention to the long- or medium-term planning essential for continued growth and survival. Consultants can assist by encouraging the manager to look to the future. For example, they can prepare current organisation charts and job descriptions and compare these with how they should look five to ten years hence, showing likely changes. New developments usually require a little inspiration, considerable incubation, and a great deal of perspiration. Therefore, the consultant should make sure that the manager plans appropriate resources and allocates the time required for future growth and development.

A noticeable feature of successful managers is that they are exceptionally well organised. This practice should be encouraged as part of the management development process by introducing systems, encouraging managers to read on management subjects, and insisting on forecasts, budgets and controls. Probably during this maturation phase an accountant (financial controller) post should be established.

The consultant will also have to draw on his knowledge of comparable enterprises to judge the productivity of the client under review. Knowledge of a range of interfirm comparisons, in the form of input/output and productivity ratios, is an invaluable asset, especially if corrective measures become necessary. The consultant must know where such information can be obtained.

Stage 4: Exit from the enterprise

Eventually the manager finds that the enterprise may have grown to a stage where it can no longer be considered small, and issues pertaining to growth, finance, corporate structure, delegation and the like will arise. The small enterprise consultant should then judiciously refer the manager to specialists capable of assisting in the new situation.

Alternatively, the manager may decide to forego the routine running of an enterprise and prefer to start something new, revert to becoming an employee, or retire. At that point, disposal of the enterprise becomes the problem of the moment.

Assessing the monetary value of an enterprise is usually done in any of three ways:

(1) *liquidation or forced sale value*, where the enterprise is virtually put up for auction and sold to the highest bidder (if any);

(2) *book value*, where items are assessed at cost less depreciation and sold piecemeal to selected markets;

(3) *market value*, where the entity is sold as a going concern and items such as goodwill are included in the price.

Varying conditions (such as the death of the owner) may determine which of these assessment methods will be used. Generally speaking, the market value method provides the best return to the seller.

The consultant is obliged to assist the client to obtain the best possible deal. Nevertheless, the consultant should keep in mind that the best sales are those involving a willing seller and a willing buyer. To arrive at this happy situation the consultant should encourage the seller to "leave something in it" for the new owner. By doing so the chances of a sale are enhanced, time is often saved and opportunities for recrimination are reduced. Trying to obtain the greatest possible amount of money from the potential new owner may well carry the sale beyond the borders of diminishing return.

Another end-of-the-road situation occurs when the manager is succeeded by a family member or someone else. With small enterprises, apart from areas of obvious equality and responsibility such as a partnership of doctors or lawyers, shared management seldom succeeds. For purposes of direction, control and responsibility it is usually better to have one identified manager than to split the authority between, say, two siblings. If it can be arranged, family succession in an enterprise should follow only after the offspring have been exposed to working in outside situations, otherwise managerial in-breeding is likely to occur.

17.4 Areas of special concern

Counselling family enterprises

The use of consultants by small family enterprises is not common. Even after initial contact, few formal consulting assignments are ever achieved. Because of the intimate relationships between family members, they are extremely reluctant to discuss business conflicts and problems. Personal and business problems become highly intertwined and in many cases they are extremely difficult for the consultant to identify, let alone resolve.

Before attempting to solve the business problems, the consultant should meet separately with each family member in order to understand the family dynamics as they relate to the operation of the business. The consultant should attempt to gain the support and trust of each family member *before* meeting them as a group to discuss the business problems.

When family ties are strong, family pride can be a major factor in resolving the conflict. In situations where family ties are weak, it may be better to propose that some members leave the business and pursue other career opportunities.

Extension services

Private consultants are not widely used by small enterprises in most developing countries. However, consulting is often provided through government-sponsored extension services to small enterprises. Extension service agents take the initiative, visit small enterprises, and provide entrepreneurs with services and advice on the spot. Such assistance may include the following activities:

-   advising on all aspects of management, work organisation and product design, development and adaptation; emphasis may be on price calculations, bookkeeping and financial planning;
-   domestic and export marketing, including sub-contracting and inventory control;
-   materials procurement;
-   choosing technology and solving technical problems including skill, space, public utility and equipment requirements and procurement methods;
-   advice on potential sources of finance and help in gaining access to finance, for example by preparing loan requests;
-   identifying training requirements for workers and owners/managers and identification of potential training sources;
-   explaining government regulations and dealing with related paperwork, including taxes and legal questions such as incorporation of enterprises, registration, licensing, grants, etc.; and
-   quality control and standardisation, particularly where sub-contracting and export promotion are important.

Only rarely is it necessary or possible for the extension service to be involved in all of these functions at the same time. Specific functions will depend on the nature of the target group, both in terms of its technical qualifications and the sub-sector to which the target entrepreneurs belong, namely manufacturing, construction, tourism, commerce, etc. There is general agreement, however, that an integrated approach has to be taken to assess and meet the needs of small enterprises. Such an approach would combine, for example, training, technological assistance, credit and, in some cases, physical infrastructure.

The extension service agent may be viewed as a "trouble-shooter" who identifies problem areas and refers the entrepreneur to specialised assistance such as chambers of commerce, professional associations, trade and artisan groups, private consultants, training institutions, or larger enterprises. To be of benefit to entrepreneurs, the value of the extension service must be judged by its ability to perceive their needs, to diagnose correctly problems that occur, and to provide timely and useful advice and support. One delivery system which has proved extremely successful is the use of a "hot-line" telephone service by means of which toll-free or reduced charges are arranged so that clients and consultants can ask for on-the-spot advice from the extension service.

CONSULTING IN PUBLIC ENTERPRISE MANAGEMENT

18

Public sector organisations, enterprises in particular, constitute an important market for management consultants in many countries owing to growing concern about the efficiency of the public sector and the quality of public services. Management consultants tend to be regarded as a useful source of ideas and expertise that could increase efficiency.

In some countries there exist public sector consulting services, including in-house consulting and management services in public utilities such as power, water supply, or railways. Independent private consultants also do a great deal of work in the public sector. Private consultants have been increasingly instrumental in transferring private sector management experience to public organisations and assisting performance improvement efforts in the public sector.

The range of consulting assignments in the public sector has been very broad. These assignments can be in any functional area of management, or deal with comprehensive issues of policy, strategy, corporate planning, organisation and overall performance improvement. They can concern individual enterprises, groups of enterprises, or even range across the whole sector. While the principles and methods of consulting discussed in our book are generally applicable to the public sector, assignments in this sector also bring in some specific factors and constraints which are absent, or which do not have the same importance, in consulting for private organisations.

A consultant who intends to work in the public sector must be aware of its specific characteristics and constraints. If not, he will be unable to orient himself and operate within the complex relationships in which every public organisation is enmeshed. A good understanding of the public sector environment, relations and procedures is required.[1] In addition to this, consultants must develop the ability to collaborate with public administrators and managers, using approaches and methods that are acceptable to the various partners involved and likely to gain their support rather than antagonising them.

The influence of the public sector environment is not the same in all consulting assignments. However, even assignments dealing with seemingly technical problems (e.g. in production management or cost accounting) often require special treatment. While the consultant may be recommending a solution that is, from a strictly technical point of view, equally applicable to a private or public enterprise, the environmental factors and forces affecting its application may be quite different.

18.1 Understanding public sector clients

First of all, it is important to find out who wants to have the consulting project carried out and for what purpose. Consultants may find that their employment has originated in one of two ways. Some governments may engage them to help in generating changes which the public enterprise managers are unable or unwilling to make. Or an enterprise may engage consultants to endorse new ideas which the government is unwilling to accept. It would therefore be useful for consultants to be aware of the circumstances and motivation leading to their engagement.

The real purpose of the project is not always that given in the terms of reference. In some countries, assignments are commissioned because there is a public demand that something should be done. At the stage of implementation, however, difficulties arise and governments sometimes lack the political will to execute measures which may be politically unpopular. Alternatively, one government agency may have a good idea, but other equally or even more influential agencies do not know about it, or do not support it. The consultant becomes trapped in interagency conflict, and his project is condemned to failure.

Assessment of the attitudes of management and staff in the public enterprise concerned is essential. If an assignment has its origin in a ministerial decision, and concerns an enterprise reporting to that ministry, it is important to find out what the management's objectives are. The battle is not lost in advance if an enterprise is reluctant to carry out a project initiated from above, but a great deal of patient explanation and persuasion will be needed in order to gain its confidence and support. It would be wishful thinking to believe that, once the supervising ministry has made up its mind, enterprise managers will simply be given orders and obey them. Experienced managers and consultants know only too well that there is a difference - sometimes a surprisingly significant one - between orders and their actual execution.

In recent years management consultants have been involved in major sectoral surveys of public enterprises, their environment and management systems. Some of these studies, particularly in Africa, have been undertaken in connection with the identification and preparation of projects for restructuring, rehabilitation and performance improvement of public-sector enterprises, for which governments have solicited loans from the development banks. Such projects involve a number of public sector partners - enterprises, ministries and agencies interested in various aspects of sectoral and enterprise management and development - in addition to the agency which is to provide finance for the project. There may be an agreed action programme and a steering committee for the co-ordination and supervision of the programme. The consultant may be requested to work primarily with this committee. In practice the relationships will always be quite complex, and it can never be taken for granted that all partners will pursue the same goal and have the same expectations of the consultant. If the use of a management consultant was suggested by a development bank or technical assistance agency, the consultant should exercise extreme care to ensure that his presence is not perceived as an imposition.

Furthermore, public sector organisations usually observe certain procedures in purchasing services. The consultant should find out about the procedure; in many countries there are publications covering government purchasing of professional and other services which provide relevant information. The procedure may be different from that which is usually applied in private enterprise. It is in the consultant's interest to comply with the procedural rules in force, even if he is not convinced of their effectiveness. For example, the format of the submission should be respected, or the structure of the fees justified as required by the regulations. Consultants who are not used to dealing with the public sector may be surprised by the lengthy selection and approval procedures, which make it impossible to keep the proposed team available until the start of the assignment, or even make it necessary to redesign the project when the decision to start has eventually been taken.

Knowledge of how public sector organisations budget and disburse funds for professional services is equally important. Many consultants might have avoided difficulties by finding out exactly what to do and whose signature is necessary in order to get paid on time.

18.2 The public sector environment

Management consultants are well aware of the need to view every organisation as part of its environment. What happens in an enterprise is often strongly affected by external factors over which the manager may have no or little control. In public enterprises, this dimension becomes even more pronounced. Most factors constituting the environment of private businesses affect public enterprises as well. In addition, there are specific institutional factors and influences:

● general public sector and civil service regulations may also apply to public economic enterprises, but in certain areas enterprises have to observe special regulations and codes;

● many management decisions about the enterprise are actually made outside it, and before a decision can be taken a lengthy consultation procedure, involving a number of units in the government structure, may be required;

● there may be a uniform planning and reporting system which applies to all enterprises and other organisations in the public sector;

● although the enterprise normally reports to one government department or agency (e.g. transport enterprises report to the ministry of transport), it also has more or less direct relations with other government departments in areas such as planning, investment, statistics, finance and accounting, auditing, regional development, foreign trade, wages and salaries, appointments to management positions, and others.

The relationships between the enterprise and the government may be relatively well defined and treated as a balanced system in official documents. The reality, however, is often different. Experience shows that co-ordination and co-operation between various government agencies is difficult and has many weaknesses in both industrialised and developing countries. In some countries various ministries pursue their own goals, and have different perceptions of what public enterprises should achieve. The demands made on enterprise management, and instructions sent to enterprises from different government departments, may be unco-ordinated, if not conflicting. In certain cases there is a conflict between various economic, financial and social objectives assigned to public enterprises. The government would like to see their profitability improve, provided that employment is maintained, tariffs for services are not increased, and unprofitable services are not discontinued. Public enterprise managers are often confused by incoherent signals coming from various government agencies, and this makes the formulation of corporate strategy all the more difficult. Furthermore, if an enterprise has to pursue a number of conflicting goals, it is very difficult, if not impossible, to assess its overall performance and establish who is actually accountable for what.

The financial relations within the public sector may represent a peculiar problem. The economy of an individual enterprise is often distorted by the fact that the government itself does not respect the financial autonomy of the enterprise and unduly delays payments for products and services, or admits that public corporations do not settle their mutual financial commitments promptly. Enterprises in turn are not able to service and repay loans received from government or commercial banks, and so on.

There is another significant aspect of the public enterprise environment. Whether it is officially admitted or not, public sector management is influenced by politics and tends to be more or less politicised. In some countries this influence is limited to the broad objectives of the sector; in setting these objectives the government is guided by basic political goals pursued by the party or coalition that is in power. In other countries politics may permeate all relations and decisions in public management, in the personnel area in particular. If this is the case, managers tend to ask themselves, "How will my decision be regarded by the politicians?"; instead of asking, "What should I decide to make the enterprise profitable and effective?" It quite often happens that when a major political change is expected in the country, say in forthcoming elections, all important decision making in the public sector is brought to a standstill.

Some very significant factors may be missing, or their role may be suppressed, in the environment of certain public enterprises. To analyse the causes and the consequences of this situation will be an essential task of the consultant. He may find out that the public enterprise is in a monopoly position and does not have to face any competition from other suppliers of goods and services. Or it may be that prices and tariffs for inputs and/or outputs are fixed by the government, and either ensure an easy profit for the enterprise, or, on the contrary, make profitability an impossible task.

The consultant should try to explore the reasons behind the absence, or weak functioning, of market and other forces that normally affect economic enterprises. He may find that the government has intentionally chosen to suppress certain forces – for example, to eliminate competition in order to shelter new national industries. It will be worth examining the impact of protectionist measures on the growth of the national enterprises concerned, as well as on the quality, price and competitiveness of their products. The consultant may often find that a distorted market and price structure is not an expression of socio-economic or political rationality, but of short-sighted and inconsistent management of the economy.

The consultant must try to understand how the system operates as a whole and what motives lie behind various measures, or behind the absence of appropriate measures. Political feasibility tends to rank high among criteria used in decision making, but such feasibility is essentially a matter of subjective judgement, reflecting the political views and priorities chosen by those who make the decisions.

Whether the consultant will be able to suggest changes in the system of public management and government-enterprise relations or not will depend essentially on the assignment objectives and on the climate in which the assignment is taking place. The consulting project may be a part of a comprehensive review of the public management system, or deal with one major aspect of this system (e.g. financing of public enterprises). If this is the case, there is an opportunity for raising fundamental questions concerning the objectives and overall effectiveness of the system, including the position of individual enterprises and conditions under which they will be able to operate as true enterprises. Several assignments recently carried out in developed countries even addressed issues such as the very existence of certain public enterprises, their transfer to the private sector, and the conditions under which this transfer should take place.[2]

18.3 Public managers, their motivation and development

Managerial attitudes and behaviour in public sector organisations constitute a key issue which consultants have to deal with in most assignments. It is very much a systems problem, as managers tend to act in accordance with the written and unwritten behavioural rules proper to the public enterprise system. Thus, if risk taking is not encouraged, most of them will avoid it. If conformity is valued more than drive and originality, most managers will be conformists. Therefore, if there are flaws in the system, these flaws inevitably affect managerial behaviour and efficiency at all levels.

But there may be other problems. For example, in many developing countries the very nature of the public manager's role is misunderstood. Managers in economic enterprises tend to be regarded as another group of civil servants. Their background and previous career may therefore be in general administration; when they are appointed to management positions in public enterprises, they may lack both the technical skills and the managerial attitudes needed for such a job. Alternatively, the importance of political loyalty may be overrated; this brings to managerial positions individuals who may be loyal, but eventually do more harm than good because they cannot master the technical aspects of the job. Excessive turnover of managerial staff in the public sector reflects a widespread misconception of individual responsibility and of the manager's role in efforts for long-term improvement of performance. A manager who knows that he will not stay in his job for more than six months is unlikely to worry about the future of the enterprise.

The lack of appropriate motivation is often referred to in this connection. The consultant should find out what motivates the managers in public enterprises and what does not. Management and performance can be improved only if individuals responsible for making and implementing decisions are predisposed towards such an improvement. If the consultant finds out that the motivation of managerial staff needs to be increased or reoriented, he should not hesitate to make appropriate suggestions. These suggestions may concern the salaries of public sector managers, the relationship between their remuneration and the actual performance of the enterprise, public recognition of the managers' role and contribution, increased job security, the possibility of taking risks, as well as other motivational factors.

Training tends to be regarded as an essential tool for improving the competence and performance of public sector managers. Indeed, many consulting assignments in the sector make recommendations for management training, or provide such training directly.

Management seminars and workshops can be used to make managers aware of the problems of their sector, of the opportunities for improving what needs to be improved, and of management experience in other countries and sectors. Public managers benefit a great deal from seminars run jointly for the private and the public sectors, in which they can learn from private managers how they deal with new challenges and problems.

Experience shows, however, that by itself even the best training programme is not enough to generate change and sustain the effort to change until a desired result is achieved in practice. Management training ought to be integrated with the identification of problems faced by public sector organisations, the analysis of the causes of these problems, and action aimed at removing those causes. If the real problems of the sector are not identified and tackled, training easily becomes an aim in itself.

18.4 Initiating and implementing programmes for performance improvement

As mentioned at the beginning of this chapter, management consultants may have an opportunity to influence the approach taken by a government or a public enterprise in order to streamline management and increase performance in the sector. The question is where and how to start an effective change process, and how to ensure that the original enthusiasm and good intentions will not die down after a few meetings and reports. It is quite difficult to provide answers, owing to the complexity of the environment and the various forces and problems involved.

The consultant can be very helpful in defining strategy and tactics for a performance improvement programme. It is necessary to identify the right starting point and method: for example, should it be an action programme prepared and presented by the management of one public enterprise as a pilot scheme, or should impetus be given by the prime minister, who would set up an inter-ministerial committee for reviewing the public enterprise management system? There is no universal recipe; each situation is different, and it is necessary to consider what approach is likely to motivate the people involved, obtain the necessary support from both the top and the bottom, and break down the barriers to improved performance (which may be quite strong). Motivation and impetus for change is unlikely to come if it is imposed by orders from the top. The chances that changes will occur are much brighter if there is involvement and participation at all levels from both management and workers, and if the changes are perceived as emerging from the whole group of practising managers.

In some countries action for improving performance in the public sector has started at the enterprise level. Various diagnostic and organisation development approaches have been applied, including the "planning for improved enterprise performance" (PIP) approach used by the ILO and several other organisations in various countries.[3] This has led to the definition of performance improvement, rehabilitation, modernisation, redressment and similar programmes, which define specific targets, set out the necessary technical, financial, marketing, personnel and other measures which will gradually be taken, outline responsibility for implementing the programme, and suggest financial and other incentives to motivate managers and employees for achieving programme objectives.

In preparing a performance improvement programme it is often useful to provide the enterprise concerned with data from comparable organisations. This can be particularly helpful if the enterprise enjoys a monopoly position, or applies government-controlled prices and tariffs, and therefore is not exposed to the influence of a free market. Ratios indicative of resource utilisation and operational efficiency achieved by other enterprises provide a basis for comparison and can suggest areas where productivity and efficiency ought to be increased.

Experience shows that even within the very complex public sector environment individual enterprises can resolve a number of management problems with their own resources and within their competence. However, a purposeful and systematic performance improvement effort is also a tool for identifying and analysing conditions and factors that are not under the control of the enterprise, but have to change if the enterprise is to implement its performance improvement programme. At that point the government departments concerned must become involved, and a performance improvement programme started by one or several enterprises has to be widened to embrace needed changes in the public management system. If there is reluctance to consider such changes, efforts generated at the enterprise level will produce modest results and enterprise managers will be discouraged from pursuing the programme.

Following the experience of public sector management in France, several countries have started using "programme contracts" to set the "rules of the game" for individual public enterprises, including mutual commitments of both enterprise and government. In some cases, management consultants have been involved. Such a programme sets out the objectives of the enterprise and the conditions under which these objectives should be achieved. It also defines conditions that the government itself has to create and observe in order to make the management of the enterprise fully responsible for the results achieved. It is too early to say whether this particular form of defining relations between enterprise and government will be suitable for wide application. However, it provides an interesting example of an approach that aims at running a public enterprise as a business and not as a civil service unit.

---

[1] See, for example, P. Fernandes: *Managing relations between government and public enterprises. A handbook for administrators and managers* (Geneva, International Labour Office, 1986), and M. A. Ayub and S. O. Hegstad: *Determinants of performance of public industrial enterprises*, Industry and Finance Series, Vol. 14 (Washington, DC, World Bank, 1986).

[2] See P. Fernandes, op. cit.; and *Privatization: Policies, methods and procedures* (Manila, Asian Development Bank, 1985).

[3] See R. Abramson and W. Halset: *Planning for improved enterprise performance: A guide for managers and consultants* (Geneva, International Labour Office, 1979); and V. Powell: *Improving public enterprise performance: Concepts and techniques* (Geneva, International Labour Office, 1986).

CONSULTING IN COMPUTER APPLICATIONS FOR MANAGEMENT

19

19.1 The computer scene in the 1980s

The fastest growing services of management consulting in the 1980s in industrialised countries concern computers and communication technologies. Improvements in computing hardware and software have expanded the markets for computer applications, and these in turn have created new challenges for management and new opportunities for consultants. These opportunities will continue because electronics, the technology behind computing and communications, is far from mature. As the price-performance of computing and communications technology continues to improve, the opportunities for managers, and in turn for management consultants, will continue to grow.

These opportunities result not from a single technological thrust but rather from the convergence of two electronic technologies — computers and telecommunications — which are changing the relative costs of moving people, goods and information. The nineteenth-century technologies such as rail transport and elevators reduced the relative cost of moving people horizontally and vertically and thereby encouraged the development of concentrated financial and commercial centres where people came together to process information. Similarly, advances in computers and communications make it cheaper for some people, equipped with workstations, to communicate with each other and with large data bases. These trends change the economics of doing business. Teleconferencing, for example, is often competitive with the cost of flying people around for meetings. Such trends also open up opportunities for delegating and decentralising business functions. Management consultants can help their clients to take advantage of reduced costs of moving information while assuring that morale and motivation of employees is kept high. Furthermore, the speed of technological change provides considerable challenges for management consultants. Unless new technologies are introduced skilfully, people suffer from stress induced by fear of redundancy, by repetitive, uninteresting work, and by the fear of not being able to cope with new systems.

In large organisations computers are no longer the sole province of the data-processing department; they are directly accessible to a new class of computer users such as secretaries, administrative staff, financial managers, office managers and so forth. Over 80 per cent of the enterprises which successfully coped with this change in the 1980s used consultants. Consultants helped with new applications made possible by a new generation of computer uses such as the electronic office concept; helped to set up training programmes so that employees could learn how to use the new machines; helped to establish and implement policies to encourage innovation while minimising confusion. The goal of this work is to help the employees of an organisation to absorb fully the new technology so that it becomes not just an administrative support and can be used to improve the organisation's competitive position.

The more employees are exposed to computers, the greater the demand for "user-friendly" resources. Many consultants find that the patterns of problems they encounter lead naturally to the development of the packages, books and training courses that their clients are eager for. In 1984 alone in the United States an estimated $3 billion of books, manuals, audiotapes, videotapes, disk tutorials and how-to classes were sold to make computers comprehensible to managers. "Fundamentals of data processing for non-data-processing professionals" is one of the most popular seminar topics offered by management consultants.

Management consultants help clients to use technologies to reduce the labour component of work, and to extend human capabilities. Reducing the labour component of work may free people from one sort of drudgery and the consultant should take care that the design of the work organisation does not subject them to another form of drudgery. For example, whereas data-processing equipment in the 1960s freed clerks from many boring paper-shuffling routines, it created armies of data-entry clerks. Today proper work organisation need not divide work into mind-deadening, machine-tending jobs. Instead work can be designed to extend the capabilities of every employee from top to bottom of the organisation. An order-entry clerk need not deal with a bewildering array of codes, but instead deal directly with clients. A production worker need not spend his life tightening one bolt, but instead be part of a team that takes responsibility for a high-quality product. In this, the consultant must help his client to see how technology can make work interesting as well as productive. Today too many consultants know only the technology, and although this expertise commands attractive fees, its narrowness often results in low productivity and poor morale.

19.2 The business functions

The main traditional business functions are all susceptible to the introduction of computers. Furthermore, consultants who specialise in these functions have long realised that micro-electronics has revolutionised some functions and that much of their work as consultants is to help businesses to keep pace and introduce technology in order to remain competitive. Some newer applications in selected business functions are reviewed below.

Production

Consultants in production or operations management face a continual computer-induced revolution. Manufacturing in most industrialised countries confronts a situation similar to that faced by agriculture in the 1940s and 1950s, when that sector's productivity rose rapidly. Many manufacturing firms will be able to survive this period of change only if all affected employees participate in the effort. Consultants can help their clients survive and prosper by applying new principles of work organisation, industrial relations and skill re-training.

Today's computer-induced revolution in manufacturing is probably more significant than the one in office data processing because in manufacturing computers are changing the rules. Before the 1970s managers generally accepted as the key to efficient manufacturing the organisation of work to produce a long series of standard items. New types of machines and handling systems, such as robots, numerically-controlled machine tools or electronically-guided transport networks, combined with new production planning and control systems, improve production efficiency of very short batches. Thus products which previously had to be made one at a time can now be turned out automatically, within limits.

An important consulting challenge will be helping clients choose and implement new production systems such as materials requirement planning (MRP), Kanban (just in time, or JIT), optimised production technology (OPT), or flexible manufacturing systems (FMS). Choosing among computer-based production management techniques requires trade-offs where a consultant's experience may be vital. MRP, for example, allows a great deal of advanced planning for medium-inventory, mass-production situations, but reduces flexibility to change those plans. Kanban can reduce inventory costs while involving employees in decision making, but requires excellent relations with suppliers and workers. OPT can clear up bottlenecks in one part of the manufacturing process, but can upset other parts. FMS promises to eliminate some of the weaknesses of the other three approaches.

These are just a few of the areas where consultants can help clients to make better use of capital invested in machinery and equipment, and at the same time help them to plan the training that workers and supervisors must have to deal with advanced technologies.

Finance

Financial management is so dependent on the rapid evolution of computer technology that many large consulting firms spend significant amounts on research and training and computers to keep their staff and clients up to date.

In the area of investing, investors can now keep track of and analyse trading activity in stocks and commodities through personal computers which receive trading information via FM broadcast transmissions. Information can be processed as well as received, so that an investor can get an up-to-the-minute tally on the worth of his portfolio. New electronic technologies are subjecting the financial sector to an upheaval in fields from EDP equipment management and electronic methods of payment to new client services. The up-to-the-minute information about a company's finances that electronic banking offers translates directly into better-managed cash balances. It can both increase the amount of money treasurers can invest for their companies and allow them to invest it on the best possible terms.

Such technology, properly applied, improves the productivity of both capital and labour. For example, one large North American company with a short-term investment portfolio averaging $80 million estimates that by using electronic banking facilities to reach the market early in the morning it earns an extra $150,000 a year. Staff productivity is improved by freeing staff from data gathering to do more analysis. One European company which carries out about 80 fund transfers a day tied up three staff members using telex. Through electronic banking these three people now spend only a small part of each day doing their old jobs and the rest of the day in more productive work.

Consultants and managers who use microcomputers and spreadsheet software (Lotus 1-2-3, Supercalc and others) can decrease the time they take to produce a budget forecast or a financial analysis. The consultant or manager can adjust the spreadsheet information to a new situation and review the results in a few minutes. A major benefit of this is that a person gains time to think about the information and to raise questions about productivity.

Marketing and distribution

When they make a consumer purchase, few people stop to think that it probably costs more to distribute the item than to manufacture it. Such has not always been the case, but today the high proportion of final product price accounted for by distribution costs also accounts for a high proportion of the distribution consultant's value to his client. The computer is partly responsible for this opportunity: first in helping the consultant to evaluate more alternatives, and second in automating the information flow that parallels the flow of goods. The speed with which inventory is turned over is crucial for many firms, and systematic co-ordination between manufacturer, wholesaler, retailer and consumer can considerably reduce distribution costs and liberate capital. Between 1980 and 1984, for example, General Motors, spurred by the competitiveness of the Japanese car industry, slashed its annual inventory-related costs from $8 billion to $2 billion using new JIT physical distribution systems which require networks of computers linking suppliers of parts with assembly plants. Transport costs can also be lowered, for example by reducing the number of times a product is handled, or by increasing the size of packages.

In physical distribution, information technology is now well past the experimental stage. Order processing, various levels of warehouse automation, inventory control, vehicle scheduling and so on are now computerised in many firms in the distribution sector. Electronic point of sale (EPOS) systems, coupled with bar-coding of goods, extend the information technology linkage to the final point of sale, allow retailers to operate with reduced levels of inventory, and bring a step nearer the ideal of physical distribution systems functioning as a pipeline rather than as a series of storage points.

Decentralised computing power with access to large-scale data bases makes direct mail a cost-effective alternative to mass-media advertising for many products. Instantaneous feedback, through information technology, of responses to changes in the marketing mix will facilitate rapid evaluation of mass-media advertising promotions, product and price changes, and so forth. Faulty marketing decisions can thus be remedied quickly. Reducing the risks of faulty decisions increases the scope for innovative and experimental adjustments to the marketing mix.

Electronic funds transfer at point of sale (EFT/POS), whereby customers' bank accounts are debited directly as they go through retailer checkouts, have been tested, but appear to be meeting consumer resistance. More success has been obtained in France with Smartcard, a credit-card-sized device incorporating a microprocessor which functions in much the same way as travellers' cheques. Teleshopping (placing orders for goods or services in response to information displayed on a domestic TV screen) has been tested with consumers, with disappointing results. It is not certain that teleshopping will soon develop into a significant sales outlet for goods. For services (financial, travel, and such) its prospects are rather brighter, once a widely-acceptable system of electronic funds transfer is developed.

Many marketing consultants use the principle of capturing data at the point of entry to help their clients to reduce costs, and speed up operations by putting data-entry terminals close to their customers — often on customers' premises. For example, many specialised wholesalers now have systems whereby retailers can easily ask a computer terminal on the retailer's premises about the availability of an item in the wholesaler's stock and place an order for it without discussing the order with the wholesaler. The consultant has several potential roles here. First, he helps his wholesaler client to work with retailers to design and implement a system that functions for both types of company. Here he is building on his consulting expertise, gained from similar experiences with other clients. He can also help the client to retrain the sales representatives and order-entry clerks whose jobs must be drastically redesigned. In most cases the context of their jobs is radically different — more professional and less mechanical. They can now use their knowledge of the technical features, quality and cost of various products to assure that the final retail consumers receive greater value.

Office management

The electronic office, heralded ever since the 1960s, is not yet a reality. Although it is not yet widespread, and present examples cry out for refinement and sophistication, the electronic office is arriving in bits and pieces. Consultants need to be able to help clients to thread their way between the fantasy woven by some equipment vendors and the reality of making things work.

Office equipment vendors would have preferred a more gradual and orderly acceptance of comprehensive office systems (of their own manufacture, naturally) and were slowly developing systems that would maximise each vendor's market share. However, the mushroom growth of the microcomputer industry, and the adaptation of its products for business use (mainly through software for spreadsheets and word processing) upset this stately pace and introduced chaos into the office equipment market, as personal computers, if they can communicate at all, can usually only communicate with a few similar machines, often expensively. Resolving the communications problem depends mostly on which vendors' communications protocols become standard. Until this issue is resolved, consultants will need to advise caution; after that, many assignments will involve helping clients to take advantage of the set of standard products.

Some functions have become standard in office automation systems: word processing, mailing list management, graphics, and spreadsheets for budgeting. In addition, a whole new range of functions is becoming electronically standardised: personal and company filing, communications, electronic mail, scheduling, mainframe information sharing, and historical record archiving.

Consultants need to advise their clients about the "misconception" that all the systems are "fully integrated". For example, a system described as fully integrating word processing, electronic mail and message distribution, and electronic filing may mainly address text manipulation and make little attempt to interface with other functions such as data processing.

Ample evidence suggests that *user involvement* is the best policy when introducing new office technology. The introduction of computers is more than putting a terminal on someone's desk. Properly designed ergonomic workstations can pay for themselves quickly in terms of increased productivity and morale. Thus a consultant is often well placed to advise managers on the advantages of detachable keyboards, adjustable chairs, footrests and wristrests that can be adapted to each person's needs, proper levels of light and non-glare screens to reduce eye fatigue, and the proper use of rest breaks to reduce errors and maintain productive output.

However, helping clients choose and install ergonomic workstations is only a small part of the challenge. The biggest gains are often associated with programmes where office workers learn to analyse their own jobs and are encouraged to work smarter, not harder. In such programmes equipment becomes the tools office workers use to gain recognition for finding better ways of working, and often to share in the gains from increased office productivity. The consultant's role here is often to set up training programmes and advise on the organisation of task forces and quality circles, and on formulae for gain sharing.

A consultant's greatest value is frequently his ability to help a client to anticipate and deal with unintended consequences. For example, organisations well advanced in installing electronic mail suddenly find that "telephone tag" has been replaced by a communications explosion. Before installing electronic mail a manager might expect to complete successfully 20 per cent of his telephone calls. With electronic mail this "hit rate" jumps to 100 per cent: every one who called left a message that needs a reply. Answering all these messages creates work and stress. Furthermore, a manager's secretary is less likely to be able to keep up with the boss's incoming mail unless the electronic mail goes to the secretary's screen, too. A consultant is more likely to discuss these problems with the client than an equipment vendor. He will be able to devise solutions that are organisational (e.g. delegating some of the answering), technical (e.g. limiting the number of messages that can accumulate) and behavioural (e.g. the courtesy of leaving only urgent messages).

19.3 Consulting and computers in small businesses

Businessmen, seeing that their consultants have personal computers, often ask for advice on which microcomputer to buy. The most common mistake consultants make in this situation is to fail to distinguish between professional and business uses of such machines. The former include what a professional person, such as a consultant, an accountant, or an engineer, does with such machines — for example, analysing client problems and producing form letters. Business uses include payroll, accounting, inventory control and so forth, which few professionals need bother with. Personal computers designed for professional applications rarely work well for small businesses.

Selecting computers for small businesses

In the United States, fewer than one tenth of the 3.2 million businesses employing under 50 people owned a computer in 1985, and this proportion was much lower outside the United States. Yet small businesses need no longer wait until they become big to use computers. Realising this, more and more entrepreneurs spend a great deal of time and money — much of it wastefully — amid a bewildering variety of products and programmes. Then they often turn to consultants, accountants and lawyers for advice because very few people who sell computer hardware and software to small businesses know much about its potential and the businessman's problems.

For example, the owner of a medium-sized business in a Mediterranean country recently visited a management consultant with whom he had dealt for many years. He was enthusiastic about the presentation by a computer salesman of a "fantastic" minicomputer system that could not only process all his data, but would also give him instant access to all kinds of management information. The consultant advised caution, pointing out that the businessman was only spending $1,000 a year on data-processing services from a well-run service bureau. Nevertheless, the businessman went ahead and two years later had spent $120,000 on hardware and software without getting much value for his money — and was still using the service bureau.

Any system should solve clearly defined business problems, which fall into two large groups: *technical support* and *core business operations*. Computer systems for the former are easy to install but rarely help much; computer applications for the latter can significantly enhance the firm's productivity but must be approached cautiously. Core business operations would seriously reduce business performance if a computer failed. A broker who cannot process transactions, a dealer whose inventory records are lost, or a bank that cannot cash cheques because of a computer breakdown are all having problems with core business operations. The consultant needs to point out that reliability does not happen by chance, and that leading brandnames may cost more but are usually backed up by reliable after-sales service. Additionally, market leaders are more likely to produce subsequent generations of equipment which is compatible with earlier models than fly-by-night low-cost computer vendors.

Technical support functions include document processing, financial analysis, engineering analysis, data base manipulation, and word and list (e.g. mailing labels) processing. With the exception of lists and data bases, the storage requirements of these applications are not important. The purpose and volume of such applications should always be questioned and the system closely examined — what may be required is a filing cabinet and not a computer. The business will not suffer much if equipment for these applications breaks down unless such applications affect core operations. Many programmes are easy to learn and are well tested, well documented and inexpensive because they are designed to appeal to large non-specialised markets.

Microcomputer software for spreadsheets, word processors and data bases are personal productivity tools that can help business people and professional managers (as well as consultants) to perform technical support tasks faster and better. These tasks fall into three main groups: calculating and forecasting; filing and retrieving; and writing reports and letters. Each of these types of task is facilitated by a type of software. Calculations such as budgeting are facilitated by spreadsheet software (e.g. Visicalc, Lotus 1-2-3, and Multiplan are popular); database management software (e.g. dBase III, or Friday) is designed for filing and retrieving; word-processing software (e.g. Wordstar, Wangwriter, Multimate) helps people to write and edit reports. "Integrated" software that combines graphics, word-processing and spreadsheets is becoming standard in many businessses.

Core business operations

Core operations are another matter. Because each business evolves its own procedures for pricing, customer service, product delivery, and similar functions, no standard computer packages will exactly match existing procedures. A computer package that forces a company to change the way it bills customers, handles invoices, or controls inventory, will create problems with customers, suppliers and employees unless carefully planned. However, good packages are flexible enough to meet a specific company's needs, and some consultants specialise in customising packages for each client's specific business.

If a client is convinced that a computer is needed, the consultant should make sure that this client fully understands the limitations of microcomputers and has considered the alternatives such as minicomputers and service bureaux.

A management consultant who is dedicated to providing good advice in small-business computing must stay up to date on the constantly changing potentials and limitations of hardware and software. This can be arranged by attending trade fairs and company demonstrations, subscribing to journals and attending training courses. For example, in the mid-1980s the main limitation of most microcomputers for small businesses is that they are single-user systems that can handle only one application at a time, and therefore the user must often wait for a report to be printed before doing anything else. Typically, as soon as a computer is installed (micro, mini or mainframe) several people want to use that resource. So a single-user system can quickly become a bottleneck rather than an aid. Furthermore, most microcomputers today use diskettes (called floppy disks) for storing programmes and files; these often have too little capacity or are too slow when processing even a small firm's customer file or inventory records. Multi-user microcomputers that can handle several thousand records are available, but these are costly.

One strategy for small business clients who are not yet "computer literate" is for them to start with a microcomputer that can immediately help with non-critical functions, such as word-processing for correspondence. At this stage the client will need help with two things:

(1) becoming comfortable with computer technology (hardware, software, documentation, good habits in storing files and so forth); and

(2) analysing his business goals and key result areas in preparation for applying computers to core business areas.

Most clients need to spend a lot of time and energy in learning the technology. A consultant can help the client to make good use of this time by setting up projects where the company learns the technology by applying it to straightforward tasks. For example, a businessman could learn to use a spreadsheet programme to analyse his key result areas, and project management software to plan a project to apply computers to core business areas. At the same time a clerk might use a data base package to create files on customers, or suppliers, for mailing lists. While some experiments might yield significant results, the main point at this stage is for the businessman and his employees to become comfortable with the technology so that it loses its aura of magic and so that the client can take the lead in the next, more serious, stage. Using the 20-80 rule, 20 per cent of the employees will make 80 per cent of the progress, and it is around them that the next stage will be built.

Eventually, the client should have a realistic view of the way data flow in his business and a rough idea of where the priorities lie. These priorities are assessed by analysing the balance sheet and income statement and calculating a variety of productivity ratios. For retailers and wholesalers, these include sales and inventory turnover per employee, floor space, and so on. For small industrialists and farmers one would look at money tied up in raw materials, land, work in progress and so forth.

Key employees should be involved, even though some of them may have lost interest and fallen behind because they failed to catch on to the computer technology. But those people may still be a vital source of ideas for improving the enterprise — which is the phase we are now in. One can involve people by helping to set up task forces, study teams, or quality circles. The client may want the consultant to organise training sessions on how to improve business performance and the consultant may want to suggest that the client should consider some profit-sharing ideas, because the employees will probably want to know how they will benefit if they participate in helping the enterprise to improve. Training of employees to use the technology can often be arranged at little or no cost by approaching companies which market hardware and software; this should not be confused with training employees how to improve the way they do their jobs.

At this point the client could be encouraged to implement a few changes for the better while investigating other long-term computer-based improvements. It is important now to look closely at "value-added resellers" or "vertical marketers". These are computer-oriented companies that specialise in particular types of business — in computer systems for lawyers, or for building contractors, for example. The client's trade association or a trade magazine should be a good source of information. If a client's core operations will depend completely on new systems, vendors must be reliable, and backstopping should be available. Other companies using the systems should be asked about their experiences.

Finally, the consultant should work out proposals with expected benefits in quantitative and qualitative terms. The solution should be flexible, able to grow with the company. "Hidden costs", such as training, should be included in the calculations. The implementation schedule should include training, information releases to keep people informed, and ceremonies or "rituals" to make sure employees feel that they are a part of the new organisation and new system. Make sure the documentation is good! Someone may even need to train the users how to become familiar with the documentation. Successful systems are characterised by people improving their skills and attitudes as the system is implemented and perfected.

Group and standard computer services

Computers can help consultants to provide better services to small and medium businesses by reducing the cost of standardised and personalised service. An example of this approach is assistance to small businesses in analysing their own performance, and finding areas of improvement through a combination of interfirm comparison and performance clinics. Basically, the consultant offers a service to a group of clients in the same type of business. These clients meet periodically to analyse their own performance ratios, calculated by the consultant, and share ideas about where and how to improve performance. Spreadsheet software is useful in reducing the effort of providing this type of service.

An example of making standardised services widely available comes from the Swedish Employers Federation which designed and promulgated a standardised accounting system among 100,000 small and medium businesses. The standard system and its variations (for construction, services, manufacturing, and so on) has made it easier for software houses to design computer-based packages that meet business needs.

These developments are rapidly changing the roles of consultants who specialise in finance and accounting services. For example, accounting packages are now appearing that apply the logic of artificial intelligence or expert systems in helping managers to choose productivity and financial ratios and compare them with sectoral standards.

Vertical marketing

By concentrating on similar types of business, some consultants go into vertical marketing of computer services and systems. Rather than simply leading clients to vertical marketers, consultants can themselves become vertical marketers. This involves choosing an industry and providing computer systems, including software and hardware, which solve critical problems occurring only in that industry. Such consultants market through special industry channels (trade fairs, professional associations and trade journals), and often know as much about the business as its practitioners.

Becoming a vertical marketer can be attractive for consultants with computer expertise, but it is risky as well. Hundreds of vertical markets can easily be defined by starting with three-digit standard industrial classifications. The biggest ones, however − banking, insurance, airlines, for example − are already served by the large equipment vendors like IBM, Burroughs and NCR. The next tier of markets, which includes hospitals and car dealerships, is often already served by specialised vertical marketers. Some "herd" markets − farmers, dentists, doctors, lawyers and accountants − have attracted hundreds of vertical marketers and are often hard to reach. Other herd markets − clothing, or food retailers, for example − often have profit margins that are too low to pay for the services of knowledgeable consultants. Some small manufacturers of computers have gone bankrupt concentrating on herd markets such as insurance agencies, law offices and farms. Thus, while vertical marketing is relatively straightforward, there is no margin for error.

19.4 Consulting and computers in large enterprises

In large organisations, what often appears to be a computer-related problem is not. It is frequently a problem in personnel policy, or a management or training problem. Thus the consultant who is about to be hired "because he is an expert in computers" should make sure that his expertise applies.

Productivity of the systems department

Consider the following brief by a chief executive: "The data processing manager and I think our computer operations department is reliable and efficient, but the systems department is not. Fewer than 10 per cent of our new applications projects are finished on time, and then only because we take staff off less critical jobs to meet the crisis. The systems manager has tried many productivity ideas — on-line programming, structured programming, structured walkthroughs — but the productivity of the systems department remains low. Some chiefs of user departments say they are planning to staff and manage their own projects."

This is a common brief because most organisations take longer and longer to design, test and implement new computer applications. Thus, many consultants take on more assignments to improve the productivity of the systems departments, but without much success. Conventional wisdom cites five major causes of unsatisfactory productivity in new systems development:

- the user keeps shifting his requirements;
- applications are growing more complex and this increases systems development time geometrically;
- similar new applications often conflict with existing applications and data bases;
- the professionalism of analysts and programmers is declining;
- criteria for measuring the performance of analysts and programmers are missing.

There is evidence to support all five points, but very few consultants have been able to help systems departments to improve productivity by trying to tackle these causes. Improvements come when consultants concentrate on helping systems managers manage better.

Oddly enough, very few systems managers believe that their area can be managed better. Many of them are ambitious ex-technicians with little real commitment to being good managers. They often exhibit a certain smugness and complacency about planning and managing their departments. One reason for this attitude is that they have implemented productivity tools over the years, without much result, primarily because analysts and programmers sense their managers' attitude. Consequently nobody really tries to make new tools and procedures work; and so of course they fail. Furthermore, many users within large organisations are aware of the systems managers' attitudes and are beginning to take responsibility for designing and implementing their own systems.

How then can a consultant help organisations to improve the productivity of the systems department? First, avoid the temptation to recommend and help install the latest productivity tool. Aim instead to develop the systems managers' skills and confidence — a "can do" attitude — and then embark on a well-structured productivity improvement programme. This stage can incorporate some productivity tools; the mistake to avoid is installing productivity tools as window dressing instead of attacking the root cause of low productivity. Most importantly, the consultant needs to help his client to ensure that the productivity programme is not sabotaged by analysts and programmers seeking to ride out just another management campaign so that they can slip back into their comfortable (and ineffectual) old ways of working.

The first step in setting up *a productivity programme* is to help the managers to measure current productivity and set achievable targets for improving it. Indicators include the proportion of projects that overrun their costs and schedules. The consultant is trying to develop managers who take pride in bringing new systems in under budget and on time, and who keep statistics and graphs to demonstrate their commitment to good management.

After the managers have set achievable targets, help them to list the factors that keep productivity low, and divide these into two groups: controllable and non-controllable. Then help them to produce action plans that concentrate on the controllable factors — those that they can do something about. Continue working as a process consultant, visiting the managers periodically and making sure that they have not lost interest in the productivity targets they set. The key here is to make improvements in productivity visible to everyone.

Systems managers who are committed to being good managers usually learn better management techniques quickly. Observe their meetings and determine whether some training in holding better meetings would help. For example, systems managers need two types of meetings: (1) status meetings where information is shared about project status, and (2) action meetings where problems are solved and solutions implemented. The consultant's role here is to help managers to learn how to ask intelligent questions at these meetings; to show them how to organise the meetings; and to help them to overcome the tendency to accept excuses too readily.

Career paths in data processing

Now consider a brief by an MIS manager: "The staff rotation policy in the information system department is designed to ensure that nobody gets stuck maintaining existing programmes for ever, but maintenance programming continues to increase compared to new work. We lose several top systems analysts every year because we do not have enough new interesting work. At the same time, users want me to transfer some systems talent to them, and I have tried to match some of my people with people in marketing, manufacturing and accounting, but my salary scale is usually higher than theirs. So I am left with several highly paid but underutilised people."

Data-processing managers often ask consultants to solve data-processing personnel problems, particularly how to attract and keep top systems professionals. This problem is usually compounded by a counter-pressure: as an organisation's installed base of computer applications grows, the proportion of programme maintenance work to new applications work grows as well.

Most systems analysts prefer the challenge of working on new applications to the routine of updating existing ones. Also, most companies prefer to develop their future managerial talent by rotating people across the organisation, but people have difficulty moving between systems and other line and staff positions because few companies have pay scales and job titles that make such movements easy.

Solutions to this problem have worked in some companies, but not in others. Rather than recommending and implementing a particular solution to this particular career-path problem, a consultant should consider helping his client to analyse several alternatives, such as how to organise work so that it is more interesting, or how to involve the employees concerned as well as the personnel department in solving the career-path problem. Having analysed the problem, the consultant briefs the client so that he knows the alternatives and can set up an internal consultative process for as many of the employees as possible. One alternative for large organisations is the information resource management (IRM) concept, which involves a combination of data processing, telecommunications and office automation. This arrangement provides more job opportunities for qualified professionals trained in systems design and development.

Intrapreneurship

Another alternative for strong systems groups is to become "intrapreneurial": that is, for the systems group to become a profit centre where the employees share in the net returns of their projects, taking on outside jobs, and giving users the right to buy systems services outside the organisation. Data-processing managers often like this idea because it can help them (in collaboration with hardware vendors) to convince top management to buy extra processing capacity to be rented out to other organisations (see also section 12.5).

A consultant can help his client to make "intrapreneurship" work by providing advice and training. First, point out that not just anyone can be an intrapreneur: if the person in charge of a new EDP profit centre is not bursting with enthusiasm for making a success of himself and his idea, it is unlikely to work. Secondly, advice on corporate funding may be welcome. Funds for this type of activity should be kept low enough to encourage a sense of urgency and to make the intrapreneur realise that he must be market-oriented. For example, in-house users might be allowed to buy services from other data processing vendors so that they do not feel they are paying premium prices for in-house services while outsiders get service at the marginal cost of otherwise unused resources. This realisation may lead the client to ask for help with keeping the internal relationships clean. The consultant can help to draft a policy statement, perhaps even to organise a briefing to make sure everyone understands the rules of the game: who controls what money, what the criteria are for success, and what the success of this venture will mean to the company. Finally, the consultant may wish to suggest entrepreneurship training. As mentioned above, data-processing managers and systems analysts may know the computer business, but they rarely possess skills in marketing, subcontracting and financial management which are often crucial for success in such ventures.

Designing management information systems (MIS)

Many senior managers, when faced with management information systems problems, turn to computer specialists too soon.

A large government ministry in Asia decided that it wanted a management information system that would predict economic problems, a task most consultants felt was impossible, and in any case one that would require professional and analytical expertise that the ministry was unable to hire or obtain. Nevertheless, the ministry hired a string of computer specialists who dutifully produced systems and procedures, none of which came close to satisfying the request.

Regardless of his background and expertise, the consultant should start by trying to find a feasible system that will actually improve the performance of the client organisation, before he takes on the task of producing a new computer-based MIS. One good way to start is to compare the performance indicators of the client organisation with those of similar organisations. The consultant can ask about the four or five most important performance indicators that the client uses to control his "key results areas". Such questions are often best asked either by general management consultants, or by consultants who specialise in the client's types of business.

For the many organisations whose top managers are vague about what business they are really in, it is often best to use a top-down process consulting approach to identify the key indicators. Then the consultant helps the management team to set targets, tackle constraints and produce an action plan. From this action plan can be deduced the performance indicators that need to be monitored to track the implementation of the action plan. The MIS that results becomes a score-keeping system that managers can use to analyse further problems and reward achievement.

The far more commonly used approaches to MIS problems when management is vague about its strategy, namely bottom-up and imposed financial or budgetary systems, can do more harm than good. The bottom-up approach, where the consultant analyses the paper flows and attempts to computerise selected operating procedures, is often a last resort, where management and the consultant engage in a sort of charade.

Designing computer applications

When a consultant is called in to help improve an information system, the consultant and the client usually agree on a conventional three-stage project with eight phases as shown in table 19.1. Most computer systems result from this conventional, linear, step-by-step process, which has its disadvantages: the typical system takes an average of a year to design, programme, test and implement. Since few organisations can afford enough experienced systems analysts and designers, most users must wait their turn, and the queue is often two years long. Systems that take a total of three years to implement are rarely what the user wanted in the first place; furthermore, his needs have probably changed as well. So most organisations supplement their in-house information systems expertise with external consultants and use several variations of the conventional project approach to develop new information systems.

Three common alternatives to the conventional project approach are packages, prototypes and user-developed systems. They are all used to shorten the

Table 19.1 Conventional systems development project

Stage	Phase
I. Definition	1. Feasibility study
	2. Information analysis
II. Physical design	3. Systems design
	4. Programme development
	5. Procedure development
III. Implementation	6. Conversion
	7. Operation and maintenance
	8. Post-audit

time, lower the cost and raise the quality of the resulting system. To be able to choose the right approach for a client, a consultant must understand the cost patterns and risks of each one.

With the conventional approach, about a quarter of the total cost is incurred in defining the functions of a proposed system and its expected costs and benefits. About half the cost is spent in the design phase, where the programmes are written, documented and tested. The remaining quarter is incurred during implementation in training users, switching over to the new system and evaluating the results (the post-audit). Of course, some steps may be repeated when the work of an earlier phase needs to be modified because of later results.

Because the costs of the conventional approach represent mostly the use of expensive skilled consultants and systems employees, much effort goes into techniques to improve their productivity (among these are structured design and programming). This has resulted in a new research area in computer science: software engineering — that is, the entire range of activities used to design and develop software (for example, programme specifications, structured programming, testing techniques).

Although application software packages have existed for decades, their rapidly increasing popularity reflects the changing economics of the computer industry. The basic idea is to reduce the total cost by spreading systems development costs over several installations by repeatedly using the same package. A good example is the use of standard payroll and transport scheduling packages by franchise retailers such as fast-food restaurants. The systems development savings of multiple-site installations also extend to software maintenance: fewer hours are needed to change one system installed in 100 sites than to change 100 different systems in those locations. For example, when payroll systems must be changed due to changes in legislation, collective agreements, or new remuneration schemes, then it is much more economical to change the same payroll system at many sites than to change many different systems.

Consultants find it relatively easy to help clients to decide whether to use packages or to develop unique systems from scratch. Furthermore, because they develop expertise by specialising in particular applications for several clients, consultants often have an advantage over in-house systems analysts who must spread their expertise over different applications for the same company. But since "canned" packages rarely fit a company's needs exactly, a consultant's main advantage often resides in his ability to help the client to manage the subtle organisational changes that are frequently required for systems to mesh well with the organisation.

Furthermore, when a user's needs have not been specified precisely, a consultant can often help his client choose a third approach — prototyping. Prototyping is a combination of systems design, user involvement and training. A prototype is a rough system put into the user's hands quickly, as opposed to a refined system that is implemented only after it has been thoroughly tested. The prototype approach exploits the fact that as hardware gets cheaper and high-level software easier to use, companies can afford to build "quick and dirty" systems and refine them over time to get an acceptable fit between user and system. Furthermore, by involving the users in refining the prototype system, one often finds that the users can do some of the easier programming tasks, such as defining functions and menus and setting out formats for documents and reports. Since the users and systems designers together identify the final requirements while the users actually work with the system, less money is spent at the outset defining the requirements. Benefits can also begin to accumulate earlier and users are often less resistant because they participate sooner.

However, these benefits can be expensive. The development of a working system within a few days is usually accomplished with a data-base management system (DBMS) with high-level query languages and report-writing packages. DBMS systems can cost more than $100,000 and require hardware expansions to run. They also run more slowly than a conventionally designed programme, written say in COBOL. Although this lack of emphasis on operating efficiency troubles many data-processing managers, the prototype approach — by concentrating on staff productivity — often cuts systems development costs by 75 per cent. This is a profitable trade-off when benefits are needed quickly, or where users' needs are likely to change often.

Training the users

Without training, any sufficiently advanced technology is indistinguishable from magic, and when technology is immature, as with computers and telecommunications, investment in training is the key to survival.

The knowledge gained through research and the expertise gained through consultancy can often be passed on to clients through training. However, all too often requests for training get turned over to computer jocks who know all about the insides of the boxes, but too little about what they are good for. A frequent complaint of managers is that they learned everything about the machines except how to use them effectively.

When training some managers in how computers can help them, remember that computers themselves are good at teaching people how to use them. The problem for the consultant is to provide the proper selection of learning tools and exercises. For microcomputers these include "electronic tutorials" — computer programmes designed to lead new users through a series of exercises on the computer, in the best tradition of computer-based training. Beyond this it is often useful to provide exercises in the business functions that a manager will frequently use. For example, financial managers appreciate training sessions using spreadsheet packages, while project managers would gravitate to sessions on project management software. The management consultant is often uniquely qualified to implement improved training approaches based on the business functions, as opposed to the conventional approach of explaining hardware and software before the applications.

For large organisations, especially those where the data processing manager is ill-equipped to assist in staff development, consultants are often asked to assist in setting up microcomputer training programmes. The first phase, lasting about a year, should involve at least 20 per cent of the staff in laboratory-based training with a variety of hardware and software which the organisation has decided to support. After that a training system should be set up whereby electronic tutorials are available for people who wish to learn about particular hardware and software. If the consultant has done his job properly, there should be enough employees in the organisation who can serve as trainers and coaches to those who want to acquire computer skills.

19.5 Future outlook: preparing for the unexpected

Notwithstanding the spectacular progress made in the last 5-10 years, computing is far from being a mature technology. Personal computer hardware and software, for example, are evolving so rapidly that management consultants are faced with radically different computer-based productivity tools about once a year.

Although there are vast numbers of computers in use today, they are still far from being pervasive. Virtually all pervasive technologies (automobiles, telephones, typewriters, and such) have passed through four evolutionary stages, starting as laboratory curiosities, then for a time being exotic tools or toys used by a few to solve special problems. In the third stage the technology is manufactured and has become well-known and quite commonplace, but is still used by a small proportion of the population. It is only in the fourth and final stage that pervasive technologies become part of the fabric of a society, where their absence is more noticeable than their presence.

Computer technology, especially personal computers, is in stage three and is unlikely to reach stage four until extensive and compatible data and communication networks are built that would make computers an effective substitute for the telephone or postal systems. In helping the technology become pervasive, computer scientists are concentrating on providing the high-performance computer architectures with interfaces that mask their internal complexity from the user.

As computers enter this fourth stage, the consultants' opportunities will be characterised by the fact that most users are beginners. For the time being, the consultant acts as an interface for many clients, helping them to reduce the amount of time required to get through cumbersome manuals and training courses, to find out how to apply what is still a relatively expensive, unreliable and awkward technology which most managers still have trouble in learning.

Since we literally do not know what will happen in the future, the best a consultant can do is to prepare for the unexpected by assuming that most things will stay the same, and by following two or three historical trends. Two trends to follow are *technological innovations* and *social demands*. The technological innovations, like networks and graphics, open up new kinds of business opportunities. Social demands concern functions and activities where considerable social and economic benefits could be drawn from computerisation (e.g. by increasing safety at work or warning of disasters).

The forward-looking consultant will want to watch how networks are changing because, for the past few decades, the types of business that applied networks of computers most successfully often radically changed their ways of operating. In doing so they usually improved productivity, especially in terms of delivering value to customers. These industry networks were often pushed by the computer vendors who encouraged the businesses to adopt certain standards. One of the earliest of these were airline passenger reservation systems, followed by linkages with hotel and car rental reservations. Bank demand-deposit clearing house systems using magnetic ink character recognition (MICR) are now being followed by electronic funds transfer (EFT) networks. The universal product code (UPC) standard was necessary for customer electronic point of sale (EPOS) systems for integrated distribution of packaged foods. Similarly the Kanban (JIT) automobile assembly systems pioneered by Japanese manufacturers are only possible with computer networks between a manufacturer and his suppliers.

A consultant with a dynamic viewpoint will develop frameworks for quickly assessing the stage each client is at and will adjust his services accordingly. In an organisation where few end users understand the technology, the client needs help in setting up education and user-support services. In a more advanced organisation, the client may need help in creating groups of change agents who can help all parts of the organisation to share innovations. The client may also need help in turning completely absorbed technology into a strategic competitive advantage. Since at each stage sensitive considerations emerge as to which department will provide certain services, a consultant's value may lie in his detachment and objectivity.

In summary, the rapid increase in computer and telecommunications capabilities is creating significant opportunities for management consultants with computer experience. These opportunities differ for consultants who specialise in different management and business functions, or serve different types of client. However, skills in involving people in client organisations in the design and use of systems are becoming increasingly important to all consultants in the computer field.

PART IV

MANAGING A CONSULTING ORGANISATION

CONCEPTUAL APPROACH TO THE MANAGEMENT OF CONSULTING

20

The previous parts of this book have shown how management consultants operate in helping to solve their clients' business and management problems. Part IV, which opens with this chapter, looks at the consultant's work from a different angle. It shows management consulting as a professional service that itself requires competent management if it is to serve clients effectively and, at the same time, achieve satisfying business results.

That management consulting itself needs to be managed may be self-evident to a large consulting firm employing hundreds of consultants and engaged in a wide range of assignments. In such a professional firm, finding work for all consultants, co-ordinating a number of varied assignments, providing operating consultants with technical and administrative support, and making sure that the firm keeps in touch with developments that affect its work all represent a formidable management challenge. However, a small consulting organisation, and even a single practitioner, also needs some management of resources, time allocation, relations with clients, administrative support, professional development and so on.

In practice this basic truth is often ignored. There are consulting organisations, including some fairly large ones, which devote all their talent and energy to finding new assignments and dealing with their clients' problems. They neglect the management of their own operation, which leads to inefficiencies, internal conflicts, and even to flaws in the services provided to clients.

Clients are not unaware of this. We often hear, "Healer, heal thyself!", or "Consultant, take your own medicine!" The message cannot be more plain. While any professional service requires management reflecting its nature and complexity, the case of management consultants is a particularly delicate one. Management is their daily bread and showing clients how to manage better is their main activity. If clients are to take such advice seriously, they must see that the consultant is able "to practise what he preaches". If this is not the case, clients become suspicious and tend to be cynical about the consultant's real ability to deal with other people's problems.

This chapter provides a brief review of those general characteristics of consulting that affect its management. Emphasis is put on the unity of two inter-related aspects: consulting as a professional service, and consulting as a business activity.

20.1 Consulting as a professional service

It is useful to start our analysis by recollecting that management consulting belongs in the service sector, and, within this sector, to the still very broad and heterogeneous sub-sector of *professional services*. Our first question will concern those characteristics of professional services that have significant implications for their organisation and management.

Intangible product

It has been pointed out many times that professional services produce intangible outputs or products.[1] In consulting, the product is the advice given to the client, or, if emphasis is put on implementation, one could say that the final product is the change that has actually occurred in the client organisation thanks to the consultant's intervention.

Such a product is difficult to define, measure and evaluate. The consultant can have his conception of the product, while the client's view of the product and its real value can be quite different. In marketing his services, what the consultant is selling is essentially a promise — a promise of help that will satisfy the client's needs. Clients cannot, to use Theodore Levitt's words, "see, touch, smell, taste or test" the product before deciding to purchase it.[2] They have to look for surrogates in assessing whether the consultant is likely to deliver what he has promised. The consultant-client relationship has to be built on confidence above all.

However, there appears to be a growing desire on both the consultants' and the clients' side to "increase the tangibility" of consulting services in order to enhance their marketing, planning, quality management and control by both the client and the consultant. Aubrey Wilson points out that certain fundamental characteristics of services, traditionally stressed in academic literature, "are far from being absolutes" and "are in fact manipulatable".[3] For example, more and more consultants are trying to define their service as a distinct product and provide clients with a specific and detailed description of this product, which could be a management model or system, or a structured methodology applicable to particular types of problem in client organisations.[4]

Link between consultant and client

The link between the consultant and his client, emphasised in earlier chapters, is a fundamental feature of consulting services. If there is no client, there is no service. The consultant cannot produce for stock, getting ready for quick delivery to future clients. In fact, the client is a direct participant in the production process. As a minimum, he has to help the consultant in defining the scope of the advice, provide needed information, and then take the advice. However, the client's involvement can be much more intensive; in genuine process consulting, it is the client who "produces", while the consultant acts as a catalyst and provides only one, though essential, ingredient in the production process.

The link between the consultant and the client is a highly individualised one. On each side of the partnership there is one person, or a small team. Whatever the size and complexity of the professional service firm, the firm puts individual professionals in direct contact with individual clients for undertaking specific assignments. Larger consulting firms can handle relatively larger and more complex assignments, involving teams of consultants, but even a very large firm operates through a number of individualised client assignments and cannot think in terms of mass production, or of distributing services through wholesalers. Even the largest consulting firm operates as a retailer. Professional consultants are used to dealing directly with clients and spend more time with clients than with colleagues within their firm.

Unity of design, production and delivery

Design, production and delivery are separate processes in many sectors. In consulting, the professional (individual or team) working within the client's organisation deals with all these functions. Production is simultaneously delivery. Elements of the design of the service may be available before starting the assignment — the consulting firm may have developed a standard planning, cost control, job evaluation, or remuneration system, and markets this system as its unique "product". Yet the design work can be completed only while working with a client, by adapting the system to his specific conditions and requirements, and putting it to work.

Some standardisation of services is both feasible and desirable because there are not only differences but also similarities in clients' needs. To determine what to standardise and sell as a "standard product" is a difficult decision. There are consultants who have spoilt their reputation by trying to sell standard service packages to clients who needed an individualised approach. On the other hand, if a standard system or methodology is applied flexibly and with imagination, it helps to increase the quality and reduce the cost of the service provided. A consultant who has developed and "owns" such a system can gain a distinct competitive advantage over other consultants.

Consulting firms try to standardise not only their products but also certain internal procedures. In a sense, part II of this book, describing the five major phases of the consulting process, can be regarded as a general standard for structuring and sequencing activities and relationships in a consulting process. Many consulting firms have developed their own standard procedures — for example, for diagnosing problems in a client organisation, or designing and introducing a management information system.

Role of professional staff

A consultant on an assignment has to make choices and decisions regarding what service to deliver. Even if he is introducing a standardised system, helped by guidelines and suggestions from his superiors, many things must be left to his discretion. In addition, his personal relationship with the client will have a strong influence on the effectiveness of the process and the outputs.

The fact that many significant technical decisions can never be fully centralised or replaced by standard guidelines underscores the professional competence and responsibility of the "operating core", as Henry Mintzberg calls it.[5] In a consulting firm this operating core is made up of highly educated and skilled professionals, who must be able to work relatively independently, and readily take decisions within general strategies and policies set out by the firm.

The firm, on the other hand, must know that it can rely on the competence and integrity of its operating core staff. In some established professions there is a well-defined path to the necessary level of competence and integrity, including university studies, attendance at a graduate school, and practical training and "indoctrination" over a number of years in a professional firm. Membership in professional institutions or special examinations may be required. The result of this process is a reasonably high degree of standardisation of skills, permitting the definition of a range of jobs that a professional should normally be able to perform either without or with limited supervision. Even the attitudes of professionals tend to become fairly standardised; thus it can be predicted how professionals will normally react and behave in typical situations in which their intervention is required.

In management consulting the situation is infinitely more complex, for several reasons. Consulting is a young profession and consultants employed by any firm usually have different educational and practical backgrounds. It is almost necessary for them to come from various schools and business environments so that the firm can handle a variety of assignments and deal with management problems requiring a multidisciplinary approach. Furthermore, the behavioural aspects of handling technical and human problems are probably more significant in management consulting than in certain other professions.

Therefore, in managing the professional staff, consulting firms face special challenges, such as:

- how to build up a homogeneous operating core with people possessing heterogeneous backgrounds and skills (e.g. finance and accounting, information science, behavioural science, sectoral economics, industrial engineering);

- how to develop a common philosophy of consulting and an esprit de corps while maintaining the diversity of personalities, attitudes and approaches needed for various assignments, which can be a source of innovation;

- how to define the right degree of decentralisation of technical decisions concerning client assignments (e.g. questions which an operating consultant on assignment can decide, and those on which a manager or partner should give an opinion or make a decision);

- how to provide consultants on assignments with technical information and support services in order to make them as effective as possible to their current clients;
- how to make sure that not only the skills, but also the personalities and work styles of consultants and clients, will be matched in order to establish a productive consultant-client relationship in every single case.

Professional culture

Despite their high level of knowledge and skill, or perhaps because of it, consultants are difficult to manage. Many of them have become used to getting on with the job for the client and deciding what to do without waiting for any instructions and controls from their superiors. They tend to have their own conception of management in a professional firm: managers are responsible for creating favourable conditions for professional work (which includes finding new work and securing finance), but should not intervene in individual projects and assignments. Some professionals resent any control or interference in their operational work, while others are prepared to accept it on condition that it comes from people whom they respect as experienced senior colleagues.

Some consultants become strong individualists and one is tempted to ask why they actually stay with the firm. Some stay because they regard themselves as technicians and do not want to be bothered with administrative and marketing problems. Others appreciate the advantages of team work and of collaboration with other professional colleagues in dealing with complex business and management problems. There is a third group of professionals for whom work in a professional firm is mainly a learning experience, and who do not feel that they must stay with the firm until retirement.

The attitudes that will prevail depend very much on the organisational culture of a particular consulting firm. Indeed, consulting firms tend to exhibit various organisational cultures. The firm may be nothing more than "a collection of individualities housed under one roof", and physically not even under the same roof, since consultants spend most of their time in client organisations. The management of the firm may act as an employment agency, whose main objective is to find work, keep consultants occupied, and ensure regular income to the firm and its employees.

In contrast, leading consulting firms in many countries emphasise a common consulting philosophy, team spirit, sharing of information, participation in management, and pride in belonging to an excellent professional firm.[6] They respect individualities, but counter centrifugal tendencies (which easily develop in decentralised organisations where the operating individual enjoys a great deal of freedom and responsibility in working with a client).

Service quality

The client has a contract with the consulting organisation, not with its employees. Under this contract the organisation accepts full responsibility for the service provided. This underlines the importance of quality management, and the need to devise a quality management system that is adapted to professional services, where detailed and continuous quality checks are unthinkable, and where quality standards are difficult to define and are prone to subjective interpretation.

In this context, probably the key issue of quality management is the consulting philosophy and self-image of the firm. If "highest possible quality of services to clients" is adopted and pursued as a basic objective, solid ground is laid down for treating service quality as a key aspect of both policy and operations. The following management approaches are then essential for putting this basic objective into effect:

(1) Consistently applying high standards in recruiting new consulting staff.

(2) Providing high-quality induction training, as well as facilities for further training and self-development throughout every consultant's professional career.

(3) Making sure that experience available anywhere within the firm will always be tapped and considered in dealing with assignments for which it may be needed.

(4) Evaluating the course and the outcome of every assignment and paying particular attention to the client's satisfaction.

(5) Treating quality of service, and self-development efforts which are aimed at higher quality, as principal factors in promoting and remunerating consultants.

(6) Demonstrating that higher management echelons in the consulting firm are continually interested in quality, and using a variety of intervention techniques to check service quality in justified cases and to help improve quality.

(7) Assigning the right role to research and product innovation and ensuring that their results will be available, in the shortest possible time, to operating consultants and to clients.

20.2 Consulting as a business activity

Management consulting is a business activity, and has to be managed as such, in all cases where an independent service is provided to clients for a fee, and where the consulting firm has to sell its services and finance its operation and growth from its earnings. This applies to the vast majority of consultants in free-market and mixed-economy countries. However, the reader knows that there are also consulting units whose financial independence is limited or nil. Not all principles of managing a professional business may be applicable to them. Yet they can greatly benefit from being organised and managed as "quasi-businesses".

Recognising that consulting is a business

It is not always easy to call a spade a spade. For many years, professional firms resented being regarded as "businesses", and even at the present time many professionals feel uneasy about "selling" their services or discussing fees, which they regard as unprofessional and beneath their dignity.[7] As one practitioner has pointed out, a management consultant is often "torn between being a professional and a commercial".

Yet in the economic system of most countries a professional service must find a buyer (client) who is able and prepared to pay an adequate price for it. There is a more or less structured market for professional services, and competition among professionals is increasingly regarded not only as acceptable, but as beneficial to the clients. The marketing of consulting and other professional services has undergone spectacular changes over the last ten years, and in many countries further changes are likely to occur in the years to come.

Like any other business, a consulting firm can and should make a profit. The size of this profit will, of course, depend on many variables, some of which are not under the firm's control (e.g. demand for consulting services), while others are (e.g. the technical level of the services provided and the efficiency of operations). Profit planning, and deciding on the use of the profits, is important in every consulting firm that wants to be in a healthy financial position and have adequate resources for further development.

As regards business ownership, most consulting firms are owned by the consultants themselves. Several legal forms of ownership are common in consulting and will be described in chapter 26. However, not all consultants working with a firm are necessarily co-owners. There can be a group of senior consultants (partners), who are co-owners of the firm, and a group of consultants who are employed by the firm without having any share in the ownership.

People-intensive business

A consulting business sells the professionals' time and expertise, including the special know-how and technical backstopping provided by the firm for its staff. Such a service is highly people-intensive (labour-intensive) and involves relatively little capital. An enterprising management professional who lacks capital may be unable to establish a manufacturing business, but may enter the consulting business relatively easily. All he needs is a small amount of working capital to cover his living and other expenses before he starts collecting fees on a regular basis. He can even borrow this money. Many sole practitioners have thus been able to enter the consulting business, although quite a few of them have had to make personal sacrifices at the beginning of their career in consulting.

The labour-intensive nature of consulting affects all areas of managing consulting businesses. The professional staff constitutes the main asset, although it has no value from a strictly accounting point of view and bankers would not normally recognise it as a collateral.[8] The cost of staff tends to be high; an optimum allocation and utilisation of staff time (staff productivity), and investment in further staff development, are therefore fundamental issues of economics of the consulting firms. Opportunities for achieving economies of scale and increasing staff productivity are limited; therefore, growth in income and profits is not normally possible without recruiting more people.

On the other hand, to change products, that is to introduce new services, is much easier in consulting than in capital-intensive businesses. Many consulting firms have been able to exploit this advantage in adapting their service portfolio to new needs of clients.

Yet it appears that at the present time management consulting is tending to become more capital-intensive. This is owing to factors such as information technology and its rapid penetration into management and administration. Management consultants have increasingly to invest in hardware, software and related staff training, but new developments in the EDP field quickly make this investment obsolete, thus forcing the firm into making further investments.

Entrepreneurship in consulting

Entrepreneurial attitudes and behaviour are essential in the consulting business. Most consultants who start their business as sole practitioners think and act as entrepreneurs: they launch new activities and seek clients in conditions of uncertainty, take considerable but calculated risk, work hard to succeed, seek independence, and pursue their business and life goals with drive and perseverance. A consulting business needs entrepreneurial thinking and behaviour even when it becomes larger and employs many consultants. It probably needs entrepreneurship much more than large businesses in some other sectors: this is explained both by the rapidly changing needs of clients and by the fact that new opportunities for consulting arise virtually every day, but the consulting firm has to perceive and take them.

Due to the individualised nature of consulting work and the daily interaction between the consultant and the client, it is impossible fully to centralise the entrepreneurial function in the hands of one owner or a small group at the top of the firm. Where this happens, many opportunities will be easily missed, because they are only visible to the consultant on an operating assignment. This is essentially a matter of defining the role of every professional in the firm, not only in terms of a specific technical function assigned to him, but also in terms of business development. Individual consultants will think and behave as entrepreneurs if they know that such behaviour is wanted, valued and stimulated by the firm's management.

When consulting is not a business

Not all management consulting units are independent businesses. Internal consulting units within governments and public or private corporations, and most consulting units in management or productivity centres in developing countries, cannot be categorised as businesses. Some of these units provide consulting services free, or for a nominal price, instead of charging the full market rate. Their budgets may be subsidised by their parent body, or from another source. Some of these units may be in competition with other consultants, but their independence may be limited in various areas:

● in recruiting, remunerating and terminating the appointments of staff;
● in fixing consulting fees;
● in expanding or scaling down activities;
● in deciding to launch new products and enter new markets; and so on.

All the principles involved in managing a professional business cannot be applied to such a unit. However, certain principles are applicable. The effectiveness of these units can be enhanced by treating them as "quasi-businesses", providing them with relative decision-making autonomy and making sure that their business results have a bearing on staff remuneration and motivation, on the expansion or reduction of operations, and the like. For example, internal consulting units may compete with external consultants for work to be done within the parent organisation, but, at the same time, be authorised to market their services to other companies.

20.3 The management matrix in a consulting organisation

Some important conclusions concerning the nature and the scope of the management of consulting activities can be drawn from this analysis. First, each of the two sides of consulting reviewed above — consulting as a professional service and consulting as a business — has its specific management requirements and justifies certain management tasks. Secondly, management tasks in a consulting organisation relate either to individual client assignments or to common and general problems of developing and operating a consulting practice as a whole. These different dimensions are shown in figure 20.1 in matrix form.

Figure 20.1   The management matrix in a consulting organisation

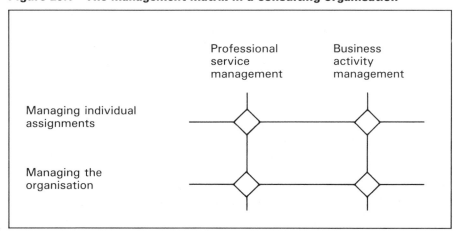

Balancing professional service and business activity management

In management consulting, the management of a professional service and of a business activity are two sides of one coin. They can be described and examined separately, but in real life they are not separated. The management of the firm deals with both of them, trying to balance them and keep under control tendencies that could overemphasise the business side to the detriment of the professional side, or vice versa.

There may be pressures that could easily destroy the delicate equilibrium. Individuals or teams sometimes foster services in which they are personally interested, but for which there is no market, or which are very costly to the firm because they do not generate enough income. Or, the management of the firm may press consultants to improve business results without maintaining quality, or even by deliberately lowering quality. This tendency can express itself in many ways. Operating consultants may be asked to increase productivity by saving on data gathering and analysis; or less experienced and less highly paid consultants are assigned to jobs requiring more expertise than they possess, and so on.

Balancing assignment and practice management

The main thing management consultants do is work on assignments in client organisations. Every assignment has a business dimension (cost, price, efficiency of execution, contribution to the firm's income and profit) in addition to the professional tasks to be carried out for the client.

Assignments constitute basic building blocks in the management system of consulting organisations. In theory, the system operates as follows. Once an assignment has been identified and a contract agreed to, the organisation has to appoint a consultant or establish an assignment team and furnish them with needed resources. A self-contained management unit is thus created within the consulting firm. As assignments normally have a limited life-span, assignment teams cease to exist when the job is completed. Individual team members are regrouped to make up new assignment teams, while other resources (e.g. equipment, stationery, finance) have been used up or are reallocated.

It could be objected that the short life-span of an assignment does not provide for continuity in organisational relations and makes the whole management system volatile. Yet the nature of consulting services underlines the importance of assignments as basic management units. During the assignment, the working time and the expertise of the operating consultants "belong" to the client, and the team leader must be able fully to control the resources and guarantee the delivery of the service. The consulting firm supports, guides and controls the assignment team in this effort. The whole operation of the firm is geared to this basic objective.

Thus, assignment management is a crucial activity in any professional consulting firm. However, even the best assignment management cannot ensure the functioning and development of the consulting organisation as a whole. It can even create conflicts and imbalance in the organisation by unduly favouring one assignment to the detriment of others, or of the global interests of the firm. Future development can be jeopardised. Here again a balanced approach is required, putting the right emphasis on global concerns and needs of the organisation in addition to dealing with specific client projects. These global concerns and organisational needs include in particular:

— the firm's professional and business culture;
— strategy for achieving growth and high professional standards;
— the development of new capabilities and products;
— market development and promotion;
— management and development of the principal resource — the professional staff;
— sound financial management and control.

In summary, the art of managing a consulting practice consists of dealing with all dimensions of the management matrix in a balanced manner, making sure that both individual client assignments and the consulting firm as a whole meet their professional goals and business objectives. What this means to various management functions will be discussed in detail in the chapters that follow.

---

[1] See T. Levitt: "Marketing intangible products and product intangibles", in *Harvard Business Review*, May-June 1981; and P. Mills, J. L. Hall, J. K. Leidecker and N. Margulies: "Flexiform: A model for professional service organisations", in *Academy of Management Review*, 1983, Vol. 8, No 1.

[2] T. Levitt, op. cit., p. 96.

[3] A. Wilson: *Practice development for professional firms* (Maidenhead, McGraw-Hill, 1984), pp. 8-9.

[4] See e.g. "How to improve selling by viewing your service as a product", in *Consultants News*, June 1985.

[5] See H. Mintzberg: *The structuring of organisations* (Englewood Cliffs, NJ, Prentice-Hall, 1979).

[6] See e.g. D. H. Maister: "The one-firm firm: What makes it successful", in *Sloan Management Review*, Fall 1985.

[7] For example, in his useful book on the marketing of professional services A. Wilson stresses that "professional practice is not a business" (A. Wilson, op. cit., p. 168).

[8] A critique of economists' and accountants' conception of the "human capital" is made, for example, by G. S. Odiorne in *Strategic management of human resources* (San Francisco, CA, Jossey-Bass, 1984).

THE CONSULTING ORGANISATION'S STRATEGY 21

In chapter 12 strategic management was shown to be one of the principal areas in which management consultants work with business clients. Thus, many consultants are familiar with the concept of strategy and the techniques of strategic planning and management. This chapter looks at the question of whether consultants should deal only with their clients' corporate strategy, or whether a strategic approach can also be useful to the management of consulting organisations.

21.1 The concept of strategy

The answer to this question lies not in the theory, but in the practice of consulting. In the past, most consultants followed no particular strategy and tried to react to any opportunity and any request from a potential client. This has changed. More and more consultants realise that they cannot be all things to all clients, and that they stand a better chance of obtaining business by offering a unique service, or by serving a market segment where they will perform better than other consultants. They behave increasingly as strategists even if the term "strategy" is not always used.

Why strategy?

This changed attitude is the result of a number of recent developments in the consulting business and its environment. These developments, which were examined in considerable detail earlier in our book, can be summarised as follows:

- The rapidly growing number of management consultants has brought competition to consulting; as a result, consultants are becoming strongly marketing oriented, and more aggressive in the marketing of their services.
- The growing complexity and pace of change in the environment in which both clients and consultants operate generate new problems with which a

consultant can help; consequently, consulting firms have to re-examine their competence and range of services with increased frequency, making sure that they are always ready to help clients with new significant problems.

● The profession itself has made considerable progress in the methods and organisation of consulting work, allowing every consultant to choose from a wide array of conceptual approaches and methodological tools.

● Every consultant faces the classic strategic dilemma of how to allocate his limited resources — he has to match them with opportunities, and plan for the development of resources so as to be ready to tackle future business, yet avoid spreading his capabilities thinly over too many problem areas.

Purpose and goals

We cannot help starting this section by quoting from Lewis Carroll's *Alice's adventures in wonderland*: "Would you tell me, please, which way I ought to go from here?" "That depends a good deal on where you want to get to," said the Cat. "I don't much care where . . .", said Alice. "Then it doesn't matter which way you go", said the Cat. ". . . so long as I get *somewhere*", Alice added as an explanation. "Oh, you're sure to do that", said the Cat, "if you only walk long enough."

As in other businesses and organisations, strategy in consulting consists in choosing a path that leads from one condition (the present) to a different one (the future). The starting point is known, or can be identified by assessing the consultant's present position, resources and capabilities. This is not very difficult if there is a will to see reality as it is and not through rose-coloured spectacles. The future is a different matter. It also requires a realistic approach — for example, it may be quite unrealistic merely to extrapolate past growth trends. But, more than that, if strategic thinking is to be applied, the basic question is: Strategy for achieving *what*? *Where* do we want to go and *when* do we want to get there? These "what", "where" and "when" questions can be answered if the consultant develops *a vision of the future* and clarifies the purpose and basic goals of his professional business.

The two dimensions of consulting discussed in the previous chapter have to be given full consideration in developing strategy. First, the consulting organisation needs to define its purpose and objectives from *a professional point of view* by trying to answer questions such as:

● What sort of professional firm do we want to be?

● What will be our professional culture, our consulting philosophy and our role in solving clients' problems, in helping clients to increase organisational performance, and in developing their learning and problem-solving capabilities?

● Do we want to become leaders in technical terms, that is consultants who are always at the forefront of progress in technology and management methods, and who are the first to offer new information and new services to their clients?

- Shall we confine ourselves strictly to consulting in management, or widen the range of our professional services? What services should we add in order to be more useful to clients?
- What new services can we afford to add to our portfolio without losing our identity and entering areas beyond our competence?

The second strategic dimension is that of *a business activity*. The key questions to ask are, for example:

- What does our consulting firm want to achieve as a business?
- Should our strategy ensure mere survival, or moderate or rapid growth?
- What is the position in the market for consulting services that we want to achieve?
- What earnings and profits should be achieved?
- What should our firm's financial strength and independence be?

Consulting units which are not independent businesses also have to address certain basic questions concerning their goals, resources, growth rate, and financial results, even if they do not have to make a profit or aim at becoming self-supporting.

The unity of these two dimensions ought to be stressed again. A consultant who viewed the future of his firm only in financial terms would lose sight of the social role and responsibility of a professional organisation, and would most probably be unable to achieve his business goals also. However, to ignore marketing and financial goals, and the need to develop successfully as a business entity, implies that even highly appropriate and realistic professional goals would not be achieved because of the consulting firm's inadequate financial objectives and results.

Competitive edge

A fundamental question in defining consulting strategy is: What is our competitive advantage, or, why should a client turn to us rather than to other consultants? The reason could lie in special technical expertise, or a unique product unavailable elsewhere, a wide range of multidisciplinary expertise required for complex business problems, an intimate knowledge of an industrial sector, speed and reliability of service delivery, low fees, good reputation and contacts among public sector agencies, or other qualities.

It is essential to know whether a consultant possesses, or can develop, any competitive edge. If it can be achieved without extravagant expenditure, it is worth trying, defining strategy accordingly, and making sure that both current and potential clients learn about it. True enough, every consultant cannot become a recognised national or international authority in his technical field. However, the range of opportunities available to consultants is so wide that most consultants can try to offer some special benefit to their clients which will differentiate them from competitors and constitute their competitive advantage.

Flexibility in applying the strategic approach

Only experience can show whether strategy has been chosen correctly. Another consultant, a competitor, may have chosen to offer the same new service, and has performed better in marketing and service delivery. Both your and your competitor's choices were correct when they were made, but your competitor has been more successful in implementing his strategy. You will have to revise your strategy, looking for one that takes the competitor's achievements into account.

However, the main reasons for flexibility in defining and redefining strategy are not management errors, or competitors' successes, but changes in the business environment. Management consulting would lose its meaning if it did not reflect alterations in technology, markets, finance, legislation, national and international politics and any other significant changes that affect clients' businesses. Consulting strategy has to follow, or preferably anticipate, these changes. Once the financial markets have been internationalised, and even smaller firms can think of borrowing on the international money market, a financial consultant's strategy cannot be restricted to the national financial market. Consultants in office management, accounting, operations control and many other areas have to provide advice on the use of computers in their technical or functional areas, and should they choose to ignore computer applications, such a "strategic choice" may put them out of business. Many other examples were given in part III, which reviewed the problems and trends in consulting in various areas of management.

The need for flexibility and imagination in defining consulting strategy cannot be overemphasised. Strategic choices tend to be decisions with long-term implications, not easy to modify. Yet strategy must never become a straightjacket. In particular, it must not inhibit innovation and entrepreneurship. A consulting firm may have defined its area of specialisation with great care and precision, but this should not prevent the staff on assignments from being alert to new kinds of problem and opportunity faced by clients. Dynamic consulting firms have always encouraged their staff to think of new work opportunities and come up with suggestions on how to tackle new problems. The relationship between long-term strategic choices and the need for flexibility and innovation may be delicate and difficult to control, but no management consultant can afford to ignore it.

Consulting firms can be more flexible in changing and up-dating their "product" and "markets" than industrial and other firms where the choice of a product and a technology implies considerable long-term investment in fixed assets and employment of specialist staff who may be difficult to reorient. In consulting, educational background, experience and training in methodology allow consultants to be flexible in tackling not only new jobs, but even new technical areas. This is facilitated, too, by staff structure and turnover. Employing consultants with varied technical backgrounds and profiles, and using multidisciplinary teams, increases the flexibility of the firm in applying new strategies.

21.2 Principal strategic choices

This section will mention several choices that consultants face in defining their strategy. It is not intended to be an exhaustive review, but points to the kinds of choice that are available rather than giving a complete checklist. We will return to the question of strategic choices in subsequent chapters, when the marketing, structuring and staffing aspects of consulting firms are discussed.

There are situations in which it is difficult to ascertain what choice has a strategic dimension. A decision intended to be operational may turn out to be strategic if it has a major impact on the orientation of the consulting firm. An operating assignment may uncover an important new market not previously considered by the consultant, generate further assignments in the same new field, and eventually change the profile of the consulting firm quite considerably.

Defining your product

A fundamental strategic choice concerns the nature and the scope of the services provided to clients. We have learned in chapter 20 that defining a consultant's product is not easy owing to the intangible nature of professional services, the unique needs of every client, and other factors. Because of these inherent technical difficulties, consultants are somehow reluctant to be explicit in defining their product. Some are worried that the definition might be unduly restrictive and prevent them from seeking and taking new opportunities in areas not covered by the definition. Others prefer to examine each opportunity for a new assignment on its own merits and decide whether or not to take it without referring to any *a priori* product definition.

Yet product definition is increasingly regarded as a basic building block of consulting strategy. It is needed for determining the consulting firm's identity and profile, for marketing services to potential clients, and for focusing the development of the firm's capabilities and resources on areas designated as strategic priority. It reacts to a significant trend in demand for consulting services, where growing emphasis tends to be placed on clearly defined, and proven, special expertise related to specific problems faced by clients.

Let us review four different ways of defining the nature and scope of the services provided (setting aside, for the time being, the definition of the client base, which will be discussed in the following section).

Alternative 1: Functional or subject areas of intervention

This alternative, common in the past and still widely applied at the present time, defines the consultant's services by functional or technical areas in which he can help clients. Emphasis is placed on broad background knowledge and past experience in the given area. Examples are: finance, marketing, production management, or general management. The definition can be kept wide, or narrowed down into sub-areas — for example, maintenance, production scheduling and control, stock control, quality control, or supervisory development, instead of production management.

While it indicates the area of competence, the definition lacks focus if the subject area is broad. It does not specify what quality is peculiar to the consultant, what his strong points are, or how he differs from other consultants. It says nothing about the consultant's method of work and about the results he aims to obtain in his interventions. The consultant's identity is blurred. He has to keep up to date in a wide area of business management (which may be feasible in a large firm, but virtually impossible for a sole practitioner or small firm).

Alternative 2: Management and business problems

This second alternative defines the services offered by referring to typical business and management problems experienced by clients. Emphasis is put on help in problem solving and on relevant special expertise. Examples are: energy savings, rationalisation of information flows, identification and negotiation of joint ventures, technology transfer agreements, mergers, turnarounds. The underlying assumption is that the consultant will analyse the problem and provide a solution beneficial to the client, combining specialist and generalist approaches as appropriate. Thus, a company turnaround consultant is offering to handle (individually or in a team) financial, commercial, technological, organisational, legal, personnel and other aspects of a turnaround.

Alternative 3: Special techniques and systems

In this case the consultant has developed and is offering to the clients his particular (often unique) approach to dealing with a problem in the form of a special management technique, model, or system. It may be (but not necessarily) a proprietary system, which is not available from any other consultant. Such an approach can be devised for dealing with problems that are common to many clients. It is, of course, understood that the consultant provides more than the installation of a standard system. As a rule, the assignment includes a preliminary diagnostic study, an adaptation of the basic standard system to the client's conditions, and assistance with implementation and related staff training. Further servicing and perfecting of the system may also be included, thus establishing a long-term consultant-client relationship.

Examples abound in various areas of consulting. Well known and widely applied are systems using predetermined time standards in setting production standards, job evaluation schemes, bookkeeping and accounting systems, stock control systems, operations control techniques applied to transport or location problems, or models used in market research. A rapidly growing number of such systems involve computerised models and other applications used in business forecasting, strategic planning and various other areas of management.

A consultant who has developed a special system may be recognised as an authority on applying a standard approach of proven effectiveness to certain kinds of problem, which are relatively easy to identify and structure. He may find it difficult to get assignments in other problem areas. He should be careful not to get a reputation of someone who tries to apply the same standard package to any problem presented by a client.

Alternatively, some consultants use standard systems, not as their main product, but as an accessory tool for dealing with a special aspect of the problem in hand (e.g. a business forecasting model used in corporate strategy assignments).

Alternative 4: Consulting methodology applied

In this instance the consultant tries to make his product more tangible and explicit by providing a description of his particular methodological approach to identifying problems in client organisations and to helping clients in planning and implementing changes. Emphasis is not put on the content and end result of the consulting process, but on the methodological approach, and on the fact that the client himself will be able to acquire a methodology for diagnosing his problem in the future. The method becomes the product offered. Clearly, its description must be detailed, specific and convincing enough for the client to understand what will be happening in each phase of the consulting process, and for him to consider whether he is prepared to accept such an approach in collaboration with the consultant.

Combining the four alternatives

The reader has certainly come to the conclusion that the four alternatives described above are not mutually exclusive and can be combined in various ways. This is what is occurring in more and more consulting firms. For example, some process consultants define their services by describing their methodological approach (alternative 4), but show how this approach is applied to distinct management problems (alternative 2).

Other services

Finally, the definition of the nature and scope of services includes choices concerning services other than consulting proper, such as management development, technical training, production of training materials, research, product design and testing, project management, data processing, and so on. Many consulting organisations have adopted the strategy of supplementing consulting by some of these services. Experience tends to show that this strategy meets with the clients' approval, and is even encouraged by a positive response from clients. Clearly, the range of choices for putting together the total service package, or portfolio, and the scope for innovation and imagination in developing it, are literally limitless.

In these cases the synergy with consulting work should be given careful consideration. Do the consulting, training and information services support and complement one another technically? Do they constitute an integrated package of services enhancing the value of assistance provided to clients? Is the consulting firm more effective because it is providing other services in addition to consulting proper? Or is it spreading its resources thinly over different services unrelated to one another?

Almost every consultant likes to have a special "product" that attracts a host of business clients. This basically healthy desire stimulates imagination, innovation and competition in consulting. Nevertheless, as *Business Week* pointed out,[1] many executives these days "seem eager to latch on to almost any new concept that promises a quick fix for their problems". While "consultants have always had a role in launching fads", they have been "working overtime to roll out new fads since the 1970s". True enough, "a little faddishness may be helpful because it makes managers think about new ways to do their job better". However, "today the bewildering array of fads pose far more serious diversions and distractions for the complex task of running a company". Are these comments of any relevance to the strategy followed by your firm?

Defining your client base

Defining the client base (that is, for whom to work) is another aspect of service specialisation, treated in formulating strategy. This includes considering whether to serve:

- organisations of different size (small, medium, large, very large);
- organisations in one or more sectors (e.g. energy, transport, health, banking, any other sector);
- private, public or mixed-ownership organisations;
- firms in a limited geographical area, in a whole country, in other countries and regions, multinational firms;
- organisations with management systems at different levels of sophistication (e.g. firms known to be very advanced in applying new manufacturing and management technologies);
- a larger or smaller number of clients.

Small businesses tend to be served by smaller local consulting firms rather than by larger national or international consultants. None the less, even some very large consulting and public accounting firms, in the United States and other countries, have recently established small-business consulting divisions.

How much work to do *for the government and for public enterprises* is an important policy issue. Most private consultants are interested in government contracts. As we have seen, governments and public enterprises need the technical services of private management consultants. However, some consulting firms have defined the share of business they want to do for the public sector, say not to exceed 20-30 per cent.

Geographical expansion has far-reaching implications for the design of the consulting firm. Single practitioners and smaller firms tend to seek clients in a smaller geographical area (unless they have developed special contacts or expertise and can get interesting contracts from more remote clients). Larger firms normally operate in a wider geographical area.

Going international is a very important strategic choice, with many implications for the structure, competence and operation of the firm. By and large, consulting firms internationalise operations for the following main reasons:

— to find new markets for services;
— to respond to demands received from foreign clients (including clients from developing countries in a growing number of cases);
— to satisfy the consultants' curiosity and need for challenging new work opportunities.[2]

The level of *the clients' sophistication* ought to be compared to the sophistication of the services that the consultant is able to provide. There are differences between clients (and countries and sectors) in terms of sophistication of their management systems, and competence of managerial and specialist staff. Not every client requires, and can use, the latest innovations in management sciences and technologies. Not every consultant can claim to operate at the cutting edge of technology and a realistic assessment of one's own level of sophistication can be one of the soundest strategic moves.

Finally, it is important to decide *how many clients to serve*. This may be crucial to a single practitioner or a small firm. Getting large contracts from a small number of clients reduces the amount of time spent on acquisition work and ensures regular income. However, it may create an excessive dependency on one or a small number of major clients, and even on individual managers in the client organisations. It may narrow down the consultant's horizon and limit his chances to learn from new clients.

Product innovation and research

Like any other product, a professional service has its life cycle; it passes through periods of design and development, testing, launching on the market, growth, maturity, saturation and decline. This process has a time dimension: some services become obsolete and have to be phased out sooner than others. As far as possible, in planning strategy the consultant should analyse the life cycle of his particular services in order to avoid their obsolescence and be ready for introducing new services at an appropriate moment.

A practical approach used by consulting firms as well as by management development institutions is to classify services in groups, using criteria such as the contribution of the service to the firm's income, the rate of growth of the service, and the cost involved in developing and marketing it. Analysis will reveal, for example:

● services that do not grow any more, but continue to generate a substantial part of the total income;
● services that grow rapidly, though their relative importance in the firm's total income is still very small;
● services whose volume tends to stagnate in certain markets, but which are in great demand in other markets;
● services where marketing and maintenance requirements are excessively high;
● services that could easily be redesigned and adapted for new markets (client groups, sectors, countries, etc.).

There is, then, the question of what *research* the consulting organisation should do for its own needs, mainly for improving and keeping its consulting (but also its training, information, and other) services up to date. In many consulting firms, the senior staff is busy negotiating and preparing new assignments, while the operating staff is busy serving client organisations. Little is done by way of research and new product development. That is why some outstanding academics have been able to compete successfully with professional consultants: basing their advice on solid research, they have been able to come up with new products which have aroused the practitioner's attention beyond all expectation.

Every consulting organisation has to decide whether or not to carry out research for product development, and if not, how to acquire the new knowledge and expertise without which product innovation is impossible. Many larger and medium-sized consulting firms have chosen to do their own research, aimed mainly, but not exclusively, on developing new services. Another major benefit, which several consulting firms have already derived from research, is the demonstration of intimate knowledge of the business and management scene which tends to enhance a firm's competitive edge.

Sole practitioners and small firms are in a different situation; their limited resources prevent them from engaging in major research projects. They can, however, keep informed about on-going research in universities and management institutes and make sure that they participate in seminars describing recent research. Joint research involving several consulting firms, and research organised by consultants' associations for the benefit of their members, are underused and deserve to be explored.

Size and growth rate of the organisation

In many countries very large consulting organisations and single practitioners operate alongside each other. Various firms have grown in their own ways and, in many cases, no particular growth strategy has been pursued. The vision and entrepreneurial spirit of the founder or principal, and competence in marketing and delivering services, have been the main factors of growth, allied with a favourable business climate.

Nevertheless, the size of the firm and the rate of growth ought to be considered when defining strategy. These questions should be examined in connection with the range of services offered, the sectoral and geographical coverage, the assessment of the market, existing and newly developing competition, the consulting organisation's resources, and its ability to sustain growth while maintaining or increasing quality.

In many cases, further growth means looking for new markets (e.g. in other countries or sectors). The firm should assess its potential for internationalising operations, and its chances of developing competence and gaining credibility in new sectors.

Some consulting organisations have deliberately opted for a limited size and do not try to grow beyond it. This is often justified by a combination of human and managerial factors — for example, the desire to maintain a coherent professional team where individuals can interact with each other and a simple management structure can be used.

Growth involves recruiting and developing new consulting staff in any case. If growth is fast, it is often difficult to find new consultants, the initial training of new recruits has to be shortened, and relatively inexperienced consultants have to be assigned to jobs that may be beyond their competence. In the 1970s quite a few consulting firms which followed a fast-growth strategy had to struggle with considerable problems of staffing, indoctrination, coherence and integrity.

A consulting firm that does not grow, or grows too slowly, faces other problems. Its staff ages, becomes more experienced, and wants to be promoted to senior positions and obtain corresponding increases in remuneration. The cost of the firm's services also grows if the higher remuneration cannot be counterbalanced by increased staff productivity. What is to be done? The firm may try to change its product-market scope, focusing on services requiring quite experienced senior (and better paid) staff.

In other cases, staff turnover helps. Some senior and even junior staff members, who see no chance of promotion if the firm does not grow, decide to leave and can be replaced by new recruits at junior level. In one sense, such problems exist in any organisation. They tend to be more acute, and to have a greater effect on strategy, in professional service organisations, both because these are limited in size and because professionals employed in them are highly competent individuals who pursue ambitious career goals. We will return to this question in chapters 27 and 28, when discussing staffing and staff development in more detail.

Collaborative relations within the profession

Consultants pursue, too, various strategies of collaboration with other professional organisations. Some consultants accept only assignments for which their firm has all the resources required and would never enter any collaborative arrangement with another professional, but many consultants are prepared to team up with other consultants. A general management or business strategy consultant would frequently co-operate with market research, quality management, technology transfer, or commercial law specialists in a comprehensive corporate-strategy or turnaround assignment. Some consultants like to stay sole practitioners, but have developed a network of technical contacts with other professionals, allowing them to tackle more important assignments, and provide more complex services, than an individual person could ever do. Even a larger consulting firm may use subcontractors or part-time staff, including persons who are not professional consultants, but can provide special expertise (and whom the firm cannot afford to employ full time).

Such collaborative arrangements tend to be more and more popular. They succeed if there is mutual confidence and if the partners see eye to eye on their consulting philosophy.

21.3 Systematic application of strategic management

We have seen that every consulting firm has a number of options in defining its market and strategy. This section will outline the main steps in applying a systematic approach to strategic management.

The need to base strategy on hard data cannot be overemphasised. It is useful to start by a thorough *self-diagnosis* (sometimes called a "strategic audit" to emphasise the focus and purpose of the exercise). The method is basically the same as that used for diagnosing client businesses, bearing in mind the nature and special problems of a professional service organisation. Many consulting organisations will be able to undertake such a diagnosis by themselves, although it may be quite painful, and require a great deal of determination and courage, to apply to one's own operation the same rigorous approach that is used when working with clients. However, only vanity prevents a management consultant from turning to another consultant for advice and help in such a diagnosis. This help could hardly be expected from a direct competitor, but may easily be obtained from consultants who are not in competition. For example, a financial management consultant may benefit from the advice of a marketing consultant in defining marketing strategy for his consulting services. A local consulting firm in a developing country may get useful advice on strategy from a similar firm in another country.

Self-assessment: your resources and capabilities

The first step is the assessment of the consultant's present position in the profession and the business. This position reflects past successes and failures. A new consultant cannot refer to any past record of achievements in consulting, but has to assess the technical and problem-solving competence that he brings to the market for consulting services.

Human resources are the critical resources in any professional firm. The following aspects are those normally looked at:

● staff structure in terms of technical profile, specialisation, educational background, management and consulting experience;

● age and grade structure;

● work capacity;

● dynamism, motivation, entrepreneurial spirit;

● flexibility and adaptability to new tasks and situations;

● adherance to the firm's consulting philosophy and preference for particular intervention techniques;

● potential for further development.

Financial resources are, as we know, a less critical factor in professional firms than human resources, but any strategy will have certain financial implications and its financial feasibility will have to be established. Therefore it is important to assess:

— the financial health of the firm;
— the sources of finance;
— the financial reserves and other resources that can be mobilised for development and growth.

Past performance ought to be reviewed in terms of the firm's pace of growth, changes in the market share, programme innovation, improvements in professional standards, resource mobilisation and utilisation, financial results and any other developments from which lessons can be drawn for future strategy. Also, if the firm had chosen some explicit strategy in the past, it is essential to evaluate whether it had been possible to follow it and, if not, why the real course of events had diverged from the strategy.

In summary, the diagnosis should help to develop a realistic view of the consulting firm's *profile*, and of its *position* in the profession and on the market for consulting services. Answers should be sought to questions such as:

● What kind of consulting organisation are we?
● What is our consulting philosophy?
● What is the quality and technical appeal of our services?
● How important is our position in the profession?
● What has our performance record been in technical terms and financially?
● Have we made full use of our capabilities in the past?
● Do we have underused resources and are we able to mobilise additional resources?
● How do we assess our strengths and weaknesses?
● What is our potential for further growth and development?

Self-assessment: your image

It is equally important to know how a professional organisation is perceived by the external environment — by its existing and potential clients, by the public authorities and, in certain cases, even by the general public. This perception is often referred to as "image". This image may be fully consistent with the consultant's real capabilities and achievements record. There are, however, instances of considerable divergence between the real profile of a professional organisation and its public image. This may be due to various reasons, such as undue publicity given by the press to one poorly executed assignment, or a wrong choice of public media for advertising. In addition, the consulting firm may have wrong information on its real image. This is understandable, since it is not always easy to find out what other people think about you.

The strategic audit provides an excellent opportunity to find out about the consulting firm's image. Even a new consultant should consider if he is entering the market without any image, or if he already has one. If an author of popular books on management decides to found a consulting firm, he clearly has an image. If a management training centre opens a consulting department, this new unit has an image affected mainly by the nature and quality of the centre's training programmes (practical or theoretical, suitable for higher or middle management, and so on).

The market for your services

The next step is the assessment of the market for consulting services. This includes both the existing market and the potential market.

The examination of the *existing market* focuses on relations between the consultant and his current clients, assessing whether the clientele has been correctly chosen, how solid are the links for co-operation with clients, and whether the existing clients would purchase more current services, or new types of services, from the consultant.

The identification and assessment of the *potential market* starts with an hypothesis as to what the market might be (bearing in mind the scope and level of the consultant's resources and capabilities). Fact-finding and market research would confirm this original hypothesis, or suggest another definition of the market, or confirm the original definition on condition that the consultant could improve his image, and so on.

The survey covers in particular:

- technico-economic characteristics and development tendencies of the sector(s) to be served: advanced or obsolete technology, growth prospects and difficulties ("smokestack" industries), position in respect to other sectors and national development strategies, inter-sectoral linkages, international competition;

- organisations in the sector: number, size, categories, leaders, monopolies, ownership pattern, traditions; more detailed information on organisations the most likely to be a prospective market (including names and addresses of organisations, and, if possible, names of owners and senior managing staff);

- the management scene: level and sophistication of management, use of management systems and technologies, prevailing attitudes and traditions, background and competence of managerial staff;

- practices concerning the use of consultants: demand, attitudes, experience with use, special requirements.

It has to be stressed that assessing a potential market involves much more than finding addresses of firms and some global information on them. It is an in-depth research effort; the consultant *must* know his potential market in considerable depth and detail. Various sources of information and research methods ought to be combined in order to develop a comprehensive picture of the market (business publications and reports, trade journals, official statistics, stock-market information, training events and management conferences, individual contacts and interviews, and so on). Information obtained directly from existing and potential clients is particularly useful.

The definition of a potential market is a particularly important but delicate matter for a new consulting firm, which does not have any clientele and faces the risk of adopting either an excessively wide or an unduly narrow definition of its market. In the first case, the firm's marketing effort will be too costly and largely unproductive, embracing organisations where there is little or no likelihood that they will become clients. In the second case, good opportunities of finding assignments will be missed by omitting certain prospective clients.

Some consultants regard *all* organisations in the field of their specialisation as a potential market, while others use a more restrictive definition and regard their market as consisting of organisations which have problems and require the consultant's help. Both approaches have their rationale. An organisation that does not have a problem today may have one tomorrow, or next year, and it will be good if it is aware of the existence and reputation of *your* consulting firm! Some marketing effort may therefore be directed at creating this awareness. At the same time, every consulting firm needs assignments that will keep it occupied today, and these will be found in organisations that *already* experience problems. This includes not only organisations in difficulties, but also prosperous firms that are seeking opportunities for developing their business and increasing efficiency.

The concept of *market segmentation* is helpful in analysing the chances of a consulting firm successfully entering a new market. Segmenting the market involves subdividing potential clients and their business and management problems into smaller groups, by one or more criteria — for example, by size, geographical location, technology used, ownership pattern, financial difficulties experienced (shortage of working capital, foreign exchange problems), market served (local market, exporting, re-export), or other issues. Such segmentation is meaningful, moreover, if it identifies some common characteristics of the organisations involved, reflected in their common consulting needs and in the kind of services required. A new consultant would be looking for a market segment, or niche, which (i) is likely to be most interested in his competence and the services he offers, and (ii) is less "occupied" by other consultants.

Your competitors

The market analysis is pursued by assessing existing and potential competitors. It is essential to find out as much as possible about other consultants' profiles, strategies and achievements:

— Who are they (names, founders, key executives)?
— How large and how well established are they?
— For what markets and organisations do they work?
— What is their technical competence and range of services?
— What are their consulting and marketing approaches and methods?

— What are their typical assignments?
— What professional image do they enjoy?
— What are their terms of business?
— What can we learn from them and what can we do better?
— Are we likely to win or lose if we compete with them?

Learning from competitors is not aping them without imagination. Less experienced consultants can easily fall into a trap by trying to do exactly what their established and experienced competitors do, although their resources are usually inadequate for this. Whether to compete or not is a fundamental strategic decision. Many consultants have decided not to compete with existing firms by offering the same service, but to *avoid* direct competition by offering a new service that is not available from other consultants. However, most consulting services cannot become legally protected intellectual property (except certain proprietary systems and software packages). Sooner or later, competitors will come up with the same or a similar service. What will your strategy be then?

The business environment and climate

Assessment of the environment has to reach beyond the market for your particular services. Various other environmental factors affect opportunities for management consulting:

● the political climate;
● promotional or restrictive government policies;
● the dynamism of the business community;
● the availability and sources of finance for new development projects;
● local cultural values and traditions;
● labour legislation and industrial relations;
● legislation governing professional services, contracting, liability, and the like;
● important trends in technology likely to affect your clients in the future;
● development tendencies of professional services, including services other than management consulting;
● facilities offered to foreign investors.

These are only examples of factors that may be important to your consulting firm. Whether a particular environmental factor is important or not, and should be examined in depth, reviewed briefly, or ignored, is a matter for the consultant's judgement. A general management consulting firm contemplating expanding international operations will be interested in different environmental factors from a marketing consultant working with small businesses serving a limited local market.

Every consultant is keenly interested in the general business climate. If business is prosperous, the markets for consulting services tend to be expanding rapidly. This often stimulates consulting firms to an equally fast expansion, even if, as mentioned above, they are not always able to maintain their professional standards. On the other hand, recession and stagnation of business has also affected consulting in many countries, but not necessarily all services in the same way. Services considered as essential for the clients' survival, and for achieving tangible improvements in productivity and efficiency, continue to sell well or even better. Other services tend to suffer. In many instances the recession, and falling demand, have forced management consultants to phase out training and other service packages that were fashionable and easy to sell in the period of general prosperity, but ceased to interest clients when austerity became the name of the game.

Developments in the profession

Although many consultants follow the developments in their profession virtually on a daily basis, a strategic audit provides an opportunity for a more thorough review of these developments and of their possible implications for future strategy. Important changes that affect the nature of consulting services deserve particular attention. These can be changes in consulting methods, the conception of ethics, the approach to marketing and advertising, the ways of combining management, technological and other consulting, the relations between consulting and training, and similar issues. Many of these trends are discussed in chapter 2 and other parts of this book.[3]

Choosing your strategies

The diagnostic and analytical work described in the previous paragraphs provide information and generate suggestions for strategy. It is a matter of principle to base any major strategic choice (e.g. a decision not to market services in certain sectors) on a thorough analysis of facts.

If such an analysis is not feasible, perhaps because information is not available, or because the firm is unable to draw conclusions from analysis, an important strategic choice might be deferred until more information becomes available. Or two or more alternatives might be pursued, with the proviso that only one will be retained when the situation becomes clearer.

Strategic choices affecting various aspects of the consulting firm are mutually related. There is a significant relationship between the basic objectives to be pursued, the services to be offered, the market segment that will be the firm's target, the image to be built up, the marketing techniques to be used, the staff to be recruited and trained, the research and product development to be undertaken, and the resources to be allocated to these activities. The purpose is to develop coherent strategy, not a set of inconsistent or even conflicting choices.

Involving staff in strategy formulation

There are valid reasons for organising strategy formulation as an exercise involving as many members of the consulting staff as possible. This can be done through task forces, meetings, special projects, and so on. Participation in strategic thinking and planning helps to build up an esprit de corps, increase the firm's cohesion, and counter the centrifugal tendencies that develop only too easily in consulting. Both senior and junior staff members thus feel associated with the strategy that is adopted, and accept it as their own choice.

In discussing common strategy every professional has the opportunity to compare his personal strategy (if any) with that of the organisation to which he belongs. If the two strategies conflict, he can consider how to resolve the conflict. This is not unusual in professional services. An individual may believe in a different mode of consulting or code of ethics from that which is practised by the organisation. He may decide to leave if he finds no way of reconciling the two approaches.

Making strategy explicit

Strategy should provide a framework and guiding principles for operating decisions made by all units and staff members in a consulting firm. Therefore they have to know the strategy chosen and understand the reasons behind it. Staff participation in formulating strategy has contributed to this understanding. It is useful to tell all staff about the strategy chosen by management and to keep people informed about any changes in it. Attention must be paid to strategy in the induction training of new staff. Making staff aware of strategy is particularly important in larger and decentralised consulting organisations with many relatively autonomous operating units, which are exposed to a permanent danger of losing sight of common objectives and strategic choices.

Some consulting firms have found it useful to have a strategic plan for 3-5 years. If such a plan has to be prepared, the firm is encouraged to make strategic choices explicit and express them in measurable and controllable terms. The plan is a tool for achieving coherence between the various choices discussed above, and rejecting strategies that are not feasible. However, it may be difficult, or even undesirable, to set targets for 3-5 years if technology changes very rapidly and future business prospects are uncertain. Many consultants prefer to confine their planning to a shorter time-scale (1-3 years).

Strategy is an internal matter and the consulting firm may treat a statement of strategy or a strategic plan as confidential documents. Yet certain aspects of strategy can be made publicly known. It may be useful to give clients, current and prospective, some information on the strategy chosen, thus helping to build up the consulting firm's image. This is done, as a rule, through information brochures, annual reports and other publications, or in describing the firm's profile when submitting proposals to clients.

Monitoring implementation

In theory, operating decisions and actions should be in harmony with strategy. Often they are not. Strategy is either ignored or for some reason cannot be applied.

An occasional deviation from strategy may be a sign of flexibility in taking opportunities and doing what the market demands. Many consultants will accept an assignment in a sector or country which they do not normally regard as their market if they feel that they possess the required competence and should not miss an attractive opportunity.

If deviations from strategy become frequent and significant, this probably indicates that the strategy was wrongly chosen or has become obsolete. It is necessary to revise it. This may have to be done immediately if the change in the environment, or the gap in strategy, is important enough. Under normal circumstances, however, strategy would be reviewed and updated periodically, say annually.

---

[1] "Business fads: What's in — and out", in *Business Week*, January 20, 1986; pp. 40-47.

[2] See D. B. Nees: "Building an international practice", in *Sloan Management Review*, Winter 1986.

[3] Some publications give a useful summary of trends in consulting. See FEACO: *A study of the management consulting profession 1960-84* (Helsinki, Mec-Rastor, 1984); J. Kennedy (ed.): *The future of management consulting* (Fitzwilliam, NH, Consultants News, 1985); and D. A. Tierno: "Growth strategies for consulting in the next decade", in *Sloan Management Review*, Winter 1986.

MARKETING CONSULTING SERVICES

22

A consulting firm can exist and prosper if it gets and keeps clients. This is what marketing is about: define your product and market, find clients, identify their requirements, sell the consulting service to them, deliver the service to the clients' satisfaction and make sure that once you have good clients you do not lose them.

In management consulting, as in some other professions, there has been a long debate on the appropriateness of marketing and of its various techniques. Even today, some consultants feel uneasy about "selling" their services; they regard it as unprofessional and beneath their dignity. Many consultants are poor at marketing and, if they have to engage in it, they do it with little enthusiasm and imagination.

Yet the marketing of consulting is as old as consulting itself. James McKinsey, one of the pioneers of management consulting, spent many hours having meals with prospective clients and other useful business contacts. Over the meal, he would engage in a technical discussion, aiming to gain the person's confidence and explain how he could be of help. His business sense was telling him that a professional must be active in marketing his services. He was, however, cautious not to oversell.[1]

Since McKinsey's time, the leaders of the profession have always exhibited competence in marketing their services. They have systematically sought opportunities to make social contacts with potential clients, to be recommended by existing clients to new prospects, to carry out quick management surveys free of charge, or to speak at management conferences. This, in addition to the firm's reputation, used to be sufficient to attract clients to the established firms as long as the market for consulting services was small, and competition was limited.

No wonder therefore that the firms established in the business did not favour the use of a wider range of marketing techniques, and of advertising in particular. The same attitude prevailed in consultants' associations. As mentioned in chapter 6, it was not until the late 1970s that advertising was admitted in the United States as a correct and acceptable means of marketing professional services in a competitive environment. Stress was laid on the point that competition in professional services ought to be encouraged, as it provides the client with the possibility of getting a better service for a lower price. In other countries, attitudes to the marketing of professional services have also started changing, although, for the time being, such marketing is less developed and uses a narrower range of techniques than in the United States.

In summary, management consultants, like other professionals, have to market their services for two main reasons:

- if you do not market in a competitive environment, you do not get the market share that you could and should get, and are thus abdicating your position in your competitors' favour;

- irrespective of competition, marketing is needed to put the right consultant in touch with the client who needs him; the client may not know about your firm, lack an understanding of what consulting is about, or just be timid and shy, so a professional approach to marketing will surmount these obstacles and establish the required collaborative relationship.

Thus, the question is no longer *whether* to market consulting services but *how* to do it in a truly professional manner, and effectively. Chapter 21 has shown that marketing considerations have a prominent place in the strategy of consulting firms. This discussion will now be pursued by reviewing the principles and methods of marketing.[2]

22.1 The marketing approach in consulting

What is to be marketed?

The marketing of consumer goods is a well-established field, using a wide range of effective techniques and channels. Even within the service sectors, there are some areas where marketing is quite well developed — for example, car rentals, tourism, or insurance. In contrast, management consulting is at the very beginning of its "marketing era". Consultants realise that they have to become better at marketing, but how should they do this, and what pitfalls should they avoid? Clearly, the marketers of consulting can learn a great deal from the experience of any sector, but nothing would be more harmful than a mechanistic application of marketing philosophies, approaches and techniques taken from elsewhere.

There are three main reasons for this. Firstly, consulting services are always provided within the business, administrative and professional culture of a particular country and organisation. This culture includes, among others, certain traditions and norms concerning the behaviour of professionals in marketing and delivering services. Therefore, in every country potential clients expect professionals to market their services in a particular way. Communication channels, advertising techniques and statements regarded as tasteful and perfectly correct in one country can make potential clients laugh and even provoke their resentment in another country. Of course, the clients' expectations concerning professional services are not static, and a consultant may be able to use tomorrow a technique that would be out of the question today.

Secondly, the "intangibility" of consulting services is another significant factor in marketing. True enough, there has been a tendency to "make tangible the intangibles", and we have shown in chapters 20 and 21 that management consultants can in certain cases develop and offer standard systems and service packages to clients. Information technology, and the advent of flexible computerised systems suitable for application in production and office management under various conditions, increase the range of consulting services that can be made more tangible. The client should be able to consider such a product or service package on its own merits. The marketing effort can be geared to making the product known to potential clients, and to arousing the interest of these clients by pointing out the benefits they can derive from this product.

However, the opportunities for making management consulting services tangible and packaging them are and will remain limited. Thus, the client must have some reason for turning to one particular consultant rather than to another (only very few potential clients would simply pick any telephone number in a directory of consultants). Since clients know that they are going to negotiate the purchase of an intangible product, and that it will be difficult (if not impossible) to compare this product directly to those offered by other consultants, they look for *surrogates* in evaluating what they are likely to get and deciding to whom to turn. This being the case, management consultants have to do the same — they also look for surrogates in showing clients that they understand and can solve their problems, and that the client will be in good hands if he turns to them.

Experience shows that the most important surrogate is the *professional reputation or image of the consultant*. We know, of course, that even the most experienced and reputable consultant may develop (for various reasons) an inadequate proposal for dealing with a given problem. No one can provide an absolute guarantee that a professional, even one of high reputation, will come up with the best possible solution in every case. Yet the probability of getting an excellent service is increased by using a consulting firm with a reputation for the quality, originality, reliability, satisfying cost/benefit ratio and other positive characteristics of its service.

Past experience looms large among these characteristics. It is, in fact, the main surrogate for which most clients are looking. "Have you done it before?" is the classic question asked by clients. It is a fully legitimate question which underlines the importance of "referrals", or the possibility of referring to past clients and assignments in showing new clients that the consultant is fully versed in their management and business problems. However, "Have you done it before?" represents a formidable marketing challenge to new consultants, and to professionals who have decided to tackle new sectors, or new kinds of management and business problem. They "have not done it before", yet they have to convince the client that they possess enough relevant knowledge and experience to serve him effectively.

Thus, in addition to marketing specific assignments to individual clients (direct marketing), a consultant has to "market" his professional reputation and image (indirect marketing). In fact, in the marketing cycle the latter precedes the former. If they know nothing about you, most potential clients will never turn to you, and may refuse to talk to you if you turn to them!

Building up a professional reputation or image is the core of marketing professional services. It is not enough if a consultant *is* fully competent to undertake certain jobs and has interesting products to offer. Potential clients must *know this*: the consultant must enjoy a reputation, or image, which is consistent with his technical competence and the products he offers, and which truly reflects what he can do for clients.

In this connection, some marketing specialists refer to *positioning*, meaning a set of measures and activities whereby a product, a commercial firm, or a professional practice, acquires a desired "position" in the prospective clients' minds. This is what a management consultant wants to acquire: an appropriate position in his current and prospective clients' minds!

Positioning has a significant public relations dimension in addition to the purely professional or technical one. The question is not only what *technical message* will build up your image and arouse potential clients' interest, but what *medium* ought to be used and what *public relations principles and techniques* apply to your marketing efforts. Clients must not be irritated or made suspicious by overselling, by advertising in wrongly chosen media, or by self-laudatory statements. For example, some consultants like to stress their unique approach and expertise in their publicity brochures, although a quick comparison reveals that this is grossly exaggerated, as they offer exactly the same service as many others! The advice of a competent public relations specialist may help to avoid these pitfalls, and put a body of knowledge about public relations at the management consultant's disposal.

Thirdly, we must remember that consulting practice involves direct interaction with the client. Even standard systems and packages will need to be adapted to fit the client's situation and for installation in the specific environment of his organisation. In marketing his services, an individual consultant also markets *his personal ability to co-operate with the client* in getting the job done. This is a major objective of the first contacts and exploratory meetings with the client and of the preliminary survey of the client's problems. The client must be convinced that he can "buy" the consultant's personality, attitudes, habits, and work methods *in addition* to the technical expertise required for the problem in hand. The consultant, in turn, is looking for similar information on the client and the staff who will be directly involved in the assignment. He knows that he will be able to deliver his product only in an atmosphere of mutual understanding, trust, support and collaboration. Not only clients take a risk. Consultants take one too. They can minimise this risk by assessing, while negotiating the assignment, whether they will be able to set up a productive collaborative relationship with the client.

This problem becomes more complex in marketing the services of larger consulting firms. A large professional service organisation uses just one or a few professional workers for a specific client project. Experienced clients are well aware of this. To some extent, they are prepared to rely on the firm's reputation, which also covers the professional attitudes and work methods that prevail in the firm. Clients normally expect that the firm will also guarantee the personalities of individual consultants who will be directly assigned to the job. A standard way of doing this is to submit the names and CVs of consultants in technical proposals to potential clients. In many instances this is not enough. As mentioned in chapter 7, in purchasing an assignment from a consulting firm the client is definitely influenced by the personality and performance of the firm's representatives (usually very competent and senior ones) who come to negotiate the assignment. Often different consultants will later be assigned for executing the assignment. They have to be "sold" to the client too, and the best way is to involve at least the future project leader in the negotiation and preliminary survey stage, before the client signs the contract. Thus, the firm will have marketed not only its professional product, but also the person who will be responsible for delivering this product in closest collaboration with the client.

The prospective client's psychology

Whether a potential client identifies himself by contacting the consultant or the consultant finds him in some other way, it is easier if the client is aware of his problem and has had at least some experience with consultants from past assignments. Often this is not the case. In marketing their services, management consultants face a great deal of ignorance and must overcome various psychological barriers. Dissipating the potential client's fears and anxieties is, in fact, as important as preparing solid technical proposals, or providing evidence of the consultant's past achievements.

Reluctance to admit that a consultant is needed. Some managers do not want to admit to themselves that they need a consultant because this would hurt their self-esteem. Often the potential client is worried that a consultant's presence will be regarded by others — by subordinates, peers, superiors, shareholders, or even by competitors and customers — as an admission of incompetence.

Doubts about the consultant's competence and integrity. It is common for clients to have doubts about an external person's ability to resolve intricate problems with which management has struggled without finding any solution. Some clients feel, too, that a consultant will not really take all the trouble needed to search out a solution that is likely to work in the long term, and that he will simply try to place one of his standard packages. Some organisations feel that consultants are too inquisitive and collect too much information that could somehow be misused in the future.

Fear of becoming dependent on a consultant. Sometimes the remark is heard that it is easy to recruit a consultant, but difficult to get rid of him. Consultants are said to structure and manage assignments in a way that inevitably leads to new assignments. This can create a permanent dependence on one consulting firm.

Fear of excessive consulting fees. This fear is quite widespread in organisations with financial difficulties and in small businesses. Owners and managers sometimes ignore how the fee is calculated and justified, and with what benefits it could be compared. They believe that using a consultant is a luxury that is beyond their means.

Repeat business

With past and current clients the situation is different. One can assume that they are already familiar with consulting in general, and with the consulting firms that have worked for them in particular. This simplifies the marketing of new assignments to these clients. One can also assume that they will be inclined to turn again to the consultant who gave them good service in the past. This leads to repeat business, which, as we already know, may amount to 70 to 80 per cent of the total income in some firms.

Yet it would be a great error to think that repeat business will be forthcoming without any marketing effort. The business environment and the consulting scene change continually. Former clients must be informed of the changes occurring in the consulting firms known to them from past assignments, so as to convince them that "their" consultant is always the right one as he keeps abreast of developments and will again be able to come up with something new. Clients know that staff turnover is quite high in consulting firms and want to be assured that the new staff members are as good or even better than those known from previous assignments. Finally, competition must never be underestimated. Any consultant can lose an excellent client if a rival consulting firm does a good marketing job and offers an attractive new product to that client!

Clients served by other consultants

The statement made in the previous paragraph implies that it is quite normal to offer a consulting service to a client who is already served by another consultant. In a competitive environment this is, indeed, fully acceptable practice. But it is necessary to consider when this is likely to be effective.

Some clients, in particular larger businesses and government agencies, prefer to use several consulting organisations rather than reserve all assignments for one consultant. Also, if you feel that you can offer a better service than your competitor, and demonstrate this to a potential new client, there is no reason why you should not try.

Six fundamental principles

Experience has shown that successful marketing of consulting services is guided by certain general principles. Although some of these principles were touched upon previously (e.g. in chapter 6), it may be useful to summarise them at this point.

Do not sell more than you can deliver! Marketing creates expectations and makes commitments. Overmarketing may create more expectations than a consulting firm is able to meet. This may be counterproductive and even unethical: some clients may need your help urgently; you promise it, but cannot deliver. Or, an excessive selling effort may force you to recruit and immediately send to clients more new staff than you can train and supervise.

Do not misrepresent yourself! The temptation to offer and sell services in which your consulting firm is not really competent is quite high in marketing. To yield to this temptation is unethical; the client's interests can be seriously damaged. This is a matter of technical judgement, too. Competence in marketing also involves your ability to realistically assess your own competence!

Refrain from denigrating other consultants! Questions concerning your competitors' approaches and achievements come up quite often in discussions with clients. Nothing should prevent you from providing factual information, if you have it. However, it is unprofessional to provide distorted information and make disparaging comments on competitors in order to influence your client. A sophisticated client is likely to regard such comments as an expression of your weakness, not of your strength.

Never forget that you are marketing a professional service! As discussed above, management consultants have to be entrepreneurial and innovative in marketing. They can learn a great deal from marketing in other sectors. Yet the professional nature of the service, the clients' sensitivity and the local cultural values and norms must not be lost from sight in deciding how to market.

Aim at an equally high technical performance in marketing and in execution! To market ineffectively, without making highly competent staff responsible for marketing, would be suicidal. However, in their effort to foster marketing some consultants have not maintained the delivery of assignments at the same quality level (in staffing, controlling quality, respecting deadlines, and similar). It is useful to view marketing as a process that does not end with the signing of the contract. The execution of assignments has a significant marketing dimension. Flawless service is marketing for repeat business, and for obtaining the references essential for building up the consultant's professional image.

Regard the clients' needs and desires as the focal point of all marketing! There is no point in selling to potential clients what they do not need, or do not want to buy. The client may be quite pleased to hear that you are a brilliant professional, but it is infinitely more important to convince him that you care for him, understand his problem, are prepared to listen to him and can help to find and implement a solution beneficial to his business. This is a golden rule of marketing professional services. Your marketing efforts must be client-centred, not consultant-centred.

22.2 Techniques for marketing the consulting firm

A wide range of techniques is available to management consultants for building up their professional reputation and image, or positioning their practice, in the clients' minds. The main techniques are reviewed in this section. Their purpose is not to market individual assignments, but to get potential clients interested in the consulting firm and its products and create opportunities for contacts with these clients. Many of the techniques simultaneously enhance the image of the consulting firm as a professional organisation, and that of the individual persons representative of its approach, style and technical expertise.

While certain techniques are aimed purely at public relations and image building (e.g. advertising), the reader will notice that other techniques aim to arouse the clients' interest by directly providing another useful technical service (e.g. information, or training). This is very significant. It places the marketing of consulting services in a truly professional context and helps the consulting organisation not only to enhance its image in the clients' eyes and minds, but to broaden and increase its own technical competence.

Working the referrals

Word of mouth is one of the oldest and yet most efficient ways in which a professional firm becomes known to new clients. Businessmen and managers are used to sharing information about professionals such as lawyers, accountants, engineers and management consultants. They exchange both favourable and negative information, so only a firm which has rendered a flawless service to a client can hope to have another useful referral. A manager looking for a consultant will often ask his business friends for advice before turning to any other source of information.

It could appear that excellent performance in serving clients is all that is necessary to get good referrals. Experience shows that it is indeed the main thing, but not the only one. Some consultants do not leave it to chance that a happy client will recommend them to colleagues. They discuss their promotional needs and policies with their clients, asking them:

● to suggest who else in the business community may be interested in similar services;

● to authorise the use of the clients' names as a reference to prospective clients;

● possibly to give permission for describing or summarising a successful assignment in a technical publication, in promotional material or in a management seminar;

● to speak about the consultant with other managers and businessmen, but also with bankers, lawyers, accountants and other persons who may be asked for a good consultant's name by their own business contacts.

This requires an excellent mutual understanding between the consultant and the client. The client must not feel ashamed that he had to pay a consultant for dealing with a problem that he should have solved by himself. Rather he should be proud that co-operation with an outstanding professional has helped him to discover new opportunities and view his problems in a wider perspective. The consultant must show his client that his concern for the client goes beyond a single contract — this is best achieved by informing past clients of the latest research and the state of the art in their sector or problem area, telling them about new services the consultant can provide, having a business lunch with them from time to time, and in general maintaining frequent communication. The client will then enjoy talking about "his" consultant and recommend him without hesitation. Happy clients become your best marketers, and do it free of charge!

Professional publications

Books for managers. Writing books that will be read by managers, or even become reference works, is becoming increasingly popular among consultants. Some recent publications based on experience and research in management consulting firms have become real bestsellers, and their impact on promoting new business has been very strong, although difficult to measure.[3]

The promotional effect depends on the nature and quality of the publication. The reader must be impressed by the width and depth of the author's innovative approach to topical management problems and conclude that his firm might also benefit from such an approach. Finding the right publisher is equally important. Publications that just repeat the same old stuff using new words may bring in a few clients, but will have little effect in the long run. Writing a really good book is an extremely difficult and time-consuming exercise, and those who say that every management consultant could try it are bad advisers. But if you feel that you have enough to say, do not hesitate!

The need for original management publications reflecting the real problems and needs of local practice is considerable in many developing countries. This is a real challenge and opportunity for management consultants.

Articles on management and industry topics. To a management consultant, writing an article presents certain advantages over publishing a book:

— the topic covered can be narrower (e.g. an interesting development in a sector served by the consultant, or an intervention technique that has helped several clients);

— the time required to write an article is much shorter;

— the readership base will be much larger if the article is published in a widely-circulated newspaper or journal;

— many busy managers do not read books unless these are recommended to them as absolutely essential, but do glance through articles on topics of concern.

To arouse interest in potential clients, articles must address important topical issues. Articles based on one or more successfully completed assignments, and outlining the approach taken, the changes achieved and the benefits to the clients, are particularly useful.

The *choice of the medium* is essential. The general public or the academic community are not the primary target. We can therefore recommend:

● professional, business and trade journals, which are normally read by a wide management public (e.g. a consultant who wants to be recognised as an authority in road transport management should be known as an author to the readers of trade publications on transport in general and road transport in particular);

- business and management pages and supplements of important daily newspapers and weeklies;
- local newspapers, in particular those preferred by the local business community.

Here again, the reputation of the publication is important. Articles in *leading* newspapers and periodicals definitely bring in more new business.

Occasional papers and pamphlets. Both existing and potential clients appreciate it very much if a management consultant shares with them some of his knowledge and experience through technical and information papers, guides, reports, briefs, pamphlets, checklists and other materials. These can deal with a relatively narrow and specialised topic, but must be of direct interest to the recipient. Therefore, you should choose a topic of concern to managers, providing suggestions and guidelines tested by experience. You do not have to divulge *all* your know how (this constitutes your competitive advantage), but you must be prepared to say something if the material distributed is not to be viewed as trivial publicity. Papers informing managers and/or specialists about the state of the art in their field, or about trends likely to affect the business, are particularly welcome.

Newsletters. A newsletter is a periodical publication whose purpose is to keep its readers abreast of developments in their field of activity on a regular basis. A management consultant can choose between a newsletter devoted entirely to news from a sector or trade, and one which also gives news from his consulting firm (completed projects, research done, new services started, articles published, and so on). If the area to be covered is well chosen and the newsletter handled professionally, it can become a highly regarded reference service, regarded as essential information by the subscribers. Several newsletters launched by consultants have achieved this standard, and have attracted many clients to the firms promoting them.[4]

All publications should include a reference to the consulting firm to which the author belongs, with some information on the firm and its products, and (if they agree to it) on client organisations from which the published experience was drawn.

Relations with public information media

Public information media such as the press, television, or radio are constantly looking for the information that their audience expects to receive. Management consultants possess, or can help to gather, organise and present, some of this information — for example, on developments in business and finance, impact of technological developments on factory and office work, new energy-saving techniques, or the likely impact of political changes on investment decisions.

Quite a few consultants have found it most beneficial to keep in touch with the media and be helpful to them. Editors and other media people have to meet imperative short deadlines, need quick help, and want to be sure that their contact is very well informed, trustworthy and reliable. They want information in a format suitable for immediate use. A consultant who understands these requirements and tries to be flexible can expect to be quoted as a source or technical authority, or be invited to give an interview. This will have a much greater promotional effect than many costly advertisements!

Being responsive to public media requirements does not mean refraining from taking any initiative. Once you understand how the media operate, and for what kind of information they are looking (and how presented), you can yourself come up with suggestions of topics, or directly offer a piece of news or a story to your contact in the media.

News or press releases are intended for wider distribution to the media. Some consultants have had good experience with them. A news release showing that you have done something interesting in an area on which media are keen to report can be most welcome and may be used by several media, or the media may get in touch with you for further information.

Some media people have a distorted picture of management consultants and look mainly for sensational information on them (e.g. on major assignments that ended up as complete failures, or on exorbitant fees charged for work that the client could have easily done by himself). Caustic articles with this kind of information have appeared in quite a few general and business journals in several countries. It is counterproductive to react aggressively and arrogantly. Helping media to do their job, and demonstrating high professional standards in dealing with them, is the best way to change their attitude to management consultants.

Management seminars

Training and information services that managers and businessmen are keen to obtain can have a very pronounced promotional function and lead to new consulting assignments. Management seminars, round tables or conferences, workshops, information sessions, executive briefings and similar events have become very popular in many consulting firms. Usually the consultant invites managers to attend a session on a topic of real concern to them — for example, how to handle industrial relations under new legislation, what is happening in international money markets, or what changes in work organisation will be required by the introduction of new manufacturing technology. The consulting firm can invite external specialists as speakers, but it is essential that its own professional staff should make a presentation to demonstrate that the firm is fully up to date and does care about vital problems that worry clients. If possible, work recently undertaken by the firm should be described, showing benefits derived by the clients. However, it is essential that participants perceive the seminar as of direct help to them and not as a selling exercise.

It is impossible to suggest one single way of organising a seminar. For example, you have to consider whether it is better tactics to offer it as a free service to the management public, or charge a relatively high fee, or charge only for the meals and printed materials provided. A seminar may be arranged by the consulting firm alone, or in collaboration with a management centre or institute, a local chamber of commerce, or a trade association. The seminar should be brief, and the time and venue must be convenient.

The participants should be potential clients. Ideally, you would use a selective mailing list and invite decision makers from organisations likely to have problems, or to be looking for opportunities in the areas that will be discussed. You will have to assess the probability of response (which may be 5-20 per cent, depending on factors such as the topic, the reputation of your firm and the speakers, the quality of the mailing list and the managers' propensity to attend seminars). It is better if invitations look very personal.

Those who attend express, by so doing, interest both in the topic and in your expertise. They may be potential clients. Their names should therefore be carefully noted. While some of them may continue to talk further with you after the seminar, or may ask for an appointment, you will also have a list of persons for future contacts (say a telephone call 2-3 weeks after the seminar, offering to meet them to discuss their specific problems in greater depth without any immediate commitment). This may generate new assignments.

Special information services

The promotional effect of special information services can be similar to that of seminars and newsletters. A consulting firm that becomes a recognised authority in a special area of information vital to decision-makers can use its information services for promoting consulting work. A periodic information report can include a description of the firm's consulting services, pointing out the relation between information and advice on how to apply it. Individual enquiries can be used to mention the availability of other services. If the information received is highly valued by the clients, many of them will also be interested in other technical services offered by the same firm.

Advertising

The purpose of advertising is to arouse the interest of a large number of potential clients by convincing them that your products or services are particularly attractive to them. Advertising is making headway in management consulting and we shall see more of it in the years to come. Therefore, management consultants should be aware of its advantages and its pitfalls. Those who also consult in marketing and distribution tend to be familiar with advertising issues and may even be able to design advertisements and advertising campaigns for their own firm. A new consultant who is not versed in advertising will be well advised to turn to a professional public relations or advertising agency before embarking on a major advertising campaign and spending a lot of money on it. Quite a few mass-advertising methods and media used for promoting goods and services that interest the wider public are not suitable for the marketing of consulting services.

Press advertisements have to meet two basic criteria. Firstly, they must be placed in journals and newspapers where potential clients are likely to see them.

It is necessary to find out what managers and businessmen read. The longer the press run and the wider the circulation of a journal, the higher the cost of advertising space will be. A consultant who has been of help to a business or trade periodical and has developed privileged relations with the editors may be offered advertising space at a special rate.

Secondly, advertisements must meet the criteria of effective design: providing a small amount of essential information rather than a lot of fragmented detail; stressing the benefits for which the client is looking rather than promoting the firm's name and background; clearly suggesting where and how to contact the consultant. If possible, the service offered and the likely special benefit to the client should be included in the heading and the advertisement should have an attraction and appeal for the client.

Advertising on radio and television has been little used by management consultants. Yet it should not be completely overlooked. For example, some stations have programmes for the local industrial and business communities on topics such as creating an enterprise, saving energy, or increasing productivity; an advertisement following such a programme may be quite effective.

Mailing publicity materials is a method which probably every consultant has thought about at some point. Many consultants reject the idea, because they feel that this so called "cold contacting" is inefficient. Those who use it include both some well-established firms and newcomers to the consulting business.

It is essential to have a good mailing list. Some consultants prefer to draw up such a list themselves, using information on organisations in the sector they want to serve (e.g. on smaller firms located in a given district likely to experience maintenance or cash-flow problems). Or there may be a trade association or a special firm from which a mailing list can be purchased.

Only well-chosen and properly designed materials should be mailed. These include information brochures and leaflets on the consulting firm, information sheets and reports on new services, annual activity reports, reprints of articles, samples of newsletters, and similar. There is no point in flooding managers with paper. They receive too much publicity material anyhow. The materials sent should therefore be succinct and brief and should give the potential client a piece of meaningful technical information, providing evidence of the consultant's approach, knowledge of the business and (if possible) work recently undertaken. This should be supplemented by a short description of the consulting firm and profiles of its senior staff.

Exhibitions of professional materials and services, organised in conjunction with trade fairs, exhibitions of computer and office equipment, professional conventions, or management and training conferences, also provide opportunities for advertising. If the consultant can be present, some clients may get in touch with him directly at the exhibition.

The manager's professional and social activities

If you are a management consultant it is in your interest to socialise with managers and be regarded as someone who belongs to management and business circles. You expect that these contacts will "make you visible" to a number of potential clients, who will prefer to deal with a person known to them from professional and social contacts rather than with a stranger. You will also get to know bankers, lawyers and other professionals who may recommend you to their own clients.

Many consultants are members of management associations and similar voluntary membership bodies, local, national, or international. They readily give talks at meetings (for free) and agree to serve on committees or working parties. They exhibit "relaxed initiative" (interest and availability), but should not overdo it by being so active that their behaviour becomes annoying and suspicious. A single practitioner has to consider in how many events he can afford to participate, while a larger consulting firm can make sure that its staff will represent it in several organisations.

Private social, cultural and sporting activities provide opportunities for informal contacts which can generate new business. More than one important consulting project has had its origin on a golf course!

Voluntary social work

Organisations involved in social work and community development are badly in need of members and advisers with administrative and management skills. While their problems may not be the most sophisticated ones from a strictly technical point of view, helping them is often a most rewarding social experience. It teaches the consultant that people in business and government organisations also have a number of private problems and interests, and engage in various social activities where different rules and criteria apply.

Voluntary social and community service gives a significant social dimension to the consultant's image. This can even be expressed through formal recognition or award. It helps to establish contacts with managers and businessmen who also engage in these activities — in some countries quite a few of them do.

Directories

In most industrialised countries, and now even in some developing countries, various directories of professional services exist and many of them include sections on management consultants. In addition to the consultant's name and address, a directory would normally also indicate his areas of competence, using either standard terms and definitions chosen by the publisher of the directory, or a description provided by the consultant himself.

It is unlikely that a potential client would select a management consultant straight from a directory listing. However, a directory may be used for establishing a short list of consultants, or for checking and completing information on them. It is therefore advisable to be listed in directories that are well known and enjoy a good reputation. This includes membership directories issued by professional consultants' associations. It is not necessary to be mentioned in every directory at all costs.

If the "yellow pages" of the area telephone directory include a section on management consultants, you should make sure that your firm is listed.

Responding to enquiries

The use of any of the marketing techniques discussed above can at some point lead to an enquiry by a prospective client. In some instances the prospects are directly invited to make an enquiry (e.g. as a follow-up to a seminar which they attended). These enquiries can cover a wide range of questions, including general questions on business and management, sources of information, profile of the consulting firm, work for other clients, or problems faced by the client who is making the enquiry.

Any such enquiry can be another effective step in preparing new business, or can spoil the emerging relationship and turn a potential client away. This risk is particularly high in large consulting firms, if the person contacted (who may be a telephone operator, but could equally well be a professional who happened to be in the office) is unable to put the client in touch with the right colleague, or to react properly to the enquiry.

It is useful to bear the following rules in mind:

- resources should be made available for handling enquiries;
- every enquiry should be handled with utmost courtesy and patience and at the right technical level (a well-informed client can be discouraged by a poor answer from a clerical assistant or a less well-informed junior professional);
- enquiries that cannot be answered immediately should be handled in the shortest possible time;
- responding to enquiries involves marketing tactics — that is, considering how far to go: merely answering a question, showing interest in the client organisation, offering a meeting, or similar;
- in certain cases the consultant will have to decide how much to reveal (it may well happen that a client could try to turn an enquiry into a free consultation);
- enquiries should be recorded in clients' files (see section 22.4), and suggestions for further follow-up should be made if appropriate.

Location and standing of office facilities

A happy medium needs to be struck between the prestigious image of a professional service and the economy of its operation. The right address is usually close to the sources of business. This tends to locate a firm in or near the financial or commercial quarter of the capital city or a major industrial centre, which in some countries is the same place. However, a "good address" is likely to be expensive and the consultant must be able to afford it.

The business-like appearance of the offices, the reception area and the meeting rooms where visitors are received, is equally important. Successful consulting firms want to show clients that they possess up-to-date office equipment, elegant but sober furniture, and efficient internal administration. Exhibiting excessive luxury may impress certain clients, but will discourage most of them. Your clients will quickly conclude that you will make them pay for the beauty and comfort of your office facilities. Owners and managers of small firms definitely feel uneasy in offices too unlike their own working environment!

Name and logo

Although many consultants are unaware of it, public relations experts confirm that the firm's name and logo have their role in communicating the firm's image to the public and to potential clients.

If the firm's name is well known and has become a part of its goodwill, it should not be changed, even if it does not any longer have a real meaning. A new firm, however, can consider alternative choices.

Names of persons. Naming a firm after the founder, owner, or main partners is very popular in professional services. It is useful to know who has the key role in the firm. If a consultant is successful as an author or conference speaker, potential clients can easily see his association with a professional practice of the same name. On the other hand, there can be some confusion. It may be difficult to maintain a clear distinction between professional and private activity undertaken under the same name.

A quick perusal of lists of important accounting and consulting firms shows that names of persons (founders or main partners) prevail in their names. However, to use a person's name is not recommended if it sounds awkward in the consultant's cultural environment, or if it can evoke bizzare associations.

Activity area. To call a firm by its activity area (e.g. International Marketing Consultants, Road Transport Management Services) is another possibility. Such a name should be carefully chosen:

- it may become too restrictive if the consultant enters a new area (e.g. adds new fields of transport to road transport) — this has, in fact, happened in many consulting firms;
- it may easily lead to confusion if it is too general and if several firms in the same business community use similar names (Resource Planning Services, Resource Management Associates, Strategic Planning Services, and similar).

Acronym. It is useful to think of the firm's acronym: in the case of some consultants the original full name has been forgotten and the acronym has replaced it completely.

Logo. The logo of a professional firm does not have the same importance as in mass advertising of consumer goods, but it can play a useful role in reminding the clients quickly that a message is coming from a particular consultant. A logo can be used, for example, on letter headings, newsletters, reports, publicity materials and printed and visual advertisements.

22.3 Techniques for marketing consulting assignments

Every consultant prefers clients to come to him. Yet many consultants, in particular newcomers to the profession, would not get enough work by merely waiting for potential clients to come. They have to find clients and market assignments to them. The main techniques are reviewed in this section.

Cold contacts

Cold contacts are visits, letters, or telephone calls whereby a consultant turns to a potential client and tries to sell him a service. A lot has been said and written about these contacts. The professional community regards them as the least effective marketing technique and some consultants never use them. Yet they are still used, and newly established consulting firms may be unable to avoid them.

Cold visits (unannounced) are least suitable. Managers resent being disturbed by unknown persons for unknown reasons. There are cultures, however, where this is acceptable.

Cold mailing of letters is a better technique. Its purpose is not to sell an assignment, but to present the consultant to the prospective client and prepare the ground for a further contact, to follow in 2-3 weeks.

Cold telephone calls have the sole purpose of obtaining an appointment with the client. They also serve for answering the immediate questions that the client may ask before deciding to receive or visit the consultant.

The effectiveness of cold contacts can be increased by observing certain rules. Firstly, the prospects have to be properly selected. They must be "target organisations", identified by researching the potential market, and the consultant must be convinced that he can do something useful for them. He should work out his own list of addresses, or, if he decides to buy one from an agent, he should screen it before using it.

Secondly, cold contacts require technical preparation. The consultant should learn as much as possible about the organisation to be contacted. The worst thing that can happen is to exhibit flagrant ignorance of basic facts about the client's business in the first conversation with him. Letters worded in general terms, or giving a lot of detailed information of no interest to the prospective client, should be avoided. Instead, individualised letters should be written, showing the client that the consultant has something specific and relevant to offer. A telephone call also needs preparation to be effective. Some consultants even have checklists for preparing and constructing the conversation over the phone.

Thirdly, the consultant should aim at getting in touch with the right person. In many (but not all!) organisations it should be the top executive. A cold letter should be addressed to him personally. In calling by telephone the consultant should try to speak with his "target person", aiming to reach him at a time of day when he is not too occupied. Busy executives do not bother to return calls unless they have a reason for this. Therefore, if he does not reach his target person, the consultant should not leave his name and number, hoping that his call will be returned. Rather he should call again at a moment suggested by the secretary.

A normal sequence in cold contacting would be (i) a letter, (ii) a telephone call following up on the letter and asking for an appointment, and (iii) an appointment with the client. To get to this third step does not guarantee a new assignment, but the possibility of getting one has increased.

It is difficult to give generally valid figures on the number of letters or phone calls needed to get one appointment. Some consultants indicate such figures, but these clearly reflect specific local conditions.[5] The better you research your potential market and the more professionally you proceed in making the contact, the smaller the number of contacts made to get one assignment will be.

Contacts based on referrals and leads

If a consultant "puts referrals to work" as discussed in section 22.2, there is no doubt that most contacts with new clients will take place thanks to referrals and leads. These occur in various ways:

● the prospective client asks for a meeting;

● the consultant is introduced to the prospect by a mutual business friend;

● the consultant gets names of potential clients from his current clients.

The fact that the consultant has been recommended, or can use referrals likely to influence the prospective client's attitude, creates a favourable atmosphere for negotiating an assignment. The prospect may know a great deal from his business friends and the discussion can quickly pass from generalities to specific issues. The consultant should find out how much information the client already has, to avoid both repeating the obvious and forgetting to provide information that the new client needs.

If the client wants no more than information, the consultant should not force him into negotiating an assignment immediately. Experience will teach him how far to go in such situations. For example, the consultant may suggest another contact in which the discussion could be pursued, and prior to which he could look − free of charge − at some data on the prospect's business. Or he can provide some detailed descriptions of assignments carried out for clients whom the prospect knows and respects. Such a contact should be followed up by a telephone call after 2-4 weeks. If the prospect has lost interest, the consultant should not persist.

In a similar vein, consulting firms which organise management seminars often make follow-up contacts with participants to find out whether they would be interested in a consulting assignment. An approach in several stages (as described above) should be applied in these instances.

Responding to invitations to submit proposals

In certain cases new contacts with potential clients can be made in response to a published announcement inviting consultants to present a technical proposal for executing a project. As a rule, the client will be a public agency or enterprise, or (less frequently) a private organisation that for some reason has chosen this selection procedure. Many of these projects are in developing countries.

In such a situation the client has not only identified himself, but probably has a fairly precise view of what he wants to be done. His own technical services, or an external consultant, will have undertaken a preliminary investigation and developed a global description (terms of reference) of the project. This description would be made available on request. Frequently the selection procedure is in two steps:

— in the first step, consultants who are interested are invited to contact the client and provide a *technical memorandum* on their firm's profile and relevant experience; those retained are included in a short list;

— in the second step, the consultants short-listed submit *technical proposals*, which are then examined and selected as described in section 7.4.

Projects thus announced are often large and financially attractive and whet the appetite of many consultants. However, before a firm decides to tender, several factors ought to be considered and relevant information carefully examined:

● the prospect may already have a short list, or even a specific firm in mind, when starting the formal selection procedure;

● several important consulting firms may be interested in the job and competition will be tough;

● the preparation of a technical memorandum and of a good technical proposal is time-consuming and costly (a fairly detailed diagnostic survey, including missions abroad, may be needed before drawing up a proposal); this work is done at a loss by those who are not chosen and sometimes its cost is not reimbursed even to the winning firm;

● the selection procedure may be long, the consultant may be asked to submit additional information, reconsider some of his terms, and pay several visits to the client; therefore he should not be in pressing need of securing the job and starting it quickly.

If the consultant decides to compete for such a project he should develop a tactical plan for winning it. For example, he may feel technically fully competent for the job, but be unknown to the client. The question is: What can be done in a short time to become known to an important new prospect? Can our former clients help? Should we organise study visits to our former clients for the prospective client's key technical staff? What else can be done?

Auditing

Audits of company accounts and financial statements (required by law in many countries) provide exceptional opportunities for direct selling of management consulting services. This has been well perceived by public accounting firms with management consulting departments; these do between 30 and 70 per cent of management consulting assignments for their audit clients.

The relationship between an audit and a consulting assignment may be more or less direct. Some audits point directly to deficiencies and a consulting service is then offered to remedy these. In other cases, the marketing approach is more subtle; the collaborative relationship already existing between the client and the accounting firm is of great help, and information collected by the auditors enables the consultants coming from another department in the same professional firm to focus on areas of vital importance to the clients.

Marketing during the entry phase

The entry phase of a consulting assignment was described in detail in chapter 7. The reader should recall that in most instances the client does not give his final agreement to the assignment until he has seen, and reviewed, a technical proposal based on preliminary problem diagnosis. The implication is clear: the marketing of a new assignment does not end at the first discussion with the prospect, but continues throughout the entry phase even if some technical work on a new assignment has already started.

The marketing dimension of the entry phase cannot be overemphasised. Whether there is competition or not, the consultant should think of the marketing effect of everything he says and does in the first meetings with the client organisation, in the preliminary diagnostic survey, in formulating and presenting the proposal to the client, and in suggesting how to staff the assignment. The proposal submitted to the client is a marketing as well as a technical document and these two dimensions must be well balanced.

Marketing during assignment execution

Furthermore, it is very useful to regard assignment execution as a set of activities during which the consultant pursues his marketing effort. This includes:

— being alert to any sign of the client's unhappiness or apprehension concerning the approach taken, the progress made, the costs incurred, or the behaviour of the assignment team;

— keeping the client fully informed about the progress of the assignment and examining all potential problems and difficulties with him as early as possible;

— keeping eyes open for further work opportunities (beyond the scope of the current assignment) and mentioning these to the client in an appropriate way;

— regarding the current assignment as a referral needed for future marketing (this will depend both on the technical quality of the job done, on the consultant's integrity, and on the relationship established with the client and his staff).

Once more we have to refer to the importance of repeat business and of solid referrals in planning for the future and in marketing professional services.

22.4 Marketing audit and programme

Marketing audit

An established consulting firm keen to improve its marketing should start by reviewing and assessing its past marketing practices. A marketing audit is a useful diagnostic tool for this purpose. It can be a totally self-diagnostic exercise if the consulting firm feels capable of examining various aspects of its own marketing, including public relations, the effect of advertising, and so on. If not, specialists in the marketing of professional services or in public relations can be asked to assist. They may be useful, for example, for interviewing clients and collecting information from other external sources in order to provide unbiased information.

Detailed outlines specifically designed for auditing the marketing of professional services are available from the literature.[6] Generally speaking, the audit would:

- examine the past and current marketing practices (organisation, information base, strategy, programme, techniques, activities, budgets and costs) and assess their contribution to the development of the firm;

- compare the findings with the marketing approach of direct competitors and other consultants;

- consider what changes in marketing will be necessary in order to meet new requirements of the market;

- suggest measures for making the marketing function more effective.

The benefits of a thorough marketing audit reach beyond the marketing function. It can identify new potential areas of business, suggest new sorts of client services, reveal gaps in the firm's technical competence, and make many other practical suggestions. It can, in fact, serve as a first step to examining overall strategy and applying strategic management systematically.

Marketing programme

A marketing programme (or plan) is a document in which a consulting firm defines its marketing objectives and strategy and determines what measures to take in putting the strategy into effect. A written marketing programme makes clear what is to be done over a definite period of time and what contribution to the total marketing effort is expected from individuals or units within the firm. Depending on its planning practices, a consulting firm can have a separate marketing programme, or treat this programme as a part of its strategic planning system.

Objectives of marketing should clearly express what is to be achieved by marketing activity over a definite period of time in both quantitative and qualitative terms. Quantitative objectives may indicate the market share to be attained and the volume of new business to be generated. Qualitative objectives concern, for example, the positioning of the consulting firm in the clients' minds and its competitive edge in terms of unique services it will be able to offer to the clients. The objectives are to be achieved some time in the future — say in one, three, or five years. This underlines the need to place all analytical and strategic considerations in a *time perspective*. For example, most of the techniques of indirect marketing used to build up a professional image will not generate new business immediately and have to be treated as an investment in future business. Yet it is advisable to determine, or at least to assess, by what time the indirect marketing activity should start bearing fruit.

The mix of marketing techniques to be used has to be consistent with the firm's existing and desired professional image and market penetration on the one hand, and its professional and financial resources on the other hand. The optimum mix is influenced by so many factors in every consulting firm that it is impossible to give other than general guidelines. Experience tends to show that:

- it is preferable to combine several marketing techniques (reinforcing each other if possible); however, it is better to avoid techniques in which you would feel uncomfortable and those for which your consulting firm lacks resources;

- although regarded as least effective, cold contacts (personal, by mail, or by telephone) are used by every second consulting firm (more often by smaller and young firms than by larger and well-established firms);

- newcomers to the consulting business cannot afford to wait until the market comes to them and have to give priority to techniques that put them rapidly in direct contact with potential clients.

Reliable data on the *volume of resources* spent on marketing by various consulting firms are not available. As we know, the area of marketing is relatively new in professional services, and marketing practices are changing rapidly. Also, a great deal of indirect marketing can simultaneously be an income-generating activity (e.g. management seminars and information services for which the clients pay). Many single practitioners have to devote 20-30 per cent of their time to marketing. Some consulting firms indicate that they spend between 5 and 25 per cent of their income on marketing. This figure is strongly influenced by the choice of marketing techniques — for example, an advertising campaign in major business journals will be a costly undertaking.

Planning the forward workload

The very nature of their services requires that consulting organisations maintain a sufficient backlog of orders for several weeks or months ahead. For any consultant there is an optimum figure that provides a reasonable safety margin and still allows new jobs to start without undue delay. Some consulting firms consider a 3-month backlog of work as ideal, while 6 weeks are regarded as a minimum. A backlog exceeding 3 months implies that the order book is lengthening and some clients will be kept waiting longer for the consultant to commence an assignment. Many consultants do not attain the 6-week backlog and are quite happy if they have one for 3-4 weeks ahead. This, however, is a small safety margin.

To maintain a satisfactory safety margin, the volume of new assignments in fee-earning days (weeks or months) negotiated in every period of time (week or month) should be equal to the average volume of consulting work performed by the firm in this period. This, of course, is theory, but it provides guidance for the firm's work planners and marketing officers. If the firm is selling at a rate below this figure, its forward load is decreasing and there may be danger ahead.

In practice, the marketing of assignments and the planning of work have to be less global. Ideally, the structure of the forward load should correspond as closely as possible to the relative numbers of consulting staff of different technical profiles. Clearly, it is easier to plan forward workloads for consultants who are relatively versatile and can undertake a wider range of different assignments.

Pacing the marketing effort

A steady control of the forward workload helps to pace the firm's marketing effort in order to avoid both under- and overselling. There must always be, in the pipeline, a number of initial meetings with prospective clients, management surveys for preparing proposals to clients, or other marketing events. If these marketing events are not generating a normal number of new assignments, it may be necessary to allocate more of the senior staff's time to marketing, or to examine the effectiveness of the marketing techniques used.

A sole practitioner must also watch his forward workload carefully. Although he would normally allocate some 20-30 per cent of his working time to marketing (as mentioned above), he may be tied up full-time by a longer assignment, thus risking not doing enough to prepare for future work. This must be avoided. If the consultant prefers to give all his working time to a current client, he must put in more hours and try to meet new prospects and do some marketing outside regular business hours.

The intensity of promotional activity should be heavily influenced by the duration of current assignments and the size and length of future assignments. If the average length is dropping, more time will be needed to find and negotiate the same total volume of business for the firm.

For example, a firm that normally undertakes 50 assignments a year to occupy its 25 consultants finds out that it has to sell 60 assignments, i.e. 20 per cent more, to maintain the same volume of work. Its records show that it normally has to make 5 initial visits to prospective clients and 1.3 management surveys to get one contract. Can it do 300 initial visits and 78 surveys instead of 250 visits and 65 surveys? A few pointers begin to emerge from this simple arithmetic: either the average assignment should be longer, or more consultants should be employed for marketing, or fewer operating consultants engaged.

The marketing information system

We have seen in this chapter, as well as in chapter 21 dealing with strategy, that marketing requires a considerable amount of information. This information may be so voluminous and diversified that it is difficult to use unless it is systematically organised. Therefore, it is useful to view and treat this information as a system intended to provide both global and detailed information on existing and potential markets, and on the consulting firm's marketing activities and capabilities.

This approach involves:

- defining the kind of information to be collected, stored and analysed;
- determining in what way and how frequently this information will be updated;
- assigning responsibility for collecting, updating and analysing information;
- choosing a convenient formula and equipment for storing, processing and retrieving information.

Information on markets for services describes the main trends and significant developments of these markets. Focus should be on developments that create a new demand for consulting services, or change the nature of this demand. Information on competitors is included.

Information on individual clients provides a detailed picture of the markets for services. It is kept in client files (card index, computer files, or similar), which are normally established on all clients — past, current and prospective — and contain:

- the client's name and address; names of key managers;
- names of contact persons;
- basic business information on the client (or an indication of files where this information is stored);
- summary information on past and current assignments, including the consultant's assessment of these assignments (and a reference to assignment files, reports and other documents containing detailed information);
- information on all past contacts with the client (what contact made, by whom, with whom, and with what result);
- information on other consultants who have worked, or tried to work, with the client;
- suggestions and information needed for future contacts (e.g. who else in the client organisation might be interested).

Client files should be screened periodically for the planning of follow-up visits and new contacts with prospective clients.

Information on specific new business opportunities should be generated by systematic screening of information on markets and clients. For example, if the consulting firm is interested in doing more work for government departments and public enterprises, its information system must detect every invitation to submit proposals for consulting services published in official journals and other periodicals.

Information on the consulting firm's own marketing activities and capabilities includes facts and figures permitting it to assess (audit) the firm's marketing effort both quantitatively and qualitatively, work out a marketing programme, and assign to marketing those members of staff who have proven marketing capabilities. These can be found among consultants at various levels of seniority and length of consulting experience. In addition to experience, the consultant's personality and marketing talents are factors that affect success in marketing, and the firm's information system must reveal this.

---

[1] See W. B. Wolf: *Management and consulting: An introduction to James O. McKinsey* (Ithaca, NY, New York State School of Industrial and Labor Relations, Cornell University, 1978), chapter III.

[2] The range of technical publications on the marketing of professional services has been rapidly growing. See, for example, E. W. Wheatley: *Marketing professional services* (Englewood Cliffs, NJ, Prentice-Hall, 1983); A. Wilson: *Practice development for professional firms* (Maidenhead, McGraw-Hill, 1984); P. Kotler and P. N. Bloom: *Marketing professional services* (Englewood Cliffs, NJ, Prentice-Hall, 1984); or R. A. Connor and J. P. Davidson: *Marketing your consulting and professional services* (New York, Wiley, 1985).

[3] A well-known example is the bestseller *In search of excellence* written by T. J. Peters and R. H. Waterman (New York, Harper and Row, 1982), based on research sponsored by the American consulting firm McKinsey.

[4] See H. Holtz: *Successful newsletter publishing for the consultant* (Washington, DC, The Consultant's Library, 1983).

[5] See, for example, L. E. Greiner and R. O. Metzger: *Consulting to management* (Englewood Cliffs, NJ, Prentice-Hall, 1983), p. 46-47.

[6] See, for example, Wheatley, op. cit., chapter 3.

COSTS AND FEES 23

We have stressed in chapter 20 that a consulting organisation ought to be run as an effective and efficient business. This includes healthy business relations with the clients: both the clients and the consultant must be convinced that the cost and the price of the service and other financial terms of the contract are correct and fair. This chapter will examine the main problems concerning costs and fees in selling consulting services and operating the financial side of a consulting practice.

23.1 Income-generating activities

A precise definition of services for which clients can be charged is essential to the costing and pricing of consulting services. If only chargeable services generate income, any other service and activity of the consulting organisation will have to be financed out of this income.

Chargeable services

Generally speaking, a chargeable service is one performed directly for a particular client. It does not have to be carried out at the client's premises: the consultant can travel and negotiate on behalf of the client, search for information in a documentation centre, or work in his own office on a business forecasting model. It should be clearly established, however, that these activities are part of a given assignment, and their results will be made available only to the client who commissioned them and who will be charged for them. This is quite understandable. Clients do not want to be charged for work not done *directly* for them.

Certain activities may or may not be treated as chargeable. *Travel time* is an example. Most consultants charge a full rate for the time spent on travelling to and from the client's location and any other travel time required by the assignment. Some consultants charge at a reduced rate, while others do not charge

Table 23.1   Chargeable time

Item	Weeks	Days
Total time	52	260
— annual leave	4	20
— public holidays	2	10
— reserved against sickness	2	10
Days available	44	220
— reserved for training and meetings	2	10
— lost time	4	20
Chargeable time	38	190

anything (e.g. if they work for local clients and travel time is negligible).

Supervision, technical guidance and assignment control may also be charged for in various ways. Here again, some consultants prefer to give their clients precise information on the amount of supervision and similar work required by the assignment and charge a corresponding fee for it. Others consider this to be an unnecessary complication of accounting procedures, for example if a senior consultant supervises several assignments during the same period of time and the cost of his time would have to be apportioned to these assignments.

In summary, the prevailing practice is to charge clients directly for all services provided under a specific client contract, with the exception of services which it is impossible or impractical to charge direct.

Free client services

Strictly speaking, in a self-supporting consulting practice there is no place for "free" client services: the consultant can work for free only if, for some reason, he has decided to do the work in his leisure time, if he accepts a reduction in his income, or if the service is subsidised by a governmental or other agency. A service that is given free to one client will normally be paid for by other clients. Someone will be charged for every free lunch offered to a potential client!

As regards diagnostic surveys, it was mentioned in chapter 7 that short surveys required for preparing an assignment proposal are done for free by some consultants and billed only if the proposal is accepted and the assignment executed. Other free services may include management seminars or information services, not charged for because they are used as marketing tools.

Fee-earning days

Services to clients are costed and in most cases also charged on the basis of consultant-days (or hours or weeks). It is essential to plan and attain the required number, which may be determined as shown in table 23.1 (assuming a five-day working week).

The 190 chargeable days represent the expectation of a consulting unit for the planned period. This is a 73 per cent utilisation of the total time, as determined by the ratio:

$$\frac{\text{Chargeable time}}{\text{Total time}} = \frac{190}{260} = 0.73$$

We have chosen a hypothetical example. It is not a standard figure; every consulting unit has to establish its own time budget based on local conditions, and the firm's experience and strategy.

An alternative way of calculating this ratio is comparing chargeable time to days available:

$$\frac{\text{Chargeable time}}{\text{Days available}} = \frac{190}{220} = 0.86$$

Consulting firms often use this second variant of the ratio. Larger firms apply differential rates to various categories of consultants. A typical utilisation is 85-95 per cent for operating staff, 60-80 per cent for senior staff (supervisors, team leaders) and 15-50 per cent for higher management staff (partners, senior partners, officers). Operating consultants can achieve high utilisation rates thanks to the marketing, planning and co-ordination done by more senior colleagues. Data from various countries indicate that single practitioners who take care of their own marketing and administration achieve utilisation rates of 55-65 per cent. As we already know, many of them have to spend as much as 20-25 per cent of their time on marketing.

Time shown as "lost" in table 23.1 will not earn any fees, but should never be spent doing nothing. It can be used for research, programme development, work on training materials, marketing, staff self-development and many other activities — preparing the firm's future, developing new products, and finding new clients. It depends on the imagination and initiative of individual consultants and their superiors as to whether "lost" time will be turned into an effective activity!

23.2 Costing chargeable services

Fee per unit of time

The time unit used by most consultants in calculating fees is one working day, but some consultants use weekly or hourly rates. The basic consideration is simple: every fee-earning day has to earn a corresponding portion of the total budgeted income. This, of course, is an average figure. The actual fee will be influenced by some other factors, as will be shown in section 23.3.

Let us use the hypothetical example of a consulting unit described in section 26.2 and assume that the time budget of the 20 operating consultants in that unit is 190 days each (table 23.1) and that the 6 senior consultants should achieve 130 chargeable days each. To keep things simple, the unit's director and the two trainees attached to the unit will not do any directly chargeable work. Let us assume, too, that the unit's income should attain $2,555,000, which corresponds to the operating budget (total income) shown in table 25.2 (chapter 25). The average daily fee rate will then be:

$$\frac{\text{Total income}}{\text{Fee-earning days}} = \frac{\$2,555,000}{(20 \times 190) + (6 \times 130)} = \$558$$

Charging the same per diem rate for all consultants irrespective of their experience and seniority could cause difficulties. Many clients would insist on having only senior consultants assigned to their projects if they could get them for the same price. In contrast, some tasks requiring less experienced consultants would be too costly. Most consulting firms therefore apply differential fee rates for various categories of consultant. In our hypothetical case the per diem rate for an operating consultant may be set at $530 and a senior consultant's fee at $700. This will permit the unit to achieve the same total income. (The projected time utilisation is attained by both categories of consultant.)

Fee/salary ratio

Another ratio used by consulting organisations (the so-called "factor" or "multiple") compares the salaries paid to the fee-earning consultants to the total fees earned as follows:

$$\frac{\text{Total fees earned}}{\text{Salaries} + \text{Social charges}} = \text{Factor}$$

The normal value of this ratio in consulting firms is between 2.0 and 3.0, but ratios higher than 3.0 are not uncommon. Tables 25.2 and 25.3 (chapter 25) show an expense structure that prevails in consulting firms in many countries, and provide data from which the "multiple" can be calculated.

A single practitioner can often achieve a lower ratio if he operates with lower overhead expenses. If he spends 25 per cent of his "days available" on marketing and administration, he may be able to earn as much as a senior staff member in a consulting organisation and still charge a lower per diem fee. For example, his total annual income may be $83,000 (salary and social charges $50,000, various overhead expenses $25,000 and profit $8,000), to be earned in 165 chargeable days. The per diem fee is $500, while the "multiple" is only 1.66.

23.3 Principles and methods of fee setting

The actual fees are not the result of a simple arithmetical operation apportioning the total income to be earned to the projected fee-earning days. Some other factors must be taken into consideration.

Marketing-policy considerations

Consulting fees are simultaneously an instrument of general, financial and marketing management policy. A consultant has to keep in mind not only how much the service sold costs him and what income he must earn, but, at the same time, what fee is appropriate on a particular market and how much the clients will be *able* and *willing* to pay.

Normal fee level. A "normal" fee level may be well established and generally known, and may even be recommended by a professional association (e.g. as minimum and maximum fees). Fees higher than the suggested maximum would then be acceptable only for certain special services, or may have to be justified in detail.

Fees charged by competitors. As in other areas, the consultant should find out how competitors calculate fees, what pricing policy they follow and what the clients think about their fees. It is equally useful to learn about the fees charged by other colleagues in the profession, who are not competitors.

Fees for different market segments. Different segments of the market served may require different fees. Typically, lower fees may be charged to small enterprises and non-profit-making social organisations than to important multinational or national business corporations. Some consultants follow this policy, while others consider it inappropriate.

Promotional fees. A promotional fee (say lower by 10-15 per cent than a normal fee) is sometimes used in launching a new type of service in order to stimulate the client's interest. It is understood that it will be increased to a normal level at the end of the promotion campaign. This is acceptable if the clients are aware of it. It is unprofessional to get clients interested in a new service and then increase the fee, to their great surprise!.

Subsidised fees. Governmental consulting services may be able, or even obliged, to charge lower fees to certain or all clients. This is possible thanks to a government subsidy, whose purpose is to promote consulting and make it available to clients who would be discouraged by high fees. In some countries even private consultants may be able to work for lower fees thanks to government subsidies under special schemes for assisting small enterprises, encouraging businesses to move to new geographical areas, helping underprivileged social groups to start new businesses, and similar.

Fees determined by clients. Government agencies or other clients may have established maximum fee levels and are unable to go beyond these in recruiting a consultant.

Congruency of fees with the consultant's image. The level of fees charged and the fee-setting technique used are an element of the consultant's professional image. Thus, a consultant who positions himself as a high-level adviser to top managers facing important strategic decisions would consistently charge higher fees than his colleague involved in routine reorganisations of office operations.

Principal fee-setting methods

Management consultants use several methods of fee setting. This reflects the differences between the jobs they do and the various views on appropriate ways of remunerating professional services. We must remember again that both the form and the level of remuneration are part of the consultant-client relationship and contract. They have to be acceptable to both parties and be consistent with local business practices.

Fee per unit of time

The most frequent and generally preferred method is to charge a fee for the time spent working for a client. The unit of time used is one working day (8 hours) in most cases, but it can be one hour, one week, or one month (in long assignments).

As mentioned in the previous section, differential fee rates are normally used for various levels or ranks of consulting staff. The ratio between the fee charged for a top-level senior expert and one charged for an operating consultant can be as high as 4 : 1. Research assistants and junior consultants may be charged for at an even lower rate than operating consultants.

Easy and clear fee calculation and billing are major advantages of this technique. The clients are billed after agreed periods of time (e.g. monthly) for time actually worked by the consulting team in the previous month. Many consultants consider this to be the only possible and correct method of charging for professional work.

Yet fees per unit of time raise objections. The client is billed for the time worked and not for the work accomplished. He therefore has to trust his consultant's professional integrity and competence. Alternatively he has to control the progress of the assignment in enough detail to convince himself that he will pay not only for the time used, but also for the product as agreed in the contract.

Some clients object that this sort of fee encourages the consultant to take more time than necessary and to try to prolong every assignment. This does occur occasionally. But it can be avoided by examining the consultant's proposal thoroughly, defining the duration of the assignment in the contract, and properly monitoring the progress of the assignment.

Flat (lump-sum) fee

In this instance the consultant is paid for completing a precisely defined project or job.

The advantages to the client are obvious. He knows how much the whole job will cost him. He can also know the amount of time to be spent on the project, hence the daily rates used in costing the assignment. Finally, he may be able to withhold payment, or the last instalment of it, if the job is not completed according to the contract.

The consultant must be able to agree to these conditions. In particular, he must be sure that the project cannot cost him more. He cannot accept this form of fee if the completion of the job depends more on the client's than on the consultant's staff. Thus, a flat fee may be charged for a market survey, a feasibility study, a new plant design, or a training course, but not for a reorganisation the completion of which depends much more on the client than on the consultant.

It does happen occasionally that a consultant who first agreed to do a job for a fixed price needs more time to complete it and prefers to do it for free rather than to ask for an additional payment not foreseen in the contract. The reason may be that the consultant himself did not plan and manage the job properly. Or the assignment has taken more time for unforeseen reasons; it is vital to complete it, but the client's financial position permits no overrunning of costs. This could mean that on such an assignment the consultant will make no profit, or may even fail to recover his costs.

The job can also require less time than has been quoted. This can easily occur if the assignment is not precisely defined and the consultant has to make a generous time allowance to avoid taking too much risk. Occasionally a smart consultant may submit a high quotation knowing that the client will have little insight into the project. In such cases the client will pay too much.

These and other drawbacks of a simple flat-fee arrangement have led to the development of several alternatives:

● to protect the client, a lump sum is set as an upper limit that must not be exceeded: within this limit, the actual fee is paid on a time basis;

● to protect the consultant, a contingency provision is included in the contract (to be used if unforeseen conditions or events occur);

● competitive bidding may be applied and the consultants asked to justify their fees in detail; the client could then analyse several bids and review them with the consultants before choosing one of them.

Fees contingent on results

Fees contingent on results, the so-called "contingency fees", have one or both of the following characteristics: (1) the fee is paid only when specific results are achieved; and (2) the size of the fee depends on the size of the results (savings, profit) achieved.

In theory, this could be *the* ideal way of remunerating and motivating consultants: the consultant is not paid for spending time at the client's offices, or for writing reports, but for achieving bottom-line results. The client pays only if the results are real and measurable and there is a healthy proportion between the payment made and the results obtained.

In practice, however, a host of problems arise:

— the consultant may be tempted to focus on easy short-term improvements, producing immediate savings, and neglect measures likely to produce benefits in the long run (such as preventive maintenance, staff development, or R and D);

— it is often very difficult to identify and measure real results; the client's and the consultant's assessment of the results may be very different, therefore friction and conflict are difficult to avoid;

— sometimes the projected results are not achieved through the fault of the client and the consultant cannot do anything about it;

401

- it is not easy to decide when to pay the consultant if the results can only be measured long after the end of the assignment;
- if the client company is in difficulties, the projected results may never be attained and the consultant will get no fee whatsoever.

Contingency fees have been one of the most controversial issues in the practice of management consulting. As mentioned in section 6.2, for many years they were banned by the consultants' codes of ethics. This ban has been lifted in most countries and contingency fees are no longer regarded as unethical. This, however, does not remove the technical objections to their use.

In current practice, most management consultants (as well as chartered accountants) continue to reject contingency fees. Some consultants use this method of payment if they feel that they can take the risk involved, that the client will get a substantial economic benefit which will be measurable, and that contingency payment is the most correct expression of the consultant's contribution to the improvement of the client's business. This tends to apply to certain special types of assignment rather than to the "classical" consulting projects. For example, a financial management consultant may be happy to work for a contingency fee when helping his client to negotiate a company merger or acquisition. Whichever side of the table the client sits, he is interested in negotiating an arrangement which is most favourable to him and acceptable to the other party. The financial results of the negotiation can be measured in this case, and the use of a contingency fee is possible. Finally, the use of contingency fees is more common in the United States, where it has increased over the last five years, than in other countries; this difference is often explained by the more entrepreneurial attitudes of American consultants, and by the influence of professions and trades where contingency fees have been common practice (the legal profession in particular).

Retainer fee

In retainer arrangements (see section 11.3), the consultant's fee is calculated on the basis of the number of days of work in a period (say four days per month) and the consultant's normal daily fee. A retainer ensures a steady income to the consultant and saves marketing time. It is, therefore, usual to apply a reduced daily rate. The retainer fee is to be charged and paid even if the client (at his discretion) uses the consultant for less time than foreseen by the contract.

Communicating fees to clients

A "fair-play" approach in consulting involves, among other things, informing the client about fees and about methods used to calculate fees. The client should have no reason to suspect that he is charged an exorbitant fee and that the consultant wants to conceal from him an unjustifiable profit. Clients do not expect consultants to provide a high quality service for a low price. Many clients are even wary of cheap consultants. Nevertheless, consulting is costly and clients have the right to know why it is so.

When and how to communicate the fee to the client is a matter of tactics, and tact. Some clients ask a direct question in their first meeting with the consultant. They should get an equally direct answer. Others make remarks which express their fears, or show ignorance about consulting fees and their justification. At a convenient moment the consultant should tell the client what his normal fee rate is and in what way he charges for the work performed. If the client asks for more information, the consultant should explain the structure of the fee. Such general information should be given at a relatively early stage in negotiating the assignment, to avoid disenchantment at a later date. Information on fees given in the written proposal to the client should not come as an unpleasant surprise. In particular, if the client believes that the consultant's standard fees are too high for him, this should become clear before a preliminary diagnostic survey and work on a detailed proposal is started. On the other hand, it may be better tactics to demonstrate professional competence and a good understanding of the client's business before starting to talk about fees.

23.4 Costing and pricing an assignment

Calculating time

The first step in costing an assignment is the calculation of the time (in work-days in most cases) needed to carry out the job. This calculation is based on an assignment plan (section 7.3) and on estimates of time required for each work operation. Reliable time estimates can be made only if the assignment plan is precise and detailed enough. For example, we know that in planning the diagnostic phase of the assignment the consultant can choose among several alternative data-gathering techniques. The time requirements of various techniques can be very different.

Considerable experience is required for correctly assessing time for all operations and phases of a consulting assignment. Such an assessment is normally made by senior members of the consulting organisation, responsible for planning and supervising assignments. Some consultants have their own tables of indicative time data to which they can refer in assignment planning (e.g. number of interviews per working day). However, such data must be applied with due regard to the specific conditions of every assignment.

There are cases where precise time assessment is difficult, if not impossible. Two kinds of situation are particularly common.

First, either the individual who assesses time may be inexperienced in consulting, or the job to be carried out may be new even to an experienced practitioner. In such a case the consultant should try to get information on the time required in comparable situations, say from other consultants. Or, instead of committing himself to completing the job in a fixed number of days, he should suggest a more flexible arrangement to the client.

The second case concerns assignments in which the initial phases can be planned with sufficient precision, while the subsequent phases can be estimated only roughly. Typically, the consultant may be able to make an accurate time assessment for the diagnostic phase, a rough assessment for action planning, and no more than a preliminary guess for the implementation phase. This is quite understandable owing to the number of factors likely to affect implementation. In these instances, it may be preferable to use a phased approach to assessing time and costing the assignment. Only orientation data would be given for the phases where duration and volume of work required are unclear at the beginning of the assignment. Clients who understand the nature of consulting will be receptive to such an arrangement.

Costing the consulting time

As mentioned in section 23.1, the tendency is to be as precise as possible in measuring the labour costs of an assignment. The cost of the time of operating consultants would therefore be treated as a direct labour cost in any case. The cost of supervisory and control work, as well as various technical and administrative support operations, can be treated as either direct or indirect costs and the consulting unit will have to decide which is more appropriate.

If different categories of consultants are assigned to the project, it is customary to calculate and indicate the time and price for each category separately, so that the client knows how much he is to pay for the junior, intermediate, senior and very senior (top) levels of direct services to his firm. As we know, the fee differentials can be significant and the cost of an assignment could rocket if a large part of the job is done by the most expensive tier of the consulting staff.

The total time required by an assignment, and the cost of this time, should be established even if a fee-setting method other than per-unit-of-time rate is applied. In such a case, instead of communicating this information to the client, the consultant will use it as internal management information in deciding for what sort and size of fee he would be able to work.

Other expenses

Expenses other than direct labour costs may be either included in the fee (as overhead expenses) or charged directly to the client. It is important to make this clear to the client, who should know precisely what kinds of expenses he will have to reimburse.

Typical "billable" or "reimbursable" expenses are travel and board and lodging expenses of consultants on assignments, and special services arranged by the consultant (e.g. testing, computing, purchase of special equipment, drawings, document reproduction, long-distance communication and document delivery). In addition to listing these items it may be necessary to indicate the values — e.g. the expenses that the consultant expects to incur in travelling to and from the client's premises, and how much the client is to pay for the consultant's board and lodging, or for local transport during the assignment.

In international consulting these "billable" expenses may be quite high, reaching 25-30 per cent of the fees. There may even be a provision for family travel and accommodation if the consultant is to work on a long assignment abroad.

Expenses defined as "billable" are not a part of the consultant's fees, but a separate additional item in the total assignment budget and in bills submitted to the client.

Discounts and contingencies

Under normal circumstances, if the cost of the assignment has been calculated correctly there is no reason for granting any discount on a consulting fee, and the consultant cannot actually afford to do so. Nevertheless, in certain situations a reduced fee may be justified and can be offered.

For example, a client can claim a "quantity discount" if the volume of work contracted notably exceeds the average size of assignments. Either the assignment can keep the consultant occupied for a fairly long time, or the assignment team will be larger than usual. The consultant may save on marketing time, administrative support expenses, and even on technical backstopping and supervision. A discount can also be arranged if a consulting firm already has an assignment with a client, and is offered an additional one by the same client for the same period of time.

On the other hand, we are living in a period of inflation and it would be difficult to ignore this fact in costing assignments. A provision for cost increases can be made in various ways, depending on the client's and the consultant's convenience. For example, the contract can include an "escalation clause", whereby the fees will be adjusted upwards in accordance with the officially recognised inflation rate. Or a contingency provision (say 5-10 per cent of the total cost) is made, to be used by common agreement of the consultant and the client for justified and inevitable cost increases, and for expenses that could not be foreseen before starting the job.

Schedule of payments

Both the client and the consultant are concerned not only about the amount of the fee to be paid, but also about the payment schedule. Many clients are interested in delaying payments. Consultants, in contrast, want to be paid as soon as possible after having completed the job or a part of it, and if they can get an advance payment before starting the job, they certainly are not opposed to it.

The most common arrangement is one whereby the consultant bills his client periodically (as a rule monthly or weekly) for work carried out in the previous period. The last bill is payable within an agreed number of days after the completion of the assignment. Payments are to be made within an agreed period of time — as a rule, 30 days after billing.

There are, then, various possible arrangements:

● In some situations (e.g. international consulting), consultants try to get an advance payment (a sort of "retainer") after the signature of the contract, but before starting the work; if the client agrees to this, he actually confirms his commitment to the assignment and his confidence in the consultant.

- If other than per-unit-of-time fees are applied, there still may be some payment of advances before the project is completed, or the consultant may propose waiting for the payment until the job is finished and the projected results achieved. For example, the payment schedule may be: 30 per cent on signature, two payments of 20 per cent each during the assignment; and 30 per cent one month after the client has received the final report and bill.

- The client may prefer to pay the same proportion of the total fee at regular intervals, even if the real progress of the assignment is not quite as regular.

- Occasionally a schedule of payments may be so important to the client that it is necessary to redesign the assignment in order to adjust the pace of the work to the client's financial position. For example, the client may prefer to stretch the assignment over a longer period of time, or the consultant can consider accepting a payment schedule that differs from the actual work schedule of the assignment, but makes the processing of payments easier for the client.

In fixing his fee the consultant should find out if the payment schedule matters to the client, and whether any particular constraints are to be observed. However, in the consulting business, it is not usual to encourage early and prompt payment by offering cash discounts to clients.

Negotiating the fee

Under what circumstances can a consultant agree to negotiate his fee with a client who wants to get the job done for a lower price? It is virtually impossible to think of universal rules. In the social and business cultures of some countries, professional fees are never challenged. In other countries everything is regarded as negotiable, and the local culture may require the consultant and the client to pass through a negotiation ritual before concluding a contract. It may even be customary to agree on a slightly lower price than originally demanded. The consultant should be aware of this and, if necessary, build in a "negotiation provision" in his first price quotation. Thus, the price agreed on after the negotiation will be the correct one, and regarded as such by both parties.

Irrespective of local habits, there may be technical reasons for negotiating consulting fees. The client may need more detailed information to convince himself that the fee is correctly set. A true professional is always prepared to give this information. Furthermore, in challenging the fee the client may actually be raising questions about the design of the assignment. This requires a thorough discussion in any event. As mentioned in section 7.4, the client may want to negotiate the consultant's proposal for various reasons. He may be thinking of a less costly alternative approach. Often the client may be able to have some tasks performed by his own personnel instead of using consultants or their technical and administrative support services. The timetable may also have to be reconsidered for financial reasons if the client wishes to use a different schedule of payments from that proposed by the consultant.

When agreeing to negotiate his fee the consultant should try to be well informed on the conditions under which the negotiation will take place. Will it be a formality, a ritual required by local culture? Does the client have alternative proposals (at different prices) from other consultants? Is he happy with the design of the assignment and the competence of the staff proposed, but not with the price? Is the price proposed prohibitive to the client, or does he merely want to save money by pressing the consultant? Thus, the consultant should prepare himself for the negotiation, trying to anticipate questions and suggestions likely to be made by the client.

23.5 Billing clients and collecting fees

Professional firms bill clients and collect fees like other businesses. They may face, however, additional problems with certain clients if these do not feel sure that they are paying the right price and that the consultant has really delivered what was promised. This confirms how important it is to be clear and consistent when negotiating the assignment and informing the client about the fee rate and the billing practice.

Bills should be issued as soon as records of work performed and expenses incurred are available. This underlines the importance of reliable and smoothly operating administration.

Information to be provided in a bill

Bills should be as detailed as necessary to avoid any misunderstanding or unnecessary query from the client. The client must know exactly what he is being charged for and why. He should be able to refer to the contract (or the attached

Table 23.2   Information provided in a bill

1. Bill number.
2. Period covered.
3. Services provided (listing, dates, volume of work by each consultant).
4. Fee rates and total charges.
5. Expenses billed separately from fees.
6. When payment is due.
7. How to make payment (currency, method of payment, account number).
8. Whom to contact for queries.
9. Date of expedition of the bill.
10. Name, address, telephone and telex numbers of the consultant.
11. Signature and courtesy formula.

terms of business) if he has any doubt. He should find no unexpected charge in a bill, e.g. no charge for a service or supplies that he thought would be provided in the agreed fee. Information normally provided in a bill is indicated in table 23.2.

Addressing and delivering the bill

Problems arise if the consultant does not know to which department and person to address the bill. This can easily happen in large businesses and in government services. The consultant should therefore find out what actually happens to the bill when it is delivered, and make sure that the right people receive copies of the bill. To deliver the bill personally may sometimes be advisable. However, there is no reason why the consultant should harass financial or other services in organisations that are known to pay their bills correctly.

Collection period

What is a normal collection period in professional services? In most countries consultants would ask for payment to be made within 30 days, and hope to receive the money not later than in 45 days. There may be local differences, and in international consulting payments may take longer.

Clearly, payments received late result in additional charges to the consultant. Rare are the consultants who can afford to extend interest-free credit to their clients! A late-paying client should first be reminded with courtesy — it may be enough to send another copy of the bill with a remark that perhaps the original was lost. If the consultant believes there is a problem, it may be wise to contact the client personally and find out the cause of non-payment. This can be done during a supervisor's visit if the assignment is still operational. A tactful reminder may be all that is necessary.

If a client still does not pay, the consulting team may be withdrawn. The client should then be told clearly what measures the consultant intends to take to collect his fees.

Whether to take a non-paying client to court or not is a delicate decision. The procedure risks being both lengthy and costly, and the result is uncertain. In many cases it is wiser to stay out of court and try to find a compromise settlement.

Uncollectable accounts

Some fees are uncollectable in any country. Well-managed consulting firms in sophisticated business environments report that they normally write off 0.5-2.0 per cent of uncollectable fees, but in certain countries this figure can be much higher. If bad debts cannot be collected, in many countries they can at least be deducted for tax purposes.

There are also countries where business clients consider it normal and ethical practice not to pay the last 5-10 per cent of the total fee for a project: if the consultant operates in such a country he must know about this!

ASSIGNMENT MANAGEMENT 24

The crucial role of assignment management was stressed in chapter 20. A number of references to various aspects of assignment management were made in other chapters of our book, in particular chapters 7-11 dealing with the main phases of the consulting process, and in chapter 23 dealing with costing, fee setting and billing. In addition, we have found it useful to include a separate chapter dealing with assignment management as a whole, focusing on principles and methods that tend to prevail in current consulting practice.

24.1 Structuring and scheduling an assignment

Defining an assignment and its management requirements

Assignments undertaken by management consultants differ in many respects. Within one firm a particular assignment pattern may predominate, but in many firms the range of assignments in which they have been or are prepared to be involved is wide indeed. It is useful to review the kinds of assignment in which the consulting organisation is involved, trying to find some common patterns between various assignments in terms of their resource requirements and management implications.

In practice, an assignment is usually defined in the proposal to the client and in the contract. The definition includes the start and the end of the assignment, the objectives, the work programme, the consultants involved, the resources required, the price to be paid, the degree and form of the client's involvement, and the supervisory responsibility. Checking the completeness and clarity of assignment definitions is an important precondition of effective assignment management. Even questions such as where the data will be processed and reports produced, or who will take care of the consultant's transport during the assignment, should be clarified. More important, however, are technical issues related to the client's problem and the approach to be taken by the consultants. Although it is true that every assignment is unique, it is equally true that there are similarities between assignments, and the consulting firm should be able to decide when to apply its standard management procedure and what assignments require special treatment (e.g. frequent progress reviews at the topmost level of the firm's management hierarchy).

Assignment team leaders and supervisors

The key role in managing operating assignments is played by *team leaders* or *project managers*. As a rule, a consulting firm would have a group of senior colleagues whose experience and achievement qualify them for this critical position. The function often includes the negotiation and preparation of new assignments as discussed in chapter 7 — the senior consultant who negotiates the assignment, does the preliminary survey of the client organisation, and co-ordinates the drafting of the proposal submitted to the client, is then charged with managing assignment execution. Interdisciplinary general management assignments would be managed by team leaders who are all-round generalists, while functional assignments are normally managed by senior specialists in marketing, finance, production or another area.

In managing the assignment, the team leader must enjoy full authority and responsibility for operating staff time-allocation, work scheduling and organisation, the method of work, and the nature of the advice given to the client. He is the line manager and must be regarded as such by both the consulting firm's higher management and the members of the team. This is a very important principle since the team often consists of consultants of different backgrounds and profiles. In addition, if specialist consultants have to contribute to several assignments during the same period of time, there is not only a scheduling and co-ordination problem, but also a problem deriving from the technical approach, intellectual involvement and commitment to one or another job.

If an assignment is small and involves only one or two operating consultants, a senior consultant is usually appointed as *supervisor* of several assignments. His supervisory responsibilities include:

- periodic visits to operating consultants on client assignments;
- control and assessment of assignment progress;
- technical guidance for operating consultants;
- review of important reports and proposals to be submitted to the client;
- liaison with clients on matters of assignment progress and mutual commitments.

It is always necessary to define clearly the working relations with the client, i.e. what matters should be discussed and agreed on with the operating consultants, or with the supervisors who come to control the assignment. For example, if the assignment does not progress because the client does not spend enough time with the operating consultant, the supervisor should raise the matter with the client. When conclusions drawn from diagnosis, or action proposals are submitted to the client, the supervisor may come to meetings and support the operating consultant with his authority.

Assignment scheduling

Ideally, a consulting firm would like to see all its consultants moving directly from completed assignments to new ones, without losing a single working day. The starting dates and the schedules of assignments are negotiated with clients in order to make this possible. An ethical approach is required, however: if the client is in a difficult situation and needs help quickly, you should never try to convince him that he can wait in order to make your work-scheduling task easier!

Before establishing detailed work plans for each assignment, the consulting firm needs to make sure that the consultants selected for the assignment will be available at the necessary times and for the periods required. This may be yet another piece in the jig-saw puzzle, to be seen in the context of the total picture of operations.

Firstly, the technical profile of the team is matched to the technical profile of the assignment. It is obvious that the choice of professional staff will vary according to the size of the consulting firm. Smaller units either have to work in more limited fields, or employ highly versatile and adaptable people. In extreme cases, the problems of a sole practitioner, or a partnership of 2-3 consultants, are plain to see.

Secondly, there is the factor of personalities. The correct matching of client's and consultant's personalities can make the difference between good, middling and poor assignments. Guidance on the client's characteristics, in terms of likes and dislikes, habits, interests and general way of life, should be provided (as confidential information) by the consultant who negotiated the contract. The consulting unit knows the personalities of its own staff.

The client and the consultant do not necessarily have to have everything in common. There are even advantages sometimes in complementing a client of one type by a consultant of another when a modifying influence appears desirable, but the consulting unit should avoid pairing two obvious incompatibles.

Up to a point, it can be expected that every consultant will adapt to normal and unavoidable differences, and matching people is only a matter of avoiding clashes at the more extreme limits of human behaviour. An operating consultant has occasionally to be chosen for his ability to hold his own in a wide range of situations.

Thirdly, it is equally important that the team leader and the team members get on well with each other. Consultants do not always see eye to eye in matters of individual preference any more than other people.

However, it should not be overlooked that, though in many cases the client will have received a suggested team structure, including the names and profiles of the team members, as part of the assignment proposal, there may be a time-lag of uncertain length between the submission of the proposal, its acceptance by the client, and the actual start of the assignment.

Various circumstances may affect the scheduling of the actual start and execution of the assignment. If waiting time cannot be avoided, it is necessary to decide who will wait. The consultant may have to choose between two or more clients, nominating one to be served first (assuming that other clients can wait and will agree to do so). Or a major assignment is scheduled to start in, say, two months, but the designated team leader is available now. Would the client agree to advance the start of the assignment? Should the team leader be assigned to another job? Should he be kept waiting? When is this justified and when not? What will the client do if he has to wait?

It frequently happens that a current assignment should have finished, but requires more time than originally scheduled, so that there is a risk of delaying a job promised to another client. As it is inconvenient to interrupt a nearly finished job, the consulting firm would probably try to negotiate a compromise with one or both clients, for example, start the new assignment gradually, as individual team members become available. These and similar situations require careful consideration and tactful negotiation with the clients concerned. Clients are not unaware of these problems, and will usually be open to a discussion of mutually convenient arrangements when work plans for an assignment are being prepared.

Lastly, assignment and individual work scheduling should follow a golden rule: never leave any consultant unoccupied! If time-lags between assignments cannot be avoided, the consultant should have other activities waiting for attention (as mentioned in the previous chapter). The consulting firm should have a backlog of jobs for this situation, and encourage individual consultants to make their own suggestions for productive use of the time that cannot be spent with clients.

Overall assignment plan

The overall assignment plan covers the whole period of the assignment. It presents the operating team's main activities against a timetable (in weeks or days). It specifies the starting and final points of these activities, the volume of work (man/weeks or man/days) in every period in the timetable, and points of time for submission of reports (interim and final) and for progress control of the assignment.

Estimates of time in the overall plan can be made:

- *top down*, when the consultant knows that he has a certain number of weeks and man/weeks available and tries to allocate them to a certain number of different activities;

- *bottom up*, when the consultant estimates the time needed for each particular activity and compares the total time thus obtained with the established deadlines and total estimates of man/weeks needed for the assignment.

Experience with the time taken for similar activities on previous assignments is useful in any case.

The length of assignments affects planning. A short assignment must obviously be planned in greater detail in order to complete it on time. A long assignment invites the temptation to neglect planning since there is no immediate time-pressure. If allowed to take this line, the consultants may suddenly become aware that half the time has been used, and only one quarter of the programme accomplished. Long assignments may also tend to lose sight of ultimate objectives, particularly as the operating team becomes more accepted and part of the scene. A clear plan and its regular control avoid this.

A well-calculated overall assignment plan allows for some contingencies and should have to be altered only when major events disturb the normal progress of the assignment. The plan can be presented as a bar chart, a table giving numerical values, a network diagram (for long and complex assignments) or a combination of these.

It is useful to enter the client inputs and activities in the assignment plan in a way which permits a separate control of client and consultant inputs.

The plan is available for assignment control both to the consulting organisation and to the client.

24.2 Preparing for an assignment

The consulting organisation may designate consultants other than those who planned and negotiated the assignment to start working with the client from the beginning of the diagnostic phase. Also, a team may be needed for the job, while the assignment was negotiated and planned by no more than one or two people. The preparatory measures may include those listed below.

Liaison officer

It is usual for the client to appoint one or more of his staff members to provide close and continuous liaison with the consultants. The term "counterpart" is sometimes used. These people are of great assistance to operating consultants and save their time, especially during the early investigational stages. Theirs may be full-time work. In some assignments, consultants train the liaison officers to maintain and develop the work after the end of the assignment.

Recruitment and training of client staff

The preliminary diagnostic·survey may have shown that there is a shortage of competent people in the client company, with no prospect of finding suitable candidates internally. The client may recruit and select additional staff himself, or may use the consulting unit's service. Either method will take some time. Client staff, possibly including the liaison officer, may need preliminary training in certain techniques. The consulting firm may assist in finding the most suitable courses for them to attend.

Special training of operating consultants

An assignment may require certain skills in which the only available consultant is short of experience. He may get intensive coaching in the consulting organisation, or gain direct experience by joining another assignment where the team is already practising the same methods.

Office accommodation

A consulting team should not have to hunt for offices when it starts an assignment. Consultants need not have the best offices, but they will not be highly regarded by the client's staff if they have only a small table in a corner of a general area. Without suitable office space consultants cannot avoid wasting some of their expensive time. Also, operating consultants on assignments need privacy for interviews, discussions with liaison officers, meetings with the supervisor, study of documents, and writing. As a rule, meeting rooms are not suitable for use as consultants' offices.

Consultant briefing

One person likely to know little about the assignment before the briefing is the operating consultant, who has probably been very busy winding up his last assignment and is in no position to give thought to a new one. If his supervisor has been involved with the entry-phase activity, that is one person who will know a great deal. Otherwise, the colleague who negotiated the assignment will brief them both. At the briefing meeting, the team takes over the accumulated documentation from the preliminary survey. All matters pertaining to the start of the assignment are then discussed. A checklist of points for the briefing (table 24.1) would guard against significant omissions.

Client briefing

Many of the points which should be raised in a final check with the client are covered in the list in table 24.1. The remaining precautions to be taken may depend on how much time has passed since the assignment was agreed to and what the pre-assignment activities were. Checks should be made to ensure:

● that the client's views and needs are still in accordance with the terms of the contract as mentioned above;

● that he has adequately explained the nature and purpose of the assignment to all managers and other employees who will be in any way affected.

Introducing the consultants

The conduct of the first days of an operating assignment is of vital importance. The client has already met senior members of the consulting firm, but may be meeting the operating team for the first time. The members of the team new to the client are introduced to his managers and other employees as appropriate. These introductions should be comprehensive and should include all staff who might resent being missed out. At the end, the consultants should ask tactfully if there are any others they should see. During introductions the consultants will sense whether the client's briefing of his staff was complete and understood. The team should be careful to remember names.

Table 24.1   Checklist of points for briefing

A. Hand over	1.	Report on preliminary problem diagnosis and proposal to the client
	2.	Internal confidential notes on the client
	3.	Working papers borrowed from the client
	4.	Published or other printed matter
B. Convey and discuss	1.	Terms of reference and contract
	2.	Source of introduction to the client
	3.	Client's experience of consultants
	4.	Client organisation's structure, personalities, general style of management, apparent centres of power and influence
	5.	Client's needs and desires, real and imagined
	6.	Probable attitudes of staff
	7.	Basis of forecast results of the assignment
	8.	Assignment strategy and plan
	9.	Client's experience in the techniques the consultants intend to use
	10.	Key facts of the client's operation
	11.	Production processes; trade jargon and terms particular to the business and the locality
	12.	Contacts made with trade unions and other bodies
	13.	Previous work in the sector (for the same client, competitors, etc.)
C. Inform on	1.	Commitments to the client in respect of various services of the consulting unit (training, recruitment, design, computing, etc.)
	2.	Arrangements for invoicing and payment of fees
	3.	Arrangements for starting date, time and place
	4.	Arrangements for office accommodation, staff liaison, secretarial and other support
	5.	Accommodation, travel arrangements and meeting place of consultants before going to client organisation

Introductions may be combined with a tour of the plant or offices. This gives a two-way opportunity — for the consultants to begin their orientation and for the employees to get their first sight of the team. The particular functional department for the assignment would be the principal stopping place, but the first tour should be comprehensive. It could end with another tactful question — "Is there anywhere we have not been?"

During introductions the team members should talk enough to show and arouse interest, but avoid any remarks that would suggest prejudgement or over-confidence. This is the start of an exercise in patient listening.

Starting work

After introductions the team should make time to talk on their own and discuss impressions. They should re-check the overall assignment plan. If there is not already a short-term plan, they should draw one up to cover the next week or two. The date of their supervisor's next visit is arranged and a copy of his own programme in the meantime is left with the operating team.

With the departure of the seniors, the operating consultant is on his own for the first time in his new surroundings. This can be a ticklish time and if there is any stage fright this is when it occurs. It is essential for the operating consultant to do something immediately and establish contacts with the client's people. Making a start is more important than what precisely is done first. The longer the delay, the harder it becomes. Experience shows the consultant what initial steps would be effective in this new environment.

24.3 Managing assignment execution

Consulting requires considerable decentralisation of operational decision making and control. Once an assignment has started, it functions on the whole as an independent project, where most matters are decided on the spot by the operating consultant (or the team leader) in consensus with the client. This section provides a number of thoughts and practical suggestions concerning the short-term control of assignments. The reader should consider what is applicable in his particular setting (e.g. the frequency of control visits to consultants on assignments will be influenced by distance and the cost of travel).

Operating consultants' self-discipline and self-control

The self-discipline and self-management of the operating consultants is a vital factor in assignment control. They are the full-time members of the team, and often the consulting firm's sole representatives for 90 per cent of the time of the assignment.

The consultants are constantly exposed in a situation where they are greatly outnumbered. They have to set an example for hard and high-quality work and intellectual integrity. It is primarily a matter of their own judgement to decide how the code of conduct and the unwritten rules of the profession should be applied in the conditions of the client organisation, and from this viewpoint every organisation has its own behavioural patterns, habits, traditions, and defects. Should questions arise, the senior consultant supervising the assignment has to help the operating team with his advice and guidance.

Assignment diary. At the end of the first day of the assignment, the operating consultant starts the assignment diary. This is an essential record of activity throughout the assignment. It is written up each evening with a summary of the day's significant events (or non-events) and of progress made. It is a necessary reference for the supervisor. Every paper or note written by the operating team should be recorded in the diary, and dated: sometimes the date proves to be its main value.

Time-keeping. The general rule is that the consultant on an assignment adjusts to the working hours of the client organisation. But the assignment programme is usually a heavy one and the operating consultant may need to work long hours to complete it on time. There may be both practical and tactical advantages in starting a little ahead of the rest of the staff in the morning and leaving a little later in the evening — so long as the consultant does not appear to make a virtue of it.

The consultant's home may be far from the client's premises and he may occasionally need to travel on a working day. If this is foreseen, it should be discussed with the client before the start of the assignment. An agreement should be reached on how the working hours and days will be counted, and whether the consultant will be authorised to take time off for travelling home if he has worked overtime.

When the assignment concerns departments working two or three shifts, the operating consultant must spend enough time on each one to find out all he needs. His reception on a night shift is often illuminating — workers may receive him warmly and appreciate that somebody is interested in their work problems.

Sensitivity, anticipation and reaction. The operating consultant has to be sensitive to all the points the supervisor would normally check. This sensitivity is allied to self-control. The consultant will encounter frustrations and must endure them with patience and good humour. Anger will only arouse opposition and the consultant may find himself being baited. At times people may put forward ill-considered views, or provide incorrect information. In rejecting these the consultant must use tact and show tolerance, taking care to give reasoned explanations. There may be attempts to use him in internal politics, or involve him in intrigues. If he has his eyes and ears open, he may be sufficiently ahead of these games to sidestep them, and be respected the more for it. Genuine appeals must always be met with ready help: goodwill and co-operation do not come unless they are deserved.

Favours offered by clients. Sometimes clients arrange for their staff to be able to purchase goods in local shops at a discount, or they may allow the purchase of the company's products at cost rather than at market price. The consultant is not a member of the client's staff, and should not expect to participate. If he is invited to join the scheme, he should consider the privilege with care and discretion.

The same rules apply to gifts from the client. There is perhaps no danger in accepting a parting gift, made as a personal gesture at the end of a satisfactory assignment, but at any other time discretion is necessary in deciding whether and how to accept gifts.

Control by supervising consultant and client

The supervisor visits the assignment as frequently as its circumstances warrant, e.g. once or twice a month. Visits are made more frequently when the operating consultant is new, or when the assignment is going through a difficult period. Dates of visits should be known in advance to all parties so that appointments and other preparations may be made.

The supervisor spends time with the operating consultant and client together, to assess the development of the relationship between them, and separately, to find out how each regards the other and the progress of the assignment. The supervisor also considers progress in relation to the wider policies and interests of both the client organisation and the consulting organisation.

With the operating consultants, the supervisor may check some or all of the following points:

- that frequent and satisfactory contacts are being maintained with client personnel;
- that assignment progress is up to date and under control;
- that the assignment diary is in good order;
- that the operating consultants are not under stress from any form of harassment by the client;
- that in their anxiety to reach an early balance between financial benefits and fees, the members of the operating team are not tempted to go for a quick return from some potentially dangerous scheme;
- that the opportunities for putting in useful interim reports to the client are being used;
- that the operating consultants' morale is high, and their enthusiasm unflagging.

The supervisor is always ready to act as a sounding board for an operating consultant's ideas and as an audience for rehearsal of presentations. He discusses the operating consultant's performance frankly and constructively with him, giving approval for work well done and guidance where improvement is necessary.

With the client, the supervisor checks:

- whether he is satisfied with the overall progress of the assignment, the contribution made by the operating team, and the relations that have developed between the consultants and the client's staff members;
- whether he has met all agreed obligations and inputs in the assignment.

To make control efficient, the client organisation has, on its side, to have its own procedure for examining the progress of operating assignments. The scheduled interim reports submitted by consultants should be studied, views of staff members collaborating with consultants collected, and the consultants' working methods and behaviour observed. Any problem should be raised with the supervisor.

There are periods, particularly in the early stages of an assignment, when the work shows no tangible results. The supervisor may notice signs of fretting, impatience, lessening interest, or simply "cold feet". The symptoms to be watched out for could be:

- people "too busy" to spend time with the consultants;
- defensive or reserved attitudes and a reluctance to talk;
- remarks like, "Your man is taking up a lot of our time"; "When are we going to see some results?"; or "You people are costing us a lot of money."

The supervisor has to take these signs for what they are worth. They are not to be ignored, nor are they grounds for panic. They have to be countered by whatever overt or covert means are appropriate. It could be that in fact the client is not being sufficiently involved and does not know enough about what is going on.

From his sessions with the operating consultants, the supervisor might find that the assignment is in fact getting behind. If so, short-term measures may be agreed.

Short-term adjustments in the work plan

Sometimes, tactics of expediency in face of unpredictable occurrences might require the imposition of a short-term plan on the overall plan of the assignment, in order to break an impasse or show the way round a knotty problem.

A short-term work schedule may be used to plan a temporary increase in the number of operating consultants beyond the originally planned figures in order to accelerate some assignment activities. However, the option of injecting more consultants to complete the work in a shorter calendar time is not always available. The addition of extra consultants does not reduce the time proportionally — as a rule, four consultants require more than one-quarter of the time that one would need. There are various reasons for this, one being the necessity to co-ordinate and sequence activities. Also, the capacity of the client to supply facts and figures and digest the consultants' ideas and proposals is limited, since they are in addition to his normal load. Additional consultants may even hinder rather than help in such a situation.

One way of gaining time is to allocate junior or trainee consultants when an assignment suits the particular stage of their personal development. They can take over parts of the plan and save time at little or no extra cost to the client. In other cases, it may be the client himself who can increase his involvement and thus speed up the assignment.

Supervisor's report

The supervisor keeps notes and gives reports to the management of the consulting firm in much the same way as the operating consultants keep the assignment diary. He may have five or more current assignments and cannot rely on his recollection of one control visit after making several others. These reports are for internal use only and can be hand-written.

It is useful to keep a duplicate book for each assignment. The bound pages are automatically filed; the tear-off pages go to inform headquarters about the assignment in the intervals between the supervisor's meetings with his own superiors.

Liaison with the operating consultants

Whether the location of the assignment raises difficulties of communication depends on the type and size of the consulting unit and the geographical spread of its operations. Many operating consultants may be working a long way from their headquarters for extended periods.

Though the consulting organisation may have a newsletter, hold regional staff meetings and perhaps an annual conference for everyone, an operating consultant may feel out on a limb for much of the time. The main line of communication between him and his organisation is through the supervisor.

The supervisor's visits are, therefore, important occasions for discussion of the consulting unit's news and achievements, interesting developments on other assignments, and for some informal talk on what is going on. The operating consultant is made to feel he still belongs to an organisation. The worst feeling a consultant could harbour is that so long as he is bringing in the fees nobody cares much about him. Supervisors thus have a responsibility to both the consulting organisation and to their operating colleagues to keep the whole as close-knit as possible. Without it, an operating consultant on a long assignment may begin to identify himself too much with his client and lose his vital independence and objectivity.

Health and morale of operating consultants

A consultant's morale is unlikely to be high if his health is not good. Consultants on assignments tend to go on working when client staff would go on sick leave. Furthermore, a hotel is not usually the most sympathetic place for someone who is ill. The supervisor watches the operating consultants' health carefully; delaying a visit to a doctor could mean a serious illness.

A drop in morale can occur without a loss of physical health. Isolation from wife and family, frustrations of the assignment, or uninspiring surroundings all contribute. One of the tell-tale signs is that a consultant begins to hate the sight of the place he has to work in.

It should not be overlooked that consultants are — or become — somewhat different from people who work under the same roof and have daily contacts with their colleagues. They are not "organisation men", but are a collection of highly individual people who have to be managed as such. Their morale is mainly sustained by dedication to their profession and bolstered by success in it. The supervisor's role is to treat each one according to his present needs and future potential.

Assignment progress control by higher management

Periodical (e.g. monthly) progress reviews of all assignments should be made by higher management in the consulting organisation — by top management in small organisations, and by divisional or regional management or by a senior partner in large organisations. They are based on reports submitted by supervisors and/or team leaders, information received from clients (complaints, additional requests), and the senior managers' own intelligence gathered through personal contacts with the clients and the consulting staff.

Assignments which are on schedule and present no technical problems do not require detailed discussion, except for those which are approaching completion, and higher management should become involved in these by studying the report, planning a visit to the client for presenting the conclusions, and preparing for the transfer of the assignment team to another project. Problematic assignments should be reviewed in more detail, in particular if the supervisor concerned is not in a position to redress the situation by measures that are within his competence, and needs help from his superiors.

Whenever necessary, assignment progress reviews by higher management should also discuss *technical* problems involved in assignments. This may be the case with assignments which are particularly difficult, where new consultants or new supervisors are employed, or where new and unfamiliar methodologies are applied. It is very important for the operating teams and the supervisors to know that someone higher up is interested, not only in smooth delivery and regular income, but also in the operating consultants' efforts to apply new approaches and improve the quality of the service.

All technical problems cannot (and should not) be referred to top management for advice or decision. Many consulting firms therefore use procedures whereby higher management would be consulted, or requested to approve the report to the client, on any assignment that exceeds a certain size (e.g. cost over $200,000); proposes an unusual solution (e.g. merging companies from different sectors); has major political and social implications (e.g. could provoke a strike); or would deviate from routine practice in some other way.

Controlling costs and budgets

Both the client and the consultant are concerned about the financial side of assignment execution. The client is certainly pleased to see that the job is making progress, but since he is also paying bills submitted by the consultant, it is normal for him to compare the progress achieved with the money that has been spent.

The consulting firm, on the other hand, has a similar concern. If the contract stipulated a lump-sum payment, both the operating consultants and the supervisor involved must watch very carefully whether the progress made is really commensurate with the time and other resources spent. It does happen that too much time is spent on fact finding and diagnosis, and the consultants are then completing the assignment under extreme presssure, or cannot finish it within the agreed time-limit and budget.

However, even if a per diem fee rate is applied and no fixed budget was agreed upon for the assignment, the consultant's responsibility to the client requires a strict control of cumulative costs and their comparison to the progress really made in the assignment. If this relationship is ignored and the client expected to pay the fees without saying anything even if the consultant is taking more time than scheduled this can lead to a major conflict and the assignment may be phased out in an unpleasant atmosphere.

The consulting firm controls assignment budgets for one more reason. It wants to know which assignments are profitable and which are not, in order to take corrective measures in respect of its service portfolio, assignment design and

421

scheduling, fee structure and work organisation. Therefore many consulting firms budget and control the complete cost and the profit made for every assignment (see also section 25.2).

24.4 Assignment records and reports

In a decentralised organisational setting, where a number of assignments are executed simultaneously and many operating decisions are taken far from the headquarters, an accurate and reliable system of records and reports is indispensable for effective assignment management, for charging clients properly, and for paying consultants their salaries and reimbursing their expenses.

Notification of assignment

At the beginning of every assignment the supervisor (or the survey consultant) prepares a form of notification, which is intended to inform many sections within the consulting organisation. It initiates or supplements a client file for the commercial aspects of the unit's work with him. The form caters for information as indicated in figure 24.1. When, during the course of an assignment, additional operating consultants, specialists, or trainees become involved, a supplementary notification is made.

Consultants' time records

These records are the source of data for invoicing clients and for much of the control information needed by management.

One standard form suffices for operating and senior consultants. It is returned to the office either weekly or monthly depending on the requirements for invoicing and control.

The form should cater for the following:
- consultant's name;
- dates of period covered;
- client names (for up to, say, five assignments, surveys, or visits);
- fee rates for paid work;
- number of fee-earning days per client;
- number of non-fee-earning days per consultant divided into:
  - leave
  - sickness
  - unassigned
  - unpaid operating
  - receiving training
  - giving training
  - supervision
  - preliminary survey
  - promotional activity
  - attending public and professional events.

Operating consultants normally enter the name of their current client, the fee-earning days to be charged and the non-chargeable days.

Figure 24.1 Notification of assignment

NOTIFICATION OF ASSIGNMENT	Assignment No.
Client	Industry
Address	Phone

Assigner (main contact)
Invoices to

Type of assignment

Preliminary survey ☐	Operating ☐	Folow up ☐
Paid survey ☐	Training ☐	Other (specify below) ☐

Fee rate	Special invoicing instructions

Expenses rechargeable to client
Operating function
Operating consultant(s)
Survey consultant or supervisor
Other (trainees, etc.)

Starting date	Planned duration	Finishing date

Briefing and special conditions	Other comments

Date	Issued by	Signature

Other consultants (supervisors, marketers, survey consultants, etc.) enter the names of all clients dealt with personally during the period, the days spent on non-chargeable work, the days of chargeable work, fee rates, and the use made of all non-fee-earning time.

Consultants' expenses

The organisation may have a standard scale of expense allowances, and rules for their application which cover an assumed normal set of conditions. This is surprisingly difficult to draw up and administer: the "every situation is different" character of operating assignments often extends to the consultants' actual expenses. As a rule, consulting organisations are prepared to consider any case of higher than standard expenses at the consultant's request.

The main sources of expenses are:

- accommodation and meals while away from home;
- travelling;
- communication (cables, telephone calls, etc);
- entertainment of client and contacts.

Whether other out-of-pocket expenses are reimbursed by the client will depend on the terms of the contract. The expenses claim form caters for any items that are to be recharged to the client.

Receipts for various expenses

Orderly administration and bookkeeping require clear rules as regards receipts for various expenses incurred both by individual consultants and by the consulting firm.

The consultants must know that certain categories of expenses will be reimbursed to them only if they submit a receipt. The firm should keep receipts for all expenses that will be charged to clients for reimbursement. If an expense item is important, it may even be good practice to provide the client with a copy of the receipt. Finally, certain receipts may be required when claiming deductions for tax purposes, or should be kept available for the eventuality of tax inspection.

If an expense item cannot be documented by a receipt, it may be useful or even necessary to establish an internal check or another document to prove that the expense was really incurred and authorised, and to make sure that it will be properly recorded in the books.

Reports to the client

The reports given to the client at various points of the assignment were discussed in chapters 7-11.

Confidential notes on the client organisation

These notes (also called "survey notes") were described in section 7.4.

Supervisors' reports

The ways in which the supervisors report on their control visits to operating assignments were described in section 24.3.

Assignment reference report

This report, called "assignment summary" by some consultants, and prepared at the end of operating assignments, is a very useful piece of information, which makes it unnecessary to read detailed client reports for single facts on past assignments. In addition, it gives comments on possibilities of further work with the client.

The report provides information on the following points:
- client company name and address;
- assigner's name and title;
- nature and size of organisation;
- operating function of the assignment;
- names of members of the consulting team;
- dates of start and finish;
- brief summary of objectives and results;
- references to all reports and documents that give details of the assignment.

In this short reference report, comments are then made on the following questions:
- Whether and why the consulting unit rates the quality of the assignment as being:
  - above standard;
  - standard;
  - below standard.
- Whether the value of the assignment for future reference is
  - A: excellent;
  - B: average;
  - C: not to be used.
- Whether the client has agreed that the consulting unit may use him as a reference to prospective clients (if the rating was A or B).
- Whether future assignment opportunities should be pursued with the same client and what should be kept in mind in negotiating new business with him.

OPERATIONAL AND FINANCIAL CONTROL

25

This chapter deals with key aspects of operational short-term management and control, emphasising those methods and indicators that help the consultant to monitor operations and prevent events that could reduce efficiency or lead to crises which would be difficult to control. We assume that the reader is familiar with the basics of financial and budgetary control and therefore the discussion focuses on specific problems of consultants and consulting organisations.

25.1 Operating work plan and budget

Operational management and control uses two basic management tools: an operating work plan and an operating financial budget. Both documents are normally prepared annually, for the next planning and budgetary year, in a monthly or quarterly breakdown. This breakdown accounts for seasonal and other variations within the twelve-month period, such as a reduced workload during the holiday period, and other events, including major payments to be made or received at a foreseeable point in time.

Operating work plan

The operating work plan should reflect the consulting organisation's strategic choices and indicate how strategy will be implemented in the forthcoming year. It therefore determines:

— the volume of consulting and other services to be sold and delivered to clients;
— changes in the service portfolio (phasing out a service, introducing a new product, starting work in a new sector, new foreign operations);
— staff recruitment and training required;
— the volume and orientation of promotional and marketing activities;
— the backlog of new assignments to be maintained;

Table 25.1 Methods of achieving efficiency and higher profits

Method	Achieved by
Sell more	Providing new types of services
	Recruiting more consulting staff
	Using staff time better
	Enhancing marketing efforts
Charge more	Increasing fees
	Charging for services provided free hitherto
Spend less	Reducing overhead (general) expenses
	Executing assignments more efficiently

- other measures needed to implement the work programme and to prepare for the future (research and development, organisational changes, investment, etc.);
- the ways in which consultants would be used effectively during the time not spent in working for clients.

Extrapolation of past trends is a useful technique for preparing an operating work plan. However, mechanistic extrapolation cannot be recommended. An analysis of business trends, and of the consulting firm's current strengths and weaknesses, helps to determine growth and other targets that are neither mere extrapolation nor unrealistic dreams.

Operating budget

The basic management tool for controlling the financial side of the consulting firm's operation is the operating budget. In preparing the budget the firm has to include all expenses it expects to incur during the budget period, and fix the projected income at a level required for recovering expenses and ensuring an adequate profit. If budget preparation reveals that the budget cannot be balanced, it is necessary to review the work plan and the planned expenditure to keep them within realistic financial limits, and re-examine the costing, pricing and other assumptions underlying the two sides of the budget.

The budgetary planning may show that the consulting firm's costs will be too high, and therefore the fees risk being excessive, or profits too low. In this case, management can look at various methods of achieving efficiency and higher profits, listed in table 25.1. Which method to adopt will depend on the market, the opportunity to recruit new consultants and find enough work for them, the unit's ability to increase efficiency in implementing assignments, and so on. Recruiting new consultants for certain technical disciplines may not be feasible; some new work could be found for the new recruits, but it would be impossible to keep them sufficiently occupied. Using short-term external collaborators, or negotiating a collaborative arrangement with another consulting firm, may be the solution.

Table 25.2   Operating budget of a consulting firm

Budget item [1]	$	%
1. Professional salaries[1]	1,004,000	39.3
2. Social charges and benefits on professional salaries	240,000	9.4
3. Administrative and support staff salaries	180,000	7.0
4. Social charges and benefits on salaries	43,000	1.7
5. Marketing and promotion expenses (other than salaries)	95,000	3.7
6. Rentals and utilities	94,000	3.7
7. Equipment, furniture, materials, stationery	100,000	3.9
8. Communications (mail, telex, telephone)	90,000	3.5
9. Taxes (other than income taxes)	65,000	2.5
10. Library, subscriptions, membership fees	60,000	2.3
11. Staff training and development	62,000	2.4
12. Other expenses (travel, entertainment, etc.)	150,000	5.8
13. Overhead expenses (3 to 12)	939,000	36.7
14. Total expenses (1 to 12)	2,183,000	85.4
15. Gross profit (before tax)	372,000	14.6
16. Total income (14 + 15)	2,555,000	100.0
17. Expenses billed to clients	485,000	19.0
19. Gross billing (16 + 17)	3,040,000	119.0

[1] Professional salaries include the following: director ($47,000) 47,000; senior consultants (6 x $39,500) 237,000; operating consultants (20 x $34,000) 680,000; trainee consultants (2 x $20,000) 40,000; total 1,004,000.

If growth in operations and income is planned, analysis should reveal how expenses will increase. The consulting firm will certainly keep the difference between fixed and variable expenses in mind, and subject each expense line to a more detailed analysis before deciding whether and how it should be allowed to grow.

An hypothetical example of an annual operating budget is shown in table 25.2. It corresponds to the (also hypothetical) consulting unit, employing 29 consultants, shown in figure 26.2 (chapter 26). The salary rates and other figures in the budget are therefore not intended as standards for remuneration policy, or for assessing the expense structure and efficiency of any particular consulting firm.

Structure of expenses

Nevertheless, the expense and income structure shown is within the broad limits of normal practice in a number of management consulting firms. These limits tend to be as shown in table 25.3.

Management consulting services are highly labour-intensive and *professional staff salaries* are therefore by far the most important single expense item in any firm. Their share in the total expense structure depends on factors such as the professional income level in a particular country and firm, and the size of the consulting firm. Single practitioners and other small firms are usually able to operate with lower overhead costs, reducing or completely eliminating certain items of expenditure without which a larger firm cannot operate. For example, a single practitioner may be able to operate without any secretarial and support staff and without renting expensive office space.

Other expenses (grouped under lines 3-12 in table 25.2) include a wide range of different items linked with operating a consulting unit of a given profile, scope and level of activity. As a rule, in this group consultants include costs that cannot be directly related to a particular client assignment; or, if they could be, it would not be practical and efficient to do so. For example, reproduction expenses can be treated as an overhead item or a direct cost item to be charged to a particular client. Routine reproduction work (e.g. reproducing consulting reports in a standard number of copies) is normally treated as an overhead cost. Reproduction of voluminous special reports, or large numbers of additional copies ordered by the client, should be charged to the client as "billable expenses". A similar choice has to be made in the case of telephone charges and for other costs.

Expenses billed to clients (billable expenses) are often not regarded by consultants as part of their business income even if these expenses pass through their accounts. Therefore, billable expenses are shown separately (line 17) in the operating budget.

Profit

Gross profit is the surplus to fees generated over the budget period. It provides for:

- a profit-share or bonus to the owners, partners, or other employees of the consulting firm;
- establishing security reserves;
- increasing the working capital;
- financing capital expenses;
- paying a profit tax.

As shown in table 25.3, in most cases the profit margin would be between 10 and 25 per cent of the total income. The actual figure will depend upon such factors as the possibility of charging fees that provide for an adequate profit, the ability to reduce and control expenses, and the firm's need to generate resources for further expansion of its services or for other purposes mentioned above.

25.2 Performance monitoring

The monitoring of operational and financial performance is an essential, yet often underestimated, management function in consulting organisations. The purpose is not to produce statistics for their own sake, but systematically to collect and evaluate key information likely to reveal negative trends (from which will spring the need for action to redress the situation) or positive trends (which may need to be reinforced so that any opportunities disclosed are not missed).

Table 25.3   Typical structure of expenses and income

Item	%
Professional staff salaries (including social charges)	30-60
Other expenses	40-60
Gross profit (before tax)	10-25
Total income	100
Billable expenses	15-30
Gross billing to clients	115-130

Using comparison

It is impossible to assess performance without making comparisons: superior or substandard performance can be identified and assessed only by referring to some other performance. Consultants use comparisons extensively when working with clients, therefore they should not hesitate to apply them to their own operation.

Comparing results achieved with planned targets can be revealing provided that the targets were based on thorough analysis and planning and not just on guesswork. The main documents to which this comparison refers in performance monitoring are the annual work plan and operating budget.

Comparing current and past performance helps to discover and analyse trends in performance, as well as changes in factors affecting it.

Comparing performance with other consultants can be most instructive. This can be done in various ways:

— Consultants who are business friends can exchange and compare data informally, as colleagues who want to learn from each other.

— There can be a formal interfirm comparison scheme, which can be run by a consultants' association or another agency. Under such a scheme, key data are collected, tabulated and distributed to participating consulting units on a regular basis, without revealing the identity of these units.[1]

— Performance achieved by a specific consulting firm can be compared with data regarded as sectoral standards. Such sectoral standards would reflect "good practice", i.e. experience of consulting firms whose management is considered competent and performance adequate. Here again, such standards can be developed by an association for the benefit of its members. Our book refers to a number of ratios collected from consulting firms and their associations. These operating ratios can be regarded as a form of standard.

In making comparisons, it is essential to determine the *causes* of superior or substandard performance: it can result from poor management of operations, but also from an unforeseen environmental change over which the consultant has no control.

Key monthly controls

Operational controls have to be established and examined on a relatively short-term basis to permit action before it is too late. In practice, this will be on a *monthly basis* in most cases. This explains why the operating work plan and budget described in section 25.1 above are prepared with a monthly breakdown of most data. Any deviation from the consulting unit's standards, or any undesirable trend, requires prompt action by management.

The list of controls given below can be used as a guide in establishing a list that suits a particular consulting firm. In fact, the meaning of most of these controls has already been explained to the reader.

- *Forward workload (backlog)*

  Most important; ideally it should be around 3 months and should not drop below $1 \, ^1/_2$ months; if it is too high, clients are kept waiting for too long.

- *Number of client visits (meetings, surveys) to number of assignments negotiated*

  Indicative of the effectiveness of promotional work; an alternative ratio is volume of new business negotiated per client visit (meeting, survey), which is more precise if assignments vary greatly in extent.

- *Actual and budgeted utilisation of total time*

  Can be computed for all consulting staff or by categories, e.g. for operating consultants, supervisors, partners and officers; shows not only whether the firm has enough to do, but also whether work is properly scheduled and organised for smooth delivery.

- *Cumulative actual fee-earning days against planned fee-earning days*

  Similar use as previous ratio.

- *Actual and budgeted fee rate*

  Can be computed for all consulting staff or by categories of consultant; helps to assess whether the firm is in a position to apply optimum fees and gives guidance in using the staff in accordance with its technical and income-generating ability.

- *Fees earned against fees budgeted (monthly and cumulative)*

  Synthetic indicator of actual programme delivery rate in financial terms.

- *Fees earned against expenses (monthly and cumulative)*

  Synthetic indicator of short-term performance in financial terms; can provide early warning of excessive expenses and cash-shortages.

- *Expenses incurred against expenses budgeted (in total and by expense budget lines; monthly and cumulative)*

  Permits detailed control by expense lines, providing suggestions for specific expense-cutting measures and for adjustments of budgets owing to price and other changes outside the consultant's control.

- *Monthly billing against monthly fees earned*

  Shows whether the firm is properly organised to process work records and bill the clients as soon as records become available.

- *Number of months of outstanding fees*

  Shows whether fees are collected within normal time limits (4-6 weeks); an alternative ratio is outstanding fees as percentage of total (annual) income.

Annual controls

All ratios do not lend themselves to short-term analysis and action and therefore not all need to be presented every month. A dropping backlog of work requires immediate action, therefore the data are needed monthly. The staff structure cannot be changed by short-term measures, and an analysis of relevant information once or twice a year may be enough.

An annual performance review, or audit, would examine the data collected on a monthly basis, plus certain additional data, such as:

- *growth rate of business*;
- *profitability (gross and/or net profits compared to total income)*;
- *profit per consultant employed (per partner, etc.)*;
- *non-collectable fees (bad debts) as part of total income*;
- *volume of work sold per consultant engaged in the marketing services*;
- *ratios indicating the structure of consulting staff (various categories)*;
- *number of consulting staff compared to number of administrative and support staff*;
- *expense and cost structure (relative magnitude of various expense lines)*.

It is often useful to analyse various other *financial ratios* which can be calculated from the annual financial statements. However, before choosing to do this it is necessary to consider whether they are as meaningful in consulting as in manufacturing industry and other sectors (owing to factors such as the small volume and role of fixed assets, etc.).

Here again, analysis should reveal causes and point to remedies. Increased income can be the result of better performance, but also of price adjustments due to inflation, while real performance in non-financial terms has not changed or has deteriorated.

Organisational level of performance monitoring

The management of the consulting firm will be interested in knowing and analysing all key controls, both monthly and annual. As a rule, operating and financial performance ratios are reviewed at regular management meetings. If it is decided to take corrective action, the precise target to be achieved and the responsibility for action to be taken should be defined.

It is good practice to keep not only partners and senior members of the firm but also other consultants informed about the performance achieved by the firm, pointing out what should be improved, and in what way individual consultants can help to make such improvements.

The key performance ratios can be calculated and analysed *by units within the firm*. This opportunity should not be missed. It can show which units are the main contributors to the total results achieved, and which "problem" units have become, or may become, a financial burden. This can stimulate the management and staff of the units to be more active and entrepreneurial.

In a similiar vein, some performance indicators (e.g. profitability) can be calculated and analysed *by projects (assignments) or products*. For example, one consulting firm found that the profitability of its consulting assignments was minimal. However, most assignments generated demand for tailor-made in-plant training programmes, and also brought participants to open training seminars scheduled on a regular basis. Since these two groups of products were highly profitable, the overall result was judged as being satisfactory and the relatively low profitability of consulting assignments acceptable.

Finally, it is often useful to know performance data for *each consultant employed*. A typical example is the ratio of volume of work sold per consultant engaged in marketing the services. Rather than calculating and examining average data per consultant, some consulting firms record and analyse the marketing performance of each individual. The same can be done in assessing programme delivery, by comparing the budgeted and the real income and profitability for individual consultants. If an individual's profitability is low, the reasons can be, for example,

— fee charged is too low in comparison to salary paid and other costs;
— chargeable time utilisation is low owing to small demand for the services of the individual concerned, or to other reasons reflecting weaknesses in service marketing, scheduling and organisation.

While performance monitoring aims at immediate improvements first of all, its strategic implications should not be overlooked. It helps to reveal changes and trends that will affect the consulting firm in the long run, such as major shifts in demand for certain kinds of service, or the increasing cost of selling services to certain markets. Adjustments to the firm's strategy can thus be based on hard data instead of mere guesses and estimates.

25.3 Bookkeeping and accounting

Like any business, a consulting organisation needs bookkeeping and accounting to control the financial side of the operation and produce information required by law. Some comments on accounting problems faced by consultants will be made in this section, which, however, is not meant as a complete review of accounting in professional firms. Such information is available from specialised publications.[2]

Choosing your system

The purpose is to have an accounting system that is fully adapted to the nature of consulting operations and will be used as a management tool. Such a system should be as simple as possible. A single practitioner who serves a few clients and has a limited range of expenditure can use a very simple system indeed. The complexity of the system will increase with the growth of the firm and the complexity of its operations, but even a larger consulting firm should try to keep its accounting simple.

A consultant who is versed in accounting can decide himself what system to use. There are, too, proprietory bookkeeping systems for smaller businesses available on the market; the consultant may be able to purchase such a system, including all forms and books, from a supplier of office equipment and stationery. In some countries, the associations of professional firms have issued accounting guidelines and recommendations for the member firms. Finally, the consultant can ask an accountant to design a tailor-made system. Often this will be the best solution, provided that the accountant does not conceive an unduly complicated system which creates an unnecessary workload.

The essential criteria to be considered include the following:

- What is the structure of the firm's income (volume, number of clients, frequency of payments, collection problems, different kinds of income)?
- What is the structure of the firm's expenses (different expense items, critical expense items, frequency of expenses)?
- What are the firm's material and financial resources (buildings, equipment, stocks of materials and spare parts, financial reserves, cash)?
- How is the firm's operation financed?
- What are the existing and potential problems as regards cash-flow and liquidity?
- What information is critical for sound financial management and how frequently should it be provided?
- What records and reports are required by law?

A smallish consulting firm may be satisfied with a simple single-entry system, using a simple cash book, though most consulting firms prefer a double-entry system. Every consultant, irrespective of the legal form of the business and the accounting system chosen, should separate his business accounts from private household accounts. This basic rule of financial management is generally recommended by management consultants to their small-business clients and consultants will be well advised to follow the same principle in their own businesses.

Another possible choice may be between cash-basis accounting (only cash transactions are recorded) and accrual-basis accounting (accounts receivable and accounts payable are recorded). In the United States, for example, professional firms prefer cash-basis accounting since under this system only income for which cash has actually been collected is taxed.[3]

What accounts to keep

In some countries there will be a suggested or even compulsory chart of accounts (called "accounting plan" in some French-speaking countries) with which both public and private business companies have to comply. In many cases, however, the consultant will be free to choose his own chart of accounts. In particular, he will be able to decide how detailed the chart should be.

The purpose has always to be kept in mind. Accounts from which statutory financial reports are produced will be needed. Accounts required for controlling important expenses (e.g. wages of administrative and support staff) should be kept separately in most cases. On the other hand, unimportant expense items do not require separate accounts, and a number of these items can usually be blocked in one account.

It is advisable to aim at coherence between budgeting and accounting to facilitate both the preparation and the control of budgets. If the firm decides to structure its operating budget as shown in table 25.2 above, its accounts for income and expenses should be structured accordingly. The accounting can be more detailed. For example, income may be recorded in several client accounts before being posted to the general ledger. However, inconsistencies should be avoided. Thus, if "marketing and promotion expenses other than salaries" are budgeted separately from any salaries, they should be shown in the same way in the respective accounts. Needless to say, to avoid errors and confusion, it is necessary to be precise in defining what is to be recorded in what account. For example, will all telephone charges (except those chargeable to clients) be consistently charged to the communications account, or should some of them be treated as marketing and promotion expenses if they concern marketing? Many such decisions will have to be made.

Financial statements

Consulting firms established as corporations (limited liability companies) have to produce financial statements which include:

- the balance sheet;
- the income statement (profit and loss account);
- the sources and uses of funds statement (funds flow statement);
- the statement of earned surplus;
- the auditor's certificate and notes on the financial statements.

Even if this is not required by law, any consulting unit, including the sole practitioner, should prepare financial reports at least once a year, for self-assessment and to keep control of the financial health of the firm. This can be quite a simple, though extremely useful and instructive, exercise.

The meaning and use of these statements are amply described in accounting and financial management literature.[4]

[1] For example, the Association of Management Consulting Firms (ACME) in the United States operates such a scheme. See *ACME survey of key operating statistics on management consulting* (published periodically).

[2] On bookkeeping and accounting in consulting firms see, for example, M. R. Altman and R. I. Weil: *Managing your accounting and consulting practice* (Albany, NY, Matthew Bender, 1978); or M. C. Thomsett: *Fundamentals of bookkeeping and accounting for the successful consultant* (Washington, DC, Bermont Books, 1980).

[3] Cf. Altman and Weil, op. cit., chapter 5.

[4] Cf. references under 2 above and ILO: *How to read a balance sheet* (Geneva, International Labour Office, 2nd (revised) edition, 1985).

STRUCTURING CONSULTING ORGANISATIONS 26

Because there is a variety of consulting organisations, these organisations use many different structural arrangements. Structure must never become a strait-jacket. Our review of structural, or organisational, arrangements, including the legal forms of business, will therefore refer to some typical arrangements, but are not a blueprint for all situations. The structure of a particular consulting firm reflects many factors, including the nature and volume of activities, personalities, the strategy chosen, traditions, and the legal and institutional environment.

26.1 Legal forms of business

In most countries consultants can choose among several legal forms of business organisation. However, this choice is not always completely free. Local legislation may include special regulations for organising and operating professional services. Therefore an international consulting firm may have to use different legal forms in various countries. Unless the consultant is sufficiently knowledgeable in legal matters, he should seek a lawyer's advice. An accountant's or tax adviser's viewpoint is equally important because the forms of business organisation differ as regards taxation, record keeping, reporting and liability.

Sole proprietorship

A sole proprietorship (sole owner) is a person who owns and operates his business. This form may involve either the single practitioner, or the owner plus a variable number of associates. While normally and legally there may be no limit to the number of staff, it is usual that the "sole owner" employs only a few associates, and perhaps only for the duration of specific assignments. The firm's net income is taxed as the owner's personal income; the owner's liability for all debts incurred by the firm is unlimited.

Sole proprietorship is a simple form, suitable for those who are starting in consulting but have some previous management experience, or who prefer to remain completely independent in their consulting career. In addition to working on assignments, the sole practitioner has to take care of marketing future assignments. The risk is quite high in the case of sickness. Even if the single practitioner has health insurance, a prolonged illness may affect his business contacts very adversely. The firm normally ceases to exist with the death or retirement of the owner (although his estate remains liable for outstanding debts).

Partnership

Partnership is a fairly common form of business in consulting and the provision of other professional services. It entails a contract between two or more persons who agree to set up a firm in which they combine their skills and resources, and share profits, losses and liabilities. Under most legal systems, the partnership does not have to be on an equal basis — for example, a consultant may enter a partnership with a junior colleague on a 60-40 basis; or one or more of the partners may wish to devote less time than the others to the partnership business and hence will accept a smaller share of both profits and losses.

The advantages of partnership include the division of labour to optimise the use of the partners' skills, the possibility of undertaking more important and complex assignments, the possibility of continuing the business in the absence of one of the partners, and a better utilisation of resources such as office space, equipment, or secretarial support.

The disadvantages include the unlimited liability of each partner for errors and obligations of all other partners arising from the business, and the need to reach an agreement on every important decision. In some legal systems it is possible to establish a *limited partnership*, which includes one or more general partners (with unlimited liability), and one or more limited partners, whose third-party liability is limited to a specific amount (which can be zero).

It is generally recommended that a clear and unambiguous partnership agreement should be drawn up, even if local legislation does not explicitly require one. Much more important, however, is the composition of the group: individuals who cannot work together and do not trust each other for any reason should avoid becoming partners.

Partnerships usually are not limited by law as to size, but in practice are often confined to a comparatively small number of people. If a unit expands beyond this number, though it may still retain something of the spirit and the title of partnership, it might be advisable to consider transforming the business into a corporation.

Corporation

Many consulting firms are established as corporations (limited liability companies). The corporation has two fundamental characteristics: (1) it is a legal entity that exists separately from the owners (i.e. does not cease to exist after an owner's death or withdrawal from business); and (2) the owners have no personal liability for the obligations and debts of the corporation (the shareholders are protected from liability incurred by the company, except in certain cases when it is established that the corporate form was abused in order to avoid personal liability).

The major advantages of incorporation include:

- considerable flexibility in doing and developing business;
- the possibility of easy changes in the number of co-owners (shareholders): there can be one sole owner, therefore even a sole practitioner can incorporate his business;
- the possibility for individuals to be simultaneously owners and employees of the corporation;
- the possibility of retaining earnings for reinvestment in the firm;
- separate taxation of personal income (salary, bonuses and dividends) and the corporation's profits, and the possibility of deducting certain employee benefits and certain types of corporate expenses from taxable income (the level of taxation is often a major factor in deciding whether to incorporate or not).

On the other hand, a firm using the corporate form must comply with a number of requirements stipulated in the company or other law of particular countries. These include:

- compulsory registration (incorporation) prior to starting business;
- a statement of corporate purposes (objects of the company), the definition of which may be very significant as in some countries the corporation is not authorised to do business outside the scope of this statement;
- accounting and other records to be kept, with periodic reporting;
- public auditing of company reports;
- the organisation and definition of responsibilities of top management (shareholders' meeting, board of directors).

Moreover, corporate directors can be personally liable both civilly and criminally for certain corporate acts of malfeasance or misfeasance.

Management consultants in various countries have adopted special arrangements in using the corporate form. With few exceptions, they do not "go public", i.e. the shares are not available on the stock market, but ownership is reserved to a group of senior consultants (officers, principals, partners, etc.). Promotion to this level in the hierarchy may include not only an entitlement, but an obligation to purchase a certain number of shares and thus invest in the firm. The maximum number of shares which can be owned by one member of the firm is often limited (in many firms the limit is between 1 and 5 per cent of the shares) and the owner must resell these shares to the company (thus recovering his money) when retiring or leaving for any other reason.

In some consulting firms there is one (or more) majority owner who actually controls the firm. Usually he would be the sole founder, or one of the partners who established the firm, who at some point decided to transform the firm into a corporation and widen the ownership base. In a small number of cases, consulting firms are owned by other business corporations (by banks, accounting firms, engineering firms, or others).

As regards the use of profits (after tax), some consulting firms use the whole profit for developing the business and creating reserves, while others distribute a part of the profit to the shareholders of the firm, or to all employees.

Other forms

As we know, not all management consulting units are independent businesses. Some units are established and operate as divisions in private corporations that have wider corporate purposes and offer other types of service (accounting, auditing, engineering consultancy, etc.) in addition to management consulting. In such a case, the legal entity may not be the consulting unit itself in its own right, but the organisation to which the unit belongs.

There are also consulting units established as, or within, associations, foundations, public agencies, and other non-profit-making organisations. However, the corporate form tends increasingly to be used for these units in order to enhance their independence, motivation, responsibility and liability. For example, a management institute can often be organised as a corporation, or a public agency can create (and own) a professional service company that sells services to clients in both the public and private sectors.

26.2 Structuring the operating core

Consultants spend most of their time working for clients on specific assignments. In the management system of a consulting organisation, individual assignments are treated as basic management units with precisely defined terms of reference, resources and responsibilities. However, assignments are temporary management units and structuring by assignments would not provide for stability and continuity of internal organisation. Most consulting organisations therefore structure their operating core — the professional staff — in more or less permanent "home" units.

Permanent organisational units

Consultants are attached to these units according to some common characteristics in their background and/or areas of intervention.

Functional units are very common in consulting organisations. They used to be organised by the basic functions of management, such as general management, finance, marketing, production and personnel. More recently, their focus has started shifting to technical problem areas, such as strategy and policy, organisation development, or management information systems. A consulting assignment may be fully within the function or problem area covered by the unit (e.g. in marketing), and the unit can therefore staff and supervise the assignment from its own resources. In other cases, the unit would "borrow" staff from other units for the duration of the assignment. This is particularly common in complex assignments dealing with various aspects of a business; these assignments tend to be mainly in the province of units dealing with general aspects of business strategy and policy.

Sectoral units (e.g. for construction, banking, international trade, road transport, health) are often established if this is justified by the volume of business done in a sector and by the need to have teams that are recognised as sectoral experts. It is impossible to suggest a minimum size for such a unit. Even a small unit with all-round experts in a sector may play a useful role in developing and managing assignments which can also make use of specialists from other units. If a certain sector generates a sizeable amount of work, a sectoral unit may become more or less self-contained and employ a wider range of specialists on a permanent basis in addition to its generalists.

Geographical (territorial) units are often established when a consulting organisation decides to decentralise in order to get closer to the clients and increase efficiency (e.g. by reducing transport and communication expenses). They exist in two basic forms:

- offices whose main purpose is marketing and liaison with clients in a delimited geographical area; these units tend to be small, staffed by a few all-round generalists, and equipped by certain services for supporting operating assignments; assignments can thus be staffed both by consultants from the unit and from headquarters;

- fully staffed local (area) branches that can take care of most assignments using their own personnel; these units are effective if the volume and structure of business done in the area concerned is relatively stable, or is regularly expanding; a major advantage, appreciated by the consultants, is that they do not have to be absent from their homes for long periods of time.

Geographically decentralised units are most common in larger consulting firms. A smaller firm must weigh the advantages of getting close to the clientele against the cost of the operation and the firm's ability to keep technical and administrative control over geographically distant units. There are, too, various combinations. For example, a decentralised geographical unit may specialise in the sector(s) featuring most prominently in the area covered by the unit.

Some examples

Figure 26.1 shows a general pattern of organisational structure used by a number of larger consulting companies in various countries.[1] In contrast, figure 26.2 shows the structure of the professional core of a consulting unit employing 29 consultants. It is a hypothetical example used to explain typical organisational considerations.

A unit of this size can make up a whole consulting company, or constitute a division in a larger company or a management development institution. The unit

Figure 26.1 Typical organisation of consulting companies

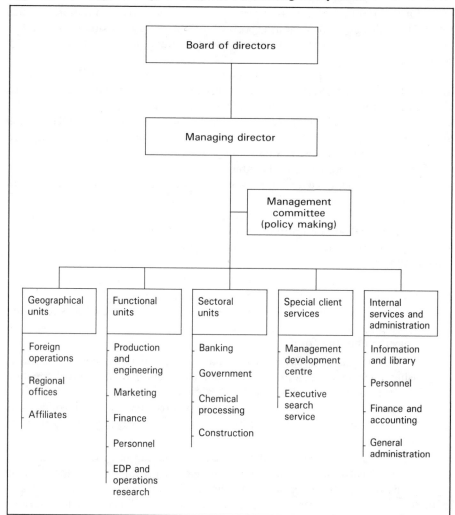

employs 6 senior consultants, of whom 4 work as team leaders and supervisors of operating assignments, and 2 concentrate on marketing and on management surveys. The 20 operating consultants will, as a rule, be specialists in various management functions. Among the supervisors in the unit 3 may also specialise in managing assignments in functional areas, while the fourth supervisor may be an all-round general management expert, able to supervise assignments covering several functional areas. The 20 operating consultants can work in assignment teams or individually on separate smaller assignments. Thus, the supervisors will either work as team leaders on larger assignments, or supervise several operating consultants working individually for different clients.

Figure 26.2   Professional core of a consulting unit

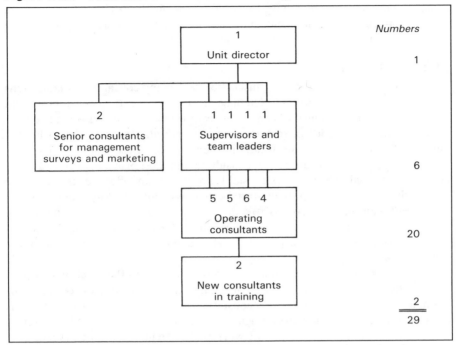

A consulting firm may never expand beyond 27 to 30 people, as the owner or manager may wish to keep personal control of all the operations and relations with clients. In this case, the top man may have a small office and staff to support the operating core.

If expansion takes place, and a unit employs more than 30 consultants, it may split into two sub-units. One senior consultant may become the manager of the second unit, which he builds up to full size. During this expansion more seniors will be required, and in time central support services may be set up. The additional seniors are needed to co-ordinate and administer these separate units, or to set up specialist units and support services.

The key factors determining expansion are market demand and the availability of operating consultants with sufficient experience and knowledge to be appointed as supervisors or team leaders. At least 3-5 years of experience, encompassing both a range of assignments with companies and a variety of techniques, are required. To replace the operating consultants as they rise to higher levels or leave, new consultants must be ready trained. For this reason a stable organisation includes 2-3 trainee-consultants in every group of 27 to 30, as shown in figure 26.2.

Another factor governing expansion is the ratio of specialist to generalist consultants. Where an assignment calls for several disciplines, the supervising consultant may accept overall responsibility but call on a specialist to oversee special techniques as required. To meet the full range of client demands, the consulting organisation may have to employ some highly specialised consultants, e.g. in productivity measurement, materials handling, or franchising. It is more difficult to find a constant demand for these types of service within a smaller unit.

Matrix management

It results from the foregoing discussion that many consulting organisations in fact practise some sort of matrix management. Both operating consultants, and their more senior colleagues who work as team leaders or supervisors, have their "home" units — functional, sectoral, or geographical. However, only a limited number of assignments remain totally in the province of these home units.

The organisational culture of a consulting firm must provide for considerable flexibility to facilitate the rapid establishment of an effective collaborative relationship and a team spirit in starting new assignments. Any member of an assignment team must accept his role in the team, and the co-ordinating role of the team leader, as soon as the team is constituted and starts tackling the job. If this were not the case, the start would be slow and costly, to the detriment of the client.

However, the role of the "home" unit extends beyond the function of a pool of specialists from which operating consultants can be drawn as necessary. For example, the head of a marketing consulting unit is also interested in what is actually happening in the assignments to which he has detached marketing consultants, even if these consultants work under the immediate supervision of a team leader from another unit. He is responsible for technical guidance and control of operating consultants in the special field of marketing. He carries out this responsibility in various ways: by organising technical meetings of marketing consultants, reviewing consulting reports, discussing progress of the work with the team leaders, visiting the marketing consultants on assignments, and so on. Such guidance and control have to be exercised in agreement with the team leaders and supervisors, and in a way that does not undermine the operating consultants' authority in the clients' eyes.

Flat structure

In addition to matrix management, most consulting organisations use a relatively flat organisational structure. The number of rungs on the management ladder between an operating consultant and the top manager of the unit is usually between none and three, depending on the organisation's size, complexity and service diversification. Such a structure encourages collaboration and interaction with peers in the operating core rather than referring matters upwards through the chain of command.

26.3 Organising for marketing

To structure the marketing function of a consulting firm effectively is not easy, for reasons explained in chapter 22. Virtually every member of the consulting staff may have some role to play in marketing, and consultants on assignments can do a lot of marketing if they keep their eyes open and think of future business for their firm. Yet some formal structuring of the marketing function is necessary.

Marketing manager

Whatever the size and complexity of the consulting firm, its management team has to pay considerable attention to marketing. Decisions on its marketing strategy and programme will normally be discussed and taken by senior management. If possible, one member of the senior management team should be appointed *marketing manager*. This can be a full-time or part-time function.

The marketing manager is responsible for preparing and submitting key market analyses, strategies, programmes and budgets. He is concerned with the marketing function in its totality. Certain marketing activities will be his direct responsibility, e.g. advertising, press relations, mailing lists, editing and distributing publicity information. He may have a small technical and administrative team for these functions. Other marketing functions are not the direct responsibility of the marketing manager, but he has to follow, evaluate and stimulate them in collaboration with other managers.

Roles in indirect marketing

Roles in indirect marketing (aimed at building up the professional image of the firm and creating opportunities for contacts with new clients) are normally shared throughout the consulting firm and assigned to those units or individuals who can use their skills to best effect. The purpose is to optimise the use of individual capabilities: not everyone can write a book or article that will promote the firm, and so on. The roles have to be precisely defined, e.g. it should be determined who will be active in what management or trade association.

Roles in direct marketing

Direct marketing of specific assignments is normally the function of senior consulting partners or managers, who would spend 30-100 per cent of their time in contacts with individual clients, trying to sell an assignment, negotiating a preliminary diagnostic survey, or following up previous work.

In some consulting firms these senior professionals are full-time marketers. They may not be the firm's top technicians, but their social, diagnostic and selling skills make them an invaluable asset to it.[2] Many consulting firms prefer changing roles, e.g. by making the marketers responsible for the co-ordination and supervision of the assignments sold by them.

Direct marketing requires excellent co-ordination and follow-up by senior management and/or by the managers of sectors and geographical areas within the consulting firm. Unco-ordinated contacting of the same client by different units of one consulting firm must be avoided.

26.4 Organising other client services

To enhance the impact of consulting and make good use of staff capabilities and other resources, many consulting organisations supplement their consulting services by training, research, information, documentation, computing, systems design, testing, quality control, and other services to clients. Organisational arrangements can be permanent or ad hoc.

Permanent arrangements

Permanent arrangements usually take the form of special units within the consulting firms. These are justified if the volume of the service is sufficiently important and stabilised, or growing regularly. To establish a new unit for a special service may be a strategic decision if the firm intends to promote that service and wants to demonstrate to the clients that adequate resources have been allocated and a suitable organisational framework created for this purpose.

Training units are very common in consulting organisations. There is a wide variety of them, ranging from smallish training sections to important management development institutes. These units tend to enjoy relative autonomy within the firm and some of their programmes may be open to external participants. Training units may market their programmes quite independently of the consulting services marketed by other divisions in the firm. Training units also contribute to consulting assignments in various ways, e.g. by providing trainers, or mounting tailor-made courses as part of consulting projects. Many of them organise internal courses and seminars for the consulting firm's own staff. The teaching staff is frequently drawn from experienced consultants, some of whom return to consulting after a period spent with the unit.

Information and documentation units providing services to clients are less common than training units. Yet some consultants have been successful in converting their internal information services into services available to clients, as discussed in sections 1.5 and 22.2. The nature of the service, including the handling of information inputs, files and outputs in a systematic matter, justify the establishment of a separate unit structured and managed as a professional information service.

Economic research and feasibility studies. As most of these studies require special skills (industrial economics, market research, operations research, business forecasting, etc.), and often may be carried out as off shoots of main assignments, some larger consulting organisations have concentrated them in specialised service units. Some firms are fully specialised in this kind of service.

Systems development and computing services. This activity has become very important in the last decade. The services range from feasibility studies for computer applications, through systems analysis and design and training of specialist staff, to computing services or facilities management provides on a temporary or continuing basis. Some consulting organisations have their own computing centres, or have established separate companies for this purpose.

Ad hoc arrangements

Often the volume and frequency of the service do not justify a permanent organisational arrangement. This concerns training programmes in particular. Many consulting assignments include some sort of management or other training, e.g. for applying a new management system proposed by the consultant. Such a service can be provided by the assignment team, or by trainers from the consulting firm's training centre, or carried out by another organisation acting as a subcontractor, and so on.

Similarly, consulting assignments can include research studies, attitude surveys, feasibility studies, information searches, systems design projects, and many other activities in support of the main task of the assignment. Management consultants tend to be increasingly ingenious in finding ways to provide a total package of services required by the client, even if special technical expertise has to be found, ad hoc, outside the consulting firm.

Specific management requirements

If a consulting firm decides to establish a special client service other than consulting, and if that service tends to expand, it is necessary to pay due attention to its specific management requirements. These should be thoroughly examined before it is decided how to integrate the service in question with the overall management structure of the firm. It may be useful to seek specialist advice on these questions from outside the consulting firm, or to consult a technical publication (see references in appendix 11).

26.5 Organising for international operations

In organising for international operations, consulting firms give consideration to factors such as the frequency, relative importance and predicted future trend of these operations, the institutional and legal setting in countries where work is to be done, the possibility of repatriating earnings, language requirements, and local practice concerning business and professional services.

Consultant missions

If work abroad is irregular and its volume small, consulting firms usually prefer to send their staff on missions from headquarters. This is how foreign operations start in most consulting firms. It can be a costly arrangement, not only because of the price of long-distance travel and living and other expenses of operating consultants, but also because of costs incurred by negotiating, preparing and supervising assignments in foreign countries.

Offices in other countries

Having gained some experience with consulting across national boundaries, a consulting firm may feel that it is more effective to have a permanent presence where the market for the services is. The establishment of a foreign (country or regional) office is often the solution. As with decentralisation within the home country, this office may start as a small one, staffed mainly for marketing, liaison with local businesses and government, and as a support for operating teams coming from headquarters to work on specific projects.

Foreign subsidiaries

Fully staffed foreign subsidiaries have been founded by many large consulting firms that regularly undertake a substantial amount of foreign business. Such a subsidiary may be quite independent of the parent company in operational matters, but there is always a provision for policy guidance and quality control. There is a growing tendency to staff foreign subsidiaries with local professionals, even in consulting companies which originally preferred to staff them by consultants detached from headquarters.

Association with local consultants

Some countries require foreign consultants to work in association with a local consulting firm. But even if there is no such regulation, consulting firms operating abroad often find it useful, for a number of reasons, to negotiate and execute assignments and to organise their foreign operations in association with local consulting firms. This association can have various forms, such as a shared ownership of a foreign company on a 50-50 basis, or an arrangement whereby the precise scope of collaboration is defined separately for every assignment. There have been, too, cases of abuse — e.g. if the association is established with the sole intention of bypassing legislation in order to get contracts and the local consultant is a man of straw. Further comments on this topic are made in chapter 29.

26.6 Organising administrative and technical support services

Many single practitioners and other smallish consulting units are proud of having minimal administrative expenses because they are able to handle many jobs personally, with the help of a spouse, or by recruiting an external collaborator from time to time for typing a major report. However, as the consulting firm grows, its administrative and support services reach a volume that justifies permanent staff.

Office staff

Because the majority of the professional staff — the operating consultants — are able to use their clients' administrative services, consulting firms usually need only a small office staff at their headquarters. The smaller the staff, the more it is necessary for its members to help in any part of the daily work. The work is straightforward, but must be done with the efficiency that befits a professional body. The office staff, therefore, needs to be rather above average in ability, versatility and discretion. In a small unit the following staff may be employed:

Secretary to the director (may also act as administrative assistant and office manager, and type confidential reports for both operational and internal matters).

Accounts clerk/cashier (would keep time and other records, invoice clients, pay salaries and expenses, and purchase office supplies).

Receptionist/telephonist/copy typist (would type routine documents such as invoices and purchase orders).

Shorthand typists (would type routine communications, and reports that should not be typed by the clients' personnel; they can also assist in various secretarial duties).

It is logical that larger units will require more office staff. At some point the establishment of an administrative service unit, headed by an administrative assistant or director, will be justified.

Organising bookkeeping and accounting

In organising bookkeeping and accounting the consultant is faced with several alternatives. Most single practitioners do their own accounting, not only to save on administrative expenses but in order to be constantly in control of their financial position and of the efficiency of their operation. Even a consultant whose main field of intervention is production or personnel may find it useful to do his own accounting.

In small consulting firms, routine bookkeeping may be done by an accounts clerk/administrative officer as mentioned above, while financial and tax reports would be prepared by one of the professionals, or by an external accountant employed on a part-time basis. Some consultants have all bookkeeping and accounting done by an external accountant, but this may be a costly arrangement.

As the firm grows, a point is reached at which it is necessary to employ a qualified accountant on a full-time basis.

Library and documentation

A dynamic and reliable information and documentation service[3] is needed for two principal reasons:

- information on new developments in management relevant to the work of the consulting organisation has to be collected and channelled to the consultants (who often work far from their headquarters, in localities where new books, professional reviews, or other information sources are not easily available, and on projects which keep them too busy to search for new information);

- information on the work methods used and results obtained in previous assignments must be available for any new assignment.

The information service has responsibility for collecting, extracting, storing and retrieving managerial and technical information contained in important publications, for use by the appropriate consultants. Suggestions are also made to consultants concerning new materials they should study. The consulting unit should have at least a reference library of the standard management handbooks, a selection of the best textbooks on general and functional management, references on special techniques, and basic books on management consulting and training concepts and methodologies.

The consulting unit should subscribe to leading management and business periodicals and also to an abstracting service. While some periodicals may be for general circulation, an information service may select and photocopy articles and abstracts that are of direct interest to particular consultants. The unit may also subscribe to those newspapers that regularly issue business or industrial supplements, or use an agency specialising in screening and copying published matter for its subscribers.

Whoever runs a periodicals or clippings service may also collect companies' annual reports, brochures, advertising and descriptive matter, government economic plans and reports, and so on. These provide useful information for initial meetings with potential clients, diagnostic surveys and operating assignments.

These are costly services, but consultants must keep up to date. Some excellent operating procedures can often be traced to an idea picked up from an article or book not necessarily directly related to the particular subject.

The organisation and use of the information service requires inputs from both ends of the information flow. The information section should take the initiative in looking for new sources and suggesting what might interest whom, while the consultants should present specific demands clearly indicating the nature and scope of the information required for their priority tasks.

The second essential part of an information service is the *reports library*. Survey reports, survey notes, and operating and follow-up reports have to be classified, indexed and filed. They grow into an invaluable reference library for the further guidance of consultants in their work. Although complete solutions cannot usually be transferred unchanged from one situation to another, the methods used and results achieved provide examples and give inspiration. Reports are also needed for training new consultants, and for the development of internal operational guides and manuals.

The reports library must have an efficient means of information retrieval and for this an *indexing system* has to be established and maintained. Reports may be indexed by client, sector, country, operating function, subject within a function, or technique applied. Thus, an enquiry as to what work has previously been done in, say, production planning in food canning with the use of EDP could result in either the extraction of a report, or the reply that no assignment of this nature has been undertaken, or that there has been one assignment, but without any EDP application.

A long-term view is needed when deciding on an indexing system. It is easier to start with something that will be suitable in twenty years' time than to change reports going back twenty years from one system to another.

Clients' reports are confidential papers and the library must be run on lines of strict security. Copies lent to consultants must not be taken into other clients' premises, nor left open in public places.

26.7 Office facilities

Headquarters accommodation

In all circumstances, headquarters accommodation should be designed round the fact that consulting is predominantly a field operation and not a head-office activity. As mentioned in chapter 22, a "good address" enhances the image of the consulting firm and has other advantages, such as the proximity of many clients. However, the total office space required can be quite small.

The accommodation needed for the internal administrative and support services is self-evident. For example, the reports library may start in a small way with a few lockable filing cabinets, but in time may need a room of its own. At the beginning it may share this room with the reference library of books and other documentation files, but with the growth of the unit more space will be needed.

As for consulting staff, the senior staff members involved in supervision and practice development need office space at headquarters. Although regular meetings with the unit's manager will probably take place in his office, operating consultants nevertheless need at least a desk each (though perhaps not individual offices). In addition, it is useful to have a meeting room, space for training workshops, and small rooms for receiving clients and other visitors.

The operating consultants' places of work are normally with their clients. Some operating work may legitimately be done off the clients' premises and a small amount of space at headquarters may be desirable. A good deal depends on how widely the consultants are dispersed.

In some situations, particularly for consulting units in management institutions in developing countries, the matter of consultants' accommodation takes on certain other aspects. There are places where almost all the operating assignments are in a compact area round about headquarters. Client companies tend to be small and assignments short, and it also happens that the consultant cannot proceed with his work as scheduled because the client is absent, documentation has not been prepared, or for other reasons. There is thus a tendency for operating consultants to spend more time at headquarters.

The number of consultants sitting at their desks instead of working with clients is generally considered to be an indicator or danger signal which requires careful examination.

Sole practitioner's office

A sole practitioner may be able to operate from his home without renting any office space. However, this is not always desirable from the client-relations viewpoint. In some countries, an office in a business area may be a necessity. To avoid excessive office accommodation and administrative costs, sole consultants and other professionals often choose to share an office, and a secretary, with colleagues.

Office equipment

Good quality office and communication equipment is a major asset in a consulting organisation. *Text-processing equipment* and *personal computers* are now within reach of most consulting organisations and plummeting costs have made them accessible even to single practitioners. If a sufficiently versatile machine is chosen it can be used for many purposes, including: record keeping; filing; bookkeeping; mail and communications; preparing proposals for clients; typing, editing and printing reports; and so on. Some *document reproduction equipment* (or easy access to such equipment) is needed in any consulting firm; high-capacity reproduction and printing equipment will probably be justified only in firms where large numbers of documents are reproduced on a regular basis.

26.8 Top management

Collective bodies

The pattern of the consulting organisation's top management depends very much upon its legal statute. In firms constituted as corporations (limited companies) there will be a *board of directors*. In a small firm the directors would generally be the general manager (managing director) and the senior consultants (partners). In a large firm there may also be external board members who, being non-executive, may play a useful role in the sense that they may preserve the same detachment in guiding the firm as the consultants have in advising their clients. They also tend to be chosen because of their range of business interests and contacts.

Consulting units that are not independent companies may have a *governing body* comprising a cross-section of managers from private and public enterprises, representatives of chambers of commerce and employers' associations, senior government officials and possibly other members in addition to one or more senior managers from the unit.

Chief executive officer

The key position in the management hierarchy is that of the *chief executive officer*, who may be called (in various countries and organisations) principal, general manager, president, managing director, managing partner, director-general, or simply manager or director. The chief executive officer may use a *management committee* in the usual way for involving other managers in dealing with issues requiring collective discussion.

The individual at the top will possibly be a career consultant with considerable experience and managerial talent. On reaching the top, he may experience problems similar to those faced by managers of research and other professional services — he must stop thinking and operating as a technician and concentrate on managing. Some consulting organisations have recruited top managers from outside, from among individuals who have been excellent business managers, but not necessarily practising consultants. There is no universal rule — the candidate's competence and personality will determine whether he will be able to cope with the challenge of the job and provide the leadership required.

---

[1] Adapted from an organisational chart developed by a FEACO research project.

[2] The situation is similar in public accounting firms. See M. Stevens: *The Big Eight* (New York, Macmillan, 1981); chapter 2.

[3] For more details see K. Vernon (ed.): *Library and information services of management development institutions: A practical guide* (Geneva, International Labour Office, 1986).

PART V

DEVELOPING MANAGEMENT CONSULTANTS

CONSULTING AS A CAREER   27

In the first four parts of this book, management consulting has been shown to be a special profession with its own objectives, methods, rules and organisation. To individuals who join this profession, consulting is a *career* in which they may spend the main part of their working lives.

27.1 Personal characteristics of consultants

To become a career management consultant is to make a major life decision. Both individuals considering the career and consulting organisations should therefore think very carefully about the characteristics which make someone a suitable candidate.

Management consultants have discussed these characteristics many times and useful advice can be found in several publications.[1] As in any profession which has attempted to prepare a profile of an ideal candidate, there is no perfect model against which every entrant can be measured, but there are certain common characteristics affecting the consultant's success and his personal job satisfaction. These common characteristics differentiate the consulting profession from other occupations that also require a high level of technical knowledge and skill, but have other objectives and use different methods of action (e.g. research, teaching, or management jobs with direct decision-making authority and responsibility). In management consulting, particular importance is attached to analytical and problem-solving abilities, as well as to special competence in the behavioural area, in communicating, and in helping other people to understand the need for change and how to implement it.

What kind of person is able to perform the multiple roles required of a management consultant appropriately? It seems that the qualities a consultant needs fall into two broad categories: On the one hand a number of distinctly *intellectual abilities*, and on the other hand a number of distinctly *personal attributes*.

Dilemma analysis ability

Intellectually, the consultant needs the ability to make a "dilemma analysis", because an organisation which uses a consultant is probably faced with a situation that appears insoluble. If the difficulty could easily be solved by the operating manager, a consultant would not be needed. The consultant must recognise that a dilemma, whether real or not, exists in the minds of those within the organisation. The consultant's role is to discover the nature of the dilemma and to determine the real cause of it, rather than what is thought to be the cause.

To accomplish this, the consultant must have a special type of diagnostic skill. He should approach a study of the organisation's dilemma by means of an existential pragmatism that takes into account the total client setting and all situational variables. It is only through skilful examination of the organisation's fabric that the structural relationships between the various sub-systems that comprise the total organisation can be seen, together with the interdependent nature of its individuals, groups, sub-structures and its environmental setting.

In order to make this kind of dilemma analysis, insight or perception and intuition are necessary. Insight or perception is vital because any dilemma requiring outside assistance will be part of a complex situation. The ability to penetrate this complexity and isolate the key situational variables is the toughest task. Unless the important factors can be sifted from the maze of detail, and cause separated from symptoms, accurate diagnosis is impossible.

Sense of organisational climate

Intuition or "sensing" must be coupled with perception in order to assess the nature of power and politics in the organisation. Experience with bureaucratic and managerial structures, both public and private, tends to indicate that these are not optimally functional. Underlying and intermingled with the functional operations the organisation performs are the crucial dynamics of internal power and politics. Invariably, people are vying with other people for organisational influence, or for some internal political reason. Very often the consultant has been asked to help, not just to provide needed assistance, but also as an instrument of a strategy designed to secure an objective related to this influence.

Unless the consultant can intuitively sense the organisational climate, he runs the risk of being only a pawn in a game of organisational politics. If he has the ability to recognise and understand the dynamics of the internal power and political relationships, the consultant can use them masterfully in pursuit of whatever change objectives client and consultant conclude are appropriate.

Apart from these diagnostic abilities, the consultant needs implementation skills. Obviously, he must have some basic knowledge of the behavioural sciences and the theories and methods of his own discipline. But more than these he needs imagination and experimental flexibility. Dilemma-resolving is essentially a creative enterprise. No real-life situation is going to fit perfectly into the mould suggested by standard techniques or textbook methods. Diversity and unique circumstances will almost always exist. The consultant must have sufficient imagination to innovate adaptations and tailor his concepts to meet real demands.

Furthermore, the consultant must be able to visualise the impact or ultimate outcome of the actions proposed or implemented. But, as happens so often, this is as much a process of experimental trial and error as it is one of *a priori* solutions. The courage to experiment and the flexibility to try as many approaches as needed to solve the problem are important ingredients in the practitioner's make-up.

Integrity is essential

The other important qualities required of the consultant are what we call his personal attributes. Above all, he must be a professional in attitude and behaviour. To be successful, he must be as sincerely interested in helping the client organisation as any good doctor is interested in helping a patient. The consultant must not conceive of himself as, or portray the image of, a huckster of patent medicines. After all, the consulting role in management and business is no different from that role in any other profession. If the concern of a consultant is primarily to make an impression or build an empire, and only secondarily to help the client organisation, the organisation's leaders will soon recognise that the individual is a phoney and deal with him accordingly. People in management generally are astute individuals. They can identify objectivity, honesty, and, above all, integrity.

When entering a client system, a strong tolerance for ambiguity is important. The consultant's first acquaintance with an organisational problem tends to be marked by a degree of bewilderment. It takes time to figure out the true situation, and during this period the consultant is going to experience a certain amount of confusion. One must expect this to occur and not be worried by it.

Coupled to this type of tolerance must be the qualities of patience and the ability to sustain a high level of frustration. Curing a client's ills is likely to be a long and trying experience. Substantive changes, full co-operation and complete success are unlikely in the short run. Inevitably, attempts to change people's relationships and behavioural patterns are going to be met with resistance, resentment, and obstructionism from those who are, or who think they may be, adversely affected. It is important for the consultant to have that kind of maturity and sense of reality which recognises that many of his actions and hopes for change are going to be frustrated. Such maturity is necessary to avoid experiencing the symptoms of defeat and withdrawal that commonly accompany the frustration of a person's sincere efforts to help others.

Sense of timing and interpersonal skills

Finally, the consulting practitioner should have a good sense of timing, a stable personality and well-developed interpersonal skills. Timing can be crucial. The best conceived and articulated plans for change can be destroyed if introduced at the wrong time. Timing is linked to an understanding of power and of the political realities existing in the change situation, and to the kind of patience that overrides the enthusiasm surrounding a newly conceived idea or training intervention that one is longing to try out immediately.

Obviously, consulting involves dealing with people rather than with machines or mathematical solutions. The consultant must have good interpersonal skills. He must be able to communicate and deal with people in an atmosphere of tact, trust, politeness, friendliness, change and stability. This is important because the impact of the consulting practitioner's personality must be minimised to keep it from becoming another variable in the existential setting and so making a contribution to the existing complexity of the situation. Beyond this, success will depend on the persuasiveness and tact the consultant uses in confronting the interpersonal relationships on which the helping situation is based.

Table 27.1 attempts to summarise the key intellectual abilities and personal attributes of a management consultant in telegraphic form.

How to interpret these requirements

It could be objected, and rightly, that only a very mature and exceptionally capable person can possess all the qualities mentioned. In recruiting a new consultant it is therefore necessary to consider what qualities he must possess on recruitment, and what qualities he will be able to acquire, or improve, through training and experience. For example, a candidate who has 5-7 years of business experience but is too shy, clearly lacks self-confidence, and has difficulties in presenting his ideas orally, is probably not a good potential management consultant, although he may be very knowledgeable in his technical subject.

27.2 Recruitment and selection

The foundations of successful careers in consulting are laid down at the moment of recruitment: only candidates who meet certain criteria will have good chances of becoming fully competent consultants and advancing up the career ladder to their own and the consulting organisation's satisfaction. Hence the extraordinary importance of a careful search and a thorough appraisal of candidates.

Recruitment criteria

Although consulting organisations apply different requirements in recruiting new consultants, the comparison of their practices allows for some general conclusions concerning personal characteristics, education, practical experience and age.

Personal qualities were discussed in the previous section and there is no need to return to them.

Education is carefully examined in every case. University (first degree) level or a higher degree (a doctorate or master's degree) is required at the present time for nearly all management consulting positions. The relevance of the field of study to the particular field of consulting is considered and in some cases candidates must have a specific educational background — for example, a doctorate in

Table 27.1   Qualities of a consultant

1. *Intellectual ability*
   — ability to learn quickly and easily;
   — ability to observe, gather, select and evaluate facts;
   — good judgement;
   — inductive and deductive reasoning;
   — ability to synthesise and generalise;
   — creative imagination; original thinking.

2. *Ability to understand people and work with them*
   — respect for other people; tolerance;
   — ability to anticipate and evaluate human reactions;
   — easy human contacts;
   — ability to gain trust and respect;
   — courtesy and good manners.

3. *Ability to communicate, persuade and motivate*
   — ability to listen;
   — facility in oral and written communication;
   — ability to teach and train people;
   — ability to persuade and motivate.

4. *Intellectual and emotional maturity*
   — stability of behaviour and action;
   — independence in drawing unbiased conclusions;
   — ability to withstand pressures and live with frustrations and uncertainties;
   — ability to act with poise and in a calm and objective manner;
   — self-control in all situations;
   — flexibility and adaptability to changed conditions.

5. *Personal drive and initiative*
   — right degree of self-confidence;
   — healthy ambition;
   — entrepreneurial spirit;
   — courage, initiative and perseverance in action.

6. *Ethics and integrity*
   — genuine desire to help others;
   — extreme honesty;
   — ability to recognise the limitation of one's competence;
   — ability to admit mistakes and learn from failure.

7. *Physical and mental health*
   — ability to sustain the specific working and living conditions of management consultants.

psychology, or a degree in computer science. The consulting organisation is equally interested in the performance of the candidates during their university studies, in particular in project assignments during which the students have practised fact finding, communication and other consulting skills.

Practical experience (a minimum of 5-10 years) used to be required by all consulting organisations, but this has changed in recent years. Some important consulting organisations have started recruiting up to 30 to 50 per cent of new consultants directly from university or business school, particularly in special fields where it is difficult to recruit experienced practitioners from business firms. The idea is that talented individuals will quickly acquire the necessary practical experience by working in teams with experienced practitioners.

The age at which candidates are recruited reflects the required education and experience. The lower age limit is usually between 25 and 30 years. In many cases there is also an upper age limit. It may be difficult for a senior manager or specialist, who has reached an interesting position in his employment, to switch over to consulting unless he is directly offered a senior position with a consulting organisation. This, however, would happen only in special cases — for example, if senior people have to be recruited from outside to start new lines of consulting and head new divisions. Consulting emphasises certain work methods and behavioural patterns and some people would find it difficult to learn these after a certain age. The upper limit for recruitment therefore tends to be between 36 and 40 years. However, if an individual decides to open his own consulting practice, it is up to him to consider at what point in his career he is ready to take this step.

Recruitment sources

It will be seen that there are two main sources: business enterprises and universities. But any other source is acceptable, provided it gives the candidate the required kinds of experience and skill. Many consulting organisations advertise job opportunities in business journals and management periodicals, thus opening their doors to any candidates who meet the criteria.

A good source might be found in the client organisations, although in most cases a consultant must not use this source for reasons explained in chapter 6. But of course there are exceptions. A client may willingly authorise a consultant to offer a job to an employee whose personal qualities would be better utilised in consulting than in his present job. Similarly, a national management centre in a developing country may need to attract talented trainers and consultants from certain enterprises with which it co-operates, in order to establish a service needed by the entire local management community.

When recruiting directly from universities and business schools, consulting firms aim at getting the best students. They may interview 20 or more candidates for one job position. In some countries, consulting careers with leading firms enjoy such a reputation that it is not difficult to get the best graduates interested. However, this practice is criticised both by some university teachers and by many consultants, who maintain that direct recruitment from university is not an appropriate path to effective consulting.

Interviewing and testing

Candidates for consultants' posts are asked to fill in the usual application forms (personnel questionnaires), supply detailed curricula vitae, and provide other evidence of professional work (articles, papers, a doctoral thesis, etc.). References given by the candidate and other references identified by the consulting organisation are carefully checked for every candidate who looks interesting (by correspondence, personal visits and telephone calls).

Applicants are subjected to multiple interviews: by the personnel officer, a manager of the consulting organisation, a supervising consultant to whom the candidate might be attached after recruitment, and one or two other consultants. Both structured and unstructured interviews are used; in both cases, emphasis is on obtaining as complete a picture as possible of the technical knowledge and experience of the candidate and of personal characteristics which are essential to consulting.

In some consulting organisations (more frequently in the United States than in Europe) tests are used as aids in selecting new consultants. These include both cognitive tests (designed mainly to measure knowledge) and psychological tests (related to personality, attitudes, interests and motivation). If personality and attitude tests are used, the evaluation of results should be made by a professional psychologist.

Tests can convey useful information about the candidate, but their importance in the choice of consultants should not be overrated. They sometimes provide distorted information because of the ambiance in which the test is administered, or because some tests that are widely used become well known and hence less effective. In general, mature candidates do not like these tests.

Medical examination

A medical examination will be required, as is usual in the case of long-term employment. This will take account of the life-style of consultants, which in most cases is more demanding on the individual's physical and mental fitness, resistance and endurance than many other jobs with a comparable technical content.

Selection

As any new entrant to the profession is to be seen as a potential career consultant who may stay with the organisation for many years, the selection of those who will be offered employment requires very careful evaluation of the applicants, based on all information provided by each applicant himself, reference checking, multiple interviews and, possibly, tests. Managers of consulting organisations should avoid making authoritative decisions on selection without consulting a number of experienced colleagues: every case of recruitment warrants a collective assessment.

27.3 Career development

The great diversity of career structures in consulting firms reflects their different history, size, technical areas covered, consulting modes used, and even personal preferences of the key decision makers. But certain common patterns tend to emerge from this diversity.[2]

In most firms, the consultants progress through four principal grades, or ranks, during their career. Some firms use only two or three grades, while more than four grades are used in some large firms.

Career progression usually implies that the consultant will take on more responsibility, which can be:

- supervisory (team leadership and supervision of assignments);
- promotional (management surveys, negotiation and selling of new assignments);
- managerial (managing organisational units in the firm; function in general and top management);
- technical (directly performing assignments that require particularly experienced and knowledgeable consultants);
- various combinations of these four alternatives.

A typical career structure can be described as follows:

Pre-operating level: trainee (junior consultant)

This level exists only in certain firms. These firms recruit new consultants as trainees (for 6-12 months), whose main task is to master the essential consulting skills as quickly as possible (see chapter 28).

First level: operating consultant (resident consultant, associate, associate consultant, consultant)

This is the actual first level in the career. The operating consultant is the front-line man who does most of the consulting work at client organisations. Every operating consultant has a special field of competence, as a rule in one management function or in special techniques. Normally the consultant would undertake a number of operating assignments in varying situations for a period of 3-5 years before being considered for promotion to the next level.

Second level: supervising consultant (team leader, project manager, senior associate, senior consultant, manager)

The main responsibilities of consultants promoted to this second level include team leadership (e.g. in assignments requiring expertise in general management and involving several functional areas) and supervision of operating consultants (e.g. a marketing supervisor may be in charge of 4-6 different assignments in marketing). A consultant at this level also continues to execute assignments directly if these require a more experienced person. Further responsibilities may include management surveys and the marketing of new assignments.

Third level: principal (manager, survey consultant)

Consultants at this level carry out a number of marketing and middle-management functions. Typically they spend most of their time in promotional work (visiting clients, doing management surveys, planning and negotiating new assignments). Some may be personally in charge of important client assignments; others head organisational units within the firm, or co-ordinate and control a number of client projects.

Fourth level: officer (director, partner, senior partner, vice-president, president)

Senior and top management responsibilities prevail at this superior level. This includes strategy and policy direction and senior management positions in the firm. Consultants at this level are also concerned with practice development, do promotional work with important clients, and may be personally in charge of very complex and important assignments. In most firms they are the owners, but there are firms where the principals (the third level) also belong to the group that owns the firm.

Factors affecting careers

It will be seen that there is a significant relationship between progression in *rank* and *role*. A higher rank means a more difficult role, and more responsibility. This relationship is not the same in all firms. Certain firms prefer a more conservative approach, whereby precisely defined functions are assigned to each rank in the consulting hierarchy. Thus, only a consultant of a higher grade would be used in negotiating with a potential client.

In contrast, many firms are increasingly flexible in deciding what a consultant can and should do irrespective of his rank. For example, a consulting project can be managed by an individual in any of the four principal grades (including the operating consultants), depending on the scope of the project and the capabilities of the individual. These firms encourage young operating consultants to assume responsibility for more difficult jobs and for managing assignments, and thus to expand their capabilities, as soon as possible after joining the firm. Even consultants whose experience is relatively short are expected to demonstrate project managers' abilities and be able to present the results of their work both to the clients and to the supervising consultant.

Career advancement is based on achievement above all. Individuals who cannot demonstrate high achievement are encouraged to move on. If they stayed, they would see many of their younger colleagues advance more rapidly, which inevitably creates jealousies and leads to frustration. It is often emphasised that every young consultant should be regarded and treated as a potential partner, and that career development to partner level should not take longer than from 6 to 12 years.

Such a fast career progression has a positive motivational effect on the consultants and creates a dynamic and competitive working environment.

467

However, a consulting firm that adopts fast career progression as a policy must be prepared to face certain problems:

- if the firm's growth is fast enough, the number of senior positions grows as well and promotions can be fast also, but if growth slows down or stops promotions become difficult;

- some firms have therefore introduced special promotion schemes for competent individuals for whom supervising and managerial jobs are not available;

- an alternative is reorienting the firm to more difficult assignments and thus increasing the demand for senior consultants – this enables the firm to change the overall ratio of operating to senior consultants (for example, instead of employing two seniors for every five operating consultants, the new mix of projects would permit the firm to employ three seniors and thus change the ratio from 5 : 2 to 5 : 3);[3]

- finally, the consultants who leave the firm are often those whose chances of promotion to higher positions are smaller than those of their colleagues.

Staff reviews

There are two reasons why systematic staff reviews (performance assessment) are probably more important in management consulting than in other sorts of organisation:

- the career patterns described above as prevailing in consulting require consultants to develop rapidly and be able to assume a widening range of responsibilities – it is difficult to find jobs for consultants whose growth potential is limited and who will not be able to keep pace with their more dynamic and ambitious colleagues;

- the operational environment in which a consultant works (individual role in an assignment, team leader, supervisor, immediate colleagues) changes frequently, and an operating consultant may be a member of three or more different teams within one year; performance evaluation must therefore be organised for collecting and assessing all information needed for managing the consultants' careers and professional development in this constantly changing work environment.

Thorough evaluation of a new consultant is therefore started during his initial training. Several reports are prepared (described in detail in the next chapter).

The second element in systematic staff evaluation is formal performance reviews at the end of each assignment. These reports are prepared by the team leader or supervisor, discussed with the consultant, and filed in his personnel record.

The third element is periodic performance appraisals, which take place in most consulting organisations once a year, in some organisations every six months.

They are based on reports from all assignments and evaluate performance and competence in areas such as:

- the technical subjects covered;
- consulting methods (diagnosis, etc.);
- team leadership, supervision, co-ordination;
- marketing and client-relations capabilities;
- training and self-development;
- special personal characteristics, interests and talents.

Every periodic performance appraisal must aim to tell, openly and clearly, both the consulting firm and the individual where to focus improvement efforts. If an individual consultant ought to start looking for a career outside consulting, a performance appraisal should reveal this and make an unambiguous recommendation!

Staff turnover

Not all consultants will stay with one firm until retirement. Staff turnover figures are quite high in consulting: an annual turnover of 15-20 per cent is considered as normal, a 5-10 per cent turnover as low. The reasons include:

- different views on how to carry out consulting;
- different views on advancement in careers;
- entrepreneurship (quite a few consultants prefer to start their own consulting practices);
- interest in other than a consulting career (business management, government administration, university careers, politics, etc.).

Large consulting firms tend to have a higher staff turnover than small firms. Many young professionals join these firms in order to gain diversified experience in a relatively short time, without intending to stay in consulting. This is less common in small firms. In addition, small firms try to be more adaptable to the needs and aspirations of individual staff members.

Sole practitioner's career

What, then, is a typical career path of a consultant who has decided to work as a sole practitioner?

Most individuals who start their own consulting business do it, for reasons already known to the reader, after some 8-15 years of practical experience in functional or general management, or after having worked for several years for a consulting firm. Only exceptionally (but more often at the present time than in the past) would they go into independent consulting directly from university. Those who go directly into independent consulting without any previous experience usually set up in special fields where technical knowledge acquired at university is in great demand and businesses are prepared to use technical experts without practical experience.

469

A sole practitioner has no one who will promote him to a more senior position. What normally happens is that, as he becomes more experienced and competent, a sole practitioner is able to undertake more complex and difficult jobs, and also to charge higher fees. Nevertheless, many sole practitioners get into situations where important career decisions have to be faced. For example, they could progress technically and take on more responsible jobs, but this would require giving up personal independence and agreeing to work in a team. One consultant will decide to expand his firm and start employing other consultants. Another will join a larger consulting firm if a senior position is offered to him. A third will reject both these alternatives and look for special assignments requiring a senior expert, but small enough to be undertaken by an individual. The consulting business offers enough opportunities to satisfy a wide range of different career aspirations.

---

[1] The first significant attempt to define these characteristics was made by ACME in the United States. See P. W. Shay: *The common body of knowledge for management consultants* (New York, Association of Consulting Management Engineers, 1974), pp. 41-42. See also G. Lippitt and R. Lippitt: *The consulting process in action* (La Jolla, CA, University Associates, 1978), chapter 7, and B. L. Johnson: *Private consulting* (Englewood Cliffs, NJ, Prentice-Hall, 1982), chapter 1.

[2] There is little published information which permits a comparison of the career patterns in various consulting firms. Interesting information from North American firms can be found in *Management consulting 82* (Boston, MA, Harvard Business School Management Consulting Club, 1981).

[3] This problem is discussed by D. H. Meister in "Balancing the professional service firm", *Sloan Management Review*, Fall 1982.

TRAINING AND DEVELOPING CONSULTANTS 28

The reader knows from chapter 27 that all entrants to the consulting profession should have an excellent educational background and that a great many will also have several years of practical experience. Yet consulting has its own special training and development requirements that are additional to whatever a new consultant may have learned at university, or at business school, and in his former job.

There are three main reasons for this. Firstly, as we have stressed many times in this book, consulting on how to do a job is different from actually doing that job. A new consultant must develop a full understanding of this difference and acquire the skills that are specific to consulting.

Secondly, the breadth and depth of technical knowledge required for advising clients usually exceeds what a new consultant has learned during his studies and previous employment. A new consultant with 5-10 years of business experience may have worked in 2-4 jobs and experienced one or several business and management contexts. This does not always provide him with enough experience for giving the best possible advice to the client. In addition, a new consultant may have to update and upgrade the technical knowledge acquired during university or business school studies.

Thirdly, the new entrant is joining a consulting firm which, it can be assumed, has chosen a particular consulting philosophy and strategy. This will concern issues such as the objectives of consulting, the consulting methods and techniques used, the ways in which clients should participate, and ethical considerations. There is a need to "indoctrinate" the new recruits to make sure that they will learn the consulting firm's particular professional approach, and identify themselves with its philosophy.

However, the consultant's education can never end with the completion of initial training. "Least of all can consultants afford to take the attitude that the old ways of doing things are good enough. Probably no group is more severely challenged by the information explosion than management consultants. Learning must be a life-long job for consultants," wrote E. M. Shays, President of the Institute of Management Consultants in the United States.[1]

How does a consultant learn? What is the most effective way of developing a competent consultant? Like managers, consultants learn from experience above all. This includes the consultant's own direct experience, on assignments in which his task is to deal with problems and situations that provide meaningful learning opportunities. In doing so the consultant also learns from his clients' experiences. In fact, learning from present clients to serve future clients more effectively is a fundamental feature of consulting. Furthermore, the consultant learns from other consultants — his colleagues in a team, his superiors, consultants who worked for the same client before him, and other members of the consulting profession.

Learning on the job, by practising consulting, is therefore the main generally recognised method of learning. This is how most consultants acquired their proficiency in the past, and even at the present time some consultants advocate that on-the-job learning is the only way of becoming competent in consultancy. However, recent experience has shown that learning on the job alone is not enough and that it should be supplemented (but not replaced!) by other learning opportunities. This is the approach that we have adopted in this chapter. Such an approach tends to be supported by professional associations of consultants. For example, the by-laws of the Management Consultants Association in the United Kingdom stipulate that "every new entrant should be provided with adequate formal training before being placed on assignment".

28.1 Training of new consultants

Objectives of training

The overall objective of an initial training programme for consultants is:

To ensure that the consultant has the ability and confidence to carry out assignments in his field of management.

As consulting is not easy, initial training must explain and demonstrate this, but at the same time provide enough guidance to the new entrant for him to start his first assignment confident of his ability and enthusiastic in his determination.

The overall objective quoted above can be broken down into four sub-objectives, as follows:

---

1. To ensure that the consultant can investigate an existing situation and design improvements.

This requires the ability to gather information and analyse it critically, to identify all aspects of the problem, and then to design practical improvements using imagination and creative ability.

> 2. To ensure that he can develop a collaborative relationship with the client, gain acceptance of the proposed changes, and implement change satisfactorily.

The ability to make contacts with people easily, an understanding of factors stimulating or inhibiting change, a sound knowledge of the techniques of communication and persuasion, and good interaction with people during implementation, are vital parts of a consultant's armoury. They are stressed and practised during initial training.

> 3. To ensure proficiency in his field or discipline.

This includes knowledge of all the technical aspects of his field, some of which he may not have encountered in his previous career, and the ability to apply them to a client's problems. At the same time, a consultant must be able to see the problems of his particular functional field in the broader context of an overall management strategy, and relate them to problems of other functional areas and to the environment in which an enterprise operates.

> 4. To satisfy the management of the consulting organisation that he is capable of working independently and under pressure to the required standard.

It would be unrealistic to require new consultants to be able to tackle any difficult assignment immediately after training. Nevertheless, by the end of the initial training period the consultant must have demonstrated to the satisfaction of his seniors his ability to handle a field assignment. At the same time, a systematic evaluation of the trainee's performance should give the consulting organisation enough information about the strengths and weaknesses of the new colleague for his supervisor to be able to help him by proper guidance and coaching during the first operation assignments.

Patterns of initial training

The design of an initial training programme depends on many variables, including the specific needs of individual trainees and the resources of the consulting organisation. The practices of consulting organisations vary. There is a broad range of initial training programmes, from precisely planned and structured programmes to totally informal programmes of undetermined duration. It is not the purpose of this chapter to prescribe one particular pattern for all conditions. There are, however, certain principles which should be reflected in any programme for new consultants and also certain patterns which have given good results in varying situations.

Individualisation. New entrants have different backgrounds in terms of knowledge and experience and different personal characteristics. There should be no uniform initial training programme, although some elements of initial training will be given to every new consultant for obvious reasons. We will show below how the training programme can be individualised without becoming too difficult and expensive for the consulting unit to organise.

Practicality. Some aspects and methods of consulting can be explained and practised during a course, but most of the training has to take the form of practice in carrying out the various steps of a consulting assignment, and in interacting with clients, under the guidance of a senior consultant. The programme must include both the observation of experienced consultants in action and the execution of practical consulting tasks or projects.

Stretching the trainee. The programme should demonstrate that consulting is demanding in time, effort and brainpower, so that the trainee is under no illusion about the responsibilities he has accepted in his newly chosen profession.

Length of programme. Although it could be argued that a new consultant will need several years of experience to become fully competent and be able to operate with little guidance and supervision, it would be impractical, and psychologically unsound, to maintain new consultants in the category of trainees for too long. Assuming normal conditions of recruitment, the period of initial training would not exceed 6 to 12 months.

Basic components of the training programme

The programme of initial training has three basic components:

- training courses for new consultants;
- practical field training at client organisations;
- individual study.

A training course for new consultants will cover those aspects of consulting which have to be given to all trainees, and can be dealt with in a classroom situation, using a variety of training methods as discussed in section 28.3 below. As a rule, this will be a full-time residential course and its total duration may be between 2 and 12 weeks. Large consulting organisations can afford longer courses, and hold them at their own headquarters or training centres. Small consulting organisations may have to send their new members to an external course for management consultants, complementing such a course by a short seminar dealing with their specific problems and work concepts.

Field training is intended to develop a range of practical skills, demonstrate consulting in action, and mould the trainee's attitudes towards his new profession on the basis of his own first-hand experience. In planning this part of the training the consulting organisation enjoys great flexibility, provided it has enough clients willing to receive trainees, and experienced consultants who have the time and the ability to train new colleagues.

Whether the trainee's time spent at a client organisation should be charged to the client is a delicate matter which should be frankly discussed with clients, without imposing arrangements that clients would accept reluctantly. While it is justifiable to ask clients to pay some fee if a trainee's work leads to measurable improvements, it is not reasonable to expect individual clients to bear directly the cost of training new consultants, as this should be a general overhead in the unit's costs. A compromise solution may be found by charging a reduced fee, or a fee paid for only a part of the trainee's time. The same applies to the trainer's time — if the trainer is an operating consultant, time spent on guiding and advising trainees should not be charged to the client.

Individual study is another component which provides for flexibility of training. A new consultant can be asked to fill some gaps in his knowledge by reading professional books and articles, final assignment reports, operating manuals and other documentation.

In an ideal situation these three components of the initial training may be combined and scheduled as follows:

(1) first (introductory) part of the course for new consultants (say between 2 and 9 weeks);

(2) field training (length as necessary and feasible);

(3) second part of the course (say 1 to 3 weeks), including seminars on operating methods, and familiarisation with technical services, people and documentation at the consulting unit's headquarters;

(4) field training continues as appropriate;

(5) no specific period is reserved for individual study — this will be done in parallel with the course and with field training (the consultant may have to make allowance for many overtime hours to be spent on this).

A consulting organisation may, however, find it impossible to follow this schedule for various practical reasons: for example, the number of trainees may not warrant an in-house course, even though no external course is available in the country. The training task may thus become more difficult for everybody concerned and a new entrant will have to pick up much more through individual reading and from discussion with the operating consultant (his field trainer).

The trainer's role

During recruitment and selection, the new consultant meets senior people in the organisation for a short time. He cannot get to know them well, nor can he obtain more than a superficial view of the work a consultant really does. The trainer is the first member of the organisation the new consultant gets to know well. He sets an example of how a consultant behaves, and how he achieves results largely without the authority to impose his ideas. The trainer therefore plays an important part in developing the characteristics that differentiate the consultant from the manager, executive, accountant, or planner. Apart from instilling knowledge, the trainer sets the tone for the new consultant in his work with clients, and helps him to identify with the consulting firm's philosophy and strategy.

The head-office trainer is a senior person with wide experience of consulting and training. He has overall responsibility for the new consultant's training, including the programming of field training. He is in charge of the central training course for new consultants and will give a number of sessions in the course himself. He may visit new consultants during field training to ensure that all is well.

In a central training course for consultant induction, each trainee is viewed as an individual who will spend much of his time as the sole operating consultant on an assignment. His behaviour within the group and ability to join in the common cause is also noted. So are his reactions to the problems and ideas discussed during the course.

The trainee may find it difficult to adjust to the course. His move may involve more than a change of job: incidental domestic problems could be a source of distraction. The trainer does not take a teacher-and-pupil attitude and the atmosphere in the course room is not that of a schoolroom. This point may seem obvious, but a trainer also has to learn to do the job for the first time and may start by being rather a pedant. A trainee should find the trainer a good friend and counsellor on whom he can rely at any time for guidance and help.

The field trainer is an operating consultant with a client. He is already practising in the field in which the new consultant will operate, and arranges for him gradually to take over a part of the assignment. He too must have training capabilities, be sympathetic to the needs of the new consultant, and be able to impart to him enthusiasm for working with a client. In particular, he has the responsibility of ensuring that the new consultant can operate successfully on completion of the training. The field trainer develops a very special relationship with the new consultant. As he will be spending some evenings with him, a strong bond of friendship is usually born, and this may persist for many years after training is completed.

The senior consultant supervising the operating consultant has a minor role to play in field training. Apart from ensuring completion of the programme on time, and approving any training reports, he makes sure that the new consultant is happy in his work and has no worries.

Both the headquarters' trainer and the field trainer have important responsibilities concerning the evaluation of the new consultant.

Evaluation of training

The new consultant's progress in training is carefully watched by those in contact with him and a series of reports is issued. The purpose is to ascertain whether the training is achieving its objectives, propose corrective measures (extension of the training programme, inclusion of new subjects for individual study and the like), and gather information on the strengths and weaknesses of the new member of the unit (this is invaluable to those who will supervise his first assignments). Needless to say, evaluation also helps to improve the training policies and programmes of the consulting unit.

Many consulting organisations use a system of confidential reports in which the trainers (both at head office and in the field) give their personal *appraisal of the trainee*. At least two reports are required:

- one at the end of the head-office training course;
- one at the end of field training.

Additional reports may be required — for example, if the initial training is broken down into several periods, or if the length of field training warrants interim progress reports.

The reports (see an example of a report form in figure 28.1) evaluate the new consultant under a number of headings. The assessments are usually on a numerical scale with supporting comments and examples. The scale can use a range of numbers or letters, a common system being a five- or three-point scale, as follows:

1. Excellent	A. Satisfactory
2. Very good	B. Satisfactory with
3. Standard	reservations
4. Poor	C. Unsatisfactory
5. Unsatisfactory	

The standard against which the new consultant is measured is the standard expected of an operating consultant on his first assignment. The question to be answered is: "On present showing, will he be ready to operate at the end of the training?" Consistency of interpretation of the standard by the central trainer, field trainers and supervisors derives from their common experience and their knowledge of current operating requirements.

The trainers review with the trainee how he is progressing, informally during work and training sessions and in formal discussions which are held when an evaluation report is prepared. The new consultant must be told of his strengths, weaknesses, and any other aspects of his work.

In addition to these discussions, senior members of the consulting organisation interview the new consultant during training. Apart from giving all the participants an opportunity to talk about the work and progress, these interviews ensure that the new consultant becomes a fully integrated member of the organisation. They show that management is interested in him, aware of his progress, and making plans for his assignment after completion of training.

The importance of open criticism and frankness need hardly be stressed. Both the future effectiveness and life of the consulting organisation, and the long-term career prospects of new consultants, depend on the excellent professional work of the individual. Any doubts about a new consultant's ability are not hidden, but are discussed with him and with the seniors in the unit. If the doubts cannot be resolved by the end of the training course, a decision is required on whether the new consultant stays or terminates his employment. On balance,

Management consulting

Figure 28.1 Training report form

TRAINING REPORT (confidential)		Report number	Date
Trainee		Trainer	
Supervisor		Client	

Type of report	Interim report ☐ Final report	Head-office training ☐ Field training

Reporting period	starting date	finishing date	duration in weeks

Description of work performed

Evaluation	A - satisfactory			
(mark x in the appropriate column; comments are required if marked other than satisfactory)		B - satisfactory with reservations		
			C - unsatisfactory	
				Comments
I. Personal attributes				
Intellectual capacity				
Professional conduct				
Physical appearance and bearing				
Initiative and energy				
Person-to-person communication				
Social behaviour				
II. Technical qualities (general)				
Diagnostic skills				
Preparing suggestions				
Techniques of introducing change				
Verbal reporting				
Written reports				
III. Specific functional or sectorial skills				

478

Figure 28.1 (continued)

Evaluation	A	B	C	Comments
IV. General observations Attendance and punctuality				
Course contribution (as individual)				
Course contribution (to group work)				
Contribution to field work				
Meeting set deadlines				
Speed and accuracy				

Overall assessment by the trainer

Supervisor's comments

Recommendations concerning first assignments and future training

Other comments or decisions

termination of employment at this early moment may be the better choice, both for the new consultant and for the organisation. However, termination should be an exception — that is, if the initial selection of candidates is carried out in a competent manner.

At the end of the total initial training programme it is useful to draw conclusions on the further training needs of the new consultant and on the best ways of meeting them (by giving preference to certain types of assignments at the beginning, by further individual study, etc.)

The design and execution of the training programme also require evaluation. Several ways of evaluating are open to trainers, and particularly the head-office trainer who has responsibility for the whole course. Trainees may be asked to comment on the course in the usual way. These can be general or specific comments on the content of individual exercises and the performance of each trainer. Care is necessary to preserve confidence — trainees may be reluctant to comment if they feel that adverse criticism may be turned against them later. However, the feedback to individual trainers can spur them to improve their sessions.

Comment and criticism may be obtained from senior consultants responsible for the early assignments. They may find the new consultants lacking in specific skills; these deficiencies may be due to omissions, or poor coverage of certain subjects, either in the initial head-office training course or during the field training. The new consultant should also be asked, both during and after field training, whether he found the practical preparation for the first assignments adequate.

28.2 Subjects covered by initial training

Although we have emphasised the individual character of initial training for new consultants, some general guidance on programme content can be given. It concerns the main areas to be covered in most cases, assuming that the planners of these training programmes make the appropriate adjustments for the individual needs of the trainees. In doing so, they will also decide on how to use the basic components of training (training course, field, on-the-job training and individual study) to deal with specific subject areas of the total programme.

While there are considerable differences in the professional profiles of new consultants when they join the consulting organisation, attempts have been made to summarise attributes which should be common to competent management consultants working with different consulting organisations. This has led to the development by some professional associations of a "body of knowledge" for management consultants; [2] some work has also been done on developing model course curricula in management consulting. [3]

By and large, the training of management consultants has to cover the various topics listed below. This list of topics is not meant to serve as a standard curriculum. Firstly, as already mentioned, different entrants have different backgrounds and training needs. Secondly, consulting organisations often find it more effective to provide training in stages: initial training is confined to topics essential for beginning to operate under the guidance of a more experienced team leader or supervisor. Further topics are dealt with later, once the new consultant has acquired some direct consulting experience and starts being involved in the marketing of services, assignment management, and other functions. This will be discussed in section 28.4.

The subject areas listed below also include some points which were mentioned in chapter 27 under the personal characteristics, or qualities, of a good consultant. Both the central course and the field component of training should provide opportunities and time for improving characteristics such as good judgement, analytical and problem-solving ability, skill in interpersonal relations, and ability to communicate and persuade. The training programmes will also aim at improving other qualities such as self-confidence, integrity and independence. These cannot be the subject of a particular session or exercise, but are an overriding objective for the trainers' and trainee's common efforts. It should be noted too that the demands of the initial training programme must not be unrealistic: most young consultants will need several years of experience to acquire fully the qualities that characterise a competent member of the profession.

Orientation to management consulting

- Nature and objectives of consulting; consultants and clients; consulting and change
- Basic consulting styles and approaches
- Types of consulting organisations and services
- Management consulting as a career
- Organisation of the profession
- Professional ethics in consulting work
- Historical development, present position and future perspectives of consulting

Overview of the consulting process

- Framework and stages of a consulting assignment (project)
- Entry
- Diagnosis
- Action planning
- Implementation
- Termination

Consulting skills I: Analytical and problem-solving

- Systematic approach to problem solving in management and business
- Methods for diagnosing organisational performance
- Data collection and recording techniques

- Techniques for data and problem analysis
- Techniques for developing action proposals
- Techniques of creative thinking
- Techniques for evaluating and selecting alternatives
- Techniques for measuring and assessing results achieved by consulting projects

Consulting skills II: Behavioural and communication

- Human and behavioural aspects of the consulting process and the consultant-client relationship
- Behavioural roles of the consultant and the client
- The client's psychology
- Consulting and culture
- Techniques for diagnosing attitudes, human relations, behaviour and management styles in organisations
- Techniques for generating and assisting change in people and in organisations
- Communication and persuasion techniques
- Team work and the conduct of meetings
- Using training in consulting; assessing training needs; designing training programmes
- Management and staff training techniques
- Courtesy and etiquette in consultant-client relations
- Effective report writing

Consulting skills III: Marketing and managing assignments

- Principles of marketing in professional services
- Marketing techniques
- Proposals to clients (planning, preparation, presentation)
- Consulting contracts and their negotiation
- Fee setting
- Structuring, planning and staffing an assignment (project)
- Managing and controlling an assignment
- Reporting to the client and to the consulting organisation

Managing and developing a consulting organisation

- Considerations in establishing a consulting organisation
- Economics and strategy of a consulting organisation
- Legal form and organisational structure

- Organisational culture and management styles
- Recruiting, developing and remunerating consultants
- Financial management
- Operational management and control; performance monitoring
- Internal administration

Theory and practice of management

As mentioned, in some cases the initial training of a new consultant will also include selected management subjects. Consulting organisations increasingly recruit specialists with an excellent technical background but a rather narrow perspective and limited knowledge of the business and management environment. Such a new recruit may require training to relate his work to other aspects and areas of management and to understand the economic, social, political and cultural contexts in which he will operate. Since computers are more and more used both by clients and by consulting firms themselves, many new recruits, including those coming from business practice, will require some training in computer applications.

28.3 Training methods

Training course methods

The training of new consultants uses a variety of training methods, with emphasis on participative methods, and on those where the trainee can adjust the pace of learning to his capabilities.

Subjects which involve mainly the imparting of knowledge may require some lecturing, but this should be supplemented by discussions, practical exercises and other techniques. In many cases, lecturing can be replaced by the reading of texts (e.g. on the origin and history of consulting, on types of specialisation of consulting organisations), or by using audio-visual learning packages (e.g. videotapes). Subjects involving skill improvement require techniques that permit practice. This can be done to some extent in a training course by using properly chosen learning situations and exercises.

Arthur Turner has summarised his experience with methods suitable to training in process consulting skills in this way:

Internal development programmes need to draw on knowledge in such fields as industrial sociology, political science, organisational behaviour, psychology, social psychology, interpersonal communication. But such programmes need to emphasise skill more than knowledge, through discussion and role-playing sessions in which the skills are acquired through practice, reflection, and experimentation. The discussion should not be about what you *should know*, nor even about what you *should do*, but about what you *are doing*, here and now, and about what you have done and will be doing, in specific interactions with members of a client organisation. In other words, process-skill development sessions should primarily consist of open discussion among colleagues of specific client case situations, supplemented by role plays of actual and desired consultant-client interactions. The sessions should be led by someone expert at facilitating this kind of experiential learning, who can bring to bear, when relevant, simple but powerful behavioural concepts to assist in understanding past events and to stimulate useful experimentation with new approaches.

The three most relevant skills to develop for an effective consulting process are, in my opinion: diagnosing behaviour, listening, and behaving authentically.

Diagnostic skill is developed by examining and discussing what is taking place within client organisations. These discussions develop hypotheses that can be tested in subsequent client contacts. In such discussions and experiments with different approaches, consultants may discover, perhaps to their discomfort, that effective diagnosis of behaviour is often in part an intuitive and not just a logical process.

Listening of a very special kind is an essential consulting process skill. Good consultants learn how to listen with understanding to what is meant as well as to what is said, to feelings as well as to facts, to what is hard to admit and not just easy to say. There is no way to develop this skill except by practising it, with the benefit of feedback from a friendly audience which has heard the same words and observed the same non-verbal signals. It is easy to tell consultants how they ought to listen and have them agree that this is desirable. But to help them to learn that they do not listen as well as they think and then to produce a worthwhile improvement in this ability, in practice, requires a series of carefully designed and effectively conducted workshop sessions. It does not happen all at once.

Behaving authentically needs to be seen as an equally necessary skill. Consultants need to be able to be themselves, to behave according to their own values, and sometimes to confront clients with unwelcome facts and opinions. Again, small group discussions and role plays of actual experiences provide the best setting in which to develop the skill of understanding oneself as well as others, and of usefully and constructively expressing one's own point of view even when the other person may not want to hear it.[4]

Case studies can introduce the new consultant to various consulting situations and provide good material for discussion; the consulting organisation should be in a position to prepare its own case studies, or histories, from previous assignments.

Practical exercises can lead the trainee consultant through various common consulting practices, such as:

- effective speaking and persuasion;
- investigational interviewing;
- analysing company accounts and preparing ratios;
- discussion leading and control;
- written communication;
- methods charting;
- designing systems and procedures;
- work measurement.

Role-playing provides an excellent way of introducing consulting practice into learning situations. It takes place in a controlled situation, i.e. in a classroom, where mistakes are used to teach and have no disastrous consequences. For example, as a large part of a consultant's work on assignment consists of presenting proposals to clients and their staff, it is useful to organise role-playing exercises in:

- interviewing staff to obtain facts about an assignment problem;

— dealing with awkward situations or complaints from staff about proposed changes;
— persuading members of the client's staff to accept a new method of operation;
— explaining to the client conclusions drawn from his financial reports;
— presenting an assignment report to the client;
— dealing with embarrassing questions from the client or members of his staff.

Role-playing exercises need to be realistic, and test the participants under conditions as near as possible to those found in everyday life. Feedback after the exercise is essential. This suggests four requirements:

● a trainee himself playing the part of a consultant;
● other trainees playing client or other roles;
● at least two trainees acting as observers, with a brief to watch for certain features of the players' behaviour;
● the preparation of thorough briefs for all participants.

Time is allowed for briefing the role-players and observers, and for the absorption of the material including the preparation of any figures. After the role-playing, observers comment and a general discussion leads to the identification of lessons to be learned. Aids such as tape recorders or closed-circuit television may be used in this connection.

Field-training methods

In field training, the consultant learns mainly by doing practical diagnostic, problem-solving and project work. As this is carried out in a real life situation, which may be very sensitive to errors and *faux pas*, the trainee will be guided and even controlled by the trainer in more detail than might be necessary in another situation. It may not, however, be easy to find situations in which the new consultant could practise not only a few, but a wide range of the techniques that should eventually make up his consulting kit.

Here again, feedback on what the consultant did and how he did it is an essential dimension of training. The team leader or supervisor acting as field trainer must provide this feedback, creating an atmosphere in which any aspect of work and behaviour can be openly discussed without embarrassing the new colleague. The whole assignment team may participate in such discussions.

Role-playing can be used to rehearse activities before the "live" show later. In this form of role-playing, the new consultant and trainer rehearse in the office or at home in the evening, and are able to anticipate and correct snags.

In certain cases a whole consulting project can be designed and used primarily as a training experience. This has been done in external courses for management consultants as well as in various types of course for managers and students of management. Such a simulation exercise can be very close to an actual situation. Yet the differences should not be lost from sight: for example, if the client agrees to the consulting project, but does not pay a normal fee for it, this may affect the participation and attitudes of the client staff when working with the trainee consultant.

28.4 Further training and development of consultants

As mentioned at the beginning of this chapter, in management consulting life-long education is a must. This idea is not new. Many consultancy organisations have gained and maintained their excellent reputations precisely because of their continual efforts to upgrade the competence of staff.

Principal directions of consultants' development

Most staff development activities in consulting organisations fall under one or more of the following four areas.

Upgrading functional proficiency. Keeping abreast of developments and making himself more knowledgeable and competent in his own field together form the basis of an operating consultant's further development. Many training and development activities in a consulting organisation are geared to this objective.

Mastering new fields. A consultant may learn new subjects complementary to his main field in order to broaden his ability to undertake assignments touching on several management functions, perhaps with a view to becoming an all-round consultant, able to lead teams of mixed functional specialists, to act as adviser on general management problems, and to undertake diagnostic surveys of business companies and other organisations. Another reason for learning new subjects may be the consulting organisation's intention to become active in new technical fields. Many consulting organisations prefer to transfer their more dynamic consultants, familiar with the organisation's philosophy and practices, to these new activities rather than staff them with new recruits.

Upgrading behavioural and process-consulting skills. Experience has amply demonstrated that initial training of a new consultant is just a first step in developing the know-how needed to perceive, diagnose, understand and influence human behaviour in organisations. Further training of all consultants (without any exception) therefore deals with the *how* of management consulting as it relates to people, including effective client-consultant relations, the consultant's role in organisational change, and the process-consulting skills required for various institutions.

Preparing for career development. This includes personal development needed for the positions of team leaders, supervisors, division heads, partners and other senior positions concerned with management and business expansion. Career advancement carries with it the need to use a broader approach and develop technical competence in several fields.

Organisation and methods of further development

There are certain features in consulting practice which make further training and development difficult to organise. For example, most consultants in the same discipline are geographically dispersed on individual assignments. To arrange a technical discussion may require a special organisational effort. Furthermore, the highly individualised character of many consulting assignments encourages consultants to become individualists, and this creates a constant problem in transferring effective work experiences from one consultant to another.

Nevertheless, the profession also has many features which facilitate the consultant's development. A consultant's energy and time are much less absorbed by routine matters and established procedures than those of a manager involved in the same technical field. He can approach every new assignment as a challenging exercise where innovation is both possible and desirable. He can thus refine his method virtually continually and is never short of opportunities for the practical application of ideas and suggestions found in the literature or other sources. Furthermore, a consultant learns a great deal from any client organisation, but to reinforce his learning he must compare, generalise, conceptualise and try to apply a new, more effective approach to successive assignments. He has to avoid the pitfall of mechanically applying past solutions to new situations. Clearly, most of the learning from experience, including the consultant's own and his colleagues' experience, as well as the clients' experience, takes place on the job: it is learning by doing and by observing how others do. It should, however, be enhanced by other learning opportunities and approaches.

Professional guidance by senior consultants. As we know, supervising consultants and team leaders, among others, are responsible for the development of operating consultants who report to them. They provide guidance when examining work progress and discussing solutions proposed by the operating consultant. Such discussions can easily be broadened to inform the operating consultant of experience from other assignments, or techniques used by colleagues. A major feature of guidance by senior consultants is that it should help operating consultants to develop their personal characteristics and communication skills. Discussions should be organised within the assignment teams on experience gained from the consulting process, and used for staff development on a regular basis.

Seminars and conferences. Short seminars and conferences for professional staff are organised in many consulting organisations. There may be an annual conference which deals with technical and methodological topics useful to all consultants, as well as policy and administrative matters. Seminars may be organised in functional divisions, on a regional basis, or in other ways. There are also various external seminars on management and consulting topics from which consultants might benefit. Such services are available from consultants' associations, management institutes, and in some countries also from private consultants who concentrate on training other consultants.

Information to consulting staff. While dissemination of information by itself does not guarantee training and development (e.g. information may be ignored or misunderstood), it is a basic input for learning in the consulting organisation. A properly organised system of information and documentation should supply operating consultants with facts and ideas which they should know and, if appropriate, apply in their assignments. Additional information may be forthcoming as a result of a consultant's membership of a professional association,

Reading. Consultants have to acquire the habit of reading the main professional periodicals, technical papers, important new publications and internal consulting reports relevant to their field.

Research and development assignments. Special project assignments, such as developing a new line of consulting, or preparing an operating manual based on the unit's past experiences, are excellent learning opportunities for senior staff members.

Training others. One of the best methods of self-development is training other people. Consultants have many opportunities to do this, either for the client's personnel during assignments, or at the consulting organisation's training centre, or as part-time teachers at management institutes and schools.

Training for supervisory functions. Promotion to the role of supervisor usually takes place after several years in an operating role. Some experience of the role is gained by seeing seniors in action, and by guiding new consultant trainees. Training on promotion is usually quite short and is provided by experienced seniors who happen to be good trainers. Training is given partly in formal sessions at head office and partly with experienced seniors in action. Head-office training and briefing require about three weeks, while training with an experienced senior may extend over some months. During this time the promoted consultant works largely on his own, with only occasional guidance and advice from his more experienced colleague.

Planning and budgeting

The diversity of individual consultants' career paths and training needs, as well as the desire to be flexible in meeting current clients' requirements, make it difficult to plan staff development and to observe what has been planned. Yet some planning is useful.

Some consulting firms use indicative standards showing the amount of formal training which, on average, a staff member would undergo in one calendar year: for example, between 40 and 60 hours of formal training. A corresponding budget can then be worked out, bearing in mind whether the training will be arranged internally or externally. As a rule, the cost of training per staff member will be higher in comparison to the cost of training per manager or staff member in many other sectors.

Individual planning is even more important. It is useful to establish training objectives which reflect career objectives and against which the consultant can measure his progress. In particular, such training objectives should be defined for the first years of operating, based on the evaluation made at the end of the initial training programme, and the subsequent periodical performance reviews. While some flexibility in deciding on participation in specific training events will always be required, training must not constantly be put off in order to cope with the current workload.

In consulting more than in many other occupations the individual bears the main responsibility for his own development. The consultant's professional development is self-development above all, and the results achieved will depend mainly on a person's ambition, determination, perseverance, and intellectual capabilities. This is self-evident to the sole practitioner, who knows very well that he takes full responsibility for his own future. However, a member of a consulting firm working on jobs assigned to him by his management can also show a great deal of initiative and interest in achieving his career goals and training objectives, and can use every opportunity for improving his competence. Thus, successful staff development in a well-managed consulting organisation is the result of a joint effort on the part of both the management and the individual concerned.

[1] E. M. Shays: "Learning must be a life-long job for consultants", in *Journal of Management Consulting*, Vol. 1, No. 2, 1983. The article provides a good summary of current thinking in the profession on further training and development of management consultants.

[2] The first important attempt was made by ACME, which published its common body of knowledge for management consultants in 1957. The Institute of Management Consultants in the United States has developed a body of knowledge for consultants who apply for accreditation by the Institute.

[3] For example, a conference on educating management consultants held in Salt Lake City, Utah, in February 1985 agreed on a "model management consulting course outline". See J. Owen Cherrington and K. D. Stocks: "Master plan for teaching consultants", in *Journal of Management Consulting*, Vol. 2, No. 3, 1985.

[4] A technical note provided by Arthur Turner.

THE CONSULTING PROFESSION IN DEVELOPING COUNTRIES 29

Our book is addressed to management consultants world-wide, in both industrialised and developing countries. However, the less developed countries face certain specific problems and constraints that affect the growth of their own consulting profession, and the ways in which local consultants acquire skills and expertise. Numerous references to consulting in developing countries have been made in earlier chapters. This chapter gives an overview of the state of the art of management consulting in developing countries and attempts to outline some action proposals for strengthening the local consulting profession.

29.1 Demand and supply

There are three main reasons which justify the creation and promotion of a management consulting profession in developing countries. Firstly, progress towards self-reliance involves, inter alia, the establishment of local professional services able to reduce dependence on foreign expertise. Secondly, no one is better placed than local professionals for adapting internationally available management know-how to specific conditions in each country. Thirdly, there is a significant financial reason: reducing the use of expensive foreign consultants permits reductions in the cost of the consultancy components of many projects, saves foreign exchange, and makes consulting services accessible to local clients, including small businessmen.

These three reasons are important and generally recognised. Nevertheless, the growth of management consulting in developing countries has been slow, slower than the growth of certain other professions, such as engineering consulting, architecture or accountancy.

Only in a few countries, such as Brazil, Egypt, India, Indonesia, Nigeria and the Philippines, is there the nucleus of a local management consulting profession; this is due mainly to the existence of a dynamic industrial sector, the availability of funds for financing consulting, and good-quality higher education facilities. In most developing countries there may be a few individuals or small firms, and a consulting unit in a local management or productivity centre, offering a limited range of management consulting services, but not an organised profession able to meet diverse needs of local management.

Clearly, demand for management consulting in a country reflects the level of industrialisation and economic development reached, and the complexity of managerial and administrative problems faced by the private and the public sectors. The need for efficiency and for meeting higher performance standards looms large among these factors: where there is no competition and no pressure for efficiency, there tend to be fewer opportunities for consulting assignments.

A considerable share of the demand for consulting in developing countries has been created by development projects, most of which are in the public sector. However, often it is not the government but the donor or lending agency which determines the need for an important consulting assignment to be carried out as part of a project design and implementation. As a rule, this demand for intervention by management consultants is at quite a sophisticated level (e.g. organisational design of a new enterprise, restructuring of a ministry, or effective scheduling and co-ordination of operations in building a power station). Many of these consulting projects are beyond the capabilities of the few local consultants, therefore foreign consultants have to be brought in to do the job. As a result, many agencies and enterprises in developing countries exhibit a preference for foreign consulting firms. In turn, consultants from developed countries regard the developing world as an important market for their services. In certain cases, a limited participation of local consultants in these projects is foreseen; to cover this, various regulations have been promulgated by several governments.

This has been, in a nutshell, the typical management consulting scene in developing countries in the last 10-15 years. The situation described has created a "chicken-and-egg" problem for the developing countries' management consultants. The assignments that are available exceed their competence in most cases, but how can local consultants increase their competence if assignments that provide learning opportunities go to foreign consultants? On the other hand, local management consultants (both private and from government-owned management institutes or productivity centres) can tackle the less sophisticated problems faced by local small businesses and some public enterprises, but in these circles the need for consulting and the benefits to be drawn from successful assignments are often poorly understood. If a consultant is brought in, this may be regarded as a favour to the consultant, not an effective service to management.

29.2 Special problems faced by consultants

The management consulting scene differs from country to country; even in some of the so-called least developed countries there are individuals and teams capable of carrying out excellent assignments. Certain problems whose existence inhibits consulting are, however, fairly common in these countries.

Demonstrating usefulness

In developing countries, many businessmen and managers do not understand why they should turn to a consultant and how a person who is not employed by the organisation can be of any use in solving business problems. There is no established tradition of using external experts. In autocratic cultures, administrators and managers are used to receiving orders from their superiors and giving orders to their subordinates, not to receiving independent advice on the course of action to take. The age of the consultant may also present a problem in cultures where older persons enjoying higher social status are not supposed to receive advice from younger persons. In addition, there is a confidence problem: businessmen are not sure whether or not information conveyed to a consultant will eventually become available to tax collectors or some other government service. In general, there is little experience with professional ethics.

Meetings with businessmen to explain the nature and advantages of consulting are certainly useful and can be organised by consultants' associations (if any), management institutions, employers' associations, chambers of commerce, or government departments. However, it is crucial to demonstrate in practice how consultants operate. Businessmen and managers should be able to hear from their peers, and preferably go and see with their own eyes, what a local consultant was able to achieve. Of course, achievement is more than a report — the example must be an assignment that included implementation and produced measurable results, such as increased sales, improved maintenance with resulting savings, or a joint venture in which foreign technology was adapted and put into effective operation locally.

An organised marketing effort is required to make such cases known, with the agreement of the client involved. Employers' organisations can be most helpful in publicising successful assignments to their members. Interfirm comparison techniques may be used, pointing out improvements that led to increased performance in companies whose performance indicators are being compared with those of other firms.[1]

Offering an effective service package

In deciding what services to offer to potential clients, a consultant in a developing country should be guided by two basic criteria:

- what service he or his team will be able to deliver;
- what service will be regarded as most helpful by the client.

The first criterion is self-evident, but its application may cause difficulties if an inexperienced consultant is not in a position to ascertain what tasks are within his competence and what tasks are too difficult for him. Indeed, some young consultants tend to overrate good education and underrate the impact of experience on the competence of the consultant. Experience is particularly important in unstructured and complex management situations for which little guidance is found even in the best textbooks. Much management consulting actually deals with issues that belong to the art of managing, and experience is necessary for finding and implementing the best solution. This may be one of the reasons why the advancement of management consulting in the developing countries has been less rapid than that of consulting in engineering, where a good education and solid knowledge of scientific principles and methods make it possible to carry out effective consulting with less experience than is necessary for consulting on how to manage complex organisations and how to solve their interdisciplinary problems.

The second criterion is often not properly considered by management consultants, who tend to offer what they like doing, not what makes life easier for the manager. For example, many organisations in developing countries are not interested in getting assistance in a narrow area only (e.g. in training supervisors or salesmen), but need complex help which may include advice on legislation, taxation, environmental protection, technology transfer, licensing, production organisation, product design or testing, credit, export, use of foreign exchange, management development and other matters. Most management consultants are not organised, or sufficiently well connected with other professionals, to provide such an assistance package. Yet even in consulting in industrialised countries a great deal has changed in the last ten years, and many consulting firms try to offer more than "pure" management consulting.

There is also the problem of the methodology used. Many assignments end with the consultant writing a report which is never implemented. Therefore consultants participate in the implementation of their proposals in only a small number of assignments; this severely curtails the opportunities for learning from the client and from one's own mistakes. Furthermore, participative or process consulting is rarely used. Many clients participate insufficiently in consulting assignments carried out in their organisations, and the consultant-client interaction remains relatively limited.

Serving the social sectors

As already mentioned in sections 1.3 and 5.3, management consultants in all countries tend to be increasingly called upon to help to solve the specific administrative, managerial, training and efficiency problems in social development programmes and organisations. This area has acquired a special dimension in the developing countries. However, the opportunities to use local consultants, and to create consulting services (external and internal) that are specialised and trained in social sector work, are far from being utilised. There are many open questions. For example, there may be some scope for "barefoot consultants" working with rural communities and in the informal sector. However, if classic management consulting is too sophisticated and unsuitable, what should be the profile, education, job specialisation, work methods and career path of the right candidate for this job? What is an effective package of services? How should this type of consultancy be organised and remunerated? These questions are waiting for answers.

Collaborating with foreign consultants

The work done by foreign consultants provides a wide range of opportunities for developing the local management consulting profession. Unfortunately, many of these opportunities are missed. Some foreign consultants are not keen to train developing countries' consultants, whom they regard as future competitors. In contrast, the better management consulting firms intervening in developing countries do not share this view and regard the local consultants as their allies and partners. Some of these firms have established local offices in several developing countries where they increasingly employ local professional staff, or have agreed on collaborative arrangements with independent local consulting firms (see also section 26.5).

Several governments and donor agencies either have adopted procedures by which foreign consultants have to team up with local consultants in every assignment, or decide case by case whether such a partnership is feasible and desirable. This approach has certainly created favourable conditions for employing local consultants and for learning from foreign consultants.

The real benefits drawn from collaboration depend on a number of factors. There are cases where, to satisfy the legislator, the local consultant is only a man of straw, or an agent who takes care of local arrangements and government contacts. Often local consultants are assigned simple and repetitive tasks from which they learn very little. Therefore joint projects, joint ventures and any other arrangements must be designed, not only to meet the legal and other formal requirements, but also to reflect a strategy for strengthening the local consulting partner by ways and means which have been discussed between the two partners and found to be fully acceptable by both of them.

Enhancing ethical standards

In making itself more professional, management consulting in developing countries is often confronted with ethical problems. As there are many young consultants with little experience, they often lack role models with which they could compare their own competence, behaviour and performance standards. Some young consultants tend to overestimate their own capabilities and misrepresent themselves when offering services to clients.

In some countries there are also "professionals" of dubious technical competence and integrity, who take advantage of the fact that many local managers and administrators lack experience in choosing, supervising and evaluating consultants. These individuals view consulting as an easy way of earning their living.

Many consultants need to increase their self-discipline in working with client organisations, respecting agreed timetables and deadlines, and helping the client to obtain full benefit from the assignment.

Clients have a contribution to make to consulting ethics, too. Late payment and even the failure to pay for contracted consultancy services quite frequently put consultants in difficulties. Local management consultants in an East African country report that on average they are unable to collect up to 20 per cent of the fees, while some less cautious firms collect hardly more than 50 per cent. This shows that certain clients attach little value to the consultant's advice and see nothing dishonest in refusing to pay, or in delaying payment as long as possible. Another problem is the use of unfair practices in choosing consultants, in particular if certain clients apply criteria other than the consultant's competence and the quality of his proposal.

Strengthening institutional and policy support

As the management consulting profession grows, it needs to organise itself in an association, not only to speak with one voice when dealing with the government and defending the consultants' common interests, but also to establish and promote a code of ethics, separate wheat from chaff and eliminate those who do not belong to the profession, educate new consultants to adopt a professional approach and help to organise their technical training.

In many developing countries an important role in promoting management training, research and consulting has been played by national management centres or institutes. Some of these institutions have taken a useful initiative by establishing consulting units and organising training programmes for new consultants, including those who want to start an independent practice, or are employed in government consulting or organisation and methods services. A management institute can encourage the establishment of a consultants' association and help it in its formative period, as did, for example, the Centre for Management Development in Nigeria.

Policy support for the growth of national consulting capabilities is required from governments and local business circles. Government and business should not have conflicting views on the usefulness and real potential of a local consulting profession and on the conditions under which this profession can grow. The policy framework to be established includes, in particular:

● promoting legislation facilitating the establishment and operation of local consulting services;

● applying fair policies for remunerating local consultants (this relates both to the fees paid and to the salaries of consultants employed in governmental management development and consulting units);

● encouraging the involvement of local consultants in assignments that have to be managed by more experienced foreign consultants;

● removing any other policies and practices that might discriminate against less experienced, though basically sound, local management consultants, firms or individuals;

● evaluating the local consultants' services objectively, and making it clear that low-quality service is not acceptable and cannot be justified by limited experience.

As many consulting assignments in developing countries are carried out as part of technical assistance loans and projects, the policies of international and bilateral aid agencies have considerable impact on the growth of the consulting profession. The World Bank, the ILO, the regional development banks and other agencies have made it their policy to encourage the use of local management consultants for jobs that are within these consultants' competence (in association with consultants from industrialised countries if necessary). This creates both work and learning opportunities. In addition, the training and development of local management consultants, and assistance to the emerging profession, has been the objective of a number of technical assistance projects aimed at strengthening management in the less developed countries.[2]

29.3 Approaches to training and development

Most individuals who have started consulting in developing countries need to increase technical knowledge and expertise in their areas of intervention. This requires a sufficient number of diversified learning opportunities and a systematic effort to develop consultants both on the job and through formal training.

Sources of recruitment

Whether they are recruited by national management institutions or by private consulting firms, the new consultants should as a minimum possess a good degree in management or a related field and a few years of practical experience in a developing country. Education at excellent foreign universities or business schools is not enough for entering consulting direct; it does not prepare the individual to face the realities in a developing country, and for adapting management know-how to local culture. That is why local practical experience is essential.

Training courses for new consultants

A new consultant should pass through an individualised training programme before he starts operating. Every consultant needs to attend a course or seminar on consulting of the type described in chapter 28. Many consultants will also need further training in their area of operation (e.g. marketing), or for broadening their knowledge of human, business and environmental issues.

Training courses for management consultants are available at management centres in several developing countries, at some other institutions specialising in management training for developing countries, and in international management consulting firms.

Training cum consulting

Many young professionals get into management consulting through training. They start consulting as trainers in a local management centre and, if the centre is keen to make its own programmes more relevant to the practitioners' needs, these trainers get increasingly involved in in-plant projects carried out by the participants, and in follow-up advice to participants who have completed the course.

Many demands for consulting assignments are actually a result of managers' participation in workshops and seminars. The trainer who gets such requests can start responding by undertaking simple assignments, dealing with rather narrow management problems or special techniques. He can tackle more complex assignments (individually or in a team) later on, after having undertaken a number of simple assignments as a follow-up to the courses taught.

The ILO and other technical assistance agencies encourage combined use of consulting and training in the projects they carry out in the developing countries. Thus the local trainers involved in these projects develop both training and consulting skills. After having practised training for several years, some of these young professionals specialise fully in consulting (but continue to carry out training as appropriate), while others stay primarily in training (but do some consulting as well). Experience shows that while combining consulting with training is a useful and increasingly applied approach in all countries (see section 1.5), in developing countries this appears to be the best approach to building up effective services to managers and to developing the skills of local professionals.

Using practitioners as part-time consultants

Where there is a shortage of cadres who could become full-time consultants, it may be possible to involve some competent managers and administrators in consulting activities by associating them with local consulting organisations on a part-time basis. This approach will help in training the younger consultants. In addition, some part-time consultants may decide to choose consulting as their full-time occupation.

Learning from foreign consultants

Several references to the role of foreign consultants were made in the previous paragraphs. It should be stressed that learning from foreign consultants does not occur automatically and that learning opportunities need to be carefully chosen, designed and supervised. For example, if there is a shortage of senior local consultants from whose work the new entrants to the profession could learn, their role can be played by senior foreign consultants, on condition that they are able and willing to adapt their intervention methods to the local environment, and guide and counsel the younger colleague to facilitate his learning.

Involvement in one or a few joint projects does not ensure that the developing country's consulting firm will have access to the broad spectrum of competencies that normally exist in an experienced and well-established consultancy. This spectrum includes competencies required for marketing and managing consulting, in addition to those needed for the execution of assignments. That is why a longer-term arrangement may be advisable, in which an experienced unit from a developed country accepts responsibility for transferring a wide range of skills through joint projects, and for helping to build up a local consulting unit.[3] This transfer can be organised in several stages, aiming at gradual enhancement of competence and sophistication in accordance with the changing needs of local industrial and managerial practice.

---

[1] See, for example, C. Guthrie: *Interfirm comparison and business clinics in road transport* (Geneva, International Labour Office, 1985, mimeographed).

[2] For example, ILO has co-operated with the Government of India on strengthening the local consulting profession and developing a strategy for improving the consultants' intervention methods. See A. Turner: "Management consulting in India", in *Business India*, June 7-20, 1982.

[3] Many useful ideas can be found in the *Discussion paper on the development of the local consulting profession in developing countries* (Washington, DC, World Bank, 1984), irrespective of the fact that this paper deals primarily with engineering consulting.

APPENDICES

THE CLIENT'S TEN COMMANDMENTS

If you are a user of management consultant services, or a potential user, you may wish to glance through this appendix. The Ten Commandments summarise, in telegraphic form, the critical points of which you need to be aware. Consulting produces good results if consultants are competent in serving clients and clients in using consultants!

---

1. Learn about consulting and consultants!
2. Define your problem!
3. Define your objective!
4. Choose your consultant!
5. Develop a joint programme!
6. Participate actively!
7. Involve the consultant in implementation!
8. Monitor progress!
9. Evaluate the results and the consultant!
10. Beware of dependence on consultants!

Now, let us look at the meaning of each Commandment.

1. Learn about consulting and consultants!

Management consulting is a young but dynamic and rapidly developing profession. You can be sure that you will find a consultant for any business or management problem that comes to your mind. But who are these consultants? How do they work? Are they really as good as one often hears? You want to get replies to these questions. Do not wait until the last moment before recruiting a consultant! Find out about consulting and consultants, try to become a well-informed client who knows the management consulting scene!

- This book is also intended for clients. It describes how consultants operate (especially parts I and II, and selected chapters in part III), market services (chapter 22), charge for services (chapter 23), and manage assignments (chapter 24). Of course, you may like to see other publications (appendix 11).

- Reading a book is not enough. Speak with business friends, follow management and business periodicals, attend meetings of a management association, ask for information from the consultants' own associations, be alert to news on consulting!

- It is essential to know who is who. Try to collect information on consultants who may interest you: what is their speciality and approach, for whom have they worked, what is their reputation, are their fees within your reach?

2. Define your problem!

The purpose of consulting is to help clients in solving their management and business problems. If you have no problem, you do not need a consultant. Therefore you should be convinced that your organisation does have a problem which warrants a consulting assignment.

- Define your problem as precisely as possible: what is or could go wrong? What do you want to improve? Why do you need a consultant — are you sure that you and your own people cannot solve the problem?

- If the idea of using a consultant comes from members of your staff who seek your approval, ask them to be explicit and precise in defining the problem. Do not accept any superficial and vague definitions!

- Keep the definition of your problem open: the consultant will in any case make his own diagnosis, and may show that your original definition was wrong, or incomplete. The final definition of the problem must be supported by both the client and the consultant.

3. Define your objective!

The aim of the consultancy will be to solve your problem, but your actual objective will have to be more specific. Two kinds of objective are important in preparing for a consulting assignment: action objectives and learning objectives.

- Consultants can intervene in various ways. Consider what you want from the consultant in planning and implementing changes in your organisation. Information that you lack? Training for your staff? A new organisational or information system? Increased production and sales? Higher profitability? Each of these choices will require a different intervention method and a different volume of consulting services. Your action objective will reflect your choice.

- Your learning objectives are equally or even more important. It has been said many times that effective consulting helps the client to learn from his own and the consultant's experience. Therefore, define what you want to learn and how you would like to learn during the assignment. This will be your learning objective.

- Write your objectives down, trying to be as precise as possible. But be flexible and be prepared to redefine these objectives after having spoken with your consultant or received his proposals. He may help to improve the definition of your objectives in your own interest.

4. Choose your consultant!

To choose the right consultant is essential, but it is not an easy matter. It requires information, an effective selection procedure, skill in assessing consultants — and patience. Some risk is always involved — but a proper approach to choice will minimise this risk. There are horses for courses and your aim is to get the right consultant for your organisation and the kind of problem you have. Remember: it is you who is choosing the consultant, not the consultant who is choosing you! But you will have to understand and like each other.

- Take the choice of a consultant very seriously. Never recruit "the guy who happens to be around", or who just sent you a flattering letter and a nice publicity brochure, unless you are sure that he is the ideal choice.

- Use short lists of consultants, screen carefully candidates to be put on the short list, get information on their capabilities, clients and past assignments, check leads and references given to you by business and social friends, your own colleagues, consultants' and management associations and any other source.

- Try to apply a rigorous (though not rigid) selection procedure including rating and evaluation of consultants' proposals; make the choice as objective as possible and minimise the risk of errors. Improve the procedure on the basis of experience!

- Never give a major assignment to an unknown consultant. If possible, test new consultants on smaller and shorter jobs.

- Be sure that you choose not only a consulting firm, but also individual consultants employed by this firm (who may be different people from those who came to propose the assignment to you). The consultants have to match personalities in your organisation as well as your technical problem.

5. Develop a joint programme!

The consultant whom you have chosen may be the best one, but he is not your employee, and his presence and intervention will create an unusual situation in your organisation. Careful planning and preparation of his assignment is a necessity.

- Review the proposals received in detail with the consultant, ask questions, suggest improvements in the approach and the work plan.
- Clarify the consulant's role and your own, the style of consulting to be used and responsibilities for all phases of the assignment. Who will do what? How will you and your people co-operate with the consultant? Are you sure that the consultant will not do work that your people can do — this can reduce cost and speed up execution.
- Reach an agreement on the programme of work to be implemented, the timetable and deadlines to be observed, measurable and controllable results to be attained, reports to be submitted to you and control sessions to be held at critical points of the assignment.
- Settle the financial side clearly and unambiguously: the fee, the reimbursable expenses, the form and frequency of payments.
- Sign a contract with the consultant in a form that is customary in your business environment.

6. Participate actively!

The modern concept of management consulting emphasises the client's active participation at all stages of the assignment. Both the consultant's and the client's best brains are needed to make the assignment a success. But your participation does not occur automatically — a real effort is required, especially since a consulting assignment is an additional job to the normal work which goes on in your organisation.

- Tell your people about the consultant's presence; introduce the consultant to everyone who should meet him.
- Make the right people available at the right time. You will gain nothing by assigning second-rate staff to work with the consultant.
- Provide readily all information related to the assignment and needed by the consultant (confidential information not required for the assignment does not have to be provided if you prefer it).
- Look for ways in which the design of the assignment can be improved, your participation increased, and the consultant's efficiency enhanced — he works for you and the ultimate benefit will be yours.
- However, participating in the asssignment does not mean irritating the consultant, holding his hand, always looking over his shoulder, delaying decisions on his proposals and not letting him proceed with the job!

7. Involve the consultant in implementation!

A universal problem faced by consultants and clients alike is that too many assignments end short of implementation. The report looks all right — but can it be implemented? Can the new scheme work? Are we able to make it work? Certain consultants are only too happy to leave the client without implementing the proposals. The true professionals do care about implementation and are sorry if they cannot participate in it.

● Make it your principle that your consultants must be involved in implementation.

● Choose a degree and form of the consultant's involvement in implementation that suit your organisation. Several alternatives are available in most cases.

● If cost is what worries you, choose a light involvement: you implement, but the consultant helps to debug the new scheme and is available if problems arise.

● In any event, avoid implementation by the consultant without the active participation of your staff!

8. Monitor progress!

There are many reasons why the real course of a consulting assignment may deviate from the path originally agreed. Because it is your assignment, and you are keen to get results, it is in your interest to monitor progress very closely and take corrective measures before it is too late.

● Your monitoring will reveal whether the consultant:
  — is taking the right technical direction;
  — is behaving as a real professional (with integrity, tact, commitment, efficiency);
  — is providing inputs of the right quality and quantity;
  — is not facing unexpected obstacles;
  — has no frictions and conflicts with your staff;
  — is likely to accomplish the agreed objectives.

● Monitor your own performance:
  — are you respecting your commitments?
  — can you keep pace with the consultant?
  — are your people helping the consultant, ignoring him, or making difficulties?

● Pay special attention to the collaborative spirit in which the assignment should be taking place!

● Do not underestimate the financial aspects of delivery:
  — is the consultant billing you regularly?
    are his bills clear and correct?
  — are you paying him without delay?

- — will the assignment remain within agreed financial limits?
- — should you budget for an additional allocation of funds?
- Conclusions from monitoring ought to be reviewed with the consultant and joint decisions taken on needed adjustments.

9. Evaluate the results and the consultant!

Many assignments end in a bizzare way. The consultant leaves the organisation, a report is submitted and accepted, bills are paid and everyone is happy. Yet the client cannot really say whether or not the assignment was worth while, and whether the benefits obtained justified the costs. No lessons are drawn for future assignments, and for the possibility of using the same consultant again.

- It is in your interest to evaluate every assignment on the basis of hard facts, not of feelings and impressions ("the consultant was a very nice guy, everyone liked his frankness and friendly behaviour").
- Evaluate the results obtained. What has changed? Will the changes be lasting? How much will they cost us? What problems remain unsolved?
- Evaluate the consultant. Has he delivered as promised? What could we learn from him? Was working with him an exciting experience? Would we use him again?
- Write your evaluation down. The consultant may contact you again and other people in your organisation will want to know how he performed when working with you. Such information must be available to your colleagues!
- Evaluate your own approach. Have you done well in this assignment? Have you become more skilful in working with consultants? Are you making effective use of them? Where do you need to improve?

10. Beware of dependence on consultants!

You and your staff may have appreciated and enjoyed the presence of a professional consultant in your organisation. However, the purpose of consulting is not only to make additional expertise available to your organisation for dealing with current problems, but to increase your skills and independence in dealing with future problems. Dependence on consultants can be a symptom of a very unhealthy state of affairs!

- Do not delegate to consultants any decisions that are your responsibility and that you have to take.
- Do not get used to always having a consultant around to whom you hand over every complicated matter.
- Make sure that you do not turn to consultants with the same task again — you and your staff should have learned how to tackle such a task.

- Develop internal consulting capabilities for dealing with problems for which an external expert is not necessary!
- Do not put all your eggs in one basket — diversify your sources of external expertise!

●

The Ten Commandments did not teach you how to use consultants, but stressed critical points in choosing consultants and in working with them. If you want to learn more about consulting, read about it and speak with people who have used consultants. And try it out — first on a smaller assignment, but one dealing with a real, not a fictitious, problem.

When you and your organisation become real experts in working with consultants, you may find it necessary to define your own *policy* for using consulting services. The Ten Commandments provide some guidance for this, but you should aim to establish a policy that reflects your specific needs and experience.

ASSOCIATIONS OF MANAGEMENT CONSULTANTS IN SELECTED COUNTRIES

AUSTRALIA	Institute of Management Consultants in Australia (IMCA) P.O. Box 2031 St. Kilda West Victoria 3182
AUSTRIA	Fachverband Unternehmensberatung und Datenverarbeitung Wiedner Haupstrasse 63 1045 Vienna
	Vereinigung Oesterreichischer Betriebs- und Organisationsberater (VOB) Strauchgasse 3 1010 Vienna
BANGLADESH	Bangladesh Association of Management Consultants 98 Malibagh (DIT Road) Dhaka 1219
BELGIUM	Association belge des conseils en organisation et gestion (ASCOBEL) Avenue Louise 430, Boîte 12 1050 Brussels
BRAZIL	Associação Brasileira de Consultores de Organização (ABCO) Rua da Lapa 180, COB 20021 Rio de Janeiro
	Instituto Brasileiro dos Consultores de Organização (IBCO) Av. Paulista, 326, 7° andar - cj. 77 CEP 01310 São Paulo
BULGARIA	Bulgarian Association of Management Consulting Firms (BAMC) 6 D Blagoev Boulevard Sofia 1000
CANADA	Canadian Association of Management Consultants (CAMC) Suite 805 121 Bloor Street East Toronto, Ontario M4W 3M5

	Institute of Certified Management Consultants of Canada Suite 805 121 Bloor Street East Toronto, Ontario M4W 3M5
CHINA	China Enterprise Management Association (CEMA) San Li He Beijing
	Consulting Association of Shanghai (CAS) c/o 81 Wu Xin Road Shanghai
CZECHOSLOVAKIA	Czech and Slovak Association for Management Consulting Slezská 7 12056 Prague 2
DENMARK	Den Danske Sammenslutning AF Konsulenter I Virksomhedsledelse (DSKV) c/o Schobel & Marholt/AIM Dyregardsvej 2 2740 Skovlunde
	Foreningen af Managementkonsulenter (FMK) Regus Housle Larsbjorsstraede 3 1454 Copenhagen K
FINLAND	Liikkeenjohdon Konsultit (LJK) Pohjantie 12A 02100 Espoo 10
FRANCE	Chambre syndicale des sociétés d'études et de conseils (SYNTEC) 3, rue Léon-Bonnat 75016 Paris
	Office professionnel de qualification des conseils en management 3, rue Léon-Bonnat 75016 Paris
GERMANY	Bundesverband Deutscher Unternehmensberater (BDU) E.V. Friedrich-Wilhelm-Strasse 2 5300 Bonn 1
HONG KONG	The Hong Kong Management Association Management House, 3rd Floor 26 Canal Road Hong Kong
HUNGARY	Association of Management Consultants in Hungary c/o SZENZOR Szt. Istán Krt. 11 1055 Budapest

ICELAND	Felag Islanskra Rekstrarradgjafa (FIRR) c/o Icelandic Management Association Ananaustrum 15 P.B. 760 Reykjavik
INDIA	Institute of Management Consultants in India M. Visvesvaraya Industrial Research and Development Centre No. 1 11th Floor, Cuffe Parade Colaba Bombay 400 0045 Management Consultants' Association of India Express Towers 11th Floor, Nariman Point Bombay 400 021
INDONESIA	Ikatan Nasional Konsultan Indonesia Jl. Bendungan Hilir Raya No. 29 Jakarta 10210
IRELAND	Association of Management Consulting Organisations (AMCO) Confederation House, Kildare Street Dublin 2 Institute of Management Consultants in Ireland (IMCI) 10-12 Lansdowne Road Ballsbridge Dublin 4
ITALY	Associazione Fra Società e Studi di Consulenza di Direzione e Organizzazione Aziendale (ASSCO) Via San Paolo 10 20121 Milano Associazione Professionale dei Consulenti di Direzione e Organizzazione Aziendale (APCO) Via Dogana 3 20123 Milano
JAPAN	All Japan Federation of Management Organizations (Zennoren) Kyoritsu Building, 3-1-22, Shibakoen, Minato-ku Tokyo 105 Association of Management Consultants in Japan Shuwashibakoen Sanchome Building 3-1-38 Shiba Park Minato-ku Tokyo 105 Chusho Kigyo Shindan Kyokai (Smaller Enterprise Consultants Association) Ginza Section of MITI, 6-15-1, Ginza, Chuo-ku Tokyo 104 Meikokukai, Japan Productivity Center 3-1-1, Shibuya, Shibuya-ku Tokyo 150

Management consulting

MALAYSIA
Yayasan Pengurusan Malaysia (Malaysian
Institute of Management)
7th Floor, Wisma H.L.A.
57 Jalan Raja Chulan
50200 Kuala Lumpur

MEXICO
Asociación Mexicana de Empresas de Consultoría (AMEC)
calz. Legaria 252
México 17, D.F.

NETHERLANDS
Ordre Van Organisatiekundigen en-Adviseurs
Koningslaan 34
1075 AD Amsterdam

Raad van Organisatie-Adviesbureaus (ROA)
34 Van Stolkweg
P.O. Box 84200
2508 The Hague

NEW ZEALAND
Institute of Management Consultants
New Zealand Incorporated
P.O. Box 4046
Auckland 1

NIGERIA
Institute of Management Consultants
14 Kagoro Close
P.O. Box 9194
Kaduna

Nigerian Association of Management Consultants
c/o Centre for Management Development
P.O. Box 7648, Ikorodu Road
Lagos

NORWAY
Norsk Forening AV Radgivere i Bedriftsledelse
c/o Hartmark-Iras
P.B. 50
1324 Lysaker

PAKISTAN
National Association of Consultants of Pakistan
(NACOP)
P.O. Box 8901
103-B, SMCH. Society
Karachi

PHILIPPINES
Institute of Management Consultants
c/o Mr. A. Figueras
P.O. Box 589
Manila

POLAND
Association of Economic Consultants
Pl. Inwalidów 10
01-552 Warsaw

PORTUGAL
Associação Portuguesa de Projectistas
e Consultores (APPC)
Av. António Augusto Aguiar 126-7°
1000 Lisbon

ROMANIA	Association of Management Consultants in Romania c/o IROMA Sos. Odai 20 Bucharest, Sectorl, Otopeni
SINGAPORE	Association of Management Consultants 151 Chin Swee Road // 03-01
SOUTH AFRICA	Institute of Management Consultants of Southern Africa P.O. Box 784-305 Sandton 2146
SPAIN	Asociación Espãnola de Empresas de Ingeniería y Consultoras (TECNIBERIA) Velásquez 94 Aptdo. 14 863 28006 Madrid
SWEDEN	Svenska Organisationkonsulters Förening (SOK) c/o Cerise Office Assistance AB Frejgatan 44 11326 Stockholm
SWITZERLAND	Association suisse des conseils en organisation et gestion (ASCO) c/o Aura AG Mühlebachstrasse 28 8008 Zürich
TURKEY	Turkish Management Consultant Firms Association Gümüssuyu Cad 44-4 Taksim Istanbul
UNITED KINGDOM	Institute of Management Consultants 5th Floor, 32/33 Hatton Gardens London ECIN 8DL Management Consultancies Association (MCA) 11 West Halkin Street London SW1X 8JL
UNITED STATES	Academy of Management P.O. Box 39 300 South Union St. Ada, Ohio 45810 Academy of Management Managerial Consultation Division c/o Joe Weiss Management Department, Bentley College Waltham, MA 02254 American Institute of Certified Public Accountants (AICPA), Management Services Division 1211 Avenue of Americas New York, NY 10036 Association of Internal Management Consultants (AIMC) Box 304 East Bloomfield, NY 14443

Management consulting

Association of Management Consulting Firms
(ACME) (division of CCO)
230 Park Avenue, Suite 544
New York, NY 10169

Council of Consulting Organisations, Inc. (CCO)
230 Park Avenue, Suite 544
New York, NY 10169

Institute of Management Consultants (IMC)
(division of CCO)
230 Park Avenue, Suite 544
New York, NY 10169

USSR

Association of Consultants in Economics
and Management (Preparatory Committee)
c.o VNESHCONSULT
Krylatskaya Street 31
Building 2, Apt. 463
Moscow 121614

YUGOSLAVIA

Association of Engineering and Consulting Companies
Trubarjeva 5
61000 Ljubljana

Yugoslav Management Consulting Organisation (YUCOR)
Kneza Milosa 9/11 (SITJ)
Belgrade

*International associations of consultants whose members are involved
in management consulting*

AFRICA

Federation of African Consultants (FEAC/FECA)
01 P.O. Box 1387
01 Abidjan

EUROPE

European Committee of Consulting Engineering
Firms (CEBI)
103, bd. de Waterloo
1000 Brussels

Fédération européenne des associations de conseils
en organisation (FEACO)
79, avenue de Cortenberg
1040 Brussels

LATIN AMERICA

Federación Latinoamericana de Asociaciones de
Consultores (FELAC)
Suipacha 552 - Piso 4° - Of. 1
1008 Buenos Aires

INTERNATIONAL

International Council of Management Consulting
Institutes
32/33 Hatton Garden
London EC1N 8DL

International Federation of Consulting Engineers (FIDIC)
P.O. Box 86
1000 Lausanne 12 Chailly

PROFESSIONAL CODES
(Examples)

Code of Conduct of the FEACO (European Federation of Associations of Management Consultants)

All member associations must subscribe to FEACO's code of conduct and practice under which it is regarded as unprofessional conduct:

- To advertise in a blatant or commercial manner.
- To accept any trade commissions, discounts or considerations of any kind in connection with the supply of services or goods to a client.
- To have interest in firms supplying goods or services to their clients, or to be under their control, or to fail to make known any kind of interest likely to affect their service.
- To calculate remuneration on any basis other than the agreed professional scale of fees.
- To disclose confidential information regarding their clients' activities.
- To pay or accept payment for the introduction of clients, except in accordance with recognised and generally accepted professional practice in the country concerned.
- To do anything which does not accord with the statutes of the profession.

Code of Ethics and Standards of Professional Practice of the ACME (The Association of Management Consulting Firms), United States

Preamble

Purposes of the Code of Ethics and Standards of Professional Practice

The Code of Ethics and Standards of Professional Practice signify voluntary assumption by members of the obligation of self-discipline above and beyond the requirements of the law. Their purpose is to let the public know that members intend to maintain a high level of ethics and public service, and to declare that — in return for the faith that the public places in them — the members accept the obligation to conduct their practice in a way that will be beneficial to the public. They give clients a basis for confidence that members will serve them in accordance with professional standards of competence, objectivity, and integrity.

The Code expresses in general terms the standards of professional conduct expected of management consulting firms in their relationships with prospective clients, clients, colleagues, members of allied professions, and the public. The Code of Ethics, unlike the Standards of Professional Practice, is mandatory in character. It serves as a basis for disciplinary action when the conduct of a member firm falls below the required standards as stated in the Code. The Standards of Professional Practice are largely aspirational in character and represent objectives and standards of good practice to which members of the Association subscribe.

The Association enforces the Code of Ethics by receiving and investigating all complaints of violations and by taking disciplinary action against any member who is found to be guilty of Code violation.

The professional attitude

The reliance of managers of private and public institutions on the advice of management consultants imposes on the profession an obligation to maintain high standards of integrity and competence. To this end, members of the Association have basic responsibilities to place the interests of clients and prospective clients ahead of their own, maintain independence of thought and action, hold the affairs of their clients in strict confidence, strive continually to improve their professional skills, observe and advance professional standards of management consulting, uphold the honor and dignity of the profession, and maintain high standards of personal conduct. This Code has evolved out of the experience of members since the Association was incorporated in 1933. In recognition of the public interest and their obligation to the profession, members and the consultants on their staffs have agreed to comply with the following articles.

I. Code of Ethics

1. Basic client responsibilities

1.1 We will at all times place the interests of clients ahead of our own and serve them with integrity, competence, and independence.

We will assume an independent position with the client, making certain that our advice to clients is based on impartial consideration of all pertinent facts and responsible opinions.

1.2 We will guard as confidential all information concerning the affairs of clients that we gather during the course of professional engagements; and we will not take personal, financial, or other advantage of material or inside information coming to our attention as a result of our professional relationship with clients; nor will we provide the basis on which others might take such advantage. Observance of the ethical obligation of the management consulting firm to hold inviolate the confidence of its clients not only facilitates the full development of facts essential to effective solution of the problem but also encourages clients to seek needed help on sensitive problems.

1.3 We will serve two or more competing clients, or clients in any known adversary relationship, on sensitive problems only with their knowledge.

1.4 We will inform clients of any relationships, circumstances, or interests that might influence our judgment or the objectivity of our services.

2. Client arrangements

2.1 We will present our qualifications for serving a client solely in terms of our competence, experience, and standing, and we will not guarantee any specific result, such as amount of cost reduction or profit increase.

2.2 We will accept only those engagements we are qualified to undertake and which we believe will provide real benefits to clients. We will assign personnel qualified by knowledge, experience, and character to give effective service in analyzing and solving the particular problem or problems involved. We will carry out each engagement under the direction of a principal of the firm who is responsible for its successful completion.

2.3 We will not accept an engagement of such limited scope that we cannot serve the client effectively.

2.4 We will, before accepting an engagement, confer with the client or prospective client in sufficient detail and gather sufficient facts to gain an adequate understanding of the problem, the scope of study needed to solve it, and the possible benefits that may accrue to the client. The preliminary exploration will be conducted confidentially on terms and conditions agreed upon by the member and the prospective client.

2.5 We will, except for those cases where special client relationships make it unnecessary, make certain that the client receives a written proposal that outlines the objectives, scope, and, where possible, the estimated fee or fee basis for the proposed service or engagement. We will discuss with the client any important changes in the nature, scope, timing, or other aspects of the engagement and obtain the client's agreement to such changes before taking action on them — and unless the circumstances make it unnecessary, we will confirm these changes in writing.

2.6 We will perform each engagement on an individualized basis and develop recommendations designed specifically to meet the particular requirements of the client situation. Our objective in each client engagement is to develop solutions that are realistic and practical and that can be implemented promptly and economically. Our professional staffs are prepared to assist, to whatever extent desired, with the implementation of approved recommendations.

2.7 We will not serve a client under terms or conditions that might impair our objectivity, independence, or integrity; and we will reserve the right to withdraw if conditions beyond our control develop to interfere with the successful conduct of the engagement.

2.8 We will acquaint client personnel with the principles, methods, and techniques applied, so that the improvements suggested or installed may be properly managed and continued after completion of the engagement.

2.9 We will maintain continuity of understanding and knowledge of clients' problems and the work that has been done to solve them by maintaining appropriate files of reports submitted to clients. These are protected against unauthorized access and supported by files of working papers, consultants' log-books, and similar recorded data.

2.10 We will not accept an engagement for a client while another management consulting firm is serving that client unless we are assured that any conflict between the two engagements is recognized by, and has the consent of, the client. We will not endeavor to displace another management consulting firm or individual consultant once we have knowledge that the client has made a commitment to the other consultant, unless we are assured that the client is aware of any conflict between the two commitments.

2.11 We will review the work of another management consulting firm or individual consultant for the same client, only with the knowledge of such consultant, unless such consultant's work which is subject to review has been finished or terminated. However, even though the other consultant's work has been finished or terminated, it is a matter of common courtesy to let the consulting firm or individual know that the work is being reviewed, provided that the client consents to such disclosures.

3. Client fees

3.1 We will charge reasonable fees which are commensurate with the nature of services performed and the responsibility assumed. An excessive charge abuses the professional relationship and discourages the public from utilizing the services of management consultants. On the other hand, adequate compensation is necessary in order to enable the management consulting firm to serve clients effectively and to preserve the integrity and independence of the profession. Determination of the reasonableness of a fee requires consideration of many factors, including the nature of the services performed; the time required; the consulting firm's experience, ability, and reputation; the degree of responsibility assumed; and the benefits that accrue to the client. Wherever feasible, we will agree with the client in advance on the fee or fee basis.

3.2 We will neither accept nor pay fees or commissions to others for client referrals, or enter into any arrangement for franchising our practice to others; provided, however, that two or more consulting firms or individuals may agree as to sharing of any fee or commission on a basis reasonably commensurate with the relative values of the services performed for the client. Nor will we accept fees, commissions, or other valuable consideration from individuals or organizations for recommending equipment, supplies, or services in the course of our service to clients.

II. Standards of Professional Practice

In order to promote highest quality of performance in the practice of management consulting, ACME has developed the following standards of good practice for the guidance of the profession. Member firms subscribe to these practices because they make for equitable and satisfactory client relationships and contribute to success in management consulting.

1. We will strive continually to advance and protect the standards of the management consulting profession. We will strive continually to improve our knowledge, skills, and techniques, and will make available to our clients the benefits of our professional attainments.

2. We recognize our responsibilities to the public interest and to our profession to contribute to the development and understanding of better ways to manage the various formal institutions in our society. By reason of education, experience, and broad contact with management problems in a variety of institutions, management consultants are especially qualified to recognize opportunities for improving managerial and operating processes; and they have an obligation to share their knowledge with managers and their colleagues in the profession.

3. We recognize our responsibility to the profession to share with our colleagues the methods and techniques we utilize in serving clients. But we will not knowingly, without their permission, use proprietary data, procedures, materials, or techniques that other management consultants have developed but not released for public use.

4. We will not make offers of employment to consultants on the staffs of other consulting firms without first informing them. We will not engage in wholesale or mass recruiting of consultants from other consulting firms. If we are approached by consultants of other consulting firms regarding employment in our firm or in that of a client, we will handle each situation in a way that will be fair to the consultant, the firm, and the client.

5. We will not solicit employees of clients for employment by us or by others, except with the consent of the client. If we are approached by employees of clients regarding employment in our firm or in that of another client, we will make certain that we have our clients' consent before entering into any negotiations with employees.

6. We will continually evaluate the quality of the work done by our staff to insure, insofar as is possible, that all of our engagements are conducted in a competent manner.

7. We will endeavor to provide opportunity for the professional development of those who enter the profession, by assisting them to acquire a full understanding of the functions, duties, and responsibilities of management consultants, and to keep up with significant advances in their areas of practice.

8. We will administer the internal and external affairs of our firm in the best interest of the profession at all times.

9. We will not advertise our services in self-laudatory language or in any other manner derogatory to the dignity of the profession.

10. We will respect the professional reputation and practice of other management consultants. This does not remove the moral obligation to expose unethical conduct of fellow members of the profession to the proper authorities.

11. We will strive to broaden public understanding and enhance public regard and confidence in the management consulting profession, so that management consultants can perform their proper function in society effectively. We will conduct ourselves so as to reflect credit on the profession and to inspire the confidence, respect, and trust of clients and the public. In the course of our practice, we will strive to maintain a wholly professional attitude towards those we serve, toward those who assist us in our practice, toward our fellow consultants, toward the members of other professions, and the practitioners of allied arts and sciences.

Adopted February 1, 1972
Amended September 19, 1978
Amended November 2, 1981

Questions about interpretations or Code violations should be sent to:

President
ACME, Inc.
230 Park Avenue
New York, New York 10169
212/697-9693

OUTLINE OF A MANAGEMENT SURVEY

This appendix provides an overview of the main subject areas to be covered by a diagnostic or management survey of a company. The checklists suggest the subjects to cover, not a sequence of steps. This sequence will have to be decided with regard to the nature of the client organisation, the kind of information that is already available, and the main functional area in which the assignment will be carried out.

In functional areas the survey consultant will look only for facts that will help him to understand the nature of the client organisation, appraise the level of performance, discover underused resources and define possible improvements. He will refrain from more detailed analysis, with the exception perhaps of the area on which the assignment is to concentrate.

The paragraphs below are restricted to a summary view of each area. Further suggestions can be found in chapters 12-19 dealing with consulting in various areas of management. Figure 1 on the following page shows the ten subject areas covered. A different structuring of the survey is possible, however. For example, in an organisation involved in an extensive investment programme this would be treated as a separate subject area.

Many consulting firms have prepared their own internal guides to diagnosing organisations in the form of detailed lists of questions to which consultants can refer in planning and undertaking a survey.

Subject area 1: General characteristics of the client organisation

Under this heading the consultant will examine key information on the nature, purpose, role and major characteristics of the client organisation. The checklist indicates the scope of the subject. The consultant will be particularly interested in factors and events which may have shaped the history of the client organisation and be the origin of various deeply rooted traditions and behavioural patterns.

Figure 1   Subject areas of a comprehensive management survey

(1.)	General characteristics of the client organisation
(2.)	Environmental factors
(3.)	Objectives and strategies — overall

(4.) Finance	(5.) Marketing	(6.) Production (operations)	(7.) Research and development	(8.) Human resources
Objectives, policies, plans				
Structure, activities				
Performance				

(9.)	Management systems and practices
(10.)	Performance — overall

Checklist 1   General characteristics

Subject	Specification
Activity	Type (sector), purpose Main functions, products, services National or multinational Complexity and sophistication of products and processes
History	When and how established Growth pattern Key events (acquisitions, mergers, technological breakthroughs, influence of wars or crises)
Importance	Volume of activity Volume and structure of resources Position in country, sector, region, local community, internationally
Ownership	Pattern (private, public, co-operative) Legal form (partnership, limited company, state agency)
Influences	Main owners Centres of control, role of board of directors Social and political influences and pressure groups
Location	Where located Number and size of units Distances, communications

Subject area 2: Environmental factors

The client organisation has to be seen in the context of a socio-economic environment with which it interacts in many ways. The checklist given below is very broad. In reality, it will be exceptional for the consultant to review all aspects; in most cases only selected environmental considerations will apply. The subjects included in the checklist will be studied from the viewpoint of the needs and opportunities of the client organisation and not in a general, all-embracing way.

Some of the environmental factors will be variables that the client organisation cannot influence. There are, however, assignments that may include proposals for changes in the environment — for example, a diagnostic survey of state import corporations may lead to a revision of the government system of import licences and customs tariffs. In another case, consumer taste may be influenced by education or advertising.

Checklist 2   Environmental factors

Subject	Specification
Economic	Broad economic setting Development level and trends Country's economic wealth Structure and state of market State of given industry in the country Financial system, availability of money, foreign debt

Checklist 2 continued

Natural resources	Raw materials
	Fuel and energy
	Water
	Land
	Climate
Human resources	Education
	Labour market
	Employment and unemployment
	Technical and business skills
	Training facilities
Socio-cultural	Structure of society (classes, ethnic groups, minorities, income distribution)
	Consumer taste
	Social, cultural and religious traditions
	Social organisations (including workers' and employers' organisations), role, influence
Government	Profile, source of power, stability
	Economic policy, including regional development
	Planning, regulation and control of economy
	Taxation
	Government services and facilities
	Local government (functions in economic development)
Political	Political system and life
	Impact of politics on management
Legal	Labour law
	Company or commercial law, etc.
Physical	Immediate physical environment
	Transport and communication facilities
	Housing facilities
	Utilities and technical services
	Pollution: environmental protection

Subject area 3: Objectives and strategies (overall)

The study of the client's business objectives, strategies, policies and plans is a key element in management surveys; it provides orientation to a more detailed analysis of various functions and activity areas, and a basis for appraising performance. The consultant examines both the methodology used (the system whereby objectives, strategies and policies are established and plans worked out) and the particular targets and other objectives established by management. Special attention is paid to conflicting objectives, strategies and policies, and to blank areas in which the client operates without objectives and plans.

Checklist 3 Objectives and strategies (overall)

Subject	Specification
Methodology	Methods of defining purpose and objectives
	Systems of strategic, operational and contingency plans
	Areas managed without objectives and plans

Purpose and objectives	Assessment of purpose and specific organisational objectives as defined by management
Strategic choices	Assessment of major choices (overall and by areas of business)
Investment	Policies and plans, main projects

Subject area 4: Finance

This is a key area of any management survey because the financial strength and results of business organisations reflect the potential and results of almost all other areas and functions.

The *financial appraisal*, as the survey in this area is frequently called, concentrates on analysis of the client's financial reports for the preceding three to five years as a means of assessing strengths and weaknesses, measuring past performance, examining the use of funds available, and establishing upward or downward trends. The findings of the financial appraisal are used to orient further investigation and remedial activities in other functions and areas of management.

What sort of thing should a consultant look for in studying a set of financial reports? First, there is the overall picture presented by the current year's figures. Is the company making enough profit? How strong is it in financial terms? Is it taking or giving too much credit? Are the stocks too high? Secondly, there is the picture that emerges from studying trends over a period of years. Is the company becoming more profitable? Is it expanding too fast? Is productivity rising or falling? Is liquidity improving or deteriorating?

In both these pictures it is necessary to distinguish between two conflicting aspects of the company's operations — profitability and solvency. A business can be highly profitable yet financially weak. Another may be financially strong but not making enough profit. The method used to interpret financial statements is to calculate certain *ratios*. Cash figures alone are almost meaningless; an increase in profit from $10,000 to $15,000 may be good or bad, depending on the amount of extra resources used in generating the extra profit. Many different ratios can be developed from a set of financial reports, but some of them are of little value or are simply variations of each other. Guidelines on the application and interpretation of ratios are provided in many publications on accounting and financial management.

A correct interpretation of the static picture presented by one year's figures requires considerable skill and care. For instance, if the fixed assets of land and buildings are undervalued in current market terms, a false impression may be given in the profit ratios. The comparison of one business with another should not be undertaken without the utmost care and unless the consultant is thoroughly familiar with both businesses. Different methods may be used to evaluate assets and calculate depreciation, policies on whether to capitalise expenditure or write it off against income may be different, the treatment of research and development costs may vary, changing price levels may invalidate attempts to compare and so on.

The main value of analysing ratios lies in studying the *trend* within one company over a period of years. Since this approach means comparing like with like, there is little risk of misinterpretation of the main trends.

Checklist 4   Finance

Subject	Specification
Financial management	Strategy and policy
	Records and reports — availability, timeliness, quality
	Staffing (numbers, competence)
	Position in corporate structure
	Relationships with banks
Balance sheet and income (profit and loss) account	Comparative analysis
	Key ratios
	Financial health and stability
Sources and application of funds	Sources and cost of funds
	Movements and uses of funds
	Profits and their use
	Cash flow
Financial planning and forecasting	Systems and techniques used
	Assessment of projections made
Auditors' reports	Existence, quality
	Comments made by auditors

Subject area 5: Marketing

In organisations that sell their products or services the marketing function provides an essential link with the environment and strongly influences other functions. The consultant tries to get a picture of the available market and of the product-market strategy followed by the client. He will examine the effectiveness of marketing strategy and activity and its impact on production, research and development, purchasing and other functions. Various components of the marketing function, such as the organisation of sales, advertising, the location and turnover of stocks, warehousing, transport, etc., will be briefly reviewed if appropriate.

Checklist 5   Marketing

Subject	Specification
Marketing management	Concept, strategy applied
	Staffing (numbers, competence)
	Position in corporate structure
Markets (local and export)	Size, trends
	Own share
	Competitors (number, importance, strategy)
	Market research
	Backlog of orders

Checklist 5 continued

Client base (customers)	Size and structure
	Principal clients
Pricing	Strategy and tactics
Sales	Distribution channels
	Organisation
	Techniques
	Sales force (size, competence, motivation)
	Reliability of delivery
	Stocks (volume, location, turnover)
	Selling expenses (volume, trend)
Client services	After-sales services
	Technical services (information, training, systems design, consulting, etc.)
Advertising	Importance, cost
	Techniques
	Impact

Subject area 6: Production (operations)

It is difficult to describe briefly the activities and problems that interest the consultant in the very large and diversified area of production. More than in other areas, the consultant's problem will be how to recognise essential information in the vast amount of data that production offers to him.

In essence, the consultant will concentrate his efforts on two issues:

- a general examination of the organisation of production and the layout of production departments, main material and product flows, relations between marketing and production, purchasing and production, and research and development and production;

- an examination of key indicators of effectiveness of production activities (capacity utilisation, lead time of main products, volume and distribution of work in progress, equipment breakdown and stoppages, utilisation of working time or production workers, waste, quality of production, various losses in the production area).

In non-productive organisations (services, social organisations, government departments) the consultant will review, in an analogous way, the services or other operations that constitute the organisation's main "products".

Checklist 6   Production (operations)

Subject	Specification
Production management	Concept
	Production strategy applied
	Staffing (numbers, competence)
	Position in corporate structure

Checklist 6 continued

Production units	Number, location Specialisation Linkages
Production capacity	Volume Utilisation Bottlenecks Free and spare capacity
Technology used	Type Level, sophistication
Land and buildings	Owned or rented Location, access Age, condition Suitability Cost of operation
Plant and machinery	Types, quantities Age, condition, breakdowns Technical sophistication — (automation, precision, speed, etc.) Suitability Maintenance (system, level) Special equipment
Production organisation	Material and product flows (process diagrams) Work in progress (volume, location, control) Materials handling New forms of organisation
Control and support functions	Planning, scheduling, co-ordination, records Operational control (system, level) Industrial engineering (work study, value analysis, etc.) Staff capabilities (engineers, technicians)
Quality management	System applied Level attained New trends
Purchasing	Organisation Procedures, regulations Main suppliers, reliability Sub-contractors
Production workers	Categories Skills, experience Remuneration, motivation Supervisory staff
Safety and health	Accidents Preventive measures
Efficiency of production system	Cost of main products Labour productivity Losses (stoppages, waste of material and energy, pilferage, etc.)

Subject area 7: Research and development

The first question on research and development (R and D) will concern its role in the development of the client organisation. If the organisation is research-oriented and operates in a technically advanced industry (such as electronics, telecommunications, or petrochemicals), the management of its research function may have a considerably greater impact on overall results than does production management. The consultant will examine relations in the total cycle of research — development — manufacturing — marketing. He will be interested in research and development expenditure and its utilisation in the relationship of R and D management to general management of the firm, in the pace and problems of the transfer of R and D results to production, in the competence of key professional staff and the main achievements of the R and D department.

Even in organisations having little or no internal research and development some relationship to external research and development may exist, e.g. licences will be purchased, or new production technologies bought in the form of equipment.

The organisation of investment (capital building) activities linked to the application of R and D results may require particular attention in organisations involved in extensive expansion or reconstruction.

Checklist 7   Research and development

Subject	Specification
R and D management	Strategy and policy definition Plan, implementation Structure Position in corporate structure Personalities
R and D staff	Numbers Qualifications, experience Achievements Motivation
Innovation potential	Product design, backlog of new designs Laboratories Prototype workshops Testing equipment, pilot plant Information and library
Collaboration with other organisations	Type of arrangements Partners Licence agreements (and similar)
Use of R and D	Results, application Impact on business Special advantage

Subject area 8: Human resources

The critical issue in the human resource area is the impact of personnel policy (i.e. criteria applied to selection, recruitment, staff development, promotion and remuneration) on the performance and development prospects of the client organisation. Although this may be difficult during a short survey, the consultant tries to get a true picture of how and by whom personnel decisions are made and how this affects the morale and motivation of people. Career planning and development, personnel performance appraisal and the role of staff training and development will then be briefly examined. In the field of remuneration and motivation, both financial instruments (wage policy, profit sharing) and other motivational factors (challenging work opportunities, employment security, social services) will be reviewed and their impact on the performance of the organisation assessed.

The consultant should in any case acquaint himself with the basic principles of labour-management relations practices in the client organisation.

Checklist 8   Human resources

Subject	Specification
Human resource management	Concept and policies
	Human resource planning
	Staffing of personnel department
	Position in corporate structure
Staff structure	Age, sex
	Competence, skills (by categories)
	Minorities, foreign workers
	Employment conditions (permanent, temporary, seasonal)
	Turnover
	Absenteeism
Recruitment and selection	Recruitment practices
	Selection practices
Training and development	Career prospects
	Expenditure on staff development
	Organisation
	Methods and techniques
	Job rotation, etc.
	Staff appraisal
Remuneration and motivation	Wage and salary systems
	Wage levels and differentials
	Payment by results
	Profit-sharing and similar schemes
	Social benefits
	Non-financial incentives
Labour-management relations	Nature, practices
	Impact on management and performance

Subject area 9: Management system and practices

Step by step, the consultant will be extending and deepening his knowledge and understanding of the client organisation's management. He will try to determine the relationship between the problems he has discovered and the ways in which decisions on important matters are taken and implemented. Special attention will be paid to the profiles and management styles of key personalities and to various questions usually embraced by the term "organisational culture".

Checklist 9   Management systems and practices

Subject	Specification
Managers	Key personalities (professional and personal profiles, attitudes to change, motivation)
Organisational structure	Form of structure, history Departments, divisions (specialisation, role, relative importance) Relations between line and staff Centralisation and decentralisation Existence, quality and use of charts and manuals
Decision making	Practice applied to main sorts of decision
Co-ordination	Methods, areas Co-ordination of key functional areas
Communication	Networks and channels (formal and informal) Methods
Internal information, planning and control system	Systems used, impact Management information system Activity and performance plans Budgetary and cost control Reporting; reports and records analysis
Modern techniques	Policy, effectiveness Preferred techniques Computer technology applications Communication technology, etc.
Organisational culture	Values and traditions Habits and rituals Prevailing management style Employee participation
Use of external expert services	Policy, importance Experience with management consultants

Subject area 10: Performance (overall)

The examination of the client's (i) resources, (ii) objectives, strategies, policies and plans, and (iii) main activities and results in particular functional areas, enables the consultant to make some judgement on the overall performance of the client organisation, assess whether this performance has been satisfactory, and point out possible and needed improvements.

Checklist 10   Performance (overall)

Subject	Specification
Performance indicators	Growth, productivity, profitability, cash-flow, return on investment, market value of shares, employment generation and other key indicators
Competitive	Special resources, achievements and capabilities advantage
Position in sector	Position attained (leadership, etc.) and image achieved with customers and general public

533

Checklist 10   continued

Subject	Specification
Trends	Factors and forces likely to affect future performance (positive and negative influences)
Performance assessment	Practices and their impact (frequency, depth of analysis, conclusions drawn)
Performance improvement	Programmes for improving performance Approaches and methods used Results achieved

TERMS OF BUSINESS

The terms of business are usually sufficiently standardised to be drawn up as a permanent document for attaching to proposals submitted to the client. This avoids having to type them afresh on each occasion. The main non-standard item may be the fee rate. This is left blank, to be filled in when the report is submitted.

The example below gives a typical list of terms. The document may or may not have a blank space at the end for entering any special conditions.

1. Our charges for this assignment are $ ..... per day per consultant employed, inclusive of supervision, but excluding travelling and subsistence when the consultant is engaged on the client's business away from the office or plant to which he is assigned.[1]

2. The fee covers all time spent on the client's work whether carried out on his premises or elsewhere. No charge is incurred during absence due to illness or leave, but no deduction is made for public or statutory holidays. Any computer bureau charges will be invoiced at cost. Charges are invoiced and payable monthly.[2]

3. We reserve the right to review our fees in the light of operating costs and to adjust them accordingly, but in the event of any change being required at least three months' notice will be given to current clients.

4. On concluding an assignment, it is our practice to maintain contact with the client, and to carry out periodic servicing visits to ensure that the benefits secured through our work are maintained.[3] Such visits are charged at $ ..... per day, including travelling, subsistence and time spent after the visit in preparing a servicing report. A charge of $ ..... per day is also made for any one-day visits prior to the start of the assignment.

5. Our work may be terminated on either side by one week's notice in writing.[4]

6. All forecasts, and recommendations in this and any subsequent report or letter are made in good faith and on the basis of the information before us at the time. Their achievement must depend among other things on the effective

co-operation of the client's staff. In consequence, no statement in a report or letter is to be deemed to be in any circumstances a representation, undertaking, warranty or contractual condition.

7. All our consultants are under special contract which protects our clients against the divulging of confidential information. Our consultants are also under agreement not to seek or accept employment with our clients, and it is a condition of the engagement of our company that you will not employ on your staff any member of our company involved in this assignment.[5]

---

[1] Some consulting units indicate a weekly rate. The cost of travel to and from the place of the assignment may be charged separately if the distance is great.

[2] In some circumstances charges may be invoiced weekly.

[3] The reference to servicing (follow-up) visits does not imply that the client has to agree to them in any case. If he so wishes, this clause will be deleted.

[4] The period of notice for premature termination of an assignment may depend on the reason for it. Some consulting units make this clause 24 hours' notice on either side.

[5] The reason for this clause is obvious. It could be argued, however, that it is an interference with individual liberty and could in time curtail a man's employment opportunities. Some consulting firms add ". . . within X years of its termination".

CASE HISTORY OF CONSULTING IN PRODUCTION MANAGEMENT
(Potomac Dryer Felt Company)

The purpose of this case study, written by Lewis S. Moore on the basis of his own consulting experiences, is to illustrate in compact form the association between the consultant and the client and the roles played by the consultant at various stages of the assignment.

The consultant is an expert in maintenance management. Nevertheless, he uses several techniques (e.g. workshops and goal setting) to involve the client's personnel and to make the whole assignment a joint effort. The study also shows that diagnosis, action planning and implementation are not necessarily distinct major phases in every assignment and improvements can be introduced step by step (each one going through diagnosis, action planning, implementation and evaluation). The consultant is consistent in emphasising the learning effect of his interventions. He also distributes short handouts on various technical aspects to help the client in self-development.

●

Dryer felts are very wide, specialised fabrics used in the paper industry. Each customer has exact specifications, and each demands flawless felts. There is no market for seconds.

Potomac management thought they could get more efficient production from their 12 huge (38 feet wide) looms. Reported efficiency was 73 per cent for the previous month, but they had no ideas on how to improve on this.

I studied the production reports, and began trying to answer two questions:

(1) Was 73 per cent the "true" productivity of these looms?

(2) How was production time lost?

I questioned the data because production reports often distort the truth. A supervisor sometimes argues, for example, that his shift should not be penalised for production time lost due to equipment breakdowns. After all, his people cannot produce when equipment is out of service.

In Potomac's reports the weaver's estimate of downtime was subtracted from scheduled production hours for each machine, and efficiency was computed from production made during the remaining hours.[1] This may seem fair to workers; but, unfortunately, it can encourage downtime because no one is accountable for it. In fact, production personnel look better if they exaggerate downtime hours - this increases their reported efficiency.

Actual production units and scheduled hours of operation are both easy to verify. From these I found that *unreported* cost efficiency for the previous month was a disappointing 36.1 per cent, even when I included the one-third of looms not scheduled for production. Surely, if *that* figure had been reported to corporate headquarters it would have caused a stir. They were unhappy with 73 per cent. Imagine their reaction to less than half as much.[2]

Downtime [3] on the eight giant looms at Potomac scheduled for production that month was 2,804 hours. I studied the downtime logs to find out why. I wanted to be thoroughly prepared for the first meeting to discuss this with management.

First meeting

That first meeting was a few days later. Present were the plant manager, production superintendent, three production supervisors, the maintenance manager and, because this was a small operation, five loom fixers who were to work with us. Twelve persons is a good number for organising projects. A very small group cannot do enough; with groups of more than 20 persons, individuals get too little attention.

I had asked the plant manager to introduce me and to explain how we would be working together at Potomac. He began, "I have asked this consultant to show us how we can better manage our operations. He has studied our records and observed us for several days, and is now ready to begin. He has shown me some remarkable conclusions on which I expect us to act."

He continued, "Mr. Moore will not solve these problems for us. His job is to show us that we can solve them. He will spend an hour or so — the time may vary greatly — with each of you at your job, observing, asking questions, and recommending how *you* should proceed. This is to guide each of you in preparing for weekly, one-hour project workshops in which we will review each man's progress and co-ordinate plans for the coming week."

The superintendent asked, "What is a project?"

I explained that a project is a part of normal job responsibilities selected for special study and improvement.

"We are always looking for ways to improve," he said.

I answered, "For the purposes of this programme each of you will single out one problem or opportunity to focus on. Do not neglect the rest of your job, but concentrate on the problem we select as much as possible until it is completely solved."

A supervisor asked, "How is this different from what we have always done?"

"It is different in that you will in every case measure the result you are trying to change. You will decide what the average is right now — that's called the "baseline", and we will use it as a benchmark against which to judge progress. I will show you how to determine what results should be if everybody does what he or she is supposed to do and the job goes just as you planned. You will try different plans by making one change at a time, and by analysing the effect on results of each change. We want to know exactly what works and why. You will make progress reports to me and to each other as often as you have something new to add — that should be every week or two. Finally, all this will be written up by you and turned in to your plant manager."

Several of the men looked uncomfortable. One said, "I'm not much for making speeches." Another said, "Sounds like a lot of extra work."

The plant manager replied, "Projects do not add any new responsibilities. You were always responsible for improvements in your job. The consultant and I discussed this earlier. Everything he just described is essential if we are to get this operation under control. We have operated out of our hip pocket too long, not planning or measuring or writing things down. Because we do not really solve the problems, the same ones keep returning. We go from crisis to crisis. As fast as one fire is put out, another springs up. As for the speeches, no one will judge you for eloquence. But I want to see first-hand what each of you is doing, and this way you can learn from each other. Talking to this group is no more difficult than talking to your people."

The plant manager did not mention another reason for the workshops. They are powerful motivators. Managers who have done good work enjoy projects with built-in opportunities for recognition. Those who have failed to do what they know they should have done face embarrassment. Since each man gives his own report, we avoid the awkward position of "informer". Before each workshop I discuss with each manager his progress, the data and what questions we will ask. One question is always what his next step should be. I help him decide. In the workshop I take notes, and read them aloud before adjourning. Everyone has an assignment. I follow up during the week to be sure each man is able to do this next step. At the next workshop I introduce each manager with, "Last time you said you would . . .". I should already know what he has done, what problems he faced, and what his results are.

"When does the project end?" asked one supervisor.

"When you have no reason to anticipate further changes in methods or improvement in results," I said. "You may wish, for example, you had no waste at all, but you know that is impossible. You know that 2 per cent waste is normal and unavoidable at changeover. Less than 2 per cent reported waste has to mean an error in the records. More than 2.5 per cent means that someone is being careless. If your project is to reduce waste, then when you get to 2 per cent and *know why*, the project is ended."

"That does not mean you can ignore waste," interjected the plant manager. "You must continue to monitor results, and I will ask you about them from time to time. If they do not stay under control, I will expect you to go back to the project and find out what went wrong."

I continued, "When one project is ended, you begin another. This 'habit of improvement' should become a routine part of everyone's work."

"Can we do team projects?" someone asked.

"Yes," I replied, "but only if each person on the team has distinct responsibilities which include analysing data, planning corrective action, etc. We want evidence that each of you is having to think for yourself; otherwise, you are simply following someone else's plan, and not making the contribution we need from you."

"What if we do not want to do projects?" asked another supervisor. "I have enough projects already."

"What you do for a project is between you and your superior. I certainly don't want any one of you doing 'busy work', just to say you have a project, or be expected to take on more projects than you can handle. After we see what you are doing already, we may recommend that you report on these projects at the workshops."

"Why?" he asked.

"Because," I replied, "if you know how to do projects already, your work will be a good way to teach others. As the projects unfold in the coming weeks, we will look for good examples of management principles which you have applied. Others may not be interested in details on bearing life or downtime cost; but they need to know how you recognised opportunities, analysed problems, set goals, and planned what to do."

The maintenance manager asked, "How do we pick projects? In other words, how do we know that a type of job or operation is a good candidate for a project — that there is real opportunity to do better and not just 'pie-in-the-sky'?"

I was glad he asked. "That's an excellent question. There are several ways to recognise opportunities. It is partly a matter of technique and partly a matter of sensitising yourself to notice them. One technique is to honestly account for lost production time."

I had begun a graph of cost efficiency by weeks. I showed this on an overhead projector so everyone could see, and explained how the numbers were calculated from reported production. "How was so much production time lost?" I asked.

The production superintendent said, "The problem is breakdowns. We can't keep the looms running."

"We fix them and you tear them up," said the maintenance manager.

"Now hold on," said the plant manager, looking slowly from face to face. "Let's just get the facts and act accordingly. We will work as a team."

I asked what caused the breakdowns.

"Operator abuse," said a loom fixer.

I wrote the word 'misuse' on the chalkboard, and asked, "What are other causes?"

"Improper maintenance," said a supervisor. The loom fixer who had just spoken glared at him, while I wrote on the chalkboard again.

Some other suggestions were made, but they all fell under "misuse" or "improper" maintenance. "Occasionally, equipment breaks down because of a defect in design or manufacture of some part of the mechanism. But all breakdowns are the result of either misuse, improper maintenance or a defective part. In a few special cases you intentionally wait for failure. We will discuss those when we see one."

"But parts wear out, don't they?" This loom fixer was clearly uncomfortable.

"Yes, they do wear out," I said. "But the purpose of preventive maintenance — or PM — is to detect worn parts before they fail, and to prevent breakdowns, isn't it? That's why you change the oil and spark plugs in your car, and why you should check the cylinder compression and test the battery. Many people are careless about these checks, and they get caught sooner or later. They think they are saving money, but it is false economy. Breakdowns are far more costly than prevention."

I continued, "Then according to what you have said about their causes, any breakdown is a failure of some type. To stop these failures, we have to determine what went wrong and do something differently in the future. How do we determine the true causes?"

The maintenance manager said, "I suppose we could do a mechanical autopsy." He paused while laughter broke the tension. "We could probably tell the difference between maintenance oversights and abuse."

"Let's look at last month's breakdown records on one, troublesome loom. This may give us a better idea of where to begin." I had studied the records and prepared transparencies beforehand. "What is the most frequent cause of breakdowns?"

There were 94 entries concerning "weft insertion". That was an outrageous problem.

"We have had a lot of trouble with weft insertion on that loom," said the production superintendent. "We can't seem to keep it running."

"Part of the problem," I explained, "is that there are no written maintenance procedures, no measured settings, no evaluation of settings to systematically find the optimum, and no clear record of what has been done. Your records say 'set this' or 'adjust that'."

"We run many different felts on that loom and have to reset it every time. Why, you would have 50 different settings for weft insertion," said a loom fixer.

Another man spoke up. "But the loom does have to be reset. If we have a record of settings, maybe we could do it right the first time, instead of ten times by trial and error, and never really getting it right, even then."

I asked, "Would you and the production supervisor of your shift" — I nodded in his direction — "be willing to begin a project on weft insertion set-up for this type of loom? That means you would measure settings, determine the optimum for each felt, and, unless you have a better idea, measure progress in terms of the number of weft insertion breakdowns."

The two men said they would do this project, and I agreed to meet with them later that day to plan what to do.

"What is the second most costly type of breakdown?" I asked, pointing to the overhead transparency.

Several men pointed out a series of repairs done on the motion protection

Figure 1   Weft insertion stops per shift (loom 11)

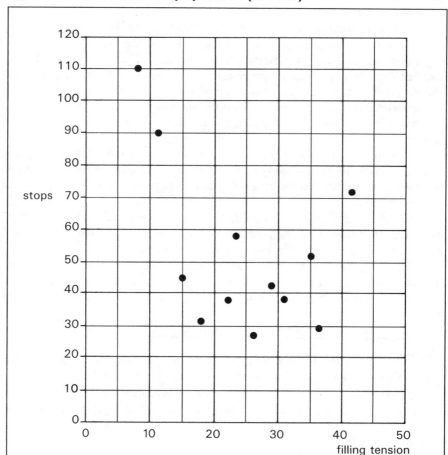

system. This consists of safety switches meant to stop the loom if the shuttle was not at the right place at the right time.

A supervisor spoke up, "I remember one evening in the middle of the second shift we began having trouble with the motion protection. The loom kept shutting down. They fooled with it all night. It was finally fixed, I see, at 11 a.m. the next day. We lost 13 hours of production."

He and the loom fixer on his shift agreed to take as their project troublesome procedures on the motion protection system. They would evaluate progress in terms of either the number of breakdowns or hours of downtime for that reason. Other mechanical downtime entries concerned random problems with clutches, picker motion, bearings and the like. There seemed to be no pattern.

I said, "Electrical problems, such as motion protection, can catch you by surprise. They represent one class of possible exceptions to prevention mentioned earlier. But we should not be surprised by most of these breakdowns. PM could have prevented them."

None of the remaining entries suggested misuse or defective parts.

"In view of that," I asked the maintenance manager, "would you be willing to take as your project to evaluate present PM deficiencies and upgrade as necessary to prevent breakdowns? Hours of mechanical downtime will be your measure of performance. Notice that includes the two other projects, but you have overall responsibility for maintenance anyway. You can judge progress by comparing with the January total of 1,170 hours. You will also need to begin reporting maintenance cost by loom; keeping separate totals for labour and parts."

Two loom fixers were normally assigned to overhaul, so they would actually do the PM legwork. The maintenance manager, as appropriate to his usual job responsibilities, would write procedures and supervise record-keeping.

Maintenance cost data would be important later for minimising unit cost. I expected an initial rise in maintenance cost, as needed repairs were done; but certainly lower total costs when legitimate savings on downtime were considered. It was not yet worth even mentioning, but I wanted to be prepared to show managers the real worth of what they had accomplished. For the time being we would try to bring simple problems under control. We could build on that after the men gained some confidence and understanding on how to be in control of these problems.

I said to the plant manager, "We need someone to impartially evaluate the cause of each breakdown, and to see that corrective action is taken. Would you make that your project?"

Of course he would. That was his job. The plant manager's participation is vital. He sets an example for others. Unless he participates, few others will. The entire improvement programme operates under his authority — the consultant merely guides and pressures people to set goals. This type of programme is genuinely a team effort that will not work if the plant manager's attitude is: "Consultant, you fix those supervisors, while I keep on doing just as before."

I wanted all managers to be actively involved in their own projects. Those not involved become bored by the training workshops and will be resented by the others. I said, "If anyone else has a project idea he would like to pursue, please speak up. If not, certainly other projects will develop as we analyse breakdown records. I will never ask you to do a 'makework' project just to say you have one."

The superintendent volunteered, "I will study the cost-effectiveness of an entirely different type of weft insertion that we could put on these looms if we have to."

"When will you be ready to give a first report?" (I always ask "when" and take notes.)

"In two weeks," he replied.

I read aloud my notes on project assignments and other commitments, and added, "The objective for the next workshop is to have baseline data for your project on a graph, and to explain how you plan to proceed. Any questions?"

A few days later

My first appointment was with the supervisor and loom fixer who had taken the weft insertion set-up project.

The supervisor said, "Explain to me how we are supposed to do this."

I replied, "What things have to be adjusted on the weft insertion mechanism?" (I took notes as he and the fixer mentioned a dozen adjustments.) "You can put a number or exact description on each of these. For instance, you have a gauge that could be used to measure filling tension." (That was one item on the list.) "How would you go about finding the best setting?"

The supervisor thought for a moment. "If the filling is too slack, it kinks. The weaver must stop the loom and take the kink out. If it is too tight, the end may be dropped and the loom stops itself. I guess we are looking for the fewest stops."

"Excellent," I said. "Set the tension by gauge. Count the number of stops during each shift, and then change the tension adjustment and try again. I will make a form for you to record the weft insertion settings, type of felt, type of filling, loom stops and data on anything else that might be a factor. Be sure to notify all weavers and fixers on this loom that you need a count of weft insertion stops. Make a note in the log book, put up a sign by the loom, and personally see the weavers to explain. This sounds like a lot of trouble, but you will get better data. Before the next meeting I will show you some simple ways to analyse your data." I assumed responsibility to ensure that each man was thoroughly prepared for the next workshop.

The next project concerned troubleshooting procedures for the motion protection system. I asked that supervisor about procedures used now. He looked sheepish.

"The only system we use is to keep replacing parts until it works. I know it is not very good. We do not waste good parts taken off, but we sure do waste time."

I got a wiring schematic from the loom's maintenance manual. "Where are you most likely to have trouble?" I began taking notes. "How can you test that part without removing it?"

After I had asked about every element in the system, I said, "I will get this typed. In the meantime, plan how to teach this to the loom fixers. An easy, enjoyable way would be to have each fixer troubleshoot a loom that you have disabled in various ways. Encourage competition by keeping score on how long it takes a fixer to repair it. That will stir up some interest. Give a prize, if you want. But, do plan the whole thing out on paper. In the next workshop, tell the other managers what you plan to do and when you will have the scores to present. I will see you again before the next meeting so that we can discuss your plan."

Next was the maintenance manager's project on upgrading preventive maintenance.

He began, "We have several problems with PM. First, my men are constantly under the gun to keep production looms running. They don't have time for PM.

The two overhaulers, who are supposed to do PM, will just get started when they get called to fix a breakdown; and they have to go."

He continued, "Another problem is that my men don't understand all the stuff on the PM checklists." (Daily, weekly, monthly and semi-annual checks were included in the manufacturer's technical manuals.) "Third, my men don't understand why they ought to fix something that is not broken. I wonder myself."

If the man in charge understands PM and is committed to it, then, one way or another, he will make it effective. This manager was admitting that he did not fully agree with it. Should I try to convince him, or simply make him do the right things long enough for results to begin improving?

I asked, "What kinds of things would have to happen to be proof positive to you that maintenance was doing a better job?"

"I am not sure," he said.

"Well, let's try it the other way. What would be evidence of worse maintenance?"

The maintenance manager pondered for a moment. "More breakdowns, I suppose." He had not kept maintenance cost records, and was not used to thinking in terms of choices that minimise unit cost. That would come later.

I said, "Do this. When the problem loom we talked about today is down for changeover to a new felt, then you and your two overhaulers plan to meticulously go through the PM checks. Since this is the first time, plan to be in there with them with your sleeves rolled up. Show the men how to follow the book exactly. That means you will need to study procedures beforehand and to make sure you have all the tools and gauges needed. If you have any questions, call the manufacturer. Arrange with the plant manager to have someone else cover your other responsibilities for as long as it takes to do this, and figure it will take two or three times as long as normal this first time. You may find a lot of worn parts to replace. Tell the production superintendent and plant manager what you plan to do. As you suggested, we will let breakdowns be the judge."

What I was trying to do here was to *make success unavoidable*. If the maintenance manager, or someone in authority, did not have first-hand knowledge of maintenance procedures, they could be in no position to supervise the fixers. I would have no way of knowing if recommended procedures were being followed. Also, while the maintenance manager worked side by side with his subordinates, he would see their strengths and weaknesses. He would find out what they did not know, and where they were likely to cut corners. He would know what to look for when checking their work in the future.

Meticulous adherence to the maintenance plan would cost plenty this time. It would delay the normal changeover, and others might press the maintenance manager for attention. I was trying to avoid any interference to getting this loom in top condition. It had better get results. If there was not a significant improvement in breakdowns or downtime hours, I would have to re-evaluate the manufacturer's recommendations. This latter prospect seemed unlikely.

The maintenance manager mentioned another possible interruption. "What should I do if the overhaulers get called for an emergency repair? It happens all the time. Should I tell production to wait?"

I answered with another question, "How do you think that situation should be handled?" Even if I were certain of the right answer, I would try to make the manager think of it himself.

"It makes the most sense to first work on the loom we can get running first. It would be silly to postpone a 10-minute repair while we finished an all-day job."

I said, "Good thinking. Tell the plant manager and production superintendent about this too, and do not let them pressure you into releasing the PM loom before it is ready. I want you to feel satisfied that every reasonable effort has been made to prevent breakdowns. This test will give you a clear idea of how far that is possible. You should expect a big improvement in mechanical downtime hours, but most likely there will still be some breakdowns. Plan to analyse their causes and then adjust PM."

I continued, "If I ask you about all this at the next project workshop, do you think you can explain it OK?" I never ask suprise questions that might embarrass anyone. Asking them beforehand is an admonition to prepare. If a manager does not prepare, that is his problem.

The day before the next workshop I followed up on the weft insertion project. Some data had been gathered during the week and I wanted to review it before the meeting.

The supervisor looked excited. "All this time everybody thought that filling tension was critical; too little and we would get kinks, too much and we would lose the pick. It is critical on the low side, but until the tension is quite high, it does not cause the pick to be dropped. We used to waste a lot of time adjusting the tension when we didn't need to. Look at this graph."

The graph showed a flat minimum number of stops over a broad range of filling tension. "This is a wonderful illustration of the value of data," I said. "What everybody 'knows' does not bear up when you measure it. I would like you to make an overhead transparency of this graph for the workshop tomorrow. I will ask you how you got the numbers and what they mean."

"What is the next step?" I asked.

"We only found one thing that does not cause weft insertion stops. We still have far too many — about 40 per shift on the types of filling that are a problem. It takes about a minute and a half to fix each stop. What do you think I should do now?" he asked.

"When you first discussed weft insertion, you mentioned ten other adjustments." I looked at my notes. "But the manual on this loom says these are not really variable. There is simply one right setting for all cases. You can try varying these settings from recommendations; but before you do that, do you have any reason to believe that there is a problem with the normal settings?"

He described how they had an identical loom with far fewer weft insertion stops. "We have tried interchanging loom parts, but the problem has always been with this one loom."

As often happens, this man's project was about to take an unexpected turn. I had thought this would be a simple matter of optimising settings. Apparently, the problem was more subtle. "Something about the two looms has to be different.

But, before interchanging any parts again, let's get a baseline count on weft insertion stops with the same felt on the good loom. At the meeting tomorrow, show the data you have already, and explain how you plan to proceed. Let us talk more about that right now."

Project workshops are a consultant's weekly reward for careful planning and organising. Client managers actually do most of the work, but a good consultant knows how to get the best out of them. Most people's limitations stem not from lack of know-how or ability, but from a lack of short-term goals and from not being asked to make commitments. Nearly everybody wants to be a "winner", but few have the self-discipline to break a big goal into daily commitments to prepare to win.

The maintenance manager wanted looms to be maintained better. Surely he had heard about preventive maintenance — loom technical manuals explained it clearly. Yet, PM was not done because it demanded action today for reward at some indefinite future time. The maintenance manager and his men could only motivate themselves to do what they *had* to do today for reward tomorrow. Thus, effective corrective action is aimed not at "theory and principles of preventive maintenance", but rather at setting up conditions that compel small, successive steps in the right direction. Weekly workshops, on-the-job meetings, and an occasional push from the plant manager are all that are needed to do this.

My intermediate objective is to help my clients see that achievement itself becomes its own reward, so that managers are less dependent on the contrivance of a "programme" to sustain motivation. The foundation of achievement is measured progress and a goal. The supervisor's excitement about the loom stop data is classic evidence of achievement motivation. He began the project to please others, but he will take the next step to please himself.

I have a "window of opportunity" at the beginning of each consultancy programme. Most people will co-operate simply because they are asked. Good will only lasts a few weeks. It is critical that initial efforts gain some measurable progress in order for the programme to sustain itself. This is why I chose to concentrate effort on narrowly defined but highly visible goals such as weft insertion stops.

Second workshop

I began the next project workshop by asking the supervisor who had been studying weft insertion stops to show a transparency of his graph. By way of an introduction, I asked questions such as: "What is the objective of your project? Why did you gather this particular information? Would you explain exactly what it is you are measuring and how you measured it?" Questions like these guide the presenter through a better presentation, and subtly teach him how to prepare a talk. I had taken notes ahead of time, and knew what points to emphasise.

I continued, "Tell us your interpretation of these numbers. Why did they surprise you? How did you decide what to do next?" A consultant should already know the answers to questions he asks in this type of meeting.

Comments were invited. The most important questions — always to be asked — are:

(1)   Based on what you have learned so far, how will you do the job differently?

(2)   What is the next step in this project? When will you take it?

(3)   What do you expect to learn from it?

Questions like these ensure that the project proceeds by plan and not by accident, that there is a clear purpose for each step in the plan, that there is a timetable for progress, and that findings are translated into specific actions on the job. Also, breaking the projects into steps (if appropriate), with a goal or discovery or sense of completion for each, helps sustain interest and prevent discouragement.

All these projects at Potomac Dryer Felt Company illustrate "technical" problems in the sense that employees did not know how to set up or maintain looms to prevent breakdowns. The weft insertion project is a classic case of collecting data by experiment. In this case the supervisor deliberately changed one variable (filling tension) and got data from ongoing production.

The maintenance manager's analysis of breakdowns shows how data can be obtained without having to deliberately change or control anything. No chart is given because the only cause of breakdowns found was maintenance error or PM omission.

---

[1] Manufacturers often use two types of production efficiency — usually called "labour efficiency" and "utilisation", or "labour efficiency" and "cost efficiency". Potomac's reports are usually called labour efficiency, meaning that some or all of downtime is subtracted from scheduled hours before computing efficiency. If a worker gets six hours' worth of work done, and can justify two hours of downtime, then he is credited with 100 per cent efficiency. Utilisation is percentage productive time. Cost efficiency does not allow for any downtime, thus it is a painfully honest measure of performance.

[2] This illustrates the importance of first digging out the facts. Opinions are worthless, except as a starting point for gathering facts. Even authentic-looking reports can greviously mislead. One indisputable fact is true cost efficiency = (weekly production)/(maximum theoretical production). Anybody can count how many units a machine can produce in an hour of faultless operation. Opportunities to increase this "standard" rate may exist, but our first goal was to be sure that machines are kept in continuous operation, except for planned maintenance.

[3] By definition, downtime is scheduled hours minus earned hours. Earned hours is actual units produced divided by standard units per hour. For example, if a machine is capable of ten units per hour, and 50 units are produced during an eight-hour shift, then five hours are earned. Downtime is $8 - 5 = 3$ hours, and cost efficiency is 62.5 per cent. In this particular case, the immediate goal was to reduce downtime; although the ultimate goal is always to reduce unit production costs. The problem with unit cost is that it is made up of so many factors that it can be difficult to compute and may obscure progress in removing causes of downtime. The purpose of measuring is to evaluate progress. Since efforts are far more effective when focused on one or two problems at a time, then determine the simplest way to measure these. When each cost factor is under control, the total will be under control.

CASE HISTORY OF PROCESS CONSULTING
(Apex Manufacturing Company)

In his book *Process consultation*, Edgar Schein [1] provides a case history of the Apex Manufacturing Company to explain the progressive steps and procedures of an assignment using the process-consulting approach.

1. Initial contact with the client and defining relationships

The contact client from the Apex Manufacturing Company was a divisional manager one level below the president. The company is a large manufacturing concern, organised into several divisions. The contact client indicated that there were communication problems in the top management group resulting from a recent reorganisation. Because the company expected to grow rapidly in the next several years, they felt they should work on this kind of problem now.

He spoke openly about his concern that the president needed help in handling certain key people, shared his worries that the president and his key subordinates were not in good communication, and indicated that recent company history suggested the need for some stabilising force in the organisation. I asked him whether the president knew he had come to me and what the president's feelings were about bringing in a consultant. The contact client indicated that the president as well as other key executives were all in favour of bringing someone in to work with them. All saw the need for some outside help.

Eventually, after many months of working with the president and his six key subordinates, I arrived at a point where all of them saw me as a potentially useful communication link. They asked me quite sincerely to report to each one the feelings or reactions of others whenever I learned anything I felt should be passed on. At the same time they were quite open with me about each other, knowing that I might well pass on any opinions or reactions they voiced to me. They did not want me to treat everything as confidential because they trusted me and each other enough.

This case was of great interest because of my own feeling that my having to

549

serve as carrier of this type of information was not an ideal role for me, and reflected an insufficient ability on their part to tell each other things directly. Hence I took two courses of action. First, I tried as much as possible to train each man to tell others in the group directly what he thought about an issue. At the same time, I intervened directly in their process by passing on information and opinions if I felt this would aid the working situation.

A simple yet critical event will illustrate what I mean. Two members, Pete and Joe, did not always communicate freely with each other, partly because they felt some rivalry. Pete had completed a study and written a report which was to be discussed by the whole group. Three days before the report was due, I visited the company and stopped in at Pete's office to discuss the report with him and ask how things were going. He said they were fine, but frankly he was puzzled about why Joe hadn't come to him to look at some of the back-up data pertaining to Joe's function. Pete felt this was just another bit of evidence that Joe did not really respect Pete very much.

An hour or so later I was working with Joe, and raised the issue of the report. Joe and his staff were very busy preparing for the meeting but nothing was said about looking at the back-up data. When I asked why they had not done anything about the data, Joe said that he was sure it was private and would not be released by Pete. Joe wanted badly to see it, but felt sure that Pete had deliberately not offered it. I decided there was no harm in intervening at this point by reporting to Joe how Pete was feeling. Joe expressed considerable surprise; and later in the day, he went to Pete, who gave him a warm welcome and turned over to him three volumes of the data which Joe had been wanting to see and which Pete had wanted very much to share with him. I had to judge carefully whether I would hurt *either* Pete or Joe by revealing Pete's feelings. In this case I decided the potential gains outweighed the risks.

Getting back to setting the proper expectations on the part of the company, I have to make it very plain that I will not function as an expert resource on human-relations problems, but that I will try to help the group solve those problems by providing alternatives and by helping them to think through the consequences of various alternatives. I also need to stress my expectation that I will gather data primarily by observing people in action, not by interviewing and other survey methods (though these methods would be used whenever appropriate). Finally, I have to point out that I will not be very active, but will comment on what is happening or give feedback on observations only as I feel it will be helpful to the group.

The fact that I will be relatively inactive is often a problem for the group because of their expectation that once they have hired a consultant they are entitled to sit back and just listen to him tell them things. To have the consultant then spend hours sitting in the group and saying very little not only violates this expectation but also creates some anxiety about what he is observing. The more I can reassure the group early in the game that I am not gathering personal data of a potentially damaging nature, the smoother the subsequent observations will go.

In summary, part of the early exploration with the contact client and any associates whom he involves is intended to establish the formal and psychological contract which will govern the consultation. I feel there should be no formal contract beyond an agreement on a per diem fee and a potential number of days to be devoted to working with the client system. Each party should be free to terminate or change the level of involvement at any time. At the psychological contract level, it is important to get out into the open as many misconceptions as possible, and to try to be as clear as possible about my own style of work, aims, methods, and so on.

2. Method of work

The method of work chosen should be as congruent as possible with the values underlying process consultation. Thus, observation, informal interviewing, and group discussions would be congruent with:

(1) the idea that the consultant does not already have pat answers or standard "expert" solutions, and

(2) the idea that the consultant should be maximally available for questioning and two-way communication.

If the consultant uses methods like questionnaires or surveys, he himself remains an unknown quantity to the respondent. As long as he remains unknown, the respondent cannot really trust him, and hence cannot really answer questions completely honestly. The method of work chosen, therefore, should make the consultant maximally visible and maximally available for interaction.

Often I choose to start a consultation project with some interviewing, but the purpose of the interview is not so much to gather data as to establish a relationship with each of the people who will later be observed. The interview is designed to *reveal myself* as much as it is designed to *learn something about the other person.* I will consider the use of questionnaires only after I am well enough known by the organisation to be reasonably sure that people would trust me enough to give direct and frank answers to questions.

In the Apex Company, the exploratory meeting led to the decision to attend one of the regular meetings of the executive committee. At this time I was to meet the president and the other key executives to discuss further what could and should be done. At this meeting, I found a lively interest in the idea of having an outsider help the group and the organisation to become more effective. I also found that the group was willing to enter an open-ended relationship. I explained as much as I could my philosophy of process consultation and suggested that a good way of getting further acquainted would be to set up a series of individual interviews with each member of the group. At the same time, I suggested that I sit in on the weekly half-day meetings of the executive committee. The interviews then would occur after several of these meetings.

At the initial meeting of the group, I was able to observe a number of key events. For example, the president, Alex, was very informal but very powerful. I got the impression initially (and confirmed it subsequently) that the relationship of all the group members to the president would be the key issue, with relationships to each other being relatively less important. I also got the impression that Alex was a very confident individual who would tolerate my presence only as long as he saw some value in it; he would have little difficulty in confronting me and terminating the relationship if my presence ceased to have value.

It was also impressive, and turned out to be indicative of a managerial style, that Alex did not feel the need to see me alone. He was satisfied from the outset to deal with me inside the group. Near the end of the initial meeting, I requested a private talk with him to satisfy myself that we understood the psychological contract we were entering into. He was surprisingly uncomfortable in this one-to-one relationship, had little that he wished to impart to me, and did not show much interest in my view of the relationship. I wanted the private conversation in order to test his reaction to taking some personal feedback on his own behaviour as the consultation progressed. He said he would welcome this and indicated little or no concern over it. As I was to learn later, this reflected a very strong sense of his own power and identity. He felt he knew himself very well and was not a bit threatened by feedback.

Part of the initial mandate was to help the group to *relate to the president*. In the interviews which I conducted with group members, I concentrated quite heavily on what kind of things went well in the relationship; what kind of things went poorly; how relationship problems with the president were related to job performance; in what way the group members would like to see the relationship change, and so on. I did not have a formal interview schedule, but rather, held an informal discussion with each member around issues of the sort I have just mentioned.

Intervention by the consultant

In the Apex Company, I found that the treasurer consistently made the operating managers uncomfortable by presenting financial information in an unintentionally threatening way. He wanted to be helpful, and he felt everyone needed the information he had to offer, but it often had the appearance of an indictment of one of the other managers; his costs were too high, his inventory control had slipped, he was too high over budget, etc. Furthermore, this information was often revealed for the first time in the meeting, so that the operating manager concerned had no forewarning and no opportunity to find out why things had gone out of line. The result was often a fruitless argument about the validity of the figures, a great deal of defensiveness on the part of the operating manager, and irritation on the part of the president because the managers could not deal more effectively with the treasurer.

As I observed this process occurring repeatedly over several weeks, I decided that merely drawing attention to the pattern would not really solve the problem because everyone appeared to be operating with constructive intent. What the group needed was an alternative way to think about the use of financial control information. I therefore wrote a memo on control systems (see section 5) and circulated it to the group.

When this came up for discussion at a later meeting I was in a better position to make my observations about the group, since a clear alternative had been presented. My feeling was that I could not have successfully presented this theory orally because of the amount of heat the issue always generated, and because the group members were highly active individuals who would have wanted to discuss each point separately, making it difficult to get the whole message across.

In working with the Apex group I found the written "theory memo" a convenient and effective means of communication. With other groups I have found different patterns to be workable. For example, if the group gets away for a half-day of work on group process, I may insert a half-hour in the middle (or at the end) of the session to present whatever theory elements I consider to be relevant. The topics are usually not selected until I observe the particular "hang-ups" which exist in the group. I therefore have to be prepared to give, on short notice, an input on any of a variety of issues.

A final method of theory input is to make reprints of relevant articles available to the group at selected times. Often I know of some good piece of theory which pertains to what the group is working on. If I suggest that such an article should be circulated, I also try to persuade the group to commit some of its agenda time to a discussion of the article.

The key criterion for the choice of theory input is that the theory must be relevant to what the group already senses is a problem. There is little to be gained by giving "important" theory if the group has no data of its own to link to the theory. On the other hand, once the group has confronted an issue in its own process, I am always amazed at how ready the members are to look at and learn from general theory.

Agenda-setting interventions may strike the reader as a rather low-key, low-potency kind of intervention. Yet it is surprising to me how often working groups arrive at an impasse on simple agenda-setting issues. In a way, their inability to select the right agenda for their meetings, and their inability to discuss the agenda in a constructive way, is symbolic of other difficulties which are harder to pinpoint. If the group can begin to work on its agenda, the door is often opened to other process discussions. Let me provide some examples of how this approach works.

In the Apex Company I sat in for several months on the weekly executive-committee meeting, which included the president and his key subordinates. I quickly became aware that the group was very loose in its manner of operation: people spoke when they felt like it, issues were explored fully, conflict was fairly openly confronted, and members felt free to contribute. This kind of climate seemed constructive, but it created a major difficulty for the group. No matter how few items were put on the agenda, the group was never able to finish its work. The list of backlog items grew longer and the frustration of group members intensified in proportion to this backlog. The group responded by trying to work harder. They scheduled more meetings and attempted to get more done at each meeting, but with little success. Remarks about the ineffectiveness of groups, too many meetings, and so on, became more and more frequent.

My diagnosis was that the group was overloaded. Their agenda was too large, they tried to process too many items at any given meeting, and the agenda was a mixture of operational and policy issues without recognition by the group that such items required different allocations of time. I suggested to the group that they seemed overloaded and should discuss how to develop their agenda for their meetings. The suggestion was adopted after a half-hour or so of sharing feelings. It was then decided, with my help, to sort the agenda items into several categories, and to devote some meetings entirely to operational issues while others would be exclusively policy meetings. The operations meetings would be run more tightly in order to process these items efficiently. The policy questions would be dealt with in depth.

Once the group had made this separation and realised that it could function differently at different meetings, it then decided to meet once a month for an entire day. During this day they would take up one or two large questions and explore them in depth. The group accepted my suggestion to hold such discussions away from the office in a pleasant, less hectic environment.

By rearranging the agenda, the group succeeded in rearranging its whole pattern of operations. This rearrangement also resulted in a redefinition of my role. The president decided that I should phase out my attendance at the operational meetings, but should plan to take a more active role in the monthly one-day meetings. He would set time aside for presentation of any theory I might wish to make, and for process analysis of the meetings. He had previously been reluctant to take time for process work in the earlier meeting pattern, but now welcomed it.

The full-day meetings changed the climate of the group dramatically. For one thing, it was easier to establish close informal relationships with other members during breaks and meals. Because there was enough time, people felt they could really work through their conflicts instead of having to leave them hanging. It was my impression that as acquaintance level rose, so did the level of trust in the group. Members began to feel free to share more personal reactions with each other. This sense of freedom made everyone more relaxed and readier to let down personal barriers and report accurate information. There was less need for defensive distortion or withholding.

After about one year the group decided quite spontaneously to try some direct confrontive feedback. We were at one of the typical monthly all-day meetings. The president announced that he thought each group member should tell the others what he felt to be the strengths and weaknesses of the several individuals. He asked me to help in designing a format for this discussion. I first asked the group members whether they did in fact want to attempt this type of confrontation. The response was sincerely positive, so we decided to go ahead.

The format I suggested was based upon my prior observation of group members. I had noticed that whenever anyone commented on anyone else, there was a strong tendency to answer back and to lock in on the first comment made. Hence, further feedback tended to be cut off. To deal with this problem I suggested that the group discuss one person at a time, and that a ground rule be established that the person being described was not to comment or respond until all the members had had a chance to give all of their feedback. This way he would be forced to continue to listen. The ground rule was accepted, and I was given the role of monitoring the group to ensure that the process operated as the group intended it to.

For the next several hours the group then went into a very detailed and searching analysis of each member's managerial and interpersonal style, including that of the president. I encouraged members to discuss both the positives and the negatives they saw in the person. I also played a key role in forcing people to make their comments specific and concrete. I demanded examples, insisted on clarification, and generally asked the kind of question which I thought might be on the listener's mind as he tried to understand the feedback. I also added my own feedback on points I had observed in that member's behaviour. At first it was not easy for the group either to give or receive feedback, but as the day wore on, the group learned to be more effective.

The total exercise of confrontation was considered highly successful, both at the time and some months later. It deepened relationships, exposed some chronic problems which now could be worked on, and gave each member much food for thought in terms of his own self-development. It should be noted that the group chose to do this spontaneously after many months of meetings organised around work topics. I am not sure they could have handled the feedback task effectively had they been urged to try sooner, even though I could see the need for this type of meeting some time before the initiative came from the group.

In this case, my intervention tended to help the group move from chaotic meetings toward a differentiated, organised pattern. In the end, the group spent more time in meetings than before, but they minded it less because the meetings were more productive. The group has also learned how to manage its own agenda and how to guide its own processes.

Feedback systems to groups and individuals

After getting to know the top-management group through several group meetings, I suggested that it might be useful to interview and give feedback to the next level below the vice-president. There was some concern on the part of the senior group that there might be a morale problem at this level. Initially I was asked merely to do an interview survey and report back to the top group. I declined this approach for reasons already mentioned: gathering data to report to a higher group would violate process-consulting assumptions because it would not involve the sources of the data in analysing their own process. I suggested instead that I conduct the interview with the ground rule that all my conclusions would first be reported back to the interviewee group, and that I would tell top management only those items which the group felt should be reported.[2] The group would first have to sort the items and decide which things they could handle by themselves and which should be reported up the line of authority because they were under higher management control. The real value of the feedback should accrue to the group which initially provided the data; they should become involved in examining the issues they had brought up, and consider what they themselves might do about them.

The above-mentioned procedure was agreed upon by the top management. One vice-president sent a memorandum to all members who would be involved in the interview programme, informing them of the procedure, his commitment to it, and his hope that they would participate. I then followed up with individual appointments with each person concerned. At this initial appointment I recounted the origin of the idea, assured the interviewee that his *individual* responses would be entirely confidential, told him that I would summarise the data by department, and told him that he would see the group report and discuss it before any feedback went to his boss or higher management.

In the interview I asked each person to describe his job, tell what he found to be the major pluses and minuses in the job, describe what relationships he had to other groups, and how he felt about a series of specific job factors such as challenge, autonomy, supervision, facilities, salary and benefits, and so on. I later summarised the interviews in a report in which I tried to highlight what I saw to be common problem areas.

All the respondents were then invited to a group meeting at which I passed out the summaries, and explained that the purpose of the meeting was to examine the data, deleting or elaborating where necessary, and to determine which problem areas might be worked on by the group itself. We then went over the summary item by item, permitting as much discussion as any given item warranted.

The group meeting had its greatest utility in exposing the interviewees, in a systematic way, to interpersonal and group issues. For many of them, what they had thought to be private gripes turned out to be organisational problems which they could do something about. The attitude "let top management solve all our problems" tended to be replaced with a viewpoint which differentiated between intra-group problems, inter-group problems, and those which were higher management's responsibility. The interviewees not only gained more insight into organisational psychology, but also responded positively to being involved in the process of data gathering itself. It symbolised to them top management's interest in them and concern for solving organisational problems. Reactions such as these are typical of other groups with whom I have tried the same approach.

Following the group meeting, the revised summary was then given to top management, in some cases individually, in others, in a group. My own preference is to give it first individually, to provide for maximum opportunity to explain all the points, and then to follow up with a group discussion of the implications of the data revealed in the interviews. Where the direct supervisor of the group is involved, I have often supplemented the group report with an individual report, which extracts all the comments made by interviewees concerning the strengths and weaknesses of the supervisor's style of management. These focused feedback items have usually proved of great value to the manager, but they should be provided only if the manager initially *asked for this type of feedback*.

In giving either individual or group feedback from the interview summary, my role is to ensure understanding of the data and to stimulate acceptance of it, so that remedial action of some sort can be effectively undertaken. Once the expectation has been built that top management will do something, there is great risk of lowering morale if the report is merely read, without being acted upon in some manner. Incidentally, it is the process consultant's job to ensure that top management *makes this commitment initially* and that high-level officials understand that when the interviews are completed there will be some demands for action. If management merely wants information (without willingness to do something about the information), the process consultant should not do the interviews in the first place. The danger is too great that management will not like what it hears and will suppress the whole effort; such a course will only lead to a deterioration of morale.

The results of interviews (or questionnaires) do not necessarily have to go beyond the group which is interested in them. One of the simplest and most helpful things a group can do to enhance its own functioning is to have the consultant interview the members individually and report back *to the group as a whole* a summary of its own members' feelings. It is a way of hauling crucial data out into the open without the risk of personal exposure of any individual if he feels the data collected about him are damaging or that the analysis of such data will result in conclusions that are overcritical of his performance.

The giving of individual feedback can be illustrated from several cases. In the Apex Company I met with each of the vice-presidents whose groups had been interviewed and gave them a list of comments which had been made about their respective managerial styles. I knew each man well and felt that he would be able to accept the kind of comments which were made. In each case we scheduled at least a one-hour session, so we could talk in detail about any items which were unclear and/or threatening.

These discussions usually become counselling sessions to help the individual overcome some of the negative effects which were implied in the feedback data. Since I knew that I would be having sessions such as these, I urged each interviewee to talk at length about the style of his boss and what he did or did not like about it. In cases where the boss was an effective manager, I found a tendency for subordinates to make only a few vague generalisations which I knew would be useless as helpful feedback. By probing for specific incidents or descriptions, it was possible to identify just what the boss did which subordinates liked or did not like.

Making suggestions

The consultant must make it quite clear that he does not propose any particular solution as the best one. However frustrating it might be to the client, the process consultant must work to create a situation where *the client's ability to generate his own solutions is enhanced*. The consultant wants to increase problem-solving ability, not to solve any particular problem.

In my experience there has been only one class of exceptions to the above "rule". If the client wants to set up some meetings specifically for the purpose of working on organisational or interpersonal problems, or wants to design a data-gathering method, then the consultant indeed does have some relevant expertise which he should bring to bear. From his own experience he knows better than the client the pros and cons of interviews or questionnaires; he knows better what questions to ask, how to organise the data, and how to organise feedback meetings; he knows better the right sequence of events leading up to a good discussion of interpersonal process in a committee. In such matters, therefore, I am quite direct and positive in suggesting procedures, who should be involved in them, who should be told what, and how the whole project should be handled.

For example, I recall that in the Apex Company the president decided at one of their all-day meetings to try to give feedback to all the members. He asked me to suggest a procedure for doing this. In this instance I was not at all reluctant to suggest, with as much force and logic as I could command, a particular procedure which I thought would work well. Similarly, when it was proposed to interview all the members of a department, I suggested exactly how this procedure should be set up; I explained that all the members had to be briefed by the department manager, that a group feedback meeting would have to be held, and so on. I have not been at all hesitant in refusing to design a questionnaire study if I thought it was inappropriate, or to schedule a meeting on interpersonal process if I thought the group was not ready.

In conclusion, the process consultant should not withhold his expertise on matters of the learning process itself; but he should be very careful not to confuse being an expert on *how to help an organisation to learn* with being an expert on *the actual management problems* which the organisation is trying to solve. The same logic applies to the evaluation of individuals; I will under no circumstances evaluate an individual's ability to manage or solve work-related problems; but I will evaluate an individual's readiness to participate in an interview survey of his group or a feedback meeting. If I feel that his presence might undermine some other goals which the organisation is trying to accomplish, I will seek a solution which will bypass this individual. These are often difficult judgements to make, but the process consultant cannot evade them if he defines *the overall health of the organisation* as his basic target. However, he must always attempt to be fair both to the individual and the organisation. If no course of action can be found without hurting either, then the whole project should probably be postponed.

3. Evaluation of results

Considerable value change and skill growth occurred over the course of the first year. During this time I spent a great deal of time in two major activities: (1) sitting in on various meetings of the top-management group; and (2) conducting interview and feedback surveys of various key groups, as managers decided they wanted such interviews done. In addition, there were periods of individual counselling, usually resulting from data revealed in the interviews.

I have already given examples of the kind of specific activities which occurred in the group meetings, interviews, and feedback sessions. It was clear that with increasing experience, the group was learning to tune in on its own internal processes (skill), was beginning to pay more attention to these and to give over more meeting time to analysis of interpersonal feelings and events (value change), and was able to manage its own agenda and do its diagnosis without my presence (skill). The group first discovered this from having to conduct some of its all-day meetings in my absence. Where such meetings used to be devoted entirely to work content, the group found that even in my absence they could discuss interpersonal process with profit. The members themselves described this change as one of "climate". The group felt more open and effective; members felt they could trust each other more; information was flowing more freely; less time was being wasted on oblique communications or political infighting.

During the second year, my involvement was considerably reduced, though I worked on some specific projects. The company had set up a committee to develop a management-development programme. I was asked to sit in with this committee and help in the development of a programme. After a number of meetings, it became clear to me that the kind of programme the group needed was one in which the content was not too heavily predetermined. The problems of different managers were sufficiently different to require that a formula should be found for discussing the whole range of problems. One of the reflections of the value change which had taken place in the managers was their recognition that they should be prime participants in any programme which they might invent. If a programme was not exciting or beneficial enough to warrant the committee's time, it could hardly be imposed on the rest of the organisation.

We developed a model which involved a series of small-group meetings at each of which the group would set its own agenda. After every third meeting or so, a larger management group would be convened for a lecture and discussion period on some highly relevant topic. Once the first group (the committee plus others at the vice-president level) had completed six to eight meetings, each member of the original group would become the chairman for a group at the next lower level of the organisation. These ten or so next-level groups would then meet for six to eight sessions around agenda items developed by themselves. In the meantime the lecture series would continue. After each series of meetings at a given organisational level, the model would be reassessed and either changed or continued at the next lower level with the previous members again becoming group chairmen.

My role in this whole enterprise was, first, to help the group to invent the idea; second, to meet with the original group as a facilitator of the group's efforts to become productive; third, to serve as a resource on topics to be covered and lecturers to be used in the lecture series; and fourth, to appear as an occasional lecturer in the lecture series or as a source of input at a small group meeting. As this procedure took form, my involvement was gradually reduced, though I still met with the original committee to review the overall concept.

In recent months I have met occasionally with individual members of the original group and with the group as a whole. My function during these meetings is to be a sounding-board, to contribute points of view which might not be represented among the members, and to help the group to assess its own level of functioning. I have been able to provide the group with some perspective on its own growth as a group because I could more easily see changes in values and skills. It has also been possible for the group to enlist my help with specific interpersonal problems. A measure of the growth of the group has been its ability to decide when and how to use my help, and to make those decisions validly from my point of view in terms of where I felt I could constructively help.

4. Disengagement: reducing involvement with the client system

The process of disengagement has, in most of my experiences, been characterised by the following features where:

(1) reduced involvement is a mutually agreed upon decision rather than a unilateral decision by consultant or client;

(2) involvement does not generally drop to zero but may continue at a very low level;

(3) the door is always open from my point of view for further work with the client if the client desires it.

In most of my consulting relationships there has come a time when either I felt that nothing more could be accomplished and/or some members of the client system felt the need to continue on their own. To facilitate a reduction of involvement, I usually check at intervals of several months to see whether the client feels that the pattern should remain as is or should be altered. In some cases where I have felt that a sufficient amount has been accomplished, I have found that the client did not feel the same way and wanted the relationship to continue on a day-a-week basis. In other cases, I have been confronted by the client, as with the Apex Company, with the statement that my continued attendance in the operational group meetings was no longer desirable from his point of view. As the president put it, I was beginning to sound too much like a regular member to be of much use. I concurred in the decision and reduced my involvement to periodic all-day meetings of the group, though the initiative for inviting me remained entirely with the group. Had I not concurred, we would have negotiated until a mutually satisfactory arrangement had been agreed upon. I have sometimes been in the situation of arguing that I should remain fully involved even when the client has wanted to reduce involvement, and in many cases I have been able to obtain the client's concurrence.

The negotiation which surrounds a reduction of involvement is in fact a good opportunity for the consultant to diagnose the state of the client system. The kind of arguments which are brought up in support of continuing (or terminating) provide a solid basis for determining how much value and skill change has occurred. The reader may feel that since the client is paying for services, he certainly has the right to make unilateral decisions about whether or not to continue these services. My point would be that if the consultation process has even partially achieved its goals, there should arise sufficient trust between consultant and client to enable both to make the decision on rational grounds. Here again, it is important that the consultant should not be economically dependent upon any one client, or his own diagnostic ability may become biased by his need to continue to earn fees.

5. Memo on control systems

In this study with the Apex Company the following memo was prepared, distributed and later discussed in a meeting:

Some ideas why internal auditing is seen as nonhelpful or as a source of tension

(1) Auditors often feel primary loyalty to the auditing group rather than the company as a whole; they tend, at times, to feel themselves outside of the organisation. Managers, on the other hand, feel primary loyalty to the organisation.

(2) Auditors are typically rewarded for finding things wrong, less so for helping people get their work done. Managers, on the other hand, are rewarded for getting the job done, whether things were wrong or not.

(3) Auditors tend to be *(a) perfectionists*, and *(b)* focused on *particular problems* in depth. Managers, on the other hand, tend to be *(a)* "*satisfiers*" rather than maximisers (they tend to look for workable rather than perfect or ideal solutions), and *(b) generalists*, focusing on getting many imperfect things to work together toward getting a job done, rather than perfecting any one part of the job.

(4) The auditor's job tempts him to *evaluate* the line operation and to propose solutions. The manager, on the other hand, wants *descriptive* (non-evaluative) feedback and to design his own solutions.

Some possible disfunctional consequences of tension between line organisation and auditing function

(1) Members of the line organisation tend to pay attention to doing well, primarily in those areas which the auditor measures, whether those are important to the organisational mission or not.

(2) Members of the line organisation put effort into hiding problems and imperfections.

(3) Management tends to use information about subordinates in an unintentionally punishing way by immediate inquiries which give subordinates the

feeling of having the boss on their back even while they are already correcting the problem.

(4) Members of the line organisation are tempted to falsify and distort information to avoid punishment for being "found out", and to avoid having their boss "swoop down" on them.

(5) Detailed information gathered by the auditing function tends to be passed too far up the line both in the auditing function and the line organisation, making information available to people who are too far removed from the problem to know how to evaluate the information.

Some tentative principles for the handling of auditing

(1) *Line involvement.* The more the line organisation is involved actively in decisions concerning *(a)* which areas of performance are to be audited, and *(b)* how the information is to be gathered and to whom it is to be given, the more helpful and effective the auditing function will be.

(2) *Horizontal rather than vertical reporting.* The more the auditing information is made available, first to the man with the problem (horizontal reporting), then to his immediate boss only if the problem is not corrected, and then only to higher levels in either the line or the auditing group if the problem is still not corrected, the more likely it is that auditing will be effective (because line organisations will be less motivated to hide or falsify information and less likely to feel punished).

(3) *Reward for helping rather than policing.* The more the managers in the auditing group reward their subordinates for being *helpful* (based on whether they are being perceived as helpful by the line) rather than being efficient in finding problem areas, the more effective the auditing function will be. (Auditing people tend to be undertrained in how to use audit information in a helpful way; an appropriate reward system should be bolstered by training in how to give help.)

(4) *Useful feedback.* The more the auditing information is *relevant* to important operational problems, *timely* in being fed back as soon after problem discovery as possible, and *descriptive* rather than evaluative, the more useful it will be to the line organisation.

---

[1] E. H. Schein: *Process consultation* (Reading, MA, Addison-Wesley, 1969). Reprinted with the kind permission of the author and the publisher.

[2] This procedure was brought to E. H. Schein's attention by R. Beckhard. See also R. Beckhard: *Organisation development: strategies and models* (Reading, MA, Addison-Wesley, 1969).

CASE HISTORY OF A COMPANY TURNAROUND
(The Scandinavian Airlines System)

The Scandinavian Airlines System (SAS) is the national air carrier of Denmark, Norway and Sweden. These countries share ownership as follows: Denmark $2/7$, Norway $2/7$ and Sweden $3/7$. SAS is a mixed-economy enterprise: in each of the three countries, 50 per cent of the shares are in private hands and 50 per cent are owned by government. The SAS Group includes the airline and a number of subsidiaries for hotels, flight kitchens, restaurants, travel agencies and other operations. In 1984-85 the Group employed on average 29,727 persons, out of whom 18,845 were in the airline. In the same year SAS operated 91 aircraft, flew 125 million scheduled kilometres and carried 10.7 million passengers. It was ranked 16th among the 120 members of IATA.

This case history [1] describes a major business turnaround which was started in 1981 and within two years reshaped the company from top to bottom. Management consultants participated in this exercise all along: in diagnosing the company's strengths and weaknesses, defining a new strategy, implementing strategic plans, developing a new corporate image, streamlining internal organisation, implementing a cost reduction programme, training employees, improving communication and staff motivation, designing new computerised systems, and various other areas. However, it is difficult to say what exactly the consultants did and whether all their ideas and proposals were accepted and used by management. The reasons are (i) that the turnaround was managed and leadership provided by the company's own management, not by external consultants, and (ii) that most of the consulting work was directly integrated with the projects launched and carried out by the company, hence the changes made were the result of joint work and not of proposals developed separately by a consultant.

In addition to external consultants, the company's internal consultants were also involved. SAS had a relatively large team of about 30 internal consultants and it was normal to use their skills and potential for the turnaround. They participated in many different jobs in a similar way to the external consultants.

1. Background

Both the expansion of the airline market and the growth of airlines were relatively smooth until the mid-1970s. This was due to increasing demand for services, the protectionist aviation policies adopted by most governments, cartel-type arrangements among the airlines and slowly rising oil prices. Dramatic changes occurred after 1975. The world economic recession led to the stagnation of demand for air transport, oil prices increased sharply in 1973-74 and again in 1978-79, deregulation of air transport became a reality in the United States and started emerging in other countries, and competition became tough in all markets.

Against this background, many airlines which were profitable, or had at least managed to break even in the past years, started experiencing financial difficulties. Some went bankrupt in the late 1970s, in the United States in particular. Others sought rescue in severe cost cutting, gradually eliminating service after service, regardless of customers' needs and wishes.

After years of relatively comfortable though not very profitable operation, SAS also got into difficulties in the latter part of 1970s. The company's market share dropped, productivity declined, capacity was underused, and punctuality and the service image became alarmingly poor. The centre point of the SAS transport system, Kastrup airport in Copenhagen, acquired the reputation of a place to be avoided whenever one could find an alternative. The last year in which SAS made some profit was 1978-79. The two following financial years ended with a loss, which reached 109 million Swedish Kroner (SEK) (i.e. over $20 million) in airline operations in 1980-81, a record in SAS history.

2. Diagnosis

In 1980, the SAS Board of Directors realised where these trends would lead the company if they were to continue for a few more years. Further cost cutting without improving service quality was still technically possible but risked being suicidal, since it could only expedite further decline of consumer satisfaction and of the market share. The situation seemed to be ripe not for "some" improvements, but for a fundamental change. The company was in a crisis and the need for change was increasingly recognised. At this point, the future President and Chief Executive Officer (CEO) of SAS was brought in by the Board. He was Jan Carlzon, who had managed, and successfully turned around, two Swedish "daughter" companies within the SAS Group — the travel agency Vingresor and the domestic air carrier Linjeflyg. In November 1980 Carlzon became the head of the airline operations. His mandate, which he himself proposed to the Board, was to "make SAS profitable in its airline operations, and to achieve this goal in a zero-growth market". The scene for the turnaround was set.

The reference to "airline operations" in Carlzon's mandate was significant. For it had become quite normal in the airline business, including SAS, to lose money in airline operations but to make up for these losses (at least to some extent) by buying and selling aircraft and by other subsidiary operations.

Intensive diagnostic, auditing and strategic planning work was started in

December 1980. For three months, there were two parallel management teams — one running the daily operations, the other working on future strategy and restructuring. Alongside the CEO, the "strategic team" included several SAS managers and two external consultants. These consultants were chosen by the CEO as individual experts. This reflected the company's established practice of using management consultants. Even if a consultant came from an important and reputable consulting firm, SAS management chose him and worked with him in his individual capacity. The "strategic team" commissioned several special studies (e.g. operating performance comparisons with other airlines, or studies of trends in airline industry) and some of these studies were made by consultants.

The strategic team completed its work and submitted proposals to the Board in March 1981. In April 1981, a new organisation was installed and the two management teams merged. Within two months, plans for putting the new strategy into effect were developed, and the Board was in a position to approve them in June 1981. Carlzon became President and CEO of SAS in August 1981.

3. Corporate strategy

SAS reports that it was relatively simple to reach consensus on the strategic approach to take. Further cost cutting as practised in the 1970s would have been, using Carlzon's own words, like "stepping on the brakes of a car that is already standing still". Therefore the only way out was to increase revenue without, of course, losing control of costs. But higher revenues meant higher quality services, new kinds of service, and more customers. In a stagnating market, more customers implied better marketing and a competitive edge over other airlines. The era of reserved markets was coming to an end and completely new attitudes to the air transport business were required. From a production-oriented organisation dominated by technological considerations the airline had to be converted into a market-oriented service organisation, which regarded the customer as the focal point of its endeavours, and the happy customer, not the most modern aircraft, as its principal asset.

The strategy chosen by SAS was to become the best airline and the first choice for "the frequent business traveller". This choice reflected the nature of the airline's principal market, which was the internal market of the three Scandinavian countries, plus the connections between Scandinavia and over 30 destinations in 17 European countries. Frequent business travellers were regular users of SAS services on this market, and, given the choice, would stay with SAS if they got excellent service. Thus, SAS could maintain and increase the share of those passengers who paid the full price. However, as distinct from other airlines that introduced a "business class" before SAS, it was decided not to increase the air fare. New and improved services had to be offered to the businessman for the same price. In addition, improvements had to be achieved in all areas and aspects of services provided by SAS to its customers. The "party line" was "let us be one per cent better in a hundred details rather than a hundred per cent better in only one detail".

This was not always possible without increasing costs. Convinced that the new strategy was right, management was prepared to take the risk and approve cost increases in justified cases in order to generate more income, and asked for specific suggestions on how to improve service, even if this implied higher costs. The investment cost of all the suggestions made, and endorsed by management, reached $40 million, and the additional annual operating costs $10 million.

Some 150 specific action proposals, or projects, were developed and gradually put into effect in implementing the "businessman's airline" strategy. The most prominent were:

— the introduction of EuroClass (within Europe) and First Business Class (on intercontinental flights) for the business traveller, for the normal price of Economy Class;

— "operation punctuality" — a set of measures to achieve punctuality, regarded as a high priority by the business traveller;

— the revision of the flight network and frequency to achieve more profitable routes and the more frequent, non-stop flights required by the business traveller;

— substantial improvements of facilities, shorter distances between connecting flights (using a new optimisation model) and accelerated service to customers at Kastrup;

— various new services on the ground and in the air (information, communication, secretariat, special booking, quicker check-in procedures, separate counters for Business Class, new service packages, etc.);

— generally increased sensitivity to the needs and wishes of the business traveller.

To supplement its basic strategy, SAS developed a "marginal" strategy in order to sell whatever capacity was left after having served the full-fare business traveller. Mini-fares for tourists on intra-Nordic routes were introduced in June 1982 and on European routes in November 1982. This was made possible by a considerable increase in the number of full-fare travellers. Mini-fares attracted a growing number of tourists — on Nordic routes about ten times more in 1981-82 than in the previous year.

Another supplementary strategy concerned the cargo market which accounted for about 15 per cent of SAS total revenue (25-35 per cent on inter-continental routes). A fast door-to-door service was introduced for cargo customers, starting in Scandinavia. However, in this case the expected results became apparent only slowly. The improvement of cargo services and profitability therefore received renewed management attention after 1983, as one of the follow-up areas of the turnaround.

4. Staff participation and development

The basic turnaround strategy was developed by a relatively small team of managers and consultants under the leadership of the new CEO. This, however, was only the first step. It was clear from the beginning that detailed action plans could never be developed and the turnaround successfully implemented without involving the total staff. Carlzon likes to refer to the "moment of truth" in operating an airline such as SAS, which occurs when an individual SAS employee is in direct contact with an individual customer. If SAS has 10 million customers a year and each customer meets approximately five employees in SAS uniform, there are 50 million "moments of truth". Therefore, 50 million times something can go wrong, or, on the contrary, the airline's image can be enhanced thanks to SAS staff competence, initiative, courtesy and care for the passenger. Thus, the objective was to help SAS front-line employees, that is those dealing directly with customers, to take the best possible course of action in these "moments of truth" and in all other situations that could not be reglemented by any instructions and that escaped routine control by management.

SAS management made a special effort to provide all employees with complete information on the company's condition, the difficulties and challenges faced, the proposed changes in strategy and policies and the responsibilities to be assumed by every individual. The objective was to help everybody to view his or her own role and activity in the light of the overall situation, and to have enough information for taking initiative with the full conviction that it was aimed in the right direction.

Various information media were used, including numerous meetings where senior management met with staff, and the famous "little red book", entitled *Let's get in there and fight!*, distributed to all employees in 1981. People were told bluntly that the company had to fight, and win, a battle for its survival and future. They were invited to engage actively in this battle and the role of every single individual was emphasised. The management's view was that the most important thing for a person was to know that he or she was needed and that a very specific contribution to SAS recovery was expected from everyone.

For example, the Operations Control Centre at the Kastrup airport was the unit that had more control over punctuality than any other unit within SAS. Its manager was asked to come up with proposals for making SAS the most punctual airline in Europe within 6 months. He came back with proposals, and with a request for an additional $1.5 million in extra operating costs. This was authorised. However, SAS became the most punctual airline in Europe within only 4 months and the additional operating cost incurred by the Centre was only about $0.1 million, because the team had found new ways of working.

But there were problems in communicating with people, too. The strong emphasis on service orientation and on the customers' demands was perceived by some skilled technicians as a strategy that no longer attached the right importance to safety and to the technical aspects of airline operations. They criticised the management's approach and there was even some staff unrest. Management drew a lesson from this and adopted a more balanced approach, stressing that safety continued to be the main objective, and experienced technical personnel a very precious resource of the whole SAS Group.

Reorganisation of the company was a significant feature of the turnaround.

The objective was to increase the decision-making authority and the responsibility of middle and lower management, and to define precisely the contributions to be made by even the smallest organisational units. In doing so, the company organisation shifted from a predominantly vertical structure, in which many rungs in the management ladder issued and controlled instructions and lower management was responsible for implementing instructions and had little possibility of taking initiative, to a flat or horizontal structure in which the role of smaller decentralised units operating as profit centres was considerably increased and higher management was responsible for providing effective support to the operating core in addition to establishing broad strategy and policy guidelines.

A number of changes in management staff could not be avoided. The very appointment of a new CEO was a starting signal and an impetus to the turnaround. This was followed by the appointment of several new divisional vice-presidents and over 200 new "results responsible" managers of units within the company's structure. Reorganisation also involved some reductions in staff. The combined effect of reorganisation and cost cutting was the elimination of about 700 posts. However, lay-offs could be avoided, and the solution found in early retirement, transfers, and leave of absence.

The active participation of managers and staff in planning and implementing the changes required by the new strategy provided many opportunities for developing people at work, through specific projects and assignments. In addition, a specially designed management training programme was organised. It included a three-week programme for senior management and key trade union officials, a two-week course for middle managers and a one-week course for supervisors. All employees serving in the front line (about 10,000) went through a two-day service programme whose main objective was to help front-line staff in providing individualised service to customers. The programme (called a "smiling course" by the press) was a great success and demonstrated that Scandinavians were able to smile when dealing with customers. This two-day service programme took about one year of expert time to develop, including contributions from psychology, pedagogy and communication consultants in addition to those made by SAS professional staff. All these training activities focused on the new philosophy, goals, strategies, organisation and work methods of the company.

5. Cost trimming

As mentioned, the previously applied cost-cutting practices which had ignored the customers' needs and had proved to be detrimental to the airline's long-term interests had to be abandoned in the new strategy. Nevertheless, it was important to control costs and seek new opportunities for reducing them, in particular by eliminating activities whose contribution to generating a revenue was nil or marginal, or which were out of proportion to the company's needs and possibilities.

Thus, SAS took a painful decision to sell or lease out four A-300 Airbuses, marvels of technology by the pilots' standards, whose capacity was excessive and did not fit the company's new business strategy. Instead, priority was given to smaller planes, like the various versions of the Douglas DC-9 or even the 40-seat Fokker F-27 in some cases, which made feasible the more frequent, non-stop flights preferred by the business traveller.

The cost-analysis and cost-reduction methodology applied throughout the company, called TRIM 82, was provided by external consultants who were involved in the turnaround. Its basic idea is that linear cuts across the board are the least suitable methodology in a business enterprise aiming at long-term efficiency and profitability. Instead, a cost-cutting programme has to reflect the company's objectives and strategies. All units within the company engage simultaneously in a cost-analysis and cost-reduction exercise in the following steps:

— task mapping (examining groups of activities and their relevance to the objectives and strategies of the organisation, and identifying tasks where major savings can be achieved);

— analysis of necessary resource levels (producing recommendations for resource allocations, reductions or increases, bearing in mind the views of the service users likely to be affected);

— task or activity redesign (including negotiation of service content and level that can be delivered with altered resource allocations);

— commitment (which can be achieved because the people involved define and carry out their own cost-saving projects and are provided with the required resources, training and management support).

TRIM 82 produced some 200 million SEK (about \$30 million) of annual savings. Every division in SAS was assisted by a consultant throughout the exercise. The consultants helped in making sure that the right methodology was used and the time schedule maintained. However, the direct responsibility for the decisions taken and the results achieved remained with the respective managers.

6. New corporate image

In a service business, it is essential to communicate a major change in strategy, based on better quality service and new types of service, to the customers, both existing and potential. The message ought to be clear and unambiguous, so that the customer can quickly perceive the difference and the new benefits offered to him. To achieve this, SAS turned to consultants in communication and launched a special project for developing a new look or identity for the airline, and a major publicity campaign aimed at reaching the target — the business traveller — first of all.

An important assignment for developing a new corporate image was entrusted to an American consulting firm. It included new aircraft livery, interiors, reservation offices, ticket desks, logotype, colours, textiles, uniforms, customer documentation and other things. SAS accepted many of the consultants' basic ideas and declined or modified others, taking into account the cultural values and preferences of Scandinavian and European business travellers. The company and the consultants then worked together on final solutions.

A major publicity campaign in several steps was designed and organised with the assistance of Swedish advertising consultants. Each step was tailored to the particular phase of the turnaround and to the principal message that the company wanted to get across. Thus the November 1981 campaign supported the introduction of EuroClass and focused on the new image of the company; in Spring 1982 the second step emphasised the upgrading of the services to the business traveller; the Fall 1982 campaign presented the First Business Class on intercontinental flights and simultaneously another campaign (addressing a different public) introduced the Mini-fares; and an important campaign started in April 1983 pursued the objective of presenting the new corporate identity to the customers in its totality.

7. Results and future prospects

From the business point of view, the turnaround was completed and its main operational and financial targets attained by the end of financial year 1982-83. Table 1 shows that profitability was in fact restored within one year. The positive trend in results was maintained over the next three years. Every year after 1982-83 the profit figure set a new record, unprecedented in SAS history. As the volume of business increased, the airline was able to create 2,469 new jobs in three years against the 693 positions eliminated during the turnaround. The increase in the whole Group was 5,600 jobs in four years.

As regards service quality, SAS became number one in punctuality in Europe in 1982, and in 1984 its new strategy was publicly rewarded when the magazine *Air Transport World* nominated SAS the Airline of the Year 1983.

The results achieved show that the change process was extremely fast and pursued very specific and tangible goals. However, it was carried out in a particular atmosphere — SAS management itself presented the turnaround as a battle for survival and for ensuring the future, one requiring full staff engagement and total mobilisation of company resources. A new corporate identity was created and foundations of a new corporate culture were laid down. This cultural change itself was considered as a major achievement since in Scandinavia service to customers was not traditionally given much status and prestige; hence traditional cultural barriers had to be overcome. However, the question was whether the company would not exhaust its energy and resources by achieving a spectacular turnaround in record time, and whether it would be able to sustain momentum and preserve its competitive edge in the years to come.

SAS management has declared that the turnaround was only a first step in an effort to achieve superior performance in the long term. Since 1984, the company has therefore engaged in new long-term projections and in studies and projects aimed at preparing the airline for coping with such forseeable changes as deregulation of the European market and the need to purchase a new generation of airplanes in the early 1990s. SAS management has labelled this process "the second wave".

Table 1   SAS Group: selected results in 1979-85

Item	1979-80	1980-81	1981-82	1982-83	1983-84	1984-85
Operating revenue (SEK million)						
Group	9 220	10 172	12 807	15 972	18 005	19 790
Income before allocations and taxes (SEK million)						
Group	−63	−51	448	601	968	1 017
Airline	−54	−109	336	462	918	807
Personnel						
Group	24 980	24 124	24 770	26 657	28 526	29 727
Airline	17 069	16 425	16 376	17 101	17 710	18 845
Average exchange rate for 1$US (SEK)	4.17	5.60	6.28	7.83	8.04	8.88

Employee motivation and satisfaction will be a significant factor in these efforts. SAS management was successful in motivating staff for the turnaround, pointing to the crisis situation, emphasising the role of every individual and developing a common vision of what could be achieved in the future. Small gifts were distributed to the staff as a token of management's recognition, but wages were adjusted upwards only in a few cases. The future will show whether and how SAS staff can be motivated for excellent performance on a permanent basis.

Management consultants continue to be associated with this forward-looking process on a selective basis — as discussion partners and a sounding board for senior management, a source of special expertise and innovative ideas, trainers, new project co-designers or performance auditors. The consultants who helped SAS to map out and implement its turnaround strategy have been authorised to present this case to potential future clients as evidence of a successfully completed assignment. SAS management has even helped them with such presentations, thus confirming its conception of the role of management consultants and of the collaborative relationship between consultant and client.

---

[1] The case history is based on written and oral information provided by SAS. The following materials were used:

SAS Annual Reports, for financial years 1978-79 to 1984-85;

Managing a corporate recovery, lecture by Jan Carlzon in September 1983 (SAS, 1983);

Leadership is like a blueprint for a cathedral, speech by Jan Carlzon in November 1985 (SAS, 1985);

Let's get in there and fight! ("the little red book") (SAS, 1981);

The fight of the century (SAS, 1982);

Now we are going to use our heads (SAS, 1983);

The challenge (SAS, 1985).

PERSON-TO-PERSON
COMMUNICATION IN CONSULTING

This appendix is intended to provide an overview of some of the essentials required in consulting practice, emphasising that the person-to-person form of communication should be viewed not simply as an art and a skill, but as a downright necessity. Mastery of person-to-person communication adds to the stature of the consultant and sets him on the path to becoming a senior and highly respected practitioner.

1. General issues and problems

Person-to-person communication is vitally important for two reasons: primarily, because it is the means of linking the consultant and the client; and secondly, because of its role in bridging the concepts and practices of change between the management and the staff within the client organisation.

Review of management consulting practices suggests that on assignments approximately 30 per cent of the time is spent on problem analysis and related matters on an individual basis, whereas 70 per cent is spent in communicating with others. Thus, for the consultant and his client, communication represents a large slice of the available time and effort.

Listening is considered to be the single most important component (accounting for 45 per cent of the total communication time). Next in importance comes speaking (30 per cent), reading (16 per cent), and writing (9 per cent).[1] A quick glance at these figures reveals that three-quarters of management's time involves person-to-person communication — listening and speaking. Considering that the consultant has to provide functional expertise coupled with its application, it is inevitable that considerable emphasis should be placed on training in this form of communication. In training programmes for consultants up to 20 per cent of the total time is devoted to this task.

Finally, it stands to reason that ease of communication facilitates comprehension and acceptance of new ideas which is, after all, the main purpose of the consulting assignment.

Communication is the vehicle for transmitting knowledge and introducing attitude change. Person-to-person communication is its most effective form and essential for counselling work. It is the basis for the preparation of written reports, which usually do no more than confirm agreements previously reached.

Communication is also the source of power for three accelerators creating the greatest impact on the management scene today, i.e. changes in technology, changes in management concepts and methods, and the interaction of different cultures. Person-to-person communication is the final link in the chain required to bring them into effect. Additionally, such communication is a vital part of the synergy phenomenon, which explains why the collaborative efforts of members of a team are often more effective than the individual efforts of those same people.

Edgar Schein has summarised the factors affecting an individual's ability to "build, maintain, improve and, if need be, repair face-to-face relationships", in the following nine points:

(1) self-insight and a sense of one's own identity;

(2) cross-cultural sensitivity — the ability to decipher other people's values;

(3) cultural/moral humility — the ability to see one's own values as not necessarily better or worse than another's values;

(4) a pro-active problem-solving orientation — the conviction that interpersonal and cross-cultural problems can be solved;

(5) personal flexibility — the ability to adopt different responses and approaches as needed by situational contingencies;

(6) negotiation skills — the ability to explore differences creatively, to locate some common ground, and to solve the problem;

(7) interpersonal and cross-cultural tact — the ability to solve problems with people without insulting them, demeaning them, or destroying their "face";

(8) repair strategies and skills — the ability to resurrect, to revitalise, and to rebuild damaged or broken face-to-face relationships;

(9) patience.[2]

The consultant should be aware that person-to-person communication possesses direct advantages and disadvantages compared with other forms of communication. Major advantages include *immediacy* and *association*. Immediacy offers opportunities to raise questions and provide answers on relevant issues as needs arise. Association permits a clearer understanding of spoken words by associating them with accompanying gestures, intonation, emphasis, etc., and so provides appropriate interpretation. Such interpretation is necessary because the 500 most frequently used words of the English language possess more than 14,000 different meanings (an average of more than 28 per word), which leaves a good deal of room for possible error.

One major drawback to this form of communication is that permanent records are not usually maintained, and residual interpretation may not be a faithful reproduction of original messages owing to problems created by distortion, omission, addition, etc. To reduce errors of this nature the following considerations should be kept in mind:

- brevity (keep the message to a minimum),
- relevance (don't confuse the audience),
- draw conclusions (don't rely on inferences being properly made),
- consider audience level (communicate to express, not impress),
- use own natural style to best advantage (you cannot pretend to be what you are not, but you should, at least, perform to the best of your ability).

Critical elements in the communication process are represented in figure 1. References to the model shown can be found in most literature on this subject. Critical areas, from a consultant's point of view, occur throughout the system and are noted in the figure. They are discussed in the next section.

2. Using communication techniques in consulting

In consulting, person-to-person communication deals with either the reception or the presentation of information. During the life-cycle of an assignment composed of a *beginning*, a *middle* and an *end*, the emphasis for the consultant usually switches from reception to presentation of information. In the initial stages the consultant is mostly fully absorbed obtaining relevant information, and the presentations at this time are usually confined to explaining his presence in the organisation.

Reception techniques at the beginning stage

Reception techniques applied at the *beginning* stage involve listening and observing, which have to do with receptivity and assimilation. They might be thought of as "passive" exercises; but this would be entirely wrong, since full concentration is called for, and expected, during this crucial stage. Most people can absorb four times more information than can be delivered verbally; thus there is the ever-present danger of distraction.

Measures to facilitate information gathering include:
- soliciting permission to write down important facts (especially figures);
- using the pregnant pause, i.e. when the speaker stops talking, don't hurry to speak yourself, but look as if you are expecting futher information − when it comes it may be most revealing;
- encourage elaboration of points by asking "Anything else?", or "Yes, go on, please!";

Figure 1 Critical elements in reception and transmission of person-to-person communication

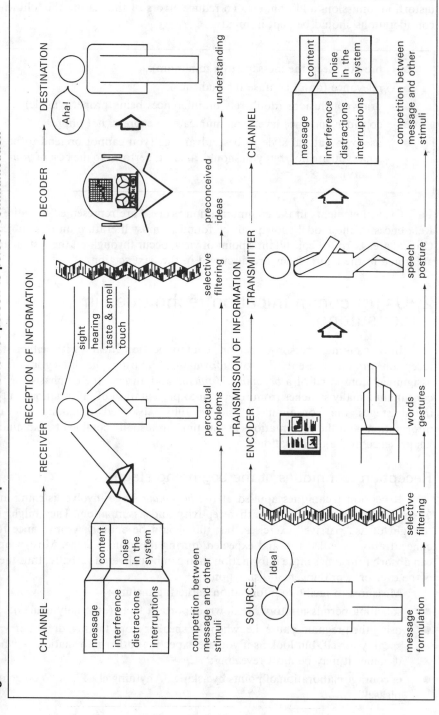

- ask for examples to illustrate generalities that are offered;
- try not to be involved in speculation, or answering questions in the fact-finding stage; advise that you will certainly give your opinion at a later stage but that you would first prefer to hear all other impressions;
- if necessary answer a question with a question, e.g. to a question put to you, reply with, "Why do you ask that?", or "Behind all good questions usually lies an answer — I would like to know your answer to your own question."

Because so much time is involved in listening and observing and the consultant may be impatient to proceed as rapidly as possible, it is quite possible that bad habits will develop. Some elementary precautions that might be taken to prevent this are indicated in table 1.

Table 1   Precautions to facilitate the listening process

Bad habits	Possible remedies
Becoming distracted	Try to analyse individual statements and evaluate them (award theoretical marks, e.g. 7 out of 10)
Taking too many notes	Select key points and write digest-style telegram notes
Making snap decisions	Record pertinent data
	Draw your conclusions after the meeting or interview
Lack of concentration	Try to anticipate the next idea, sentence or phrase
Selective listening	Look for new or hidden meanings
Interrupting the speaker	Wait until there is a natural break in the delivery

Case-building during the middle stage

In the *middle* stage of the communication process a large percentage of time becomes allocated to building a case for the proposed changes and preparing the necessary supporting documents and material. There can be insufficient time allowed for preparation, but only rarely can too much time be allocated; material which is not used can always be discarded.

Preparation involves the development of a structure for the presentation of conclusions and proposals whether it be for formal or informal presentation. There is no guarantee that your presentation will be heard in its entirety, so prepare summaries for delivery at its commencement, during its course, and on its conclusion so that early-leavers and late-comers (who may be important persons) can be provided with some idea of the total scope of your case.

An outline of your presentation may be in note form, on cards, etc., but should be available. If time and conditions permit, it is advisable to use audio-visual aids. Rehearsal will improve performance, and opportunities should be taken, whenever possible, to practise before a critical audience.

Delivering the presentation: the end stage

The *end* stage of the process usually revolves around presentations by the consultant. Critical elements to be kept in mind at this stage are:

- introduce the presentation with a summary outline of what is to follow;
- at the conclusion of discrete sections of your delivery, reference to the outline might usefully be repeated, e.g. "Let's see where we are, up to this stage";
- if you are delivering a tightly knit presentation, advise that questions will be handled only after the presentation has been completed or at set times during your delivery; in many cases you will probably have answered likely queries during the course of your presentation, and continuity of delivery and timing will not suffer;
- unless specifically warranted, do not commence with an apology: there is always a chance that it might not be accepted; confidence and a positive approach are priority personal qualities required to induce change;
- most people have an "image" of what they expect to see in a consultant in much the same way as they view doctors, lawyers, engineers and other professionals; by and large, neat but "neutral" clothing styles and a highly organised presentation are expected, and anything else may detract from the presentation;
- when handling questions, answer them one at a time; if objections are raised, deal with them as recommended in section 4.4;
- always make due acknowledgements to persons who have assisted you in your work — it may be necessary to make this a "thank you" to the whole organisation;
- if delivering from a written, fully prepared text, try to read each sentence to yourself, pause, look at your audience and say it aloud; pause, glance at the next sentence again silently and then repeat it aloud to your audience while looking at them; with practice, a flowing style can be developed which will convert a script-reading session into an imposing delivery;
- if the consultant is convinced that his proposal will supply the changes necessary to assist the organisation, he must have the strength and the will to fight for his case; this does not mean that he should seek to humiliate any opposition if there is room for compromise; however, he should resist it by every possible means.

Consultants bring a wealth of education and experience in communication with them to the profession. A young consultant should have his particular style observed and analysed by experienced colleagues and subsequently try to capitalise on his acknowledged strengths and take appropriate steps to remedy weaknesses.

Selected literature on person-to-person communication in consulting is listed in appendix 11.

[1] H. and Z. Roodman: *Management by communication* (Toronto, Methuen Publications, 1973), p. 146.

[2] Reproduced with acknowledgement from E. H. Schein "Improving face-to-face relationships" in *Sloan Management Review*, Winter 1984.

CONSULTANT REPORT WRITING

The reports written by consultants for their clients are mentioned in various chapters of the book according to the occasions and purposes that call for them. The purpose of this appendix is to review the essential factors in the writing and production of all reports used in consulting. The consultant's general strategy should be to make report writing as easy for himself as possible. Ease of writing leads to ease of reading.

1. Reports in perspective

In consulting work written communication complements oral communication, but in some special cases the written report may become the main communication channel. In addition to conveying information, reports to clients have other important functions. They contribute by their quality and presentation to the impact the consultant makes during the assignment. They also affect the consultant's general reputation. When the personal contacts between consultant and client are limited (for example, if the client obtains written survey reports from several consultants and will select one on the basis of those reports), persuasion may be a vital feature of a report.

As a matter of principle, consulting reports do not repeat information obtained from the client or well known to him, with the exception of information which directly justifies proposals. The essence of information is *news*. Thus, the information content of reports should be on:

- facts discovered for the first time by the consultant;
- newly discovered significance of known facts;
- newly found connections between known effects and hitherto unknown causes;
- solutions to the problems, and their justification.

For his own check, the consultant should ask himself about the *necessity* and *purpose* of any report he intends to produce:

— why is the report necessary?
— what will it achieve?
— is there a better way of achieving this purpose?
— is now the time for it?

It is not a bad thing to try drafting an introduction, starting with "The purpose of this report is . . . ". If there is any difficulty in finishing the sentence there is some doubt about the need for the report. The length of time since the last report does not matter, as long as the assignment has progressed satisfactorily in the meantime and the client knows it.

2. Structuring the report

The contents need to be arranged in the best *sequence* for the nature and purpose of the report and for the desired reaction to it. This may be difficult. Although the author hopes the reader will start at the beginning and read through to the end, there is no guarantee that he will. This is one of the hazards of written communication. Persuasion requires careful build-up through a reasoned sequence — which the reader may not choose to follow.

A solution to this may be in a well-presented *summary* at the beginning of the report. Many busy executives will read the summary for overall guidance to the structure of the report even if they do not read all chapters.

A *table of contents* is essential (except in very short reports); it is regrettable that many reports do not have one. The best place for the table of contents is at the very beginning of the report, i.e. preceding an introduction, a preface, a summary, or any other sections. In some countries it is customary to give a table of contents at the very end.

The whole report should be carefully planned. It will contain certain main ideas and topics, some of which will have subdivisions. It may help to write headings and sketch the subject matter on separate sheets or cards. The sheets may then be sorted into the best order for deciding the outline and for drafting.

Marshalling the body of a report into a logical structure is aided by having a formal system of numbers and/or letters for main headings, sub-headings and so on. The wording after each number may be typed or printed in a different style.

A decimal system may be used, as in the example on the left, or numbers and letters, as in the example on the right:

1. MAIN HEADING	I.	MAIN HEADING
1.1. SUB-HEADING	1.	Sub-heading
1.1.1. Sub-sub-heading	A.	Sub-sub-heading
	(i)	listed item
	(ii)	listed item

The advantage of such a scheme is that it makes the writer think about his priorities and determine which topics are genuine subdivisions of others. It promotes the orderly organisation of the structure and points the way to economy of layout and avoidance of repetition.

For example, a report covering three subject areas, Buying, Stores, and Production, deals with three statements about them: Findings, Conclusions, and Recommendations. Which of the three layouts below may be the best?

1. *Findings*	1. *Buying*	1. *Buying*
1.1 Buying	1.1 Findings	1.1 Findings
1.2 Stores	1.2 Conclusions	1.2 Conclusions
1.3 Production	1.3 Recommendations	
		2. *Stores*
2. *Conclusions*	2. *Stores*	2.1 Findings
2.1 Bying	2.1 Findings	2.2 Conclusions
2.2 Stores	2.2 Conclusions	
2.3 Production	2.3 Recommendations	3. *Production*
		3.1 Findings
3. *Recommendations*	3. *Production*	3.2 Conclusions
3.1 Buying	3.1 Findings	
3.2 Stores	3.2 Conclusions	4. *Recommendations*
3.3 Production	3.3 Recommendations	4.1 Buying
		4.2 Stores
		4.3 Production

For any particular report one of these may prove easiest, but if "Findings" tell the client nothing new, there is no point in belabouring them. "Conclusions" usually lead straight into "Recommendations". It could even be that the whole report needs to be written as for section 4 in the third column above, the recommendations themselves being written so as to make the findings and conclusions quite clear.

Everything depends on priorities, weights, balance and purpose; a scheme of marshalling helps to sort them out.

Appendices are useful for taking out of the body of a report detailed tables, charts, diagrams, etc., that would break up the continuity of reading and would be difficult to fit in. The body of the report is essentially for reading and quick examination of summary data. Appendices can take items which, though they make a contribution, require a more lengthy examination. It does not help to make a case if the reader is suddenly confronted with several pages of closely tabulated figures. A small table or diagram, however, is not disturbing.

If a report included, for example, the complete specification of an office system, this would almost certainly be in an appendix. Such an appendix may later become part of a general manual of procedures for the client, while the report may remain confidential.

Acknowledgements have to be made, especially in final reports on consulting. This may require some tact. If names are mentioned there must be no obvious omissions: every genuine helper likes to see his name on the list. At the same time, to include someone who has been more hindrance than help — and knows it — may cause mixed feelings all round. If the list would be too long, it is better to leave it out and settle for general thanks and the remark that "it would be an impossible task to mention everyone who . . .".

Table 1   Principles of clear writing

---

1. Keep the report as short as possible.
2. Consider your reader, his outlook and experience.
3. Write to express, not to impress.
4. Write naturally: style that flows smoothly and does not draw attention to itself is the most effective.
5. Keep sentences short; vary their length but let the average be under 20 words.
6. Avoid complex sentences and carefully blend short and long words.
7. Use familiar words, avoiding rare or far-fetched ones.
8. Avoid jargon unless it is sure to be familiar to the reader and you know what it means.
9. Avoid unnecessary words that give an impression of padding.
10. Use terms the reader can picture: call a crane a crane, not "a lifting facility".
11. Put action into your verbs; use the force of the active voice; use the passive voice to vary the style.
12. Keep every item of a report relevant to the purpose.
13. Ensure the contents include all the points necessary to the purpose.
14. Keep a proper balance, giving space and emphasis to each item according to its importance.
15. Keep a serious "tone" as befits a serious purpose: do not tempt the reader to read between the lines: if you do you are at the mercy of his imagination.
16. Be careful in the use of numbers: figures tend to draw attention to themselves; decide when absolute values have more significance than percentages, and vice versa; when quoting figures from other sources, be exact; when estimating, consider the order of accuracy and round off.

---

3. Writing the report

At the present time executives are flooded with reports and hate long and badly written ones. It is useful, therefore, to observe certain principles, which have been summarised in table 1.[1]

When the author has the time, the first complete draft should be put aside for a day or two, after which anything wrong is more easily seen and revised. When it looks right to the author, someone else should read it. An operating consultant's draft will certainly be read by his supervisor, who usually has a knack of finding things a less experienced consultant never suspected. There are, however, some dangers at this point: any report can always be improved, and the temptation to work on it until it is "perfect" may be hard to resist. As with most things, there is a point of diminishing returns.

When working on his report the consultant may find out that the report outline originally chosen is not the best one. There is no point in sticking to an ineffective outline. However, if the client agreed to that outline beforehand, he should also be asked to agree to a modified outline to avoid a possible misunderstanding when presenting the report.

If the report is a collective piece of work and the co-authors are known to have different personal styles, final editing should be foreseen. Consistency and homogeneity are key characteristics of well-presented reports.

4. Typing and printing the report

The report must look professional in every respect. Its cover and binding should give a good first impression. Inside, the typescript should allow a generous binding margin, be impeccably typed on a well-adjusted machine and free from extraneous marks or alterations. Any graphs, charts and diagrams must be well drawn and in every respect up to the standard of the typescript.

The consulting unit may have its own standard format that not only distinguishes its report but caters for filing and control in its report library. Within the covers, the body of the report may also have a standard layout for division and subdivision of the contents.

The final draft prepared for reproduction should leave the typist in no doubts as to precisely what is required. The author should take the trouble to lay out the text as he wants to see it typed. He is also completely responsible for ensuring that no mistakes remain.

The use of *text processing* for typing, editing, reproducing and storing executive and consultancy reports became common in industrialised countries during the 1970s and is rapidly making headway in many developing countries.

Selected literature on report writing is listed in appendix 11.

---

[1] Some of the principles are adapted from R. Gunning: *The technique of clear writing* (New York, McGraw-Hill, 1952).

SELECTED BIBLIOGRAPHY
FOR MANAGEMENT CONSULTANTS

Part I. Management consulting in perspective

Albert, K. J.: *How to be your own management consultant* (New York, McGraw-Hill, 1978); 256 pp.

APO: *Development of management consultancy in APO member countries* (Tokyo, Asian Productivity Organisation, 1978); 185 pp.

Argyris, Ch.: *Intervention theory and method: A behavioural science view* (Reading, MA, Addison-Wesley, 1970); 374 pp.

Argyris, Ch.; Schön, D. A.: *Organisational learning: A theory of action perspective* (Reading, MA, Addison-Wesley, 1978); 344 pp.

Barcus, S.W.; Wilkinson, J.W.: *Handbook of management consulting services* (New York McGraw-Hill, 1986); 440 pp.

Beckhart, R.; Harris, R. T.: *Organisational transitions: Managing complex change* (Reading, MA, Addison-Wesley, 1977); 110 pp.

Bell, Ch. R.; Nadler, L. (eds.): *The client-consultant handbook* (Houston, TX, Gulf Publishing Co., 1979); 278 pp.

Bennett, R.: *Management research: Guide for institutions and professionals* (Geneva, International Labour Office, 1983); 245 pp.

Bentley, T. J. (ed.): *The management services handbook* (London, Holt, Rinehart and Winston, 1984); 527 pp.

Bermont, H.: *How to become a successful consultant in your own field* (Washington, DC, Bermont Books, 1978); 157 pp.

Bermont, H.: *Psychological strategies for success in consulting* (Washington, DC, The Consultants Library, 1983); 68 pp.

Blake, R.; Mouton, J. S.: *Solving costly organisational conflicts* (San Francisco, CA, Jossey-Bass, 1984); 327 pp.

Block, P.: *Flawless consulting: A guide to getting your expertise used* (Austin, TX, Learning Concepts, 1981); 215 pp.

Cody, T. G.: *Management consulting: A game without chips* (Fitzwilliam, NH, Consultants News, 1986).

Cohen, W. A.: *How to make it big as a consultant* (New York, AMACOM, 1985); 304 pp.

Fuchs, J. H.: *Making the most of management consulting services* (New York, AMACOM, 1975); 214 pp.

Fuchs, J. H.: *Management consultants in action* (New York, Hawthorn Books, 1975); 216 pp.

Gallessich, J.: *The profession and practice of consultation* (San Francisco, CA, Jossey-Bass, 1982); 490 pp.

Goodman, P. S.: *Change in organisations* (San Francisco, CA, Jossey-Bass, 1982); 446 pp.

Goodstein, L. D.: *Consulting with human service systems* (Reading, MA, Addison-Wesley, 1978); 172 pp.

Gowan, V. Q.: *Consulting to government* (Cambridge, MA, Infoscan, 1979); 368 pp.

Greiner, L. E.; Metzger, R. O.: *Consulting to management* (Englewood Cliffs, NJ, Prentice-Hall, 1983); 368 pp.

Guttmann, H. P.: *The international consultant* (New York, McGraw-Hill, 1976); 193 pp.

Harris, P. R.; Moran, R. T.: *Managing cultural differences* (Houston, TX, Gulf Publishing Co., 1979); 418 pp.

Hersey, P.; Blanchard, K. H.: *Management of organisational behaviour: Utilising human resources* (Englewood Cliffs, NJ, Prentice-Hall, 1977); 384 pp.

Holtz, H.: *How to succeed as an independent consultant* (New York, Wiley, 1983); 395 pp.

Hunt, A.: *The management consultant* (New York, Ronald Press, 1977); 159 pp.

Johnson, B. L.: *Private consulting: How to turn experience into employment dollars* (Englewood Cliffs, NJ, Prentice-Hall, 1982); 147 pp.

Kadushin, A.: *Consultation in social work* (New York, Columbia University Press, 1977); 236 pp.

Katz, D.; Kahn, R. L.: *Social psychology of organisations* (New York, Wiley, 1978); 838 pp.

Kelley, R. E.: *Consulting: The complete guide to a profitable career* (New York, Charles Scribner's Sons, 1981); 258 pp.

Kennedy, J. (ed.): *The future of management consulting* (Fitzwilliam, NH, Consultants News, 1985); 99 pp.

Kishel, G. F.; Kishel, P. G.: *Cashing in on the consulting boom* (New York, Wiley, 1985); 180 pp.

Klein, H. J.: *Other people's business: A primer on management consultants* (New York, Mason-Charter, 1977); 202 pp.

Leavitt, H. J.: *Managerial psychology* (Chicago, IL, University of Chicago Press, 1978); 386 pp.

Lippitt, G. L.; Hoopes D. S. (eds.): *Helping across cultures* (Washington, DC, International Consultants Foundation, 1978); 76 pp.

Lippitt, G. L.; Lippitt, R.: *The consulting process in action* (La Jolla, CA, University Associates, 1978); 130 pp.

Lippitt, G. L.; Langseth, P.; Mossop, J.: *Implementing organisational change* (San Francisco, CA, Jossey-Bass, 1985); 185 pp.

Lippitt, G. L.: *Organization renewal: A holistic approach to organisation development* (Englewood Cliffs, NJ, Prentice-Hall, 1982); 418 pp.

Moore, G. L.: *The politics of management consulting* (New York, Praeger, 1984); 176 pp.

Moran, R. T.; Harris, P. R.: *Managing cultural synergy* (Houston, TX, Gulf Publishing Co., 1982); 399 pp.

Schein, E. H.: *Organisational psychology* (Englewood Cliffs, NJ, Prentice-Hall, 1980); 274 pp.

Schein, E. H.: *Process consultation: Its role in organisation development* (Reading, MA, Addison-Wesley, 1969); 150 pp.

Shay, P. W.: *How to get the best results from management consultants* (New York, Association of Consulting Management Engineers, 1974); 60 pp.

Sinha, D. P., (ed.): *Consultants and consulting styles* (New Delhi, Visions Books, 1979); 248 pp.

Smith, B.: *The country consultant* (Fitzwilliam, NH, Consultants News, 1982); 300 pp.

Steele, F.: *Consulting for organisational change* (Amherst, MA, University of Massachusetts Press, 1975); 202 pp.

Steele, F.: *The role of the internal consultant* (Boston, MA, CBI Publishing Co., 1982); 158 pp.

Stevens, M.: *The Big Eight* (New York, Macmillan, 1981); 270 pp.

Stewart, V.: *Change: The challenge for management* (Maidenhead, McGraw-Hill, 1983); 166 pp.

Stryker, S.: *Guide to successful consulting (with forms, letters and checklists)* (Englewood Cliffs, NJ, Prentice-Hall, 1984); 272 pp.

Tisdall, P.: *Agents of change: The development and practice of management consulting* (London, Heinemann, 1983); 163 pp.

Walsh, J. E.: *Guidelines for management consultants in Asia* (Tokyo, Asian Productivity Organisation, 1973); 210 pp.

Weinberg, G. M.: *The secrets of consulting* (New York, Dorset, 1986); 228 pp.

Wolf, W. B.: *Management and consulting: An introduction to James O. McKinsey* (Ithaca, NY, Cornell University Press, 1978); 112 pp.

Part II. The consulting process

Barish, N. N.; Kaplan, S.: *Economic analysis for engineering and managerial decision making* (New York, McGraw-Hill, 1978); 791 pp.

Bennett, R.: *Management research: Guide for institutions and professionals* (Geneva, International Labour Office, 1983); 245 pp.

Bentley, T. J. (ed.): *The management services handbook* (London, Holt, Rinehart and Winston, 1984); 527 pp.

Block, P.: *Flawless consulting: A guide to getting your expertise used* (Austin, TX, Learning Concepts, 1981); 215 pp.

Bowlin, O. D., Martin J. D., Scott D. F.: *Guide to financial analysis* (New York, McGraw-Hill, 1980); 335 pp.

Buffa, E. S.; Dyer, J. S.: *Essentials of management science; operations research* (New York, Wiley, 1978); 528 pp.

Clark, J. J.; Clark, M. T.: *A statistics primer for managers* (New York, The Free Press, 1983); 258 pp.

Clover, V. T.; Balsey, H. L.: *Business research methods* (Columbus, OH, Grid Publishing Co., 1979); 385 pp.

Consultants News: *25 "best" proposals by management consulting firms* (Fitzwilliam, NH, Consultants News, 1984); 510 pp.

Dunham, R. B.; Smith, F. J.: *Organisational surveys: An internal assessment of organisational health* (Glenview, IL, Scott, Foresman and Co., 1979); 179 pp.

Emory, C. W.: *Business research methods* (Homewood, IL, Irwin, 1976); 483 pp.

Greenberg, L.: *A practical guide to productivity measurement* (Washington, DC, Bureau of National Affairs, 1973); 77 pp.

Greiner, L. E.; Metzger, R. O.: *Consulting to management* (Englewood Cliffs, NJ, Prentice-Hall, 1983); 368 pp.

Harnett, D. L.: *Statistical methods* (Reading, MA, Addison-Wesley, 1982); 730 pp.

Harrison, I. W.: *Capital investment appraisal* (London, McGraw-Hill, 1973); 90 pp.

Holtz, H.: *Government contracts: Proposalmanship and winning strategies* (New York, Plenum Press, 1979); 288 pp.

ILO: *How to read a balance sheet*, Second (revised) edition (Geneva, International Labour Office, 1985); 213 pp.

ILO: *Introduction to work study*, Third (revised) edition (Geneva, International Labour Office, 1979); 442 pp.

Kepner, C. H.; Tregoe, B. B.: *The new rational manager* (Princeton, NJ, Kepner-Tregoe, 1981); 224 pp.

Lopez, F. M.: *Personnel interviewing: Theory and practice* (New York, McGraw-Hill, 1971); 356 pp.

Margerison, Ch.: *Managerial problem solving* (Bradford, MCB Publications, 1982); 166 pp.

Maynard, H. B.: *Industrial engineering handbook* (New York, McGraw-Hill, 1971); 1,980 pp.

Nierenberg, G. I.: *The art of negotiating* (New York, Pocket Books, 1984); 254 pp.

Oxenfeldt, A. R.: *Cost-benefit analysis for executive decision making: The danger of plain common sense* (New York, AMACOM, 1979); 432 pp.

Payne, T. A.: *Quantitative techniques for management: A practical approach* (Hemel Hempstead, Prentice-Hall, 1981); 452 pp.

Platt, C. J.: *Survey of company reports: An analysis of current practices in presenting information* (Farnborough, Wieton Publications, 1978); 125 pp.

Rawlinson, J. G.: *Creative thinking and brainstorming* (Farnborough, Gower, 1981); 128 pp.

Reeves, T. K.; Harper, D.: *Surveys at work: A practitioner's guide* (Maidenhead, McGraw-Hill, 1982); 259 pp.

Shenson, H. L.: *How to strategically negotiate the consulting contract* (Washington, DC, Bermont Books, 1980); 107 pp.

Wagner, H. R.: *Principles of management science; With applications to executive decisions* (Englewood Cliffs, NJ, Prentice-Hall, 1975); 612 pp.

Warren, R.: *How to understand and use company accounts* (London, Business Books, 1983); 221 pp.

Weisbord, M. R.: *Organisational diagnosis* (Reading, MA, Addison-Wesley, 1978); 180 pp.

Westwick, C. A.: *How to use management ratios* (Aldershot, Gower, 1973); 284 pp.

White, D. J.: *Decision methodology* (London, Wiley, 1975); 274 pp.

Wolf, W. B.: *Management and consulting: An introduction to James O. McKinsey* (Ithaca, NY, Cornell University Press, 1978); 112 pp.

Part III. Consulting in various areas of management

Chapter 12. Consulting in general management

Ansoff, H. I.: *Strategic management* (London, Macmillan, 1979); 236 pp.

Deal, T. E.; Kennedy, A. A.: *Corporate cultures: The rites and rituals of corporate life* (Reading, MA, Addison-Wesley, 1982); 232 pp.

Drucker, P.: *Innovation and entrepreneurship: Practice and principles* (New York, Harper and Row, 1985); 277 pp.

Drucker, P.: *Management* (New York, Harper and Row, 1973); 840 pp.

Drucker, P.: *The practice of management* (London, Pan Books, 1970); 480 pp.

Gilder, G.: *The spirit of enterprise* (New York, Simon and Schuster, 1984); 272 pp.

Goodman, S. T.: *How to manage a turnaround* (New York, The Free Press, 1984); 279 pp.

Hussey, D. E. (ed.): *The truth about corporate planning: International research into the practice of planning* (Oxford, Pergamon Press, 1983); 586 pp.

Koontz, H.; O'Donnell, C.; Weihrich, H.: *Management* (New York, McGraw-Hill, 1980); 832 pp.

Kotter, J. P.: *The general managers* (New York, The Free Press, 1982); 221 pp.

McGregor, D.: *The human side of the enterprise* (New York, McGraw-Hill, 1960); 246 pp.

Mintzberg, H.: *Power in and around organisations* (Englewood Cliffs, NJ, Prentice-Hall, 1983); 700 pp.

Mintzberg, H.: *Structures in fives: Designing effective organisations* (Englewood Cliffs, NJ, Prentice-Hall, 1983); 312 pp.

MIT: *Global technological change: A strategic assessment* (Cambridge, MA, MIT, 1983).

Newman, W. H; Warren, E. K.; Schnee, J. E.: *The process of management* (Englewood Cliffs, NJ, Prentice-Hall, 1982); 578 pp.

O'Toole, J.: *Vanguard management* (New York, Doubleday, 1985); 432 pp.

Pascale, R. T.; Athos, A. G.: *The art of Japanese management* (New York, Warner Books, 1981); 363 pp.

Peters, T.; Austin, N.: *A passion for excellence: The leadership difference* (New York, Random House, 1985); 437 pp.

Peters, T.; Waterman, R. H.: *In search of excellence* (New York, Warner Books, 1982); 360 pp.

Pinchot, G.: *Intrapreneuring: Why you don't have to leave the corporation to become an entrepreneur* (New York, Harper and Row, 1985); 368 pp.

Porter, M. E.: *Competitive advantage: Creating and sustaining superior performance* (New York, The Free Press, 1985); 557 pp.

Schein, E. H.: *Organisational culture and leadership* (San Francisco, CA, Jossey-Bass, 1985); 370 pp.

Steiner, G A.; Miner, J. B.: *Management policy and strategy* (New York, Macmillan, 1982); 357 pp.

Steiner, G. A.: *The new CEO* (New York, Macmillan, 1983); 133 pp.

Stewart, R.: *Choices for the manager* (Englewood Cliffs, NJ, Prentice-Hall, 1982); 165 pp.

Chapter 13. Consulting in financial management

Anthony, R. N.: *Accounting: Text and cases* (Homewood, IL, Irwin, 1983); 974 pp.

Auerbach, R. D.: *Money, banking and financial markets* (New York, Macmillan, 1985); 650 pp.

Bean, D. G.: *Financial strategy in the acquisition decision* (Farnborough, Gower, 1975); 175 pp.

Bierman, H.; Smidt, S.: *The capital budgeting decision* (London, Macmillan, 1975); 482 pp.

Bradley, J. W.; Korn, D. H.: *Acquisition and corporate development* (Lexington, MA, Lexington Books, 1981); 252 pp.

Clark, J. J.; Hindelang, T. J.; Pritchard, R. E.: *Capital budgeting: Planning and control of capital expenditures* (Englewood Cliffs, NJ, Prentice-Hall, 1979); 468 pp.

Ensor, R.; Muller, P.: *The essentials of treasury management* (London, Euromoney Publications, 1981); 259 pp.

Franks, J.; Broyles, J.: *Modern managerial finance* (New York, Wiley, 1979); 376 pp.

Glautier, M. W. E.; Underdown, B.: *Accounting theory and practice* (London, Pitman, 1976); 741 pp.

Grass, M. (ed.): *Control of working capital* (Farnborough, Gower, 1972); 151 pp.

Gray, J.; Johnston, K. S.: *Accounting and management action* (New York, McGraw-Hill, 1973); 574 pp.

Heywood, J.: *Foreign exchange and the corporate treasurer* (London, A. and C. Black, 1978); 163 pp.

Horngren, C. T.: *Cost accounting: A managerial emphasis* (Englewood Cliffs, NJ, Prentice-Hall, 1982); 997 pp.

Hovers, J.: *Expansion through acquisiton* (London, Business Books, 1973); 178 pp.

Kettell, B.: *The finance of international business* (London, Graham and Trotman, 1979); 275 pp.

Kirkman, P. R. A.: *Accounting under inflationary conditions* (London, George Allen and Unwin, 1974); 266 pp.

McCarthy, G. D.; Healey, R. E.: *Valuing a company: Practices and procedures* (New York, Ronald Press, 1971); 521 pp.

Mehta, D. R.: *Working capital management* (Englewood Cliffs, NJ, Prentice-Hall, 1974); 182 pp.

Merrett, A. J.; Sykes, A.: *The finance and analysis of capital projects* (London, Longman, 1973); 573 pp.

Morell, J.; Ashton, R.: *Inflation and business management* (London, Economic Forecasters Publications, 1975); 194 pp.

Pocock, M. A.; Taylor, A. H.: *Handbook of financial planning and control* (Farnborough, Gower, 1981); 423 pp.

Rodriguez, R. M.; Carter, E. E.: *International financial management* (Englewood Cliffs, NJ, Prentice-Hall, 1979); 686 pp.

Tennent, M.: *Practical liquidity management* (Farnborough, Gower, 1976); 201 pp.

Van Horne, J.: *Financial management and policy* (Englewood Cliffs, NJ, Prentice-Hall, 1980); 809 pp.

Walker, T.: *A guide for using the foreign exchange market* (New York, Wiley, 1981); 372 pp.

Weston, J. F.; Brigham, E. F.: *Managerial finance* (Hinsdale, IL, Dryden Press, 1978); 1030 pp.

Winkler, J.: *Company survival during inflation* (Farnborough, Gower, 1975); 168 pp.

Chapter 14. Consulting in marketing management

Best, A.: *When consumers complain* (New York, Columbia University Press, 1981); 232 pp.

Buell, G.: *Handbook of modern marketing* (New York, McGraw-Hill, 1970); 1400 pp.

Elliot, K.; Christopher, M.: *Research methods in marketing* (London, Holt, Rinehart and Winston, 1973); 250 pp.

Enis, B. M.; Cox, K. K.: *Marketing classics: A selection of influential articles* (Boston, MA, Allyn and Bacon, 1981); 533 pp.

Gattorna, J.: *Handbook of physical distribution management* (Aldershot, Gower, 1983); 528 pp.

Green, P. E.; Tull, D. S.: *Research for marketing decisions* (Englewood Cliffs, NJ, Prentice-Hall, 1978); 673 pp.

Gronroos, C.: *Strategic management and marketing in the service sector* (Helsinki, Swedish School of Economics and Business Administration, 1982).

Kotler, P.: *Marketing essentials* (Englewood Cliffs, NJ, Prentice-Hall, 1984); 556 pp.

Kotler, P.: *Marketing management: Analysis, planning and control* (Englewood Cliffs, NJ, Prentice-Hall, 1984).

Kotler, P.: *Principles of marketing* (Englewood Cliffs, NJ, Prentice-Hall, 1983); 640 pp.

Levitt, T.: *The marketing imagination* (New York, The Free Press, 1983); 203 pp.

McCarthy, E. J.: *Basic marketing: A managerial approach* (Homewood, IL, Irwin, 1981); 762 pp.

Nash, E. L.: *The direct marketing handbook* (New York, McGraw-Hill, 1984); 946 pp.

Ogilvy, D.: *Ogilvy on advertising* (New York, Crown, 1983); 224 pp.

Robeson, J. F.; House, R. G.: *The distribution handbook* (New York, The Free Press, 1985); 970 pp.

Sammon, W. L.; Kurland, M. A.; Spitalnic, R.: *Business competitor intelligence: Methods for collecting, organising and using information* (New York, Wiley, 1984); 357 pp.

Seibert, J. C.: *Concepts of marketing management* (New York, Harper and Row, 1973); 570 pp.

Staudt, T.; Taylor, D. A.: *A managerial introduction to marketing* (Englewood Cliffs, NJ, Prentice-Hall, 1970); 576 pp.

Willemin, J. H.: *The handbook of professional service management* (Lund, Studentliteratur, 1984); 275 pp.

Chapter 15. Consulting in production management

Biegel, J. E.: *Production control, a quantitative approach* (Englewood Cliffs, NJ, Prentice-Hall, 1971); 295 pp.

Birchdale, D.: *Job design: A planning and implementation guide for managers* (Epping, Gower, 1975); 141 pp.

Brown, J. K. (ed.): *Manufacturing: New concepts and new technology to meet new competition* (New York, The Conference Board, 1984); 47 pp.

Buffa, E.: *Meeting the competitive challenge: Manufacturing strategies for US companies* (Homewood, IL, Irwin, 1984); 190 pp.

Buffa, E.: *Operation management: The management of productive systems* (New York, Wiley, 1976); 686 pp.

Butera, F.; Thurman, J. E. (eds.): *Automation and work design* (Amsterdam, North Holland, 1984); 758 pp.

Greene, J.: *Production and inventory control handbook* (New York, McGraw-Hill, 1970); 800 pp.

Hutchinson, D.: *Quality circles handbook* (New York, Nichols, 1985); 272 pp.

ILO: *Introduction to work study*, Third (revised) edition (Geneva, International Labour Office, 1979); 442 pp.

Ishikawa, K.: *Guide to quality control* (Tokyo, Asian Productivity Organisation, 1986); 225 pp.

Juran, J. M.; Gryna, F. M.; Bingham, R. S.: *Quality control handbook*, Third edition (New York, McGraw-Hill, 1974); cca 1600 pp.

Kanawaty, G. (ed.): *Managing and developing new forms of work organisation*, Second (revised) edition (Geneva, International Labour Office, 1981); 206 pp.

Larson, S.: *Inventory systems and control handbook* (Englewood Cliffs, NJ, Prentice-Hall, 1976); 288 pp.

Lawlor, A.: *Productivity improvement manual* (Aldershot, Gower, 1985); 306 pp.

Luck, D. J.: *Product policy and strategy* (Englewood Cliffs, NJ, Prentice-Hall, 1972); 118 pp.

Mayer, R. R.: *Production and operations management* (New York, McGraw-Hill, 1975); 660 pp.

Maynard, H.: *Handbook of modern manufacturing management* (New York, McGraw-Hill, 1971); 1,100 pp.

Maynard, H.: *Industrial engineering handbook* (New York, McGraw-Hill, 1971); 1980 pp.

Morris, A.: *Analysis for materials handling management* (Homewood, IL, Irwin, 1962).

Muther, R.: *Practical plant layout* (New York, McGraw-Hill, 1955); 370 pp.

Riggs, J. L.: *Production systems: Planning, analysis and control* (New York, Wiley, 1970); 604 pp.

Robson, M.: *Quality circles: A practical guide* (Aldershot, Gower, 1982); 204 pp.

Ross, J. E.: *Managing productivity* (Reston, VA, Reston Publishing Co., 1977); 190 pp.

Shen, G. C.: *Productivity measurement and analysis* (Tokyo, Asian Productivity Organisation, 1985); 59 pp.

Sink, D. S.: *Productivity management: Measurement and evaluation, control and improvement* (New York, Wiley, 1985); 518 pp.

Skinner, W.: *Manufacturing: The formidable competitive weapon* (New York, Wiley, 1985); 330 pp.

Starr, M. K.: *Production management, systems and synthesis* (Englewood Cliffs, NJ, Prentice-Hall, 1972); 525 pp.

Tersine, R. J.: *Materials management and inventory systems* (New York, Elsevier North-Holland, 1976); 425 pp.

Thomas, A. B.: *Stock control in manufacturing industries* (Farnborough, Gower, 1980); 221 pp.

Walters, R. W. et al.: *Job enrichment for results: Strategies for successful implementation* (Reading, MA, Addison-Wesley, 1975); 307 pp.

Chapter 16. Consulting in human resource management and development

Armstrong, M.: *A handbook of personnel management practice* (London, Kogan Page, 1984); 416 pp.

Courtis, J.: *Cost effective recruitment* (London, Institute of Personnel Management, 1976); 92 pp.

Craig, R. L. (ed.): *Training and development handbook: A guide to human resource development* (New York, McGraw-Hill, 1976); 866 pp.

Edwards, S.; Leek, C.; Loveridge, R.; Lumley, R.: *Manpower planning; Strategy and techniques in an organizational context* (Chichester, Wiley, 1983); 208 pp.

Eichel, E.; Bender, H. E.: *Performance appraisal: A study of current techniques* (New York, American Management Association, 1984); 64 pp.

Fombrun, C. J.; Tichy, N. M.; Devanna, M. A.: *Strategic human resource management* (New York, Wiley, 1984); 499 pp.

Gladstone, A.: *The manager's guide to international labour standards* (Geneva, International Labour Office, 1986).

Glueck, W. F.: *Personnel: A diagnostic approach* (Plano, TX, Business Publications, 1982).

Gorlin, H.; Schein, L.: *Innovations in managing human resources* (New York, The Conference Board, 1984); 38 pp.

Hamner, W. C.; Schmidt, F. L. (eds.): *Contemporary problems in personnel* (Chicago, St. Clair Press, 1977); 510 pp.

Henderson, R. I., *Compensation management: Rewarding performance* (Reston, VA, Reston Publishing Co., 1985); 788 pp.

Hill, N. C.: *Counselling at the workplace* (New York, McGraw-Hill, 1981); 282 pp.

ILO: *Job evaluation* (Geneva, International Labour Office, 1986); 203 pp.

ILO: *Payment by results* (Geneva, International Labour Office, 1984); 164 pp.

Janger, A. R.: *The personnel function: Changing objectives and organisation* (New York, The Conference Board, 1977); 133 pp.

King, P.: *Performance planning and appraisals: A how-to book for managers* (New York, McGraw-Hill, 1984); 160 pp.

Loughran, C. S.: *Negotiating a labor contract; A management handbook* (Washington, DC, Bureau of National Affairs, 1984); 473 pp.

Managing manpower in Europe (Geneva, Business International, 1982); 192 pp.

McBeath, C.; Rands, D.: *Salary administration* (London, Business Books, 1976); 320 pp.

McKinnon, R.: *Headhunters* (London, Scope Books, 1982); 172 pp.

Nadler, L.: *Corporate human resources development: A management tool* (New York, Van Nostrand Reinhold, 1980); 199 pp.

Nadler, L. (ed.): *The handbook of human resource development* (New York, Wiley, 1984); 845 pp.

Odiorne, G. S.: *Strategic management of human resources: A portfolio approach* (San Francisco, CA, Jossey-Bass, 1984); 356 pp.

Paterson, T. T.: *Job evaluation,* Vols. 1 and 2 (London, Business Books, 1972); 428 pp.

Perry, R. H.: *How to answer a headhunter's call: A complete guide to executive search* (New York, AMACOM, 1984); 249 pp.

Pigors, P.; Myers, C. A.: *Personnel administration: A point of view and a method* (London, McGraw-Hill, 1981); 588 pp.

Plumbley, P. R.: *Recruitment and selection* (London, Institute of Personnel Management, 1985); 176 pp.

Schein, E. H.: *Career dynamics: Matching individual and organizational needs* (Reading, MA, Addison-Wesley, 1978); 276 pp.

Stewart, V.; Stewart, A.: *Practical performance appraisal* (Farnborough, Gower, 1978); 192 pp.

Taylor, A. R.: *How to select and use an executive search firm* (New York, McGraw-Hill, 1984); 173 pp.

Thomason, G.: *A textbook of personnel management* (London, Institute of Personnel Management, 1981); 619 pp.

Tracey, W. R. (ed.): *Human resources management and development handbook* (New York, AMACOM, 1985); 1550 pp.

Truell, G. F.: *Coaching and counselling: Key skills for managers* (Buffalo, NJ, PAT Publications, 1981); 77 pp.

Chapter 17. Consulting in small enterprise management

APO: *Productivity through consultancy in small industrial enterprises* (Tokyo, Asian Productivity Organisation, 1974); 500 pp.

Baumback, C. M.: *Basic small business management* (Englewood Cliffs, NJ, Prentice-Hall, 1983); 540 pp.

Coleman, B.: *The small business survival guide* (London, Norton, 1984); 350 pp.

Guidelines for management consulting programmes for small-scale enterprise (Washington, DC, Peace Corps, 1981); 212 pp.

Harper, M.: *Consultancy for small businesses (the concept; training the consultants)* (London, Intermediate Technology Publications, 1976); 254 pp.

Harper, M.: *Small business in the third world: Guidelines for practical assistance* (Chichester, Wiley, 1984); 211 pp.

How to set up and run your own business (London, Daily Telegraph, 1984); 207 pp.

Jones, S.; Cohen, M. B. (eds.): *The emerging business: Managing for growth* (New York, Wiley, 1983); 425 pp.

Kline, J. B.; Stegall, D. P.; Steinmetz, L. L.: *Managing the small business* (Homewood, IL, Irwin, 1982); 466 pp.

McClelland, D. C.; Winter, D. G.: *Motivating economic achievement* (New York, The Free Press, 1969); 410 pp.

Neck, P.; Nelson, R. (eds.): *Small enterprise development: Policies and programmes*, Second (revised) edition (Geneva, International Labour Office, 1987)

Rosenblatt, P. C. et al.: *The family in business* (San Francisco, CA, Jossey-Bass, 1985); 321 pp.

Steinhoff, D.: *Small business management fundamentals* (New York, McGraw-Hill, 1978); 512 pp.

Stillman, R. J.: *Small business management: How to start and stay in business* (Boston, MA, Little, Brown and Co., 1983); 275 pp.

White, R. M.: *Entrepreneur's manual; Business start-ups, spin offs, and innovation management* (Radnor, PA, Chilton Book Co., 1977); 419 pp.

Woodcock, C. (ed.): *The Guardian guide to running a small business* (London, Kogan Page, 1984); 248 pp.

Chapter 18. Consulting in public enterprise management

Abramson, R.; Halset, W.: *Planning for improved enterprise performance: A guide for managers and consultants* (Geneva, International Labour Office, 1979); 178 pp.

ADB: *Privatization: Policies, methods and procedures* (Manila, Asian Development Bank, 1985); 380 pp.

Ahmed, Z. U. (ed.): *Financial profitability and losses in public enterprises* (Ljubljana, International Centre for Public Enterprises in Developing Countries, 1982); 167 pp.

Fernandes, P.: *Managing relations between government and public enterprises: A handbook for administrators and managers* (Geneva, International Labour Office, 1986).

ICPE: *Essays on relations between governments and public enterprises* (Ljubljana, International Centre for Public Enterprises in Developing Countries, 1985); 248 pp.

Powell, V.: *Improving public enterprise performance: Concepts and techniques* (Geneva, International Labour Office, 1986).

Shirley, M. M.: *Managing state-owned enterprises,* Staff working paper No 577 (Washington, DC, World Bank, 1983); 101 pp.

Suárez, R. A. (ed.): *The management of interlinkages* (Ljubljana, International Centre for Public Enterprises in Developing Countries, 1985); 272 pp.

United Nations: *Performance evaluation of public enterprises in developing countries: Criteria and institutions* (New York, United Nations, 1984); 295 pp.

Chapter 19. Consulting in computer applications for management

Beck, P.: *How to choose and use business micro-computers and software* (London, Telegraph Publications, 1984); 207 pp.

Businessman's guide to microcomputers (London, Deloitte, Haskins and Sells, 1984); 148 pp.

Diebold, J.: *Managing information* (New York, AMACOM, 1985); 144 pp.

Ein-Dor, P.; Jones, C. R.: *Information systems management: Analytical tools and techniques* (Amsterdam, North-Holland, 1985); 230 pp.

Gaydasch, A.: *Principles of EDP management* (Reston, VA, Reston Publishing Co.); 300 pp.

Giertz, E.: *Creative computer usage: Eight case histories from Sweden* (Stockholm, Swedish Employers' Confederation, 1982).

Lucas, H. C.: *Information systems: Concepts for management* (New York, McGraw-Hill, 1982); 515 pp.

Murdick, R. G.: *MIS: Concepts and designs* (Englewood Cliffs, NJ, Prentice-Hall, 1980); 610 pp.

Rosenberg, J. M.: *Dictionary of computers, data processing and telecommunications* (New York, Wiley, 1984); 614 pp.

Ruprecht, M. M.; Wagoner, K. P.: *Managing office automation* (New York, Wiley, 1984); 680 pp.

Sanders, D. H.; Birkin, J. S.: *Computers and management in a changing society* (New York, McGraw-Hill, 1980).

Sanders, D. H.: *Computers today* (Maidenhead, McGraw-Hill, 1985); 672 pp.

Stair, R. M.: *Learning to live with computers: Advice for managers* (Homewood, IL, Dow-Jones Irwin, 1983); 190 pp.

The whole-earth software catalogue (Sausalito, CA, Steward-Brand, 1985).

Williams, F.; Dordick, H. S.: *The executive's guide to information technology: How to increase your competitive edge* (New York, Wiley, 1983); 314 pp.

Windsor, D. B. (ed.): *Developing a computerised personnel system: The manager's and buyer's guide* (London, Institute of Personnel Management, 1985); 226 pp.

Part IV. Managing consulting organisations

ACME: *Survey of key operating statistics on management consulting* (New York, Association of Management Consulting Firms, 1984); 51 pp.

ACME: *Survey on fee arrangements, compensation and employee benefits in management consulting firms* (New York, Association of Management Consulting Firms, 1983); 255 pp.

Altman, M. A.; Weil, R. I.: *Managing your accounting and consulting practice* (New York, Matthew Bender, 1978).

Bakewell, K. G. B.: *How to organise information* (Aldershot, Gower, 1984); 225 pp.

Batten, W. E. (ed.): *Handbook of special librarianship and information work* (London, ASLIB, 1975); 430 pp.

Bennett, R.: *Management research: Guide for institutions and professionals* (Geneva, International Labour Office, 1983); 245 pp.

Braun, I.: *Building a successful professional practice with advertising* (New York, AMACOM, 1981); 289 pp.

Connor, R. A.; Davidson, J. P.: *Marketing your consulting and professional services* (New York, Wiley, 1985); 219 pp.

Consultants News: *Fees and expense policies/statements of 24 management consulting firms* (Fitzwilliam, NH, Consultants News, 1984); 55 pp.

Consultants News: *The news release idea book for management consultants* (Fitzwilliam, NH, Consultants News, 1981); 296 pp.

Consultants News: *Public relations for management consultants: A practical compendium* (Fitzwilliam, NH, Consultants News, 1980); 83 pp.

Consultants News: *25 "best" proposals by management consulting firms* (Fitzwilliam, NH, Consultants News, 1984); 510 pp.

Daniells, L. M.: *Business information sources* (Berkeley, CA, University of California Press, 1985); 673 pp.

Greiner, L. E.; Metzger, R. O.: *Consulting to management* (Englewood Cliffs, NJ, Prentice-Hall, 1983); 368 pp.

Hameroff, E. J.; Nichols, S. S.: *How to guarantee professional success: 715 tested, proven techniques for promoting your practice* (Washington, DC, The Consultant's Library, 1982); 183 pp.

Holtz, H.: *The consultant's edge: Using the computer as a marketing tool* (New York, Wiley, 1985); 364 pp.

ILO: *How to read a balance sheet*, Second (revised) edition (Geneva, International Labour Office, 1985); 213 pp.

Kennedy, J. H. (ed.): *Public relations for management consultants* (Fitzwilliam, NH, Consultants News, 1981); 83 pp.

Kotler, P.; Bloom, P. N.: *Marketing professional services* (Englewood Cliffs, NJ, Prentice-Hall, 1984); 296 pp.

Kubr, M. (ed.): *Managing a management development institution* (Geneva, International Labour Office, 1982); 277 pp.

Kubr, M., Vernon, K. D. C. (eds.): *Management, administration and productivity: International directory of institutions and information sources* (Geneva, International Labour Office, 1981); 318 pp.

Lant, J. L.: *The consultant's kit: Establishing and operating your successful business* (Cambridge, MA, JLA Publications, 1981); 203 pp.

McCaffrey, M.: *Personal marketing strategies* (Englewood Cliffs, NJ, Prentice-Hall, 1983); 219 pp.

Pyeatt, N.: *The consultant's legal guide* (Washington, DC, Bermont Books, 1980); 145 pp.

Shenson, H. L.: *The successful consultant's guide to fee setting* (Washington, DC, Bermont Books, 1980); 167 pp.

Thomsett, M. C.: *Fundamentals of bookkeeping and accounting for the successful consultant* (Washington, DC, Bermont Books, 1980); 134 pp.

Vernon, K. D. C.: *Information services in management and business*, Second edition (London, Butterworth, 1984); 346 pp.

Vernon, K. D. C. (ed.): *Library and information services of management development institutions: A practical guide* (Geneva, International Labour Office, 1986).

Webb, S. G.: *Marketing and strategic planning for professional service firms* (New York, AMACOM, 1982); 304 pp.

Wheatley, E. W.: *Marketing professional services* (Englewood Cliffs, NJ, Prentice-Hall, 1983); 205 pp.

Wilson, A.: *Practice development for professional firms* (London, McGraw-Hill, 1984); 232 pp.

Part V. Developing management consultants

AICPA: *University education for management consulting* (New York, American Institute of Certified Public Accountants, 1978); 144 pp.

Boydell, T.: *Management self-development: A guide for managers, organisations and institutions* (Geneva, International Labour Office, 1985); 267 pp.

Harvard Business School Management Consulting Club: *Management consulting 1982* (Boston, MA, HBS Management Consulting Club, 1982).

IMC: *A body of knowledge for the accreditation of management consultants* (New York, Institute of Management Consultants, 1979); 75 pp.

Katz, A. S.: *Professional personnel policies development guidebook* (Reading, MA, Addison-Wesley, 1982); 256 pp.

King, P.: *Performance planning and appraisals: A how-to book for managers* (New York, McGraw-Hill, 1984); 160 pp.

Nadler, L. (ed.): *The handbook of human resource development* (New York, Wiley, 1984); 845 pp.

Tracey, W. R. (ed.): *Human resource management and development handbook* (New York, AMACOM, 1985); 1550 pp.

Truell, G. F.: *Coaching and counselling: Key skills for managers* (Buffalo, NY, PAT Publications, 1981); 77 pp.

Appendix 1 (on choosing and using consultants)

ACME: *How to select and use management consultants* (New York, Association of Management Consulting Firms, 1987); 33 pp.

Easton, T. A.; Conant, R. W.: *Using consultants: A consumer's guide for managers* (Chicago, IL, Probus Publishing Co., 1985); 200 pp.

Fuchs, J. H.: *Making the most of management consulting services* (New York, AMACOM, 1975); 214 pp.

Golightly, H. O.: *Consultants: Selecting, using and evaluating business consultants* (Danbury, CT, Watts, Franklin, 1985); 256 pp.

Holtz, H.: *Utilising consultants successfully: A guide for management in business, government, the arts and professions* (Westport, CT, Quorum Books, 1985); 221 pp.

Management consultants: Friends or enemies? (London, Transport and General Workers Union, 1983); 30 pp.

McGonagle, J. J. Jr.: *Managing the consultant: A corporate guide* (Radnor, PA, Chilton, 1981); 210 pp.

Taylor, A. R.: *How to select and use an executive search firm* (New York, McGraw-Hill, 1984); 173 pp.

UNIDO: *Manual on the use of consultants in developing countries* (New York, United Nations, 1972); 160 pp.

Appendices 9 and 10 (on communication and report writing)

Executive's guide to effective writing (New York, Alexander Hamilton Institute, 1980); 109 pp.

Gowers, E.: *The complete plain words* (Harmondsworth, Penguin Books, 1968); 270 pp.

Gunning, R.: *The technique of clear writing* (New York, McGraw-Hill, 1968).

Honey, P.: *Face to face: A practical guide to interactive skills* (London, Institute of Personnel Management, 1976); 150 pp.

Munter, M.: *Guide to managerial communication* (Englewood Cliffs, NJ, Prentice-Hall, 1982); 170 pp.

Nierenberg, G. I.: *The art of negotiating* (New York, Pocket Books, 1984); 254 pp.

Leech, T.: *How to prepare, stage, and deliver winning presentations* (New York, AMACOM, 1985); 417 pp.

Poe, R. W.: *The McGraw-Hill guide to effective business reports* (New York, McGraw-Hill, 1982); 209 pp.

Rockey, E. H.: *Communicating in organizations* (Cambridge, MA, Winthrop, 1977); 156 pp.

Schneider, A. E.; Donaghy, W. C.; Newman, P. J.: *Organisational communications* (New York, McGraw-Hill, 1975); 367 pp.

Sigband, N. B.: *Communication for management and business* (Glenview, IL, Scott Foresman Co., 1976); 657 pp.

Simpkin, R.; Jones, R.: *Business and the language barrier* (London, Business Books, 1976); 291 pp.

Strunk, W.: *The elements of style* (New York, Macmillan, 1959); 70 pp.

Sussams, J. E.: *How to write effective reports* (Aldershot, Gower, 1983); 109 pp.

Zinsser W.: *On writing well: An informal guide to writing non-fiction* (New York, Harper and Row, 1980); 187 pp.

Periodicals

Consultants News (Fitzwilliam, NH, Kennedy and Kennedy)
Consultation (New York, Human Sciences Press)
Journal of Management Consulting (Amsterdam, Elsevier Science Publishers)
The Professional Consultant and Seminar Business Report (Woodland Hills, CA, Howard L. Shenson)

Bibliography

ACME 1988 annotated bibliography of selected resource materials (New York, Association of Management Consulting Firms, 1988); 84 pp.

INDEX